T0237815

# Lecture Notes in Artificial Intelligence 1314

Subseries of Lecture Notes in Computer Science
Edited by J. G. Carbonell and J. Siekmann

# Lecture Notes in Computer Science

Edited by G. Goos, J. Hartmanis and J. van Leeuwen

# Springer

*Berlin*
*Heidelberg*
*New York*
*Barcelona*
*Budapest*
*Hong Kong*
*London*
*Milan*
*Paris*
*Santa Clara*
*Singapore*
*Tokyo*

Stephen Muggleton (Ed.)

# Inductive
# Logic Programming

6th International Workshop, ILP-96
Stockholm, Sweden, August 26-28, 1996
Selected Papers

 Springer

Series Editors
Jaime G. Carbonell, Carnegie Mellon University, Pittsburgh, PA, USA
Jörg Siekmann, University of Saarland, Saarbrücken, Germany


Volume Editor

Stephen Muggleton
University of York, Dept. of Computer Science
Y01 5DD Heslington, York, UK
E-mail: stephen@cs.york.ac.uk

Cataloging-in-Publication Data applied for


**Die Deutsche Bibliothek - CIP-Einheitsaufnahme**


**Inductive logic programming** : 6th international workshop ; selected
papers / ILP-96, Stockholm, Sweden, August 26 - 28, 1996. Stephen
Muggleton (ed.). - Berlin ; Heidelberg ; New York ; Barcelona ;
Budapest ; Hong Kong ; London ; Milan ; Paris ; Santa Clara ;
Singapore ; Tokyo : Springer, 1997
  (Lecture notes in computer science ; Vol. 1314 : Lecture notes in
  artificial intelligence)
  ISBN 3-540-63494-0


CR Subject Classification (1991): I.2, D.1.6

ISBN 3-540-63494-0 Springer-Verlag Berlin Heidelberg New York

© Springer-Verlag Berlin Heidelberg 1997
Printed in Germany

Typesetting: Camera ready by author
SPIN 10545832      06/3142 – 5 4 3 2 1 0     Printed on acid-free paper

# Preface

The Sixth International Workshop on Inductive Logic Programming (ILP-96) was held in Stockholm in conjunction with the Sixth International Workshop on Logic Program Synthesis and Transformation (LOPSTR-96) from 28th to 30th August 1996. These two research fields have a common basis in logic programming and also share an interest in program synthesis and refinement. For this reason the co-location of the ILP-96 and LOPSTR-96 workshops led to a productive interchange of ideas between the two research communities. This revolved around plenary sessions involving invited talks (given by Michael Lowry from the LOPSTR community and Raymond Mooney from the ILP community), as well as tutorial introductions (given by Luc De Raedt from the ILP community and Maurizio Proietti from the LOPSTR community) and an open forum for discussion on research topics of common interest to the two worskhops.

It was pleasing to see that the papers presented at ILP96 divide almost equally between experimental applications, implementations and theory. The diverse set of applications included natural language learning, drug design, NMR and ECG analysis, glaucoma diagnosis and even analysis of piano performances. Among the implementation papers authors presented various efficiency measures for logical constructions and database interaction, as well as issues related to program synthesis. Advances in theoretical underpinnings of ILP included an existence demonstration of least generalizations under the implication ordering, as well as methods for dealing with proof encodings and learning in the absence of negative data and in the presence of noise.

I would like to thank the programme committee for their help in the reviewing process. ILP-96 was hosted by the Department of Computer and Systems Sciences at Stockholm University and the Royal Institute of Technology, Sweden. My thanks go to the local chair, Carl-Gustaf Jansson and also Helene Karlsson and Hendrik Boström for an extremely efficiently run and pleasant workshop. I would also like to thank MLnet and Compulog (European networks of excellence) for their generous sponsorship of the joint event.

Oxford, 1997.                                                      Stephen Muggleton

# Program chair ILP-96

Stephen Muggleton, Oxford University Computing Laboratory, United Kingdom.

# Program chair LOPSTR-96

John Gallagher, Department of Computer Science, University of Bristol, United Kingdom.

# Local chair

Carl-Gustaf Jansson, Department of Computer and Systems Sciences at Stockholm University and the Royal Institute of Technology, Sweden.

# Local organisation

Helene Karlsson, Henrik Boström, Department of Computer and Systems Sciences at Stockholm University and the Royal Institute of Technology, Sweden.

# Program Committee ILP-96

| | |
|---|---|
| F. Bergadano (Italy) | H. Boström (Sweden) |
| I. Bratko (Slovenia) | L. De Raedt |
| S. Dzeroski (Slovenia) | P. Flach (Netherlands) |
| N. Lavrac (Slovenia) | S. Matvin (USA) |
| R. Mooney (USA) | S. Muggleton (UK) |
| M. Numao (Japan) | C.D. Page (UK) |
| J.R. Quinlan (Australia) | C. Rouveirol (France) |
| C. Sammut (Australia) | A. Srinivasan (UK) |
| S. Wrobel (Germany) | |

# Table of Contents

# Implementations

# Theory

# Invited Talk

# Inductive Logic Programming
# for Natural Language Processing

Raymond J. Mooney

Department of Computer Sciences
University of Texas, Austin TX 78712-1188, USA

**Abstract.** This paper reviews our recent work on applying inductive logic programming to the construction of natural language processing systems. We have developed a system, CHILL, that learns a parser from a training corpus of parsed sentences by inducing heuristics that control an initial overly-general shift-reduce parser. CHILL learns syntactic parsers as well as ones that translate English database queries directly into executable logical form. The ATIS corpus of airline information queries was used to test the acquisition of syntactic parsers, and CHILL performed competitively with recent statistical methods. English queries to a small database on U.S. geography were used to test the acquisition of a complete natural language interface, and the parser that CHILL acquired was more accurate than an existing hand-coded system. The paper also includes a discussion of several issues this work has raised regarding the capabilities and testing of ILP systems as well as a summary of our current research directions.

## 1 Introduction

Developing a system capable of communicating in natural language is one of the long-standing goals of computing research. Although significant progress has been made in the last forty years (Allen, 1995), developing a natural language processing (NLP) system for a particular application is still an extremely difficult and laborious task. However, a promising approach is to use machine learning techniques to help automate the development of NLP systems.

In recent years, there has been an increasing focus in computational linguistics on *empirical* or *corpus-based* methods that obtain much of their knowledge by training on large corpora of speech or text (Church & Mercer, 1993; Charniak, 1993; Brill & Church, 1996). Almost all of this work has employed statistical techniques such as *n-gram models*, *hidden Markov models* (HMMs), and *probabilistic context free grammars* (PCFGs). The computational linguistics community has focused on these techniques largely due to their successful application in prior work on speech recognition (Waibel & Lee, 1990). There has also been a fair amount of recent research on applying neural-network techniques, such as *simple recurrent networks*, to natural language processing (Reilly & Sharkey, 1992; Miikkulainen, 1993). However, there has been relatively little recent work using symbolic machine learning techniques for language applications, although some recent systems have employed decision trees (Magerman,

1995; Anoe & Bennett, 1995), transformation rules (Brill, 1993, 1995), and other symbolic methods (Wermter, Riloff, & Scheler, 1996).

However, all of these approaches are limited to examples represented as fixed-length feature vectors and are therefore subject to the standard limitations of propositional representations. Language processing, on the other hand, seems to require a very rich knowledge representation language that includes relations, recursion, and unbounded structural representations. Current empirical NLP systems employ carefully-engineered processing architectures and sets of features laboriously constructed by the system developer in order to circumvent these issues. The richness of first-order logic employed in inductive logic programming (ILP) can hopefully provide advantages for NLP applications by increasing flexibility and limiting the amount of feature-engineering required. Despite this fact, other than our own work, there has apparently been no application of ILP methods to language processing, with one early exception (Wirth, 1988, 1989).

Over the last four years, we have explored the application of ILP to NLP. In particular, we have developed and extended the CHILL system for acquiring natural language parsers (Zelle & Mooney, 1993b, 1994b, 1996a, 1996b; Zelle, 1995). [1] This system has learned both syntactic and "semantic" parsers that map a natural language database query directly into an executable Prolog query that will answer the question. Specifically, CHILL uses a training corpus of parsed sentences to induce heuristics that control and specialize an initial overly-general shift-reduce parser. CHILL has learned syntactic parsers for the ATIS corpus of airline information queries, and the results were comparable to current statistical methods. It has also acquired semantic parsers that process and answer English queries about a simple database on U.S. geography. The learned system was more accurate than a hand-built program for this application. The current paper reviews this previous research, attempts to draw some broader implications for ILP, and discusses our directions for future research.

## 2  Using ILP for Parser Acquisition

The primary task of most natural language systems is parsing. In this paper, the term "parser" should be interpreted broadly as any system for mapping a natural language string into an internal representation that is useful for some ultimate task, such as answering questions, translating to another natural language, summarizing, etc.. Parsing can range from producing a syntactic parse tree to mapping a sentence into unambiguous logical form. Figure 1 shows examples of three types of parses, a syntactic parse of a sentence from the ATIS corpus, a case-role (agent, patient, instrument) analysis of a simple sentence, and an executable logical form for a database query about U.S. geography. CHILL is able to learn parsers that produce each of these types of analyses.

---

[1] These and additional papers, software, and data are available through our web site at http://www.cs.utexas.edu/users/ml.

## Syntactic Parse Tree

Show me the flights that served lunch departing from San Francisco on April 25th.

```
s:[np:[*],
   vp:[show,
       np:[me],
       np:[np: [np:[the, flights],
                sbar:[that,
                      s:[np:[t],
                         vp:[served,
                             np:[lunch]]]]],
           vp:[departing,
               pp:[from,
                   np:[san, francisco]],
               pp:[on,
                   np:[april, '25th']]]]]]
```

## Case-Role Analysis

The man ate the pasta with the fork.

```
[ate,agt:[man,det:the],pat:[pasta,det:the],inst:[fork,det:the]]
```

## Executable Logical Form

What is the capital of the state with the largest population?

```
answer(C, (capital(S,C), largest(P, (state(S), population(S,P))))).
```

**Fig. 1.** Examples of Several Types of Parses

Frequently, language learning has been interpreted as simply acquiring a syntactic recognizer, a unary predicate that simply returns "yes" or "no" to the question: "Is this string a syntactically well-formed sentence in the language." However, such a syntactic recognizer is of limited use to an NLP system, except perhaps a limited grammar checker or a speech recognizer entertaining several word sequences as possible interpretations of an utterance. Language learning has also been interpreted as acquiring a set of production rules (e.g. S → NP VP) that define a formal grammar that recognizes the positive strings. This is more useful than a black-box recognizer since it allows a standard syntactic parser to produce parse trees that are useful for further processing. However, most natural language grammars assign multiple parses to sentences, most of which do not correspond to useful, meaningful interpretations. For example, any syntactic grammar of English will produce an analysis of "The man ate the pasta with a fork" that attaches the prepositional phrase "with a fork" to "pasta" as well as to "ate" despite the fact that people generally do not consume eating utensils (i.e. compare "The man ate the pasta with the cheese"). In fact, any standard syntactic English grammar will produce more than $2^n$ parses of sentences ending in $n$ prepositional phrases, most of which are usually spurious (Church & Patil, 1982).

A truly useful parser would produce a unique or limited number of parses that correspond to meaningful interpretations of a sentence that a human would actually consider. As a result, the emerging standard for judging a syntactic parser in computational linguistics is to measure its ability to produce a unique parse tree for a sentence that agrees with the parse tree assigned by a human judge (Periera & Shabes, 1992; Brill, 1993; Magerman, 1995; Collins, 1996; Goodman, 1996). This approach has been facilitated by the construction of large *treebanks* of human-produced syntactic parse trees for thousands of sentences, such as the Penn Treebank (Marcus, Santorini, & Marcinkiewicz, 1993) which consists primarily of analyses of sentences from the Wall Street Journal. If ILP is to be taken as a serious approach to constructing NLP systems, it must be tested on such problems and compared to the existing statistical methods.

## 2.1 Parser Acquisition by Generic ILP

A straight-forward application of ILP to parser acquisition would be to give a generic ILP system a corpus of sentences paired with representations as a set of positive examples of the predicate parse(Sentence, Representation) that takes a sentence as input and produces a syntactic or semantic analysis as output. However, it should be noticed that negative examples of sentence/representation pairs will generally not be available and that using a closed-world assumption to explicitly generate negative examples is intractable given the large space of possible sentences and representations. [2] In addition, it is generally agreed that when children acquire language they are exposed to little if any negative feedback (Bloom, 1994). Consequently, a method is needed for learning without explicit negative tuples. Fortunately, several ILP methods have been proposed for learning from only positive tuples when the target predicate represents a function (Bergadano & Gunetti, 1993; Quinlan, 1996) or when the training data is in some sense complete (De Raedt & Bruynooghe, 1993; Zelle, Thompson, Califf, & Mooney, 1995). If the goal is to construct a parser that produces a unique analysis for each sentence, then the parse/2 predicate can be treated as a function and any outputs other than the preferred analysis of a training sentence can be treated implicitly as negative examples. If it is desired that the parser produce several preferred outputs for truly ambiguous sentences, a more general assumption of *output completeness* can be used to specify that the analyses provided for each training sentence are the only correct ones and that all other potential outputs are implicitly negative (Zelle et al., 1995; Mooney & Califf, 1995). Using these techniques, a generic ILP system can be used to construct parsers from only positive sentence/representation pairs.

However, it seems unlikely that an uninformed ILP system could produce a program that generalizes well to novel sentences. Parsers are complex programs, the space of possible logic programs is very large, and providing the appropriate set of background predicates is difficult. It is generally agreed that human

---

[2] Explicit generation of negative examples using a closed-world assumption is performed automatically in many systems such as FOIL (Quinlan, 1990).

language acquisition exploits fairly restrictive constraints or biases in order to learn complex natural languages from limited data (Pinker, 1994). Of course, evaluating the success of this approach is, ultimately, an empirical question. In this paper, we compare the generic approach with a specific alternative, namely CHILL, which acquires parsers by specializing a general parsing architecture by learning control rules.

## 2.2 Parser Acquisition as Control-Rule Learning

Rather than using ILP techniques to directly learn a complete parser, CHILL begins with a well-defined parsing framework and uses ILP to learn control strategies within this framework. Treating language acquisition as a control learning problem is not in itself a new idea. Berwick (1985) used this approach to learn control rules for a Marcus-style deterministic parser (Marcus, 1980). When the system came to a parsing impasse, a new rule was created by inferring the correct parsing action and creating a new rule using certain properties of the current parser state as trigger conditions for its application. In a similar vein, Simmons and Yu (1992) controlled a simple shift-reduce parser by storing example contexts consisting of the syntactic categories of a fixed number of stack and input buffer locations. New sentences were parsed by matching the current parse state to the stored examples and performing the action performed in the best matching training context. Finally, Miikkulainen (1996) presents a connectionist approach to language acquisition that learns to control a neural-network parsing architecture that employs a *continuous stack*. Like the statistical approaches mentioned above, these control acquisition systems used feature-vector representations. CHILL is the first system to use ILP techniques rather than less flexible propositional approaches.

The input to CHILL is a set of training instances consisting of sentences paired with the desired parses. The output is a shift-reduce parser in Prolog that maps sentences into parses. Figure 2 shows the basic components of the system. CHILL employs a simple deterministic, shift-reduce parser with the current parse state represented by the content of the stack and the remaining portion of the input buffer (Tomita, 1986). Consider producing a case-role analysis (Fillmore, 1968) of the sentence: "The man ate the pasta." Parsing begins with an empty stack and an input buffer containing the entire sentence. At each step of the parse, either a word is shifted from the front of the input buffer onto the stack, or the top two elements on the stack are popped and combined to form a new element that is pushed back onto the stack. The sequence of actions and stack states for our simple example is shown Figure 3. The action notation *(x label)*, indicates that the stack items are combined via the role *label* with the item from stack position $x$ being the head.

In the Prolog parsing shell, parsing operators are program clauses that take the current stack and input buffer as input arguments and return a modified stack and buffer as outputs. During Parser Operator Generation, the training examples are analyzed to extract all of the general operators that are required to produce the the analyses. For example, an operator to reduce the

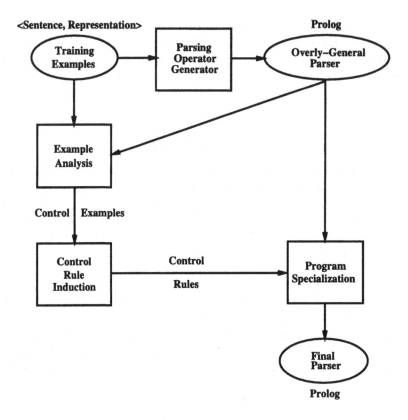

**Fig. 2.** The CHILL Architecture

| Action | Stack Contents |
|--------|----------------|
| | [] |
| (shift) | [the] |
| (shift) | [man, the] |
| (1 det) | [[man, det:the]] |
| (shift) | [ate, [man, det:the]] |
| (1 agt) | [[ate, agt:[man, det:the]]] |
| (shift) | [the, [ate, agt:[man, det:the]]] |
| (shift) | [pasta, the, [ate, agt:[man, det:the]]] |
| (1 det) | [[pasta, det:the], [ate, agt:[man, det:the]]] |
| (2 obj) | [[ate, obj:[pasta, det:the], agt:[man, det:the]]] |

**Fig. 3.** Shift-Reduce Case-Role Parsing of "The man ate the pasta."

top two items on the stack by attaching the second item as an agent of the top is represented by the clause op([Top,Second|Rest],In,[NewTop|Rest],In) :- reduce(Top,agt,Second,NewTop). The reduce/4 predicate simply combines Top and Second using the role agt to produce the new structure for the top of the stack. In general, one such operator clause is constructed for each case-role slot in the training examples. The resulting parser is severely over-general, as the operators contain no conditions specifying when they should be used; any operator may be applied to virtually any parse state resulting in many spurious parses.

In Example Analysis, the overly-general parser is used to parse the training examples to extract contexts in which the various parsing operators should and should not be employed. These contexts form sets of positive and negative *control examples* from which the appropriate control rules can be subsequently induced. A control example is a "snapshot" of the subgoal to which a particular operator clause may be applied in the course of parsing an example. Examples of correct operator applications are generated by finding the first correct parsing of each training pair with the overly-general parser; any subgoal to which an operator is applied in this successful parse becomes a positive control example for that operator.

For the agent operator shown above, the sentence "the man ate the pasta," would produce a single positive control example: op([ate,[man, det:the]], [the,pasta], A, B). This is the only subgoal to which this operator is applied in the correct parsing of the sentence. A and B are uninstantiated variables since they are outputs from the op/4 clause and are not yet bound at the time the clause is being applied. The sentence generates the following negative control examples for this operator:

op([man,the],[ate,the,pasta],A,B)
op([the,[ate,agt:[man,det:the]]],[pasta],A,B)
op([pasta,the,[ate,agt:[man,det:the]]],[],A,B)
op([[pasta,det:the],[ate,agt:[man,det:the]]],[],A,B)

Note that there are additional parse states such as op([], [the,man,ate,the, pasta], A, B) that do not appear in this list. This is because the agent clause of op/4 requires that its first argument be a list containing at least two items. Since the clause cannot match these other subgoals, they will not be included as negative examples.

The Control-Rule Induction phase uses a general ILP system to learn a *control rule* for each operator. This control rule comprises a definite-clause definition that covers the positive control examples for the operator but not the negative. CHILL's ILP algorithm combines elements from bottom-up techniques found in systems such as CIGOL (Muggleton & Buntine, 1988) and GOLEM (Muggleton & Feng, 1992) and top-down methods from systems like FOIL (Quinlan, 1990), and is able to invent new predicates in a manner analogous to CHAMP (Kijsirikul, Numao, & Shimura, 1992). Details of the CHILL induction algorithm together with experimental comparisons to GOLEM and FOIL are presented by Zelle and Mooney (1994a) and Zelle (1995). Given our simple example, a control rule that can be learned for the agent operator is

```
op([X,[Y,det:the]], [the|Z], A, B) :- animate(Y).
animate(man). animate(boy). animate(girl) ....
```

Here the system has invented a new predicate to help explain the parsing decisions. Of course, the new predicate would have a system generated name. It is called "animate" here for clarity. This rule may be roughly interpreted as stating: "the agent reduction applies when the stack contains two items, the second of which is a completed noun phrase whose head is animate." The output of the Control-Rule Induction phase is a suitable control-rule for each clause of **op/4**. These control rules are then passed on to the Program Specialization phase.

The final step, Program Specialization, "folds" the control information back into the overly-general parser. A control rule is easily incorporated into the overly-general program by unifying the head of an operator clause with the head of the control rule for the clause and adding the induced conditions to the clause body. The definitions of any invented predicates are simply appended to the program. Given the program clause:

```
op([Top,Second|Rest],In,[NewTop|Rest],In) :-
        reduce(Top,agt,Second,NewTop).
```

and the control rule:

```
op([X,[Y,det:the]], [the|Z], A, B) :- animate(Y).
animate(man). animate(boy). animate(girl) ....
```

the resulting clause is

```
op([A,[B,det:the]],[the|C],[D],[the|C]) :-
        animate(B), reduce(A,agt,[B,det:the],D).
animate(boy). animate(girl). animate(man)...
```

The final parser is just the overly-general parser with each operator clause suitably constrained. This specialized parser is guaranteed to produce all and only the preferred parses for each of the training examples.

## 3 Learning Syntactic Parsers for the ATIS Corpus

In section 2.1, we noted that the generic application of ILP to parser acquisition would induce a program directly from the examples of the **parse/2** relation. The advantage gained by the control-rule framework can be assessed by comparing CHILL to the performance achieved by CHILL's ILP component trying to learn the **parse/2** relation directly. These two approaches were compared by choosing a random set of test examples and learning and evaluating parsers trained on increasingly larger subsets of the remaining examples. Since only positive tuples of **parse/2** are available, the generic ILP approach employed a version of the induction algorithm that exploits the output-completeness assumption to learn in the context of *implicit* negative examples (Zelle et al., 1995) as outlined in section 2.1.

The experiment was carried out using a portion of the ATIS corpus from a preliminary version of the Penn Treebank. The first example in Figure 1 is taken from this corpus. We chose this particular data because it represents realistic input from human-computer interaction, and because it has been used in a number of other studies on automated parser acquisition (Brill, 1993; Periera & Shabes, 1992) that can serve as a basis for comparison to CHILL. The corpus contains 729 sentences with an average length of 10.3 words. The experiments reported here were performed using strings of lexical categories rather than words as input. Tagging words with their appropriate part of speech can be performed with high accuracy using various techniques (Church, 1988; Brill, 1995). Zelle and Mooney (1994a) and Zelle (1995) present results both with and without part-of-speech information.

Our initial experiments used a straightforward set of syntactic shift-reduce parsing operators (Zelle & Mooney, 1994b). However, better results were obtained by making the operators more specific, effectively increasing the number of operators, but reducing the complexity of the control-rule induction task for each operator. The basic idea was to index the operators based on some relevant portion of the parsing context. In these experiments, the operators were indexed according to the syntactic category at the front of the input buffer. For example, the general "shift" operator op(Stack, [Word|Words], [Word|Stack], Words) becomes multiple operators in slightly differing contexts such as:

```
op(Stack, [det|Ws], [det|Stack], Ws)
op(Stack, [nn|Ws], [nn|Stack], Ws)
op(Stack, [np|Ws], [np|Stack], Ws)
```

The operators in the initial parser were placed in order of increasing frequency of use as indicated by the training set. This allows the learning of control rules to take advantage of "default" effects where specific exceptions are learned first before control falls through to the more generally applicable operators.

Obviously, the most stringent measure of accuracy is the proportion of test sentences for which the produced parse tree exactly matches the human parse for the sentence. Sometimes, however, a parse can be useful even if it is not perfectly accurate; the treebank itself is not completely consistent in the handling of various constructs.

To better gauge the partial accuracy of the parser, we adopted a procedure for returning and scoring partial parses. If the parser runs into a "dead-end" while parsing a novel test sentence, the contents of the stack at the time of impasse is returned as a single, flat constituent labeled S. Since the parsing operators are ordered and the shift operator is invariably the most frequently used operator in the training set, shift serves as a sort of default when no reduction action applies. Therefore, at the time of impasse, all of the words of the sentence will be on the stack, and partial constituents will have been built. The contents of the stack therefore reflect the partial progress of the parser in finding constituents.

Partial scoring of trees is based on the overlap between the computed parse and the correct parse as recorded in the treebank. Two constituents are said to match if they span exactly the same words in the sentence. If constituents match and have the same label, then they are identical. The overlap between the computed parse and the correct parse is computed by trying to match each constituent of the computed parse with some constituent in the correct parse. If an identical constituent is found, the score is 1.0, a matching constituent with an incorrect label scores 0.5. The sum of the scores for all constituents is the overlap score for the parse. The accuracy of the parse is then computed as $Accuracy = (\frac{O}{Found} + \frac{O}{Correct})/2$ where $O$ is the overlap score, $Found$ is the number of constituents in the computed parse, and $Correct$ is the number of constituents in the correct tree. The result is an average of the proportion of the computed parse that is correct and the proportion of the correct parse that was actually found.

Another accuracy measure that has been used in evaluating systems that bracket the input sentence into unlabeled constituents, is the proportion of constituents in the parse that do not cross any constituent boundaries in the correct tree (Black & et. al., 1991; Goodman, 1996). We have computed the number of sentences with parses containing no crossing constituents, as well as the proportion of constituents that are non-crossing over all test sentences. This gives a basis of comparison with previous bracketing results, although it should be emphasized that CHILL is designed for the harder task of actually producing labeled parses, and is not optimized for bracketing.

Learning curves averaged over 5 random trials using independent testing sets of 204 sentences are shown in Figure 4. *Correct* is the percentage of test sentences with parses that matched the treebanked parse exactly. *Partial* is partial correct-

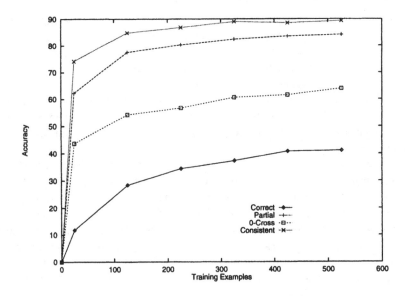

**Fig. 4.** CHILL ATIS Results

ness using the overlap metric. *0-Cross* is the proportion of test sentences having no constituents that cross constituent boundaries in the correct parsing. Finally, *Consistent* shows the overall percentage of constituents that are consistent with the treebank (i.e. cross no constituents in the correct parse).

The results are quite encouraging. After training on 525 sentences, CHILL constructed completely correct parses for 41% of the novel testing sentences. Using the partial scoring metric, CHILL's parses garnered an average accuracy of over 84%. The figures for 0-cross and consistent compare favorably with those reported in previous studies of automated bracketing for the ATIS corpus. Brill (1993) reports 60% and 91.12%, respectively. CHILL scores higher on the percentage of sentences with no crossing violations (64%) and slightly lower (90%) on the total percentage of non-crossing constituents. This is understandable as Brill's transformation learner tries to optimize the latter value, while CHILL's preference for complete sentence accuracy tends to improve the former.

Figure 5 shows the results for the partial accuracy metric for both CHILL and generic ILP. CHILL has an overwhelming advantage, achieving 84% accuracy compared to the 20% accuracy of generic ILP. Clearly, providing the shift-reduce parsing framework significantly eases the task of the inductive component. Trying to learn a complete parser from scratch is obviously much more difficult.

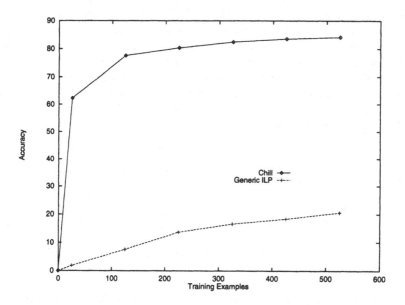

**Fig. 5.** CHILL vs. Generic ILP on the ATIS Corpus

# 4 Learning a Complete Natural-Language Interface

The previous experiment demonstrates that ILP techniques as implemented in CHILL can produce results comparable to other empirical approaches for constructing syntactic parsers using a standard treebank. However, syntactic parsing is only a small part of the larger problem of natural language understanding. Consequently, parsers are usually compared on the "artificial" metrics presented above. Unfortunately, it is unclear how well these metrics translate to performance on actual language processing tasks.

As argued in the introduction, one of the major attractions of the ILP approach is its flexibility. The type of representation produced by CHILL's parsers is controlled only by the parsing operators employed. In an effort to assess the utility of CHILL in constructing a complete natural language application, an operator framework was devised that allows the parsing of natural language queries directly into executable Prolog queries. The input to CHILL in this case task consists of sentences paired with executable database queries, where the query language used is a logical form similar to the meaning representation typically produced by logic grammars (Warren & Pereira, 1982; Abramson & Dahl, 1989). The semantics of the representation is grounded in a query interpreter that executes queries and retrieves relevant information from the database.

The chosen database concerns United States geography for which a handcoded natural-language interface already exists. The system, called *Geobase* was supplied as a sample application with a commercial Prolog, specifically Turbo Prolog 2.0 (Borland International, 1988). This system provides a database already coded in Prolog and also serves as a convenient benchmark against which CHILL's performance can be compared. The database contains about 800 Prolog facts asserting relational tables for basic information about U.S. states, including: population, area, capital city, neighboring states, major rivers, major cities, and highest and lowest points along with their elevation. Figure 6 shows some sample questions and associated query representations in addition to the example already presented in Figure 1.

What is the highest point of the state with the largest area?
`answer(P, (high-point(S,P), largest(A, (state(S), area(S,A)))))`.

What are the major cities in Kansas?
`answer(C, (major(C), city(C), loc(C,S), equal(S,stateid(kansas))))`.

**Fig. 6.** Sample Database Queries

The language data for the experiment was gathered by asking uninformed subjects to generate sample questions for the system. An analyst then paired the questions with appropriate logical queries to generate an experimental corpus of 250 examples. Experiments were then performed by training on subsets of the corpus and evaluating the resulting parser on the unseen examples. The parser was judged to have parsed a new sentence correctly when the generated query produced exactly the same final answer from the database as the query provided by the analyst. Hence, the metric is a true measure of the performance for a complete database-query application in this domain.

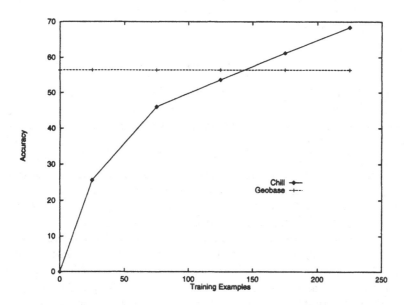

**Fig. 7.** CHILL Accuracy on Database Query Domain

Figure 7 shows the accuracy of CHILL's parsers over a 10 trial average. The line labeled "Geobase" shows the average accuracy of the hand-coded system. The curves show that CHILL outperforms the existing system when trained on 175 or more examples. In the best trial, CHILL induced a parser from 225 examples comprising 1100 lines of Prolog code in approximately 25 minutes on a SPARCstation 5 and achieved 84% accuracy in answering novel queries. Most of the "errors" CHILL makes on novel questions are due to an inability to parse the query rather than generation of an incorrect answer. After 225 training examples, only slightly over 2% of novel questions on average are actually answered incorrectly. Zelle and Mooney (1996b) and Zelle (1995) provide additional details on the Geobase application and results.

## 5   Lessons and Challenges for ILP

Applying ILP to natural language processing has highlighted several broader issues in developing and evaluating ILP systems. Natural language problems present a number of interesting challenges for ILP systems, many of which may have counterparts in other complex applications. In addition to parser acquisition, we have also applied ILP to natural language morphology, specifically to generating the past tense of English verbs. English past-tense generation has become a benchmark problem in the computational modeling of human language acquisition (Rumelhart & McClelland, 1986; Ling & Marinov, 1993). Mooney and Califf (1995) showed that a particular ILP system, FOIDL, could learn this transformation more effectively than previous neural-network and decision-tree methods. This section discusses several issues in ILP that our work on CHILL and FOIDL have uncovered.

## 5.1 Learning to Control Existing Programs

Inducing a complex logic program completely from examples is a difficult task. The standard way of easing the problem has been to supply an ILP system with relevant background knowledge (subroutines) and induce only the top-level clauses (Lavrač & Džeroski, 1994). Another approach has been to revise an existing program that is partially correct (De Raedt, 1992; Richards & Mooney, 1995). CHILL illustrates a third approach: specializing an existing program by learning control rules that restrict the application of specific clauses.

Induction of control rules has a fairly long history in learning and problem solving (Mitchell, 1983; Langley, 1985) and more recent work has applied ILP to this task (Cohen, 1990; Leckie & Zuckerman, 1993; Zelle & Mooney, 1993a; Estlin & Mooney, 1996). These systems focus on learning control rules that improve the *efficiency* of an existing program, such as transforming an $O(n!)$ naive sorting program into an $O(n^2)$ insertion sort (Zelle & Mooney, 1993a). CHILL illustrates that this approach can also be used to improve the *accuracy* of an initial (extremely) overly-general program. Other problems may also lend themselves to providing or constructing an initial overly-general program that can be appropriately specialized by inducing control rules.

## 5.2 Improving Generic ILP Systems

Initial attempts to apply existing ILP systems such as FOIL and GOLEM to parser construction and past-tense generation met with important difficulties. Limitations such as requiring extensional background and negative examples, lack of predicate invention, inability to handle functions or cuts (!), and search limitations (e.g. local minima, combinatorial explosions) prevented existing systems from performing well or even being applicable to these problems. Consequently, we had to develop new ILP systems such as CHILLIN (Zelle & Mooney, 1994a) and FOIDL (Mooney & Califf, 1995) to overcome these limitations by using techniques that integrate bottom-up and top-down search, incorporate predicate invention, eliminate the need for explicit negative examples, and allow restricted use of cuts. Existing techniques had to be improved and integrated in order to build ILP systems that could handle natural language problems.

Consequently, there is still an need for flexible, robust, efficient ILP systems that incorporate a range of abilities and features. Generic ILP systems are still unable to handle many large, complex problems such as those that arise in NLP. Statistical language learning systems have been trained on real corpora of up to

40,000 sentences (Magerman, 1995; Collins, 1996). Current ILP techniques are incapable of handling such large problems.

## 5.3 Training and Testing for Programs that Generate Output

Most ILP systems have been tested on their accuracy of classifying ground tuples as positive or negative examples of the target predicate. However, many applications such as parsing and morphological analysis require computing outputs rather than testing ground tuples. In these applications, ILP systems need to be tested on their ability to generate correct outputs from novel inputs.

With respect to training, an ILP system needs to guarantee that it will generate a program that will terminate and generate ground outputs when it is queried with the outputs uninstantiated. Most ILP systems cannot provide these guarantees; those that guarantee termination (Quinlan, 1990) do not guarantee ground outputs. The use of an output completeness assumption and implicit negatives is one way to guarantee ground outputs (Zelle et al., 1995).

With respect to testing, experiments need to specifically evaluate the ability of the learned program to generate correct outputs given only novel inputs. Unlike evaluations of other ILP systems, experiments with CHILL and FOIDL specifically tested this ability. Also, in many applications, exactly matching the output specified in the test data may not be the best measure of performance. Induced programs may generate complex outputs that are more or less similar to the "correct" output (as with parse trees) or there may be multiple correct outputs that are semantically equivalent (as with database queries). Therefore, one may want to measure various types of partial correctness of outputs, such as the number of bracketing errors for parse trees, or use some other procedure for judging the correctness of the output, such as whether it produces the same answer from a database as the "correct" output. In general, appropriate testing of logic programs generated for complex applications may require measuring something other than their accuracy at classifying ground tuples.

## 6 Ongoing Research

Our current research concerns using learning techniques such as ILP to develop a larger natural language application. We hope to field an application on the world-wide-web that will attract a significant number of users and therefore serve as an automatic source of larger amounts of language data. The specific application we are considering is a system that can process the computer job announcements posted to the USENET newsgroup misc.jobs.offered, extract a database of available jobs, and then answer natural language queries such as "What jobs are available in California for C++ programmers paying over $100,0000 a year?"

This application will involve using learning techniques to build two major components. The first is an *information extraction* system that processes individual messages and extracts specific pieces of information for the database such as the type of job, the location, the salary, the starting date, etc.. Such natural-language information extraction systems have been hand-built as part of ARPA's MUC (Message Understanding Conference) program (Lehnert & Sundheim, 1991; ARPA, 1993) and several projects have used learning techniques to automatically acquire rules for this task (Riloff, 1993; Soderland & Lehnert, 1994; Huffman, 1996). We plan to develop a system that uses ideas from ILP to learn patterns for extracting information from newsgroup postings. Examples of messages paired with filled templates will be used to train the system, and the learned rules will then be used to extract a database of information from the newsgroup postings.

The second major component is a query system for answering natural-language questions about the database built by the information extraction module. CHILL will be used to learn this component by training on sample pairs of English/Prolog job queries in the same manner used to construct the geography database interface discussed in section 4. After building a prototype system from an initial training set, we plan to put it on line and collect additional query examples. Questions that the system cannot parse will be collected, annotated, and used to retrain the system to improve its coverage. In this way, learning techniques can be used to automatically improve and extend a system based on data collected during actual use.

## 7 Conclusions

Constructing natural language systems is a complex task, and machine learning is becoming an increasingly important tool in aiding their development. This paper has summarized research on employing inductive logic programming to learn natural language parsers, and presented results illustrating that such methods can successfully learn syntactic parsers as well as complete natural language interfaces. In addition, the ILP-constructed systems were shown to perform as well as if not better than existing hand-built and statistically-trained systems.

Unfortunately, current learning research in computational linguistics is focused on alternative statistical methods. Convincing computational linguists of the utility of ILP for constructing NLP systems will not be an easy task. However, by clearly demonstrating the ability of ILP systems to easily and flexibly build real systems from large amounts of real language data without laborious feature engineering, a convincing case for ILP can be made. The research reviewed in this paper is a first step in this direction, and will hopefully encourage and assist additional research in the area.

**Acknowledgments** Much thanks to John Zelle, CHILL's primary developer. This research was supported by the National Science Foundation under grant IRI-9310819.

## References

Abramson, H., & Dahl, V. (1989). *Logic Grammars*. Springer-Verlag, New York.

Allen, J. F. (1995). *Natural Language Understanding (2nd Ed.)*. Benjamin/Cummings, Menlo Park, CA.

Anoe, C., & Bennett, S. W. (1995). Evaluating automated and manual acquisition of anaphora resolution strategies. In *Proceedings of the 33rd Annual Meeting of the Association for Computational Linguistics*, pp. 122–129 Cambridge, MA.

ARPA (Ed.). (1993). *Proceedings of the Fifth DARPA Message Understanding Evaluation and Conference*, San Mateo, CA. Morgan Kaufman.

Bergadano, F., & Gunetti, D. (1993). An interactive system to learn functional logic programs. In *Proceedings of the Thirteenth International Joint Conference on Artificial Intelligence*, pp. 1044–1049 Chambery, France.

Berwick, B. (1985). *The Acquisition of Syntactic Knowledge*. MIT Press, Cambridge, MA.

Black, E., & et. al. (1991). A procedure for quantitatively comparing the syntactic coverage of English grammars. In *Proceedings of the Fourth DARPA Speech and Natural Language Workshop*, pp. 306–311.

Bloom, P. (1994). Overview: Controversies in language acquisition. In Bloom, P. (Ed.), *Language Acquisition: Core Readings*, pp. 5–48. MIT Press, Cambridge, MA.

Borland International (1988). *Turbo Prolog 2.0 Reference Guide*. Borland International, Scotts Valley, CA.

Brill, E. (1993). Automatic grammar induction and parsing free text: A transformation-based approach. In *Proceedings of the 31st Annual Meeting of the Association for Computational Linguistics*, pp. 259–265 Columbus, Ohio.

Brill, E. (1995). Transformation-based error-driven learning and natural language processing: A case study in part-of-speech tagging. *Computational Linguistics*, *21*(4), 543–565.

Brill, E., & Church, K. (Eds.). (1996). *Proceedings of the Conference on Empirical Methods in Natural Language Processing*. University of Pennsylvania, Philadelphia, PA.

Charniak, E. (1993). *Statistical Language Learning*. MIT Press.

Church, K. (1988). A stochastic parts program and noun phrase parser for unrestricted text. In *Proceedings of the Second Conference on Applied Natural Language Processing*. Association for Computational Linguistics.

Church, K., & Mercer, R. L. (1993). Introduction to the special issue on computational linguistics using large corpora. *Computational Linguistics*, *19*(1), 1–24.

Church, K., & Patil, R. (1982). Coping with syntactic ambiguity or how to put the block in the box on the table. *American Journal of Computational Linguistics*, *8*(3-4), 139–149.

Cohen, W. W. (1990). Learning approximate control rules of high utility. In *Proceedings of the Seventh International Conference on Machine Learning*, pp. 268–276 Austin, TX.

Collins, M. J. (1996). A new statistical parser based on bigram lexical dependencies. In *Proceedings of the 34th Annual Meeting of the Association for Computational Linguistics*, pp. 184–191 Santa Cruz, CA.

De Raedt, L. (1992). *Interactive Theory Revision: An Inductive Logic Programming Approach*. Academic Press, New York, NY.

De Raedt, L., & Bruynooghe, M. (1993). A theory of clausal discovery. In *Proceedings of the Thirteenth International Joint Conference on Artificial Intelligence*, pp. 1058–1063 Chambery, France.

Estlin, T. A., & Mooney, R. J. (1996). Multi-strategy learning of search control for partial-order planning. In *Proceedings of the Thirteenth National Conference on Artificial Intelligence* Portland, OR.

Fillmore, C. J. (1968). The case for case. In Bach, E., & Harms, R. T. (Eds.), *Universals in Linguistic Theory*. Holt, Reinhart and Winston, New York.

Goodman, J. (1996). Parsing algorithms and metrics. In *Proceedings of the 34th Annual Meeting of the Association for Computational Linguistics*, pp. 177–183 Santa Cruz, CA.

Huffman, S. B. (1996). Learning information extraction patterns from examples. In Wermter, S., Riloff, E., & Scheler, G. (Eds.), *Connectionist, Statistical, and Symbolic Approaches to Learning for Natural Language Processing*, pp. 246–260. Springer, Berlin.

Kijsirikul, B., Numao, M., & Shimura, M. (1992). Discrimination-based constructive induction of logic programs. In *Proceedings of the Tenth National Conference on Artificial Intelligence*, pp. 44–49 San Jose, CA.

Langley, P. (1985). Learning to search: From weak methods to domain specific heuristics. *Cognitive Science, 9*(2), 217–260.

Lavrač, N., & Džeroski, S. (Eds.). (1994). *Inductive Logic Programming: Techniques and Applications*. Ellis Horwood.

Leckie, C., & Zuckerman, I. (1993). An inductive approach to learning search control rules for planning. In *Proceedings of the Thirteenth International Joint Conference on Artificial Intelligence*, pp. 1100–1105 Chamberry, France.

Lehnert, W., & Sundheim, B. (1991). A performance evaluation of text-analysis technologies. *AI Magazine, 12*(3), 81–94.

Ling, C. X., & Marinov, M. (1993). Answering the connectionist challenge: A symbolic model of learning the past tense of English verbs. *Cognition, 49*(3), 235–290.

Magerman, D. M. (1995). Statistical decision-tree models for parsing. In *Proceedings of the 33rd Annual Meeting of the Association for Computational Linguistics*, pp. 276–283 Cambridge, MA.

Marcus, M. (1980). *A Theory of Syntactic Recognition for Natural Language*. MIT Press, Cambridge, MA.

Marcus, M., Santorini, B., & Marcinkiewicz, M. (1993). Building a large annotated corpus of English: The Penn treebank. *Computational Linguistics, 19*(2), 313–330.

Miikkulainen, R. (1996). Subsymbolic case-role analysis of sentences with embedded clauses. *Cognitive Science, 20*(1), 47–73.

Miikkulainen, R. (1993). *Subsymbolic Natural Language Processing: An Integrated Model of Scripts, Lexicon, and Memory*. MIT Press, Cambridge, MA.

Mitchell, T. (1983). Learning and problem solving. In *Proceedings of the Eighth International Joint Conference on Artificial Intelligence*, pp. 1139–1151 Karlsruhe, West Germany.

Mooney, R. J., & Califf, M. E. (1995). Induction of first-order decision lists: Results on learning the past tense of English verbs. *Journal of Artificial Intelligence Research, 3*, 1–24.

Muggleton, S., & Buntine, W. (1988). Machine invention of first-order predicates by inverting resolution. In *Proceedings of the Fifth International Conference on Machine Learning*, pp. 339–352 Ann Arbor, MI.

Muggleton, S., & Feng, C. (1992). Efficient induction of logic programs. In Muggleton, S. (Ed.), *Inductive Logic Programming*, pp. 281–297. Academic Press, New York.

Periera, F., & Shabes, Y. (1992). Inside-outside reestimation from partially bracketed corpora. In *Proceedings of the 30th Annual Meeting of the Association for Computational Linguistics*, pp. 128–135 Newark, Delaware.

Pinker, S. (Ed.). (1994). *The Language Instinct: How the Mind Creates Language*. William Morrow, N.Y.

Quinlan, J. R. (1996). Learning first-order definitions of functions. *Journal of Artificial Intelligence Research, to appear*.

Quinlan, J. (1990). Learning logical definitions from relations. *Machine Learning, 5*(3), 239–266.

Reilly, R. G., & Sharkey, N. E. (Eds.). (1992). *Connectionist Approaches to Natural Language Processing*. Lawrence Erlbaum and Associates, Hilldale, NJ.

Richards, B. L., & Mooney, R. J. (1995). Automated refinement of first-order Horn-clause domain theories. *Machine Learning, 19*(2), 95–131.

Riloff, E. (1993). Automatically constructing a dictionary for information extraction tasks. In *Proceedings of the Eleventh National Conference on Artificial Intelligence*, pp. 811–816.

Rumelhart, D. E., & McClelland, J. (1986). On learning the past tense of English verbs. In Rumelhart, D. E., & McClelland, J. L. (Eds.), *Parallel Distributed Processing, Vol. II*, pp. 216–271. MIT Press, Cambridge, MA.

Simmons, R. F., & Yu, Y. (1992). The acquisition and use of context dependent grammars for English. *Computational Linguistics, 18*(4), 391–418.

Soderland, S., & Lehnert, W. (1994). Wrap-Up: A trainable discourse module for information extraction. *Journal of Artificial Intelligence Research, 2*, 131–158.

Tomita, M. (1986). *Efficient Parsing for Natural Language*. Kluwer Academic Publishers, Boston.

Waibel, A., & Lee, K. F. (Eds.). (1990). *Readings in Speech Recognition*. Morgan Kaufmann, San Mateo,CA.

Warren, D., & Pereira, F. (1982). An efficient easily adaptable system for interpreting natural language queries. *American Journal of Computational Linguistics, 8*(3-4), 110–122.

Wermter, S., Riloff, E., & Scheler, G. (Eds.). (1996). *Connectionist, Statistical, and Symbolic Approaches to Learning for Natural Language Processing*. Springer Verlag, Berlin.

Wirth, R. (1988). Learning by failure to prove. In *Proceedings of the Third European Working Session on Learning*, pp. 237–251. Pitman.

Wirth, R. (1989). Completing logic programs by inverse resolution. In *Proceedings of the Fourth European Working Session on Learning*, pp. 239–250. Pitman.

Zelle, J. M. (1995). *Using Inductive Logic Programming to Automate the Construction of Natural Language Parsers*. Ph.D. thesis, University of Texas, Austin, TX.

Zelle, J. M., & Mooney, R. J. (1993a). Combining FOIL and EBG to speed-up logic programs. In *Proceedings of the Thirteenth International Joint Conference on Artificial Intelligence*, pp. 1106–1111 Chambery, France.

Zelle, J. M., & Mooney, R. J. (1993b). Learning semantic grammars with constructive inductive logic programming. In *Proceedings of the Eleventh National Conference on Artificial Intelligence*, pp. 817–822 Washington, D.C.

Zelle, J. M., & Mooney, R. J. (1994a). Combining top-down and bottom-up methods in inductive logic programming. In *Proceedings of the Eleventh International Conference on Machine Learning*, pp. 343–351 New Brunswick, NJ.

Zelle, J. M., & Mooney, R. J. (1994b). Inducing deterministic Prolog parsers from treebanks: A machine learning approach. In *Proceedings of the Twelfth National Conference on Artificial Intelligence*, pp. 748–753 Seattle, WA.

Zelle, J. M., & Mooney, R. J. (1996a). Comparative results on using inductive logic programming for corpus-based parser construction. In Wermter, S., Riloff, E., & Scheler, G. (Eds.), *Connectionist, Statistical, and Symbolic Approaches to Learning for Natural Language Processing*, pp. 355–369. Springer, Berlin.

Zelle, J. M., & Mooney, R. J. (1996b). Learning to parse database queries using inductive logic programming. In *Proceedings of the Thirteenth National Conference on Artificial Intelligence* Portland, OR.

Zelle, J. M., Thompson, C., Califf, M. E., & Mooney, R. J. (1995). Inducing logic programs without explicit negative examples. In *Proceedings of the Fifth International Workshop on Inductive Logic Programming*, pp. 403–416 Leuven, Belgium.

# Experiments and Applications

# An Initial Experiment into Stereochemistry-Based Drug Design Using Inductive Logic Programming

**Stephen Muggleton**
**David Page**
**Ashwin Srinivasan**
Oxford University Computing Laboratory
Wolfson Building
Parks Road
Oxford, OX1 3QD
United Kingdom

**Abstract.** Previous applications of Inductive Logic Programming to drug design have not addressed stereochemistry, or the three-dimensional aspects of molecules. While some success is possible without consideration of stereochemistry, researchers within the pharmaceutical industry consider stereochemistry to be central to most drug design problems. This paper reports on an experimental application of the ILP system P-Progol to stereochemistry-based drug design. The experiment tests whether P-Progol can identify the structure responsible for the activity of ACE (angiotensin-converting enzyme) inhibitors from 28 positive examples, that is, from 28 molecules that display the activity of ACE inhibition. ACE inhibitors are a widely-used form of medication for the treatment of hypertension. It should be stressed that this structure was already known prior to the experiment and therefore is not a new discovery; the experiment was proposed by a researcher within the pharmaceutical industry to test the applicability of ILP to stereochemistry-based drug design. While the result of the experiment is quite positive, one challenge remains before ILP can be applied to a multitude of drug design problems.

## 1 Introduction

Previous applications of inductive logic programming (ILP) to molecular biology and organic chemistry (for example, [2, 3]) have used either a "one-dimensional" (1D) attribute-value representation or a "two-dimensional" (2D) atom and bond representation of molecules. Consequently these applications did not take into account *stereochemistry*, or the three-dimensional aspects of molecules. Stereochemistry is central to many problems in molecular biology and organic chemistry, including drug design. Because drugs generally are small organic molecules that "dock" into specific locations on proteins, a drug derives its behaviour from a substructure of the molecule with a specific geometry. The substructure responsible for the molecule's activity is referred to within the pharmaceutical industry as a *pharmacophore*. The prediction of a pharmacophore is an instance of a more general problem, called "structure-activity prediction".

This paper describes an experiment into the stereochemistry-based application of ILP to pharmacophore prediction. In this experiment, the ILP system P-Progol is given three-dimensional representations of molecules that act as "ACE inhibitors"—one of the main types of medication for hypertension—and it is asked to find a substructure common to all these molecules.[1] The molecular substructures sought are described in terms of atoms and the geometric relationships among them, rather than their bonding relationships.

We wish to emphasize that a generally-accepted pharmacophore for ACE inhibition was known prior to the performance of this experiment, and therefore the contribution of this experiment is not to provide new knowledge about ACE inhibition. Rather, this experiment was proposed by a researcher within the pharmaceutical industry (who prefers to remain anonymous) as a test of the applicability of ILP to stereochemistry-based pharmacophore prediction.

While this paper is primarily an "application" paper, it also describes an extension to the ILP system P-Progol and thus might be considered an "implementation" paper as well. The extension provides the user with more control over P-Progol's search, so that the search can be based on general knowledge about the application domain. Without this extension the application of P-Progol described in the paper would have been infeasible, in part due to time complexity. The extension is relatively general-purpose—we currently are using it within the domain of protein secondary-structure prediction as well—and further extensible in a way suggested in Section 5.

The paper is organized as follows. Section 2 reviews previous applications of ILP to structure-activity prediction using 1D and 2D representations. Section 3 discusses the issues involved in using a 3D representation. Section 4 describes the extension of P-Progol to allow it to use a 3D representation efficiently; this section also describes the experiment and results. Section 5 presents conclusions from the experiment and proposes a further extension to P-Progol to help meet a remaining challenge of drug design applications.

## 2  Background

### 2.1  Learning with 1D representation

The first major success in applying ILP to structure-activity prediction was reported in [2]. The ILP program Golem [7] was applied to the problem of modelling the structure-activity relationships of trimethoprim analogues binding to

---

[1] The reader may question why researchers do not simply look at the protein docking site in question and deduce the pharmacophore from the structure of the docking site. The reason is that the three-dimensional structure of a docking site is difficult to determine; the ability to determine the structures of docking sites is a motivation for the well-known "protein folding problem", or the problem of predicting protein secondary and tertiary structure.

dihydrofolate reductase. The training data consisted of 44 trimethoprim analogues and their observed inhibition of *Escherichia coli* dihydrofolate reductase. A further 11 compounds were used as unseen test data. Golem obtained rules that were statistically more accurate on the training data and also better on the test data than a previously published linear regression model. Figure 1 illustrates the family of analogues used in the study.

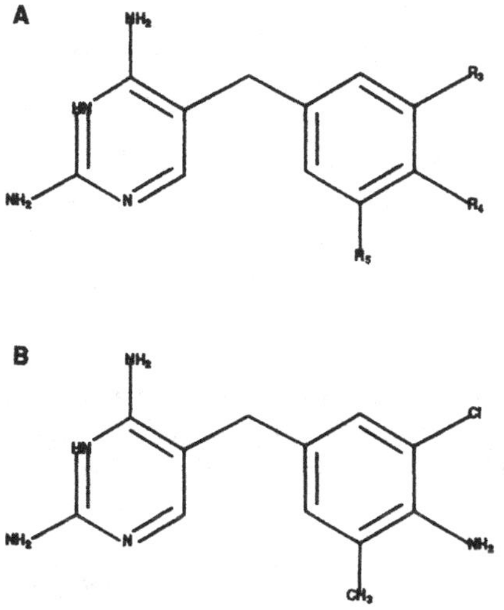

**Fig. 1.** The family of analogues in the first ILP study. A) Template of 2,4-diamino-5(substituted-benzyl)pyrimidines R3, R4, and R5 are the three possible substitution positions. B) Example compound: $3 - Cl$, $4 - NH_2$, $5 - CH_3$

## 2.2 Learning with 2D representation

In a more recent study [3] the 2D bond-and-atom molecular descriptions of 229 aromatic and heteroaromatic nitro compounds taken from [1] were given to the ILP system Progol [6]. It is of considerable interest to the pharmaceutical industry to determine which molecular features result in compounds having mutagenic activity. Besides directing the development of less hazardous new compounds, it also has applicability in areas such as antimicrobial agents where it is not possible to determine mutagenicity using standard tests (this is because of the toxicity of the agents to test organisms). The compounds studied were considerably more diverse than any studied previously (see Figure 2), emphasising the need to determine common properties at a structural level. The study was confined to the problem of obtaining structural descriptions that discriminate drugs with positive mutagenicity from those which have zero or negative mutagenicity. **Training and test data.** Of the 229 drugs, 139 drugs display positive levels of mutagenicity (as reported in [1]). The drugs were randomly divided into training

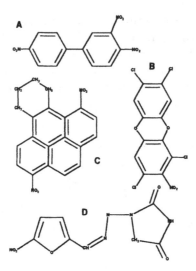

**Fig. 2.** Examples of the diverse set of aromatic and heteroaromatic nitro compounds used in the mutagenesis study. A) 3,4,4'-trinitrobiphenyl B) 2-nitro-1,3,7,8-tetrachlorodibenzo-1,4-dioxin C) 1,6,-dinitro-9,10,11,12-tetrahydrobenzo[e]pyrene D) nitrofurantoin

(160 drugs) and testing sets (69 drugs). Drugs with positive mutagenicity were labelled active, and the rest inactive. The aim of the learning process was to obtain properties of drugs in the 'active' class.

A set of 8 optimally compact rules were automatically discovered by Progol. These rules suggested 3 previously unknown features leading to mutagenicity. Figure 3 shows the structural properties described by the rules in the Progol theory. The description of these patterns are as follows. 1) Atom type 195 flags 3 fused benzyl rings. The drug also has a pair of atoms connected by a single bond, and a pair connected by an aromatic bond. 2) The drug has 2 pairs of atoms connected by a single bond, and a pair connected by an aromatic bond as shown. 3) An aromatic carbon with a partial charge of $+0.191$ is only possible if the drug has three $NO_2$ groups substituted onto a biphenyl template (two benzine rings connected by a single bond).

An interesting feature is that in the original regression analysis of the drugs by [1], a special 'indicator variable' was provided to flag the existence of three or more fused rings (this variable was then seen to play a vital role in the regression equation). The first rule (drug pattern 1 in Figure 3), expressing precisely this fact, was discovered by Progol without access to any specialist chemical knowledge. Further, the regression analysis suggested that electron-attracting elements conjugated with nitro groups enhance mutagenicity. A particular form of this pattern was also discovered by Progol (drug pattern 3 in Figure 3).

Previous published results for the same data [1] used linear discriminant techniques and hand-crafted features. The ILP technique allowed prediction of 49 cases which were statistical outliers not predictable by the linear discriminant

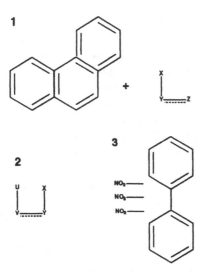

**Fig. 3.** Structural properties discovered by Progol

algorithm. Combination of rules from linear discrimination and ILP produced a 5% increase (80-85%) in accuracy over linear discrimination alone. In addition the Progol-generated rules are small and simple enough to provide insight into the molecular basis of mutagenicity.

# 3 Incorporating Stereochemistry into the ILP Approach to Structure-Activity Prediction

We have seen that ILP has been applied successfully to structure-activity prediction problems using 1D and 2D representations of both the molecules and the hypotheses. Nevertheless, because of the importance of stereochemistry in determining molecular activity, widespread successful application of ILP to structure-activity prediction—in particular to pharmacophore prediction—requires a 3D representation. There are three issues to consider in changing to a 3D representation, which correspond to the basic representational issues in ILP: the representation of molecules (examples), the representation pharmacophores (hypotheses), and the choice of appropriate background knowledge.

## 3.1 Molecule Representation

We have adopted a representation of molecules that is similar to the 2D representation used for mutagenicity, except that a fact describing an atom within a molecule also gives $x$, $y$, and $z$ coordinates of the molecule. Atoms are represented by Prolog-style facts, or ground atomic formulae, such as

$$atm(m1, a3, o, 2, 7.026500, -2.042500, 0.023200)$$

The first three arguments of this fact assert that molecule $m1$ has an oxygen atom $a3$. The fourth argument specifies that the orbitals of the atom $a3$ are "sp2-hybridized". A discussion of orbital hybridization can be found in any standard chemistry textbook; we will gloss over it in the remainder of this paper because in the end it did not play a role in the results presented here. The remaining arguments provide the novel information for use by an ILP system. They state that atom $a3$ in molecule $m1$ is at the coordinate position $\langle 7.026500, -2.042500, 0.023200 \rangle$. Given the coordinates for each atom in the molecule, via facts of this form, it is possible to compute the distances and angles among the various atoms in a molecule. In fact, to completely specify the geometry of any subset of three to five atoms within a molecule, it is enough to describe the distances between all pairs of atoms in the subset.[2] For example, given three atoms in a triangle, the triangle is completely specified by the distances between all pairs of atoms.

In addition to facts about atoms, bonds are described via facts of the form

$$bond(m1, a2, a3, 2)$$

This fact states that molecule $m1$ contains a bond between atoms $a2$ and $a3$; the fourth argument specifies that this bond is a double bond. It will be seen later that bond information is used only for determining whether an atom is a "hydrogen donor". Hydrogen donors are hydrogen atoms that are not bonded to carbon atoms.

Information of the form described above—most notably the 3D information in the form of $x,y,z$ coordinate positions for atoms—can be generated by any of a number of molecular modelling packages, such as "Sybyl" by Tripos or "Cerius II" by MSI. Converting the output of one of these programs into ground atomic formulae of first-order logic can be accomplished by a simple C program.[3]

For the experiment described in this paper, the data consisted of descriptions of 28 molecules which differ dramatically from one another but all of which act as ACE inhibitors; this set of molecules is presented in [4]. Molecular descriptions were generated by a researcher within the pharmaceutical industry, using Tripos' Sybyl program. They were converted into Prolog form by a simple C program written by the authors. The authors expect to make the data publicly available in the near future.

## 3.2 Pharmacophore Representation

Our use of a 3D representation was prompted by discussions with experts from a leading pharmaceutical company. According to one expert in particular, a pharmacophore typically consists of three to five "pieces", where a piece is a hydrogen donor (hydrogen atom bonded to a non-carbon), a hydrogen acceptor (oxygen,

---

[2] For more than five atoms, not all distances are needed, but we are interested only in subsets of at most five atoms.

[3] We are happy to make available such a program for use with "Sybyl" (MOL2 format), on request.

sulphur, or nitrogen as part of an amide structure), or a functional group (e.g., benzene ring, carboxylic acid, etc.) believed to be potentially relevant to the activity in question. For example, for ACE inhibitors it has long been known that in addition to hydrogen acceptors and hydrogen donors, a particularly effective zinc-binding functional group is necessary (there are several possible such groups).

In addition to the "pieces", a pharmacophore description includes the distances between each pair of pieces. These distances completely specify the geometry of the pharmacophore. Of course, some small variation in distances is acceptable. The typical acceptable level of variation is 0.5 to 1.0 Angstrom. A pharmacophore is completely specified by a description of the pieces (such as hydrogen donor, hydrogen acceptor, or zinc binding site) and the distances among them, with a tolerance level for the distances. For example, the following is a description of a four-piece pharmacophore.

```
Molecule A is an ACE inhibitor if:
    molecule A contains a zinc-binder B, and
    molecule A contains a hydrogen acceptor C, and
    the distance between B and C is 7.899 +/- 0.750 Angstroms, and
    molecule A contains a hydrogen acceptor D, and
    the distance between B and D is 8.475 +/- 0.750 Angstroms, and
    the distance between C and D is 2.133 +/- 0.750 Angstroms, and
    molecule A contains a hydrogen acceptor E, and
    the distance between B and E is 4.891 +/- 0.750 Angstroms, and
    the distance between C and E is 3.114 +/- 0.750 Angstroms, and
    the distance between D and E is 3.753 +/- 0.750 Angstroms.
```

In fact, the pharmacophore above is the output of P-Progol (with a "pretty-print" option to print pharmacophores in English form) for the ACE inhibitor data, as described in the next section. In standard Prolog syntax, the description is as follows.

```
active(A) :-
    zinc-inhibitor(A,B), hacceptor(A,C), dist(A,C,B,7.899,0.750),
    hacceptor(A,D), dist(A,D,B,8.475,0.750),
    dist(A,D,C,2.133,0.750), haccecptor(A,E),
    dist(A,E,B,4.891,0.750), dist(A,E,C,3.114,0.750),
    dist(A,E,D,3.753,0.750).
```

Notice that the body of this clause has ten literals. Ordinarily P-Progol would take over a week to find a clause this long. The extension to P-Progol described in the next section allowed this clause to be found in only seconds.

## 3.3 Background Knowledge

The background knowledge necessary for learning pharmacophores, from molecular descriptions of the type we have chosen, consists of clauses to identify hydrogen acceptors, hydrogen donors, other relevant atoms or groups (in this experiment, the zinc binding group), as well as code to compute the distance between any pair of atoms or groups. This background knowledge is relatively brief, so we present it here. Note that the definition of a zinc binding site is particularly simple because the data came with this site denoted by a designated dummy atom; otherwise, the background knowledge would have been more complex, since functional groups that bind to zinc would have to be described, as would be their binding geometries. It is also worth noting that we tried several error (distance tolerance) values. Results with these are described in the next section.

```
%error(0.5).
error(0.75).
%error(1.0).

hacceptor(M,A):- atm(M,A,o,2,_,_,_).
hacceptor(M,A):- atm(M,A,o,3,_,_,_).
hacceptor(M,A):- atm(M,A,s,2,_,_,_).
hacceptor(M,A):- atm(M,A,n,ar,_,_,_).

zinc_binder(M,A):-
        atm(M,A,du,_,_,_,_).

hdonor(M,A) :- atm(M,A,h,_,_,_,_), not(carbon_bond(M,A)), !.

carbon_bond(M,A):-
        atm(M,B,c,_,_,_,_), symmetric_bond(M,A,B,_).

symmetric_bond(M,A,B,_) :- bond(M,A,B,_).
symmetric_bond(M,A,B,_) :- bond(M,B,A,_).

dist(Drug,Atom1,Atom2,Dist,Error):-
        var(Error), !,
        Atom1 @< Atom2,
        coord(Drug,Atom1,X1,Y1,Z1),
        coord(Drug,Atom2,X2,Y2,Z2),
        euc_dist(p(X1,Y1,Z1),p(X2,Y2,Z2),Dist),
        error(Error).

dist(Drug,Atom1,Atom2,Dist,Error):-
        number(Error),
        coord(Drug,Atom1,X1,Y1,Z1),
        coord(Drug,Atom2,X2,Y2,Z2),
        euc_dist(p(X1,Y1,Z1),p(X2,Y2,Z2),Dist1),
        Diff is Dist1 - Dist,
```

```
        absolute_value(Diff,E1),
        E1 =< Error.

absolute_value(X,X):- X >= 0, !.
absolute_value(X,Y):- X < 0, Y is -X.

coord(Drug,Atom,X,Y,Z):-
        atm(Drug,Atom,_,_,X,Y,Z), !.

euc_dist(p(X1,Y1,Z1),p(X2,Y2,Z2),D):-
        Dsq is (X1 - X2)^2 + (Y1 - Y2)^2 + (Z1 - Z2)^2,
        D is sqrt(Dsq).
```

Note the two definitions of the *dist* (distance) predicate. The first computes the distance between two atoms and attaches the specified error or tolerance value (from the top of the background theory), and the second (when values are already provided for the distance and the error) checks whether the actual distance is within the error tolerance of the given distance.

Finally, we should note that for P-Progol we also put the *atm* and *bond* facts describing the 28 molecules into the background theory. This allows the examples to be of the following simple form.

```
active(m1).
active(m2).
        .

        .

        .

active(m28).
```

## 4  The Experiment

### 4.1  Materials and Method

**The ILP system used** We use a Prolog implementation of *Progol*, called *P-Progol (Version 2.1)*, developed by the third author. The first author has also implemented a version called *CProgol* in the C language. Details of how to obtain this version can be found in [6]. *P-Progol* is available on request from the third author. The implementation includes on-line documentation that clarifies the points of difference with the C version. The theory underlying both versions is the same and is described fully in [6]. However, differences in search strategies and pruning facilities imply that given the same language and resource restrictions, the two versions can compute different answers. For convenience, in the rest of this paper, we shall refer to *P-Progol* as *Progol*.

The experiment in pharmacophore prediction uses no negative examples. (No barriers exist to using negative examples in pharmacophore prediction; it simply happens that the dataset provided to us from a researcher within the pharmaceutical industry contains no negative examples.) Under such circumstances Progol ordinarily would return a hypothesis that classifies every example as *positive*, such as *active(X)*. To avoid this, as well as to vastly improve computational efficiency, two additions were made to Progol. The first is the addition of integrity constraints which specify that some clauses are unacceptable as hypotheses. This is similar to the use of integrity constraints in Clint and Claudien [9], due to De-Raedt, and in Tracy and Filp (see the discussion of forbidden clauses in [8]), due to Bergadano and Gunetti. For the purpose of this experiment, hypotheses (potential pharmacophores) are unacceptable which have fewer than three "pieces" or which do not specify the distances between all pairs of pieces. An integrity constraint is simply a clause that proves *false* if the constraint is violated. The precise integrity constraints used in this experiment, with the supporting code, are as follows.

```
false:-
        hypothesis(Head,Body,_),
        has_pieces(Body,Pieces),
        length(Pieces,N),
        N =< 2.
false:-
        hypothesis(_,Body,_),
        has_pieces(Body,Pieces),
        incomplete_distances(Body,Pieces).

has_pieces((zinc-binder(M,A),T),[A|L]) :- !, has_pieces(T,L).
has_pieces((hacceptor(M,A),T),[A|L]) :- !, has_pieces(T,L).
has_pieces((hdonor(M,A),T),[A|L]) :- !, has_pieces(T,L).
has_pieces((H,T),L) :- !, has_pieces(T,L).
has_pieces(zinc-binder(M,A),[A]):- !.
has_pieces(hacceptor(M,A),[A]):- !.
has_pieces(hdonor(M,A),[A]):- !.
has_pieces(_,[]).

incomplete_distances(Body,Pieces):-
        piece_pairs(Pieces,[],L),
        element(A1/A2,L),
        not(has_distance(A1,A2,Body)).

has_distance(A1,A2,(dist(_,X,Y,_,_),_)):-
        A1 == X, A2 == Y, !.
has_distance(A1,A2,(dist(_,X,Y,_,_),_)):-
        A1 == Y, A2 == X, !.
has_distance(A1,A2,(_,T)):-
        has_distance(A1,A2,T).
has_distance(A1,A2,dist(_,X,Y,_,_)):-
```

```
        A1 == X, A2 == Y, !.
has_distance(A1,A2,dist(_,X,Y,_,_)):-
        A1 == Y, A2 == X, !.


piece_pairs([],A,A).
piece_pairs([A1|T],PairsSoFar,PiecePairs):-
        get_pair(A1,T,PairsSoFar,Pairs),
        atm_pairs(T,Pairs,PiecePairs).

get_pair(_,[],P,P).
get_pair(A1,[A2|T],P1,P):-
        get_pair(A1,T,[A1/A2|P1],P).

element(X,[X|_]).
element(X,[_|T]):- element(X,T).
```

An integrity constraint merely specifies that a violating clause is unacceptable as a hypothesis, but it does not specify that refinements of that clause (in particular, extensions to the clause by adding literals) will also be unacceptable. Nevertheless, for some clauses it is known that all refinements are also unacceptable. Because Progol searches a refinement lattice, its efficiency would be helped greatly if it could prune the search at each such clause. For example in the current experiment, every extension of a clause representing a pharmacophore with six pieces (but to which the distances have not yet been added) is unacceptable, given the assumption that pharmacophores have three to five pieces. The search should be pruned at such a clause. That is, such a clause should be entirely abandoned. This is specified within the extended Progol using an *abandon* predicate, as opposed to *false*, as follows.

```
abandon:-
        hypothesis(Head,Body,N),
        violates_constraints(Body).

violates_constraints(Body):-
        has_pieces(Body,Pieces),
        violates_constraints(Body,Pieces).

violates_constraints(Body,[_,_,_,_,_,_]).
```

Several points of procedure should be specified. We wanted Progol to find the largest pharmacophore that appeared in all of the molecules (a larger pharmacophore is less likely to appear in all molecules due to chance alone), and we also wanted to know if there was more than one such pharmacophore. Consequently we ran Progol three times, once specifically searching for five-piece pharmacophores, once for four-piece pharmacophores, and once for three-piece pharmacophores. In each case Progol was set to *explore* mode. In explore mode,

Progol does not stop with the first hypothesis that covers all examples (the first potential pharmacophore that appears in all examples), but continues to search for all such hypotheses. In addition, based on consultation with our pharmaceutical expert, Progol was run with allowed distance errors (tolerances) of 1.0 Angstrom, 0.75 Angstrom, and 0.5 Angstrom.

**The Data** The examples consisted of 28 molecules having the activity of ACE (angiotensin-converting enzyme) inhibition, taken from [4]. A detailed description of each molecule was generated by a researcher within the pharmaceutical industry, whose interest was in testing the applicability of Progol to pharmacophore prediction; descriptions were generated using the Sybyl package by Tripos. Molecules were represented in the manner described in the last section. As stated earlier, no negative examples were provided. In addition, Progol was provided with the background knowledge described at the end of the last section.

## 4.2   Results

At all error levels, Progol returned the 4-piece pharmacophore shown below (which we showed in the last section), which appears in all 28 molecules. Below the pharmacophore is shown with error set to 0.75. This pharmacophore appears in all 28 molecules at both the 1.0 and 0.75 error level, and it appears in 27 of the 28 molecules at the 0.5 error level. No other four-piece pharmacophore appeared in all 28 molecules even at the 1.0 error level. This four-piece pharmacophore also has an estimated accuracy from leave-one-out cross-validation of 100%. Moreover, this pharmacophore was judged by our pharmaceutical expert to be equivalent to the generally-accepted pharmacophore for ACE inhibition.

```
Molecule A is an ACE inhibitor if:
    molecule A contains a zinc-binder B, and
    molecule A contains a hydrogen acceptor C, and
    the distance between B and C is 7.899 +/- 0.750 Angstroms, and
    molecule A contains a hydrogen acceptor D, and
    the distance between B and D is 8.475 +/- 0.750 Angstroms, and
    the distance between C and D is 2.133 +/- 0.750 Angstroms, and
    molecule A contains a hydrogen acceptor E, and
    the distance between B and E is 4.891 +/- 0.750 Angstroms, and
    the distance between C and E is 3.114 +/- 0.750 Angstroms, and
    the distance between D and E is 3.753 +/- 0.750 Angstroms.
```

Figures 4 and 5 show two of the 28 molecules with the pieces of this pharmacophore labeled.

Even at the 1.0 error level, no potential five-piece pharmacophore appears in more than 10 of the 28 molecules. The one that appears in 10 of the 28 results from adding one piece to the four-piece pharmacophore. No other five-piece pharmacophore appears in more than 4 of the 28 molecules.

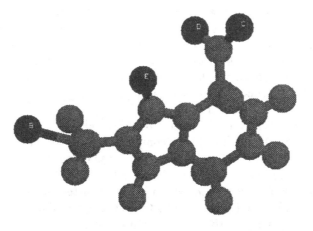

**Fig. 4.** ACE inhibitor number 1 with highlighted 4-piece pharmacophore.

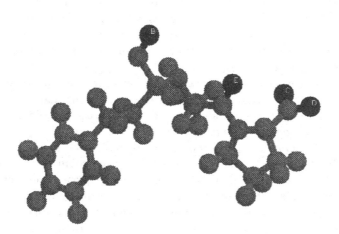

**Fig. 5.** ACE inhibitor number 10 with highlighted 4-piece pharmacophore.

Four three-piece potential pharmacophores were found to appear in all 28 molecules, but these are each simply the result of omitting one of the pieces from the four-piece pharmacophore. In general, when a four-piece pharmacophore is present, one expects also to find four three-piece potential pharmacophores. When a five-piece pharmacophore is present, one expects also to find five four-piece potential pharmacophores and ten three-piece potential pharmacophores. It is encouraging that no additional three-piece potential pharmacophores were found to occur in all 28 molecules due to chance alone.

We have not yet mentioned time complexity, which is perhaps the most surprising result. The preceding pharmacophore was found in 2.21 seconds of CPU time on a SPARC 20 workstation. As already noted, Progol would ordinarily take in excess of a week to find such a clause with ten body literals. Thus not only did the addition of integrity constraints and the *abandon* predicate make the experiment possible with positive examples only, it made it computationally efficient. This efficiency is crucial because the next section describes extensions to the current experiment which will be more demanding computationally.

## 5  Conclusions

The overall conclusion from the preceding experiment is that without reasoning about the details of ACE inhibition, but looking only for common substructures of a form specified by a domain expert, Progol finds the correct pharmacophore, and no other potential pharmacophore looks nearly so acceptable. Moveover, Progol does this very quickly. Nevertheless, ILP is not yet ready to give the pharmaceutical industry a useful new technique for drug design, because an interesting challenge remains.

Most organic molecules can arrange themselves in a number of 3D *conformations*, purely by rotating around bonds without breaking and reforming bonds. Two molecules with the same atom-and-bond structure but different conformations are called *conformational isomers* or *conformers*.[4] Every conformer has an associated *energy* level, and molecules "prefer" to be in low energy conformations. Nevertheless, at body temperature or even room temperature enough energy is available that molecules typically shift frequently between conformations, and a sample of a given substance (molecule) at a given time will usually contain a variety of conformers. Yet it is usually the case that only one conformation is responsible for a given activity of a molecule. For example, each of the 28 molecules in the experiment described in this paper is an ACE inhibitor when in one of its conformations but not when in other conformations. In this experiment Progol was provided with the "active" conformation for each molecule. But in future applications Progol will not be so fortunate. Instead, it will have to examine multiple conformations that have relatively low energy, without knowing which one is actually the active conformation.[5]

---

[4] Conformational isomers are not to be confused *stereoisomers*, which cannot interconvert without breaking and reforming bonds.

[5] The reader may question whether individual conformers can be isolated, thereby

One possible approach to the challenge of multiple conformations is to describe each compound or molecule as a set of stable conformations, each labelled by probability of occupancy. These probabilities can be directly computed with existing techniques since they are logarithmically related to the energy of the conformation. The following type of pharmacophore would then be sought, for example.

```
Molecule A is an ACE inhibitor if it has any conformation X with
probability at least 0.05 such that:
    molecule A contains a zinc-binder B, and
    molecule A contains a hydrogen acceptor C, and
    the distance between B and C in conformation X is
        7.899 +/- 0.750 Angstroms, and
    molecule A contains a hydrogen acceptor D, and
    the distance between B and D in conformation X is
        8.475 +/- 0.750 Angstroms, and
    the distance between C and D in conformation X is
        2.133 +/- 0.750 Angstroms, and
    molecule A contains a hydrogen acceptor E, and
    the distance between B and E in conformation X is
        4.891 +/- 0.750 Angstroms, and
    the distance between C and E in conformation X is
        3.114 +/- 0.750 Angstroms, and
    the distance between D and E in conformation X is
        3.753 +/- 0.750 Angstroms.
```

The *abandon* predicate which was added to Progol for the experiment described in this paper can be thought of as asserting that some class of clauses (all the clauses that are refinements of the given clause) have probability 0 of being the target hypothesis. One addition to Progol that might prove valuable for use with multiple conformations is a weakened version of the abandon predicate, which asserts that all refinements of a given clause have at most some given (nonzero) probability of being the target. For example a clause built based on a high-energy, low-probability conformation should have low probability compared with a clause based on a low-energy, high-probability conformation. These probability statements could be used to direct the search to the more highly probable part of the search space first. Such an extension might be vital in cases where many possible conformations must be considered.

We have recently begun work toward a related experiment with multiple conformations. We suggest this direction of work as a significant one for researchers interested in the application of ILP to drug design or other problems within organic chemistry or molecular biology.

---

making it possible to determine experimentally which conformer exhibits the desired activity. To quote from a popular organic chemistry textbook, "...different conformers can't usually be isolated, because they interconvert too rapidly.[5]"

# 6   Acknowledgements

This research was supported partly by the Esprit Basic Research Action ILP2 (project 20237), the EPSRC project 'Experiments with Distribution-Based Machine Learning', the SERC project 'Experimental Application and Development of Inductive Logic Programming' and a SERC Advanced Research Fellowship held by Stephen Muggleton. Stephen Muggleton is also supported by a Research Fellowship at Wolfson College, Oxford.

# References

1. A.K. Debnath, R.L Lopez de Compadre, G. Debnath, A.J. Schusterman, and C. Hansch. Structure-activity relationship of mutagenic aromatic and heteroaromatic nitro compounds. correlation with molecular orbital energies and hydrophobicity. *Journal of Medicinal Chemistry*, 34(2):786 – 797, 1991.
2. R. King, S. Muggleton, R. Lewis, and M. Sternberg. Drug design by machine learning: The use of inductive logic programming to model the structure-activity relationships of trimethoprim analogues binding to dihydrofolate reductase. *Proceedings of the National Academy of Sciences*, 89(23), 1992.
3. R. King, S. Muggleton, A. Srinivasan, and M. Sternberg. Structure-activity relationships derived by machine learning: the use of atoms and their bond connectives to predict mutagenicity by inductive logic programming. *Proceedings of the National Academy of Sciences*, 93:438–442, 1996.
4. D. Mayer, C.B. Naylor, I. Motoc, and G.R. Marshall. A unique geometry of the active site of angiotensin-converting enzyme consistent with structure-activity studies. *Journal of Computer-Aided Molecular Design*, 1:3–16, 1987.
5. J. McMurry. *Organic Chemistry (4th edition)*. Brooks/Cole Publishing Company, Pacific Grove, 1996.
6. S. Muggleton. Inverse entailment and Progol. *New Generation Computing*, 13:245–286, 1995.
7. S. Muggleton and C. Feng. Efficient induction of logic programs. In *Proceedings of the First Conference on Algorithmic Learning Theory*, Tokyo, 1990. Ohmsha.
8. C. Nédellec, C. Rouveirol, H. Adé, F. Bergadano, and B. Tausend. Declarative bias in ilp. In L. De Raedt, editor, *Advances in Inductive Logic Programming*, pages 82–103. IOS Press, Amsterdam, 1996.
9. Luc De Raedt. *Interactive Theory Revision: An Inductive Logic Programming Approach*. Academic Press, London, 1992.

# Applying ILP to Diterpene Structure Elucidation from ¹³C NMR Spectra

Sašo Džeroski[1,2], Steffen Schulze-Kremer[3],
Karsten R. Heidtke[4], Karsten Siems[4] and Dietrich Wettschereck[5]

[1] FORTH-ICS, P.O.Box 1385, 711 10 Heraklion, Crete, Greece
[2] Department of Intelligent Systems, Jožef Stefan Institute
Jamova 39, 1000 Ljubljana, Slovenia
Email: Saso.Dzeroski@ijs.si
[3] Max-Planck Institute for Molecular Genetics
Otto-Warburg-Laboratorium, Department Lehrach
Ihnestrasse 73, 14195 Berlin, Germany
[4] AnalytiCon GmbH
Gustav-Meyer-Allee 25, 13335 Berlin-Wedding, Germany
[5] GMD, FIT.KI, Schloss Birlinghoven, 53745 Sankt Augustin, Germany

**Abstract.** We present a novel application of ILP to the problem of diterpene structure elucidation from ¹³C NMR spectra. Diterpenes are organic compounds of low molecular weight that are based on a skeleton of 20 carbon atoms. They are of significant chemical and commercial interest because of their use as lead compounds in the search for new pharmaceutical effectors. The structure elucidation of diterpenes based on ¹³C NMR spectra is usually done manually by human experts with specialized background knowledge on peak patterns and chemical structures. In the process, each of the 20 skeletal atoms is assigned an atom number that corresponds to its proper place in the skeleton and the diterpene is classified into one of the possible skeleton types. We address the problem of learning classification rules from a database of peak patterns for diterpenes with known structure. Recently, propositional learning was successfully applied to learn classification rules from spectra with assigned atom numbers. As the assignment of atom numbers is a difficult process in itself (and possibly indistinguishable from the classification process), we apply ILP, i.e., relational learning, to the problem of classifying spectra without assigned atom numbers.

## 1 Introduction

### 1.1 NMR

Structure elucidation of compounds isolated from plants, fungi, bacteria or other organisms is a common problem in natural product chemistry. There are many useful spectroscopic methods of getting information about chemical structures, mainly nuclear magnetic resonance (NMR) and mass spectroscopy. The interpretation of these spectra normally requires specialists with detailed spectroscopic knowledge and experience in natural products chemistry. NMR-spectroscopy is the best method for complete structure elucidation (including stereochemistry) of non-crystalline samples. For structure elucidation of secondary natural products (not proteins) only $^1$H-NMR- and $^{13}$C-NMR-spectroscopy, including combined methods such as 2D-NMR-spectroscopy, are important because hydrogen and carbon are the most abundant atoms in natural products. In structure elucidation of peptides and proteins $^{15}$N-NMR is sometimes helpful [2].

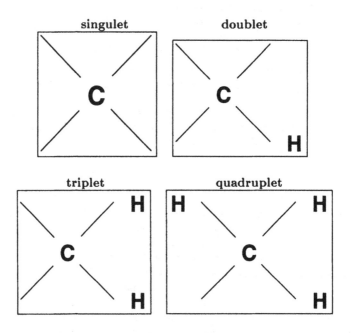

**Fig. 1.** Multiplicity of Carbon Atoms.

$^1$H-NMR- and $^{13}$C-NMR-spectroscopy are quite different: in a $^{13}$C-NMR-spectrum every carbon atom occurs as a separate signal in most cases, while in $^1$H-NMR-spectra many signals overlap and are therefore difficult to interpret [17]. $^1$H-NMR- spectra are logically decomposable and the specialist could get direct information about the structure (including stereochemistry) from the resonance frequency and shape of the signals, provided a sufficiently high resolution of resonance signals can be experimentally achieved. In ordinary $^{13}$C-NMR-spectra only the resonance frequency is observed and no signal splitting (decomposition) is possible. However, the absolute value of the resonance frequency provides more information about chemical structure and (important for prediction and database maintenance purposes) is not as sensitive to varying experimental conditions (such as the magnetic strength of the NMR-spectrometer or the type of solvent) as $^1$H-NMR-spectroscopy is.

Additional measurements can be used to determine the number of hydrogens directly connected to a particular carbon atom. This number is the so-called multiplicity of the signal: **s** stands for singulet, which means there is no proton (i.e., hydrogen) connected to the carbon; **d** stands for a doublet with one proton connected to the carbon; **t** stands for a triplet with two protons and **q** for a quartet with three protons bound to the carbon atom. Figure 1 shows each of the four situations in the order listed above. Because of the simpler nature of [13]C-NMR-data as compared to [1]H-NMR-data, the former are easier to handle and therefore remain the preferred basis for automatic structure elucidation [9].

## 1.2 Diterpenes

Diterpenes are one of a few fundamental classes of natural products with about 5000 members known [13]. The skeleton of every diterpene contains 20 carbon atoms. Sometimes there are additional groups linked to the diterpene skeleton by an oxygen atom with the possible effect of increasing the carbon atom count to more than 20 per diterpene. About 200 different diterpene skeletons are known so far, but some of them are only represented by one member compound. Most of the diterpenes belong to one of 20 common skeleton types.

The problem of structure elucidation of diterpenes requires knowledge about biosynthesis, the way in which biological organisms synthesize natural products. Not every combination of carbons, protons and oxygens that is feasible from a chemical point of view actually occurs in nature, as biosynthesis in biological organisms is limited to a characteristic subset of chemical reactions that constrain the structure space. Structure elucidation of diterpenes from [13]C-NMR-Spectra can be separated into three main stages: 1) identification of residues (ester and/or glycosides), 2) identification of the diterpene skeleton, and 3) arrangement of the residues on the skeleton.

This work deals with the second stage, the identification of the skeleton. A skeleton is a unique connection of carbon atoms each with a specific atom number and, normalized to a pure skeleton molecule without residues, a certain multiplicity (s, d, t or q). Figure 2 shows the [1]H-NMR- and [13]C-NMR-Spectra of a diterpene belonging to the skeleton type Labdan. The structure of the diterpene is also depicted, giving the arrangement and numbering of the 20 skeletal carbon atoms.

The task we address is to identify the skeleton (type) of diterpenoid compounds, given their [13]C-NMR-Spectra that include the multiplicities and the frequencies of the skeleton atoms. This task is usually done manually by human experts with specialized background knowledge on peak patterns and chemical structures. In the process, each of the 20 skeletal atoms is assigned an atom number that corresponds to its proper place in the skeleton and the diterpene is classified into one of the possible skeleton types. We address the problem of learning classification rules from a database of peak patterns for diterpenes with known structure. Recently, propositional methods were successfully applied to classifying spectra with assigned atom numbers [7]. As the assignment of atom

44

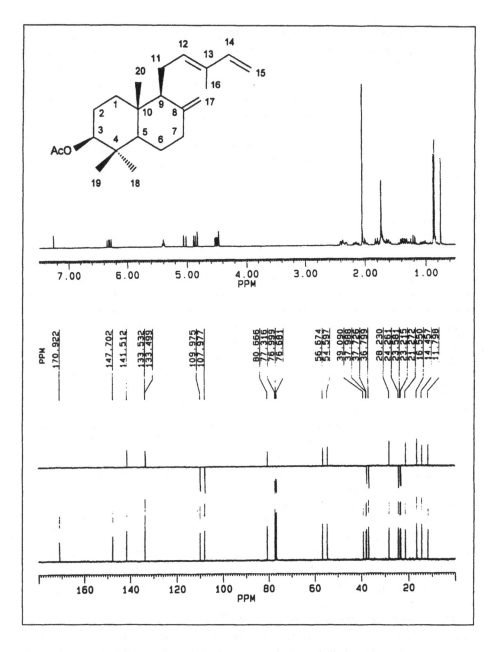

**Fig. 2.** ¹H-NMR (top) and ¹³C-NMR (bottom) Spectra of a diterpene belonging to the skeleton type Labdan, with acetyl as a residue. The additional measurements (above the ¹³C-NMR Spectrum) show 25 signals (s=5, d=5, t=7, q=5). At positions 76.681, 76.999, and 77.316 is the signal of the solvent.

**Table 1.** Facts describing the $^{13}$C-NMR spectrum of a particular molecule that belongs to skeleton type Labdan (52).

```
nmr(v1,52,v1_1,1,t,39.00).
nmr(v1,52,v1_2,2,t,19.30).
nmr(v1,52,v1_3,3,t,42.20).
nmr(v1,52,v1_4,4,s,33.30).
nmr(v1,52,v1_5,5,d,55.60).
nmr(v1,52,v1_6,6,t,24.30).
nmr(v1,52,v1_7,7,t,38.30).
nmr(v1,52,v1_8,8,s,148.60).
nmr(v1,52,v1_9,9,d,57.20).
nmr(v1,52,v1_10,10,s,39.70).
nmr(v1,52,v1_11,11,t,17.60).
nmr(v1,52,v1_12,12,t,41.40).
nmr(v1,52,v1_13,13,s,73.50).
nmr(v1,52,v1_14,14,d,145.10).
nmr(v1,52,v1_15,15,t,111.40).
nmr(v1,52,v1_16,16,q,27.90).
nmr(v1,52,v1_17,17,t,106.30).
nmr(v1,52,v1_18,18,q,33.60).
nmr(v1,52,v1_19,19,q,21.60).
nmr(v1,52,v1_20,20,q,14.40).
```

numbers is a difficult process in itself (and possibly indistinguishable from the classification process), we apply ILP, i.e., relational learning, to the problem of classifying spectra without assigned atom numbers.

The rest of the paper is organized as follows: Section 2 describes the database and the pre-processing of the data, then summarizes recent work on applying propositional learning in this domain that uses data with assigned atom numbers. When the atom numbers are not available, but only multiplicities and frequencies, we have an ILP problem. Section 3 describes several formulations of this problem and gives the results of applying the FOIL ILP system to these formulations. Section 4 gives a comparison to C4.5, nearest neighbor classification and backpropagation networks applied to different propositionalizations of the problem. Section 5 presents the results of applying RIBL, a relational instance-based learner to the ILP problem formulations. Finally, Section 6 concludes with a discussion and an outline of directions for further work.

## 2 The data and propositional learning results

### 2.1 The database

AnalytiCon GmbH maintains a database of diterpenoid compounds. This is done using the ISIS (Integrated Scientific Information System), a product of MDL Information Systems, Inc., on IBM PCs under MS Windows. The relational database contains information on 1503 diterpenes with known structure, stored in three relations - **atom**, **bond**, and **nmr**.

The first relation specifies to which element an atom in a given compound belongs. The second relation specifies which atoms are bound and in what way in a given compound. The **nmr** relation stores the measured $^{13}C$-NMR-Spectra. For each of the 20 carbon atoms in the diterpene skeleton, it contains the atom number, its multiplicity and frequency. For each compound, the skeleton type which it represents is also specified within the database. Table 1 gives an excerpt from the **nmr** relation describing molecule **v1**. The relation schema is `nmr(MoleculeID,SkeletonType,AtomID,AtomNumber,Multiplicity,Frequency)`.

## 2.2 Pre-processing

Every substituent or residue connected to a carbon atom exerts a characteristic shift on the resonance frequency signal of the carbon atom and sometimes also changes its multiplicity. Simple rules based on expert knowledge can be used to take this effect into account.

**Table 2.** Rules for generating reduced multiplicities from observed multiplicities.

| |
|---|
| IF ObservedM = s AND Frequency in [ 64.5, 95 ] THEN ReducedM = d |
| IF ObservedM = s AND Frequency in [ 96, 114 ]  THEN ReducedM = t |
| IF ObservedM = s AND Frequency in [ 115, 165 ] THEN ReducedM = d |
| IF ObservedM = s AND Frequency in [ 165, 188 ] THEN ReducedM = q |
| IF ObservedM = s AND Frequency in [ 188, inf ] THEN ReducedM = t |
| IF ObservedM = d AND Frequency in [ 64.5, 95 ] THEN ReducedM = t |
| IF ObservedM = d AND Frequency in [ 105, 180 ] THEN ReducedM = t |
| IF ObservedM = d AND Frequency in [ 96, 104 ]  THEN ReducedM = q |
| IF ObservedM = d AND Frequency in [ 180, inf ] THEN ReducedM = q |
| IF ObservedM = t AND Frequency in [ 59, 90 ]   THEN ReducedM = q |
| IF ObservedM = t AND Frequency in [ 90, inf]   THEN ReducedM = q |

They transform the raw, measured, NMR-multiplicities into the so-called reduced multiplicities, which carry more information about the skeleton types, as shown below. These rules are given in Table 2. They leave the measured frequencies unchanged. The reduced multiplicities that correspond to those in Table 1 are given in Table 3. Note that the multiplicities of atoms 8, 13, 14, 15, and 17 are changed.

## 2.3 Propositional learning: experiments and results

Given the above data, Džeroski et al. [7] formulate several propositional learning problems. Twenty-three different skeleton types are represented in the whole set of 1503 compounds: there are thus 23 possible class values. The attributes are

**Table 3.** Pre-processed facts describing the $^{13}$C-NMR spectrum of molecule **v1**.

---

```
red(v1,52,v1_1,1,t,39.00).
red(v1,52,v1_2,2,t,19.30).
red(v1,52,v1_3,3,t,42.20).
red(v1,52,v1_4,4,s,33.30).
red(v1,52,v1_5,5,d,55.60).
red(v1,52,v1_6,6,t,24.30).
red(v1,52,v1_7,7,t,38.30).
red(v1,52,v1_8,8,d,148.60).
red(v1,52,v1_9,9,d,57.20).
red(v1,52,v1_10,10,s,39.70).
red(v1,52,v1_11,11,t,17.60).
red(v1,52,v1_12,12,t,41.40).
red(v1,52,v1_13,13,d,73.50).
red(v1,52,v1_14,14,t,145.10).
red(v1,52,v1_15,15,q,111.40).
red(v1,52,v1_16,16,q,27.90).
red(v1,52,v1_17,17,q,106.30).
red(v1,52,v1_18,18,q,33.60).
red(v1,52,v1_19,19,q,21.60).
red(v1,52,v1_20,20,q,14.40).
```

---

the multiplicities and frequencies of each of the 20 skeleton atoms. For instance, attribute **A1M** is the multiplicity of atom number 1, and **A7F** is the frequency of atom number 7. There are thus 40 attributes, twenty discrete (multiplicities) and 20 continuous (frequencies). At a suggestion from the domain experts, a version of the problem is also considered where only the multiplicities are used as attributes. Four series of experiments are performed, with the following sets of attributes: observed multiplicities and frequencies, reduced multiplicities and frequencies, observed multiplicities only and reduced multiplicities only.

Three different machine learning approaches were used: backpropagation networks [19, 18], nearest neighbor classification [4, 20], and decision tree induction [14, 16]. Table 4 gives a summary of the accuracies on unseen cases for the three approaches and the four different problems as estimated by ten-fold cross-validation on the same folds.

**Table 4.** Classification accuracy on unseen cases when learning from classified $^{13}$C-NMR spectra with assigned atom numbers.

| Problem/Approach | Backpropagation networks | Nearest neighbor | C4.5 |
|---|---|---|---|
| Observed | 89.6% | 96.7% | 96.4% |
| Reduced | 95.5% | 99.3% | 97.6% |
| Observed - No Frequencies | 83.9% | 94.4% | 93.1% |
| Reduced - No Frequencies | 97.1% | 98.8% | 98.4% |

While the accuracies achieved are very high and the problem may be considered solved at first sight, one should bear in mind that the propositional formulation specified above crucially depends on the atom number information. The assignment of atom numbers is a very difficult and important part of the classification process, and classification rules that do not rely on atom number assignments need to be derived for practical purposes. Without atom number information, there is no obvious propositional representation of the problem and more careful representation engineering (feature construction) or the use of more powerful techniques, such as ILP seems necessary. In the remainder of the paper, we describe experiments that apply each of these approaches separately, as well as their combination.

**Table 5.** The classes, their chemical names and number of instances in the database.

| Code | Chemical name | Number of instances |
|------|---------------|---------------------|
| c2   | Trachyloban   | 9                   |
| c3   | Kauran        | 353                 |
| c4   | Beyeran       | 72                  |
| c5   | Atisiran      | 33                  |
| c15  | Ericacan      | 2                   |
| c18  | Gibban        | 13                  |
| c22  | Pimaran       | 155                 |
| c28  | 6,7-seco-Kauran | 9                 |
| c33  | Erythoxilan   | 9                   |
| c36  | Spongian      | 10                  |
| c47  | Cassan        | 12                  |
| c52  | Labdan        | 448                 |
| c54  | Clerodan      | 356                 |
| c71  | Portulan      | 5                   |
| c79  | 5,10-seco-Clerodan | 4              |
| c80  | 8,9-seco-Labdan | 6                 |

# 3 Applying FOIL

As we are dealing with a learning problem where 23 different classes exist, there are 23 target relations classC(MoleculeID), where C ranges over the possible classes. For example, the target relation class52(MoleculeID) corresponds to the skeleton type Labdan, most common among the 1503 diterpenes in the database (448 instances). The correspondence between the chemical names and the codes in the data is given in Table 5 together with the number of instances of each class. Only classes with more than one instance are listed.

## 3.1 Using multiplicities and frequencies

Given that much better results were obtained using the reduced multiplicities in earlier experiments, we decided to use only these (and not the observed multiplicities) for our experiments with ILP. After one takes the atom number information away, the background relation red can be simplified to a three argument relation red(MoleculeID,Multiplicity,Frequency). A particular fact of this relation states that the $^{13}$C-NMR spectrum of a given molecule contains a peak of a given multiplicity and frequency. For example, the fact red(v1,t,39.00) states that the $^{13}$C-NMR spectrum of molecule v1 has a peak at frequency 39.00 ppm with multiplicity t (a triplet).

The background relation red is nondeterminate, as there are 20 tuples for each molecule. This prevents the use of ILP systems like GOLEM [12] or DINUS [10]. While PROGOL [11] would be applicable, preliminary experiments showed it has prohibitive time complexity if longer rules/clauses are needed. Therefore, we used FOIL [15], in particular FOIL6.4. Except for a variable depth limit of one, all other settings were left in their default state.

We first used FOIL to induce rules on the entire data set, and then performed ten-fold cross validations on the same partitions of training examples as used for the propositional case by Džeroski et al. [7]. For each experiment, FOIL was run 23 times, i.e., once for each target relation. The rules from the 23 runs were then taken together to produce a rule set. Before classification, the rules from the rule set were checked against the training set to record the number of examples of each class that they cover, as well as to note the majority class in the training set. This information is then used when classifying new examples, e.g., when testing the accuracy of the rule set.

For classification, we implemented a procedure analogous to that of CN2 [3]: when an example is classified, all clauses that cover it are taken into account. The distributions of examples of each class are summed for all rules that match and the majority class is assigned to the example. If no rule matches, the majority class (from the training set) is assigned.

Given the background relation red(MoleculeID,Multiplicity,Frequency), FOIL induced 90 rules from the entire data set, comprising 607 literals in their bodies. At first sight, the rules are quite specific, covering relatively few examples. Also, many examples are left uncovered. Thus, even on the training set, these rules only achieve 51.6% accuracy. The ten-fold cross-validation yields 46.5% accuracy on unseen cases as the average over the ten runs. It seems that the background knowledge is sufficient to distinguish among the different classes (the rules typically cover examples of one class only), but FOIL induces too specific rules. The most general rule class52(A) :- red(A,d,B), B=<73.7, red(A,C,D), D>38.5, D=<44.6, B>73.2 covers 43 examples of class 52.

## 3.2 Using multiplicities only

According to the domain expert (Karsten Siems), the multiplicities should suffice for correct classification, at least when atom numbers are available [7]. If we remove the Frequency argument from the relation red, all the information left about a particular molecule is captured by the number of atoms which have multiplicity s, d, t, and q, respectively. We store this information in the relation `prop(MoleculeID,SAtoms,DAtoms,TAtoms,QAtoms)`. For our molecule **v1**, we have the fact `prop(v1,2,4,8,6)`.

Given the entire data set, the 23 target relations and the background relation `prop`, FOIL induced 17 rules with 52 literals in the bodies. Same settings were applied in FOIL as for the experiments with **red**. The rules induced in this case are much more general than the ones obtained with **red**. The most general rule `class52(A) :- prop(A,B,C,D,E)`, `E>5`, `C>3`, `D>7`, `B>1` covers 429 examples (of which 355 of class 52, 72 of class 54). Many rules cover examples of several classes. It seems that the background knowledge is insufficient to completely distinguish among the different classes and FOIL is forced to induce overly general rules. This, however, has positive effect on accuracy as compared to the experiments with **red**. Using `prop`, FOIL achieves 69.0% accuracy on the entire data sets, and 70.1% accuracy on unseen cases (ten-fold cross-validation).

At this point, note that we have in fact applied FOIL to a propositional problem. Namely, from the nondeterminate representation with the **red** relation, we have constructed a four-feature representation of each molecule. We postpone the comparison to propositional learners to the next section.

### 3.3 Combining engineered features and a relational representation

Having introduced the four new features with the `prop` relation, which seem to capture some general properties of the molecules, we repeated the experiment with the nondeterminate relational representation. This time FOIL was given both the relation **red** and the relation **prop**. The same settings of FOIL were applied as in the previous two subsections.

Given the entire data set, the 23 target relations and the background relations **red** and **prop**, FOIL induced 68 rules with 401 literals in the bodies. The rules were more general than rules induced using **red** only, but were more specific than rules induced using **prop** only. In most cases, each rule covers examples of one class only. The most general rule `class52(A) :- prop(A,B,C,D,E)`, `E>5`, `C>3`, `D>7`, `B>1`, `red(A,d,F)`, `F>54.8`, `F=<72.3` covers 227 examples of the correct class. The induced rules achieve 83.2% accuracy on the entire data set and 78.3% accuracy on unseen cases (ten-fold cross-validation). Combining the engineered features with the relational representation thus has a positive effect.

## 4 Comparing FOIL to propositional approaches

### 4.1 C4.5 using multiplicities only

As mentioned above, the relation `prop` defines a propositional version of our classification problem. We therefore applied a propositional learner, C4.5 [16], to this problem. The same experimental setting (tree induced on whole data set first, then ten-fold cross-validation) and the default settings of C4.5 were used.

The induced tree achieves 80.4% accuracy on the entire data set. The leaves of the tree typically contain examples of several different classes, confirming the suspicion that the four features do not suffice for completely correct classification. The classification accuracy on unseen cases as measured by ten-fold cross-validation (same folds as above) is 78.5%, which is almost the same as the accuracy achieved by FOIL using both red and prop.

### 4.2 Nearest neighbor using multiplicities only

We also applied nearest neighbor classification [4, 20] to the propositional problem defined by the relation prop. The same experimental setting (cross-validation folds) was used. Training on the entire dataset gives 100% accuracy.

Cross-validation on the number of neighbors used in classification was tried out, as well as two different forms of feature weighting, but the basic nearest neighbor method performed best. The classification accuracy on unseen cases (average over the ten folds) is 79.0%, which is almost the same as the accuracy of C4.5 and the accuracy achieved by FOIL using both red and prop.

### 4.3 Backpropagation networks

Various network architectures were explored to see how in comparison backpropagation networks would perform at the classification of skeletons based on unassigned $^{13}$C NMR data. This was done independently of the above experimental setup, but using the same partitions for cross-validation.

A standard backpropagation network [19, 18] with 960 input neurons, no hidden units and 23 output units was trained with the same input data as for the ILP experiments. We divided the 960 input neurons into four equally large sets of 240 nodes, one each for singulets, doublets, triplets and quadruplets. The best representation was to have for each multiplicity 24 frequency intervals (0 - 10 ppm, 11 - 20 ppm, ..., 231 - 240 ppm) with 10 nodes each and to feed the value of 1 for each frequency in the spectrum into the next unoccupied input neuron of the appropriate interval. All remaining input nodes are filled with zeros. Thus, the artificial neural net sees a discretized distribution of multiplicity signals.

During cross-validation, accuracy on the training set (average for the 10 runs) reached 97.9%, while accuracy on unseen cases reached 79.9%. Other network variations, e.g., feeding the actual frequency value into the appropriate neuron instead of 1 or using a 4 x 15 architecture that receives the sorted frequencies for each multilicity as input did not produce better results.

## 5 Applying RIBL

RIBL (relational instance-based learning) [8] generalizes the nearest neighbor method to a relational representation. RIBL first constructs cases by putting together all facts that relate to (in this case) a single molecule. Training cases are stored for further reference. When a new molecule has to be classified, RIBL calculates the similarities between it and each of the training cases, then assigns it the class of the nearest training case.

The similarity measure used in RIBL is a generalization of similarity measures used in propositional instance-based learners. In fact, given a propositional problem, RIBL becomes the classical nearest neighbor method and has the same performance as the latter. This is a very desirable property for a relational learner.

We used the same formulations and experimental methodology as for FOIL (Section 3). As it stores all training cases, RIBL achieves 100% accuracy given the entire data set for both training and testing. To estimate accuracy on unseen cases, ten-fold cross validations on the same folds as above were performed.

**Table 6.** Accuracies of different approaches when classifying NMR spectra without assigned atom numbers.

| Problem/System | FOIL | C4.5 | RIBL |
|---:|:---:|:---:|:---:|
| red | 46.5% | NA | 86.5% |
| prop | 70.1% | 78.5% | 79.0% |
| red+prop | 78.3% | NA | 91.2% |

Table 6 gives the accuracies on unseen cases achieved by FOIL, C4.5 and RIBL on the three different formulations of the problem. Given only the **red** relation, RIBL achieved 86.5% classification accuracy (average over the ten partitions) on unseen cases. This is an increase of 40% over the accuracy achieved by FOIL. Note that propositional approaches (C4.5) are not applicable to this formulation of the problem.

Given only the **prop** relation, RIBL behaves identically to the nearest neighbor method, thus yielding 79.0% accuracy on unseen cases, a performance equivalent to that of C4.5. When provided with both the **red** and the **prop** relations, RIBL achieves 91.2% accuracy on unseen cases. Using the engineered features improves RIBL's performance by roughly 5%, pushing further the best result achieved at classifying diterpene NMR spectra without assigned atom numbers. Again, propositional approaches (C4.5) are not applicable to this formulation of the problem.

# 6 Discussion

For practical purposes, $^{13}$C-NMR spectra of diterpenes without assigned atom numbers have to be classified. This is a problem that is not directly transformable to propositional form and calls for either representation engineering or the use of inductive logic programming. We explored both approaches separately and in combination. Adding the engineered features to the natural relational representation improved the performance of both relational learning systems used.

Using the engineered features only, propositional approaches (in particular C4.5, nearest neighbor and neural networks) achieve around 79% accuracy on unseen cases. This is roughly 20% less than the accuracies achieved when classifying $^{13}$C-NMR spectra of diterpenes with assigned atom numbers.

Using FOIL on the natural relational representation yields unsatisfactory results. Combining the relational representation with the engineered features greatly improves FOIL's performance. However, given the engineered features only FOIL performs much worse than C4.5, so that the best performance of FOIL (combining the relational representation and the engineered features) is comparable to that of C4.5. The reason for FOIL's poor performance is that the rules induced are overly specific as indicated by their coverage and confirmed by expert comments. However, the rules found by FOIL are quite short, indicating that the problem lies in the search heuristic: it directs the search to short rules with small coverage, despite the fact that longer rules with higher coverage exist.

From the above it is clear that a desirable property of relational learning systems is the following: given a propositional problem, a relational learning system should perform comparably to propositional systems. RIBL, which extends the nearest neighbor approach to a relational framework has this property. Given the engineered features only, it achieves 79% accuracy on unseen cases. Given the relational representation only, RIBL performs much better than FOIL (86% vs 46% accuracy on unseen cases). Finally, combining the relational representation and the engineered features it achieves 91% accuracy on unseen cases, 11% better than the best propositional result of 80% (backpropagation networks with 960 features).

The 91% accuracy achieved by RIBL is in the range of the accuracies with which experts classify diterpenes into skeleton types given $^{13}$C NMR spectra only. That number can actually only be estimated since it is expensive to have an expert carry out a statistically significant number of structure predictions without using other additional information that often becomes available from heterogeneous sources (such as literature, and $^1$H NMR spectra). This basically means that $^{13}$C NMR is not completely sufficient for classifying diterpenes and that great improvements of classification accuracy are not to be expected.

The main direction for further work thus is to provide classification accuracy at the level already achieved in conjunction with satisfactory explanation. RIBL can offer only the neirest neighbor used to classify a given instance as an explanation of that classification, but no general knowledge can be offered for inspection by domain experts. Newer versions of RIBL (based on Aha's IB3 [1]), which store only a fraction of all train cases, may offer a small number of prototypes as explanations. Alternatively, one might apply mFOIL [6, 10] and use the $m$-estimate to guide the search towards more general rules (larger $m$ in the estimate of the accuracy prefers rules that cover more examples). ICL [5] is also an interesting candidate ILP system to apply to this problem.

### Acknowledgements

Sašo Džeroski is an ERCIM (European Research Consortium for Informatics and Mathematics) fellow at ICS-FORTH. This work started during his visit to GMD (German National Research Center for Information Technology) supported by the same ERCIM fellowship. This work is also supported in part by the ILP2 project (ESPRIT IV LTR Project 20237 Inductive Logic Programming 2).

# References

1. Aha, D., Kibler, D., and Albert, M. Instance-based learning algorithms. *Machine Learning*, 6: 37–66, 1991.
2. Abraham, R.J., Loftus, P. *Proton and Carbon 13 NMR Spectroscopy, An Integrated Approach*. Heyden, London, 1978.
3. Clark, P. and Boswell, R. Rule induction with CN2: Some recent improvements. In *Proc. Fifth European Working Session on Learning*, pages 151–163. Springer, Berlin, 1991.
4. Cover, T.M., and Hart, P.E. Nearest neighbor pattern classification. *IEEE Transactions on Information Theory*, 13: 21–27, 1968.
5. De Raedt, L., and Van Laer, V. Inductive constraint logic. In *Proc. Sixth International Workshop on Algorithmic Learning Theory*, pages 80–94. Springer, Berlin, 1995.
6. Džeroski, S. Handling imperfect data in inductive logic programming. In *Proc. Fourth Scandinavian Conference on Artificial Intelligence*, pages 111–125. IOS Press, Amsterdam, 1993.
7. Džeroski, S., Schulze-Kremer, S., Heidtke, K., Siems, K., Wettschereck, D. Diterpene structure elucidation from $^{13}$C NMR spectra with machine learning. In *Proc. ECAI'96 Workshop on Intelligent Data Analysis in Medicine and Pharmacology*, 1996.
8. Emde, W., Wettschereck, D. Relational instance-based learning. In *Proc. Thirteenth International Conference on Machine Learning*, pages 122–130. Morgan Kaufmann, San Mateo, CA, 1996.
9. Gray, N. A. B. *Progress in NMR-spectroscopy, Vol. 15*, pp. 201–248, 1982.
10. Lavrač, N., Džeroski, S. *Inductive Logic Programming: Techniques and Applications*. Ellis Horwood, Chichester, 1994.
11. Muggleton, S. Inverse entailment and PROGOL. *New Generation Computing*, 13: 245–286, 1995.
12. Muggleton, S., and Feng, C. Efficient induction of logic programs. In *Proc. First Conference on Algorithmic Learning Theory*, pages 368–381. Ohmsha, Tokyo, 1990.
13. *Natural products on CD-ROM*. Chapman and Hall, London, 1995.
14. Quinlan, J.R. Induction of decision trees. *Machine Learning* 1(1): 81–106, 1986.
15. Quinlan, J.R. Learning logical definitions from relations. *Machine Learning*, 5(3): 239–266, 1990.
16. Quinlan, J.R. *C4.5: Programs for Machine Learning*. Morgan Kaufmann, San Mateo, CA, 1993.
17. Schulze-Kremer, S. *Molecular Bioinformatics - Algorithms and Applications*. de Gruyter, Berlin, 1995.
18. *Stuttgart Neural Network Simulator*. Computer code available from the University of Stuttgart, Germany, via anonymous ftp ftp://ftp.informatik.uni-stuttgart.de/pub/SNNS, 1995.
19. Tveter, D. R. *Fast-Backpropagation*. Computer code available from the author. Address: 5228 N Nashville Ave, Chicago, Illinois, 60656, drt@chinet.chi.il.us, 1995.
20. Wettschereck, D. A study of distance-based machine learning algorithms. PhD Thesis, Department of Computer Science, Oregon State University, Corvallis, OR, 1994.

# Analysis and Prediction of Piano Performances Using Inductive Logic Programming

Erika Van Baelen and Luc De Raedt

Department of Computer Science, Katholieke Universiteit Leuven
Celestijnenlaan 200A, B-3001 Heverlee, Belgium
Email: Luc.DeRaedt@cs.kuleuven.ac.be

**Abstract.** Starting from the work of Matthew Dovey on analysing Rachmaninoff's piano performances using inductive logic programming, we show how to apply the clausal discovery engine Claudien to induce theories for predicting MIDI files from the musical analysis of a score.

This extends Dovey's work in several directions: MIDI-encodings are used instead of the older Ampico, a richer musical analysis within LaRue's SHMRG-model is applied, a much finer qualitative analysis of features is learned (making it nearly quantitative), and predictions are made.

The application is not only relevant as yet another inductive logic programming benchmark, but also as a demonstration of the need for multiple predicate learning, sequence prediction and number handling in inductive logic programming. Furthermore, the results presented here can be considered the first original application of the clausal discovery engine Claudien.

## 1 Motivation and Introduction

The motivation for this research comes from the paper by Matthew Dovey on *Analysis of Rachmaninoff's Piano Performances using Inductive Logic Programming* [6]. The starting point of Dovey's study were Ampico recordings of two Piano performances by Rachmaninoff in the 1920's, i.e. of Rachmaninoff's Prelude in C Sharp Minor, op. 3 no. 2 (Ampico Roll Number 57504) and of Mendelssohn's Song Without Words, op. 67 no. 4 (Ampico Roll Number 59661). Ampico recordings capture a performance of a piano player by encoding the notes, duration and tempo, as well as the dynamics of the key pressure and pedalling. Starting from Ampico recordings and knowledge about the musical structure of the piece being performed, Dovey produced two datasets (one for each piece) and analysed them using the inductive logic programming system Progol [9]. This enabled Dovey to induce some general rules underlying piano performances by Rachmaninoff. Dovey's work did not only show that music is an interesting application area for inductive logic programming, it also potentially contributes to the analysis of music.

Despite these contributions, Dovey's work was severely limited. Firstly, Dovey only used the melody notes of the pieces, which is in the case of piano rather awkward. Secondly, the rules induced were all qualitative, and hence could not be used for reconstructing (or predicting) Ampico recordings. Thirdly, the musical analysis employed by Dovey is rather simple. Furthermore, Dovey suggested that the use of MIDI (Musical Instrument Digital Interface), which is the current information medium for encoding performances on synthesizers, could be more useful.

In this work, an attempt is made to improve the results of Dovey. To this aim, Dovey's setting was adapted in the following manner. First, instead of using the older Ampico recordings, we also use MIDI. Secondly, all notes will be taken into account. Thirdly, an extended musical analysis, using Jan LaRue's SHMRG model [7] is employed. Finally, and most importantly, rather than discovering qualitative regularities which capture some intuitions about piano performance, it was our aim to discover regularities that can be used to generate MIDI encodings starting from the musical analysis of a piece. So, we try to generate the performance data from the musical analysis of the piece, which means that the musical score (with some background information) is actually being interpreted. It is our hope that this would help to improve upon the current performances that are generated automatically by software programs.

These issues were addressed in two steps. In the first step, we started from Dovey's Ampico data (which were kindly supplied by Dovey), but extended it with new musical knowledge as well with quantitative aspects. In the second step, we used a MIDI encoding[1] (performed by Carl Verbraeken) of Mendelssohns's Lied Ohne Worte together with the musical analysis. In both steps, the first half of the data was used as a learning set. Rules were then induced by the Claudien system [2, 5] and applied on the musical analysis of the second part in order to produce an interpretation of this second part (whether MIDI or Ampico). In addition to the interpretation (on MIDI or Ampico), which represents the musical result of this work, several performance aspects were also analysed using more traditional machine learning techniques, which results in a number of statistics and graphs.

Viewed from inductive logic programming, this work represents a true application of multiple predicate learning, and hence demonstrates the relevance of this type of learning (cf. [4]). Also, it contains the first *novel* application realised with the clausal discovery engine Claudien [5], and in this respect, it shows the possibilities of the underlying data mining approach to inductive logic programming.

The paper is structured as follows: Section 2 presents the extended representation format used in the Ampico studies, Section 3, presents the representation needed for MIDI, Section 4 presents the prediction algorithm employed, Section 5 contains some results of the empirical evaluation, and finally Section 6 presents some conclusions and discusses further work.

## 2  Ampico recordings

As stated in the introduction, the first part of our study starts from Dovey's representation of the Ampico recordings. However, his representation was mod-

---

[1] There exist no original MIDI encodings of Rachmaninoff's performances.

ified significantly, the most important modification being the use of an enriched musical theory based on the SHMRG-model of Jan LaRue [7]. SHMRG stands for Sound, Harmony, Melody, Rhythm and Growth. LaRue provides recommendations for describing each of these different musical aspects. The model used by Dovey can be considered a simpler SHMRG-model, as Dovey uses this only for Rhythm, Sound and Melody. In this paper, we will employ knowledge about Sound, Harmony, Melody and Rhythm. The aspect Growth is less important as this investigation concerns a single (small) piece for piano, and not for instance a complicated symphony. In addition to also addressing Harmony, we also contribute many new features for Rhythm, Sound and Melody.

On the other hand, we did not include in our investigation more advanced musical analysis techniques such as those of Schenker and Meyer, nor models from cognitive musicology (such as Narmour and Lehrdals and Jackendoff) which are quite popular in artificial intelligence studies of music. The main reason for not applying these, is that we wished to keep the representation as simple and understandable as possible. This could however be handled in further work on this topic.

We now present in detail the descriptions we used in the SHMRG-model. While doing so, we indicate where we deviate from Dovey, and in what manner. We also assess the objectiveness of each feature.

## 2.1 Sound

Sound captures the tone or colour of the music. For our purposes (the use of piano only), this issue reduces to information about accentuation, force and touch of the different notes, as found on the score.

- *Touch* (source : score, changed w.r.t. Dovey) : staccato (S), legato (L), portato (P), leggiero (LG) or normal (). Dovey uses terms such as pizzicato and portamento, which do not really apply to piano.
- *Accent* (source : score, slightly changed w.r.t. Dovey): sforzando (S), sforzato (>), fermate (F).
- *Expected Force* (source: score, taken from Dovey) in a range from 1 to 14.
- *Actual Force* (source: Ampico, taken from Dovey) in a range from 1 to 14.
- *Expected Cresc./Dim.* : (source : score, new parameter, subjective for what concerns the end of each cresc./dim.): cresendo (C) or diminuendo (D).

## 2.2 Harmony

Harmony is the study of chords and intervals, of the ways in which chords and intervals are related to one another, and the ways in which one interval or chord can be connected to another. Harmony is not really addressed by Dovey, as he treats harmony and melody alike. We apply Cope's SPEAC-model on Harmony here. The SPEAC encoding stands for Statement, Preparation, Extension, Antecedent and Consequence. It is devised according to linguistic principles. In the

SPEAC model every note is assigned one of S,P,E,A, or C, in order to character-ize the function of the note. A linguistic example, due to Dovey, is the sentence 'I am going to the store', in which 'I' maps to a *Statement* (something which exists by itself), 'am going' maps to an *Antecedent* (which requests a response), 'store' maps to *Consequence* (which represents the answer to the request), and 'to the' maps to *Preparation*. Dovey applied the SPEAC model in a non-hierarchical manner to the melodic structure of the piece. Here we apply it on the harmonic structure of the piece.

This results in modified SPEAC feature for each note:

- *SPEAC*: (source: score, changed from Dovey, subjective).

## 2.3  Melody

This concerns the melodic theme of the work. For each note, we keep track of :

- *Phrase position* : (source : score, as for Dovey, subjective), beginning (B) end (E), or left blank for a note in the middle of a phrase.
- *Phrase shape*: (source: score, new parameter), indicates the form of the global melodic sentence, i.e. rising (R), falling (F), level (L), waveform (W), saw-tooth (S), undulating (U).
- *QA*: (source : score, new parameter) which indicates (when applicable) whether two voices are in dialogue, question (Q) or answer (A).
- *Phrase stress*: (source : score, new parameter, subjective), the note with the strongest accent in a melodic sentence is marked with an S[2].

## 2.4  Rhythm

Rhythm is concerned with everything that concerns tempo (the global level) and metrics (at the local level).

- *Tempo density* (source: score, new, subjective) : on a scale from 1 (broad) to 5 (dense).
- *Rhythmic stress* (source: score, new, subjective) : the note with the strongest accent in a rhythmic sentece is marked with an S.
- *Expected gap*: (source: score, as Dovey) the expected gap between one note and the previous one, in 1/120 beats.
- *Actual gap* (source: Ampico, as Dovey) the actual gap between one note and the previous one, in 1/120 beats.

---

[2] This feature goes back to Rachmaninoff (cf. Rachmaninoff, The complete recordings, RCA, Victor Golden Seal, BMG Music, 1992.) Rachmaninoff approached the litera-ture of the piano as only a composer could. He described his method in these words: " 'You must take the work apart, peer it into every corner, before you can assemble the whole'. He shared with his friend Feodor Chaliapin, ..., the interpretative method of determining the climax or 'point' of a piece. Once that was determined, the structure of the piece proceeded to and receded from the 'the point' with inexorable logic." .

- *Expected duration*: (source: score, as Dovey) the expected duration of a note, in 1/120 beats.
- *Actual duration* (source: Ampico, as Dovey) the actual duration of a note, in 1/120 beats.
- *Pitch* (source : score, as for Dovey) the pitch of the note. C0 represented middle C, C-1, the C one octave below middle C, C1 one octave above and so on.
- *Bar* (source : score, as for Dovey) the bar number of the note.
- *Beat* (source : score, as for Dovey) the beat number within the bar of the note.
- *Offset* (source : score, as for Dovey) the offset of the note w.r.t. the previous beat.

These last four features are not employed in the learning phase, as they precisely encode what is on the score. They are irrelevant for prediction purposes in our context, though some derivatives are used, such as e.g. pitch-descending, ...

The sequence of the notes is encoded in the following predicate:

- *Pre(Note1,Note2)* (source: score, as for Dovey), which denotes that Note1 comes immediately before Note2.

## 2.5 Representation

The above SHMRG features are first represented in a table using a kind of attribute-value representation. For instance the first 6 notes of the Prelude in C Sharp Minor correspond to :

A-1, , >, 1,1,0,0,120,11,0,87,12,P,B,F,A,,2,
G-1#,,>,1,2,0,0,120,11,3,97,11,A,,F,A,,2,
C-1#,,>,2,1,0,0,720,11,4,402,13,C,E,F,A,S,2,
C1#,P,,3,1,60,-180,60,1,-158,65,1,S,B,W,Q,,2,
E1,P,,3,2,0,0,60,1,0,61,2,P,,W,Q,S,2,
D1#,P,,3,2,60,0,60,1,2,55,1,S,E,W,Q,,2,

where the features include Pitch, Touch, Accent, Bar, Beat, Offset, Expected Gap, Expected Duration, Expected Force, Actual Gap, Actual Duration, Actual Force, SPEAC, Phrase Position, Phrase Stress, Tempo Density, Expected Cres/Dim.

Notice however that this representation is misleading as some of the relevant relations are implicit in this table. This includes the sequence of the notes, as well as the differences between expected and actual values, which actually makes this a typical *relational* or *inductive logic programming* problem.

The above table can be automatically translated into a relational representation (cf. below for an example). Such a representation was employed by Dovey in order to predict in a qualitative manner the following properties of a note : duration, duration of the gap w.r.t. the previous note, and force [3].

---

[3] Dovey actually named these predicates differently.

- *duration*, which provides information about the actual duration of the Note as compared to the expected duration.
- *detach, overlap*, which provide information about the duration of the actual detach or positive gap (resp. overlap or negative gap) of a Note as compared to the expected detach (resp. overlap).
- *timing(Note)*, which indicates how the time between the start of the given note and the preceding note varies between performance and score.
- *dynamic-actual(Note), dynamic-expected(Note)* which indicate the difference in actual (resp. expected) force between this note and the previous one.
- *dynamic-force(Note)*, which indicates the difference between the actual force of this note and the expected force.

All of the above aspects were encoded qualitatively, using 3 to 5 different values for each aspect. Using this type of representation, Dovey was able to discover 75 qualitative rules capturing some of the intuitions behind Rachmaninoff's performances in these pieces.

Though we also performed experiments on the qualitative data (see [11] for more information), we found it more interesting to try to induce rules which could be employed for predictive purposes. However, this requires the use of a finer scale for representing the numeric information.

## 2.6  Quantitative Information

We need to model 4 different aspects: force, duration, detaches and overlaps.

Let us start by force, which is encoded on a scale from 1 to 14. A straightforward way of encoding this aspect, would employ two predicates, one for the expected force and one for the actual force, e.g. *exp-force(Note,Int)* and *act-force(Note,Int)* where Note is the number of the note, and Int a number between 1 and 14. As the relative difference is more important than the specific forces, we choose to encode this aspect using a predicate

- *dynamics-ch(Note,RelInt)* where *RelInt* can now take a value between -13 and +13, indicating the difference between the actual and expected force. E.g. when the expected force of note19 is 11 and the actual is 13, this corresponds to *dynamics-ch(note19,-2)*.

Whereas force is represented on a scale from 1 to 14 (due to the nature of the Ampico rolls), time and hence duration, detaches and overlaps are represented on a much more detailed scale (1/120 of a beat). Due to the number handling problems of current inductive logic programming systems, we did not represent these aspects in the same manner as for force. Furthermore, such a fine grained division is hardly noticeable for the human. Therefore, we used as features the actual time divided by the expected time, and discretized this into 23 different intervals. This yields the following predicates:

- *duration-factor(Note,Class)* where class takes one of the following intervals: less than 0.1, between 0.1 and 0.2, between 0.2 and 0.3, ..., between 0.8 and

0.9, between 0.9 and 0.95, between 0.95 and 1, between 1 and 1.05, between 1.05 and 1.1, between 1.1 and 1.2, ..., between 1.9 and 2, more than 2. E.g. when the expected duration of note202 is 120 units, and the actual is 20, this would be noted as *duration-factor(note202,.10-.20)*

- *detach-factor(Note,Class)* and *overlap-factor(Note,Class)* similarly, where it is assumed that expected detaches (resp. overlaps) are actual played as detaches (resp. overlaps).

- *zero-gap(Note,Class)* this is to avoid divisions by 0 in case the expected gap is 0, and is only used for small actual gaps and detaches (i.e. less than 4/120 of a beat). Here, Class takes the value ok (real gap of 0), small-detach (real gap between 1 and 4) or small-gap (real gap between -1 and -4). E.g. when the expected gap between note132 and note 133 is 0 units, and there is a gap of 4 units, this is encoded as *zero-gap(note133,small-detach)*

- *zero-detach-factor(Note,Class)* and *zero-overlap-factor(Note,Class)* are used when the expected gap is 0, and the actual gap is larger than 4/120 of a beat. Then Class denotes the actual detach (resp. overlap) divided by the duration of the note, for encoding the relative time of an overlap (detach). E.g. when the expected gap between note133 and note34 is 0 units, and there was a gap of 15 units while the expected duration of note134 is 120 units, we have *zero-detach-factor(note134,.1-.2)*

When the aim is to induce the definitions of these predicates, we are actually facing a *multiple-predicate learning* task, as these predicates are possibly mutually dependent.

# 3  MIDI data

MIDI stands for Musical Instrument Digital Interface, first published in 1983 by International MIDI Association (IMA). MIDI does not have the same quality of a CD, as its encoding is much simpler. The encodings are also specific for each instrument or synthesizer. W.r.t. Ampico MIDI is a significant advance, it has e.g. 128 levels to encode the force instead of 14 for Ampico, and it applies not only to piano, but to any digital instrument. However, the ideas are very similar. It is because we did not have any Ampico device available that we employed MIDI.

Our experiments with MIDI, were all carried out on a performance by Carl Verbraeken of Mendelssohn's Lied Ohne Worte. Two important changes were made w.r.t. the Ampico data. First, the data were extended to include also the non-melody notes. Just playing the melodic notes on a piano is not interesting. Second, the right pedal of the piano was taking into account. When this pedal is applied, the strings are not damped. As the left pedal was always applied in our case study, we did not do anything special for this pedal. Other changes were made so that the Ampico data format could be reused. Beats on MIDI (in our study) were counted in 384 ticks, Ampico in 120 ticks. Velocity in MIDI is connected with volume and is counted in 128 levels, Ampico's force is encoded in 14 levels. We found it convenient to reduce these 384 ticks to 120 and the

128 levels to 14. This is useful for recycling the encoding and for comparing the results. (In this respect, our work is closer to Ampico than to MIDI, despite the fact that our predictions are used to generate a MIDI file).

New predicates were defined to capture the pedal and the non-melodic notes. Otherwise the same data representation format as above was employed.

- *pedal(MelNote,State)* (source MIDI, new), where State is one of : on, off, initiated, terminated.
- *melody-note(Note)* (source : score, new), which denotes that Note is a melody note
- *related-to-melodynote(Note1,Note2,How)* (source : score, new), where Note1 is a non-melodynote, Note2 a melody note, and How is one of chord, filler note , and grace note. At present, a non-melody-note is only related to one melody note.

Otherwise the same representation is used for melody-notes as for non-melody notes.

An example of the real representation of some notes is given below:

melody-note(note328).
pedal(note328,on).
staccato(note328).
no-accent(note328).
antecedent-function(note328).
middle-phrase(note328).
melody-undulating(note328).
pitch-descending(note328).
no-melodic-stress(note328).
no-rhythmic-stress(note328).
triplet-quaver(note328).
duration-factor(note328,< .1).
exp-gap(note328,zero-gap).
zero-detach-factor(note328,.6-.7).
exp-force(note328,5).
no-cresc-or-dim(note328).
dynamics-ch(note328,-1).
pre(note326,note328).

related-to-melody-note(note329,note328,chord).
triplet-semiquaver(note329).
duration-factor(note329,.8-.9).
exp-gap(note329,zero-gap).
zero-gap(note329,small-gap).
exp-force(note329,5).
dynamics-ch(note329,1).

related-to-melody-note(note330,note328,chord).

triplet-semiquaver(note330).
duration-factor(note330,.6-.7).
exp-gap(note330,zero-gap).
zero-gap(note330,small-detach).
exp-force(note330,5).
dynamics-ch(note330,2).

## 4 Clausal Discovery

Using the above datasets several experiments were performed with the clausal discovery engine Claudien [5, 2], cf. [11]. First, rules were derived with a similar purpose as Dovey, i.e. to get insight in the performance characteristics of Rachmaninoff. So, the aim here was to generate understandable and intuitive regularities. This was quite succesful, however, due to space restrictions we do not further elaborate on this. Secondly, it was our aim - and this contrasts our work from that of Dovey - to be able to use the induced hypothesis in order to predict MIDI [4] performance data. To realize this, we choose to induce rules on the first half of a piece (both Mendelssohn's Lied Ohne Worte, and Rachmaninoff's Prelude in C Sharp Minor were considered) and to apply the induced hypothesis to predict the Ampico performance data of the second half of the piece. We soon discovered that the naive approach, which consists of selecting a subset of the rules produced by Claudien[5] would not work. The reason is that only few predictions are made. For instance, with Claudien's accuracy parameter set to 80 per cent, only for 3 per cent of the notes the force could be predicted, only 10 percent for duration, and 5 per cent for detaches and gaps. Lowering Claudien's accuracy parameter results in more predictions, but is not a solution. The problem is that many rules induced by Claudien are recursive and rely on the performance characteristics of the previous note(s), which is often also not known. What is needed is a number of simple non-recursive rules. We therefore used the following strategy:

1. induce rules that use the features about the current melody note itself, e.g. dynamics-ch(X,0) :- strong-accent(X), cresc-expected(X).
2. induce rules that use only the features of the previous melody note, e.g. dynamics-ch(X,0) :- pre(Y,X), staccato(Y)
3. induce rules about the previous melody note and the current melody note, e.g. dynamics-ch(X,0) :- pre(Y,X), staccato(Y), conclusion-function(X)
4. (only for MIDI) : induce rules for non-melody notes.
5. (only for MIDI) : induce rules for right pedal[6].

---

[4] As said before, we actually predict a kind of Ampico data, but transform it to MIDI.
[5] When running Claudien, which is a kind of first order data mining system, many rules are generated. These are usually filtered before being applied for prediction purposes, cf. [5, 2].
[6] These rules were not used in the prediction process due to the doubtfull quality of the induced rules.

Notice that throughout, as different aspects are being learned, and as one predicate may use the other predicates, this is a multiple predicate learning task. Furthermore, many of the rules induced are recursive or even mutually recursive. Though we induced rules taking into account only two notes, the use of recursion makes that this induction problem is *not* easily transformable into attribute value form ! Also, further investigations might want to consider longer chains, done by Dovey, who considered chains of up to 4 notes.

It is our intention to make the data, the generated MIDI-file as well as the settings employed in Claudien publicly available by ftp. For more details, please contact the authors.

# 5 Prediction

To predict the different aspects of each note needed for performance, we employ a kind of forward reasoning procedure. The reason for using forward reasoning is that the induced hypotheses are highly recursive and typically consist of many rules. This makes a classical backward chaining procedure very inefficient (using Prolog as is, termination problems did arise). Secondly, the prediction process employs two meta-rules in order to handle double predictions and missing predictions. Double predictions arise when for a given note and aspect, two (or more) different values are predicted, missing predictions arise when for a given note and aspect no prediction is made. The meta-rules applied in this case represent general musical knowledge.

The prediction process can be summarized as follows. A typical forward reasoning procedure is stepwise applied. In forward reasoning, whenever the body matches the background knowledge, the corresponding head is asserted.

1. apply the rules induced in step 1 for predicting the melody notes, (forward reasoning)
2. repeatedly apply the rules induced in step 2 for predicting the melody notes (using forward reasoning, i.e. until no new predictions are made)
3. repeatedly apply the rules induced in step 3 for predicting the melody notes (using forward reasoning, i.e. until no new predictions are made)
4. (a) remove double predictions with the continuity rule
   (b) repeatedly apply the default rule to predict missing features of melody notes, and the rules induced in step 2 and 3 to predict missing features of melody notes. (until all features of melody notes are predicted)
5. (a) repeatedly apply the rules induced in step 4 for predicting the non-melody notes
   (b) apply the first default rule for non-melody notes
   (c) apply the second default rule for non-melody notes
   (d) apply the continuity rule for non-melody notes

The meta-rules are described below :

**default rule for melody notes:** if there exists a prediction for a note but not its successor, then apply the existing prediction also to the successor.

**continuity rule for melody notes:** if there exists a double (resp. no) prediction for a note, then select that prediction that is closest to the average of its predecessor(s) and successor(s).

**first default rule for non-melody notes:** if there exists a non-melody note that is related to the same melody-note (in the same way) as a non-melody note for which there is a missing prediciton, then predict the same values for both non-melody notes.

**second default rule for non-melody notes:** if all of the non-melody notes that are related to a melody note in a certain way have a missing feature, then select the value of a non-melody note that is related to the previous melody-note in the same way.

All of these rules are based on a kind of continuity principle which states that the music typically evolves in a continuous manner. The current meta-rules have been kept as simple as possible.

# 6   Experimental results

The above prediction procedure was applied to the two Ampico rolls (melody notes only), and to the MIDI file (all notes) generated by Carl Verbraeken. For reasons of space, we only present the latter results here (for more details about the Ampico rolls, cf. [11]). Before discussing these results, we should point at a fundamental difficulty in evaluating our results. To this aim, we quote Gerard Widmer [12], when describing a similar evaluation.

> It is difficult to analyze the results in a quantitative way. One should compare the system's performance of a piece with a human performance of the same piece and measure the average differences between the two curves. However, the results would be rather meaningless. For one thing, there is no single correct way of playing a piece. And second, relative errors or deviations cannot simple be added: some notes and structures are more important than others, and thus errors are more or less grave.

There are thus at least two different ways to evaluate our results. First, there is the classical machine learning perspective, which prescribes that individual predictions should be compared with actual values, and their accuracy measured. Secondly, and as Widmer argues, more importantly, one should also evaluate the way the music sounds.

Let us first look at the machine learning perspective. The results of the prediction process are shown in Figures 1, 2 and 3, each focussing on one feature needed for MIDI, i.e. duration of notes, duration of gaps, and force. In these figures, the x-axis represents the sequence of notes played, and the y-axis the actual values, respectively the predicted values.

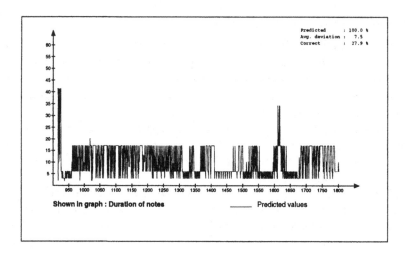

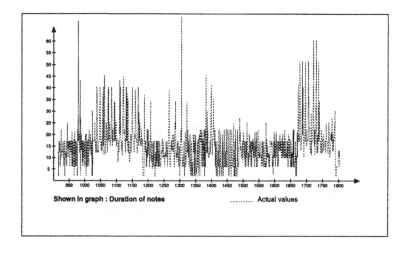

**Fig. 1.** Duration

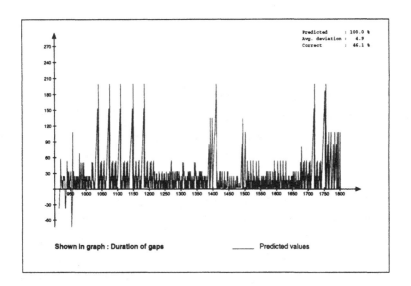

Shown in graph : Duration of gaps       _____ Predicted values

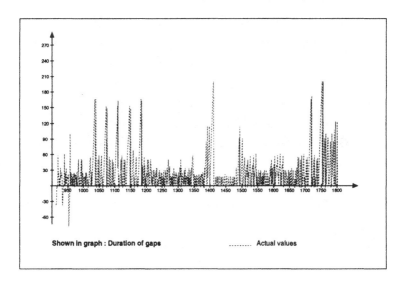

Shown in graph : Duration of gaps       .......... Actual values

**Fig. 2.** Gaps

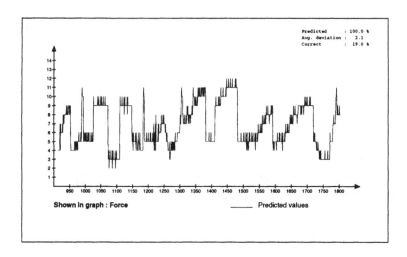

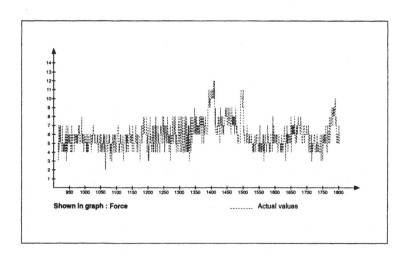

**Fig. 3.** Force

First, duration of the notes is predicted rather well, the deviation being on the average only 7.5 on a scale of 120 per beat, which can hardly be observed by the human ear. However, important differences arise when looking at the peaks, which are predicted rather poorly. An explanation for this could be that there are too few peaks in the training data and hence that the peaks are considered to be noise by the clausal discovery engine.

Second, duration of the gaps is quite well predicted, the average deviation being smaller than for duration of the notes.

Thirdly, the force. Again the trends are predicted rather well, and the peaks are much harder. However, for force the average deviation is relatively larger than for duration, which indicates that force is much harder to predict, a finding confirmed also by Dovey's experiments. For force, it also turns out that especially the second default rule for non-melody notes contributed many predictions (about 40 per cent of the notes). The other meta-rules were less used.

Fourth, when looking at the individual rules obtained (like Dovey did), it is easily seen that they make sense though they are sometimes quite specific. This is probably due to the use of a single musical piece.

Though the above three figures may be significant from the machine learning point of view, the real issue is how well the predicted performance sounds. To this aim, the predicted features for all the notes were encoded on a MIDI file, so that the human ear could judge. When listening to the MIDI file (which we intend to make available by ftp), there are some interesting observations to make. First, at the global level, the results are rather disappointing. We believe the generated performance is similar to a (not so good) student that just started to practice playing Mendelssohn's Lied Ohne Worte. However, at the level of small parts (a few bars), the sound is sometimes quite good. Secondly, the listener gets the impression that the force is predicted very well but there is often something wrong with the rhythm. This is interesting as it contradicts the machine learning perspective, where according to the curves, force was predicted much worse than duration. Probably the human ear is more sensitive to rhythm than to force. One possible cause for this is the default rules, which take into account only the previous note. In practice, it would be better to also use the next note and compute some kind of average (as with the continuity rule), which we are currently investigating.

When combining the machine learning results with the musical ones, it is easily observed that we are facing a very hard and challenging task. This is so because the learning task involves multiple predicate learning as well as sequence prediction. Indeed, consider a bar of a piece. In order to make the bar sound good, we need to predict the different predicates of each individual note in the bar (sequence) well. This means that the quality of the predictions of a bar crucially depends on many different predictions. Whenever one of these predictions is predicted very poorly, the whole bar (and maybe even more than a bar) will be affected and will sound erroneous.

In sum, we believe that the task addressed in this paper is an extremely challenging problem for inductive logic programming. It is also important, in that it demonstrates the need for multiple predicate learning and sequence prediction. These are two problems, which are hard to solve with propositional learning techniques, but which have received some atttention within inductive logic programming. Hopefully, our study will motivate further research in this direction.

Another conclusion, we could draw is based on comparing the MIDI results with those of the Ampico rolls, the first produced by Carl Verbraeken, and the second by Rachmaninoff. The results for Ampico are sligthly worse than those for MIDI. A plausible explanation for this is that Rachmaninoff's playing is less predictable than that of Carl Verbraeken, because Rachmaninoff is the better piano player.

## 7    Conclusions and Further Work

Starting from an initial study by Matthew Dovey aimed at analysing Rachmaninoff's Piano Performances using inductive logic programming techniques, we have obtained several new results. Most importantly, rather than deriving rules for the qualitative interpretation (by a human), we have shown how to induce rules that can be used to generate music performances on MIDI. This required the use of a significantly enriched and modified representation of the performance and structural data used to train the induction engine. Secondly, we have also shown that this learning task (including the prediction) is challenging and motivating for inductive logic programming as it requires multiple predicate learning, sequence prediction, and potentially also number handling. Thirdly, we have demonstrated the use of the clausal discovery engine Claudien.

There are several directions for further research. First, our results could definitely be improved by employing more musical background knowledge. As already indicated by Dovey, models of the human listener, such as those advocated by Narmour or Lerdahl [10, 8] could be useful. Second, the results could also be improved by employing more powerful inductive logic programming techniques. This would include more advanced multiple predicate learners and sequence prediction algorithms, as argued above. Furthermore, number handling techniques would allow to predict the actual values of the features instead of their range. Finally, it might be better - with the current encoding - to use induction algorithms aimed at classification, such as ICL [3], instead of the clausal discovery engine employed.

## Acknowledgements

The authors would like to thank Gerard Widmer for pointing us to the work of Matthew Dovey and comments on this work, Matthew Dovey for kindly supplying us with his data and information, Carl Verbraeken for his interest and musical help, and to the members of the Leuven ILP team, in particular to Hilde Ade and Wim Van Laer. This work is also part of the ESPRIT IV project no.

20237 on Inductive Logic Programming II, funded by the European Union. Luc De Raedt is supported by the Belgian National Fund for Scientific Research.

# References

1. D. Cope. Experiments in Music Intelligence, In *Proceedings of the International Computer Music Conference*, Computer Music Association, 1987.
2. L. De Raedt and M. Bruynooghe. A theory of clausal discovery. In *Proceedings of the 13th International Joint Conference on Artificial Intelligence*, pages 1058–1063. Morgan Kaufmann, 1993.
3. L. De Raedt and W. Van Laer. Inductive constraint logic. In *Proceedings of the 5th Workshop on Algorithmic Learning Theory*, Lecture Notes in Artificial Intelligence. Springer-Verlag, 1995.
4. L. De Raedt, N. Lavrač, and S. Džeroski. Multiple predicate learning. In *Proceedings of the 13th International Joint Conference on Artificial Intelligence*, pages 1037–1042. Morgan Kaufmann, 1993.
5. L. De Raedt and L. Dehaspe. Clausal Discovery, Technical Report, Dept. of Computer Science K.U.Leuven, 1995, Submitted to *Machine Learning*.
6. M.J. Dovey. *Analysis of Rachmaninoff's Piano Performances using Inductive Logic Programming*, Oxford University Computing Lab, 1995. An extended abstract was published in *Proceedings of the 8th European Conference on Machine Learning*, Lecture Notes in Artificial Intelligence, Springer Verlag, 1995.
7. J. LaRue, *Guidelines for Style Analysis*, W.W.Norton and Co., 1970.
8. F. Lerdahl and R. Jackendorff. *A generative theory of tonal music*. MIT Press, 1983.
9. S. Muggleton. Inverse entailment and progol. *New Generation Computing*, 13, 1995.
10. E. Narmour. *Beyond Schenkerism: the need for alternatives in music analysis*. Chicago University Press, 1983.
11. E. Van Baelen. Analyse van piano-uitvoeringen met behulp van inductie (in Dutch). Master's Thesis, Dept. of Computer Science, K.U.Leuven, 1996.
12. G. Widmer. The synergy of music theory and artificial intelligence: learning multi-level expressive interpretation. In *Proceedings of the 11th AAAI*, 1994.

# Noise Detection and Elimination Applied to Noise Handling in a KRK Chess Endgame

Dragan Gamberger[1] and Nada Lavrač[2]

[1] Rudjer Bošković Institute, Bijenička 54
10000 Zagreb, Croatia
tel. +385 1 4561142, fax +385 1 425497, gambi@lelhp1.irb.hr
[2] Jožef Stefan Institute, Jamova 39
1000 Ljubljana, Slovenia
tel. +386 61 1773272, fax +386 61 219385, nada.lavrac@ijs.si

**Abstract.** Compression measures used in inductive learners, such as measures based on the MDL (Minimum Description Length) principle, provide a theoretically justified basis for grading candidate hypotheses. Compression-based induction is appropriate also for handling of noisy data. This paper shows that a simple compression measure can be used to detect noisy examples. A technique is proposed in which noisy examples are detected and eliminated from the training set, and a hypothesis is then built from the set of remaining examples. The separation of noise detection and hypothesis formation has the advantage that noisy examples do not influence hypothesis construction as opposed to most standard approaches to noise handling in which the learner typically tries to avoid overfitting the noisy example set. Experimental results in a KRK (king-rook-king) chess endgame domain show the potential of this novel approach to noise handling.

## 1    Introduction

In an ideal inductive learning problem, an induced concept description (hypothesis $H$) will 'agree' with the classifications of the descriptions of all concept instances (training examples $E$). In practice, however, it frequently happens that data given to the learner contains various kinds of errors, either random or systematic. Random errors are usually referred to as *noise.*

The problem of noise handling has been solved in different ways. Noise handling mechanisms can be incorporated in search heuristics (e.g., [15]) and in stopping criteria (e.g., [2]) used in hypothesis construction. Hypotheses fulfilling stopping criteria may further be evaluated according to some quality measure, giving a preferential order of hypotheses. In addition, induced hypotheses can be subjected to some form of postprocessing, such as postpruning and simplification of decision trees (e.g., [1, 14, 19]). Systems employing such techniques can be called *noise-tolerant* synce they try to avoid overfitting the possibly noisy training set.

The problem of noise handling has been extensively studied in attribute-value learning. Successful approaches have been adapted to noise handling in inductive logic programming (ILP) [11, 13, 20]. Recently, compression measures [17, 20] that are theoretically based on the Minimum Description Length (MDL) principle [21] have gained much attention. These measures provide a theoretically justified basis for grading candidate hypotheses, integrating a measure of complexity (simplicity or understandability) and correctness (expected accuracy) into a single heuristic measure for hypothesis evaluation.

Compression based induction turns out to be appropriate also for handling of noisy data [17]. This paper shows that a simple compression measure can be used also for explicit detection of noisy examples. A technique is proposed in which noisy examples are detected and eliminated from the training set, and a hypothesis is then built from the set of remaining examples.

The basic idea of this work is to separate noise handling from hypothesis formation. This has the following advantages.

- Noisy examples do not influence the hypothesis construction, as opposed to standard approaches to noise handling in which a learner tries to avoid overfitting the noisy example set. In postpruning of decision trees, for example, only noise occurring in the leaves of the generated decision tree can be detected and the pruned tree is a part of the original tree that was built from the training set that included noise. Similarly, in top-down ILP systems using the covering approach, stopping clause construction depends both on the current hypothesis and the current training set. Moreover, in bottom-up ILP learners, explicit detection of noisy examples may turn out to be even more crucial since the generalization of noisy examples by a bottom-up learner will necessarily result in inappropriate hypotheses.
- Explicit detection of potentially noisy examples can contribute to a better understanding of the problem domain. It can help an expert to decide whether the detected 'potentially noisy' example is actually erroneous or whether it is correct and should be treated as an exception by adding it to the hypothesis generated from a 'noiseless' training set.
- Explicit detection and elimination of noisy examples enables the construction of hypotheses with specific properties. This can be interesting for special domains, for example medical domains, in order to ensure predictions with a small number of false positive cases and predictions of high reliability even in cases when data is expected to be inaccurate [6].

In the proposed approach to noise detection and elimination we assume a learning setting, described in Section 2, that involves a LINUS-like preprocessing step, described in Section 3. The proposed approach to noise detection and elimination is presented in Section 4. Section 5 presents experimental results in the KRK (king-rook-king) chess endgame domain corrupted with noise.

## 2 The learning setting

The learning setting, studied in this paper, consists of three steps:

1. preprocessing of the training set
2. noise detection and elimination, resulting in a reduced example set
3. hypothesis formation from the reduced example set

Noise detection and elimination is the main topic of this paper (Section 4), whereas hypothesis formation from a reduced example set of 'noiseless' examples is out of the scope of this paper. In order to describe the proposed approach to noise detection and elimination, we need to briefly describe the preprocessing step as well (Section 3).

The learning task being studied can be defined as follows: Given a set of training examples $E$, background knowledge $B$, language bias $\mathcal{L}_H$ and a quality criterion for evaluating hypotheses, find a hypothesis $H = H(E, B) \in \mathcal{L}_H$ satisfying the quality criterion.

The hypothesis language $\mathcal{L}_H$ and the background knowledge $B$ (together with some explicit definitions and/or implicit assumptions) define the basic language elements that constitute the hypothesis space, for example $Attribute = Value$, $\neg(Attribute = Value)$, $Attribute \leq Value$, $\neg(Attribute \leq Value)$, $PredicateName(ArgumentValues)$, $\neg(PredicateName(ArgumentValues))$. These language elements will be called *literals*.

In this paper, given the hypothesis language $\mathcal{L}_H$ and background knowledge $B$, the set of literals $L$ is determined in preprocessing. Since $\mathcal{L}_H$ and $B$ define the space of literals $L$ to be searched in hypothesis formation, we may define the learning setting so that the task of finding a hypothesis depends on $E$ and the literal space $L$, such that $H = H(E, L)$.

## 3  Preprocessing

Preprocessing consists of two steps: First, the transformation of the relational learning task into an attribute-value learning task by the LINUS [9, 11] transformer: by taking into account the types of the arguments of the target predicate, the applications of utility predicates and functions are considered as attributes for learning by an attribute-value learner. This step is illustrated below. The second step is the generation of negative literals: for each positive literal $l$ generated by LINUS, a negative literal $\bar{l}$ is generated and added to the literal set. This step is trivial and is therefore not described.

The LINUS transformer is illustrated on a simple example [10]. Consider the problem of learning illegal positions on a chess board with only two pieces, white king and black king. The target relation *illegal(WKf, WKr, BKf, BKr)* states that the position in which the white king is at *(WKf, WKr)* and the black king at *(BKf, BKr)* is illegal. Arguments *WKf* and *BKf* are of type *file* (with values a to h), while *WKr* and *BKr* are of type *rank* (with values 1 to 8). Background knowledge is represented by two symmetric predicates *adjacent_file(X, Y)* and *adjacent_rank(X, Y)*, which can be applied on arguments of type *file* and *rank*, respectively. The built-in symmetric predicate equality $X=Y$, which works on arguments of the same type, may also be used in the induced clauses. Given are one positive example (illegal endgame position, labelled ⊕) and two negative examples (legal endgame positions, labelled ⊖):

$$illegal(\textit{ WKf, WKr, BKf, BKr})$$

$$illegal(a, 6, a, 7). \oplus$$
$$illegal(f, 5, c, 4). \ominus$$
$$illegal(b, 7, b, 3). \ominus$$

The given facts are transformed into attribute-value tuples. The algorithm first determines the possible applications of the background predicates on the arguments of the target relation, taking into account argument types. Each such application is considered as an attribute. In our example, the set of attributes determining the form of the tuples is the following:

$$\langle \textit{WKf=BKf, WKr=BKr, adjacent\_file(WKf,BKf), adjacent\_rank(WKr,BKr)} \rangle$$

Since predicates *adjacent_file/2* and *adjacent_rank/2* are symmetric, their other two possible applications *adjacent_file(BKf, WKf)* and *adjacent_rank(BKr, WKr)* are not considered as attributes for learning.

It should be noted that the arguments of the target predicate, *WKf*, *WKr*, *BKf* and *BKr*, may be included in the selected set of attributes for learning, so that the form of the tuples could be as follows: ⟨*WKf*, *WKr*, *BKf*, *BKr*, *WKf=BKf*, *WKr=BKr*, *adjacent_file(WKf,BKf)*, *adjacent_rank(WKr,BKr)*⟩. In our experiments we have excluded these arguments from the transformed tuples in order to facilitate the comparison with FOIL [20] whose concept description language does not allow for literals of the type *Attribute = Value*.

The tuples, i.e., the values of the attributes, are generated by calling the corresponding predicates with argument values from the ground facts of predicate *illegal*. In this case, the attributes can take values *true* or *false*. The generated tuples can be viewed as the generalizations (relative to the given background knowledge) of the individual facts about the target relation. For the given examples, the following tuples are generated:

$$\langle \textit{WKf=BKf, WKr=BKr, adjacent\_file(WKf,BKf), adjacent\_rank(WKr,BKr)} \rangle$$

$$\langle true, false, false, true \rangle \oplus$$
$$\langle false, false, false, true \rangle \ominus$$
$$\langle true, false, false, false \rangle \ominus$$

In the second preprocessing step, negative literals are added to the set of literals, resulting in extended tuples of truth values of the following literal set:
$$WKf = BKf, \quad WKr = BKr, \quad adjacent\_file(WKf, BKf),$$
$$adjacent\_rank(WKr, BKr), \quad \neg(WKf = BKf), \quad \neg(WKr = BKr),$$
$$\neg(adjacent\_file(WKf, BKf)), \quad \neg(adjacent\_rank(WKr, BKr)).$$
These tuples are the input for the noise elimination algorithm.

# 4   Detection and elimination of noisy examples

This section describes the detection and elimination of noisy examples, where noise is a consequence of random errors.

## 4.1   Literals and $p/n$ pairs

Let us assume a fixed set of literals $L$ and the training set $E$ described by tuples of truth values of literals $L$. For noise detection, we will investigate the properties of literals that hold on individual pairs of training examples, each pair consisting of a positive and a negative example.

**Definition 1.** Let $E = P \cup N$, where $P$ are positive and $N$ are negative examples. A $p/n$ pair is a pair of two examples $e_i$ and $e_j$ such that $e_i \in P$ and $e_j \in N$. When appropriate, we will use the notation $p_i/n_j$ for a $p/n$ pair consisting of $p_i \in P$ and $n_j \in N$.

**Definition 2.** Let $L$ denote a set of literals. A literal $l \in L$ covers a $p_i/n_j$ pair if the literal has value *true* for $p_i$ and value *false* for $n_j$.

In the standard machine learning terminology we may reformulate the definition of coverage of $p/n$ pairs as follows: literal $l$ covers a $p_i/n_j$ pair if $l$ covers the positive example $p_i$ and does not cover the negative example $n_j$.

The notion of $p/n$ pairs can be used to prove important properties of literals for building complete and consistent concept descriptions [5].

**Theorem 3.** *Assume a training set $E$ and a set of literals $L$ such that a complete and consistent hypothesis $H$ can be found. Let $L' \subseteq L$. A complete and consistent hypothesis $H$ can be found using only literals from the set $L'$ if and only if for each possible $p/n$ pair from the training set $E$ there exists at least one literal $l \in L'$ that covers the $p/n$ pair.*

**Proof:**
*Proof of necessity:* Suppose that the negation of the conclusion holds, i.e., that a $p/n$ pair exists that is not covered by any literal $l \in L'$. Then no rule built of literals from $L'$ will be able to distinguish between these two examples. Consequently, a description which is both complete and consistent can not be found.

*Proof of sufficiency:* Take a positive example $p_i$. Select from $L'$ the subset of all literals $L_i$ that cover $p_i$. A constructive proof of sufficiency can now be presented, based on $k$ runs of a covering algorithm, where $k$ is the cardinality of the set of positive examples ($k = |P|$). In the $i$-th run, the algorithm learns a conjunctive description $h_i$, $h_i = l_{i,1} \wedge \ldots \wedge l_{i,m}$ for all $l_{i,1}, \ldots l_{i,m} \in L_i$ that are true for $p_i$. Each $h_i$ will thus be *true* for $p_i$ ($h_i$ covers $p_i$), and *false* for all $n \in N$. After having formed all the $k$ descriptions $h_i$, a resulting complete and consistent hypothesis can be constructed: $H = h_1 \vee \ldots \vee h_k$.

$\square$

As will be shown in Section 4.4, this theorem plays a central role in noise elimination. Namely, if the set $L$ is sufficient for describing a target theory $T$, then a number of different complete and consistent hypotheses $H$ can be generated from $E$. Among these, one may prefer the simplest according to some complexity measure. One possible measure of complexity of a hypothesis $H$ is the number of different literals that appear in it. Given the sets $E$ and $L$, the minimal complexity of a hypothesis that uses literals from $L$ and is complete and consistent w.r.t. $E$ is denoted by $q(E, L)$. In fact, $q(E, L) = |L'|$, where $L'$ is the smallest subset of $L$ that allows the construction of a hypothesis $H$ consistent and complete w.r.t. $E$. As Theorem 3 suggests, one can compute $q(E, L)$ without actually constructing the hypothesis $H$. This idea plays a central role in noise elimination.

## 4.2 Background

Let us assume that for the given training set $E$ and the given set of literals $L$ a consistent and complete hypothesis $H$ (an approximation to an unknown target theory $T$) can be found. This means that the set $L$ is sufficient for describing the target theory $T$. This also means that there are no contradictions in the training set, i.e., examples with same truth values of literals belonging to two different classes, since, as a consequence of Theorem 3, no complete and consistent hypothesis $H$ can be built from a training set that contains contradictions.

Let $q(E, L)$ represent the complexity of the simplest hypothesis complete and consistent with training examples in $E$ and built of literals from $L$ (as Section 4.1 suggests, a simple complexity measure can be defined as $q(E, L) = |L'|$). Let us initially fix the set of literals $L$ and study $q$ only as function of $E$, i.e. $q(E, L) = q(E)$.

Given the sets $E$ and $L$, assume that the training set $E$ contains enough training examples to induce/identify a correct hypothesis $H$. (Correctness of $H$ means that $H$ is complete and consistent for all, including unseen, examples of the unknown target theory $T$. In other words, $H$ represents the same concept as $T$.) If the set of examples is large enough to identify the correct hypothesis $H$ then, by adding examples to $E$, the complexity of the simplest hypothesis that can be generated from the enlarged training set will not increase. Let $m = |E|$. This means that for training examples $e_{m+1}, e_{m+2}, \ldots$ that were not included in the initial training set $E$ it holds that:

$$q(E) = q(E \cup \{e_{m+1}\}) = q(E \cup \{e_{m+1}, e_{m+2}\}) = \ldots$$

But if we add to $E$ an example that is inconsistent with the target domain theory, i.e., an example $f$ that is noisy, then the complexity of the hypothesis will increase:

$$q(E \cup \{f\}) > q(E).$$

Let us first illustrate this observation by a simple graph which shows the complexity of a hypothesis as a function of the number of examples in the training set, and then formalize the claim in Theorem 2.

Figure 1 shows a graph for a sequence of training sets, obtained by adding correct examples to previous example sets and by including of a single noisy example. In the graph, the point $m_0$ denotes the minimal number of examples needed to enable the generation of a correct hypothesis (that is consistent and complete also for yet unseen examples of the target theory $T$). In a sequence of training sets, the point $m_f$ denotes the number of training examples after inclusion of a noisy example $f$.

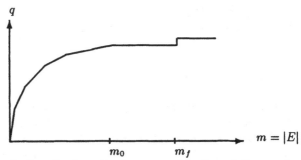

**Fig. 1.** The complexity of a hypothesis $q$ as a function of the number of training examples $m = |E|$; at point $m_f = |E \cup \{f\}|$ a noisy example $f$ is added to the noiseless training set $E$.

**Theorem 4.** *Suppose that the set of examples $E$ is non-noisy and is large enough to enable a unique simplest correct hypothesis $H$ to be generated. By adding an example to the training set, a new training set is generated $E' = E \cup \{e\}$. If $e$ is consistent with the unknown target theory $T$ ($e$ is non-noisy), then $q(E') = q(E)$. If $e$ is inconsistent with $T$ ($e$ is noisy), then $q(E') > q(E)$.*

**Proof:**
For a 'large enough' training set $E$ consisting of all correct training examples it must be true that $H$ is the simplest hypothesis that is complete and consistent with $E$. If this is not true then either set $E$ is not large enough or $H$ is not the simplest hypothesis, both being in contradiction with the assumptions of the theorem. Let $q_H$ denote the complexity of $H$. Then for every $E$ consisting of non-noisy examples: $q(E) \leq q_H$. For the large enough non-noisy $E$: $q(E) = q_H$. If $e$ is non-noisy, then $E'$ is a non-noisy set as well and $q(E') = q_H = q(E)$. This proves the first part of the theorem.

The condition of unique induction of the correct hypothesis $H$ from large enough $E$ assumed by the theorem means that for $E$ no other complete and consistent hypothesis of complexity $q_H$ exists. If $e$ is a noisy example then $H$ is not a complete and consistent hypothesis for $E'$. A different hypothesis must be constructed and for this, according to the condition of uniqueness of the hypothesis $H$, $q(E') > q_H = q(E)$ must hold. Note that it is supposed that for $E'$ a complete and consistent hypothesis can be constructed. If this is not true it means that $e$ is in contradiction with some training example from $E$. In this case the presence of noise can be detected by the existence of contradictions in the training set. □

Theorem 4 presents the basis for the suggested noise elimination algorithm. But it must be noted that the theorem makes use of the definition of a large enough training set $E$. In practice it is very hard to verify whether a training set $E$ is large enough. In practice, there need not exist a unique simplest correct hypothesis $H$. The consequence is that the claims of the theorem need not necessarily hold, which results in imperfect noise detection. The assumption is that with the increase of the number of non-noisy examples in $E$, the conditions of the theorem will be better satisfied thus increasing the probability of successful noise detection. The correctness of the theorem does not depend on the definition of the hypothesis complexity function $q(E)$, but the sensitivity of this function can influence the value $m$, the number of training examples necessary for the applicability of the theorem.

## 4.3   An exhaustive noise elimination algorithm

In this section we assume that the training set $E$ does not contain contradictory examples, i.e., identical examples belonging to different classes. Contradictory examples are potentially noisy, therefore, if $E$ contains contradictions, these need to be resolved by eliminating some, or all, training examples that constitute contradictions. This can be done in preprocessing.

Now we can try to answer the following question: Does a training set $E$ contain noise? Based on Theorem 4 we can answer the question in the following way. If it holds that

$$q(E) = q(E \setminus \{e\})$$

for all possible examples $e \in E$ then there is no noise in the domain and the domain is large enough that the correct hypothesis $H$ can be induced. If this is not the case and an example $e$ enables complexity reduction, i.e., $q(E) > q(E \setminus \{e\})$, then the example $e$ is potentially incorrect. If there is more than one example whose elimination can lead to complexity reduction, it is advisable to eliminate only the one that reduces the complexity the most. The elimination of 'suspicious' examples is an iterative process where one example is eliminated in each iteration until no elimination can result in further complexity reduction.

Algorithm 1 presents a general solution of the noise elimination problem. Its drawback is that it requires $m$ complexity computations per one example elimination, which is the most time consuming part of the algorithm.

**Algorithm 1: Exhaustive noise elimination**

**Given:** set of literals $L$, quality function $q$, noise sensitivity parameter $\varepsilon$
**Input:** example set $E$ with $m$ examples
**Output:** pruned example set $E$

> **repeat**
>> compute the estimate of the complexity of the least complex hypothesis that is complete and consistent with all training examples in $E$:
>> $q_H = q(E)$
>> **repeat for all examples** $e_i \in E$ $(i = 1 \ldots m)$
>>> compute the estimate of the complexity of the least complex hypothesis that is complete and consistent with the training examples in $E \setminus \{e_i\}$: $q_i = q(E \setminus \{e_i\})$
>> **endrepeat**
>> select $e_i$ with smallest $q_i$
>> **if** $(q_H - q_i) > \varepsilon$ **then** eliminate $e_i$ from $E$ and begin a new iteration with $E = E \setminus \{e_i\}$ and $m = m - 1$
>> **else** stop example elimination
> **endrepeat**

## 4.4 A heuristic noise elimination algorithm

Theorem 3 can now be used as a basis for the implementation of a more efficient algorithm for noise elimination. The basic idea of the algorithm is to use the minimal subset $L' \subseteq L$ and to ask the following question: Can any of the literals in $L'$ be made unnecessary for building a complete and consistent hypothesis if one (or a few) training example(s) are eliminated? The practical applicability of the proposed approach follows from the observation that, in most cases, for a noisy example $e_i$ a set $L'_i$ can be found such that $L'_i \subset L'$, where $L'_i$ covers all $p/n$ pairs of the set $E \setminus \{e_i\}$. The noisy examples that do not have this property will not be detected by the noise elimination algorithm. The heuristic noise elimination algorithm (Algorithm 2), which employs the heuristic literal minimization algorithm (Algorithm 3) is presented.

The complexity of Algorithm 2 is

$$\mathcal{O}((s+1) \cdot (\text{complexity-of-Algorithm3} + |L'| \cdot \text{complexity-of-Procedure1})) =$$

$$\mathcal{O}((s+1)(|L||L'||E|^2 + |L'||E|^2)) = \mathcal{O}(|E|^2)$$

where $s$ is the number of suspicious examples eliminated by the algorithm.

## Algorithm 2: Heuristic noise elimination

**Given:** set of literals $L$, quality function $q(E, L) = |L'|$ (the number of literals in the minimal set $L'$), noise sensitivity parameter $\varepsilon_h$
**Input:** training set $E$ with $m$ examples
**Output:** pruned example set $E$

> **repeat**
>> find by heuristic search a minimal subset $L'$ of $L$ such that a complete and consistent hypothesis $H(E, L')$ can be built (Algorithm 3)
>> **for** all examples $e_i \in E$ $(i = 1 \ldots m)$ set weight $w(e_i) = 0$
>> **repeat** for all literals $l \in L'$
>>> find the minimal subset $E'$ of examples by whose elimination the literal $l$ can be made unnecessary (Procedure 1)
>>> for all examples $e_i \in E'$ compute $w(e_i) = w(e_i) + 1/|E'|$
>> **endrepeat**
>> select the example $e_i$ with greatest weight $w(e_i)$
>> **if** $w(e_i) > \varepsilon_h$ **then** eliminate $e_i$ from $E$ and begin a new iteration with $E = E \setminus \{e_i\}$ and $m = m - 1$
>> **else** stop example elimination
> **endrepeat**

Algorithm 2 uses the noise sensitivity parameter $\varepsilon_h$ that determines the sensitivity of the algorithm. The parameter can be adjusted by the user in order to tune the algorithm according to the domain characteristics. Reasonable values are between 0.25 and 2. For instance, the value 1.0 guarantees elimination of every such example by whose elimination the set $L'$ will be immediately reduced for at least one literal. The lower values mean greater algorithm sensitivity (i.e., elimination of more examples): lower $\varepsilon_h$ values should be used when the domain noise is not completely random, and when dealing with large training sets (since statistical properties of noise distribution in large training sets can have similar effects). The default values of $\varepsilon_h$ are determined based on the number of training examples in the smaller of the two subsets of $E$: either the set of positive examples $P$ or the negative examples $N$.

| Number of examples | Default $\varepsilon_h$ |
|---|---|
| 2-50 | 1.5 |
| 51-100 | 1.0 |
| 101-200 | .75 |
| more than 201 | .50 |

The literal minimization algorithm (Algorithm 3) employing heuristic search is outlined below.

## Algorithm 3: Heuristic minimization of literals

**Input:** set of literals $L$, set of all $p/n$ pairs $PN$
**Output:** minimal set of literals $L'$
    initialize the set of $p/n$ pairs that are not yet covered by any literal $PN':= PN$
    initialize the minimal set of literals $L' := \emptyset$
    for each $p/n \in PN'$ compute the weight $v(p/n) = 1/z$ where $z$ is the number of literals that cover the pair
    **while** not covered $p/n$ pairs exist **do**
        select an uncovered $p/n$ pair from $PN'$ (called $p_s/n_s$) with the maximal value of $v(p/n)$ (i.e. $p/n$ pair covered by the least number of literals)
        for each $l \in L$ covering $p_s/n_s$, compute $w(l) = \sum v(p/n)$ where summation is over all yet uncovered $p/n$ pairs from $PN'$ covered by literal $l$
        select the literal $l_s$ with the maximal $w(l)$ value and include it in the set of selected literals $L' := L' \cup \{l_s\}$
        remove from the set of uncovered $p/n$ pairs $PN'$ all $p/n$ pairs covered by the selected literal $l_s$
    **endwhile**

The algorithm results in a list of selected literals $L'$ which is the heuristically selected minimal literal set. The complexity of Algorithm 3 is

$$\mathcal{O}(|L||E|^2 + |L'|(|E|^2 + |L||E|^2 + |L| + |E|^2)) = \mathcal{O}(|L||L'||E|^2)$$

Algorithm 2 calls another procedure which, for the given subset $L'$ and some literal $l \in L'$, determines the minimal subset of examples that must be eliminated in order to make $l$ unnecessary when building a complete and consistent hypothesis.

## Procedure 1: Finding the mininal example set for elimination

**Input:** a set of literals $L'$ such that a complete and consistent hypothesis $H(E, L')$ can be generated, a literal $l \in L'$
**Output:** the minimal set of examples $E'$ that should be eliminated in order to make $l$ unnecessary
    find all $p_i/n_j$ pairs that are covered by $l$ and not covered by any other literal from $L'$
    form set $P'$ consisting of all $p_i$ examples
    form set $N'$ consisting of all $n_j$ examples
    **if** $|P'| < |N'|$ **then** $E' = P'$ is the minimal example set
    **else** $E' = N'$ is the minimal example set

The complexity of Procedure 1 is $\mathcal{O}(|E|^2 + |E| + |E|) = \mathcal{O}(|E|^2)$.

# 5 Experimental results

The presented noise elimination algorithm is implemented in the ILLM (Inductive Learning by Logic Minimization) system [5]. This section presents the results of its application within the LINUS framework on the KRK domain for learning illegal positions in a chess endgame.

## 5.1 Learning illegal positions in a chess endgame

In the chess endgame domain White King and Rook versus Black King, described in [16] and [20], the target relation $illegal(WKf, WKr, WRf, WRr, BKf, BKr)$ states whether the position where the White King is at $(WKf, WKr)$, the White Rook at $(WRf, WRr)$ and the Black King is at $(BKf, BKr)$ is not a legal White-to-move position.

In FOIL [20], background knowledge is represented by two relations, $adjacent(X, Y)$ and $less\_than(X, Y)$, indicating that rank/file $X$ is adjacent to rank/file $Y$ and rank/file $X$ is less than rank/file $Y$, respectively. The arguments of these background predicates are not typed and the same predicates are used for both types of arguments. In LINUS [9, 11], each of these predicates is replaced by two predicates, one for each type of arguments. Thus, LINUS uses the following relations: $adjacent\_file(X, Y)$ and $less\_file(X, Y)$ with arguments of type $file$ (with values $a$ to $h$), $adjacent\_rank(X, Y)$ and $less\_rank(X, Y)$ with arguments of type $rank$ (with values 1 to 8), and equality $X = Y$, used for both types of arguments.

## 5.2 Noise detection in small datasets with random noise

A natural way to test noise handling is to select a noiseless domain and measure the accuracy of the hypotheses generated with different levels of intentionally introduced noise in the examples. This approach has been already applied to test the performance of some ILP algorithms in the presence of noise [10, 4, 11].

The experiments with LINUS [9, 11] and FOIL (FOIL0) [20] were performed on the same training and testing sets, all of which were used in [16]. Various amounts of noise were added to the examples from the chess endgame domain. Five sets of 100 examples were used as training sets, and classification accuracy was tested on 5000 examples (merged 5 sets of 1000 examples each).

In what follows, $x$ % of noise means that in $x$ % of examples, the class values were replaced by random values. For example, 5 % of classification noise means that class value was changed to a random value in 5 out of 100 example.[3] The percentage of introduced noise varied from 5 % to 30 % as follows: 5 %, 10 %, 15 %, 20 % and 30 %. No noise was introduced into the background knowledge.

---

[3] It is important to be aware of the fact that 5% of noise means that in 5% of examples the class value was randomly replaced by 0 or 1. Thus 5% noise does not mean 5 noisy (incorrect) examples but rather less than 5.

First we tried to repeat some of the experiments reported in [10, 4, 11] using the same domain with exactly the same training and test sets. We repeated the experiment with 5 sets of 100 training examples in which 0–30% of noise was introduced in the values of the class variable. Tests were made on a separate set of 5000 examples. Table 1 compares the accuracies obtained by two noise tolerant systems, LINUS-ASSISTANT and FOIL, with LINUS-ILLM which employs the heuristic noise elimination algorithm (Algorithm 2, Section 4.4) using $\varepsilon_h = 1.5$ (the default value for sets of 100 training examples). The column with LINUS-ILLM results includes the accuracy, the mean value of the number of eliminated examples, and numbers of eliminated examples in each individual training set. In Table 1 (as well as in Tables 2 and 3), a column LINUS-ILLM' is included, giving the results obtained with LINUS-ILLM without example elimination.

| Noise level in % | Accuracy | | | |
|---|---|---|---|---|
| | LINUS ASSISTANT | FOIL0 | LINUS ILLM | LINUS ILLM' |
| 0 | 95 | 92 | 97 (0.0 - 0,0,0,0,0) | 97 |
| 5 | 91 | 88 | 95 (0.8 - 1,2,0,1,0) | 92 |
| 10 | 88 | 85 | 90 (2.2 - 1,4,0,1,5) | 87 |
| 15 | 89 | 87 | 90 (3.6 - 4,6,2,1,5) | 85 |
| 20 | 89 | 88 | 87 (4.8 - 3,9,4,2,6) | 83 |
| 30 | 85 | 83 | 77 (3.4 - 2,4,3,5,3) | 77 |

**Table 1.** Comparison of results for different levels of classification noise on 5 domains with 100 training examples each.

Results show that LINUS-ILLM with noise elimination has a slightly better prediction accuracy for low noise levels than LINUS-ASSISTANT and FOIL. On the other hand, for higher noise levels LINUS-ASSISTANT and FOIL seem to be more appropriate. It can be also noticed that the numbers of eliminated examples by noise elimination are relatively small compared to the numbers that could be expected based on the level of inserted noise. An intuitive conclusion is that noise elimination is more successful for domains with a small number of random errors.

## 5.3 Noise detection in small datasets with controlled noise

In order to better investigate this property we used the same 5 noiseless domains of 100 training examples and intentionally inserted individual noisy examples. Besides the prediction accuracy, we were interested also in the total number of eliminated (potentially noisy) examples and the number of correctly detected noisy examples.

| Number of | LINUS-ILLM | | | | | | LINUS-ILLM' |
|---|---|---|---|---|---|---|---|
| introduced | $\varepsilon_h = 1.5$ | | | $\varepsilon_h = 0.75$ | | | |
| class errors | Total Corr. | | | Total | Corr. | | |
| | elim. | elim. | Acc. | elim. | elim. | Acc. | Acc. |
| 0 | 0.0 | 0.0 | 97.4 | 2.0 (1,0,4,5,0) | 0.0 (0,0,0,0,0) | 96.6 | 97.4 |
| 1 | 0.6 | 0.4 | 95.0 | 3.2 (2,1,5,8,1) | 0.6 (1,1,1,0,0) | 95.2 | 94.1 |
| 2 | 1.6 | 1.4 | 95.4 | 4.4 (3,2,6,9,2) | 1.8 (2,2,2,1,2) | 96.0 | 90.8 |
| 3 | 2.0 | 1.2 | 92.3 | 5.2 (3,2,7,10,4) | 1.8 (2,1,2,3,1) | 92.1 | 91.1 |
| 4 | 2.2 | 1.2 | 91.4 | 5.6 (4,3,7,9,5) | 2.4 (3,2,3,2,2) | 92.1 | 88.5 |
| 5 | 2.6 | 1.4 | 91.0 | 5.6 (5,4,8,5,6) | 2.6 (3,3,4,2,1) | 91.6 | 87.6 |

**Table 2.** Results of LINUS-ILLM on 5 domains with 100 training examples with controlled noise insertion.

Table 2 shows that although the accuracy was again very high, the numbers of correctly detected noisy examples, together with the total number of eliminated examples, were relatively small. That is the consequence of the relatively high value of parameter $\varepsilon_h = 1.5$ which is the default value for 100 training examples. In order to show the effects of the change in $\varepsilon_h$ values, the same measurements were repeated also for value $\varepsilon_h = 0.75$. These results are also given in Table 2. It can be seen that the accuracy did not change significantly but that the total number and the number of correct eliminations have both increased. Moreover, the ratio of correct and total eliminations has decreased.

Despite the satisfactory results of LINUS-ILLM in Tables 1 and 2, especially when compared to the results ILLM-ASSISTANT and FOIL, the described approach to noise elimination could not show all its potential on this learning domains with only 100 training examples. The problem is the following. Having only 100 examples in the training set, the learner is in the growing part of the curve presented in Figure 1, where the number of training examples $|E|$ is smaller than the minimal number of examples $m_0$ needed to be able to learn a correct theory. This is in contrast with the assumptions of the algorithm.

## 5.4 Noise detection in large datasets with controlled noise

To test the performance of the LINUS-ILLM noise elimination algorithm on more appropriate domains, we selected five domains with 1000 training examples and repeated the experiments with inserted noisy examples. Also, in order to make the experiment more similar to real-life applications and in contrast to previous experiments, background knowledge was expanded with 180 additional literals of the form *Attribute = Value*, *Attribute ≠ Value*, *Attribute ≤ Value*, *Attribute > Value*. The selected noise elimination value for 1000 example datasets was $\varepsilon_h = 0.5$ (i.e., the default value for datasets consisting of more than 200 training examples). Test sets consisted of 4000 examples.

The results are given in Table 3. It can be seen that in each experiment some (but a relative small number of) correct examples were detected as noisy. For each experiment this number can be calculated as a difference between the total number of eliminated examples and the number of correctly eliminated examples. For up to 30 inserted noisy examples all inserted noise has been completely correctly detected. The consequence is that for up to 3% of inserted noise the prediction accuracy has been constant and equal to the accuracy achieved by LINUS-ASSISTANT and FOIL from non-noisy training sets of 1000 examples [4]. It can be seen that the reported accuracies for more than 3% of intentionally inserted noise are very high as well. This confirms our hypothesis that with large training sets, where $|E| \gg m_0$, noise detection becomes much more reliable than with small training sets $E$ where $|E| < m_0$.

| Number of introduced class errors | LINUS-ILLM | | | LINUS-ILLM' |
|---|---|---|---|---|
| | Total number of eliminated examples | Correctly eliminated ex. | Acc. | Acc. |
| 0 | 3.6 (5,4,2,3,4) | 0.0 (0,0,0,0,0) | 99.8 | 99.5 |
| 10 | 13.3 (15,14,12,13,14) | 10.0 (10,10,10,10,10) | 99.8 | 97.7 |
| 20 | 24.0 (25,24,22,25,24) | 20.0 (20,20,20,20,20) | 99.8 | 95.1 |
| 30 | 36.2 (38,38,32,33,35) | 30.0 (30,30,30,30,30) | 99.8 | 93.6 |
| 40 | 41.4 (58,44,43,19,43) | 35.0 (40,40,40,16,39) | 98.4 | 92.2 |
| 50 | 39.2 (31,40,46,39,40) | 33.0 (26,36,33,33,37) | 95.9 | 90.2 |

Table 3. Results of LINUS-ILLM on 5 domains with 1000 training examples with controlled noise insertion.

# 6 Conclusion

The basic idea of this work is to separate noise handling from hypothesis formation. The paper presents an algorithm that uses a simple compression measure to detect noisy examples. Experimental results indicate that in terms of accuracy the proposed approach to noise handling is comparable to other algorithms with noise handling capabilities.

The results on small datasets of 100 examples with random (Section 5.2) or controlled noise (Section 5.3) indicate that the noise detection and elimination algorithm is particularly well suited for datasets with a relatively small amount of erroneous examples, whereas with larger amounts of noise noise detection becomes less reliable. The achieved results are good, despite the fact that these datasets do not fulfil the requirement that the dataset should contain enough training examples to induce the correct hypothesis $H$ (a hypothesis $H$ which is complete and consistent also for yet unseen examples of an unknown target theory $T$). In recent work, not presented in this paper, the heuristic noise elimination algorithm was successfully applied also in the problem of early diagnosis of rheumatic diseases [8]. Although the rheumatology domain is very noisy, noise elimination resulted in improved performance of CN2 when learning from a training set with eliminated noise. This shows the utility of the noise elimination algorithm also for real-life domains with large amounts of noise.

In this paper, good performance of the algorithm was confirmed on large datasets of 1000 examples (Section 5.4), a domain fulfilling the theoretical requirements for the applicability of the noise elimination algorithm.

Compared to other algorithms that successfully deal with noisy data, the technique proposed in this paper has the following advantages. First, noisy examples can be detected and shown to the user for inspection. Second, noise handling is not hypothesis biased, i.e., the separation of noise detection and hypothesis formation has the advantage that noisy examples do not influence the hypothesis construction (as opposed to standard approaches to noise handling in which in the hypothesis formation process the learner tries to avoid overfitting the noisy example set). Third, having eliminated potentially noisy examples, hypothesis formation can be done by any algorithm that generates complete and consistent hypotheses. Finally, explicit detection and elimination of noisy examples enables the construction of hypotheses with specific properties. This can be interesting for special domains, for example medical domains, since noise elimination can be used to ensure predictions with a small number of false positive cases and predictions of high reliability even when the inaccuracy of input values is expected [6].

A disadvantage of the proposed technique is its time and space complexity. Although significant savings can be obtained by the heuristic noise elimination algorithm as compared to the exhaustive algorithm, noise elimination is significantly more complex than noise handling by noise tolerant methods. In ILLM, the current practical upper bound is about 1000 training examples.

# Acknowledgements

This work has been financially supported by the Slovenian Ministry of Science and Technology, the Croatian Ministry of Science, and the ESPRIT IV project Inductive Logic Programming II.

# References

1. B. Cestnik and I. Bratko. On estimating probabilities in tree pruning. In *Proc. 5th European Working Session on Learning*, 138–150, 1991.
2. P. Clark and T. Niblett. The CN2 induction algorithm. *Machine Learning*, 3(4):261–283, 1989.
3. K.A. De Jong and W.M. Spears. Learning concept classification rules using genetic algorithms. In *Proceedings of the 12th International Joint Conference on Artificial Intelligence (IJCAI-91)*, Morgan Kaufmann, (1991) 651–656.

4. S. Džeroski, N. Lavrač. Inductive learning in deductive databases. *IEEE Transactions on Knowledge and Data Engineering*, 5(6), 939–949, 1993.

5. D. Gamberger. A minimization approach to propositional inductive learning. In *Proceedings of the 8th European Conference on Machine Learning (ECML-95)*, Springer, (1995) 151–160.

6. D. Gamberger. Specific rule induction for medical domains. In *Proc. Computer-Aided Data Analysis in Medicine, CADAM-95*, 136–145. IJS Scientific Publishing IJS-SP-95-1, 1995.

7. D. Gamberger and N. Lavrač. Towards a theory of relevance in inductive concept learning. *Technical report IJS-DP-7310*. J. Stefan Institute, Ljubljana, 1995.

8. D. Gamberger, N. Lavrač and S. Džeroski. Noise elimination in inductive concept learning: A case study in medical diagnosis. In *Proc. Seventh International Workshop on Algorithmic Learning Theory ALT'96*, Springer 1996 (in press).

9. N. Lavrač, S. Džeroski and M. Grobelnik. Learning nonrecursive definitions of relations with LINUS. In *Proc. Fifth European Working Session on Learning*, pages 265–281, Springer, Berlin, 1991.

10. N. Lavrač and S. Džeroski. Inductive learning of relations from noisy examples. In S. Muggleton (ed.) *Inductive Logic Programming*, 495–516. Academic Press, 1992.

11. N. Lavrač and S. Džeroski. *Inductive Logic Programming: Techniques and Applications*. Ellis Horwood (Simon & Schuster), Ellis Horwood Series in Artificial Intelligence. UK: Chichester, 1994.

12. N. Lavrač, D. Gamberger and S. Džeroski. An approach to dimensionality reduction in learning from deductive databases. In *Proceedings of the 5th International Workshop on Inductive Logic Programming (ILP-95)*, Technical report, Katholieke Universiteit Leuven, 1995.

13. N. Lavrač, S. Džeroski and I. Bratko. Handling imperfect data in inductive logic programming. In L. De Raedt (ed.) *Advances in Inductive Logic Programming*, 48–64. IOS Press, 1996.

14. J. Mingers. An empirical comparison of pruning methods for decision tree induction. *Machine Learning*, 4(2):227–243, 1989.

15. J. Mingers. An empirical comparison of selection measures for decision-tree induction. *Machine Learning*, 3(4):319–342, 1989.

16. S.H. Muggleton, M. Bain, J. Hayes-Michie and D.Michie. An experimental comparison of human and machine learning formalisms. In *Proc. Sixth International Workshop on Machine Learning*, 113–118, Morgan Kaufmann, San Mateo, CA, 1989.

17. S. Muggleton, A. Srinivasan and M. Bain. Compression, significance and accuracy. In *Proc. 9th International Conference on Machine Learning*, 338–347. Morgan Kaufmann, 1992.

18. T. Niblett T and I. Bratko. Learning decision rules in noisy domains. In M. Bramer (ed.) *Research and Development in Expert Systems III*, 24–25. Cambridge University Press, 1986.

19. R. Quinlan. Simplifying decision trees. *International Journal of Man-Machine Studies*, 27(3):221–234, 1987.

20. J.R. Quinlan. Learning logical definitions from relations. *Machine Learning*, 5(3): 239–266, 1990.

21. J. Rissanen. Modeling by shortest data description. *Automatica*, 14: 465–471, 1978.

# Feature Construction with Inductive Logic Programming: A Study of Quantitative Predictions of Biological Activity by Structural Attributes

Ashwin Srinivasan[1] and Ross.D. King[2]

[1] Oxford University Computing Laboratory,
Wolfson Building, Parks Road, Oxford
[2] Biomolecular Modelling Laboratory,
Imperial Cancer Research Fund, Lincoln's Inn Fields, London

**Abstract.** Recently, computer programs developed within the field of Inductive Logic Programming (ILP) have received some attention for their ability to construct restricted first-order logic solutions using problem-specific background knowledge. Prominent applications of such programs have been concerned with determining "structure-activity" relationships in the areas of molecular biology and chemistry. Typically the task here is to predict the "activity" of a compound, like toxicity, from its chemical structure. Research in the area shows that: (a) ILP programs have been restricted to qualitative predictions of activity ("high", "low" etc.); (b) When appropriate attributes are available, ILP programs have not been able to better the performance of standard quantitative analysis techniques like linear regression. However ILP programs perform creditably when such attributes are unavailable; and (c) When both are applicable, ILP programs are usually slower than their propositional counterparts. This paper examines the use of ILP programs, not for obtaining theories complete for the sample, but as a method of "discovering" new attributes. These could then be used by methods like linear regression, thus allowing for quantitative predictions and the ability to use structural information as background knowledge. Using structure-activity tasks as a test-bed the utility of ILP programs in constructing new features was evaluated by examining the prediction of chemical activity using linear regression, with and without the aid of ILP learnt logical attributes. In three out of the five datasets examined the addition of ILP attributes produced statistically better results (P ¡0.01). In addition six important structural features that have escaped the attention of the expert chemists were discovered.

## 1  Introduction

In principle, there is no restriction to the functions that can be learnt within the theoretical framework provided by Inductive Logic Programming (ILP). It is a measure of the promise offered by this setting that ILP programs have already been applied with some success on non-trivial problems in molecular biology [14, 15, 21], stress analysis in engineering [7], electronic circuit diagnosis [10], environmental monitoring [9], software engineering [2], and natural language processing [29]. These results were all achieved using problem-specific background knowledge encoded as logic programs, and without recourse to other methods of statistical analysis. While in theory the effect of all such methods *could* be implemented within the logical setting, practical constraints placed on ILP programs ensure that it is rarely the case.

Rather than re-implementing widely used methods of statistics, could ILP programs be better utilised in conjunction with such techniques? This paper investigates this issue on problems concerned with predicting the chemical activity of small molecules. These problems serve as a good test-bed for the following reasons. First, the established method of prediction is by regression on attributes identified by an expert chemist. This has partly resulted from a need for quantitative predictions. Second, much effort is invested into obtaining good attributes for the regression. Any assistance towards this end could potentially aid a chemist.

The results of applying ILP programs, supplied with the chemical structure of the molecules, to obtain logical descriptions relating structure to activity. can be summarised as follows: (a) ILP programs have been restricted to qualitative predictions of activity ("high", "low" etc.); (b) When appropriate attributes are available, ILP programs have not been able to better the performance of standard quantitative analysis techniques like linear regression. However ILP programs perform creditably when such attributes are unavailable; and (c) When both are applicable, ILP programs are usually slower than their propositional counterparts.

In this paper we adopt the position that propositional prediction methods like regression should exploit the fact that ILP programs can extract structural relationships: and in turn, ILP programs can rely on well-established quantitative methods for predicting the value of a numerical response variable. In short we propose a synergy between ILP and numerical propositional methods. On this basis, we examine a role for ILP programs that extract potentially useful attributes from problem-specific background knowledge. These "new" attributes are boolean-valued and augment any existing attributes that are thought to be relevant. The utility of using ILP programs for this purpose is examined on structure-activity problems that fall into the following cases:

**Case A.** Expert's attributes are thought to be sufficient to support whatever predictivity is attainable for the given SAR problem (using an appropriate algorithm);

**Case B.** Expert's attributes exist, but are thought to need augmenting to achieve improved predictivity; and

**Case C.** Expert's attributes are completely inadequate for prediction of biological activity.

The problems considered in this paper are: inhibition of E. Coli Dihydrofolate Reductase by pyrimidines and triazines (Case A), calcium channel agonists (Case

B), mutagenic activity of nitroaromatics (Cases A and C). The paper is organised as follows. Section 2 clarifies the scope of this study. Materials available are described in Section 3, the design of experiments in Section 4, and results in Sections 5. Section 6 concludes this study.

## 2 Experimental Aim

Using structure-activity tasks as a test-bed, the utility of ILP programs in constructing new features is evaluated by examining the prediction of biological activity using linear regression, with and without the aid of logical attributes that represent the features extracted by an ILP program.

## 3 Materials

### 3.1 Data

Five data sets are used in this study, and are summarised in Figure 1. The data sets are concerned with the following problems: the inhibition of E. Coli Dihydrofolate Reductase by the enzymes pyrimidine and triazine (PYR, TRIA); modulating transmembrane calcium movement (CCA); and the mutagenicity of nitroaromatic compounds, belonging to two disparate groups of 188 and 42 compounds. Those in the former (MUT1) form a sort of "regression-friendly" class, given the attributes identified as being useful. Of the 42 compounds in the latter set, actual activity values are only available for 20. These form the MUT2 data in Figure 1. Qualitative predictions of activity have been obtained using ILP algorithms on all except the CCA data.

| Case | Data | Number of examples | Number of expert attributes |
|------|------|--------------------|-----------------------------|
|      | PYR  | 55                 | 6                           |
| A    | TRIA | 186                | 11                          |
|      | MUT1 | 188                | 5                           |
| B    | CCA  | 36                 | 2                           |
| C    | MUT2 | 20                 | 5                           |

**Fig. 1.** Characteristics of data sets used in experiments.

### 3.2 Expert attributes for regression

For each data set the chemical literature describes empirical structure-activity relationships (SARs) derived by regression analyses. The variables used to obtain the regressions are listed below. We caution the reader that we have not attempted detailed descriptions of each data set. For these, we refer the reader to the specific papers cited for each problem.

**PYR.** The chemical structures of all compounds used to induce the SAR can be considered to have a common template. To this template, chemical groups can be added at three possible substitution positions, 3, 4, and 5 of the basic phenyl ring. Activity is measured as $log(1/K)$ where $K$ is the inhibition constant as experimentally assayed. The following attributes were used in obtaining the SARs [11].

| Attribute | Description |
|---|---|
| $MR'_{3,5}$ | Composite molar reflectivity of substituents at positions 3,5 |
| $MR'_{3,4}$ | Composite molar reflectivity of substituents at positions 3,4 |
| $MR'_4$ | Molar reflectivity of substituent at position 4 |
| $\pi_{3,4,5}$ | Composite hydrophobicity of substituents at positions 3,4,5 |
| $\pi_{3,4}$ | Composite hydrophobicity of substituents at positions 3,4 |
| $log_{10}(1.318 \cdot 10^{\pi_{3,4,5}} + 1)$ | Attribute constructed by chemists |

**TRIA.** Like the pyrimidines, the compounds here can also be considered to have a common template structure. However, the chemical groups substituted onto the template are much more complicated. Further, many of the substituting groups can more naturally be considered as sub- templates with substitutions. There are seven regions where a substituent might be present: the 2, 3, and 4 positions of the phenyl ring. Each substituent can in turn, itself contain a ring structure. In this case, further substitutions are possible into positions 3 and 4 of these rings. Activity is measured as $log(1/C)$ where $C$ represents the molar concentration which produces 50% reversible inhibition of Dihydrofolate Reductase as experimentally assayed. The following attributes were used in obtaining the SARS [1, 24].

| Attribute | Description |
|---|---|
| $\pi_3$ | Hydrophobicity of substituent at position 3 |
| $\pi_4$ | Hydrophobicity of substituent at position 4 |
| $MR_3$ | Molar reflectivity of substituent at position 3 |
| $MR_4$ | Molar reflectivity of substituent at position 4 |
| $\sigma_{3,4}$ | Composite $\sigma$ effect of substituents at positions 3,4 |
| $I_1$ | Logical attribute: 1 if compound contains Walker's enzyme |
| $I_2$ | Logical attribute: 1 if compound contains an ortho-substitution |
| $I_3$ | Logical attribute: 1 if compound a rigid group to position 3 |
| $I_4$ | Logical attribute: 1 if compound a rigid group to position 4 |
| $I_5$ | Logical attribute: 1 if compound has flexible bridges between phenyl rings |
| $I_6$ | Logical attribute: 1 if compound has other (non-flexible) bridges |

**CCA.** The compounds are a class of calcium-channel activators and have a template based on mthyl 2,5-dimethyl-4-1H-pyrrole-3-carboxylate. Activity is measured as $log(F)$ where $F$ is the potency of the compound relative to an accepted standard calcium-channel activator ($EC_{50}$). The attributes below were used in obtaining the SARS [5]. Experiments show that incorporating structural information using the CoMFA methodology [5] can significantly improve activity predictions over just the simple attributes below. CoMFA is a a very complex chemical/statistical process that involves aligning compounds to a 3-D grid, the calculations of many interaction energies, formation of hundreds of new attributes, and resampling.

| Attribute | Description |
|---|---|
| $CLOGP$ | Hydrophobicity of compound |
| $CMR$ | Molar reflectivity of compound |

**MUT1,2.** Compounds used here have no particular template, although all compounds are nitro-aromatic compounds. Activity is measured using the Ames test for mutagenicity. The following attributes have been used to obtain SARs [6].

| Attribute | Description |
|---|---|
| $\epsilon_{LUMO}$ | Energy level of lowest unoccupied molecular orbital in compound |
| $log(P)$ | Hydrophobicity of compound |
| $I_1$ | Logical attribute: 1 if compound contains 3 or more benzyl rings |
| $I_a$ | Logical attribute: 1 if compound is an acenthrylene |
| $log_{10}(10^{(log(P)-5.48)} + 1)$ | Attribute constructed by chemists |

## 3.3 Background knowledge for ILP

Potentially useful background information concerning each data set is available for use by an ILP program. This is as follows.

**PYR.** The existence of a template with only three possible substitution positions gives the pyrimidine problem a relatively small structural component. The background knowledge consists of predicates that define the chemical structures substituted at each position. For example, a Prolog fact of the form:

struc(d55, cl, nh2 ch3)

is intended to represent that drug 55 has a chlorine atom substituted at position 3, a amino group ($NH_2$) group substituted at position 4, and a methyl ($CH_3$) group at position 5. Also included are properties of the different structures, and arithmetic predicates for comparison of values. More details of these predicates used can be found in [13, 15].

**TRIA.** More than one *struc*-like predicate is used to encode the structure of the triazines. For example, consider the following Prolog facts:

struc3(d217, cl, absent).
struc4(d217, (ch2)24, subst14).
subst(subst14, so2f, cl).

The first clause represents substitutions at position 3 on the basic template: a $Cl$ is present and there is an absence of a further phenyl ring. The second clause represents substitutions at position 4 on the basic template: there is a $(CH_2)4$ bridge to a second phenyl ring (implicit in the representation). This second phenyl ring has a $S0_2F$ group substituted at position 3 and a $Cl$ group substituted at position 4. This is represented using the linker constant subst14 to the third clause. There is no substitution at position 2 on the basic template. As in the pyrimidines, background also includes basic properties of the substituent groups: we refer the reader to [13] for details.

**CCA, MUT1,2.** Primitive structural descriptions of the molecules and generic chemical knowledge of structural templates. The former include the atom and bond structures in each molecule, along with typing information automatically obtained from the modelling program QUANTA. This results in the structure being represented by sets of facts of the form:

atom(127, 127_1, c, 22, 0.191)
bond(127, 127_1, 127_6, 7)

which states that in compound 127, atom number 1 is a carbon atom of QUANTA type 22 with a partial charge of 0.191, and atoms 1 and 6 are connected by a bond of type 7 (aromatic). The generic structural definitions used provide definitions of methyl groups, nitro groups, aromatic rings, hetero-aromatic rings, connected rings, ring length, and the three distinct topological ways to connect three benzene rings. These definitions are generic to the field of organic chemistry Complete listings of these definitions can be found in [27].

All predicates also have "mode" annotations indicating input and output argument positions (see [20, 22] for details on mode annotations)

## 3.4 Algorithms

The propositional engine used here is the stepwise linear regression procedure implemented within the SPSS package [23]. Experience has shown that this is a robust statistcal method, even when logical attributes are involved [19]. This sequential method is the standard procedure for searching for a subset of variables (attributes) from a large set of possible candidates that may exhibit large deviations from orthogonality (linear independence). Two ILP programs have been used to extract structural constructs from the background knowledge. The program Golem [22] is used on the data sets PYR and TRIA. This is in keeping with earlier ILP experiments on these data sets. Golem is incapable of reasoning with the type of background knowledge available for the CCA and MUT data sets. For these the Progol program [20] is used. We use the Prolog implementation of *Progol*, called *P-Progol (Version 2.0)*. At the time of writing this paper S.H. Muggleton has implemented a version called *CProgol* in the C language. Details of obtaining this version can be found in [20]. *P-Progol* is available on request from Ashwin Srinivasan (electronic mail: ashwin@comlab.ox.ac.uk). The implementation includes on-line documentation that clarifies the points of difference with the C version. The theory underlying both versions is the same and is described fully in [20]. However, differences in search strategies and pruning facilities imply that given the same language and resource restrictions, the two versions can compute different answers.

## 4 Method

For reference, we term all attributes available prior to any ILP analysis as "expert attributes". Those obtained from an ILP analysis are termed "ILP attributes".

Two issues arise in a study such as this one. The first concerns the sequential selection of attributes by the regression procedure. This selection is controlled by settings of the significance levels used for including and excluding attributes. These parameters thus constrain the variables that can appear in an equation, and the regression procedure *per se* provides no guidance on "good" settings for a data set. Secondly, having decided on some "good" setting, a quantitative assessment of the gains obtained from augmenting expert attributes with ILP extracted ones has to performed. In this paper, we adopt the following two stage design to address each of these issues:

**Stage 1: Explore.** Using expert attributes only, and both expert and ILP attributes, determine "good" significance levels for each data set. One way of determining such levels is to be guided by estimates obtained from cross-validation. The use of cross-validation for parameter estimation has been preferred over distribution-based tests, such as the F-test, as they directly consider predictive performance (see, for example, [28]). This procedure is adopted here and described in Section 4.1.

**Stage 2: Assess.** For each data set where the predictive power of equations with and without ILP attributes appear worthy of further investigation (in Stage 1), perform quantitative assessments for improvement in prediction. While useful in directing parameter estimation, it is not apparent that the cross-validation estimates obtained in Stage 1 could reliably be used for this assessment. In particular, repeated re-use of the sample within the cross-validation procedure could introduce dependencies that may violate assumptions of distribution-based tests of significance. Consequently, we adopt the classical statistical procedure as described in Section 4.2.

### 4.1 Stage 1: significance levels for regression

Consider a number of settings $S_1, S_2, \ldots, S_n$ for the stepwise regression equation. The following $k$-fold cross-validation design is adopted for the data sets.

1. Randomly assign the compounds in the set to $k$ (approximately) equal partitions. Each partition will, in turn, be withheld to form a "test" set. The compounds in the other partitions will provide the "training" data for constructing the equation for predicting the activity of a compound.
2. With each of the $k$ training data sets and each setting $S_i$:
   (a) Construct an equation $E_{exp}$ relating activity to expert attributes.
   (b) Divide the range of activities in the (training) data set into $I$ intervals. For all experiments here, $I = 2$. The activity value 0 is chosen as the point of division into 2 intervals (namely, "active" and "inactive").
   (c) For each of the $I$ intervals, use an ILP system and background information available, to obtain clauses describing compounds in that interval. It is not required that all examples in the training set need be explained by these clauses.
   (d) Each input-output connected subset of literals in the clauses obtained maps to a new (ILP) attribute. That is, all examples for which a subset of literals is true get the value 1 for the corresponding attribute. All other examples get the value 0 for that attribute. Select at most $N$ such new attributes. For all experiments here $N$ is restricted to 200. The selection of attributes is done by evaluating the "compression" (as defined in [20]) of the corresponding ILP clauses.
   (e) Obtain values for the ILP attributes selected for every data item in the training and test set.
   (f) Construct an equation $E_{exp+ilp}$ relating activity to all attributes available (i.e. expert and ILP attributes)
   (g) Record predictions of $E_{exp}$ and $E_{exp+ilp}$ on the test data set.
3. For each setting $S_i$, from records of actual and predicted values of biological activity on the $k$ test data sets, evaluate the correlation coefficent between $E_{exp}$ and $E_{exp+ilp}$. This is termed $rpred_{exp}$ and $rpred_{exp+ilp}$.

We clarify further some issues raised by Steps 2b–2d:

**Qualitative values (Step 2b)** . The division here of the biological activity scale into 2 qualitative values, denoted "active" and "inactive", is in concordance with the cited research that has used ILP programs on some of the data. In principle, there is no restriction on the number of such intervals that may be considered, and a more detailed approach could use a finer division by examining the histogram of activity values.

**Learning clauses (Step 2c)** . We first draw attention to the fact that clauses are constructed for each of the $I$ qualitative values using the following training data. Compounds whose activity map to each such value constitute positive examples for that value, and all others constitute negative examples for that value. Further, since the aim here is to find *some* interesting structural concepts, we do not require that the clauses obtained derive all the positive examples in the training data.

**Construction and selection of attributes (Step 2d)** . Given a clause constructed by an ILP program, any subset of literals could be selected to mapped to new attribute. The input-output connected subsets selected here represent those literals that are clearly dependent on each other, and is in accordance with other transformational approaches that construct propositions from clauses within a given first-order language [3].

As mentioned earlier, significance settings for the stepwise regression procedure control the inclusion and exclusion of variables in the equation. These parameters relate to the level of significance that has to be achieved above (or below) which a variable is retained in the model (or removed from the model). There is no prescribed setting for these parameters (termed $PIN$ and $POUT$ respectively in SPSS). Experimental results in this paper explore two settings: $S_1 = (PIN, POUT) = (0.05, 0.10)$ (default settings for SPSS) and $S_2 = (PIN, POUT) = (0.01, 0.05)$. These settings are not unreasonable, given that the settings refer to significance values.

The value of $k$ depends on the data set. For PYR, $k = 5$, TRIA and CCA, $k = 6$, and MUT1 $k = 10$. These are in keeping with other experiments that have been performed on these data sets both with and without ILP. No crossvalidation is needed for MUT2. The reason for this is described later.

## 4.2 Stage 2: quantitative assessment

Some basic concepts used in assessing goodness of fit of linear models, and a method of evaluating the relative contribution of a set of attributes in that model is given in Appendix A. The following procedure is followed to isolate the utility of the ILP attributes:

1. Data sets for which the difference between $rpred_{exp}$ and $rpred_{exp+ilp}$ values are non-significant are removed from further consideration. For these data sets, ILP attributes are assumed to contribute nothing, and no further quantitative assessment is required.
2. For data sets for which the difference between $rpred_{exp}$ and $rpred_{exp+ilp}$ values appear significant, find ILP attributes for *all* of the data using Steps 2b–2d in Section 4.1 above.
3. For each data set in Step 2, using the setting that yielded the highest correlation $rpred_{exp+ilp}$ at Step 3 in Section 4.1 above, obtain an equation $E_{exp+ilp}$ using all attributes.
4. Partition the variables in $E_{exp+ilp}$ into a set containing only expert attributes, and a set containing only ILP attributes. Using the concepts in Appendix A record changes in goodness of fit, and determine if the change caused by addition of the ILP attributes is significant using the partial F-test.

# 5 Experimental results and discussion

Complete tabulations from the exploratory cross-validatory stage are in Figure 2. Results suggesting further analysis are highlighted, and a quantitative assessment of the effect of the ILP attributes for these data sets is in Figure 3.

| Case | Data | $(PIN, POUT) = (0.05, 0.10)$ | | $(PIN, POUT) = (0.01, 0.05)$ | |
|------|------|-------------------|-----------------------|-------------------|-----------------------|
|      |      | $rpred_{exp}$ | $rpred_{exp+ilp}$ | $rpred_{exp}$ | $rpred_{exp+ilp}$ |
|      | PYR  | **0.77** | **0.83** | 0.77 | 0.77 |
| A    | TRIA | 0.63 | 0.64 | 0.64 | 0.64 |
|      | MUT1 | 0.89 | 0.89 | 0.89 | 0.89 |
| B    | CCA  | 0.80 | 0.81 | **0.80** | **0.87** |
| C    | MUT2 | $-^{\dagger}$ | **0.64$^{\ddagger}$** | $-^{\dagger}$ | 0.64$^{\ddagger}$ |

† no equation obtained

‡ resubstitution estimate

**Fig. 2.** Results from the exploratory cross-validation stage. Here $PIN, POUT$ are parameters controlling the regression; $rpred$ stands for the correlation of predicted to actual values as ascertained from the test data in the cross-validation. For MUT2, it is evident that prediction is only possible with the ILP attributes. It is therefore unnecessary to perform cross-validation.

We first draw attention to the fact that for data sets TRIA and MUT1, ILP attributes appear to have little to contribute, and further experimentation suggests that this would continue to hold even for other settings of $PIN$ and $POUT$. This in itself is not surprising, given that these two data sets fall in Case A, where expert attributes were thought to be sufficient. It is of interest however that the tabulations in Figure 2 suggest that the other Case A data set (PYR), and data sets in Cases B and C, all appear to benefit from having access to a mechanism of augmenting existing attributes with ones that capture structural features. Thus, the results appear to suggest that there are potential gains under all three scenarios presented by Cases A, B, and C. That this benefit may be non-trivial is supported by the tabulation in Figure 3, which shows that a significant proportion of variation in biological activity (the response variable) appears to explained by the ILP attributes. In fact, in the case of MUT2, the attributes transform what was "regression-unfriendly" data to a somewhat more "regression-friendly" form.

It is sometimes a matter of concern that equations obtained from a regression analysis could be overly complex, and that including more attributes could potentially exacerbate this problem. One way to ensure that the models constructed remain understandable is to employ fairly strict constraints on the inclusion of variables (the $PIN$ parameter here), and reasonably loose restrictions on their exclusion (the $POUT$ parameter). It is also worth noting that here that all ILP attributes are logical ones. In their application to determining SARs, a value of 1 for an ILP attribute in an example indicates the presence of some structural

| Case | Data | $r^2_{exp}$ | $r^2_{exp+ilp}$ | $r^2_{ch}$ | $Pr_{ilp}\%$ | Significance |
|------|------|-------------|-----------------|------------|--------------|--------------|
| A | PYR | 0.54 (0.53) | 0.84 (0.82) | 0.30 | 65 | $P < 0.01$ |
| B | CCA | 0.69 (0.68) | 0.84 (0.82) | 0.15 | 48 | $P < 0.01$ |
| C | MUT2 | – | 0.40 (0.37) | 0.40 | 40 | $P < 0.01$ |

**Fig. 3.** Assessing the contribution made by ILP attributes. Here $r^2_{exp}$ and $r^2_{exp+ilp}$ are the coefficients of multiple determination before and after inclusion of the ILP attributes that appear in the final equation (adjusted values are in parentheses); $r^2_{ch}$ measures the relative importance of the ILP attributes; $Pr_{ilp}$ measures (as a percentage) the proportion of unexplained variation that the change in $r^2$ constitutes; and the final column is the result of testing that the true population value for change in $r^2$ on adding the ILP attributes is 0.

relationship for that example. It is relatively straightforward to interpret the coefficients of such attributes in a regression equation: all other attributes being the same, the magnitude of the coefficient of an ILP attribute indicates the contribution of the presence of the corresponding structural feature. This should be borne in mind when examining Figure 4 which shows the equations obtained for the data sets in Figure 3. The figure also tabulates the number of terms (including the constant) in the regression equation obtained by using expert attributes only. Comparison against this number suggests that complexity (as measured by number of terms) changes little by inclusion of the ILP attributes, although several expert attributes are replaced by indicators of structural features.

The descriptions of the features used are in Figure 5. These descriptions are straightforward translations of the six new (program-derived) structural concepts, all of demonstrated importance but apparently unknown to chemists.

The attribute *ILP026* in the CCA dataset describes oxygen atoms in the carboxylate group of the template. It is both of interest that groups added to the template are seen to modify the properties of the template, and that this region of the template is far from the region postulated to be important by CoMFA [5]. The best regression equation found using CoMFA has an $r^2$ value of 0.86 which is not significantly different from the results obtained using the ILP attributes. However the ILP model is considerably simpler as the CoMFA model is a function of hundreds of attributes formed by estimating interaction energies using computational chemistry. Finally it is of more than passing interest to note that for the MUT2 data, the ILP attribute found most relevant represents the same structural feature that has been reported elsewhere as a new structural alert discovered by an ILP program [14, 26].

We close this discussion with the comment that data sets other than those considered here may require the exploratory cross-validation stage to examine different settings for *PIN* and *POUT*. What the results here suggest is that if, for any such settings, inclusion of ILP attributes yielded higher predictive correlations than otherwise possible, then selecting the best such setting could result in better fitting linear models.

| Data | Equation with ILP attributes | Number of terms in "expert-only" equation |
|---|---|---|
| PYR | $Act = 1.68MR'_{3,5} - 1.66ILP009 + 1.15ILP017$ $-0.70ILP010 - 0.69ILP018 + 6.03$ | 6 |
| CCA | $Act = 0.92CLOGP - 0.89ILP026 + 2.84$ | 3 |
| MUT2 | $Act = 1.84ILP008 - 0.24$ | – |

**Fig. 4.** Equations obtained when ILP attributes augment expert attributes. The last column refers to the number of terms (including the constant) in the equation that is forced to use the expert attributes only.

| Data | Feature | Description |
|---|---|---|
| PYR | $ILP009$ | Compound has hydrogen at position 4 and the substituent at position 3 is not hydrogen |
| | $ILP017$ | Compound has hydrogen at positions 4,5 and the substituent at position 3 is not hydrogen |
| | $ILP010$ | Compound has hydrogen at position 4 and the substituent at position 3 is at least a level 1 hydrogen donor |
| | $ILP018$ | Compound has hydrogen at positions 4,5 and the flexibility at position 3 is at least 7 |
| CCA | $ILP026$ | Compound has an type 2 oxygen (that occur mainly in the common carboxylate group) with partial charge at least -0.252 |
| MUT2 | $ILP008$ | Compound has a double bond conjugated to a 5-membered aromatic ring via a carbon atom |

**Fig. 5.** Descriptions of the previously unknown ILP-discovered structural features used in constructing equations for predicting biological activity.

# 6 Conclusion

Broadly termed "constructive induction" [18],the idea of augmenting an existing set of attributes is not new. Collins [4] describes a heuristic method of incorporating polynomial terms into a regression analysis. The AQ program [17] implements the capacity to introduce new attributes by specific combinations of existing ones. The idea is fundamental to the LINUS family of algorithms [16], where all possible attributes that can be constructed within a set of language restrictions are provided to a propositional learner. The use of problem-specific background knowledge in conjunction with regression analysis also appears in various ways in [8, 12, 25]. This paper adds to this research by providing a systematic assessment of the utility of structural features extracted by an ILP program. While the features obtained could in principle be used by any propositional learner (like classification or regression trees), the experiments in this paper have been restricted to their use with linear regression.

The results here should be of potential interest to practitioners concerned with extracting quantitative structure-activity relationships. Significant effort and expertise are usually invested in identifying useful indicators of biological activity, and a general purpose method of extracting interesting structural alerts could usefully aid an expert chemist involved in the enterprise of rational drug design. The new structural features reported in this paper also serve as a demonstration of the use of ILP programs as tools for aiding the process of scientific discovery. That such programs were able to identify useful structural concepts that have escaped the attention of experienced practitioners, some that significantly improve predictions on cases where it was generally assumed that no further improvement was possible (Case A in this paper), greatly strengthens the case for their inclusion when attempting to obtain solutions to difficult scientific problems.

### Acknowledgements

This research was supported by the EPSRC project 'Experimental Application and Development of ILP' At the time of conducting these experiments, Ross King was supported by the Imperial Cancer Research Fund. The CCA dataset was provided by Darren R. Flower of ASTRA. Finally thanks are due to Donald Michie for his guidance and advice, Steve Moyle for generous use of his personal computer, and to Penny Moyle for bringing to our attention facilities within the SPSS package for performing the statistical tests used here.

# References

1. T.A. Andrea and H. Kalayeh. Applications of Neural Networks in Quantitative Structure-Activity Relationship of Dihydrofolate Reductase. *Journal of Medicinal Chemistry*, 34:2824 – 2836, 1991.

2. I. Bratko and M.Grobelnik. Inductive learning applied to program construction and verification. In *Third International Workshop on Inductive Logic Programming*, pages 279–292, 1993. Available as Technical Report IJS-DP-6707, J. Stefan Inst., Ljubljana, Slovenia.

3. W. Cohen and C.D. Page. Polynomial learnability and inductive logic programming: Methods and results. *New Generation Computing*, 13(3,4):369–409, 1995.

4. J.S. Collins. A regression analysis program incorporating heuristic term selection. In E. Dale and D. Michie, editors, *Machine Intelligence 2*. Oliver and Boyd, 1968.

5. A.M. Davis, N.P. Gensmantel, E. Johansson, and D.P. Marriott. The Use of the GRID Program in the 3-D QSAR Analysis of a series of Calcium-Channel Agonists. *Journal of Medicinal Chemistry*, 37:963–972, 1994.

6. A.K. Debnath, R.L Lopez de Compadre, G. Debnath, A.J. Schusterman, and C. Hansch. Structure-Activity Relationship of Mutagenic Aromatic and Heteroaromatic Nitro compounds. Correlation with molecular orbital energies and hydrophobicity. *Journal of Medicinal Chemistry*, 34(2):786 – 797, 1991.

7. B. Dolsak and S. Muggleton. The application of Inductive Logic Programming to finite element mesh design. In S. Muggleton, editor, *Inductive Logic Programming*, pages 453–472. Academic Press, London, 1992.

8. S. Dzeroski. *Numerical Constraints and Learnability in Inductive Logic Programming*. University of Ljubljana, (PhD. Thesis), Ljubljana, 1995.

9. S. Dzeroski, L. Dehaspe, B. Ruck, and W. Walley. Classification of river water quality data using machine learning. In *Proceedings of the Fifth International Conference on the Development and Application of Computer Techniques Environmental Studies*, 1994.

10. C. Feng. Inducing temporal fault dignostic rules from a qualitative model. In S. Muggleton, editor, *Inductive Logic Programming*, pages 473–486. Academic Press, London, 1992.

11. C. Hansch, R.Li, J.M. Blaney, and R. Langridge. Comparison of the inhibition of Escherichia coli and Lactobacillus casei Dihydrofolate Reductase by 2,4-Diamino-5-(Substituted-benzyl) pyrimidines: Quantitative Structure-Activity Relationships,X-ray Crystallography, and Computer Graphics in Structure-Activity Analysis. *Journal of Medicinal Chemistry*, 25:777 – 784, 1982.

12. A. Karalic. Relational regression: first steps. Technical report ijs-dp-7001, J. Stefan Institute, Ljubljana, Yugoslavia, 1994.

13. R.D. King, A.Srinivasan, and M.J.E. Sternberg. Relating chemical activity to structure: an examination of ILP successes. *New Gen. Comput.*, 13(3,4), 1995.

14. R.D. King, S.H. Muggleton, A. Srinivasan, and M.J.E. Sternberg. Structure-activity relationships derived by machine learning: The use of atoms and their bond connectivities to predict mutagenicity by inductive logic programming. *Proc. of the National Academy of Sciences*, 93:438–442, 1996.

15. R.D. King, S.H. Muggleton, and M.J.E. Sternberg. Drug design by machine learning: The use of inductive logic programming to model the structure-activity relationships of trimethoprim analogues binding to dihydrofolate reductase. *Proc. of the National Academy of Sciences*, 89(23):11322–11326, 1992.

16. N. Lavrac and S. Dzeroski. *ILP: Techniques and Applications*. Ellis Horwood, London, 1994.

17. R. Michalski, I. Mozetic, J. Hong, and N. Lavrac. The AQ15 inductive learning system: an overview and experiments. In *Proceedings of IMAL 1986*, Orsay, 1986. Université de Paris-Sud.

18. R.S. Michalski. Understanding the nature of learning: issues and research directions. In R. Michalski, J. Carbonnel, and T. Mitchell, editors, *Machine Learning: An Artificial Intelligence Approach*, volume 2, pages 3–25. Kaufmann, Los Altos, CA, 1986.
19. D. Michie, D.J. Spiegelhalter, and C.C. Taylor, editors. *Machine Learning, Neural and Statistical classification*. Ellis-Horwood, New York, 1994.
20. S. Muggleton. Inverse Entailment and Progol. *New Gen. Comput.*, 13:245–286, 1995.
21. S. Muggleton, R. King, and M. Sternberg. Predicting protein secondary structure using inductive logic programming. *Protein Engineering*, 5:647–657, 1992.
22. S.H. Muggleton and C. Feng. Efficient induction of logic programs. In *Proceedings of the First Conference on Algorithmic Learning Theory*, Tokyo, 1990. Ohmsha.
23. M.J. Norusis. *SPSS: Base System User Guide. Release 6.0*. SPSS Inc., 444 N Michigan Ave, Chicago, Illinois 60611, 1994.
24. C. Silipo and C. Hansch. Correlation analysis. its Application to the Structure-Activity Relationship of Triazines Inhibiting Dihydrofolate Reductase. *Journal of Medicinal Chemistry*, 19:6849 – 6861, 1976.
25. A. Srinivasan and R.C. Camacho. Experiments in numerical reasoning with inductive logic programming. In D. Michie S. Muggleton and K. Furukawa, editors, *Machine Intelligence 15*. Oxford University Press, Oxford, 1996. to appear.
26. A. Srinivasan, S.H. Muggleton, R.D. King, and M.J.E. Sternberg. Mutagenesis: ILP experiments in a non-determinate biological domain. In S. Wrobel, editor, *Proceedings of the Fourth International Inductive Logic Programming Workshop*. Gesellschaft fur Mathematik und Datenverarbeitung MBH, 1994. GMD-Studien Nr 237.
27. A. Srinivasan, S.H. Muggleton, R.D. King, and M.J.E. Sternberg. Theories for mutagenicity: a study of first-order and feature based induction. *Artificial Intelligence*, 1995. to appear.
28. S. Wold. Cross-validatory estimation of the number of components in factor and principal components models. *Technometrics*, 20:397–404, 1978.
29. J. Zelle and R. Mooney. Learning semantic grammars with constructive inductive logic programming. In *Proceedings of the Eleventh National Conference on Artificial Intelligence*, pages 817–822. Morgan Kaufmann, 1993.

# A  Assessing goodness of fit and relative contributions of variables

This appendix describes some commonly used concepts when performing multiple linear regression: more details can be found in [23]. In keeping with terminology in the field, the term attributes as used in this paper, refers to "variables", and "examples" are synonymous with "cases". The regression problem is concerned with predicting the value of a response, or dependent, variable using a number of predictor, or independent, variables. This prediction is obtained from the sample regression equation.

When the relationship between response and predictor variables is modelled by an equation that is linear in the latter, a measure of linear relationship between response and predictor variables is given by the *multiple correlation coefficient* $r$. A measure of goodness of fit of a linear model is given by $r^2$ or *coefficient of multiple determination*). This measures the proportion of variation in the response variable explained by the model. Typically the $r^2$ value is an optimistic estimate as the model usually does not fit the population as well as it fits the sample. The statistic *adjusted* $r^2$ attempts to correct $r^2$ to reflect this, and is given by:

$$r^2_a = r^2 - \frac{p(1 - r^2)}{N - p - 1}$$

where $N$ is the number of cases, and $p$ is the number of variables in the equation.

Consider now two regression equations for a dependent variable $Y$. The first, called $E_{v_1}$, is an equation for $Y$ in terms of the variables $v_1$. The second, $E_{v_1 + v_2}$ is an equation for $Y$ in terms of the variables $v_1$ and $v_2$. One method of evaluating the relative importance of $v_2$ is to consider the increase in $r^2$ (or $r_a^2$) when that set is entered into an equation that already contains the $v_1$ variables. That is:

$$r^2_{ch} = r^2_{v_1 + v_2} - r^2_{v_1}$$

where $r_{v_1 + v_2}$ is the value of $r$ after the set $v_2$ have been entered, and $r_{v_1}$ is the value of $r$ before their entry. This value of $r^2_{ch}$ does not indicate the proportion of unexplained variation accounted for by the new set of variables. This is given by the partial correlation coefficient:

$$Pr_{v_2} = \frac{r^2_{ch}}{1 - r^2_{v_1}}$$

It is possible to test for the null hypothesis that the change in $r^2$ value from including the $v_2$ variables is 0 using the "partial F-test" :

$$F_{ch} = \frac{r^2_{ch}(N - p - 1)}{q(1 - r^2_{v_1 + v_2})}$$

where $N$ is the number of cases, $p$ is the total number of variables in the equation, and $q$ is the number of variables in set $v_2$. $F_{ch}$ is F-distributed with $q, N - p - 1$ degrees of freedom.

# Polynomial-Time Learning in Logic Programming and Constraint Logic Programming

Michèle Sebag[1] and Céline Rouveirol[2]

(1) LMS – URA CNRS 317,
Ecole Polytechnique
F-91128 Palaiseau Cedex
Michele.Sebag@polytechnique.fr

(2) LRI – URA CNRS 410,
Université Paris Sud,
F-91405 Orsay Cedex
Celine.Rouveirol@lri.fr

**Abstract.** Induction in first-order logic languages suffers from an additional factor of complexity compared to induction in attribute-value languages: the number of possible matchings between a candidate hypothesis and a training example.

This paper investigates the use of a stochastic bias to control this factor of complexity: the exhaustive exploration of the matching space is replaced by considering a fixed number of matchings, obtained by random sampling. One thereby constructs from positive and negative examples a theory which is only approximately consistent. Both the degree of approximation and the computational cost of induction are controlled from the number of samples allowed.

This approach is illustrated and validated on the mutagenesis problem. An ad hoc sampling mechanism has been purposely designed, and experimental results fully demonstrates the power of stochastic approximate induction, in terms of both predictive accuracy and computational cost. Furthermore, this approach applies for learning both logic programs (as it is usually the case in ILP) and constrained logic programs, i.e. extended logic programs that can naturally handle numerical information. The gain of learning constrained logic programs for the mutagenesis problem is evaluated by comparing the predictive accuracy of the theories induced in both languages.

## 1 Introduction

The framework of Inductive Logic Programming (ILP) [21] allows induction to handle relational problems. This very expressive formalism however raises two major questions: that of dealing with numerical values, and that of mastering the computational complexity pertaining to first-order logic.

Handling numbers in ILP has mainly been tackled via transformation of relational problems into propositional ones *a la LINUS* [15] (see also [37]), or by using adequate "numerical knowledge", be it built-in as in *FOIL* [25] or provided in declarative form as in *PROGOL* [20]. A third possibility is based on Constraint Logic Programming (CLP), which both subsumes logic programming (LP) and allows for the interpretation of predefined predicates, in particular predicates involving numerical variables [8]. An earlier work [30] has presented a learner named *ICP* for *Inductive Constraint Programming*, which uses constraints to prevent negative examples from matching candidate hypotheses.

This paper is concerned with bridging the gap between the above theoretical approach and real-world problems. A major difficulty is that of computational complexity. This general difficulty of induction is usually handled through language biases (e.g. GOLEM considers $ij$-determinate clauses [22]; *PROGOL* sets an upper bound on the number of literals in a candidate clause [20]) or search biases, (e.g. *FOIL* considers one literal at a time [25]; *FOCL* restricts the amount of look-ahead [24]; *FOIL* and *PROGOL* respectively use the quantity of information and the MDL principle to sort the candidate hypotheses). However, adjusting these biases requires a precise *a priori* knowledge, which is often far from available.

This is the reason why our previous works [26, 29, 30] were based on a variant of the "bias-free" Version Space framework [18], called *Disjunctive Version Space* (DiVS) [28]. However, this gets intractable on truly relational problems, for the number of possible matchings between a hypothesis and a negative example is exponential in the size of the examples; e.g. in the mutagenicity problem, where molecules involve up to 40 atoms, the number of possible matchings goes to $40^{40}$.

We therefore propose a new algorithm that builds approximate version spaces with polynomial complexity. This algorithm, named *STILL* for *Stochastic Inductive Learner*, combines Disjunctive Version Spaces with a sampling mechanism: it only considers *some samples of the possible matchings* between a hypothesis and a negative example. It thereby constructs a theory which is only approximately consistent with linear complexity in the number of samples allowed. Besides, classification heuristics taken from the propositional *DiVS* [28] can directly be adapted for *STILL* to cope with noisy and sparse data, while keeping a polynomial classification.

The sampling mechanism allows the expert to control both the computational cost of induction and the degree of approximation of the induced theory, via the number of samples allowed. This heuristics can be used whenever several (many) matchings between a hypothesis and a training example are possible. We study its effects on learning either definite or constrained programs.

The paper is organized as follows. Next section briefly reviews the *Disjunctive Version Space* approach. As the computational pitfall in first-order logic becomes obvious, section 3 discusses how to restrict the matching search space, and introduces the sampling mechanism implemented in *STILL*. The algorithms of induction and classification in *STILL* are given, together with the corresponding polynomial complexity results. Section 4 is devoted to experimental validation on the mutagenicity problem; *STILL* results compare favorably to those of *PROGOL* and *FOIL*, reported from [33]. Finally, some avenues for further research are discussed in section 5.

# 2 Disjunctive Version Spaces in LP and CLP

This section illustrates the Disjunctive Version Space approach on a problem pertaining to organic chemistry [11]: the mutagenicity problem is one most famous testbed in ILP [33, 10]. A more detailed presentation of Disjunctive Version Spaces in the frame of attribute-value and CLP languages can be found in [28] and [30].

## 2.1 Data and language of examples

The mutagenicity problem consists in discriminating organic molecules (nitroaromatic compounds) depending on their mutagenic activity (*active* or *inactive*). This still open problem is of utmost practical interest, for these compounds occur in car exhaust fumes, and high mutagenic activity is considered carcinogenic.

The description of molecules considered in this paper includes the description of atoms and bonds, augmented with non structural information (five boolean and numerical attributes) measuring the hydrophobicity of the molecule, the energy of the molecule lowest unoccupied molecular orbital, and so on. A molecule $a$ is thus described by a ground clause, an excerpt of which is:

$$tc(a) :- atom(a, a_1, carbon, 22, -0.138), \cdots, atom(a, a_{26}, oxygen, 40, -0.388), \cdots$$
$$bond(a, a_1, a_2, 7), \cdots, bond(a, a_{24}, a_{26}, 2),$$
$$logp(a, 4.23), lumo(a, -1.246).$$

where $tc$ stands for the target concept (*active* or *inactive*) satisfied by $a$.

Literal $atom(a, a_1, carbon, 22, -0.138)$ states that in compound $a$, atom $a_1$ is a carbon, of type 22, with partial charge $-0.138$. Literal $bond(a, a_1, a_2, 7)$ expresses that there exists a (unique) bond between atoms $a_1$ and $a_2$ in $a$, the type of which is 7. This problem typically involves numerical and relational features.

## 2.2 Overview

*DiVS* basically combines the Version Space framework and the divide-and-conquer strategy [16]. Examples are generalized one at a time; and the star *Th(Ex)* generalizing the seed *Ex* is the version space covering *Ex*, that is, the set of all hypotheses covering *Ex* and rejecting all examples $Ce_1, \ldots Ce_n$ that do not belong to the same target concept as *Ex*, called *counter-examples* to *Ex*[1].
The elementary step in the construction of star *Th(Ex)* consists in building the set $D(Ex, Ce)$ of hypotheses that cover *Ex* and discriminate a counter-example *Ce*: *Th(Ex)* is defined as the conjunction of $D(Ex, Ce)$ for *Ce* ranging over the counter-examples to *Ex*.

---

[1] The counter-examples to a positive example *Ex* are the negative examples, and vice versa.

The overall theory *Th* built by *DiVS* is the disjunction of the version spaces *Th(Ex)* for *Ex* ranging over the training set.

---

**Disjunctive Version Space Algorithm**

> $Th = false$.
> **For each** $Ex$ **training example**
>     $Th(Ex) = True$
>     **For each** $Ce$ **counter-example to** $Ex$
>         Build $D(Ex, Ce)$         *(section 2.3,2.5)*
>         $Th(Ex) = Th(Ex) \land D(Ex, Ce)$
>     $Th = Th \lor Th(Ex)$.

---

*DiVS* differs from other divide-and-conquer algorithms in one main respect. For most authors [16, 20], seeds are selected among positive examples only: e.g. the different versions of *AQ*, and *PROGOL* as well, only learn the target concept. In contrast, *DiVS* generalizes positive and negative examples; it thereby learns both the target concept and its negation. This hopefully allows the effects of noisy positive and negative examples to counterbalance each other.

Another key difference between *DiVS* and all other learners, as far as we know, is that *DiVS* does not set any restriction on the number of candidate solutions: it retains all hypotheses partially complete (covering at least one seed) and consistent. In opposition, *FOIL*, *FOCL* and *PROGOL*, among others, aim at finding "the" best hypothesis covering a training example, according to the more or less greedy optimization of a numerical criterion (quantity of information for *FOIL* and *FOCL*, MDL principle for *PROGOL*). To a lesser extent, *ML-Smart* [1, 3] and *REGAL* [7] also look for concise theories.

Let us focus now on building the set $D(Ex, Ce)$ of hypotheses generalizing $Ex$ and rejecting $Ce$, depending on the hypothesis language.

## 2.3 Attribute-value learning

In an attribute-value language, the construction of $D(Ex, Ce)$ is straightforward. Consider for instance the positive and negative atoms given in Table 1:

Table 1: Seed and Counter-example

|      | element type | electric charge | Concept |
|------|--------------|-----------------|---------|
| *Ex* | carbon   22  | 3.38            | *positive* |
| *Ce* | hydrogen  3  | -.33            | *negative* |

Let hypotheses be conjunctions of selectors $(att = V)$ [16], where $V$ denotes an interval in case *att* is linear (e.g. the *type* or *electric charge* of atoms), and a value otherwise.

The set of hypotheses $D(Ex, Ce)$ is given by the disjunction of maximally discriminant selectors, i.e. of the maximally general selectors that cover $Ex$ and reject $Ce$:

$$D(Ex, Ce) = (element = carbon) \vee (type > 3) \vee (charge > -.33)$$

Star *Th(Ex)*, given by the conjunction of $D(Ex, Ce)$ for $Ce$ ranging over the counter-examples to $Ex$, is built with linear complexity in the number $N$ of examples and the number $P$ of attributes. And finally the complexity of *DiVS* is in $\mathcal{O}(N^2 \times P)$ [28].

## 2.4   First-order logic learning

All positive and negative examples of the target concept are represented via Horn clauses. Since there exists no "standard" semantics for the negation in Logic Programming and even less in Constraint Logic Programming, we explicitly introduce the negation of the target concept *tc*, denoted *opp_tc*: a negative example is a clause the head of which is built on *opp_tc*.

Consider two examples of molecules satisfying the opposite target concepts *active* and *inactive*:

> *Ex : active(ex)   :- atom(ex, a, carbon, 3.38), atom(ex, b, carbon, 1.24).*
>
> *Ce : inactive(ce) :- atom(ce, c, hydrogen, -.33), atom(ce, d, carbon, 2.16).*

We first decompose the seed $Ex$ into a clause $C$ and a substitution $\theta$, respectively the most general clause and the most specific substitution such that

$$Ex = C\theta \tag{1}$$

In our toy example, $C$ stores the structural information of $Ex$, i.e., that $Ex$ is an *active* molecule having two atoms:

$$C : active(X) : -atom(X', Y, Z, T), atom(X'', U, V, W)$$

and $\theta$ carries all other information in $Ex$:

$$\theta = \{X/ex,\ X'/ex,\ X''/ex,\ Y/a,\ Z/carbon,\ T/3.38,\ U/b,\ V/carbon,\ W/1.24\}$$

This decomposition allows induction to simultaneously explore two search spaces:

– The space of definite clauses generalizing $C$. Exploring this space is fairly simple: all variables in $C$ must be distinct for $C$ to be the most general clause satisfying equation (1); hence, the only way to generalize $C$ is by dropping literals.

– A space $\mathcal{F}$ of logical functions on the variables of $C$. Depending on whether $\mathcal{F}$ is the set of substitutions on $C$, or the set of constraints on $C$, *DiVS* either constructs definite clauses [29] or constrained clauses [26, 30]. Note that substitutions on $C$ are particular cases[2] of constraints on $C$ [8].
  In this paper, $\mathcal{F}$ is restricted to a subset of constraints on $C$, to be made more precise later on.

---

[2] Variable grounding amounts to domain constraint $(X = X.\theta)$, where $X.\theta$ denotes the constant $X$ is substituted by according to $\theta$; similarly, variable linking amounts to binary constraint $(X = Y)$.

Building the set $D(Ex, Ce)$ of hypotheses that cover $Ex$ and reject $Ce$ amounts here to finding out all pairs $(C, \rho)$, where $C$ generalizes $\mathcal{C}$ (e.g. describes a molecule satisfying the same target concept as $Ex$ and including at most the same number of atoms and bonds) and $\rho$ is a constraint on $C$ that generalizes $\theta$. Furthermore, $C$ and $\rho$ must be such that $C\rho$ discriminates $Ce$.

In the general case, discrimination can be based on predicates: if $C$ involves a predicate that does not appear in $Ce$, $C$ discriminates $Ce$. Predicate-based discrimination is not considered in the following: it does not apply for the considered description of the mutagenesis problem since all molecules involve the same predicates (*atom, bond,..*). Besides, it presents no difficulty and can be formalized as a boolean discrimination problem [30].

Constraint-based discrimination takes place when the body of $\mathcal{C}$ (or of the current hypothesis) generalizes that of $Ce$. Then there exists at least one substitution $\sigma$ such that $body(\mathcal{C}).\sigma \subseteq body(Ce)$. We then say that $\mathcal{C}$ *matches the negative example* and $\sigma$ is called *negative substitution*. For instance, in our previous example, negative substitution $\sigma$ respectively maps the first and second atoms in $\mathcal{C}$ onto the first and second atoms in $Ce$:

$$\sigma = \{X/ce,\ X'/ce,\ X''/ce,\ Y/c,\ Z/hydrogen,\ T/{-}.33,\ U/d,\ V/carbon,\ W/2.16\}$$

Whenever a negative substitution exists, $\mathcal{C}$ is inconsistent: its body generalizes the bodies of both $Ex$ and $Ce$, which yet satisfy opposite target concepts. Constraint-based discrimination prevents such inconsistencies by specializing $\mathcal{C}$: it adds constraints to the body of $\mathcal{C}$ such that negative substitution $\sigma$ does not satisfy these constraints. For instance, constraint

$$\rho = (Z = carbon)$$

is incompatible with $\sigma$, since $Z.\sigma = hydrogen$. By the way, $\rho$ must also generalize the substitution $\theta$ derived from $Ex$, in order for $C\rho$ to still generalize $Ex$; e.g. $\rho' = (Z = oxygen)$ is also incompatible with $\sigma$, but $C\rho'$ does not generalize $Ex$.

A formal presentation of constraint entailment and generalization order will be found in [8]; roughly, constraint $\rho_1$ generalizes $\rho_2$ (equivalently, $\rho_2$ *entails* $\rho_1$) iff all substitutions satisfying $\rho_2$ also satisfy $\rho_1$.

Note that building constraints that generalize $\theta$ and are incompatible with a negative substitution $\sigma$ amounts to an attribute value discrimination problem. This is particularly clear if we restrict our language of constraints to domain constraints, of the form $(X = \mathcal{V})$, where $\mathcal{V}$ is a subset of the domain of $X$ (see section 2.5). This is also true when binary logical and arithmetic constraints are considered (e.g. $(X \neq Y)$, $(Z < T + 10)$, $(S > U - 20)$), by introducing auxiliary variables (this point is detailed in [30]). However, binary constraints will not be further considered here, for two reasons. First of all, introducing binary constraints does not significantly modify the complexity of induction (it only affects its polynomial part), which is our primary concern in this paper. Second, unary constraints turned out to be sufficient to reach a good level of predictive accuracy on the mutagenesis problem.

Finally, our language of constraints is restricted to unary constraints of the form $(X = \mathcal{V})$, where

- $\mathcal{V}$ is an interval if $X$ is a real or integer-valued variable;
- $\mathcal{V}$ is a value if $X$ is a nominal variable.

In particular, if all variables are considered nominal, the language of hypotheses is a restriction of that of logical clauses (only grounding-based specialization applies).

## 2.5 Characterizing $D(Ex, Ce)$

Let $Ex = C\theta$ be the seed and let $Ce$ be a counter-example to the seed. Let $\sigma$ be a negative substitution on $C$ derived from $Ce$ and let us first assume that $\sigma$ is the only negative substitution derived from $Ce$.

Building a maximally discriminant domain constraint $\rho_{X,\sigma}$ on variable $X$ that generalizes $\theta$ and is incompatible with $\sigma$ amounts to building a maximally discriminant selector in the attribute-value case (section 2.3). Constraint $\rho_\sigma$ is defined as the disjunction of maximally discriminant constraints $\rho_{X,\sigma}$, for $X$ ranging over discriminant variables (e.g. $V$ is not discriminant since $V.\theta = V.\sigma$). In our toy example, variables $X$, $X'$, $X''$, $Y$ and $U$, which respectively identify the molecule and the atoms, are not considered as they are irrelevant for discrimination purposes:

| | $X$ | $X'$ | $Y$ | $Z$ | $T$ | $X''$ | $U$ | $V$ | $W$ |
|---|---|---|---|---|---|---|---|---|---|
| $\theta$ | $ex$ | $ex$ | $a$ | $carbon$ | $3.38$ | $ex$ | $b$ | $carbon$ | $1.24$ |
| $\sigma$ | $ce$ | $ce$ | $c$ | $hydrogen$ | $-.33$ | $ce$ | $d$ | $carbon$ | $2.16$ |

$$\rho_\sigma = (Z = carbon) \vee (T > -.33) \vee (W < 2.16)$$

It is shown that any constraint generalizing $\theta$ discriminates $\sigma$ iff it entails (is generalized by) $\rho_\sigma$ [30]. A clause $C\rho$ therefore belongs to $D(Ex, Ce)$ iff $C\rho$ generalizes $Ex$ and $\rho$ entails $\rho_\sigma$.

In the general case, let $\Sigma_{Ex, Ce}$ be the set of negative substitutions on $C$ derived from $Ce$. A constraint $\rho$ must be incompatible with *all* negative substitutions derived from $Ce$, in order for $C\rho$ to be consistent with $Ce$. $D(Ex, Ce)$ can thus be characterized as follows [30]:

**Proposition 1.** $C\rho$ belongs to $D(Ex, Ce)$ iff $C\rho$ generalizes $Ex$ and $\rho$ entails $\rho_\sigma$ for all $\sigma$ in $\Sigma_{Ex, Ce}$.

To sum up, $D(Ex, Ce)$ is computationally described by $C$ and the set of constraints $\{\rho_\sigma \ s.t. \ \sigma \in \Sigma_{Ex, Ce}\}$.

This characterization can be used to reach the two main goals of machine learning: that of explicitly characterizing the constructed theory and that of classifying further instances of the problem domain. Some results and a method addressing the first aim of learning were presented in our previous work [30]. We therefore concentrate here on the second aim of learning, that is, classification.

## 2.6 Classifying further examples

As a matter of fact, computational descriptions as above are sufficient to classify unseen instances of the problem domain, via a nearest neighbor-like decision process:

• An unseen instance $E$ is termed *neighbor* of a training example $E$ iff $E$ belongs to $Th(Ex)$, that is, is covered by a hypothesis in $Th(Ex)$.

• By construction, $E$ belongs to $Th(Ex)$ iff $E$ belongs to all $D(Ex, Ce)$, for $Ce$ ranging over the counter-examples to $Ex$.

• The computational characterization of $D(Ex, Ce)$ is sufficient to check whether an unseen instance $E$ belongs to $D(Ex, Ce)$ [30]:

**Proposition 2.** $E$ belongs to $D(Ex, Ce)$ iff $E$ can be expressed as $C\tau$, where $C$ generalizes $\mathcal{C}$ and $\tau$ entails $\rho_\sigma$ for all $\sigma$ in $\Sigma_{Ex, \, Ce}$.

Let $\Sigma_{Ex, \, E}$ denote the set of substitutions on $\mathcal{C}$ matching $E$. Then, proposition 2 is translated as:

```
Belongs(E, D(Ex, Ce))

    For each τ in Σ_Ex, E
        If τ entails ρ_σ for all σ in Σ_Ex, Ce,
            return true.
    return false.
```

And

```
Neighbor (E, Ex) :                    (E belongs to Th(Ex))

    For each Ce counter-example to Ex
        if NOT Belongs(E, D(Ex, Ce))
            return false
    return true.
```

Simply put, our approach constructs an oracle rather than an explicit theory. This oracle is made of theory $Th$, stored as the list of

$$D(Ex_i, Ex_j) = (\mathcal{C}_i, \{\rho_\sigma \ s.t. \ \sigma \in \Sigma_{Ex_i, Ex_j}\})$$

for $Ex_i$ and $Ex_j$ training examples satisfying different target concepts. Theory *Th*, interpreted according to Proposition 2, allows one to compute the boolean *Neighbor(E, Ex)* function, and this function together with a standard nearest neighbor algorithm, achieves the classification of any further instance $E$.

This approach can be compared to that of *RIBL* [5] which is also based on nearest neighbors. The essential difference is the following: in *RIBL*, the similarity between $E$ and a training example $Ex$ only depends on $E$ and $Ex$ (this is true also for the even more sophisticated first-order similarity used in KBG [2]). But here, the neighborhood of $Ex$ (and the fact that $E$ is neighbor of $Ex$ or not) depends on $E$, $Ex$ and the counter-examples $Ce_1, \ldots Ce_n$ to $Ex$: the underlying similarity is driven by discrimination.

## 2.7 Complexity

Under the standard assumption that the domain of any variable is explored with a bounded cost, the complexity of building $\rho_\sigma$ is linear in the number of variables in $\mathcal{C}$ (it would be quadratic if binary constraints were also considered). Let $\mathcal{X}$ and $\mathcal{S}$ respectively denote upper-bounds on the number of variables in $\mathcal{C}$ and on the number of substitutions in $\Sigma_{Ex_i, Ex_j}$. The characterization of $D(Ex_i, Ex_j)$ is then in $\mathcal{O}(\mathcal{X} \times \mathcal{S})$.

Let $N$ be the number of training examples. Since all $D(Ex_i, Ex_j)$ must be characterized, the complexity of learning in *DiVS* is

$$\mathcal{O}(N^2 \times \mathcal{X} \times \mathcal{S})$$

And, since checking whether an instance $E$ belongs to *Th(Ex)* requires to consider all substitutions in $\Sigma_{Ex, E}$, the number of which is upper-bounded by $\mathcal{S}$, the complexity of classification in *DiVS* is

$$\mathcal{O}(N^2 \times \mathcal{X} \times \mathcal{S}^2)$$

The crux of complexity lies in factor $\mathcal{S}$, which is exponential in the number of literals built on a predicate symbol in the examples [29]. This shows up in the mutagenesis problem, as the number of atoms in a molecule ranges up to 40. $\mathcal{S}$ thus is $40^{40}$...

# 3 Polynomial Approximate Learning

The presented approach suffers from two major drawbacks: first, it is intractable for truly relational problems. Second, inasmuch it stems from the Version Space framework, it is ill-prepared to deal with noisy and sparse data.

The tractability limitation is first addressed via a stochastic bias: the idea consists in sampling, rather than exhaustively exploring, the set of substitutions $\Sigma_{Ex, Ce}$. We again illustrate the stochastic sampling mechanism on the mutagenesis problem.

Second, two heuristics, taken from the propositional version of *DiVS* [28], are used to relax the standard consistency and generality requirements of Version Spaces, and cope with noise and sparseness.

## 3.1  Stochastic Bias

Let us have a closer look at the negative substitutions explored by *DiVS*.

In the mutagenesis problem, the semantics of a molecule is not modified by changing the identifiers of the atoms (nominal constants $a_1, a_2, \ldots a_i$). These identifiers can thus be arbitrarily set to $1, 2, \ldots, n$, if $n$ denotes the number of atoms in $Ex$. A negative substitution $\sigma$ on $\mathcal{C}$ is completely defined by associating each atom in $\mathcal{C}$, which corresponds to a given atom $i$ in $Ex$ w.r.t. $\theta$, to an atom in $Ce$ denoted $\sigma(i)$ by abuse of notation. The intractability of *DiVS* follows from the fact that the number of such substitutions is in $n'^{\,n}$, if $n'$ denotes the number of atoms in $Ce$.

Let us concentrate on atoms for the sake of readability. Discriminating $\sigma$ from $\theta$ requires to discriminate at least one atom $i$ in $Ex$ from atom $\sigma(i)$ in $Ce$. The more "similar" atoms $i$ in $Ex$ and $\sigma(i)$ in $Ce$, the more difficult it is to discriminate them, and the more informative the negative substitution $\sigma$ is: this notion parallels that of near-misses in attribute-value languages. Formally, a partial order can be defined on the substitutions in $\Sigma_{Ex,Ce}$, and it is shown that non-minimal substitutions can soundly be pruned with regards to discriminant induction [26, 29]: this pruning is analogous to the pruning of non near-misses examples in the propositional case [32, 27]. Unfortunately, building the set of such minimal substitutions turns out to be intractable too.

Another possibility would be to consider *the best* substitution $\sigma$, defined as minimizing some distance to $\theta$ in the line of the structural similarity developed in [2]. For instance, the best substitution in $\Sigma_{Ex,Ce}$ would minimize the sum of the distances between atom $i$ in $Ex$ and atom $\sigma(i)$ in $Ce$.

As noted in [33], the description of an atom can be handled as a single tree-structured feature since the element of an atom commands its atom type (e.g. the atom type of a *hydrogen* atom is in [1,3] whereas the atom type of a carbon atom is in [21,24]) and the atom type similarly commands its electric charge. Defining a distance between any two atoms thus is straightforward: the distance of two atoms having same atom type is the difference of their electric charges; otherwise, if the atoms are of the same element, their distance is the difference of their atom type, augmented by a sufficiently large constant (twice the maximal electric charge); otherwise (the atoms are of different elements), their distance is set to another constant (twice the maximal electric charge plus the maximal atom type).

However, using an optimization approach to determine which substitution to consider in $\Sigma_{Ex,Ce}$ raises several problems: first of all, we feel that a single substitution, even optimal, cannot be representative of the whole set $\Sigma_{Ex,Ce}$; second, this combinatorial optimization problem is itself computationally expensive...

Finally, we decided to consider several substitutions, the number of which to be supplied by the user.

These substitutions could have been purely randomly defined, except that, as stated above, substitutions nearer to $\theta$ are more informative. When constructing a substitution $\sigma$, one thus associates to any atom $i$ in $Ex$ the atom $j$ in $Ce$ which is most similar to $i$, provided that $j$ is not yet associated to another atom in $Ex$: atom $j$ in $Ce$ has same electric charge as atom $i$ in $Ex$, if possible; otherwise, it has same atom type; otherwise, it is of same element.

Let $n$ and $n'$ respectively denote the number of atoms in $Ex$ and $Ce$. The sampling mechanism of the substitutions in $\Sigma_{Ex,\,Ce}$ is currently implemented as follows:

```
Select σ in Σ_{Ex, Ce}

    while possible
        Select i in {1,...,n} not yet selected
            Select j in {1,...,n'} not yet selected such
            that atom j in Ce is as close as possible
            to atom i in Ex,
                Do σ(i) = j.
```

Note that index $j$ is deterministically selected depending on $i$, and $i$ is stochastically selected with uniform probability in $\{1, \ldots, n\}$. This way, any atom $i$ in $Ex$ will in average be associated to a similar atom in $Ce$, provided the sampling mechanism is run a sufficient number of times.

More precisely, the above stochastic sampling mechanism ensures that a set of samples captures an arbitrarily precise representation of $\Sigma_{Ex,\,Ce}$ with high probability, provided the number of samples allowed is "sufficient". Further work is concerned with formalizing this intuition, as well as improving the selection mechanism via taking into account also the bonds between atoms.

## 3.2  Overview of *STILL*

The *STILL* algorithm combines the general approach of *DiVS* and the above sampling mechanism. This stochastic bias is used to make both induction and classification tractable.

**Approximate Learning** Remember that *DiVS* constructs the set $Th(Ex)$ of consistent hypotheses that cover $Ex$, through exploring the whole sets of substitutions $\Sigma_{Ex,\,Ce}$ for $Ce$ ranging over the counter-examples to $Ex$. Instead of that, *STILL* only processes $\eta$ substitutions, where $\eta$ is a positive integer supplied by the user. This way, it constructs a set of hypotheses $Th_\eta(Ex)$ that cover $Ex$ and are only partially ensured to be consistent, since only sampled substitutions are ensured to be discriminated.

Concretely, the set of hypotheses $Th_\eta(Ex)$ is characterized by clause $C$ (with $Ex = C\theta$) and a set of constraints $\mathcal{R}$, including $\eta$ discriminant constraints built as follows. Let $n$ be the number of counter-examples to $Ex$; for each counter-example $Ce$, $\frac{n}{n}$ samples of substitutions are selected in $\Sigma_{Ex,\,Ce}$. $\mathcal{R}$ is composed of the constraints $\rho_\sigma$ discriminating the selected samples of substitutions derived from all counter-examples.

This heuristics ensures that the specificity of star $Th_\eta(Ex)$ does not depend on whether the seed $Ex$ belongs to the minority or the majority class (this would not be the case if the number of constraints in $\mathcal{R}$ were proportional to the number of counter-examples to $Ex$).

It was adopted for reasons of empirical accuracy, as examples in the mutagenesis application are distributed two active to one inactive.

```
Characterize Thη(Ex):

    R = φ.
    n = Number of counter-examples to Ex
    For Ce counter-example to Ex
        For j = 1 ... n/n ,
            Select σ in ΣEx, Ce ,
            Build ρσ
            Do R = R ∪ { ρσ }
    return (C, R).
```

The disjunction $Th_\eta$ of theories $Th_\eta(Ex)$ for $Ex$ ranging over the training set, is termed *approximate theory*; the number $\eta$ of allowed samples is termed *rate of approximation*. Note that $Th_\eta$ is more general than $Th$ and tends toward $Th$ as $\eta$ increases.

**Approximate classification.** The classification process in $DiVS$ is based on checking which training examples are neighbors of the instance $E$ to classify (section 2.6). In order to check whether $E$ is neighbor of $Ex$, i.e. belongs to $Th(Ex)$, $DiVS$ explores the set $\Sigma_{Ex,\,E}$ of substitutions on $\mathcal{C}$ (where $Ex = \mathcal{C}\theta$), matching $E$. The size of this set similarly makes classification intractable.

*STILL* again addresses this limitation via the sampling mechanism: instead of exhaustively exploring $\Sigma_{Ex,\,E}$, it only considers $K$ substitutions in this set, where $K$ is a positive integer supplied by the user. $E$ is termed *approximate neighbor* of $Ex$ if at least one in $K$ samples of $\Sigma_{Ex,\,E}$ entails all constraints in $Th(Ex)$:

```
Approx_Neighbor (E, Ex) :

    (C, R) = Characterize Thη (Ex)
    For i = 1 ... K
        Select τ in ΣEx,E
            If τ entails all ρ in R
                return true
    return false
```

The classification in *STILL* is finally done according to the standard nearest neighbor algorithm, based on the above *Approx_Neighbor* function.

Note the above function corresponds to an "interpretation" of $Th_\eta(Ex)$ that is more specific than $Th_\eta(Ex)$ itself; this over-specificity decreases as $K$ increases.

Parameter $K$ controls the number of trials allowed to get an answer from theory $Th_\eta$; metaphorically speaking, $K$ corresponds to the "patience" of the constructed expert.

## 3.3 Coping with noisy and sparse examples

$Th(Ex)$ (which is the theory $Th_\eta(Ex)$ tends toward as $\eta$ increases) includes consistent hypotheses only, and maximally general consistent hypotheses in particular. No doubt this approach is ill-suited to real-world datasets: when erroneous examples are encountered, strictly consistent hypotheses have few predictive accuracy [4]. And when examples are sparse, maximally general consistent hypotheses are too general: most instances come to be covered by a hypothesis in most $Th_\eta(Ex_i)$, and therefore get unclassified, or classified in the majority class.

These limitations were already encountered in the attribute-value version of *DiVS*, and have been addressed by two heuristics [28], which simply extend to first-order logic owing to the computational characterization of the constructed theory.

The presence of noise in the data is classically addressed by relaxing the consistency requirement. This is done at classification time, via modifying the test of neighborhood. By definition, $E$ is considered as neighbor of $Ex$ iff it belongs to $D(Ex, Ce)$ for all $Ce$ counter-example to $Ex$. This definition is simply relaxed as: $E$ is from now on considered as neighbor of $Ex$ iff it belongs to $D(Ex, Ce)$ for all $Ce$ counter-example to $Ex$, except at most $\varepsilon$ of them, where $\varepsilon$ is a positive integer supplied by the user. The greater $\varepsilon$, the wider the neighborhood of $Ex$ is.

The sparseness of the data is addressed by increasing the specificity of the produced theory. This modification also takes place during classification, and regards the test of constraint entailment. By construction, constraint $\rho_\sigma$ is the maximally general constraint that discriminates $\sigma$ and generalizes $\theta$; it is the disjunction of domain constraints $\rho_{X,\sigma}$ for $X$ ranging over the variables of $\mathcal{C}$. A given substitution $\tau$ hence entails $\rho_\sigma$ iff there exists at least one variable $X$ such that $X.\tau$ satisfies $\rho_{X,\sigma}$.

The specificity of the theory is tuned by considering from now on that $\tau$ entails $\rho_\sigma$ iff $\tau$ satisfies at least $M$ domain constraints $\rho_{X,\sigma}$ (instead of one), where $M$ is a positive integer supplied by the user. This amounts to considering $\rho_\sigma$ as an $M - of - N$ concept. The greater $M$, the smaller the neighborhood of $Ex$ is.

Note that the constructed theory does not depend in any way on the values of parameters $\varepsilon$ or $M$. In particular, *STILL* requires no *a priori* knowledge regarding the rate of noise and representativity of the data. Parameters $M$ and $\varepsilon$ can be adjusted from the experimental classification results — but with no need to restart induction. See [28] for a discussion about the advantages of such *a posteriori* biases.

## 3.4 Complexity

As expected, the stochastic bias cuts down the complexity of learning and classification.

Let $\mathcal{X}$ still denote an upper-bound on the number of variables in $\mathcal{C}$. The complexity of building $\rho_\sigma$ is still linear in $\mathcal{X}$. The construction of one sample $\sigma$ is quadratic in $\mathcal{X}$ (this is a large over-estimation). Hence, the complexity of learning $Th_\eta(Ex)$ is in $\mathcal{O}(\mathcal{X}^3 \times \eta)$. Finally, the computational complexity of induction in *STILL* is linear in the rate of approximation and in the number of training examples, and cubic in the number of variables in one example:

$$\mathcal{O}(N \times \mathcal{X}^3 \times \eta)$$

In the mutagenicity problem, $N$ is 188, $\mathcal{X}$ is less than 200. The rate of approximation $\eta$ was set to 300, to be compared with the typical size of a set $\Sigma_{Ex, Ce}$, that is $30^{30}$.

The complexity of classification is that of induction increased by factor $K$, which was set to 3 in our experiments:

$$\mathcal{O}(N \times \mathcal{X}^3 \times \eta \times K)$$

Note that the heuristics designed to cope with noise and sparseness do not modify the computational complexity of classification.

## 4 Experimentation

This section presents an experimental validation of the algorithms described above on the well-studied mutagenicity problem (see [33] for a detailed presentation of this problem).

### 4.1 The data

The dataset is composed of 125 active molecules and 63 inactive molecules. Four levels of description of these molecules have been considered in the literature [33, 10]: Background knowledge $\mathcal{B}_1$ includes the description of atoms and bonds in the molecules. Background knowledge $\mathcal{B}_2$ stands for $\mathcal{B}_1$ augmented with definition of numeric inequalities. Background knowledge $\mathcal{B}_3$ is $\mathcal{B}_2$ augmented with a non structural description of the molecules (five numerical and boolean attributes). Background knowledge $\mathcal{B}_4$ stands for $\mathcal{B}_3$ augmented with the definition of simple chemical concepts (e.g. benzenic or methyl group).

The reference results obtained by *PROGOL* and *FOIL* on this problem (reported from [33] and [34]), are given in Table 1. The run times (in seconds) are measured on HP-735 workstations.

| Background knowledge | Accuracy | | Time | |
|:---:|:---:|:---:|:---:|:---:|
| | FOIL | PROGOL | FOIL | PROGOL |
| $B_1$ | $60 \pm 4$ | $76 \pm 3$ | 5 000 | 117 000 |
| $B_2$ | $81 \pm 3$ | $81 \pm 3$ | 9 000 | 64 350 |
| $B_3$ | $83 \pm 3$ | $83 \pm 3$ | .5 | 42 120 |
| $B_4$ | $82 \pm 3$ | $88 \pm 2$ | .5 | 40 950 |

Table 1: Results of FOIL and PROGOL on the 188-compound problem:
Average predictive accuracy on the test set

In this paper, all experiments conducted with *STILL* only consider background knowledge $B_3$. The 11 264 ground facts composing $B_3$ are partitioned in 188 ground clauses, each clause including all information relevant to a given compound.

## 4.2 Experimental Aim

Previous experiments with *STILL* conducted with background knowledge $B_2$ [31] have shown the validity of this approach in terms of predictive accuracy. Nevertheless, the reason why *STILL* obtains such good results is still unclear.

A first explanation is related to the powerful formalism of constraint logic programming, and the use of inequality constraints relative to either the electric charge or type of element of the atoms, or the non structural description part of molecules (attributes *logp* and *lumo*). The use of numerical inequalities is typically responsible for the increase of performance of *FOIL* from $B_1$ to $B_2$ (Table 1).

The influence of the hypothesis language is evaluated with two experiments. In the first one, *STILL* handles all information in the examples as if it were nominal; only constraints such as $(X = X.\theta)$ are learned, which means that *STILL* constructs pure definite clauses. In the second experiment, inequality constraints can be set on numerical variables and *STILL* thus constructs constrained clauses.

A second explanation is related to the redundancy of the constructed theory. It has been suggested that redundant classifiers tend to be more robust and reliable than concise ones [6, 23]. *STILL* involves two kinds of redundancy. First, it both constructs the theory of mutagenic activity and that of inactivity; in opposition, *PROGOL* only constructs the theory of activity. Second, *STILL* generalizes all examples, whereas both *PROGOL* and *FOIL* remove the examples covered by previous hypotheses.

To check to what extent redundancy is a key factor of accuracy in our approach, *STILL* is compared to a variant denoted *AQ-STILL*, which does include some selection of the seeds. More precisely, *AQ-STILL* only generalizes those examples which are not yet correctly classified at the time they are considered.

In summary, four variants of $STILL$ are implemented[3] and compared:

- $STILL^{CLP}$, which corresponds to the approach described throughout this paper, where all examples are generalized and inequality constraints can be set on numerical variables;
- $STILL^{ILP}$, where all examples are generalized but specialization is limited to variable grounding;
- $AQ\text{-}STILL^{CLP}$, which differs from $STILL^{CLP}$ in the selection of seeds; and
- $AQ\text{-}STILL^{ILP}$, which similarly differs from $STILL^{ILP}$ in the selection of seeds.

## 4.3 Experimental Settings

The parameters controlling the stochastic biases are constant in the following experiments:

The rate of approximation $\eta$, that ensures the tractability of induction, is set to 300.

The parameter $K$, that ensures the tractability of classification, is set to 3.

Parameter $M$ used to control the specificity of the theory varies from 1 to 10. Parameter $\varepsilon$, which corresponds to the maximal number of inconsistencies of a hypothesis, varies from 0 to 4.

All results are averaged over 15 independent runs, where each run consists in learning from 90% of the 188 compounds (randomly selected such that the ratio of active/inactive compounds in the training set is same as in the global data, i.e. about two to one) and classifying the remaining 10% of the data. This protocol of validation is similar to the ten-fold cross validation used in [33]; the number of runs is only slightly increased (from 10 to 15), as suggested for stochastic approaches [9].

For each setting of parameters $\varepsilon$ and $M$, the average percentage of test examples correctly classified, unclassified[4] and misclassified are indicated (labels *Accur*, *?* and *Misclass*), together with the standard deviation of the accuracy (label $\pm$). The average run time on HP-735 workstations, including the construction of the theory and the classification of the test examples, is also given (in seconds).

Last, the average number of seeds is also indicated in the case of $AQ\text{-}STILL^{CLP}$ and $AQ\text{-}STILL^{ILP}$; in the case of $STILL^{CLP}$ and $STILL^{CLP}$, the number of seeds exactly is the number of training examples (170), and has been omitted.

## 4.4 CLP versus ILP

Table 2 shows the results obtained by $STILL^{CLP}$ and $STILL^{ILP}$. Remember the only difference lies in the possibility for $STILL^{CLP}$ to set inequality constraints

---

[3] In $C^{++}$.

[4] An example gets unclassified if either it admits no neighbor in the seeds, or if the majority vote ends up in a tie.

on the type of atom and electric charge of atoms, and on the numerical attributes *logp* and *lumo*.

As noted by [12], one cannot conclude from the presence of numbers in a problem, that this problem needs a learner with numerical skills: many learning problems with numbers include in fact very few distinct values, and can therefore be handled by purely symbolic means. But Table 2 witnesses that the mutagenesis problem does benefit from a CLP formalism.

| $\varepsilon$ | | $STILL^{ILP}$ | | | | | | $STILL^{CLP}$ | | | | |
|---|---|---|---|---|---|---|---|---|---|---|---|---|
| | M | Accur. | ? | Miscl. | ± | Time | M | Accur. | ? | Miscl. | ± | Time |
| 0 | 1 | 86.7 | 0.74 | 12.6 | ± 6.9 | 51 | 4 | 88.5 | 0.37 | 11.1 | ± 6.1 | 73 |
| | 2 | 83.3 | 3.3 | 13.3 | ± 7.7 | 57 | 5 | 91.1 | 0 | 8.89 | ± 7.3 | 78 |
| | 3 | **86.7** | 3 | 10.4 | ± 8.1 | 59 | 6 | 90.7 | 1.1 | 8.15 | ± 4.6 | 82 |
| | 4 | 81.1 | 9.6 | 9.26 | ± 5.4 | 60 | 7 | **91.5** | 1.1 | 7.41 | ± 3.8 | 86 |
| | 5 | 77.4 | 14 | 8.52 | ± 11 | 60 | 8 | 86.7 | 3.7 | 9.63 | ± 8.1 | 90 |
| | 6 | 68.9 | 19 | 12.2 | ± 12 | 59 | 9 | 91.1 | 2.2 | 6.67 | ± 5.8 | 93 |
| | 7 | 64.4 | 26 | 9.63 | ± 7.7 | 58 | 10 | 85.2 | 4.1 | 10.7 | ± 7.3 | 97 |
| 2 | 1 | 83.3 | 0.74 | 15.9 | ± 7.7 | 49 | 4 | 89.3 | 1.3 | 9.4 | ± 7.7 | 69 |
| | 2 | 83.7 | 1.1 | 15.2 | ± 4.6 | 55 | 5 | 88.9 | 0 | 11.1 | ± 7.3 | 74 |
| | 3 | **83.7** | 1.9 | 14.4 | ± 12 | 58 | 6 | **92.5** | 0.4 | 7.14 | ± 5 | 77 |
| | 4 | 80.4 | 3.7 | 15.9 | ± 6.5 | 60 | 7 | 91.5 | 0 | 8.52 | ± 5.4 | 81 |
| | 5 | 79.6 | 4.8 | 15.6 | ± 7.3 | 59 | 8 | 91.9 | 0.37 | 7.78 | ± 5.4 | 85 |
| | 6 | 80.7 | 4.8 | 14.4 | ± 10 | 59 | 9 | 87.4 | 0.37 | 12.2 | ± 6.1 | 88 |
| | 7 | 75.2 | 9.6 | 15.2 | ± 6.5 | 58 | 10 | 87.4 | 0.74 | 11.9 | ± 6.5 | 92 |
| 4 | 1 | 82.6 | 0.74 | 16.7 | ± 8.9 | 47 | 4 | 81.1 | 0 | 18.9 | ± 5 | 66 |
| | 2 | **85.6** | 1.1 | 13.3 | ± 6.1 | 53 | 5 | 85.6 | 1.5 | 13 | ± 8.5 | 71 |
| | 3 | 79.6 | 1.9 | 18.5 | ± 11 | 57 | 6 | 85.9 | 0.37 | 13.7 | ± 8.5 | 75 |
| | 4 | 78.5 | 2.6 | 18.9 | ± 7.3 | 59 | 7 | **89.3** | 0.37 | 10.4 | ± 8.9 | 78 |
| | 5 | 81.1 | 3 | 15.9 | ± 14 | 59 | 8 | 88.9 | 1.5 | 9.63 | ± 6.6 | 82 |
| | 6 | 77 | 5.6 | 17.4 | ± 8.1 | 59 | 9 | 84.8 | 1.1 | 14.1 | ± 6.1 | 85 |
| | 7 | 75.6 | 11 | 13 | ± 14 | 58 | 10 | 85.9 | 0.37 | 13.7 | ± 7.7 | 89 |

(a) Without inequality constraints  (b) With inequality constraints

Table 2: Results of STILL on $\mathcal{B}_3$, $\eta = 300$, $K = 3$

Note that the optimal accuracy for $STILL^{CLP}$ corresponds to higher values of $M$ ($M = 6$-$7$), than for $STILL^{ILP}$ ($M = 2$-$3$). This could be explained as follows. Hypotheses constructed by $STILL^{CLP}$ are more general than those constructed by $STILL^{ILP}$, for numerical inequalities are more often satisfied than equalities. But the specificity of hypotheses also increases with parameter $M$, which offsets the extra generality permitted by the CLP language.

The most striking fact is that the best result of $STILL^{CLP}$ (accuracy 92.5% ± 5 for $\varepsilon = 2$ and $M = 6$) outperforms that of *PROGOL* (Table 1) and *FORS* (with accuracy 89% ± 6) [10], despite the fact that *FORS* explores a language of hypotheses (including linear expressions of the numerical variables) much richer than that of $STILL^{CLP}$.

Of course, a fair comparison would require to see how the predictive accuracy of other learners varies with their control parameters; e.g. [33] only indicates the results obtained with *PROGOL* for a maximal number of inconsistencies set to 4, and a maximal number of literals in a clause set to 5.

This asks the question of how to automatically adjust the parameters of *STILL*. On-going experiments are concerned with using the training set to tune $M$ and $\varepsilon$ in the line of [13].

## 4.5 Pruning the seeds: Pros and Cons

Table 3 shows the results obtained by $AQ\text{-}STILL^{CLP}$ and $AQ\text{-}STILL^{ILP}$. Remember that the only difference between *STILL* and *AQ-STILL* lies in the selection of the seeds: *STILL* generalizes all examples whereas *AQ-STILL* only generalizes examples that are not correctly classified at the time they are considered.

| $\varepsilon$ | | \multicolumn{7}{c}{$AQ\text{-}STILL^{ILP}$} | | \multicolumn{7}{c}{$AQ\text{-}STILL^{CLP}$} |
|---|---|---|---|---|---|---|---|---|---|---|---|---|---|---|---|
| | M | Accur. | ? | Miscl. | ± | Time | Seeds | M | Accur. | ? | Miscl. | ± | Time | Seeds |
| | 1 | **83.3** | 7 | 9.63 | ± 11 | 59 | 36.3 | 2 | 79.3 | 12 | 8.52 | ± 10 | 27 | 21.4 |
| | 2 | 82.6 | 7 | 10.4 | ± 8.9 | 86 | 43.9 | 3 | **87.8** | 5.6 | 6.67 | ± 7.3 | 30 | 17.6 |
| | 3 | 79.3 | 10 | 10.4 | ± 11 | 117 | 54.9 | 4 | 81.9 | 9.3 | 8.89 | ± 6.9 | 39 | 17.6 |
| 0 | 4 | 74.1 | 17 | 8.52 | ± 7.3 | 139 | 65.3 | 5 | 81.9 | 8.9 | 9.26 | ± 9.6 | 48 | 18.7 |
| | 5 | 77 | 17 | 5.93 | ± 8.9 | 161 | 77.5 | 6 | 80.7 | 9.3 | 10 | ± 8.1 | 65 | 23.7 |
| | 6 | 68.1 | 26 | 6.3 | ± 10 | 179 | 90.4 | 7 | 82.6 | 11 | 5.93 | ± 9.2 | 89 | 29.5 |
| | 7 | 60.4 | 34 | 5.19 | ± 14 | 189 | 99.3 | 8 | 84.1 | 10 | 5.56 | ± 7.3 | 113 | 34.8 |
| | 1 | **80** | 8.5 | 11.5 | ± 10 | 54 | 39.5 | 3 | 84.8 | 6.3 | 8.89 | ± 8.5 | 42 | 32 |
| | 2 | 78.5 | 7.8 | 13.7 | ± 12 | 74 | 41.2 | 4 | 79.3 | 7 | 13.7 | ± 6.5 | 44 | 26.8 |
| | 3 | 74.8 | 14 | 10.7 | ± 9.2 | 95 | 47 | 5 | 84.4 | 7.4 | 8.15 | ± 9.6 | 50 | 25.5 |
| 2 | 4 | 75.2 | 12 | 13 | ± 9.2 | 120 | 57.9 | 6 | 84.4 | 8.1 | 7.41 | ± 7.7 | 62 | 27.2 |
| | 5 | 69.6 | 17 | 13.3 | ± 12 | 133 | 64.6 | 7 | 84.1 | 8.5 | 7.41 | ± 8.1 | 70 | 27.4 |
| | 6 | 69.6 | 20 | 10.7 | ± 10 | 147 | 73.5 | 8 | **86.3** | 5.9 | 7.78 | ± 10 | 82 | 31.4 |
| | 7 | 72.2 | 20 | 7.41 | ± 11 | 156 | 82.3 | 9 | 80.7 | 6.7 | 12.6 | ± 7.3 | 95 | 33.9 |
| | 1 | 82.2 | 6.7 | 11.1 | ± 8.5 | 49 | 40.3 | 4 | 85.2 | 5.2 | 9.63 | ± 8.5 | 47 | 31.8 |
| | 2 | **83.3** | 4.8 | 11.9 | ± 6.1 | 69 | 42.1 | 5 | 84.8 | 6.3 | 8.89 | ± 8.1 | 51 | 28.9 |
| | 3 | 81.1 | 5.9 | 13 | ± 11 | 94 | 48.8 | 6 | 85.2 | 5.9 | 8.89 | ± 8.1 | 60 | 28.3 |
| 4 | 4 | 77.8 | 9.6 | 12.6 | ± 2.4 | 113 | 56.5 | 7 | **85.6** | 5.6 | 8.89 | ± 8.9 | 67 | 29.5 |
| | 5 | 72.6 | 15 | 12.6 | ± 7.3 | 124 | 61.4 | 8 | 83.3 | 5.6 | 11.1 | ± 7.3 | 76 | 30.1 |
| | 6 | 70 | 19 | 11.1 | ± 11 | 138 | 69.5 | 9 | 82.2 | 4.8 | 13 | ± 6.8 | 88 | 31.1 |
| | 7 | 64.8 | 23 | 11.9 | ± 9.6 | 147 | 77.2 | 10 | 81.1 | 8.5 | 10.4 | ± 10 | 105 | 36 |

| (a) Without inequality constraints | (a) With inequality constraints |

Table 3: Results of AQ-STILL on $\mathcal{B}_3$, $\eta = 300$, $K = 3$

Again, the use of inequality constraints appears beneficial as $AQ\text{-}STILL^{CLP}$ outperforms $AQ\text{-}STILL^{ILP}$.

In what regards the number of seeds, it increases with $M$ in $AQ\text{-}STILL^{ILP}$: as hypotheses get more and more specific, more and more training examples are unclassified at the time they are considered, and they are therefore generalized.

In $AQ$-$STILL^{CLP}$, the same trend is observed for high values of $M$. The number of seeds also increases for small values of $M$, but for another reason: when $M$ is small, stars constructed by $AQ$-$STILL^{CLP}$ are overly general; more and more examples are therefore misclassified and generalized.

The important fact is that the best predictive accuracy of $AQ$-$STILL^{CLP}$ appears lower than that of $STILL^{CLP}$ ($87.8 \pm 7$ against $92.5 \pm 5$). This tends to support our claim that redundancy is a key factor of predictive accuracy [30, 28].

Moreover, the benefit of pruning is unclear with regards to the computational cost: $AQ$-$STILL$ includes the classification of training examples (in order to check whether they can be pruned), which means that the computational complexity of learning is in $\mathcal{O}(N^2 \times \mathcal{X}^3 \times \eta \times K)$, whereas it is $\mathcal{O}(N \times \mathcal{X}^3 \times \eta)$ for $STILL$. Factually, the computational cost strongly depends on the number of seeds: when the number of seeds is high, as it is the case for $AQ$-$STILL^{ILP}$, pruning globally hinders learning.

## 4.6 General remarks and further experiments

As shown in Tables 2 and 3, the run-times of $STILL$ range from 50 to 180 seconds (these include the construction of the theory and the classification of the test examples on HP-735 workstations). Similar run-times were obtained with background knowledge $\mathcal{B}_1$ and $\mathcal{B}_2$ [31]. This fully demonstrates the potential of the stochastic bias presented in this paper, to master the combinatorial complexity of induction in first order languages.

However, these good results could be due to the ad hoc sampling mechanism designed for the mutagenicity problem (section 3.1). On-going research is concerned with a pure random sampling mechanism.

The influence of parameters $\eta$ and $K$ must also be studied. Preliminary experiments with $\eta = 700$ on background knowledge $\mathcal{B}_2$ show the expected increase in the computational cost (linear in $\eta$) but only bring a slight improvement of the best predictive accuracy.

## 5 Conclusion

We have experimentally demonstrated the potential of the stochastic approximate learner $STILL$ for classification purposes.

The main interest of this work, in our sense, is to show how stochastic processes can be engineered to cut down the combinatorial complexity pertaining to ILP. Further research is concerned with improving the sampling mechanism (e.g. to take into account also the bonds between atoms), while preserving an acceptable complexity.

Note that this sampling mechanism supports, rather than replaces, induction. This is a strong difference with the genetic side of machine learning and ILP [14, 36]: what is sampled here is related to examples rather than to solutions.

Another interest lies in the non-standard use of the Version Space framework: the computational representation of the constructed theory sidesteps the intrinsic combinatorial complexity of Version Spaces. Further, it allows one to relax at no additional cost the consistency and generality requirements, whenever this is required by the defects, noise and sparseness of the data. Moreover, experiments demonstrate the benefit of learning redundant theories; and Version Spaces are indeed maximally redundant theories.

The main weakness of our learning approach is that it constructs nothing like an intelligible theory. Further work is concerned with pruning and compacting the inarticulate theory underlying the classification process; the challenge lies in providing a readable version of this theory *having same predictive accuracy*. The key question is that of the long debated trade-off between intelligibility and predictive accuracy.

This approach will also be given a learnability model, be it based on PAC-learnability [35] or U-learnability [19]. In particular, in the *Probably Approximately Correct* (PAC) framework, parameter $\eta$ used to sample the substitutions naively corresponds to the probability of getting the desired theory, whose approximate correction is $\epsilon$.

**Acknowledgments.** We are grateful to S. Muggleton, A. Srinivasan and R. King, who formalized, studied and made available the mutagenicity problem: this nice problem was determinant for the orientation of the presented work. The work of the authors has been partially supported by the ESPRIT BRA 6020 Inductive Logic Programming and by the ESPRIT LTR 20237 $ILP^2$.

# References

1. F. Bergadano and A. Giordana. Guiding induction with domain theories. In Y. Kodratoff and R.S. Michalski, editors, *Machine Learning : an artificial intelligence approach*, volume 3, pages 474–492. Morgan Kaufmann, 1990.
2. G. Bisson. Learning in FOL with a similarity measure. In *Proceedings of $10^{th}$ AAAI*, 1992.
3. M. Botta and A. Giordana. Smart+ : A multi-strategy learning tool. In *Proceedings of IJCAI-93*, pages 937–943. Morgan Kaufmann, 1993.
4. P. Clark and T. Niblett. Induction in noisy domains. In I. Bratko and N. Lavrac, editors, *Proc. of European WorkShop on Learning*, pages 11–30. Sigma Press, 1987.
5. W. Emde and D. Wettscherek. Relational Instance Based Learning. In L. Saitta, editor, *Proceedings of the $13^{th}$ International Conference on Machine Learning*, pages 122–130, 1996.
6. M. Gams. New measurements highlight the importance of redundant knowledge. In K. Morik, editor, *Proceedings of EWSL-89*, pages 71–80. Pitman, London, 1989.
7. A. Giordana and L. Saitta. REGAL: An integrated system for learning relations using genetic algorithms. In *Proceedings of $2^{nd}$ International Workshop on Multistrategy Learning*, pages 234–249. Harpers Ferry, 1993.
8. J. Jaffar and J. L. Lassez. Constraint Logic Programming. In *Proc. of the fourteenth ACM Symposium on the Principles of Programming Languages*, pages 111–119, 1987.

9. K. E. Kinnear. A perspective on GP. In K. E. Kinnear, editor, *Advances in Genetic Programming*, pages 3–19. MIT Press, Cambridge, MA, 1994.

10. A. Karalic. *First Order Regression*. PhD thesis, Institut Josef Stefan, Ljubljana, Slovenia, 1995.

11. R.D. King, A. Srinivasan, and M.J.E. Sternberg. Relating chemical activity to structure: an examination of ILP successes. *New Gen. Comput.*, 13, 1995.

12. R. Kohavi. The power of decision tables. In N. Lavrac and S. Wrobel, editors, *Proceedings of ECML-95, European Conference on Machine Learning*, pages 174–189. Springer-Verlag, 1995.

13. R. Kohavi and G.H. John. Automatic Parameter Selection by Minimizing Estimated Error. In A. Prieditis and S. Russell, editors, *Proceedings of ICML-95, International Conference on Machine Learning*, pages 304–312. Morgan Kaufmann, 1995.

14. M. Kovacic. MILP: A stochastic approach to ILP. In S. Wrobel, editor, *Proceedings of ILP-94, International Workshop on Inductive Logic Programming*, 1994.

15. N. Lavrac, S. Dzeroski, and M. Grobelnick. Learning non recursive definitions of relations with LINUS. In *Proceedings of EWSL'91*, 1991.

16. R.S. Michalski. A theory and methodology of inductive learning. In R.S Michalski, J.G. Carbonell, and T.M. Mitchell, editors, *Machine Learning : an artificial intelligence approach*, volume 1. Morgan Kaufmann, 1983.

17. R.S. Michalski, I. Mozetic, J. Hong, and N. Lavrac. The AQ15 inductive learning system: an overview and experiment. In *Proceedings of IMAL*, 1986.

18. T.M. Mitchell. Generalization as search. *Artificial Intelligence*, 18:203–226, 1982.

19. S. Muggleton. Bayesian inductive logic programming. In M. Warmuth, editor, *Proceedings of COLT-94, ACM Conference on Computational Learning*, pages 3–11. ACM Press, 1994.

20. S. Muggleton. Inverse entailment and PROGOL. *New Gen. Comput.*, 13:245–286, 1995.

21. S. Muggleton and L. De Raedt. Inductive logic programming: Theory and methods. *Journal of Logic Programming*, 19:629–679, 1994.

22. S. Muggleton and C. Feng. Efficient induction of logic programs. In *Proceedings of the 1st conference on algorithmic learning theory*. Ohmsha, Tokyo, Japan, 1990.

23. R. Nok and O. Gascuel. On learning decision committees. In A. Prieditis and S. Russell, editors, *Proceedings of ICML-95, International Conference on Machine Learning*, pages 413–420. Morgan Kaufmann, 1995.

24. M. Pazzani and D. Kibler. The role of prior knowledge in inductive learning. *Machine Learning*, 9:54–97, 1992.

25. J.R. Quinlan. Learning logical definition from relations. *Machine Learning*, 5:239–266, 1990.

26. M. Sebag. A constraint-based induction algorithm in FOL. In W. Cohen and H. Hirsh, editors, *Proceedings of ICML-94, International Conference on Machine Learning*. Morgan Kaufmann, J1994.

27. M. Sebag. Using constraints to building version spaces. In L. De Raedt and F. Bergadano, editors, *Proceedings of ECML-94, European Conference on Machine Learning*. Springer Verlag, 1994.

28. M. Sebag. Delaying the choice of bias: A disjunctive version space approach. In L. Saitta, editor, *Proceedings of the 13$^{th}$ International Conference on Machine Learning*, pages 444–452. Morgan Kaufmann, 1996.

29. M. Sebag and C. Rouveirol. Induction of maximally general clauses compatible with integrity constraints. In S. Wrobel, editor, *Proceedings of ILP-94, International Workshop on Inductive Logic Programming*, 1994.

30. M. Sebag and C. Rouveirol. Constraint inductive logic programming. In L. de Raedt, editor, *Advances in ILP*, pages 277–294. IOS Press, 1996.

31. M. Sebag, C. Rouveirol, and J.F. Puget. ILP + stochastic bias = polynomial approximate learning. In *Proceedings of $3^{rd}$ International Workshop on MultiStrategy Learning*. MIT Press, 1996, to appear.

32. B.D. Smith and P.S. Rosembloom. Incremental non-backtracking focusing: A polynomially bounded generalization algorithm for version space. In *Proceedings of AAAI-90*, pages 848–853. Morgan Kaufmann, 1990.

33. A. Srinivasan and S. Muggleton. Comparing the use of background knowledge by two ILP systems. In L. de Raedt, editor, *Proceedings of ILP-95*. Katholieke Universiteit Leuven, 1995.

34. A. Srinivasan, personal communication.

35. L.G. Valiant. A theory of the learnable. *Communication of the ACM*, 27:1134–1142, 1984.

36. M.L. Wong and K.S. Leung. Combining genetic programming and inductive logic programming using logic grammars. In D. B. Fogel, editor, *Proceedings of the Second IEEE International Conference on Evolutionary Computation*, pages 733–736. IEEE Press, 1995.

37. J.-D. Zucker and J.-G. Ganascia. Selective reformulation of examples in concept learning. In W. Cohen and H. Hirsh, editors, *Proc. of $11^{th}$ International Conference on Machine Learning*, pages 352–360. Morgan Kaufmann, 1994.

# Analyzing and Learning ECG Waveforms

Gabriella Kókai[1], Zoltán Alexin[2], and Tibor Gyimóthy[3]

[1] Institute of Informatics, József Attila University
Árpád tér 2, H-6720 Szeged, Hungary
Phone: (36) +(62) 311184, Fax: (36) +(62) 312292
e-mail: kokai@inf.u-szeged.hu

now visiting the Chair of Programming Languages,
Department of Computer Science,
Friedrich-Alexander University of Erlangen-Nürnberg
Martenstr. 3. D-91058 Erlangen, Germany
e-mail: kokai@informatik.uni-erlangen.de

[2] Department of Applied Informatics, József Attila University
Árpád tér 2, H-6720 Szeged, Hungary
Phone: (36) +(62) 311184, Fax: (36) +(62) 312292
e-mail: alexin@inf.u-szeged.hu

[3] Research Group on Artificial Intelligence
Hungarian Academy of Sciences,
Aradi vértanuk tere 1, H-6720 Szeged, Hungary
Phone: (36) +(62) 454139, Fax: (36) +(62) 312508
e-mail: gyimi@inf.u-szeged.hu.

**Abstract.** In this paper we present a system which integrates an ECG waveform classifier (called PECG) with an interactive learner (called IMPUT). The PECG system is based on an attribute grammar specification of ECGs that has been transformed to Prolog. The IMPUT system combines the interactive debugging technique IDT with the unfolding algorithm introduced in SPECTRE. The main result achieved in the new version of the PECG system is that an ILP method can be used to improve the effectiveness of a real size Prolog application. Applying the IMPUT method, the extended PECG system is able to suggest a correct solution to the user to replace the buggy clause recognized during the debugging process. [4]

## 1 Introduction

In this paper we present a system which integrates an ECG waveform classifier (called PECG) with an interactive learner (called IMPUT). With the help of this system not only the place of the error can be located in the program but in many cases starting from a *buggy* Prolog program we can infer a *correct* program

---

[4] This work was supported by the grant OTKA T14228 and the project PHARE TDQM 9305-02/1022 ("ILP2/HUN").

using an unfolding transformation and the IDT debugger. Applying the IMPUT method, the extended PECG system is able to suggest a correct solution to the user to replace the buggy clause recognized during the debugging process.

The main result achieved in the new version of the PECG system presented in this paper is that an ILP method can be used to improve the effectiveness of a real size Prolog application. The work of this integrated method is presented in an example in Section 4. Using the IMPUT system we can effectively assist in preparing the correct description of the basic structures of ECG waveforms.

The PECG system contains three main parts: the ECG processing, the IDT and graphic viewer modules. It is based on an attribute grammar approach of ECG waveform analysis published by Skordalakis et al [16, 17].

Skordalakis's system can classify the recognized ECG waveforms according to certain synthesized attributes. It contains a preprocessing part which produces a linguistic representation from an ECG signal. This linguistic representation is used as the input for the PECG system. The basic idea of PECG, introduced in [8], is to integrate the ECG classifier program (implemented in Prolog) with the IDT algorithmic debugger module [7, 13] and a graphic viewer. This integrated tool can recognize if any modification in the classifier program is needed. If the system cannot analyze the input then the user is helped by the built-in IDT (Interactive Diagnosis and Testing) debugger to find the false clause. The IDT improves the Shapiro's original debugging method [15] and can be employed in the debugging and testing of Prolog programs [7, 13]. The graphic viewer module helps the users to decide whether the program with a given input works correctly or not, by displaying the steps of debugging phase.

The learning part of the PECG based on an Inductive Logic Programming (ILP) [9, 11] method called IMPUT introduced in [1]. The IMPUT system combines the interactive debugging technique IDT with the specialization algorithm SPECTRE presented in [2]. The main points behind the IMPUT method is that the identification of a clause to be unfolded has a crucial importance in the effectiveness of the specialization process. If a negative example is covered by the current version of the initial program there is supposedly at least one clause which is responsible for this incorrect covering. The debugging system IDT is used to identify a buggy clause instance. This clause is removed from the initial program. If a derivation of a positive example contains this clause, then those resolvents of the clause which appeared in this derivation are added to the initial program. A modified version of the impurity measure strategy is used to determine the literal to be unfolded [1]. The former version of the IMPUT system was modified such that it can analyze a Prolog program written in DCG form containing recursive predicates.

Sections 2 and 3 contain, respectively short descriptions of the PECG and IMPUT systems. In Section 4 the workings of the integrated system is demonstrated. Finally, in Section 5 a brief summary and comments on possible future studies are presented.

## 2 The PECG system

In this section we give a short overview of the PECG system. A more detailed description can be found in [8].
The structure of the system can be seen in Figure 1.

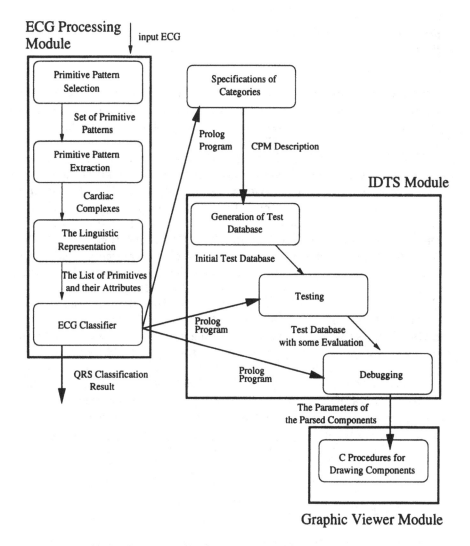

**Fig. 1.** The structure of the PECG system

The main parts are the following:

- *the ECG processing module:* this part of the system uses a syntactic approach to recognize an electrocardiographic pattern.

- *the IDT module:* this part is an interactive debugging and testing tool that is based on the Shapiro's Interactive Diagnosis Algorithm [15] and Category Partition Testing Method [12].
- *the graphic viewer module:* this part makes visible the current state of the debugging process.

The ECG processing module is built up from the following modules:

- *primitive pattern selection*
- *primitive pattern extraction*
- *the linguistic representation*
- *the ECG classifier*

In the *primitive pattern selection* part an ECG waveform can be considered as a composite pattern which can be decomposed as soon as possible into primitive patterns (straight line, peak, parabola). The main task of the *primitive pattern extraction* is to select the peaks. This part is based on recognition of the noisy peaks. The real peaks are found from the difference between the set of all peaks and the noisy ones. In the *linguistic representation* part the result of the last two steps are represented as a string of symbols from an alphabet. The *ECG classifier* module recognizes the ECG waveforms from their linguistic representations.

The IDT part can be divided into three submodules. The *test database* module generates the initial test database from a CPM specification. In the *testing* part a predicate can be chosen and the user can give a representing element of the testframe generated for this predicate. Then he or she can decide whether, for the given input, the output is correct or not. The *debugging* part is based on the idea that if the program has already been tested then the test results can be directly applied without asking the user "difficult" questions.

In the PECG system the algorithmic debugger IDT has been extended by adding a graphic viewer. This graphic module shows the ECG waveform being analyzed and in this way provides effective assistance for the user to answer the questions invoked by the debugger. At the beginning of the debugging phase the whole ECG waveform is displayed (see Figure 2) and in each step of the debugging process the current component of the input is presented.

In the Figure 3 it can be seen, that the graphic viewer draws out the whole recognized QRS waveform in a different graphic form. This module contains C routines.

## 3   The IMPUT system

In this section the IMPUT system is briefly presented. It consists of two main parts. The specialization algorithm comes from the SPECTRE system while the interactive debugger part is imported from the IDT. The original specialization algorithm was extended in order to be able to revise multiple predicates simultaneously, to be able to read in DCG rules and to handle recursive predicates. This

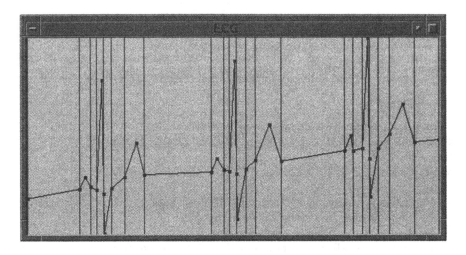

**Fig. 2.** The representation of the input ECG

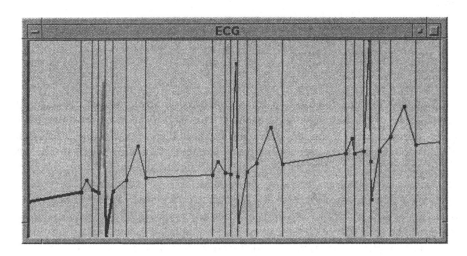

**Fig. 3.** The graphical representation of the recognized QRS part

modification initiated some further improvements and these are incorporated in IMPUT as well.

The algorithm SPECTRE [2] specializes logic programs with respect to positive and negative examples by applying the transformation rule *unfolding* [18] together with clause removal. The choice of which literal to unfold upon is made using a computation rule, which is given as input to the algorithm. A detailed description of SPECTRE can be found in [2].

**Input:** An initial program $P = \{p_1, \ldots, p_u\}$, background knowledge $B = \{b_1, \ldots, b_v\}$ (a set of clauses that is not changed during the learning process), sets of ground atoms $E^+$, $E^-$ (the positive and the negative examples).
**Output:** Series of programs $P'^{(0)}, P'^{(1)}, \ldots, P'^{(n)}$ $(P'^{(0)} = P)$, where $P'^{(i+1)} = \tilde{\mathcal{U}}(P'^{(i)})$ $(0 \leq i < n)$, $\tilde{\mathcal{U}}$ is the unfolding operator extended with clause removal.

*The Algorithm:*

Check if the program $P$ terminates on all $e^+ \in E^+$.
if fails then stop "Initial program should cover all positive examples."
let $i = 0$.
while there is an $e^- \in E^-$ such that $P'^{(i)}$ does not fail on $e^-$ do
begin
    Find a buggy clause $c \in P'^{(i)}$ using the IDT debugger
    Perform unfolding on $c$ using a computation rule.
    let $C = \{c_1, \ldots, c_s\}$ be the resolvents of $c$.
    Remove from $C$ all those clauses that does not occur in
        refutations of positive examples.
    let $P'^{(i+1)} = P'^{(i)} \setminus \{c\} \cup C$
    let $i = i + 1$
end

**Fig. 4.** The basic algorithm of IMPUT

The IDT method is based on the algorithmic program debugging technique introduced by Shapiro [15]. This method can isolate an erroneous procedure, given a program and an input on which it behaves incorrectly. A major drawback of this debugging technique is the great number of queries made to the user about the correctness of intermediate results of procedure calls. An improvement in the bug localization process is realized in IDT by combining the *category partition testing method* [6], with the algorithm introduced in [15]. The main idea basically as follows: If the program has already been tested, the test results for the procedures of the program can be directly applied in the debugging process without consulting the user. The IDT interactive debugging environment was presented in [7, 13] and a similar system for imperative languages was introduced in [6].

The IMPUT system integrates the SPECTRE and the IDT methods. The main idea of IMPUT is that the identification of the next clause to be unfolded has a crucial importance in the effectiveness of the specialization process. The specialization steps are invoked by the negative examples that are covered by the target predicate. We assume that when a negative example is covered by the current version of the program, then there is at least one clause which is responsible for this incorrect covering. IMPUT uses the IDT debugging algorithm to identify a buggy clause of the program. The clause identified in this process will be unfolded in the next step of the specialization algorithm.

The basic algorithm of IMPUT system is presented in Figure 4. A more detailed descriptions of the system can be found in [1].

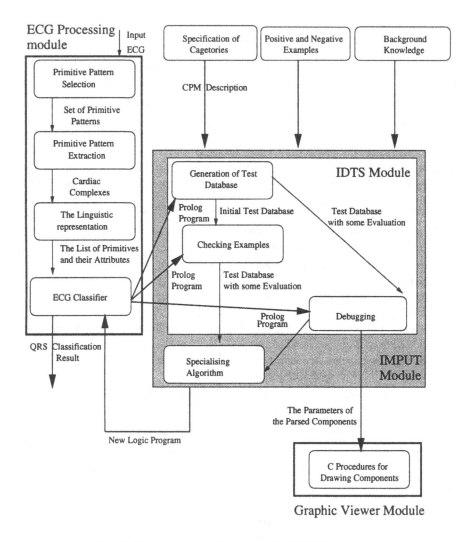

**Fig. 5.** The structure of the extended PECG system

# 4 Integration of PECG and IMPUT

In the following the extended PECG system is presented. We explain how the integrated system can learn an ECG description. The structure of the extended

PECG system is shown in Figure 5. As mentioned earlier, the debugger is extended with a graphic viewer to trace the history of the traversing of the proof tree of the ECG analyzer program, but to keep our example as simple as possible here we do not present the results any of these displays.

## 4.1 The syntax of ECG grammar

In Skordalakis's paper [17] an attribute grammar was presented for recognition of ECG waveforms. A part of this description is selected to demonstrate the learning of one cardiac cycle of a normal ECG. The syntactic part of the grammar in Prolog representation is presented in Appendix 6.1.

The syntax of the attribute grammar which we use here is basically the one by Udupa [19] for the normal ECGs. The ECG waveform is encoded as a string of pairs. The first element of each pair is a slope symbol and the second element is a number representing the duration of the corresponding line subsegment.

The terminal symbols of the grammar are the following:

$l$  denoting line segment of unit length and large positive slope,
    unit length $= 0.25$ mm and slope $= (75°, 90°)$
$nl$ denoting line segment of unit length and large negative slope,
    unit length $= 0.25$ mm and slope $= (-75°, -90°)$
$i$  denoting line segment of unit length and intermediate positive slope,
    unit length $= 0.25$ mm and slope $= (35°, 75°)$
$ni$ denoting line segment of unit length and intermediate negative slope,
    unit length $= 0.25$ mm and slope $= (-35°, -75°)$
$s$  denoting line segment of unit length and small positive slope
    unit length $= 0.25$ mm and slope $= (5°, 35°)$
$ns$ denoting line segment of unit length and small negative slope,
    unit length $= 0.25$ mm and slope $= (5°, 35°)$
$h$  denoting horizontal line segment e.g. slope $= (-5°, 5°)$

The nonterminal symbols to be used are the following:

| | |
|---|---|
| $cardiac\_cycle$ | denoting a cardiac cycle |
| $Q, RS, T, P$ | denoting a Q, RS, T, P wave, respectively |
| $ST, PR, TP$ | denoting a ST, PR, TP segment, respectively |
| $C, D, E, F, G,$ | denoting auxiliary nonterminals |
| $H, I$ | $, K, L, M$ |

Our approach is based on the attribute grammar given in [17] but we use a logical program representation for the recognition of the cardiac cycle. The attribute grammar presented in [19] was used as a starting-point and was rewritten in Prolog. The difference between an attribute grammar representation and a Prolog program, however made the rewriting process non-trivial. The main difficulties came from the imperative features of the computational rules for the attribute values. We used definite clause grammar (DCG) [14] representation for that [4].

## 4.2 The learning process

In the following we present how the IMPUT learning system refines the initial DCG program. To demonstrate the work of IMPUT some changes were made in the ECG grammar.

- A new version of the nonterminal *l* was added to the description;

```
l --> negative_intermediate_slope.
l --> negative_large_slope.
l --> negative_small_slope.
```

- A new nonterminal *n* was introduced;

```
n --> large_slope.
n --> intermediate_slope.
```

- The *large_slope* nonterminal was replaced by *n* in the following DCG rules;

```
e --> n, e.
e --> {true}.
c --> n, c.
c --> n.
```

- The *negative_large_slope* nonterminal was changed to *l* in the following DCG rules.

```
d --> l, d.
d --> l.
```

The input description contains the program for classifying cardiac cycles, the background knowledge, the positive and negative examples (see Appendix 6.2). The task of our integrated system was to find the correct program which can recognize only the positive examples. The main issues of the session are the following. The user starts the program by entering **start** then enters the name of the file to be processed. All clauses read are numbered. The clauses obtained by unfolding are numbered by pairs of numbers i-j where the first number denotes the parent, the second denotes the substituted clause.

```
| ?- start.
Welcome to IMPUT learning system.
Please enter the filename to be processed: ecg_description.

 The background knowledge is:
38: negative_large_slope(A,B):-C(A,nl,B)
...
44: horizontal_slope(A,B):-C(A,h,B)

 The theory needs to be specialized is:
0: main(A,[]):-cardiac_cycle(A,[])
1: cardiac_cycle(A,B):-q(A,C),rs(C,D),st(D,E),t(E,F),
                      tp(F,G),p(G,H),pr(H,B)
```

```
2: q(A,B):-1(A,C),q(C,B)
3: q(A,B):-B=A
...

36: pr(A,B):-i(A,C),pr(C,B)
37: pr(A,B):-B=A

 The positive examples are:
45: main([ni,ni,l,l,nl,...],[])
...
51: main([ni,nl,l,nl,nl,...],[])

 The negative examples are:
52: main([ns,ni,ni,l,l,...],[])

57: main([nl,ni,l,l,nl,...],[])
```

The positive and negative examples are checked. At the beginning, both the positive and negative examples have to be covered by the initial description. Firstly, the system checks if the sets of positive and negative examples are distinct, secondly if there exist clauses which are not necessary to deduce the positive examples. If such clauses are exist then those will be removed from the program. In this case the program found that the following clause

```
6: 1(A,B):-negative_small_slope(A,B)
```

is superfluous in the description. It means that the extended PECG system recognized the first error which we made. The superfluous clause was left out and the remaining clauses were listed.

```
Checking input examples:

The sets of positive and negative examples are distinct.

Checking positive examples:

Clauses were found, that are not needed to cover positive examples.
- clauses were removed from the initial theory.

The remained clauses are:
0: main(A,[]):-cardiac_cycle(A,[])
1: cardiac_cycle(A,B):-q(A,C),rs(C,D),st(D,E),t(E,F),
                       tp(F,G),p(G,H),pr(H,B)
2: q(A,B):-1(A,C),q(C,B)
3: q(A,B):-B=A
4: 1(A,B):-negative_intermediate_slope(A,B)
5: 1(A,B):-negative_large_slope(A,B)
7: rs(A,B):-c(A,C),d(C,D),e(D,B)
....
```

After this PECG checks for the negative examples. If the system finds such a negative example that is covered by the initial program then the learning phase

is begun, otherwise the system will stop. Only the covered negative examples
are displayed.

The first step of the learning is to find the basis of the unfolding by the
debugger. The questions asked by the system can be answered with *yes* or *no*.
The answer *no* means that the debugger has found the false clause, the debugging
process is finished and the unfolding process can be started. In the opposite case
the debugging goes on to the next predicate. In this example the last question
is

```
Is it ok [c([i,1,nl,1,ns,i,h,ns,ns,ns,ni,ns,ns,i,h,ns,ns,ns,ni,ns,s],
   [nl,1,ns,i,h,ns,ns,ns,ni,ns,ns,i,h,ns,ns,ns,ni,ns,s])] (y/n) n
```

The answer is *no* because in the correct classification the *c* can contain only
*large_slope* values. It is the second change made that allows the deduction of
*intermediate_slope* from *c* too.

```
Checking negative examples:
54: main([ni,nl,ni,nl,1,...],[])   covered.
55: main([nl,nl,1,1,i,...],[])     covered.
56: main([ni,nl,1,1,nl,...],[])    covered.
57: main([nl,ni,1,1,nl,...],[])    covered.
```

```
The fact main([ni,nl,ni,nl,1,...],[]) is covered by the theory.
Starting the false proc. algorithm to determine the basis of the unfolding.
```

```
Is it ok [ 1([ni,nl,ni,nl,1,...],[nl,ni,nl,1,i,...]) ] (y/n) y
Is it ok [ 1([nl,ni,nl,1,i,],[ni,nl,1,i,1,...]) ] (y/n) y
...
Is it ok [ c([i,1,nl,1,ns,...],[nl,1,ns,i,h,...]) ] (y/n) n
```

The most complex part of the system is the unfolding part. As mentioned
earlier, it is supposed that if a negative example is covered by the current version
of the initial program, then there is at least one clause which is responsible for
this incorrect covering. We have found that the clause $c(A, B) : -n(A, C), c(C, B)$
is incorrect. This clause cannot be removed from the initial program because the
derivation of a positive example contains this clause. The resolvents of this clause
are: $c(A, B) : -$large_slope$(A, C), c(C, B)$ and $c(A, B) : -$intermediate_slope$(A, C)$,
$c(C, B)$ The second clause $c(A, B) : -$intermediate_slope$(A, C), c(C, B)$ is removed,
because there is no positive example whose derivation contains it. The system
displays the clause to be unfolded and the result of the unfolding.

```
Unfolding at the clause instance:
   8: c([i,1,nl,1,ns,...],[nl,1,ns,i,h,...]):-
         n([i,1,nl,1,ns,...],[1,nl,1,ns,i,...]),
         c([1,nl,1,ns,i,...],[nl,1,ns,i,h,...])
```

```
- trying resolvent(s): [8-1] actual minimum is:  6.877840558577583.
- trying resolvent(s): [8-2] actual minimum is: 11.344977967946406.
```

```
The result of the unfolding is:
0: main(A,[]):-cardiac_cycle(A,[])
```

```
1: cardiac_cycle(A,B):-q(A,C),rs(C,D),st(D,E),t(E,F),
                       tp(F,G),p(G,H),pr(H,B)
2: q(A,B):-1(A,C),q(C,B)
3: q(A,B):-B=A
4: 1(A,B):-negative_intermediate_slope(A,B)
5: 1(A,B):-negative_large_slope(A,B)
7: rs(A,B):-c(A,C),d(C,D),e(D,B)
8-12: c(A,B):-large_slope(A,C),c(C,B)
9: c(A,B):-n(A,B)
...
```

The new program will not cover the four first negative examples, but only covers the fifth and the sixth ones. By repeatedly using the debugger we can find an other erroneous clause. The answer *no* given by the user to the question

```
Is it ok [d([ni,nl,1,ns,ns,...],[1,ns,ns,i,h,...])] (y/n) n
```

means that the third modification was recognized: we used $d--> 1, d$ instead of $d--> $ negative_large_slope.

```
Checking positive examples:

Checking negative examples:
56: main([ni,nl,1,1,nl,...],[]) covered.
57: main([nl,ni,1,1,nl,...],[]) covered.

The above theory:
   cover   7 positive samples from 7 (100.00%) and
   fail on 4 negative samples from 6 (66.67%).

The fact main([ni,nl,1,1,nl,...],[]) is covered by the theory.
Starting the false proc. algorithm to determine the basis of the unfolding.

Is it ok [1([ni,nl,1,1,nl,...],[nl,1,1,nl,ni,...])] (y/n) y
Is it ok [1([nl,1,1,nl,ni,...],[1,1,nl,ni,nl,...])] (y/n) y
...
Is it ok [d([ni,nl,1,ns,ns,...],[1,ns,ns,i,h,...])] (y/n) n
```

The next false clause was recognised. The clause found is spezialized by the unfolding. The resolvents of the clause are:

```
d(A,B):- negative_large_slope(A,C),d(C,B)
d(A,B):- negative_intermediate_slope(A,C),d(C,B)
d(A,B):- negative_small_slope(A,C),d(C,B)
```

In the derivation of positive examples the clauses

```
d(A,B):-negative_intermediate_slope(A,C),d(C,B)
d(A,B):-negative_small_slope(A,C),d(C,B)
```

do not occur, therefore they are removed from the set of clauses. The result of this unfolding is presented below.

```
10: d([ni,nl,l,ns,ns,...],[l,ns,ns,i,h,...]):-
      l([ni,nl,l,ns,ns,...],[nl,l,ns,ns,i,...]),
      d([nl,l,ns,ns,i,...], [l,ns,ns,i,h,...])
```

- trying resolvent(s): [10-1] actual minimum is: 0.
- trying resolvent(s): [10-2] actual minimum is: 4.141709450076293.

```
The result of the unfolding is:
0: main(A,[]):-cardiac_cycle(A,[])
1: cardiac_cycle(A,B):-q(A,C),rs(C,D),st(D,E),t(E,F),
                        tp(F,G),p(G,H),pr(H,B)
2: q(A,B):-l(A,C),q(C,B)
3: q(A,B):-B=A
4: l(A,B):-negative_intermediate_slope(A,B)
5: l(A,B):-negative_large_slope(A,B)
7: rs(A,B):-c(A,C),d(C,D),e(D,B)
8-12: c(A,B):-large_slope(A,C),c(C,B)
9: c(A,B):-n(A,B)
10-5: d(A,B):-negative_large_slope(A,C),d(C,B)
11: d(A,B):-l(A,B)
...
```

Checking positive examples:

Checking negative examples:

The above theory:
    cover   7 positive samples from 7 (100.00%) and
    fail on 6 negative samples from 6 (100.00%).

The learning process is finished because the program above has covered all positive examples and failed on all negative ones. The complete result can be found in Appendix 6.3.

# 5   Conclusion, Further Work

In this paper an integrated system has been presented which can classify and learn ECG waveforms. Combining the IMPUT method with the PECG system the integrated system was able to suggest a correct clause for the user which replaced the buggy clause recognized during the debugging process.

In general the graphic viewer helps to find bugs, and in our case shows the ECG subpattern is currently being analyzed. This module was implemented in C, the C routines are UNIX portable and work together with the Prolog interpreter.

The main advantage of our system comparing with Skordalakis' approach is that our integrated tool can positively assists the developer (user) working with the ECG classifier program because the program itself is "self-correcting".

Applying the IMPUT learning method to the ECG domain we found that correct DCG programs can be inferred for the basic structures of complex ECG waveforms. In these approaches the user only needs to prepare very general initial DCG programs. The extended PECG system is able to specialize these programs into the correct ones in a very effective way. However, our general experiences has shown for us that this method is not really suitable for the learning rules which describe the computation of the values of the arguments of these structures. For this task we are going to try to apply other ILP techniques (Progol [10], LINUS [5], CLAUDINE [3]). In general it is concluded that the effective employment of the ILP method for real like applications may require the combination of different ILP techniques.

The current version of the PECG system is about 3500 lines in SICStus Prolog, and 500 lines written in C for the implementation of the graphic viewer. The IDT module is about 1400 Prolog lines, containing 150 predicates while the classifier program is more than 2000 lines in Prolog. The IMPUT system itself contains more than 800 lines without the IDT module. [5]

We are going to extend our system in the following way:

At present the PECG system does not contain any preprocessing module for the linguistic representation of ECG waveforms. Therefore we could test the performance of our system with only preprocessed data presented in the literature. To make our system a complete ECG recognizer we plan to implement these preprocessing modules. We also plan to ensure an interactive connection between the graphic viewer and the user. It means that the user may control the analyzing process from the graphic window by marking the subparts of the waveforms to be analyzed.

At present, the PECG system is able to analyse a large set of ECG waveforms. We plan to apply ILP methods to transformations of the classifier program, such that the transformed programs can recognize further ECG waveforms appearing in actual clinical situations. We are working on this task in conjunction with ECG medical experts from the Medical University in Szeged.

# References

1. Alexin, Z., Gyimóthy, T., Boström, H.: Integrating Algorithmic Debugging and Unfolding Transformation in an Interactive Learner in Proceedings of the 12th European Conference on Artificial Intelligence ECAI-96 ed. Wolfgang Wahlster, Budapest, Hungary (1996) 403–407 John Wiley & Son's Ltd. 1996.
2. Boström, H., Idestam-Almquist, P.: Specialization of Logic Programs by Pruning SLD-trees., Proc. of the Fourth International Workshop on Inductive Logic Programming (ILP-94) Bad Honnef/Bonn Germany September 12-14. (1994) 31–47
3. De Raedt, L., Bruynooghe, M.: A theory of clausal discovery Proc. of the 13th International Joint Conference on Artificial Intelligence Morgan Kaufmann (1993)
4. Deransart, P., Małuszyński, J.: Relating Logic Programs and Attribute Grammars Journal of Logic Programming 2, (1985) 119–156
5. Džeroski, S., Lavrač, N.: Inductive Learning in Deductive Databases, IEEE Transactions on Knowledge and Data Engineering 5 (6): (1994) 939–949

---

[5] The implementation language currently is SICStus Prolog Version 3.0 #3 running on a SUN SPARCStation.

6. Fritzson, P., Gyimóthy, T., Kamkar, M., Shahmeri, N.: Generalized Algorithmic Debugging and Testing in Proceedings of ACM SIGPLAN '91 Conference on Programming Language Design and Implementation, Toronto, Ontario 1991. ACM SIGPLAN Notices 26, 6, (1991) 317–326

7. Kókai, G., Alexin, Z., Kocsis, F.: The IDT System and its Application for Learning Prolog Programs. Proc. of the Sixth International Conference on Artificial Intelligence and Information Control Systems of Robots (AIICSR-94) Smolenice Castle Slovakia September 12-16. (1994) 315–320

8. Kókai, G., Alexin, Z., Gyimóthy, T.: Classifying ECG Waveforms in Prolog Proc. of the Fourth International Conference on The Practical Application of PROLOG (PAP96) London, United Kingdom April 23-25, (1996) 193–221

9. Lavrač, N., Džeroski, S.: Inductive Logic Programming: Techniques and Applications Ellis Horwood, (1994)

10. Muggleton, S.: Inverse entailment and Progol, New Generation Computing Vol 13. (special issue on Inductive Logic Programming) Ohmsha, (1995) 245–286

11. Muggleton, S., De Raedt, L.: Inductive Logic Programming: Theory and methods, Journal of Logic Programming 19 (20) (1994) 629–679

12. Ostrand, T. J., Balker, M. J.: The Category-Partition Method for Specifying and Generating Functional Tests CACM 31:6 June (1988) 676–686

13. Paakki, J., Gyimóthy, T., Horváth T.,: Effective Algorithmic Debugging for Inductive Logic Programming. Proc. of the Fourth International Workshop on Inductive Logic Programming (ILP-94) Bad Honnef/Bonn Germany September 12-14. (1994) 175–194

14. Pereira, F. C. N., Warren, D. H. D.: Definite clause grammars for language analysis - a survey of the formalism and a comparison with augmented transition networks Artificial Intelligence 13: 231-278, (1980)

15. Shapiro, E. Y.: Algorithmic Program Debugging MIT Press (1983)

16. Skordalakis, E.: ECG Analysis in Syntactic and Structural Pattern Recognition Theory and Applications ed. Bunke, H. and Sanfeliu, A. World Scientific (1990) 499–533

17. Skordalakis, E., Papakonstantinou G.: Towards an Attribute Grammar for the Description of ECG Waveforms 7th International Conference on Pattern Recognition (1984).

18. Tamaki, H., Sato, T.: Unfold/Fold Transformations of Logic Programs, Proceedings of the Second International Logic Programming Conference, Uppsala University, Uppsala, Sweden (1984) 127–138

19. Udupa J.K., Murthy I.S.N.: Syntactic Approach to ECG Rhythm analysis IEEE Transactions on Biomedical Engineering, vol. BME-27, No.7 pp 370-375, July 1980

# 6 Appendix

## 6.1 The syntactic part of the original description for a cardiac cycle of an ECG

```
main(Inp,[])     :-     cardiac_cycle(Inp,[]).

cardiac_cycle    -->    q, rs, st, t, tp, p, pr .

q                -->    l, q.
```

```
q               -->     {true}.

l               -->     negative_intermediate_slope.
l               -->     negative_large_slope.

rs              -->     c, d, e.

c               -->     large_slope, c.
c               -->     large_slope.

d               -->     negative_large_slope, d.
d               -->     negative_large_slope.

e               -->     large_slope, e.
e               -->     intermediate_slope, e.
e               -->     {true}.

st              -->     i,st.
st              -->     {true}.

i               -->     horizontal_slope.
i               -->     small_slope.
i               -->     negative_small_slope.

t               -->     f,g,h.

f               -->     k,f.
f               -->     {true}.

k               -->     intermediate_slope.
k               -->     small_slope.
k               -->     horizontal_slope.

g               -->     i,g.
g               -->     {true}.

h               -->     m ,g.
h               -->     {true}.

m               -->     negative_intermediate_slope.
m               -->     negative_small_slope.

tp              -->     i,tp.
tp              -->     {true}.

p               -->     t.

pr              -->     i, pr.
pr              -->     {true}.
```

```
negative_large_slope        --> [nl].
negative_intermediate_slope --> [ni].
negative_small_slope        --> [ns].
large_slope                 --> [l].
intermediate_slope          --> [i].
small_slope                 --> [s].
horizontal_slope            --> [h].
```

## 6.2  The input description for our system

```
main(Inp,[])    :-    cardiac_cycle(Inp,[]).

cardiac_cycle   -->   q, rs, st, t, tp, p, pr .

q               -->   l, q.
q               -->   {true}.

l               -->   negative_intermediate_slope.
l               -->   negative_large_slope.
l               -->   negative_small_slope.

rs              -->   c, d, e.

c               -->   n, c.
c               -->   n.

n               -->   large_slope.
n               -->   intermediate_slope.

d               -->   l, d.
d               -->   l.

e               -->   n, e.
e               -->   {true}.

st              -->   i,st.
st              -->   {true}.

i               -->   horizontal_slope.
i               -->   small_slope.
i               -->   negative_smal

t               -->   f,g,h.

f               -->   k,f.
f               -->   {true}.

k               -->   intermediate_slope.
k               -->   small_slope.
k               -->   horizontal_slope.
```

```
g              -->   i,g.
g              -->   {true}.

h              -->   m,h.
h              -->   {true}.

m              -->   negative_intermediate_slope.
m              -->   negative_small_slope.

tp             -->   i,tp.
tp             -->   {true}.

p              -->   t.

pr             -->   i, pr.
pr             -->   {true}.

background negative_large_slope        --> [nl].
background negative_intermediate_slope --> [ni].
background negative_small_slope        --> [ns].
background large_slope                 --> [l].
background intermediate_slope          --> [i].
background small_slope                 --> [s].
background horizontal_slope            --> [h].


positive main([ni,ni,l,l,nl,l,ns,ns,ns,ns,ns,ns,i,h,ns,ns,ns,ni,ns,
              ns,ns,ns,ns,ns,ns,ns,ns,i,h,ns,ns,ns,ni,ns,s,s,s],[]).
positive main([nl,nl,l,nl,i,s,s,s,s,s,s,s,i,s,s,s,s,s,ns,ns,s,s,s,s,s,
              s,s,s,i,s,s,s,s,ns,ns],[]).
positive main([ni,nl,l,l,nl,l,ns,ns,ns,ns,ns,ns,i,h,ns,ns,ns,ni,ns,
              ns,ns,ns,ns,ns,ns,ns,ns,i,h,ns,ns,ns,ni,ns,s,s,s],[]).
positive main([nl,ni,l,l,nl,nl,i,l,h,s,ns,h,s,ns,s,h,h,s,ns,ns,ni,
              h,s,ns,h,s,ns,h,s,s,h,h,s,ns,ns,ni,h,s,ns,h],[]).
positive main([ni,nl,ni,nl,l,l,nl,l,ns,ns,ns,ns,ns,ns,i,h,ns,ns,ns,ni,
              ns,ns,ns,ns,ns,ns,ns,ns,i,h,ns,ns,ns,ni,ns,s,s,s],[]).
positive main([nl,nl,l,l,l,nl,i,l,i,ns,h,s,ns,h,s,h,i,ns,h,s,ns,ns,
              ns,h,s,ns,h,s,ns,h,s, h,i,ns,h,s,ns,ns,ns,h,s,ns] ,[]).
positive main([ni,nl,l,nl,nl,nl,l,i,l,h,s,ns,h,s,ns,h,s,h,s,ns,ni,ns,
              h,s,ns,h,s,ns,h,s,h,s,h,s,ns,ni,ns,h,s,ns,h],[]).

negative main([ns,ni,ni,l,l,nl,l,ns,ns,ns,ns,ns,ns,i,h,ns,ns,ns,ni,ns,
              ns,ns,ns,ns,ns,ns, ns,ns,i,h,ns,ns,ns,ni,ns,s,s,s],[]).
negative main([ns,ns,nl,nl,l,nl,i,s,s,s,s,s,s,s,i,s,s,s,s,s,ns,ns,s,s,s,s,
              s,s,s,s,i,s,s,s,s,ns,ns],[]).
negative main([ni,nl,l,l,nl,ni,nl,l,ns,ns,ns,ns,ns,ns,i,h,ns,ns,ns,ni,
              ns,ns,ns,ns,ns,ns,ns, ns,ns,i,h,ns,ns,ns,ni,ns,s,s,s],[]).
negative main([nl,ni,l,l,nl,ni,ni,nl,i,l,h,s,ns,h,s,ns,s,h,h,s,ns,ns,
              ni,h,s,ns,h,s,ns,h,s,s,h,h,s,ns,ns,ni,h,s,ns,h],[]).
negative main([ni,nl,ni,nl,l,i,l,nl,l,ns,ns,ns,ns,ns,ns,i,h,ns,ns,ns,ni,
```

```
                  ns,ns,ns,ns,ns,ns,ns,ns,ns,i,h,ns,ns,ns,ni,ns,s,s,s],[]).
negative main([nl,nl,l,l,i,i,l,nl,i,l,i,ns,h,s,ns,h,s,h,i,ns,h,s,ns,ns,
             ns,h,s,ns,h,s,ns,h,s, h,i,ns,h,s,ns,ns,ns,h,s,ns] ,[]).
```

## 6.3   The output of the extended PECG system

```
0: main(A,[]):-cardiac_cycle(A,[])
1: cardiac_cycle(A,B):- q(A,C),rs(C,D),st(D,E),t(E,F),
                        tp(F,G),p(G,H),pr(H,B)
2: q(A,B):- l(A,C),q(C,B)
3: q(A,B):- B=A
4: l(A,B):-negative_intermediate_slope(A,B)
5: l(A,B):-negative_large_slope(A,B)
7: rs(A,B):-c(A,C),d(C,D),e(D,B)
8-12: c(A,B):-large_slope(A,C),c(C,B)
9: c(A,B):-n(A,B)
10-5: d(A,B):-negative_large_slope(A,C),d(C,B)
11: d(A,B):-l(A,B)
12: n(A,B):-large_slope(A,B)
13: n(A,B):-intermediate_slope(A,B)
14: e(A,B):-n(A,C),e(C,B)
15: e(A,B):-B=A
16: st(A,B):-i(A,C),st(C,B)
17: st(A,B):-B=A
18: t(A,B):-f(A,C),g(C,D),h(D,B)
19: f(A,B):-k(A,C),f(C,B)
20: f(A,B):-B=A
21: g(A,B):-i(A,C),g(C,B)
22: g(A,B):-B=A
23: h(A,B):-m(A,C),h(C,B)
24: h(A,B):-B=A
25: m(A,B):-negative_intermediate_slope(A,B)
26: m(A,B):-negative_small_slope(A,B)
27: k(A,B):-intermediate_slope(A,B)
28: k(A,B):-small_slope(A,B)
29: k(A,B):-horizontal_slope(A,B)
30: i(A,B):-horizontal_slope(A,B)
31: i(A,B):-small_slope(A,B)
32: i(A,B):-negative_small_slope(A,B)
33: tp(A,B):-i(A,C),tp(C,B)
34: tp(A,B):-B=A
35: p(A,B):-t(A,B)
36: pr(A,B):-i(A,C),pr(C,B)
37: pr(A,B):-B=A
```

# Learning Rules That Classify Ocular Fundus Images for Glaucoma Diagnosis

Fumio Mizoguchi[1], Hayato Ohwada[1], Makiko Daidoji[1] and Shiroteru Shirato[2]

[1] Science University of Tokyo
Noda, Chiba 278, Japan
[2] Department of Ophthalmology,
University of Tokyo, Japan

**Abstract.** This paper provides an empirical study of an Inductive Logic Programming (ILP) method through the application to classifying ocular fundus images for glaucoma diagnosis. Key issues in this study are not only dealing with low-level measurement data such as image, but also producing diagnostic rules that are readable and comprehensive for interactions to medical experts. For this purpose, we develop a constraint-directed ILP system, GKS, that handles both symbolic and numerical data, and produce Horn clauses with numerical constraints. Furthermore, we provide GKS with a "sequential" learning facility where GKS repeatedly generates a single best rule which becomes background knowledge for the next learning phase. Since the learning target for this application is the abnormality of each segment in image, generated rules represent the relationships between abnormal segments. Since such relationships can be interpreted as qualitative rules and be used as diagnostic rules directly, the present method provides automatic construction of knowledge base from expert's accumulated diagnostic experience. Furthermore, the experimental result shows that induced rules have high statistical performance. The present study indicates the advantage and possibility of the ILP approach to medical diagnosis from measurement data.

## 1  Introduction

Inductive Learning methods has been used to solve the knowledge acquisition bottleneck in knowledge-based systems such as medical consultation systems and fault-finding systems [Kitazawa, 1981]. The promising feature of such methods is providing automatic construction of diagnostic rules from past experts' decision cases. In general, it is needed that diagnostic rules are readable and comprehensive for experts, because most experts tend to interpret and modify the produced rules in comparison with their own decision rules. Inductive Logic Programming provides a reasonable method for this requirement where produced rules are of the form of first-order logic, yielding knowledge-level descriptions for diagnosis [Muggleton, 1991].

However, knowledge systems often handle quantity involved in measurement data [Hiraki, 1991]. Medical diagnosis needs interpreting images of human body directly. Such image analysis generates a set of numerical data, yielding low-level descriptions for medical diagnosis.

In this paper, we provide an empirical study of an Inductive Logic Programming method through the application to classifying ocular fundus images for glaucoma diagnosis. Key issues in this study are not only dealing with low-level descriptions obtained from image analysis, but also producing diagnostic rules that are readable and comprehensive for interactions (*ex.* interpretation and modification) to medical experts. For this purpose, our constraint-directed ILP system, GKS, is introduced in order to handle both symbolic and numerical data, and to produce Horn clauses with numerical constraints [Mizoguchi, 1994] [Mizoguchi, 1995]. Furthermore, we employ a new method called "sequential " learning where GKS repeatedly generates a single best rule which becomes background knowledge for the next learning phase. Since the learning target for this application is the abnormality of each segment in image, the generated rules represent the relationships between abnormal segments. Such relationships can not be obtained by the decision-tree based learning system C4.5 [Quinlan, 1992].

The paper is organized as follows. Section 2 describes what is the learning task in the present study. Section 3 shows our learning method based on GKS and Section 4 describes the sequential learning approach. Section 5 shows how we experiment on learning from ocular fundus images and its result using GKS. In Section 6, the resultant performance of GKS is shown. Section 7 describes conclusion.

## 2   Learning Task

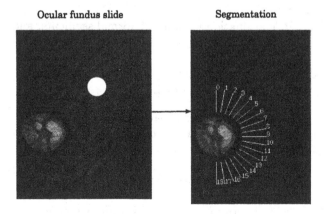

Fig. 1. Ocular fundus image and its segmentation

Since glaucoma causes the vision loss, early detection of optic nerve damage and assessment of its progression are key clinical issues. Ocular fundus images are important clue for glaucoma diagnosis. Such images involve specific optic nerve parameters (*e.g.*, rim-disc ratio and neuroretinal rim area), and medical experts necessarily use measurement data obtained from image analysis in order to improve the accuracy of clinical evaluation.

The learning task in the present study is automatically constructing diagnostic rules from image analysis and expert's analysis. Image analysis produces a set of numerical parameters, while expert's analysis provides a set of expert's interpretations. These analyses are done for each segment of the image as shown in Figure 1. The image is circularly divided into 18 segments. This segmentation reflects expert's heuristics in image analysis, and the expert specifies the abnormality of each segment.

Figure 2 shows the relationship between image analysis and expert's analysis. Each analysis is done for each segment where image analysis produces the values of numerical parameters and expert's analysis labels the normal or the specific abnormality (*e.g.*, undermining and notching) for each segment. In this setting, numerical data becomes background knowledge, and labeling becomes a set of positive and negative examples. Although this setting can be simply captured within the decision tree learning system C4.5, we shall concern with the relationship between abnormal segments. For example, the following statement should be produced:

(1) If a certain segment is abnormal, then adjacent segments are also abnormal.

This statement contains the target predicate to be learned in both left- and right-hand sides, and represents inter-relations between abnormal segments. For a clinical point of view, such relationships may indicate the structural description of the underlying optic nerve damage.

The learning target is expert's evaluation rules for abnormal segments, and is described as follows:

`class(Image,Segment,normal)`, stating that the expert's evaluation about segment `Segment` in image `Image` is normal.

`class(Image,Segment,undermining)`, stating that the expert's evaluation about segment `Segment` in image `Image` is undermining, which is a specific abnormality of ocular damage.

Image analysis provides background knowledge as shown below.

`rd(Image,Segment,RealNumber)`, stating that rim-disc ratio of segment `Segment` in image `Image` is `RealNumber`.

`color(Image,Segment,Color, RealNumber)`, stating that color information of segment `Segment` in image `Image` is `RealNumber`.

Also, topological relationships between segments are included in the background knowledge as follows:

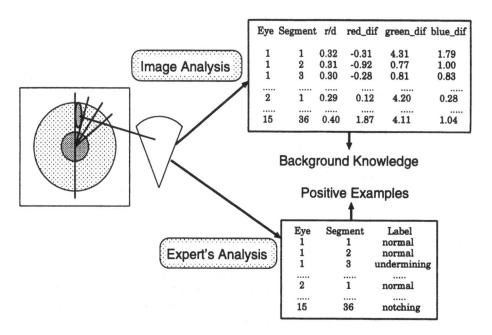

| Eye | Segment | r/d | red_dif | green_dif | blue_dif |
|-----|---------|------|---------|-----------|----------|
| 1 | 1 | 0.32 | -0.31 | 4.31 | 1.79 |
| 1 | 2 | 0.31 | -0.92 | 0.77 | 1.00 |
| 1 | 3 | 0.30 | -0.28 | 0.81 | 0.83 |
| ..... | ..... | ..... | ..... | ..... | ..... |
| 2 | 1 | 0.29 | 0.12 | 4.20 | 0.28 |
| ..... | ..... | ..... | ..... | ..... | ..... |
| 15 | 36 | 0.40 | 1.87 | 4.11 | 1.04 |

**Background Knowledge**

**Positive Examples**

| Eye | Segment | Label |
|-----|---------|-------|
| 1 | 1 | normal |
| 1 | 2 | normal |
| 1 | 3 | undermining |
| ..... | ..... | ..... |
| 2 | 1 | normal |
| ..... | ..... | ..... |
| 15 | 36 | notching |

**Fig. 2.** Image data and positive examples

**clockwise(Segment,Adjacent,Distance)**, stating that the clockwise adjacent segment of segment **Segment** is **Adjacent** where the distance between the segments is **Distance**.

**counterclockwise(Segment,Adjacent,Distance)**, stating that the counterclockwise adjacent segment of segment **Segment** is **Adjacent** where the distance between the segments is **Distance**.

These background knowledge can be viewed as initial background knowledge in the sequential learning method proposed here. Once a rule is produced, it is added into background knowledge for the next learning phrase. To differentiate produced rules from the learning target, the rules are described as follows:

**class_confirmed(Image,Segment,Class)**, stating that the evaluation of segment **Segment** in image **Image** is **Class**

In this setting, statement (1) can be described below.

```
class(Image,Segment,undermining) :-
          clockwise(Segment,Adjacent,1),
          class_confirmed(Image,Adjacent,undermining).
```

It is not straightforward to construct such a rule using C4.5 and current ILP systems.

# 3  GKS algorithm

Before showing the sequential learning method, we outline our ILP system, GKS[3], which can be regarded as a constraint-based generalization of ILP, because it allows users to produce a constraint logic program whose domain is real numbers and linear constraints.

While efficient ILP systems have been developed (e.g. FOIL [Quinlan, 1993] and Progol [Muggleton, 1995]), GKS learning strategy has novel features: First, it combines "bottom-up" and "top-down" search without using heuristic functions in FOIL; thus exhaustive search is employed. Second, unlike Progol, it does not need the depth of variable connectivity in a hypothesis. These features increase the expressive power of Inductive Logic Programming. GKS is implemented in Prolog languages, and is comparable with Progol system (see Appendix A).

In "top-down" search, GKS starts with a most general clause and adds literals until certain condition is satisfied. The search strategy is characterized by an objective function and constraints. An objective function indicates "goodness" of a hypothesis. Intuitively, a good hypothesis covers positive examples as many as possible and covers negative examples as small as possible. In addition, a simpler hypothesis is more preferrable based on a compression measure such as Minimum Description Length Principle. As an objective function, Progol adopted a linear combination between the number of positive and negative examples covered. Since these numbers are inversely proportional, the function does not satisfy the monotonicity property of hypothesis search. If a new literal is added and the resulting clause is specialized, it is impossible to generally say whether the function increases.

To guarantee the monotonicity property, GKS supports the objective function of the number of positive examples $(p)$ and the rule length $(l)$, and negative-examples are treated as a constraint. More specifically, GKS search is formulated as follows:

$$Objective function\ Minimizing\quad f(p,l)$$
$$Constraint\qquad g(n) \leq Err$$

where function $f$ is linearly combined with respect to $p$ and $l$. Parameter $Err$ indicates the permissible number of negative examples covered.

"Bottom-up" search is employed for learning from numerical data. Top-down search is sufficient for logic programs on Herbrand domain.

Constraints on numerical data cannot be obtained by combining variables based on modes. Thus, they are directly constructed from a set of positive examples. Based on this observation, the learning algorithm of GKS is shown in Figure 3.

In the algorithm, "compression" means the objective function. $\rho(SUB)$ produces rules that explain a set of positive examples $(SUB)$. $Specialize(c, SUB)$

---

[3] GKS is in short *GaKuShu* which means "learning" in Japanese.

1. Let $E^+$ and $B$ be positive examples and background knowledge.
2. $LEFT := E^+$, $SUB := \phi$, $CS := \phi$.
3. If $LEFT = \phi$, then return $CS$.
4. Let $e$ be the first element in $LEFT$.
5. $LEFT := LEFT - \{e\}$.
8. $M' := greedy(e, LEFT, \{e\})$.
9. $CS := \{M'\} \cup CS$.
10. $LEFT := LEFT - \{e' \in LEFT \mid M' \wedge B \vdash e'\}$.
11. Go to 3.


FUNCTION $greedy(M, LEFT, SUB)$
    If $LEFT = \phi$, then return $M$.
    Let $e$ be the first element in $LEFT$.
    $LEFT := LEFT - \{e\}$.
    $M' := mcc(\{e\} \cup SUB)$.
    If $M'$ has greater compression than $M$, then
        return $greedy(M', LEFT, \{e\} \cup SUB)$.
    Otherwise return $greedy(M, LEFT, SUB)$.

FUNCTION $mcc(SUB)$
    Let $c$ be a most general clause.
    $S := \{c\}$ and $S' := S - \{c\}$.
    DO
        Find $c$ which has a maximal compression in $S$.
        If $terminated(c)$, then return $c$.
        Let $S := \{c \vee \neg l \mid l \in mpc(c, SUB)\} \cup S'$.
        If $S = \phi$, then return false.
    WHILE true.

FUNCTION $mpc(c, SUB)$
    $L := \{l \mid l$ is a new mode-consistent literal produced by
        variables in $c$ and background knowledge $\}$.
    $S := \{s \mid s$ is a least general constraint set
        on variables in $c$ with respect to $SUB\}$.
    Return $L \cup S$.

**Fig. 3.** Learning Algorithm

produces a set of constraints on $SUB$ and also a set of mode-consistent literals. $\rho(SUB)$ employs top-down search until the search constraint is satisfied.

The algorithm does not specify how to select positive examples. For example, greedy algorithm should be used for producing good rules under given sample size. GKS repeatedly generalizes examples in the user-specified order for getting the efficiency.

# 4 Sequential Learning

Sequential learning exploits the ordering relation between hypotheses. This relation is based on the model theory in logic programming. Given a logic program $P$ and an interpretation $I$, the semantics of $P$ is specified by mapping $T_P$ as shown in the Logic Programming textbook [Lloyd, 1984]:

$$T_P(I) = \{A_0 | A_0 \leftarrow A_1, \ldots, A_n \text{ are ground clauses in } P, \{A_1, \ldots, A_n\} \subseteq I\}$$

This can be replaced by

$$T_P(I) = I \cup New$$

where mapping $T_P$ constructs $New$, which is a set of new atoms that do not belong with interpretation $I$.

As is similar to the fact that $T_P$ is a monotonic function, sequential learning incrementally constructs background knowledge. Let $E^+$, $B_0$ and $H$ be a set of positive examples, initial background knowledge and a set of clauses as hypotheses, respectively. Sequential learning can be formulated as follows:

$$B_i \wedge h_i \models E_i^+$$
$$B_{i+1} = B_i \cup \{h_i\}$$

where $H = \cup_i \{h_i\}$ and $E^+ = \cup_i E_i^+$.

The procedure of sequential learning is shown in Figure 4. If GKS can generate rules compressing positive examples, then it selects a rule with maximal compression. After adding the rule to background knowledge, GKS repeatedly generates rules until no more rules are useful.

Note that sequential learning has a distinctive feature for hypothesis search. Let $B_1$, $h_1$ and $E_1^+$ be the initial background knowledge, a hypothesis and positive examples, respectively. GKS first finds hypothesis $h_1$ such that

$$B_1 \wedge h_1 \models E_1^+.$$

At the next learning phase, we add hypothesis $h_1$ into the background knowledge , yielding the following condition:

$$B_1 \wedge h_1 \wedge h_2 \models E_2^+ \tag{1}$$

where $h_2$ is a new hypothesis learned. Due to the increment of the assumption set, larger set of positive examples $E_2^+$ can be covered.

In using GKS, the predicate of the heads in hypotheses ($h_1$ and $h_2$) is substituted to unique predicates, because of the explicit ordering between hypotheses. Thus, new vocabularies are added into GKS. This implies that sequential learning must search for progressively larger hypotheses, and gives birth to the following principle:

**Principle 1 (Principle of Sequential Learning)** *If the learning system provides exhaustive search for hypothesis generation, sequential learning produces more preferable hypotheses than those obtained from the previous learning phase.*

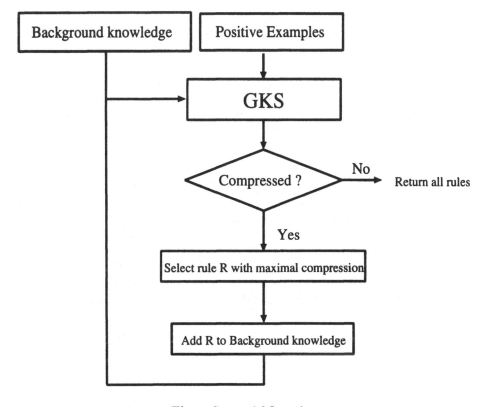

**Fig. 4.** Sequential Learning

GKS supports admissible search based on a compression measure which can be reasonable for selecting preferable hypothesis from a large number of hypotheses. The performance result described below demonstrates how such measure is effective.

The learning target of our application is the abnormality of a given segment, and learned rules are expected to represent the structural relationships between such abnormalities. Thus, at the first learning phase, GKS finds the relationship between the abnormality and measurement data of a specific segment. Then GKS may generate relational rules between the abnormalities that are already detected by the previously obtained rules.

Note that sequential learning is very similar to the work on predicting protein secondary structure in [Muggleton, 1992], where the ILP system GOLEM repeatedly generalize the three levels of rules. While GOLEM generated all rules at each level, GKS selects the best rule from a set of induced rules.

## 5 Experiment

This section shows how sequential learning is applied to classifying ocular fundus images, and its experimental result. A set of examples are taken from 15 pictures where each picture is divided into 36 segments. One of the authors, a specialist of glaucoma diagnosis, categorize 540 examples to a normal type and three types of ocular damages. "Undermining" is a typical one, and there are 433 examples that are either normal or undermining segments. A set of examples and an initial background knowledge are shown in Figure 5. Each argument in predicates has a type and a mode where "+" and "-" means input and output variables. Argument description "-real" is special in that the output variable takes a real number and its value is constrained by a set of linear constraints.

| Positive and negative examples | Number of clauses |
|---|---|
| class(+image, +segment, undermining) | 80 |
| \+ class(+image, +segment, undermining) | 353 |
| Background knowledge | Number of clauses |
| rd(+image, +segment, -real) | 433 |
| color(+image, +segment, red, -real) | 433 |
| color(+image, +segment, green, -real) | 433 |
| color(+image, +segment, blue, -real) | 433 |

Fig. 5. Examples and initial background knowledge

| Background knowledge | Number of clauses |
|---|---|
| rd(+image, +segment, -real) | 433 |
| color(+image, +segment, red, -real) | 433 |
| color(+image, +segment, green, -real) | 433 |
| color(+image, +segment, blue, -real) | 433 |
| clockwise(+segment, -adjacent, #) | 420 |
| counterclockwise(+segment, -adjacent, #) | 420 |
| class_confirmed(+image, #, undermining) | ??? |
| class_confirmed(+image, +adjacent, undermining) | ??? |

Fig. 6. Background knowledge for sequential learning

Since sequential learning increments background knowledge, relational predicates for segments are added as shown in Figure 6. Argument description "#" specifies ground instantiation. For instance, the third argument in predicate clockwise must be instantiated to ground terms. The number of clauses for predicate class_confirmed is unknown, because rules for this predicate may be incrementally added.

We introduce a variety of performance measures that are taken from [Weiss, 1990] and are shown in Appendix B. Although predictive accuracy is widely used in

ILP community, we also pay attention to "sensitivity" which means how much true hypotheses are covered by induced rules. For example, medical diagnosis needs high sensitivity, *i.e.* very few false negatives. However, accuracy and sensitivity may move in opposite directions. Increasing sensitivity tends to cover more negative examples; thus accuracy becomes lower.

GKS allows user to specify the permissible ratio of negative examples covered. Induced rules depends on this ratio, and we investigate what ratio is reasonable in the light of sensitivity and accuracy.

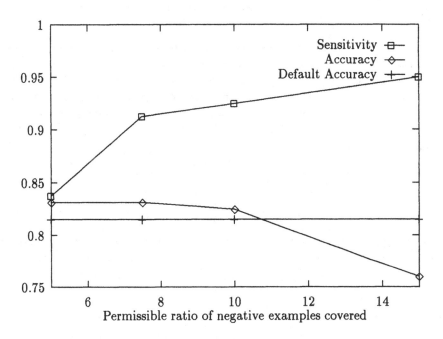

**Fig. 7.** Performance on different permissible ratio

Figure 7 shows the result of normal learning mode using the initial background knowledge mentioned above. We put from 5 and 15% as permissible ratios. This figure indicates a general trend where learning for greater ratio yields higher sensitivity but lower predictive accuracy. At the extreme case 15%, accuracy is lower than default accuracy. This result recommends that 5 and 10% ratios are reasonable for testing the performance of sequential learning.

Setting 5% ratio, GKS produces seven clauses as shown in Appendix C. The rule produced at the first learning is as follows:

```
% {Pos=50/80, Neg=17/353}
class(A, B, undermining) :-
        color(A, B, blue, C), C =< 0.0514370203,
        color(A, B, red, D), D >= -0.500916,
        rd(A, B, E), E =< 0.244362.
```

where **Pos** and **Neg** are the ratios of positive and negative examples covered by the rule. Each real number in the right-hand size of an inequality is found within a positive example using GKS algorithm.

At the second learning phase, GKS produces the following rule:

```
% {Pos=64/80, Neg=14/353}
class(A, B, undermining) :-
        class_confirmed(A, 11, undermining),
        rd(A, B, C), C =< 0.286746.
```

where predicate **class_confirmed** is a renamed version of the clause obtained from the previous learning. Note that the second argument of the condition **class_confirmed(A, 11, undermining)** is ground. This means that a particular abnormal segment leads to abnormalities of other segments. Such rule can be interpreted as a "absolute" relationship between abnormal segments.

On the other hand, the rule produced at the third learning phase is of the "relative" form shown below.

```
% {Pos=52/80, Neg=15/353}
class(A, B, undermining) :-
        clockwise(B, C, 1),
        class_confirmed(A, C, undermining).
```

The rule says that if a certain segment is undermining, adjacent segments are also undermining. The rule implies a structural relationship between abnormal segments, yielding a high-level description for glaucoma diagnosis.

# 6   Performance

Performance results of sequential learning are listed in Figure 8, which illustrate the advantage of sequential learning in comparison with normal learning and C4.5. Typical two permissible ratios (5% and 10%) are chosen as reasonable setting. Performance measures such as sensitivity and accuracy are obtained from 10-fold cross-validation. Taking a training set of examples, sequential learning repeatedly generates a set of rules from this training set and incremental background knowledge. The number of rules are 6 or 7 that are repeating times, and the performance measures are calculated by applying the rules to the residual examples.

The figure shows that sequential learning increases the both sensitivity and accuracy of induced rules. This indicates that hierarchically structured hypotheses provide a high performance classifier. This is due to the expressive power of the first-order clausal form in the ILP-based approach.

| Permissible ratio = 5 % | | | | | |
|---|---|---|---|---|---|
| | Sensitivity | Accuracy | Predictive(+) | $\chi^2$ | Error |
| Normal learning | 87.5 | 84.8 | 56.6 | 16.75 | 5.82 |
| Sequential learning | 93.8 | 87.7 | 62.0 | 21.5 | 4.86 |

| Permissible ratio = 10 % | | | | | |
|---|---|---|---|---|---|
| | Sensitivity | Accuracy | Predictive(+) | $\chi^2$ | Error |
| Normal learning | 91.3 | 77.4 | 45.3 | 12.47 | 6.28 |
| Sequential learning | 96.3 | 84.5 | 55.8 | 18.95 | 5.38 |

| C4.5 | | | | | |
|---|---|---|---|---|---|
| | Sensitivity | Accuracy | Predictive(+) | $\chi^2$ | Error |
| | 86.5 | 74.1 | 86.4 | 5.50 | 4.64 |

**Fig. 8.** Performance of sequential learning and C4.5

## 7 Conclusion

This paper demonstrates how to apply an ILP method to classifying ocular fundus images for glaucoma diagnosis. The motivation was the difficulty of the automatic acquisition of diagnostic rules from measurement data such as images. We adopt a constraint-based generalization, which allows to produce clauses with numerical constraints. GKS is designed and implemented to handle measurement data directly. Furthermore, we introduce sequential learning, which is a kind of incremental learning where learned hypotheses are added into background knowledge progressively. Such hypotheses take a form of high-level descriptions, because relationships between abnormalities can be represented in this form. We also show the performance result of sequential learning which increases both the sensitivity and accuracy of the learned hypotheses. The result indicates a great advantage and possibility of the ILP approach to learning from measurement data.

## References

[Quinlan, 1992] Quinlan.J.R., C4.5: Programs for Machine Learning, Morgan Kaufmann, San Mateo,California, 1992.

[Quinlan, 1993] Quinlan.J.R.,Cameron-Jones.R.M, FOIL: A midterm report, *Proc. of European Conference on Machine Learning*, Springer Verlag, pp.3-20, 1993.

[Kitazawa, 1981] Kitazawa Y., Shirato S., Mizoguchi F., A new Computer-Aided Glaucoma Consultation System (G4-Expert), *Royal Society of Medicine International Congress and Symposium Series*, No.44, pp.161-168, 1981.

[Lloyd, 1984] *Foundations of Logic Programming*, Springer-Verlag, 1984.

[Mizoguchi, 1994] Mizoguchi F., Ohwada H., Constrained Relative Least General Generalization for Inducing Constraint Logic Programs, *New Generation Computing*, Vol.13, No.3,4, pp. 335-368, 1995.

[Mizoguchi, 1995] Mizoguchi F., Ohwada H., Using Inductive Logic Programming for Constraint Acquisition in Constraint-based Problem Solving, *Proc. of the 5th International Workshop on Inductive Logic Programming*, Vol.13, 1995.

[Muggleton, 1991] Muggleton, S., Inductive Logic Programming, *New Generation Computing*, Vol. 8, No. 4, pp.295-318, 1991.

[Muggleton, 1992] Muggleton, S., King, R. and Sternberg, M., Protein secondary structure prediction using logic-based machine learning, *Protein Engineering*, Vol. 5, No. 7, pp. 647-657, 1992.

[Muggleton, 1995] Muggleton, S., Inverse Entailment and Progol, *New Generation Computing*, Vol. 13, No.3,4, pp.245-286, 1995.

[Hiraki, 1991] Hiraki K., J. Genneri, Yamamoto Y., Anzai Y., Learning Spatial Relations from Images, *Proc. of 8th International Workshop on Machine Learning*, pp.407-411, 1991.

[Weiss, 1990] Weiss, S. M., Galen, R. S. and Tadepalli, P., Maximizing the Predictive Value of Production Rules, *Artificial Intelligence*, Vol. 45, pp. 47-71, 1990.

# A  Learning Time (in sec.)

| Data set | $|E^+|$ | $|E^-|$ | $|B|$ | Progol | GKS |
|----------|------|------|-----|--------|-------|
| animals  | 16   | 6    | 105 | 0.183  | 0.090 |
| arch     | 4    | 4    | 17  | 0.149  | 0.083 |
| krki     | 341  | 655  | 51  | 17.281 | 7.500 |
| train    | 5    | 5    | 257 | 0.100  | 0.083 |

# B  Performance Measure

|  | Rule Positive($R^+$) | Rule Negative($R^-$) |
|---|---|---|
| Hypothesis Positive($H^+$) | True Positive($TP$) | False Negative($FN$) |
| Hypothesis Negative($H^-$) | False Positive($FP$) | True Negative($TN$) |

| | |
|---|---|
| Sensitivity | $= TP/H^+$ |
| Specificity | $= TN/H^-$ |
| Predictive value(+) | $= TP/R^+$ |
| Predictive value(-) | $= TN/R^-$ |
| Accuracy | $= (TP + TN)/((H^+) + (H^-))$ |

# C  Induced Rules

```
% 1st %
% {Pos=50/80, Neg=17/353}
class(A, B, undermining) :-
        color(A, B, blue, C), C =< 0.0514370203,
        color(A, B, red, D), D >= -0.500916,
        rd(A, B, E), E =< 0.244362.

% 2nd %
% {Pos=64/80, Neg=14/353}
class(A, B, undermining) :-
        class_confirmed(A, 11, undermining),
        rd(A, B, C), C =< 0.286746.

% 3rd %
% {Pos=52/80, Neg=15/353}
class(A, B, undermining) :-
        clockwise(B, C, 1),
        class_confirmed(A, C, undermining).

% 4th %
% {Pos=42/80, Neg=17/353}
class(A, B, undermining) :-
        class_confirmed(A, 22, undermining),
        rd(A, B, C), C =< 0.240727.

% 5th %
% {Pos=34/80, Neg=13/353}
class(A, B, undermining) :-
        class_confirmed(A, 6, undermining),
        color(A, B, red, C), C >= -0.151857018,
        rd(A, B, D), D =< 0.29496.

% 6th %
% {Pos=23/80, Neg=8/353}
class(A, B, undermining) :-
        color(A, B, blue, C), C =< -0.909224,
        rd(A, B, D), D =< 0.279323.

% 7th %
% {Pos=10/80, Neg=3/353}
class(A, B, undermining) :-
        color(A, B, green, C), C >= 1.46823204,
        rd(A, B, D), D =< 0.302881.
```

# Implementations

# A New Design and Implementation of Progol by Bottom-Up Computation

Hiroshi FUJITA[1], Naoki YAGI[2]*, Tomonobu OZAKI[2] and
Koichi FURUKAWA[2]

[1] Kyushu University, Kasuga, Fukuoka 816, JAPAN
[2] Keio University, Fujisawa, Kanagawa 252, JAPAN

**Abstract.** This paper describes a parallel version of Progol based on
MGTP which is a theorem prover employing bottom-up inference suitable for parallel implementation. Hypothesis formation in Progol, which
is performed by top-down computation with Prolog in the sequential implementation, will be performed more efficiently by bottom-up computation with MGTP in the new implementation. For the Progol's general-
to-specific search for hypotheses through the subsumption lattice, we
developed a new way of calculating a heuristic function for the A*-like
algorithm, which was also implemented with MGTP. Since MGTP already has very efficient parallel implementations on parallel inference
machines, an efficient implementation of parallel-Progol will readily be
realized as well.

## 1 Introduction

Progol [Mug95] is one of the most successful ILP systems. It has been used for
many nontrivial applications with significant results. However, the more complex
problems Progol is to deal with, the more computational power it will need to
solve them very efficiently. For this one promising approach would be to make a
parallel version of Progol and run it on parallel machines.

Current implementations of Progol are based on Prolog technology which is
a first-order theorem proving method using top-down inference, or linear input-
resolution, restricted to Horn clauses. The success of sequential Progol is largely
due to many efficient implementation techniques developed for Prolog. On the
other hand, we have an efficient parallel inference system named MGTP (Model
Generation Theorem Prover) [FH91] which is written in concurrent logic programming language KL1 [UC90] and runs on the parallel inference machine PIM.
MGTP is a first-order theorem prover based on bottom-up inference, or hyper-
resolution, which is not restricted to Horn clauses but works as well on non-Horn
clauses. The success of MGTP in parallel theorem proving strongly motivated
us to apply the technology to building a parallel version of Progol.

Given an example and background knowledge the primary task of Progol
is to construct the *most specific hypothesis* (MSH) for the example. According

---

* Current affiliation: Fujitsu Ltd.

to Muggleton's *inverse entailment*, MSH can be constructed deductively. This computation can be performed naturally and efficiently by using a bottom-up inference system such as MGTP. Sometimes MGTP would be inefficient due to introduction of *dom* predicate for satisfying *range-restrictedness* condition imposed upon MGTP input clauses. However, this problem can be solved by employing the powerful *magic-set* method [BR91]. Fortunately, in the case of Progol, *mode declaration* of predicates simplifies the use of magic-set.

The second important task of Progol is to find the best hypothesis among possible candidates lying between the most general and the most specific. To do this we develop a more accurate analysis than that of the original Progol. The task can be performed also by using MGTP.

In this paper, we describe only the key techniques developed for the new design and just a part of implementation details of the parallel-Progol. For more details and overall description of the system refer [Yag96]. In Sects. 2 and 3, Progol and MGTP are over-viewed respectively. In Sect. 4, the hypothesis formation by MGTP is described. In Sect. 5, an analysis in the A*-like search is described. We conclude the paper in Sect. 6.

## 2 Overview of Progol

Progol is an ILP system which given examples and background knowledge constructs hypotheses on the basis of Inverse Entailment and general-to-specific search through the subsumption lattice.

### 2.1 Inverse Entailment

Let $B$ be a background knowledge, $E$ a positive example, $\overline{\perp}$ a set of all ground literals which are the consequence of $B$ and $\overline{E}$, then according to Muggleton's inverse entailment,

$$B \wedge \overline{E} \models \overline{\perp} \models \overline{H}.$$

This implies $H \models \perp$, and $\perp$ is called the *most specific hypothesis*. Here we assume that $\perp$ is a Horn clause.

Since, in general, $\overline{\perp}$ comprises infinite number of ground literals, we need an idea to restrict it finite somehow. In Progol the idea is to have some upper limit with respect to the *derivation-depth* and *depth-of-variable*. Furthermore, Progol introduces the idea of *mode declaration* to predicates in background knowledge in order to make the search space as small as possible while keeping the result as practical enough.

### 2.2 Mode declaration

Each argument to a predicate is restricted to one of input, output, or some fixed value. At the same time, argument type is also specified by the declaration. For instance, the following declarations may be given:

$$\leftarrow modeh(1, reverse(+list, -list))?$$
$$\leftarrow modeb(1, append(+list, [+int], -list))?$$
$$\leftarrow modeb(1, any = \#any)?$$

where + denotes input, − output and # fixed value; *modeh* (*modeb*)[3] declares the admissible mode and type for a specified head (body) literal.

The mode declaration is requisite for the algorithm 40 in [Mug95] constructing MSH. The mode declaration will also play an important role in the MSH construction by bottom-up approach as described later.

## 2.3 Search in the subsumption lattice

In the next step, Progol searches from general to specific through the subsumption lattice of single clause hypothesis $H$ such that $\square \preceq H \preceq \perp_i$ using A* algorithm. To do this, Progol employs some heuristic function for deciding the "goodness" of a candidate hypothesis. The function depends on the analysis on several properties of the candidate hypothesis, in particular the minimal number of body literals required for making the hypothesis *I/O-complete*.

The details of the analysis in our design will be elaborated in the later section.

## 3 MGTP as a bottom-up inference engine

MGTP is a model-generation based theorem prover for first-order logic. An MGTP input clause (henceforth MG-clause) is represented with an implicational form:

$$A_1, \ldots, A_n \rightarrow B_1; \ldots; B_m.$$

where $A_i, B_j$ are literals; '$\rightarrow$' denotes *implies*; ',' denotes *and*; ';' denotes *or*.

## MGTP proof procedure.

1. Set up an initial model candidate $M_0 := \phi$.
2. Find a *violated MG-clause* such that $\forall i.\ M_k \models A_i$ and $\forall j.\ M_k \not\models B_j$.
   (a) If no violated MG-clause is found, then $M_k$ turns out to be a model.
   (b) If a violated MG-clause is found of which consequent is empty ($m = 0$), then $M_k$ leads to a contradiction and be rejected.
   (c) If a violated MG-clause is found of which consequent is not empty ($m > 0$), then extend $M_k$ to $M_{k+1}^j := M_k \cup \{B_j\}$, and for each $M_{k+1}^j$ continue the procedure from 2.
3. If all $M_k$'s are rejected (that means there is no model), then the MG-clause set turns out to be unsatisfiable.

---

[3] The first argument of *modeh* and *modeb* will be used for limiting the number of alternative solutions for the specified literal.

Most of the time in executing the procedure will be spent at the test $\forall i. M_k \models A_i$ in step 2, which we call *conjunctive matching*. The conjunctive matching does not need full-unification with occurs-check if the *range-restrictedness* condition[4] [MB88] is met by the MG-clause. This makes it possible to build simpler and more efficient inference engines than the usual full-unification based approach, especially when they are written in a concurrent logic programming language such as KL1 and run on parallel inference machines such as PIM.

Currently we have several variations of MGTP implementation such as:

**Ground-MGTP:** for range-restricted problems,

**Non-Ground-Horn-MGTP:** for non-range-restricted but only Horn problems, employing a sound unification procedure (with occurs-check),

**C-MGTP:** for handling negative literals, or "constraints," with additional procedures for *unit-refutation* and *unit-simplification*,

and more. For each variation we have KL1-coded parallel versions running on PIM as well as Prolog versions running on standard sequential machines. Since we need to deal with negative literals in Progol, C-MGTP would be the best choice. However, as far as negative literals only appear as the head litaral of a hypothesis clause and never be targeted either by unit-refutation or unit-simplification procedure, just Ground-MGTP suffices.

## 4    MSH construction by MGTP

Background knowledge is normally given as a set of Horn clauses that can basically be taken just as MG-clauses. However, they are not necessarily range-restricted. Indeed it is often the case that the condition is violated and *dom* predicates are needed to remedy the situation. For instance, the MG-clauses for *append* should be written as:

$$dom(X) \to append([], X, X).$$
$$append(T, L1, L2), dom(H) \to append([H|T], L1, [H|L2]).$$

Since *dom*-defining clauses are essentially to create the whole Herbrand universe for the clause set, it would be very difficult to obtain a meaningful result by MGTP without an appropriate control for suppressing the "*dom*-explosion."

However, we can avoid this serious problem by employing the powerful magic-set method which would often make naive bottom-up inference as clever as top-down inference while keeping the superiority of the former over the latter. In the following, we will demonstrate with small examples the way of representing mode declarations and background knowledge by the MG-clauses with magic-sets.

---

[4] An MG-clause is said to be range-restricted if every variable of the MG-clause has at least one occurrence in its antecedent. To ensure range-restrictedness, *dom* predicates may be added to the antecedent of the MG-clause. This transformation does not change the satisfiability status of the original set of MG-clauses.

## 4.1 MG-clauses for mode declaration

The MG-clauses corresponding to the mode declarations for *reverse* and *append* are as follows:

$% \leftarrow modeh(1, reverse(+list, -list))$?
$-reverse(A, B), list(A), list(B) \rightarrow head(reverse(A, B)), in\_list(A)$.

$% \leftarrow modeb(1, reverse(+list, -list))$?
$reverse(A, B), list(B) \rightarrow body(reverse(A, B)), in\_list(B)$.
$in\_list(A) \rightarrow magic\_reverse(A)$.

$% \leftarrow modeb(1, append(+list, [+int], -list))$?
$append(A, [B], C), list(C) \rightarrow body(append(A, [B], C)), in\_list(C)$.
$in\_list(A), in\_int(B) \rightarrow magic\_append(A, [B])$.

For each *modeh* declaration, an MG-clause is provided whose antecedent is the conjunction of the negated positive example and type-checking literals for each argument of it, and whose consequent is the conjunction[5] of *head* which denotes the head literal of $\bot$ and *in_Type* which denotes "input-value" of the specified type. The information stored in *in_Type* literals will be used as the "seed" for computing magic-sets[6].

For each *modeb* declaration, an MG-clause is provided whose antecedent is the conjunction of a predicate in background knowledge and type-checking literals for each argument of it, and whose consequent is the conjunction of *body* which denotes a body literal of $\bot$ and *in_Type* which denotes "output-value" of the specified type.

## 4.2 MG-clauses for background knowledge

Given the above mode declarations, the MG-clauses for *append* are written as follows:

$magic\_append([], [A]) \rightarrow append([], [A], [A])$.
$magic\_append([A|B], [C]), append(B, [C], D) \rightarrow append([A|B], [C], [A|D])$.
$magic\_append([A|B], [C]) \rightarrow magic\_append(B, [C])$.

where *magic_append/2* is introduced for *append/3* which has two input-mode arguments. For the non-recursive clause of *append*, just one *magic_append* literal is added to the antecedent of it. For the recursive clause of *append*, one *magic_append* literal is added to the antecedent of it, and another recursive clause for *magic_append* is created for the recursive call of *append*.

Thus, the system will be able to derive only those *append* literals whose input arguments are given by the computed magic-set $\{magic\_append(X, Y)\}$.

---

[5] An MG-clause $(A \rightarrow B, C)$ is logically equivalent to, but procedurally more efficient than, two MG-clauses $(A \rightarrow B)$ and $(A \rightarrow C)$.

[6] If the type checking predicate *list* is user-defined just as background knowledge, then *magic_list* predicate and its "seed-generating" MG-clause are necessary.

## 4.3 MSH construction with the MG-clauses

The MG-clauses corresponding to mode declarations describe how to compute necessary literals for $\overline{\bot}$. First, input to the $\bot$ head, is extracted from the positive example according to a *modeh* declaration. Second, a predicate is looked for in background knowledge, such that it computes some output from the above extracted input, according to a *modeb* declaration. The step is repeated until finally some predicate in the background knowledge is found, such that it computes the output of the $\bot$ head.

The *dom*-explosion can be avoided with the help of magic-sets because the variables appearing in the consequent of an MG-clause will be appearing in the antecedent magic-literal that corresponds to the consequent.

It is easy to implement in MGTP the task of generalization which derives $\bot$ from $\overline{\bot}$. To do this there are two ways; one is a post-process manner where $\overline{\bot}$ is rescanned to generate a hush table of value-variable pairs; the other is to do the same job on the fly by embedding "side-effect" literals into the MG-clauses which is allowed in MGTP and called *external-call mechanism*.

For example, given the positive example $reverse([1], [1])$, background knowledge *append*, *list* and the non-recursive clause for *reverse*, $reverse([], [])$, the result of MGTP execution will be as follows:

$$\overline{\bot} = [head(reverse([1], [1])),$$
$$body([1] = \#[1]), body([1] = [1]), body(1 = \#1), body([] = \#[]),$$
$$body(reverse([], [])), body(append([], [1], [1]))].$$

after 10 rounds[7] of the MGTP execution and 22 literals (including magic-, type- and *in_Type*-literals) generated. If the (well-controlled) *dom*-approach is taken, the number would be 4 rounds, but 71 literals.

After the generalization (replacing the ground-terms by variables) the MSH is obtained as:

$$\bot = (reverse(X, X) \leftarrow X = [1], X = [Y|Z], Y = 1, Z = [],$$
$$reverse(Z, Z), append(Z, [Y], X)).$$

## 4.4 Compiling mode information into MG-clauses

The magic-set method is indeed a general and powerful means for performing bottom-up derivation of consequences while simulating top-down propagation of the goal information.

As a matter of fact, however, in the case of Progol, another approach could be taken which would provide simpler MG-clauses and result in more efficient MSH construction. Here we write MG-clauses for *append* as follows:

$$in\_int(Y) \rightarrow append([], [Y], [Y]), in\_list([Y]).$$
$$in\_list(T), in\_int(Y), in\_any(H), append(T, [Y], L2)$$
$$\rightarrow append([H|T], [Y], [H|L2]), in\_list([H|L2]).$$

---

[7] The counter "round" advances by one when all the violated clauses under the current model candidate has been processed.

The additional literals $in\_list(Y)$ etc. are used to constrain the input arguments of the *append* in the antecedent of a clause, and to assert the output terms of the *append* in the consequent.

Thus, only such *append* literals are computed that take previously computed terms as their input arguments. Each time a new *append* literal is computed, new terms are added to the set of computed terms. MGTP execution with this code will result in 4 rounds and 19 atoms to generate $\perp$ for the same example above.

## 4.5 Compiling depth control into MG-clauses

Both derivation-depth and depth-of-variable restrictions can be compiled into each MG-clause for background knowledge. For instance, on the basis of the above "mode-compilation" approach, we provide the following MG-clauses:

$$in\_int(Y) + J, \{J < \#i, J1 := J + 1\}$$
$$\to append([], [Y], [Y]) + 1, in\_list([Y]) + J1.$$

$$in\_list(T) + J, in\_int(Y) + K, in\_any(H) + L, append(T, [Y], L2) + G,$$
$$\{J < i, K < i, L < i, G < h, G1 := G + 1, min1([J, K, L], M)\}$$
$$\to append([H|T], [Y], [H|L2]) + G1, in\_list([H|L2]) + M.$$

where $P(Args) + X$ is the KL1 macro meaning $P(Args, X)$; **h** and **i** are the integers representing the derivation-depth limit and the depth-of-variable limit respectively; $\{\ldots\}$ denotes external-call of predicates for doing arithmetics; $min1(List, M)$ returns in $M$ the value "minimum of the elements in $List$ plus one." Thus, the extended argument of a $in\_Type$ literal is used to indicate the depth-of-variable of the term, the extended argument of a background-knowledge literal to indicate the derivation-depth of it.

# 5 An analysis for the best hypothesis search

This section describes an analysis performed during the second phase of Progol after MSH is constructed.

## 5.1 Graph representation of MSH

First, the connectivity of variables in the MSH will be examined. Some terms will be defined for this. A variable appearing in the head of MSH is called a *head-variable*. A variable appearing in the body, but not in the head, of MSH is called a *body-variable*. A head-variable appearing at the input-mode argument position in the head is called a *root-variable*. A head-variable appearing at the output-mode argument position in the head and also appearing in the body of MSH is called a *goal-variable*.

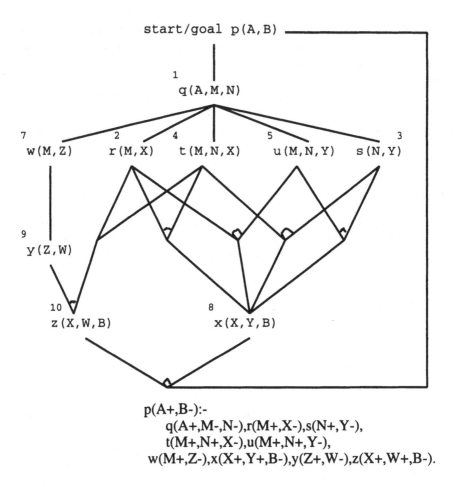

start/goal p(A,B)

1  q(A,M,N)

7  w(M,Z)    2  r(M,X)    4  t(M,N,X)    5  u(M,N,Y)    3  s(N,Y)

9  y(Z,W)

10  z(X,W,B)    8  x(X,Y,B)

p(A+,B-):-
 q(A+,M-,N-),r(M+,X-),s(N+,Y-),
 t(M+,N+,X-),u(M+,N+,Y-),
 w(M+,Z-),x(X+,Y+,B-),y(Z+,W-),z(X+,W+,B-).

**Fig. 1.** AND-OR graph representing MSH

### Root-connectivity of a variable.

1. A variable $v$ is root-connected if $v$ is a root-variable.
2. An output-mode variable $v_o^-$ in a body literal is root-connected if all input-mode variables $v_{i_1}^+, \ldots, v_{i_m}^+$ in the literal are root-connected.

By construction of MSH, every literal in the MSH should have some connections to other literals in the MSH. Further, in the MSH, there should be some paths from root-variables to body literals containing goal-variables. Thus MSH can be represented as the AND-OR graph as depicted in Fig.1 on the basis of connections between literals. It is sometimes difficult to calculate the function $h_s$, which is one of the auxiliary functions from Def. 41 in [Mug95], strictly by using only information about "depth" of nodes, because, for example, paths to reach a node may have some common nodes. To calculate $h_s$ strictly, it is necessary to use information about set of nodes needed to reach a node.

## 5.2 Candidate clause evaluation using AND-OR graph

Our new method first constructs sets of literals needed to compute all output-mode variables in the head of MSH, and then calculates $h_s$ for a candidate clause. Construction of this set of literals corresponds to calculating paths from the start to the goal node in the AND-OR graph.

**A path of a variable.** Let all input-mode variables in the $k$-th body literal $l_k$ be $A_1, \ldots, A_m$ and an output-variable in it be $B$. In order to compute $B$, it is necessary to compute all $A_1, \ldots, A_m$. A path of a variable is defined as a set of literals in the body of MSH needed to compute this variable. Let paths for $A_1, \ldots, A_m$ be $P_{A_1}, \ldots, P_{A_m}$, then $B$'s path $P_B$ can be calculated as the sum of paths needed to compute all $A_1, \ldots, A_m$ and $l_k$ itself. A path needed to compute $A_1, \ldots, A_m$ can be calculated by performing inclusive-OR on all of them.

$$P_B = (P_{A_1} \cup P_{A_2} \ldots \cup P_{A_m}) \cup l_k . \tag{1}$$

In general, each variable in MSH may have several paths. To deal with the case we introduce the following.

**Path-set of a variable.**

1. The path-set for a root-variable is empty. $\{PS_{root} = []\}$.
2. Let all literals which contain an output-mode body-variable $B$ be $\{l_1, \ldots, l_j\}$. Let the path-set for $B$ in $l_i$ be $P_{B_{l_i}}$. Let the input-mode variables in $l_i$ be $\{A_{i_1}, \ldots, A_{i_m}\}$, and the corresponding path-set for them be $PS_{A_{i_1}}, \ldots, PS_{A_{i_m}}$, respectively. Then, the path-set for $B$ in $l_i$ will be obtained as follows:

$$PS_{B_{l_i}} = (PS_{A_{i_1}} \dot{\times} \ldots \dot{\times} PS_{A_{i_m}}) \oplus l_i , \tag{2}$$

where $\dot{\times}$ denotes inclusive-OR and $PS_x \dot{\times} PS_y$ combines every pair of the path-sets from $PS_x$ and $PS_y$, $\oplus$ denotes "multiple-"addition and $PS_z \oplus l$ adds $l$ to all the elements of the path-set $PS_z$. Finally the path-set for $B$ is obtained as follows:

$$PS_B = (PS_{B_{l_1}} \cup \ldots \cup PS_{B_{l_j}}) . \tag{3}$$

For example, consider the following MSH.

$p(A^+, B^-, C^-) \leftarrow$
  $q(A^+, M^-, N^-), r(M^+, X^-), s(N^+, Y^-), t(M^+, N^+, X^-), u(M^+, N^+, Y^-),$
  $v(M^+, Z^-), w(X^+, Y^+, B^-), x(Z^+, W^-), y(X^+, W^+, B^-), z(W^+, C^-).$

The path-set for $B$ is calculated as follows.

$PS_M = PS_N = PS_A \cup q = [q]$
$PS_X = \{PS_M \oplus r\} \cup \{(PS_M \dot{\times} PS_N) \oplus t\} = \{[q, r], [q, t]\}$
$PS_Y = \{PS_N \oplus s\} \cup \{(PS_M \dot{\times} PS_N) \oplus u\} = \{[q, s], [q, u]\}$
$PS_Z = PS_M \cup v = [q, v]$
$PS_W = PS_Z \cup x = [q, v, x]$
$PS_B = \{(PS_X \dot{\times} PS_Y) \oplus w\} \cup \{(PS_X \dot{\times} PS_W) \oplus y\}$
  $= \{[q, r, s, w], [q, r, u, w], [q, s, t, w], [q, t, u, w], [q, r, v, x, y], [q, t, v, x, y]\}$

Now we can introduce the following notion as an important property of the candidate clauses being searched for the hypothesis.

**Definition I/O-completeness of a clause.** *A clause is I/O-complete if and only if every goal-variable in it is root-connected.*

If the candidate clause is to be I/O-complete then there should be a path from the start node to the goal node in the AND-OR graph for the MSH. To describe the situation more precisely, we need the following.

## Path-set of a clause.

1. A path-set of a clause is empty $PS_{cl} = []$ if the clause is not I/O-complete or there is no output-mode variable in the head of the clause.
2. Otherwise let all output-mode variables in the head of the clause be $\{v_1^-, \ldots, v_m^-\}$, and corresponding path-sets for them be $\{PS_{v_1^-}, \ldots, PS_{v_m^-}\}$ respectively. Then the path-set of a clause is the following.

$$PS_{cl} = (PS_{v_1^-} \dot\times \ldots \dot\times PS_{v_m^-}) . \tag{4}$$

For instance, the path-set of the above MSH will be calculated as follows.

$$\begin{aligned}
PS_C &= PS_W \cup z = [q, v, x, z]\\
PS_{cl} &= PS_B \dot\times PS_C\\
&= \{[q, r, s, v, w, x, z], [q, r, u, v, w, x, z], [q, s, t, v, w, x, z],\\
&\quad [q, t, u, v, w, x, z], [q, r, v, x, y, z], [q, t, v, x, y, z]\}
\end{aligned}$$

Once the path-set for MSH is calculated, it is easy to calculate $h_s$ for each candidate clause.

## Calculation of $h_s$ for a candidate clause.

1. Calculate the path-set $PS_{cl}$ for given MSH.
2. For a candidate clause, make a new path-set by removing the body literals of the candidate clause from each element of $PS_{cl}$.
3. Return as the value of $h_s$ the minimum length of elements in the new path-set.

For instance, given a candidate clause:

$$p(A, B) \leftarrow q(A, M, N), r(M, X), v(M, Z).$$

with the above MSH, the new path-set is calculated as:

$$NewPS_{cl} = \{[s, w, x, z], [u, w, x, z], [s, t, w, x, z], [t, u, w, x, z], [x, y, z], [t, x, y, z]\}$$

and $h_s = \|[x, y, z]\| = 3$.

## 5.3 Path-set calculation by MGTP

A pair of a variable $a$ and its path $X$ will be represented by an atom $var(a, X)$ in MGTP. A different path $Y$ of the same variable $a$ will be represented by another atom $var(a, Y)$. For the $k$-th body literal $p(P_1^+, \ldots, P_m^+, Q_1^-, \ldots, Q_n^-)$ in MSH having both input- and output-mode variables the following MG-clause is provided:

$$var(p_1, X_1), \ldots, var(p_m, X_m), \{or([X_1, \ldots, X_m], Z), not(member(k, Z))\}$$
$$\rightarrow var(q_1, [k|Z]), \ldots, var(q_n, [k|Z]).$$

where the external predicates $or/2$ and $member/2$ are used for performing inclusive-OR on $X_1, \ldots, X_m$, and loop-checking for a path, respectively. This MG-clause corresponds to (1) defining a path for a variable. The clause will be fired more than once if the input variables have several paths. As a consequence, we can obtain a path-set of a variable according to (2).

For the head-literal of MSH $s(A_1^+, \ldots, A_m^+, B_1^-, \ldots, B_n^-)$ the following two MG-clauses will be provided:

$$true \rightarrow var(a_1, []), \ldots, var(a_m, []).$$
$$var(b_1, X_1), \ldots, var(b_n, X_n), \{or([X_1, \ldots, X_n], Z)\} \rightarrow goal(Z).$$

The first clause is for setup the path-set calculation, and the second clause corresponds to (4). A set of atoms $goal(Z)$ represents the path-set of a clause. Thus for the above mentioned MSH example all the MG-clauses required for the analysis are as follows:

$$true \rightarrow var(a, []).$$
$$var(a, X), \{not(member(q, X))\} \rightarrow var(m, [q|X]), var(n, [q|X]).$$
$$var(m, X), \{not(member(r, X))\} \rightarrow var(x, [r|X]).$$
$$var(n, X), \{not(member(s, X))\} \rightarrow var(y, [s|X]).$$
$$var(m, X), var(n, Y), \{or([X, Y], Z), not(member(t, Z))\} \rightarrow var(x, [t|Z]).$$
$$var(m, X), var(n, Y), \{or([X, Y], Z), not(member(u, Z))\} \rightarrow var(y, [u|Z]).$$
$$var(m, X), \{not(member(v, X))\} \rightarrow var(z, [v|X]).$$
$$var(x, X), var(y, Y), \{or([X, Y], Z), not(member(w, Z))\} \rightarrow var(b, [w|Z]).$$
$$var(z, X \qquad\qquad\qquad), \{not(member(x, X))\} \rightarrow var(w, [x|X]).$$
$$var(x, X), var(w, Y), \{or([X, Y], Z), not(member(y, Z))\} \rightarrow var(b, [y|Z]).$$
$$var(w, X), \{not(member(z, X))\} \rightarrow var(c, [z|X]).$$
$$var(b, X), var(c, Y), \{or([X, Y], Z)\} \rightarrow goal(Z).$$

Given these MG-clauses MGTP will output as the $goal$ elements the path-set $PS_{cl}$ of the clause MSH shown above in 5 rounds and 21 atoms being generated.

## 6 Conclusion

We described a new design and implementation of Progol using the bottom-up inference engine MGTP. So far, we showed how to use MGTP in hypothesis formation and evaluation function calculation in A*-like search.

In the original Progol, $\overline{\bot}$ is constructed by repeatedly issuing many Prolog goals each of which is evaluated in a top-down manner one by one. In contrast, MGTP derives many consequent literals at the same time in a bottom-up manner. Therefore, it is expected that significant amount of computation for duplicated (sub-)goals in the Prolog execution is saved in the MGTP execution.

Since the new heuristic function $h_s$ performs more strict analysis for the I/O-completeness of a candidate clause than the original, the search for the best hypothesis could be improved in its accuracy.

To complete the implementation and verify the effectiveness of the parallel-Progol is the most urgent issue on which we are working intensively.

Besides, we are also working on another MGTP-based ILP system, so called "Inductive-MGTP," in which we will not use MGTP just as an implementation tool but modify and extend it to do ILP within its own framework. The Inductive-MGTP would have some generalization mechanism built in, and perform *rlgg*-like operation on model elements being generated. The expected merits of such a system would include effective uses of non-Horn clauses in hypotheses, background knowledge and examples.

# References

[BR91]    Beeri, C. and Ramakrishnan, R.: On the Power of Magic. *J. Logic Programming,* Vol.10, (1991) 255–299

[FH91]    Fujita, H. and Hasegawa, R.: A Model Generation Theorem Prover in KL1 Using a Ramified-Stack Algorithm. *Proc. of the 8th ICLP,* (1991) 535–548

[MB88]    Manthey, R. and Bry, F.: SATCHMO: A theorem prover implemented in Prolog. *Proc. of the 9th CADE,* (1988) 415–434

[Mug95]  Muggleton, S.: Inverse Entailment and Progol. *New Generation Computing,* Vol.13, (1995) 245–286

[UC90]    Ueda, K. and Chikayama, T.: Design of the kernel language for the parallel inference machine. *The Computer Journal,* 33(6) (1990) 494–500

[Yag96]   Yagi, N.: On the Construction of parallel ILP Model. Master's thesis, Keio University, (1996)

# Inductive Logic Program Synthesis
## with DIALOGS

Pierre Flener

Department of Computer Engineering and Information Science
Faculty of Engineering, Bilkent University, 06533 Bilkent, Ankara, Turkey
Email: pf@cs.bilkent.edu.tr  Voice: +90/312/266-4000 ext. 1450

**Abstract.** DIALOGS (Dialogue-based Inductive and Abductive LOGic program Synthesizer) is a schema-guided synthesizer of recursive logic programs; it takes the initiative and queries a (possibly computationally naive) specifier for evidence in her/his conceptual language. The specifier *must* know the answers to such simple queries, because otherwise s/he wouldn't even feel the need for the synthesized program. DIALOGS can be used by any learner (including itself) that detects, or merely conjectures, the necessity of invention of a new predicate. Due to its foundation on a powerful codification of a "recursion-theory" (by means of the template and constraints of a divide-and-conquer schema), DIALOGS needs very little evidence and is very fast.

## 1   Introduction

This paper results from a study investigating (*i*) what is the minimal knowledge a specifier must have in order to want a (logic) program for a certain concept, and (*ii*) how to convey exactly the corresponding information, and nothing else, to a (logic) program synthesizer (be it automated or not). I argue that "knowing a concept" means that one can act as a decision procedure for answering certain kinds of simple queries [1] about that concept, but that it doesn't necessarily imply the ability to actually write such a decision procedure. More provocatively, I could argue [13] that writing a complete formal specification is often tantamount to writing such a decision procedure (because it actually features a naive or inefficient algorithm), and is thus often beyond the competence of a "computationally naive" specifier. But the reader need not agree on the latter claim, so let's assume, for whatever reasons, that some specifier wants to, or can only, give incomplete information about a concept for which s/he wants a (logic) program. This is an innovative program development technique, especially aimed at two categories of users:

- *experienced programmers* would often rather just provide a few carefully chosen examples and have a synthesizer "work out the details" for them;
- *end users* are often computationally naive and cannot provide more than examples, but this should allow them to do some basic programming tasks, such as the recording of macro definitions, etc.

As this project is not about natural language processing, let's also assume that the specification language is nevertheless formal.

The synthesizer must thus be of the inductive and/or abductive category. However, many (but not all) such synthesizers have the drawback of requiring large amounts of ground positive (and negative) examples of the intended concept, especially if the resulting program is recursive. The reasons are that ground examples are a poor means of communicating a concept to a computer, and/or that the underlying "recursion theory" is poor. To address the first reason, some researchers have successfully experimented with non-ground examples [18], if not Horn clauses [9, 12] or even full clauses [6], as evidence language. To address the second reason, schema-guided synthesis has been proposed [9, 12].

Especially since the advent of ILP (Inductive Logic Programming), the learning/synthesis of non-recursive programs (or concept descriptions) has made spectacular progress, but not so the synthesis of recursive programs. I have therefore decided to focus on the latter class of programs, to the point where my synthesizers even *assume* that there exists a recursive logic program for the intended concept. Even though this seems counterproductive, because a synthesizer can't decide in advance whether a concept has a recursive program or not, there are two good reasons for this focus and assumption. First, as advocated by Biermann [3], I believe it is more efficient to try a suite of fast and reliable class-specific synthesizers (and, if necessary, to fall back onto a general-purpose synthesizer) than to simply run such a slow, if not unreliable, general-purpose synthesizer. It is thus worthwhile to study the properties of any sub-class of programs and hardwire its synthesis. Second, as the recent interest in constructive induction [10, 20] shows, necessarily-invented predicates have recursive programs. It is thus worthwhile to study the class of recursive programs, because any learner (even a general-purpose one) can use such a specialized recursion-synthesizer once it has detected, or merely conjectured, the necessity of a new predicate.

Finally, let's assume that our specifier is "lazy," that is s/he doesn't want to take the initiative and type in evidence of the intended concept without knowing whether it will be "useful" to the synthesizer or not. So we need an interactive synthesizer, and even one that takes the initiative and queries the specifier only for strictly necessary evidence. This is actually another solution to the mentioned example voraciousness of many learners. The query and answer languages need to be carefully designed, though, so that even a computationally naive specifier can use the system. For instance, during the synthesis of a sorting program, the specifier cannot be queried about an insertion predicate (assuming the synthesis "goes towards" an insertion-sort program), because this is an auxiliary concept that is not necessarily known to the specifier, her/his "mental" sorting algorithm being not necessarily the insertion-sort one. Also note that such an interaction scenario does not necessarily assume a human specifier.

I plan to combine all of the mentioned ideas into one system. So, in summary, I aim at an interactive, inductive/abductive, schema-guided synthesizer of recursive programs, that takes the initiative and minimally queries a (possibly computationally naive) specifier for evidence in her/his conceptual language.

*Example 1.* After analyzing my previous work (in a different mindset [9, 10, 12]), I decided on the following target scenario. Assume a (possibly computationally naive) specifier somehow has (an equivalent of) the following informal specification in mind:
  sort(L,S) iff S is a non-decreasing permutation of L,
        where L, S are integer-lists.
Now imagine a logic program synthesizer that takes this specifier through the following annotated dialogue, where questions are in teletype font, default answers (if any) are between curly braces "{...}", the specifier's actual answers are in *italics*, the comma "," stands for conjunction, and the semi-colon ";" stands for disjunction:
  Predicate declaration? $sort(L : list(int), S : list(int))$
If the specifier is ever to use a logic program for sort, s/he *must* be able to give such a predicate declaration, because the predicate symbol, the sequence of formal parameters, and their types must be known to her/him. Minimal knowledge about the system, its syntax, and its type system is thus unavoidable.
  Induction parameter? {L} *L*
  Result parameter? {S} *S*
  Decomposition operator? {L=[HL|TL]} $L = [HL|TL]$
The last three queries seem to require some programming knowledge (see Section 2 for the terminology), which would go counter a scenario with a computationally naive specifier. However, note that the system proposes default answers, so that such a specifier may indeed ignore these queries by simply accepting their default answers.
  What conditions on <S> must hold such that sort([],S) holds?
  $S = []$
The specifier *must* know what the sorted version of the empty list is, because otherwise s/he wouldn't even have the need for a sort program.
  What conditions on <A,S> must hold such that sort([A],S) holds?
  $S = [A]$
Also, the specifier *must* know what the sorted version of the one-element list is.
  What conditions on <A,B,S> must hold such that sort([A,B],S)
  holds? $S = [A, B], A \leq B; S = [B, A], A > B$
Finally, the specifier *must* know *what* the sorted version of a two-element list is, and *why* it is so. The answer may look complicated (due to the use of variables, conjunction, and disjunction), but note that it only embodies minimal knowledge about sort, which is *independent* of any sorting algorithms. Note how the specifier was "forced" to use the $\leq/2$ and $>/2$ predicates, as they are essential to the concept of number sorting. Soon afterwards, the system reports:
  A possible logic program for sort is:
```
    sort(L,S) ← L=[],S=[]
    sort(L,S) ← L=[HL|TL],sort(TL,TS), insert(HL,TS,S)
    insert(I,L,R) ← L=[],R=[I]
    insert(I,L,R) ← L=[HL|TL],I≤HL, R=[I,HL|TL]
    insert(I,L,R) ← L=[HL|TL],I>HL, insert(I,TL,TR),R=[HL|TR]
```
This is insertion-sort. Obviously (to us), the implicit informal specification of insert is as follows:

`insert(I,L,R)` iff R is L with I inserted into it,

> where I is an integer and L, R are non-decreasing integer-lists.

But the specifier need not know this. The system doesn't know this either, and actually uses predicate symbol `dpcSort` instead (see the naming scheme in Section 2), as well as other parameter names.

> **Do you want another logic program for sort?** {**yes**} *Yes, please!*
> **Backtracking** ...
> **Decomposition operator?** {L=[HL|T],partition(T,HL,TL$_1$,TL$_2$)}
> $L = [HL|T], partition(T, HL, TL_1, TL_2)$

Assume that **partition** is a system primitive (whose program is known to the system) informally specified as follows:

`partition(L,P,S,B)` iff S (resp. B) contains the elements of L that are smaller
> than (resp. bigger than or equal to) P,

> where L, S, B are integer-lists and P is an integer.

After a short while, the system announces:

> **A possible logic program for sort is:**
> `sort(L,S) ← L=[],S=[]`
> `sort(L,S) ← L=[HL|T], partition(T,HL,TL`$_1$`,TL`$_2$`), sort(TL`$_1$`,TS`$_1$`),`
> `            sort(TL`$_2$`,TS`$_2$`), combine(HL,TS`$_1$`,TS`$_2$`,S)`
> `combine(E,A,B,C) ← A=[],C=[E|B]`
> `combine(E,A,B,C) ← A=[HA|TA], combine(E,TA,B,TC),C=[HA|TC]`

This is the quick-sort program. The implicit informal specification of **combine** is as follows:

`combine(E,A,B,C)` iff append(A,[E|B],C),
> where A, B, C are lists and E is a term.

Again, the system actually uses predicate symbol `dpcSort` instead of **combine**. Also note that no further queries were posed to the specifier, and yet the system came up with a completely different program.

> **Do you want another logic program for sort?** {**yes**} *Yes, sure!*
> **Backtracking** ...
> **Decomposition operator?** {L=[_,_|_],halves(L,TL$_1$,TL$_2$)}
> $L = [-, -|-], halves(L, TL_1, TL_2)$

Assume that **halves** is a system primitive informally specified as follows:

`halves(L,F,S)` iff F is the first half of L, and S is the second half of L, such
> that S has maximum one element more than F, where L, F, S are lists.

Soon, the system proclaims:

> **A possible logic program for sort is:**
> `sort(L,S) ← L=[],S=[]`
> `sort(L,S) ← L=[_],S=L`
> `sort(L,S) ← L=[_,_|_],halves(L,TL`$_1$`,TL`$_2$`),sort(TL`$_1$`,TS`$_1$`),`
> `            sort(TL`$_2$`,TS`$_2$`),merge(TS`$_1$`,TS`$_2$`,S)`
> `merge(A,B,C) ← C=[],A=[],B=[]`
> `merge(A,B,C) ← C=[HC|TC],merge(TA,TB,TC),TB=[],A=[HC|TA],B=TB`
> `merge(A,B,C) ← C=[HC|TC],merge(TA,TB,TC),TB=[H|_],HC≤H,`
> `               A=[HC|TA],B=TB`
> `merge(A,B,C) ← C=[HC|TC],merge(TA,TB,TC),TA=[],A=TA,B=[HC|TB]`

```
merge(A,B,C) ← C=[HC|TC],merge(TA,TB,TC),TA=[H|_],H>HC,
              A=TA,B=[HC|TB]
```

This is the merge-sort program. The implicit informal specification of **merge** is as follows:

**merge(A,B,C)** iff C is the merger of A and B,
    where A, B, C are non-decreasing integer-lists.

The system actually uses the predicate symbol **dpcSort** instead of **merge**. Again note that although no further queries were posed to the specifier, the system produced yet another completely new program.

**Do you want another logic program for sort? {yes}** *No*
This ends the target scenario. ◇

In the remainder of this paper, I first discuss, in Section 2, the notion of logic program schema, and then, in Section 3, I show how such schemata are the key to building the DIALOGS system (Dialogue-based Inductive and Abductive LOGic program Synthesizer), such that it has all the wanted features. The refinement of DIALOGS is incremental, introducing more advanced features only as the need arises and as the basic mechanism is already explained. Finally, in Section 4, I look at related work, outline future work, and conclude.

## 2  Logic Program Schemata

Programs can be classified according to their synthesis methodologies, such as divide-and-conquer, generate-and-test, top-down decomposition, global search, and so on, or any composition thereof. Informally, a *program schema* consists, first of all, of a *template* program with a fixed dataflow, but without specific indications about the actual computations, except that they must satisfy certain *constraints*, which are the second component of a schema. A program schema thus abstracts a whole family of particular programs that can be obtained by instantiating the place-holders of its template to particular computations, using the program synthesized so far and the specification, so that the constraints of the schema are satisfied. It is therefore interesting to guide program synthesis by a schema that captures the essence of some synthesis methodology. This reflects the conjecture that experienced programmers actually instantiate schemata when programming, which schemata are summaries of their past programming experience. For a more complete treatise on this subject, please refer to my survey [11]. In ILP, for instance, schemata are used as a form of declarative bias by XOANON [22], MOBAL [16], CLINT/CIA [6], GRENDEL [5], SYNAPSE [9, 12], MISST [21], CILP [17], METAINDUCE [15], and others.

For the purpose of illustration only, I will focus on the divide-and-conquer synthesis methodology (which yields recursive programs), and I will restrict myself to predicates of maximum arity 3.

A *divide-and-conquer program* for a predicate R over parameters X, Y, and Z works as follows. Assume X is the induction parameter, Y the (optional) result parameter, and Z the (optional) auxiliary parameter. If X is minimal, then Y is directly computed from X, possibly using Z. Otherwise, that is if X is non-minimal, decompose (or: *divide*) X into a vector **HX** of $hx$ heads HX$_i$ and a vector **TX** of $t$ tails TX$_i$, the tails TX$_i$ being each of the same type as X, as well as smaller than X according to some well-founded relation. The tails **TX** are recursively associated with a vector **TY** of $t$ tails TY$_i$ of Y, the auxiliary parameter Z being unchanged in recursive calls (this is the *conquer* step). The heads **HX** are processed into a vector **HY** of $hy$ heads HY$_i$ of Y, possibly using Z. Finally, Y is composed (or: *combined*) from its heads **HY** and tails **TY**, possibly using Z. For X non-minimal, it is sometimes unnecessary or insufficient (if not wrong) to perform a recursive call, because Y can be directly computed from **HX** and **TX**, possibly using Z. One then has to discriminate between such cases, according to the values of **HX**, **TX**, Y, and Z. If the underlying relation is non-deterministic given X, then such discriminants may be non-complementary. In the non-recursive non-minimal case, several (say $v$) subcases with different solving operators may emerge; conversely, in the recursive case, several (say $w$) subcases with different processing and composition operators may emerge: one then has to discriminate between all of these subcases.

Each of the $1+v+w$ clauses of logic programs synthesized by this divide-and-conquer methodology is covered by one of the second-order clause templates of Template 1. Note that an "accidental" consideration of a parameter W as a result parameter rather than as an auxiliary parameter does not prevent the *existence* of a program (but the converse is true): W will be found to be always equal to its tail TW, and post-synthesis transformations can yield the version that would have been synthesized with W being considered as an auxiliary parameter. For convenience, if $hx$, $t$, $hy$, $v$, or $w$ is particularized to constant 1, then I will often drop the corresponding indices. Also, I will often refer to the predicate variables, or their instances, as *operators*.

```
R(X,Y,Z) ←
    Minimal(X),
    SolveMin(X,Y,Z)
R(X,Y,Z) ←
    NonMinimal(X),
    Decompose(X,HX,TX),              % HX=HX₁,...,HX_hx
    Discriminateⱼ(HX,TX,Y,Z),        % TX=TX₁,...,TX_t
    SolveNonMinⱼ(HX,TX,Y,Z)
R(X,Y,Z) ←
    NonMinimal(X),
    Decompose(X,HX,TX),
    Discriminateₖ(HX,TX,Y,Z),
    R(TX₁,TY₁,Z),...,R(TX_t,TY_t,Z),
    Processₖ(HX,HY,Z),              % HY=HY₁,...,HY_hy
    Composeₖ(HY,TY,Y,Z)            % TY=TY₁,...,TY_t
```

*Template 1*: Divide-and-conquer clause templates $(1 \leq j \leq v,\ v < k \leq v + w)$

The constraints to be verified by first-order instances of this template are listed elsewhere [11]. The most important one is that there must exist a well-founded relation "<" over the domain of the induction parameter, such that the instance of **Decompose** guarantees that $TX_i$ "<" X, for every $1 \leq i \leq t$. Other important constraints will be seen in Section 3.2.

Note that, at the logic program level (and at the schema level), I'm not interested in the control flow: these are *not* Prolog programs, and there is complete independence of the execution mechanism.

*Example 2.* The insertion-sort program of Example 1 is a rewriting of the program obtained by applying the second-order substitution
    { R/λA,B,C.sort(A,B), % projection: no auxiliary parameter!
    Minimal/λA.A=[], SolveMin/λA,B,C.B=[],
    NonMinimal/λA.∃H,T.A=[H|T], Decompose/λA,H,T.A=[H|T],
    Discriminate/λH,T,B,C.true,
    Process/λA,B,C.B=A, Compose/λH,T,B,C.insert(H,T,B) }
to the $\{v/0, w/1, hx/1, t/1, hy/1\}$-particularization of Template 1. This means that there is no non-recursive non-minimal case, and one recursive case, which features decomposition of the induction parameter L into one head, HL, and one tail, TL, the latter giving rise to one tail, TS, of the result parameter S. There is no auxiliary parameter. ◇

*Example 3.* The **insert** program of Example 1 is a rewriting of the program obtained by applying the second-order substitution
    { R/λA,B,C.insert(C,A,B), % re-ordering of formal parameters!
    Minimal/λA.A=[], SolveMin/λA,B,C.B=[C],
    NonMinimal/λA.∃H,T.A=[H|T], Decompose/λA,H,T.A=[H|T],
    Discriminate₁/λH,T,B,C.C≤H, SolveNonMin/λH,T,B,C.B=[C,H|T],
    Discriminate₂/λH,T,B,C.C>H,
    Process/λA,B,C.B=A, Compose/λH,T,B,C.B=[H|T] }
to the $\{v/1, w/1, hx/1, t/1, hy/1\}$-particularization of Template 1. This means that there is one non-recursive non-minimal case and one recursive case, both featuring decomposition of the induction parameter L into one head, HL, and one tail, TL, the latter giving rise to one tail, TR, of the result parameter R. Auxiliary parameter I is used in the discriminants and in the solving operators, and passed around unchanged in the recursive calls; it is however not used in the process and compose operators of the recursive case. ◇

A more general template is needed to cover the **combine** program of Section 1; it would cover logic programs for *n*-ary predicates with arbitrary numbers of result parameters and auxiliary parameters. Such a template is actually to be used by any serious implementation of the synthesis mechanism exposed hereafter.

In the following, Template 1 will turn out to have too much information, as we will not be able to distinguish between the instances of the operators in the first two clause templates, nor between the instances of **NonMinimal**, the **Discriminate**$_k$, the **Process**$_k$, and the **Compose**$_k$ in the third clause template: I'll thus unite these operators into $DS_j$ (with parameters X, Y, Z) and $DPC_k$ (with parameters **HX**, **TY** , Y, Z; note that **HY** has disappeared altogether, and that discrimination must now be on **TY**), respectively. Moreover, I will want to identify the predicate, say R, in whose logic program a certain operator appears, and this by just looking at the predicate symbol of that operator: therefore, I'll keep every operator name short and suffix their names by "-R" or "R", at the template level and at the instance level. Since nothing in $\lambda$-calculus mechanizes such a naming scheme when moving to the instance level, I will enforce it manually. Also note the convenient naming scheme of the internal variables of each clause: every head or tail of some formal parameter has a name syntactically dependent on the name of that parameter (heads are prefixed by "H" and tails by "T"); this helps tracing the role of each variable. If a predicate is declared by the specifier as r(A,B,C), then I will automatically apply the renaming substitution {X/A, Y/B, Z/C, **HX**/HA, **TX**/TA, **TY**/TB} to instances of the template (assuming A is chosen as induction parameter, B as result parameter, and C as auxiliary parameter), so that the specifier (and reader) can relate to such instances. All this yields Template 2 as a version that is more adequate for my present purposes. I'll refer to instances of its first clause template as *primitive cases*, and to instances of the other one as *non-primitive cases*.

$$R(X,Y,Z) \leftarrow$$
$$\quad DS\text{-}R_j(X,Y,Z)$$
$$R(X,Y,Z) \leftarrow$$

| | |
|---|---|
| $DecR(X, \mathbf{HX}, \mathbf{TX})$ | % $\mathbf{HX} = HX_1, \ldots, HX_{hx}$ |
| $R(TX_1, TY_1, Z), \ldots, R(TX_t, TY_t, Z),$ | % $\mathbf{TX} = TX_1, \ldots, TX_t$ |
| $DPC\text{-}R_k(\mathbf{HX}, \mathbf{TY}, Y, Z)$ | % $\mathbf{TY} = TY_1, \ldots, TY_t$ |

*Template 2*: Divide-and-conquer clause templates ($1 \leq j \leq v$, $1 \leq k \leq w$)

*Example 4.* The insertion-sort program of Example 1 is a slight rewriting of the program obtained by applying the second-order substitution
{ R/$\lambda$A,B,C.sort(A,B), DS-R/$\lambda$A,B,C.A=[],B=[],
DecR/$\lambda$A,H,T.A=[H|T], DPC-R/$\lambda$H,T,B,C.dpcSort(H,T,B) }
to the {$v/1, w/1, hx/1, t/1$}-particularization of Template 2, provided the first-order renaming substitution {X/L,Y/S,HX/HL,TX/TL,TY/TS} is indeed automatically applied in this process. ◇

*Example 5.* The **insert** program of Example 1 is a slight rewriting of the program obtained by applying the second-order substitution
{ R/$\lambda$A,B,C.insert(C,A,B), DS-R$_1$/$\lambda$A,B,C.A=[],B=[C],
DS-R$_2$/$\lambda$A,B,C.$\exists$H,T.A=[H|T],B=[C,H|T],C$\leq$H,
DecR/$\lambda$A,H,T.A=[H|T], DPC-R/$\lambda$A,B,C,D.$\exists$H,T.B=[H|T],C=[A,H|T],D>A }
to the {$v/2, w/1, hx/1, t/1$}-particularization of Template 2. ◇

## 3  The DIALOGS System

A DIALOGS synthesis is divided into two phases. The first phase performs a *full particularization* of Template 2 (instantiation of *all* its form variables, namely

$hx$, $t$, $v$, and $w$, which yields a second-order logic program) and an instantiation of *some* of its predicate variables (all except the DS-R$_j$ and the DPC-R$_k$), and is explained in Section 3.1. The second phase performs an instantiation of the DS-R$_j$ and the DPC-R$_k$ (that is the computations constructing the result parameter in each case), and is explained in Section 3.2.

## 3.1 Full Particularization and Partial Instantiation of the Template

*Predicate declaration.* DIALOGS first prompts the specifier for a predicate declaration. Assume, without loss of generality, that the specifier answers with a predicate declaration for a ternary predicate, say p(A:T$_1$,B:T$_2$,C:T$_3$), where p is a new predicate symbol, A, B, C are different variable names, and the types T$_i$ are in the set {atom, int, nat, list(_),...}. The actual type system is of no importance here, and the reader may guess the meanings of these type names.

*Dialogue issues.* DIALOGS needs to obtain a full particularization of Template 2. This means that the form variables $hx$, $t$, $v$, and $w$ need to be bound to integers. These are technical decisions, but they must be feasible without technical knowledge, because the specifier might be computationally naive or might not even exist (which is an extreme case of naiveté)! Let me explain: the need for a program for p might arise during the synthesis/learning of a program that uses p, in which case nobody can answer queries phrased in terms of p. (Of course, giving a predicate declaration for p is always possible.) This situation arises when a synthesizer/learner detects or conjectures the necessity of a new predicate p; for instance, a Compose$_k$ operator of a divide-and-conquer program might itself have a recursive program, so the synthesizer could call itself to find this program. So I need to devise a dialogue mechanism, for this first phase, with at least three features: (*i*) the provision of "reasonable" default answers; (*ii*) the runnability in two modes, namely *aloud* (where a computationally naive specifier may simply select the default answers, and any other specifier may answer with personal preferences) and *mute* (where a non-existing specifier is simulated by automatic selection of the default answers), and (*iii*) backtrackability, because there might be several reasonable default answers to certain queries, or because an answer may lead to failure at the second phase.

*Choice of the parameter roles.* The first step towards particularization of $hx$ and $t$ is the choice of the roles of the parameters: one of them must be the induction parameter, the others may be either result or auxiliary parameters, if any. Choosing an induction parameter can be done heuristically: any parameter of an inductively defined type such as nat or list(_) is a good candidate. From the predicate declaration, DIALOGS can create a sequence of potential induction parameters, keep the first one as the (first) default answer, and the remaining ones as default answers upon backtracking. Similarly for the result parameter (if any), which is also likely to be of an inductively defined type: from the remaining parameters (if any), DIALOGS can create a sequence of potential result parameters, keep the first one as the (first) default answer, and the remaining ones as default answers upon backtracking. Finally, DIALOGS can propose as the auxiliary parameter (if any) the remaining parameter (if any). Note that an auxiliary parameter is likely, but not certain, not to be of an inductively defined type, a good counter-example being I of **insert**, which is an integer, but has nothing to do with the "inductive nature" of inserting something into a list. Also remember, from Section 2, that an auxiliary parameter may inadvertently be considered as a result parameter, without any influence on the existence of a correct program (but the synthesis is likely to be a bit slower). In the following, I will implicitly drop all occurrences of Z in Template 2 in case there is no auxiliary parameter.

*Instantiation of* R. Assuming, without loss of generality, that B is chosen as induction parameter, C as result parameter, and A as auxiliary parameter, DIALOGS can now apply the second-order substitution $\{R/\lambda U,V,W.p(W,U,V)\}$ and the renaming substitution $\{X/B,Y/C,Z/A,HX/HB,TX/TB,TY/TC\}$ to Template 2, hence (partly) instantiating the heads and the recursive calls of the templates.

*Instantiation of* DecR *and particularization of* $hx$ *and* $t$. The choice of an instance of DecR will finally particularize $hx$ and $t$. DIALOGS can simply use a type-specific predefined sequence of potential instances of DecR, keep the first one as the (first) default answer, and the remaining ones as default answers upon backtracking. Assuming induction parameter B is of type **list(int)**, the sequence could be

$$\text{DecR}/\lambda \text{L,H,T.L=[H|T]} \qquad\qquad hx/1,\ t/1$$
$$\text{DecR}/\lambda \text{L,H}_1,\text{H}_2,\text{T.L=[H}_1,\text{H}_2|\text{T]} \qquad\qquad hx/2,\ t/1$$
$$\ldots \qquad\qquad\qquad\qquad\qquad\qquad\qquad \ldots$$
$$\text{DecR}/\lambda \text{L,H,T}_1,\text{T}_2.\exists \text{T.L=[H|T]},\text{partition(T,H,T}_1\ ,\text{T}_2) \qquad hx/1,\ t/2$$
$$\text{DecR}/\lambda \text{L,T}_1,\text{T}_2.\text{L=[\_,\_|\_]},\text{halves(L,T}_1,\text{T}_2) \qquad\qquad hx/0,\ t/2$$
$$\ldots \qquad\qquad\qquad\qquad\qquad\qquad\qquad \ldots$$

Similar sequences are pre-defined for every type, such that they enforce the well-foundedness constraint.

*Particularization of* $v$ *and* $w$. Definitely the hardest particularization is to decide, in advance, how many subcases there are for each case. A safe approach is to conjecture that there is one primitive case $(v = 1)$, as well as one non-primitive case $(w = 1)$, and to have the remainder of synthesis refine this: if either of these cases turns out to have subcases, which means that the instance of DS-R or DPC-R is a disjunctive formula, then set $v$ or $w$ to the number of disjuncts in this instance and rewrite the overall program accordingly.

*So far so good.* This terminates the first phase: in Template 2, all form variables and all predicate variables except DS-R and DPC-R are by now instantiated. From a programming point of view, all creative decisions have been taken, but alternative decisions are ready for any occurrence of backtracking (either because some decision leads to failure of the second phase, or because the specifier wants another program after successful completion of the second phase). The remaining instantiations are performed by the second phase, which is discussed in the next subsection.

## 3.2 Instantiation of the Solving Computations

The instantiation of the remaining predicate variables (namely DS-R and DPC-R) also is interactive and is based on the notions of abduction through (naive) unfolding and querying, and induction through computation of most-specific generalizations (or: least-general generalizations). [1]

*Basic principle.* In a nutshell, the basic principle is as follows. Assume, for concreteness and simplicity, that the first phase produced the following instantiation of Template 2 (without auxiliary parameter), with list A being the induction parameter, divided by head-tail decomposition, and B being the result parameter:

$$p(A,B) \leftarrow DS\text{-}p(A,B)$$
$$p(A,B) \leftarrow A=[HA|TA], p(TA,TB), DPC\text{-}p(HA,TB,B)$$

The possible computation "traces" for various most-general values of the induction parameter are:

$$p([],D_1) \leftarrow DS\text{-}p([],D_1)$$
$$p([E_1],F_1) \leftarrow DS\text{-}p([E_1],F_1)$$
$$p([E_1],F_1) \leftarrow p([],F_1), DPC\text{-}p(E_1,F_1,F_1)$$
$$p([G_1,G_1],H_1) \leftarrow DS\text{-}p([G_1,G_1],H_1)$$
$$p([G_1,G_1],H_1) \leftarrow p([G_1],H_1), DPC\text{-}p(G_1,H_1,H_1)$$

. . .

The strategy is to (*a*) query the specifier for an instance of the last atom of each trace, using previous answers to resolve recursive calls, (*b*) inductively infer an instance of DS-p from some of the answers, and (*c*) inductively infer an instance of DPC-p from the other answers. The criterion of how to establish such a partition of the answers follows from the dataflow constraints of the schema (see below).

The specifier *must* know what B is when A is the empty list. A query is generated by instantiating the first clause to

$$p([],D_1) \leftarrow DS\text{-}p([],D_1) \tag{1}$$

Unfolding of second-order atoms is impossible, so the unfolding process stops here. The query

**What conditions on <$D_0$> must hold such that $p([],D_0)$ holds?**

can be extracted from this clause. The answer should thus be a formula $\mathcal{F}[D_0]$, where only $D_0$ may be free, explaining how to compute $D_0$ from $[]$ such that $p([],D_0)$ holds. In other words, DS-$p([],D_0)$ should be "equivalent" to $\mathcal{F}[D_0]$. Instantiating the second clause when A is the empty list would lead to failure of the unfolding process at the equality atom.

The specifier *must* also know what B is when A has one element. A query is generated by instantiating the second clause to

$$p([E_1],F_1) \leftarrow [E_1]=[HA|TA], p(TA,TB), DPC\text{-}p(HA,TB,F_1)$$

Unfolding the equality atom gives

---

[1] Term *g* is *more general than* term *s* if there is a substitution $\theta$ such that $s = g\theta$. We also say that *s* is *more specific than g*. The *most-specific generalization* (abbreviated msg) of terms *a* and *b* is a term *m* that is more general than both *a* and *b*, and such that no term more specific than *m* (up to renaming) is more general than both *a* and *b*. The msg of a non-empty set of terms is defined similarly. See [19] for more details.

$p([E_1],F_1) \leftarrow p([],TB),DPC-p(E_1,TB,F_1)$

Unfolding the p atom, using clause (1) with the newly obtained evidence of DS-p as a "shortcut," gives

$p([E_1],F_1) \leftarrow F[TB],DPC-p(E_1,TB,F_1)$

Recursively unfolding all the atoms in $\mathcal{F}[TB]$ eventually reduces this clause to

$$p([E_1],F_1) \leftarrow DPC-p(E_1,tb_1,F_1) \tag{2}$$

where $tb_0$ represents the value of TB after this "execution" of $\mathcal{F}[TB]$. The query

**What conditions on $<E_1,F_1>$ must hold such that $p([E_1],F_1)$ holds?**

can be extracted from this clause. The answer should thus be a formula $\mathcal{G}[E_1,F_1]$, where only $E_1$ and $F_1$ may be free, explaining how to compute $F_1$ from $[E_1]$ such that $p([E_1],F_1)$ holds. In other words, $DPC-p(E_1,tb_0,F_1)$ should be "equivalent" to $\mathcal{G}[E_1,F_1]$. Instantiating the first clause when A is a one-element list would yield the same query, so we can directly establish that $DS-p([E_1],F_1)$ should also be "equivalent" to $\mathcal{G}[E_1,F_1]$.

Next query the specifier for what B is when A has two elements. Again, s/he *must* know the answer. A query is generated by now instantiating the second clause to

$p([G_1,G_1],H_1) \leftarrow [G_1,G_1]=[HA|TA],p(TA,TB),DPC-p(HA,TB,H_1)$

Unfolding the equality atom gives

$p([G_1,G_1],H_1) \leftarrow p([G_1],TB),DPC-p(G_1,TB,H_1)$

Unfolding the p atom, using clause (2) with the newly obtained evidence of DPC-p as a "shortcut," gives

$p([G_1,G_1],H_1) \leftarrow G[G_1,TB],DPC-p(G_1,TB,H_1)$

Recursively unfolding all the atoms in $\mathcal{G}[G_2,TB]$ will reduce this clause to

$p([G_1,G_1],H_1) \leftarrow DPC-p(G_1,tb_1,H_1)$

where $tb_1$ represents the value (possibly using $G_2$) of TB after this "execution" of $\mathcal{G}[G_2,TB]$. The query

**What conditions on $<G_1,G_2,H_2>$ must hold such that $p([G_1,G_2],H_2)$ holds?**

can be extracted from this clause. The answer should thus be a formula $\mathcal{H}[G_1,G_2,H_2]$, where only $G_1$, $G_2$, and $H_2$ may be free, explaining how to compute $H_2$ from $[G_1,G_2]$ such that $p([G_1,G_2],H_2)$ holds. In other words, $DPC-p(G_1,tb_1,H_2)$ should be "equivalent" to $\mathcal{H}[G_1,G_2,H_2]$. Instantiating the first clause when A is a two-element list would yield the same query, so we can directly establish that $DS-p([G_1,G_2],H_2)$ should also be "equivalent" to $\mathcal{H}[G_1,G_2,H_2]$.

One may continue like this for an arbitrary number of times, gathering more and more evidence of DS-p and DPC-p. As of now, I do not have a clear heuristic for when to stop gathering evidence. The current implementation simply goes through the loop a constant number of times and lets the specifier give "skip" answers (at her/his risk!) when tired or bored. Overcoming this is considered future work. Sooner or later thus, some inductive inference has to be done from this evidence. For example, if $\mathcal{G}$, $\mathcal{H}$, ... are conjunctions of literals (for other situations, see below), then it "often" (see below) suffices to compute the most-specific generalization of an "adequate" subset of the tuple set (considering all predicate symbols and the connectives "," and "¬" as functors)

$\{\langle \mathtt{E}_1, tb_0, \mathtt{F}_1, \mathcal{G}\rangle, \langle \mathtt{G}_1, tb_1, \mathtt{H}_2, \mathcal{H}\rangle, \ldots\}$, say $\langle ha, tb, b, \mathcal{M}\rangle$, and the binding of DPC-p to $\lambda \mathtt{T}, \mathtt{U}, \mathtt{V} . \mathtt{T}{=}ha, \mathtt{U}{=}tb, \mathtt{V}{=}b, \mathcal{M}$ can then complete the synthesis of the second clause. Similarly, compute the msg of the "counterpart complementary subset" of the tuple set $\{\langle [], \mathtt{D}_0, \mathcal{F}\rangle, \langle [\mathtt{E}_1], \mathtt{F}_1, \mathcal{G}\rangle, \langle [\mathtt{G}_1, \mathtt{G}_2], \mathtt{H}_2, \mathcal{H}\rangle, \ldots\}$, say $\langle a, b, \mathcal{M}\rangle$, and the binding of DS-p to $\lambda \mathtt{T}, \mathtt{U} . \mathtt{T}{=}a, \mathtt{U}{=}b, \mathcal{M}$ can then complete the synthesis of the first clause. I call this (and its refinement hereafter) the *MSG Method* [9, 12, 8].

This presentation of the basic principle is of course very coarse, as it sidetracks or leaves open many important issues, which will be discussed next. In any case, notice how query generation and answering actually *abduce* evidence of the still missing operators.

*Unfolding issues.* In general thus, the principle of query generation is to successively instantiate every clause for most-general values of the induction parameter and to unfold its first-order body atoms (until only a second-order atom remains), so that a query in terms of the target predicate only can be extracted, hiding the fact that the specifier actually has to answer a query about the second-order atom. Answers to previously posed queries are made available during this unfolding process as shortcuts, avoiding thus that the same query is generated twice. Naive unfolding is sufficient here, as I am only interested in the logic, not in the control, of logic programs. Also, I assume there is a system program for every primitive (such as $=/2$).

As usual, unfolding uses *all* applicable clauses (except when shortcuts are available, in which case only the shortcut clauses are used), so that several clauses may result from an unfolding step; unfolding then continues from *all* of these clauses, with the same stopping criterion and the same spawning process. Moreover, it is sometimes unnecessary to recursively unfold until only a second-order atom is left.

*Example 6.* Both of these phenomena can be illustrated by means of the delOdds predicate, which is informally specified as follows:
   delOdds(L,R) iff R is L without its odd elements, where L, R are integer-lists.
Suppose L is chosen as induction parameter, which is divided by head-tail decomposition, and R is chosen as result parameter. The following first two queries are posed to the specifier:
   What conditions on <$R_0$> must hold such that delOdds([],$R_0$) holds? $R_0 = []$
   What conditions on <$A_1, R_1$> must hold such that delOdds([$A_1$],$R_1$) holds? $odd(A_1), R_1 = []; \neg odd(A_1), R_1 = [A_1]$
Note that the second answer is disjunctive, and that it not only says *how* the result is computed, but also *when/why* it is so. Now, during the generation of the query about what happens when L has two elements, the following clauses are obtained after some unfolding:
   delOdds([$B_1, B_1$],$R_1$) $\leftarrow$ odd($B_1$),DPCdelOdds($B_1$,[],$R_1$)
   delOdds([$B_1, B_1$],$R_1$) $\leftarrow$ $\neg$odd($B_1$),DPCdelOdds($B_1$,[$B_1$],$R_1$)
Note that the unfolding yielded two clauses (using the shortcuts established from the second query). The primitive predicate odd being introduced by the specifier, we need not unfold it. Therefore, the queries

What conditions on $\langle B_1, B_2, R_2 \rangle$ must hold such that
delOdds($[B_1, B_2], R_2$) holds, assuming odd($B_2$)?
$odd(B_1), R_2 = []; \neg odd(B_1), R_2 = [B_1]$
What conditions on $\langle B_1, B_2, R_2 \rangle$ must hold such that
delOdds($[B_1, B_2], R_2$) holds, assuming $\neg$odd($B_2$)?
$odd(B_1), R_2 = [B_2]; \neg odd(B_1), R_2 = [B_1, B_2]$

should be extracted: note the new sub-sentences introduced by the keyword
**assuming**. ◇

*Instantiation of* DS-R *and* DPC-R *through the MSG Method.* Above, I wrote that
it "often" suffices to compute msgs in order to help instantiate DS-R and DPC-R
(in case their evidence involves only conjunctions of literals); so what is the
criterion for doing so? And how to choose the "adequate" tuple subsets over
which msgs are computed? To answer these, we first have to analyze the dataflow
of divide-and-conquer programs in even greater detail than so far, namely *inside*
the DS-R and DPC-R operators [9, 12, 8].

Let's start with the discriminate-process-compose operator. Essentially, it is
Y that is "constructed from" **HX**, **TY**, and **Z**. "Constructing" a term "from"
others means that its constituents (constants and variables) are taken from the
constituents of these other terms; functors can safely be ignored here, due to
their "decorative" role in logic programming. For example, in insert(HL,TS,S),
which is the DPC-R operator of the insertion-sort program in Section 1, result S is
constructed from HL and TS. But we know more: *all* the constituents of **TY** *must*
be used for constructing Y or for discriminating between different constructions of
Y, because otherwise the recursive computations of **TY** would have been useless;
but the constituents of **HX** and **Z** only *might* be used in this construction of Y. For
example, in insert(HL,TS,S), result S is indeed constructed from the "entire"
TS, but also from HL; however, in R=[HL|TR], which is the DPC-R operator of the
insert program in Section 1, result R is indeed constructed from TR, and from HL,
but not from auxiliary parameter I; and there are programs with constructions
of Y that involve **TY** and **Z** but not **HX**, or even only **TY**. Finally: Y can *only*
be constructed from the constituents of **HX**, **TY**, and **Z**, but may not "invent"
other constituents, except maybe for the type-specific constants (such as 0, nil,
...), although this is not always the case. All these observations can be gathered
in the following definition (which is a particular case of Erdem's version [8],
which itself is a powerful and generic extension of my old version [9, 12]): a
tuple $\langle \mathbf{hx}, \mathbf{ty}, y, z, \mathcal{F} \rangle$ is *admissible* (for building a discriminate-process-compose
operator) iff

$$constituents(\mathbf{ty}) \subseteq constituents(\langle y, \mathcal{F} \rangle) \land$$
$$constituents(y) \subseteq constituents(\langle \mathbf{hx}, \mathbf{ty}, z \rangle) \cup \{0, nil, \ldots\}$$

where terms **ty**, $y$, and $z$ are optional, and first-order formula $\mathcal{F}$ is a conjunction of literals without any equality atoms. From such an admissible tuple, we
can build an *admissible instance* of DPC-R by binding this predicate variable to
$\lambda \mathbf{T}, \mathbf{U}, \mathbf{V}, \mathbf{W}. \mathbf{T}=\mathbf{hx}, \mathbf{U}=\mathbf{ty}, \mathbf{V}=y, \mathbf{W}=z, \mathcal{F}$.

Let's continue with the discriminate-solve operator. Essentially, it is Y that is constructed from X and Z. But the constituents of X and Z only *might* be used in this construction of Y. Finally, Y may even "invent" new constituents: I here restrict invented constituents to the type-specific constants $(0, \texttt{nil}, \ldots)$, although this is not always the case. All these observations can be gathered in the following definition [8]: a tuple $\langle x, y, z, \mathcal{F} \rangle$ is *admissible* (for building a discriminate-solve operator) iff

$$constituents(y) \subseteq constituents(\langle x, z \rangle) \cup \{0, nil, \ldots\}$$

where terms $y$ and $z$ are optional, and first-order formula $\mathcal{F}$ is a conjunction of literals without any equality atoms. From such an admissible tuple, we can build an admissible instance of DS-R by binding this predicate variable to $\lambda\texttt{T},\texttt{U},\texttt{V}.\texttt{T}{=}x,\texttt{U}{=}y,\texttt{V}{=}z,\mathcal{F}$.

Admissibility of the instances of the DS-$\texttt{R}_j$ and the DPC-$\texttt{R}_k$ gives us thus other (dataflow) constraints of the divide-and-conquer schema. They are enforced as follows:

1. partition the tuple set for DPC-R into a minimal number of subsets (called *cliques*) of which any two elements have an admissible msg;
2. analyze every such clique: if the msg of the counterpart subset of the tuples for DS-R is also admissible, then delete the clique from the tuples for DPC-R; otherwise delete that counterpart subset from the tuples for DS-R;
3. take the msgs of the remaining cliques for building admissible instances of the DPC-$\texttt{R}_k$, and set $w$ to the number of these cliques;
4. partition the remaining tuple set for DS-R into a minimal number of cliques, build admissible instances of the DS-$\texttt{R}_j$ from their msgs, and set $v$ to the number of these cliques.

This is essentially my old MSG Method [9, 12], but run with the extended definitions of admissibility.

*Example 7.* The synthesis of delOdds, as started in Example 6, continues as follows. The first answer abduces the following evidence of DSdelOdds (left column) and DPCdelOdds (right column):

1. $\langle \square, \square, \texttt{true} \rangle$                                     (not applicable)

The second answer abduces the following evidence of DSdelOdds and DPCdelOdds:

2. $\langle [\texttt{A}_1], \square, \texttt{odd}(\texttt{A}_1) \rangle$                         $\langle \texttt{A}_1, \square, \square, \texttt{odd}(\texttt{A}_1) \rangle$
3. $\langle [\texttt{A}_1], [\texttt{A}_1], \neg\texttt{odd}(\texttt{A}_1) \rangle$                  $\langle \texttt{A}_1, \square, [\texttt{A}_1], \neg\texttt{odd}(\texttt{A}_1) \rangle$

The third and fourth answers abduce the following evidence of DSdelOdds and DPCdelOdds:

4. $\langle [\texttt{B}_1, \texttt{B}_2], \square, (\texttt{odd}(\texttt{B}_1), \texttt{odd}(\texttt{B}_2)) \rangle$      $\langle \texttt{B}_1, \square, \square, \texttt{odd}(\texttt{B}_1) \rangle$
5. $\langle [\texttt{B}_1, \texttt{B}_2], [\texttt{B}_1], (\neg\texttt{odd}(\texttt{B}_1), \texttt{odd}(\texttt{B}_2)) \rangle$    $\langle \texttt{B}_1, \square, [\texttt{B}_1], \neg\texttt{odd}(\texttt{B}_1) \rangle$
6. $\langle [\texttt{B}_1, \texttt{B}_2], [\texttt{B}_2], (\texttt{odd}(\texttt{B}_1), \neg\texttt{odd}(\texttt{B}_2)) \rangle$    $\langle \texttt{B}_1, [\texttt{B}_2], [\texttt{B}_2], \texttt{odd}(\texttt{B}_1) \rangle$
7. $\langle [\texttt{B}_1, \texttt{B}_2], [\texttt{B}_1, \texttt{B}_2], (\neg\texttt{odd}(\texttt{B}_1), \neg\texttt{odd}(\texttt{B}_2)) \rangle$    $\langle \texttt{B}_1, [\texttt{B}_2], [\texttt{B}_1, \texttt{B}_2], \neg\texttt{odd}(\texttt{B}_1) \rangle$

Note that tuples 4 and 5 for `DPCdelOdds` are just variants of its tuples 2 and 3, respectively; they could thus be eliminated. In fact, DIALOGS detects this during query generation and never even poses the third query to the specifier; the corresponding tuples are non-interactively abduced using the answer to the second query as shortcut. At step (1), the msg of all the tuples for `DPCdelOdds` is $\langle$HL,TR,R,P$\rangle$. Since there is a predicate variable in the fourth slot, namely P, this tuple is not admissible. So we should partition the tuple set into a minimal number of cliques of which any two elements have an admissible msg. A partition into two cliques of three elements each (with tuples 2, 4, 6, and 3, 5, 7, respectively) achieves this, with the following msgs:

$\langle$[HL|TL],R,P$\rangle$          $\langle$HL,TR,TR,odd(HL)$\rangle$

$\langle$[HL|TL],R,Q$\rangle$          $\langle$HL,TR,[HL|TR],¬odd(HL)$\rangle$

There are no other partitions yielding two cliques. The partitions yielding three to six cliques are obviously uninteresting, as each of their cliques is properly contained in some clique of the bi-partition.

At step (2), the counterpart six pieces of evidence of `DSdelOdds` can be deleted, because their two msgs (in the left column above) are not admissible (due to the presence of predicate variables).

At step (3), $w$ is set to 2, and `DPCdelOdds`$_1$ is bound to $\lambda$T,U,V.T=HL,U=TR, V=TR,odd(HL), while `DPCdelOdds`$_2$ is bound to $\lambda$T,U,V.T=HL,U=TR,V=[HL|TR], ¬odd(HL).

At step (4), $v$ is left to be 1, and `DSdelOdds` is bound to $\lambda$T,U.T=[],U=[], true, using the only remaining evidence for `DSdelOdds`. ◇

What if the answers to the queries are not conjunctions of literals? For simplicity, and without loss of power, I restrict the answer language to the connectives *not* ("¬"), *and* (","), and *or* (";"), and I require answers to be in disjunctive normal form, with the variables appearing in the query being implicitly free, all others being implicitly existentially quantified. Therefore, it suffices to break up disjunctive answers into their conjunctions of literals, and to apply the MSG Method. This was actually illustrated in the `delOdds` example.

*Instantiation of* DPC-R *through recursive synthesis.* Instantiating DPC-R via the MSG Method assumes that there is a finite non-recursive axiomatization of that operator. But such is not always the case; take for example the `insert` predicate used in the insertion-sort program in Section 1: its program is recursive and hence not synthesizable through the MSG Method. So another method needs to be devised for detecting and handling such situations of necessary predicate invention [20, 10]. Since the MSG Method has been devised to always succeed (indeed, in the worst case, it partitions a tuple set into cliques of one element each), a heuristic is needed for rejecting the results of the MSG Method and thus conjecturing the necessity of predicate invention. A good candidate heuristic is [9, 8]: if there are "too few" cliques for DPC-R, then reject the results of the MSG Method. The interpretation of "too few" is implementation-dependent, and could be user-controlled by system-confidence parameters; the current implementation only rejects when $w$ is 0.

*Example 8.* After the three queries of the insertion-sort synthesis of Example 1 (assuming L is chosen as induction parameter, which is divided by head-tail decomposition, and S is chosen as result parameter), the abduced tuples for DSsort and DPCsort respectively are (after some renaming):

| | |
|---|---|
| $\langle [], [], \texttt{true} \rangle$ | (not applicable) |
| $\langle [A_1], [A_1], \texttt{true} \rangle$ | $\langle A_1, [], [A_1], \texttt{true} \rangle$ |
| $\langle [B_1,B_2], [B_1,B_2], B_1 \leq B_2 \rangle$ | $\langle B_1, [B_2], [B_1,B_2], B_1 \leq B_2 \rangle$ |
| $\langle [B_1,B_2], [B_2,B_1], B_1 > B_2 \rangle$ | $\langle B_1, [B_2], [B_2,B_1], B_1 > B_2 \rangle$ |

The MSG Method partitions, at step (1), the three tuples for DPCsort into three cliques of one element each; at step (2), these tuples are removed because their counterparts for DSsort are admissible as well; at step (3), no evidence is left for DPCsort, so $w$ is set to 0; finally, at step (4), the four tuples for DSsort are partitioned into three cliques, so $v$ is set to 3. This result is however rejected by the heuristic above: it is conjectured that DPCsort cannot be instantiated through the MSG Method (that is, a program for insert cannot be found by this way). ⋄

So how to proceed? This is a situation of necessary predicate invention, which is precisely one of the situations targeted by DIALOGS, which is a recursion-synthesizer (due to its foundation on Template 2). So the idea is for DIALOGS to re-invoke itself, under the assumption that a divide-and-conquer program exists for the missing operator.

The instantiations done by steps (3) and (4) of the MSG Method need to be undone. The latter is thus revised as follows: steps (3) and (4) only *create* the instances, but the actual bindings are deferred until acceptance by the rejection heuristic.

Using Template 2 and the declaration of the current predicate (see below), the variable DPC-R is bound to $\lambda T,U,V,W. \texttt{dpcR}(T,U,V,W)$, and the predicate declaration $\texttt{dpcR}(H:T_4,T:T_3,R:T_3,A:T_1)$ is elaborated (assuming that the elements of induction parameter $B:T_2$ are of type $T_4$, that $hx = t = 1$, and that $C:T_3$ is the result parameter and $A:T_1$ the auxiliary parameter). Indeed, under these assumptions, the call to the new predicate will be $\texttt{dpcR}(HB,TC,C,A)$. Note that this doesn't necessarily create a predicate of maximum arity 3, but, as said earlier, a generalization of Template 2 should be used for any serious implementation. Moreover, the variable DS-R is instantiated according to the msgs of the tuples that have no counterparts among the tuples for DPC-R. For the insertion-sort synthesis, this gives the declaration $\texttt{dpcSort}(I:\texttt{int},L:\texttt{list(int)},R:\texttt{list(int)})$, while variable DSsort is bound to $\lambda A,B,C. A=[], B=[]$, and variable DPCsort is bound to $\lambda H,T,B,C. \texttt{dpcSort}(H,T,B)$, just like in Example 4.

The first phase of the sub-synthesis *must* be run in mute mode, as the specifier doesn't know what kind of program the system is synthesizing and therefore can't be expected to answer queries about its operators, let alone about the operators used in synthesizing these operators.

However, some hints for the first phase of this sub-synthesis could be expressed: in general, it seems reasonable to hint at T as induction parameter, R as result parameter, and H, A as auxiliary parameters. A reasonable hint could also be expressed for instantiation of DecR, but I do not go into these details here. In any case, these hints beg a fourth feature of the dialogue mechanism (see "Dialogue issues" above), namely: (iv) preference of hints (if any) over defaults in mute mode. In general, DIALOGS is thus also called with a possibly empty hint list, rather than with only a predicate declaration.

The second phase of this sub-synthesis should not generate queries about the new predicate. It shouldn't even synthesize a program for the new predicate by explicit induction on the parameter hinted at, because not every value of that induction parameter is "reachable" by values of the induction parameter of the super-synthesis: queries about the new predicate can't always be formulated in terms of the old one. For example, a factorial program needs to invent a multiplication predicate, but actually only uses a sparse subset of the multiplication relation [17]. The "trick" to make DIALOGS generate queries about the top-level predicate (see below) such that the answers actually pertain, unbeknownst to the specifier, to that new predicate is quite simple: the first phase of the sub-synthesis should *add* the obtained clauses to those of the super-synthesis, rather than work with these new clauses only.

Thus, in general, DIALOGS is called with a *start program* as an additional argument: this is the empty set in the case of a new synthesis (for the *top-level predicate*), or a set of clauses for a (unique) *top-level predicate* and its (directly or indirectly) used predicates, in case DIALOGS is used (possibly by itself) for a necessary invention of a predicate that is (directly or indirectly) used by the top-level predicate. The first phase gets a predicate declaration for the *current predicate* and builds the *current program* by adding the new clauses to the start program. Query generation in the second phase is always done for the top-level predicate, but unfolding will eventually "trickle down" to a missing operator of the current predicate and extract a question for it in terms of the top-level one. The answers to queries help instantiate a missing operator of the current predicate, through either the MSG Method or further recursive synthesis.

*Example 9.* Let's continue the synthesis of the insertion-sort program (from Example 1 and Example 8). DIALOGS calls itself recursively in mute mode with

```
sort(L,S) ← L=[],S=[]
sort(L,S) ← L=[HL|TL],sort(TL,TS),dpcSort(HL,TS,S)
```

as start program, sort as top-level predicate, dpcSort(I:int,L:list(int), R:list(int)) as declaration for current predicate dpcSort, parameter L as preferred induction parameter, parameter R as preferred result parameter, and parameter I as preferred auxiliary parameter. Assume the first phase builds the current program by adding to the start program the following clauses:

```
dpcSort(I,L,R) ← DSdpcSort(I,L,R)
dpcSort(I,L,R) ← L=[HL|TL],dpcSort(I,TL,TR),DPCdpcSort(HL,TR,R,I)
```

In the second phase, query generation for most-general one-element and two-element lists as induction parameter L of the top-level predicate **sort** leads, without interaction (due to the second and third queries of the super-synthesis), to the following tuples for **DSdpcSort** and **DPCdpcSort**, respectively:

$\langle A_1, [], [A_1], true \rangle$         (not applicable)

$\langle B_1, [B_2], [B_1, B_2], B_1 \leq B_2 \rangle$      $\langle B_2, [B_1], [B_1, B_2], B_1, B_1 \leq B_2 \rangle$

$\langle B_1, [B_2], [B_2, B_1], B_1 > B_2 \rangle$      $\langle B_2, [B_1], [B_2, B_1], B_1, B_1 > B_2 \rangle$

This is scanty evidence to continue from, so one could decide to generate a query about what happens when induction parameter L of the top-level predicate **sort** has three elements. This would yield an extension to the target scenario of Example 1; the ensuing computations are too long to reproduce here, but they eventually lead to the correct binding (just as in Example 5) of **DSdpcSort**$_1$ to $\lambda A, B, C. A=[], B=[C]$, of **DSdpcSort**$_2$ to $\lambda A, B, C. \exists H, T. A=[H|T], B=[C, H|T], C \leq H$, and of **DPCdpcSort** to $\lambda A, B, C, D. \exists H, T. B=[H|T], C=[A, H|T], D>A$. Note that $v$ is 2, and $w$ is 1. A more "daring" move would be to directly infer these instances from the tuples above, and thus to stay within the targeted scenario. Indeed, the first tuple can directly lead to the instantiation of **DSdpcSort**$_1$, based on the observation that there is no counterpart evidence of **DPCdpcSort**; the second tuple can directly lead to the instantiation of **DSdpcSort**$_2$ (by generalization of constant **nil** to a variable), based on the observation that the counterpart evidence of **DPCdpcSort** forces the "breaking up" of the second parameter in order to construct the third one; conversely, the third tuple can directly lead to the instantiation of **DPCdpcSort** (by generalization of constant **nil** to a variable), based on the observation that the counterpart evidence of **DSdpcSort** forces the "breaking up" of the second parameter in order to construct the third one. Formalizing this, and hence reducing dialogues, is considered future work. ◇

A high-level DIALOGS algorithm can be found in the Appendix.

## 4   Conclusion

In this paper, I have first motivated and then incrementally reconstructed the reasoning that led to the design of the DIALOGS system, which is a dialogue-based, inductive/abductive, schema-guided synthesizer of recursive logic programs, that takes the initiative and minimally queries a (possibly computationally naive) specifier for evidence in her/his conceptual language. DIALOGS can be used by any learner (including itself) that detects, or merely conjectures, the necessity of invention of a new predicate.

Queries are kept entirely in terms of the specifier's conceptual language, and are simple, because they only ask what "happens" when some parameter has a finite number of "elements." Even better, the specifier *must* know the answers to such queries, because otherwise s/he wouldn't even feel the need for the synthesized program. Answers are thus also in the specifier's conceptual language, and are *independent* of the synthesized program. Answers are stored so that synthesis can proceed with minimal querying. Indeed, a query can be generated more than once, albeit with different "intentions" (that is, aiming at gathering evidence of different operators): the aimed-at operators are either the ones of the top-level predicate or the ones of the current predicate (when the top-level predicate needs to invent the current predicate).

A *competent specifier assumption* only holds in the second phase, because of the backtrackability feature of the dialogue in the first phase: the specifier (if any!) can answer just about anything during the first phase, because wrong answers will lead to failure in the second phase.

Note the elegant ways by which DIALOGS avoids the "background knowledge re-use bottleneck" [13]: first, it only tries to re-use the $=/2$ primitive (by the MSG Method); moreover, other primitives (such as $\leq/2$ or odd) used by the specifier in answers to queries end up in the synthesized program (which prevents the sometimes automa-g-ic flavor of inductive synthesis); finally, the system re-uses the primitives occurring in its knowledge base for DecR. Overall thus, these primitives do not "compete" in re-use situations.

Due to its foundation on an extremely powerful codification of a "recursion-theory" (by means of the template and constraints of a divide-and-conquer schema), the current prototype implementation needs very little evidence and is very fast. An even faster and more powerful implementation is planned.

The time-complexity of synthesis is essentially linear in the complexity of the synthesized program, due to the repeated unfolding of the synthesized program for various most-general values of some parameter. Steps (1) and (4) of the MSG Method amount to partitioning a graph into a minimal number of cliques, which is known to be an NP-complete problem; however, this should not be an issue, as the graphs under investigation only have a few nodes.

The class of synthesizable programs is a subset of the class of divide-and-conquer programs. It seems to depend on the knowledge base for DecR, but a "Devil's Advocate" argument against its completeness with respect to that class may be countered by appealing to the ingenuity of a non-naive specifier when answering the DecR question. The current (relaxable) assumptions are that DS-R is non-recursively defined, and that DPC-R has a divide-and-conquer instance, *if* a new predicate needs to be invented for it.

DIALOGS falls into the category of *trace-based inductive synthesizers* [9] (such as [3], GRENDEL [5], SYNAPSE [9, 12], METAINDUCE [15], CILP [17], ...), because it first explains its examples in terms of computation traces (that fit a certain template), and then generalizes these traces into a recursive program. The main innovation here is that DIALOGS generates its own, generalized examples. Note that SPECTRE [4] and TRACY [2] are *not* trace-based synthesizers, as they don't construct their candidate clauses in a truly schema-guided way. However, they do use a form of declarative bias to enumerate and analyze (that is, accept or reject) potential clauses, and they also feature unfolding/resolution in the process of verifying the coverage of examples.

DIALOGS is most closely related to SYNAPSE [9, 12]: this non-interactive schema-guided inductive/abductive synthesizer expects some positive (ground) examples as well as Horn clause equivalents (called *properties*) of at least the answers that DIALOGS would query for. In other words, DIALOGS is a simplification of SYNAPSE, without any loss of power, but with less burden on the specifier and with faster synthesis. The Proofs-as-Programs Method (which should have been called Abductive Method) of SYNAPSE has disappeared, as it has become the driving synthesis mechanism of the second phase of DIALOGS.

The CILP [17] and METAINDUCE [15] systems essentially feature subsets of the functionality of SYNAPSE and DIALOGS, in the sense that they have only examples as input language, rely on a simpler divide-and-conquer schema, and use less powerful MSG Methods, which cannot infer disjunctively defined operators.

The CLINT [6] and CLINT/CIA systems [7], although they are *model-based inductive synthesizers* [9], are also related to DIALOGS, in the sense that they are also interactive, sometimes guided by (mono-clausal) templates, and have an extended evidence language (full clauses, called *integrity constraints*). However, these integrity constraints are not used constructively during a synthesis, but only to accept or reject candidate programs.

As said before, a stopping criterion for the dialogue loop of the second phase needs to be identified. Co-routining the abduction, induction, and evaluation steps of that phase seems an approach towards this, as the loop can then be exited when the msgs stop changing.

Future work will also aim at increased schema independence (it's already largely achieved in the second phase, except for the hardwired verification of the constraints), at least via the coverage of an even more powerful divide-and-conquer schema (with support of compound induction parameters, . . . ) and of other schemata (tupling generalization [14], descending generalization [14], . . . ). Ideally, the schema would be a parameter of the system, and thus constitute a real declarative bias.

Another plan is to integrate DIALOGS with a post-synthesis transformation/optimization tool; the preference will of course go to using schema-guided transformers [14], as these can exploit much of the additional information (such as "what is the instance of each operator?") generated by DIALOGS.

### Acknowledgments
Many thanks to Esra Erdem for numerous stimulating discussions about the MSG Method. The anonymous reviewers were constructive in suggesting some improvements of the presentation. Esra Erdem, Halime Büyükyıldız, and Serap Yılmaz provided useful feedback on an earlier version of this paper, and contributed to the implementation of a first prototype of the DIALOGS system, as well as to the ordeal of typesetting this document in LaTeX.

# References

1. Angluin, D.: Queries and concept learning. *Machine Learning* 2(4):319–342, 1988.
2. Bergadano, F., Gunetti, D.: Learning clauses by tracing derivations. In S. Wrobel (ed), *Proc. of ILP'94*, pp. 11–29. GMD-Studien Nr. 237, Sankt Augustin, 1994.

3. Biermann, A.W.: Dealing with search. In A.W. Biermann, G. Guiho, and Y. Kodratoff (eds), *Automatic Program Construction Techniques*, pp. 375–392. Macmillan, 1984.

4. Boström, H., Idestam-Almquist, P.: Specialization of logic programs by pruning SLD-trees. In S. Wrobel (ed), *Proc. of ILP'94*, pp. 31–48. GMD-Studien Nr. 237, Sankt Augustin, 1994.

5. Cohen, W.C.: Compiling prior knowledge into an explicit bias. In *Proc. of ICML'92*, pages 102–110. Morgan Kaufmann, 1992.

6. De Raedt, L., Bruynooghe, M.: Belief updating from integrity constraints and queries. *Artificial Intelligence* 53(2-3):291–307, February 1992.

7. De Raedt, L., Bruynooghe, M.: Interactive concept learning and constructive induction by analogy. *Machine Learning* 8:107–150, 1992.

8. Erdem, E.: *An MSG Method for Inductive Logic Program Synthesis.* Senior Project Final Report, Bilkent University, Ankara (Turkey), May 1996.

9. Flener, P.: *Logic Program Synthesis from Incomplete Information.* Kluwer, 1995.

10. Flener, P.: *Predicate Invention in Inductive Program Synthesis.* TR BU-CEIS-9509, Bilkent University, Ankara (Turkey), 1995. Submitted.

11. Flener, P.: *Synthesis of Logic Algorithm Schemata.* TR BU-CEIS-96xx, Bilkent University, Ankara (Turkey), 1996. Update of TR BU-CEIS-9502. In preparation.

12. Flener, P., Deville, Y.: Logic program synthesis from incomplete specifications. *Journal of Symbolic Computation* 15(5-6):775–805, May/June 1993.

13. Flener, P., Popelínský, L.: On the use of inductive reasoning in program synthesis. In L. Fribourg and F. Turini (eds), *Proc. of META/LOPSTR'94*. LNCS 883:69–87, Springer-Verlag, 1994.

14. Flener, P., Deville, Y.: *Logic Program Transformation through Generalization Schemata.* TR BU-CEIS-96yy, Bilkent University, Ankara (Turkey), 1996. In preparation. Extended abstract in M. Proietti (ed), *Proc. of LOPSTR'95.* LNCS 1048:171–173, Springer-Verlag, 1996.

15. Hamfelt, A., Fischer-Nilsson, J.: Inductive metalogic programming. In S. Wrobel (ed), *Proc. of ILP'94*, pp. 85–96. GMD-Studien Nr. 237, Sankt Augustin, 1994.

16. Kietz, J.U., Wrobel, S.: Controlling the complexity of learning in logic through syntactic and task-oriented models. In S. Muggleton (ed), *Inductive Logic Programming*, pp. 335–359. Volume APIC-38, Academic Press, 1992.

17. Lapointe, S., Ling, C., Matwin, S.: Constructive inductive logic programming. In S. Muggleton (ed), *Proc. of ILP'93*, pp. 255–264. TR IJS-DP-6707, J. Stefan Institute, Ljubljana (Slovenia), 1993.

18. Muggleton, S., Buntine, W.: Machine invention of first-order predicates by inverting resolution. In *Proc. of ICML'88*, pages 339–352. Morgan Kaufmann, 1988.

19. Plotkin, G.D.: A note on inductive generalization. In B. Meltzer and D. Michie (eds), *Machine Intelligence* 5:153–163. Edinburgh University Press, 1970.

20. Stahl, I.: *Predicate invention in ILP: An overview.* TR 1993/06, Fakultät Informatik, Universität Stuttgart (Germany), 1993.

21. Sterling, L.S., Kirschenbaum, M.: Applying techniques to skeletons. In J.-M. Jacquet (ed), *Constructing Logic Programs*, pp. 127–140. John Wiley, 1993.

22. Tinkham, N.L.: *Induction of Schemata for Program Synthesis.* Ph.D. Thesis, Duke University, Durham (NC, USA), 1990.

# Appendix: The DIALOGS Algorithm

```
% Interactive synthesis of a recursive (divide-and-conquer) pgm.
dialogs <-
  set interaction mode to `aloud´,
  read(PredDecl), % declaration for r, the top-level predicate
  Hints = {},
  StartPgm = {},
  dialogs(PredDecl,Hints,StartPgm,Pgm),
  write(Pgm),
  if the specifier wants more programs then fail else true.


% Synthesis (in case of detected or conjectured necessary
% predicate invention) of a recursive (divide-and-conquer) pgm
% for the current predicate declared in PredDecl, using Hints
% (if any), which program is used by and thus added to the
% context program StartPgm to yield the final program Pgm.
dialogs(PredDecl,Hints,StartPgm,Pgm) <-
 % phase 1
  NewClauses = a set of divide-and-conquer clauses (according to
    Template 2) for the current predicate (which is declared in
    PredDecl), where only the DecR operator has been instantiated,
    according to Hints (if any),
  CurrPgm = StartPgm union NewClauses,
 % phase 2
  abduce(CurrPgm,DSev,DPCev),
  induce(DSev,DPCev,DSinsts,DPCinsts),
  evaluate(DSinsts,DPCinsts,CurrPgm,Pgm).


% Interactive abduction of evidence sets DSev and DPCev for the
% uninstantiated operators DS-R and DPC-R in program Pgm.
abduce(Pgm,DSev,DPCev) <-
  DSev = {}, DPCev = {},    % initializations
  as often as ``needed´´ do
    construct Goal, % a goal for the top-level predicate
    demo(Pgm,Goal,Assumptions,Residue),
    ask(Goal,Assumptions,Residue,DS-exs,DPC-exs),
    DSev = DSev union DS-exs,
    DPCev = DPCev union DPC-exs
  od.


% An SLD-refutation of <- Goal in theory Pgm (augmented with
% shortcut clauses from previous queries) generates the conj
% Assumption, but is blocked by the unresolvability of the
% unit-goal Residue, because it has a predicate variable.
demo(Pgm,Goal,Assumption,Residue) <- ...
```

```
% The set DS-exs (resp. DPC-exs) contains the tuples for the
% predicate variable DS-R (resp. DPC-R) in second-order atom
% Residue, which tuples are extracted from the answer (by the
% specifier or by an oracle based on previous answers) to the
% query under what conditions atom Goal must hold, assuming
% that conjunction Assumption holds.
ask(Goal,Assumption,Residue,DS-exs,DPC-exs) <- ...


% Inductive generalization of the evidence sets DSev and DPCev
% into lists of ``plausible'' instances (according to the
% admissibility criteria) DSinsts and DPCinsts for the operators
% DS-R and DPC-R.
induce(DSev,DPCev,DSinsts,DPCinsts) <-        % revised MSG Method
  partition(DPCev,DPCcliques),                % step 1 (as in text)
  prune(DPCcliks,NewDPCcliks,DSev,NewDSev),   % step 2 (as in text)
  buildInsts(NewDPCcliks,DPCinsts),           % step 3 (revised)
  partition(NewDSev,DScliks),                 % step 4 (revised)
  buildInsts(DScliks,DSinsts).                % step 4 (cont´d)


% Heuristic-based acceptance or rejection of the induced
% instances DSinsts and DPCinsts for the uninstantiated operators
% DS-R and DPC-R in second-order logic program CurrPgm, so as to
% instantiate the latter into a first-order program Pgm.
evaluate(DSinsts,DPCinsts,CurrPgm,Pgm) <-
  if #DPCinsts=0 then  % reject!
    construct NewPredDecl    % decl. for dpcR, the new curr. pred.
    construct NewHints,      % hints for dpcR
    in the last two clauses of CurrPgm do
      instantiate the DS-Rj (as described in text),
      particularize v accordingly,
      instantiate DPC-R to dpcR,
      particularize w to 1
    yielding NewStartPgm,
    set interaction mode to `mute´,
    dialogs(NewPredDecl,NewHints,NewStartPgm,Pgm) % recursion!
  else   % accept!
    in the last two clauses of CurrPgm do
      particularize v to #DSinsts,
      for 1<=j<=v do instantiate DS-Rj using DSinsts[j],
      particularize w to #DPCinsts,
      for 1<=k<=w do instantiate DPC-Rk using DPCinsts[k]
    yielding Pgm.
```

# Relational Knowledge Discovery in Databases

Hendrik Blockeel and Luc De Raedt

Katholieke Universiteit Leuven
Department of Computer Science
Celestijnenlaan 200A
3001 Heverlee
e-mail: {Hendrik.Blockeel, Luc.DeRaedt}@cs.kuleuven.ac.be

**Abstract.** In this paper, we indicate some possible applications of ILP or similar techniques in the knowledge discovery field, and then discuss several methods for adapting and linking ILP-systems to relational database systems. The proposed methods range from "pure ILP" to "based on techniques originating in ILP". We show that it is both easy and advantageous to adapt ILP-systems in this way.

## 1 Introduction

It is common knowledge that in the machine learning field, ILP has turned out to be very useful for classification problems in structured domains. Similar problems can be found in the knowledge discovery field. For instance, finding integrity constraints holding in a database closely corresponds to finding classification rules with ILP, as we will show later on in this paper.

In the past, research on knowledge discovery in databases (KDD) has focused mainly on propositional techniques; this implies that relationships between the attributes of one tuple can be found, but no relationships between several tuples of one or more relations. It seems that this is an important limitation, since problems such as finding integrity constraints cannot be solved using propositional techniques (at least not in an easy way).

In this paper, we show that some problems in knowledge discovery are closely related to typical ILP classification problems, and that therefore ILP or ILP-like methods are useful to solve them (section 2). We then show in section 3 how ILP can be adapted for this kind of problems, and eventually (in section 4) arrive at an algorithm for KDD that searches for regularities expressed in relational algebra instead of logic. Such an algorithm strictly does not fall in the class of ILP algorithms but it does use techniques based on ILP. In section 5, finally, we present some conclusions.

## 2 What ILP can offer to relational databases

In the machine learning field, the advantages and disadvantages of ILP vs. other techniques are well-known, and the subject of hot debates. Typical for non-ILP systems is that they try to find rules involving several attributes of an example. Each example is described using a fixed number of attributes for which values are given. The representational power of these techniques corresponds to that of propositional logic. Therefore, we will also use the term "propositional techniques".

When rules have to be found that involve several examples, or when the examples do not have a fixed number of attributes, these propositional techniques are no longer applicable, as they lack the required representational power. ILP systems, on the other hand, can represent this kind of data and rules, since they use first order predicate logic as a representation formalism, which is more powerful.

If we translate these properties to database terminology, then we can say that propositional systems find rules involving one relation, while ILP systems can also find rules involving several relations.

As a database typically contains more than one relation, it seems clear that a lot of interesting rules are simply not considered when using propositional techniques. Nevertheless, research in the data mining community has focused mainly on these techniques (see e.g. [5]). Finding inter-relation rules can sometimes be simulated by computing the universal relation (i.e. joining all the relations into one relation), but this may be a very costly operation, and the universal relation can be very large. For this reason, it seems that ILP offers interesting opportunities to data mining.

We will now analyze in more detail one problem where ILP is useful for KDD, and on which our group is currently working. We address the following questions: in what way is some relation $R$ related to a set of relations $\mathcal{R} = \{R_1, \ldots, R_n\}$? Can $R$ be computed from $\mathcal{R}$, and if so, what is the exact way of computing it? If it cannot, are there any other interesting relationships between $R$ and $\mathcal{R}$?

These questions are interesting because if $R$ can be expressed in terms of $\{R_1, \ldots, R_n\}$, then it is redundant; instead of listing it explicitly, it is probably better to define it in terms of the other relations. If $R$ cannot be expressed exactly in terms of $R_1, \ldots, R_n$, it may still be interesting to find some expression that defines a (preferably large) *subset* of $R$ in terms of the other relations; in that case, we could say the expression is an overly specific description of the relation $R$. Analogously, an overly general description of $R$ (an expression that computes a superset of $R$) may be of interest, if a correct one cannot be found. Such relationships may not enable the system to compute $R$ from $R_1, \ldots, R_n$, but they do impose certain integrity constraints on the database. They identify new relations $R'$, computed from $R_1, \ldots, R_n$, for which an inclusion constraint holds between $R$ and $R'$ (in one direction or another).

We will from now on use the following terminology to distinguish relations that are computed from other relations, from those that are defined by listing all their tuples.

**Definition 1.** A relation is defined *extensionally* if it is defined by exhaustively listing all its tuples.

**Definition 2.** A relation is defined *intensionally* if it is defined in terms of other relations by a relational algebra expression.

In relational databases, relations defined extensionally are usually called *tables*, while relations defined intensionally are called *views*. Intensional definitions have the advantage that some redundancy is removed, and possible inconsistencies are avoided; on the other hand, answering queries about the relation becomes more expensive because (part of) the relation has to be computed instead of being retrieved from storage. In many cases, an intensional definition will nevertheless be preferred. However, finding such an intensional definition requires establishing the correct relationship between the relation and other relations, and expressing it in some way (e.g. relational algebra or SQL).

A theoretical answer to whether $R$ can at all be expressed in terms of a set of relations $\mathcal{R}$ using the relational algebra, was given years ago, see for instance [10]. However, there does not seem to be an easy way of computing the answer to this question (i.e. one that is significantly faster than just trying to find such an expression and eventually failing if none exists). Therefore, the algorithms we will consider later on in this text will not try to check beforehand whether an intensional definition of a relation exists or not, but just hope there is one, and try to find it.

## Corresponding problems in ILP

Two settings can be distinguished in ILP. In the classical setting, logical clauses are induced that together form a complete and consistent hypothesis defining a concept. Formally, if $H$ is the induced hypothesis, $B$ is background knowledge that may be available, and $E^+$ and $E^-$ are sets of positive and negative examples, then the following two statements must hold:

$$\forall e^+ \in E^+ : H \cup B \models e^+$$
$$\nexists e^- \in E^- : H \cup B \models e^-$$

The hypothesis can then be used for classification of unseen examples. Most ILP systems (e.g. Progol [9], FOIL [11]) use this setting.

Another setting is what we call *characteristic* ILP. Clauses are induced that are valid for the given data; this means that there should not exist a substitution for which the clause is false. Formally, if $c$ is a clause, $B$ is the background knowledge and $E$ a set of examples (we do not distinguish positive and negative examples in this setting), then $c$ is valid iff

$$c \text{ is true in } \mathcal{M}(B \cup E)$$

(where $\mathcal{M}(B \cup \mathcal{E})$ denotes the minimal Herbrand model of $B \cup E$).

Every clause describes the data in some way, and the set of all valid clauses forms a maximally informative description of the data. ILP systems using this setting exist (e.g. CLAUDIEN[1], ICL[2]) but are far less numerous than systems using the classical setting.

There is a straightforward relationship between finding an intensional definition for a relation, and classification of tuples. If $R$ is considered to represent some class of tuples $(v_1, \ldots, v_k)$, then the expression of $R$ in terms of $\{R_1, \ldots, R_n\}$

gives a means of deciding whether a specific tuple $(v_1, \ldots, v_k)$ belongs to $R$ (i.e. classifying the tuple), using only the information in the relations $R_1, \ldots, R_n$. We can therefore conclude that the problem of finding intensional definitions is closely related to the classification setting within ILP.[1]

On the other hand, if an intensional definition cannot be found, but the expressions that are induced are considered as integrity constraints, then we would like to find as many such constraints as possible (in order to describe the allowed database instance as precisely as possible). This corresponds to the characteristic ILP setting.

We have hereby established a link between typical ILP problems and finding intensional definitions or integrity constraints in databases. ¿From this we can expect that ILP can easily be adapted for the tasks considered. It is also clear that the kind of relationships discussed here cannot be discovered using propositional techniques, as they involve several relations. Thus, we conclude that ILP is not only well fit for the applications we consider, it is crucial that a technique of comparable power be used.

# 3 Simple bridges between ILP and relational databases

In this and the following sections, we discuss several ways in which ILP systems can be linked to databases, in increasing order of adaptation of the ILP system to the database. We first consider some rather trivial methods.

## 3.1 Conversion of data

ILP systems use logic to represent the data, the hypotheses, etc. The data are usually presented to the system in Prolog syntax, i.e. as a text file containing a number of facts in the form $\mathtt{pred}(arg_1, \ldots, arg_n)$.

When the data are available in a relational database, they can easily be transformed to Prolog syntax (for each relation, a set of facts is written with each fact corresponding to one tuple), and are then ready to be processed by an ILP system. This transformation can be seen as a pre-processing tool for the ILP system. This is the easiest way to use ILP for knowledge discovery in a relational database: nothing has to be changed to the ILP engine itself.

## 3.2 A link to databases at the Prolog level

As they work with a logical representation, many ILP systems are implemented in Prolog (e.g. CLAUDIEN[1], ICL[2]), or, when they are implemented in another

---

[1] It should be mentioned here that most ILP systems work with positive and negative examples, while in a database only positive examples are given. The closed world assumption has to be made in this case. Recently, however, more attention has been given to ILP systems that learn from positive examples only (this is often called learning in a non-monotonic setting; see for instance [1]). These systems are the ones for which the analogy holds best.

language, use libraries that implement many features of a Prolog system (e.g. [9]). Some Prolog systems can be linked to relational databases. This means that part of the knowledge base is not read from a Prolog file, but is assumed to be in the database to which the Prolog system is linked. The internal database of the Prolog system is then augmented with the external database in a transparent way. When a literal $p(a, b)$ occurs somewhere, and the predicate $p$ corresponds to a relation $P$ in the relational database, then Prolog will send a query to the relational database system to determine wether the tuple $(a, b)$ is in relation $P$. If this is the case, the literal succeeds; otherwise it fails.

When an ILP system runs in a Prolog environment that supports this kind of link, it is not necessary to write the data in the database to a text file in the correct format, and then load this file into the system; it is sufficient to tell the system that those predicates can be found in the relational database.

This method to use ILP for knowledge discovery in a relational database is very straightforward; if the Prolog system underlying the ILP system supports links with database systems, the ILP system can work with the database without any changes at all, except some declarations to open and close the database. If the ILP system is not implemented in Prolog, or if the underlying Prolog system does not support links with databases, a significant extension of the system is of course required.

When compared with the first method, this method has the disadvantage that it is probably slower, as access to a relational database is needed for every literal that is to be tested, while with the first method one conversion is done beforehand, and afterwards all the data will be loaded in memory. On the other hand, a database may be too large to be loaded into the Prolog system; in that case, this method offers a simple alternative.

### 3.3 A link to databases at the clause level

We know that there is a straightforward relationship between first order logic and relational databases: a predicate is just a relation between its arguments. Similarly, there is a relationship between logical clauses and relational database queries (at least for the usual query languages, e.g. relational algebra, SQL). For ease of discussion, we will restrict ourselves here to the SQL query language.

In a clause, every literal corresponds to a tuple of a relation. The conjunction of a number of literals can be computed as a join, where the conditions on the join are given by the variables that the literals have in common. For instance: the query

```
?- parent(X,Y), parent(Y,'Laure').
```

is written in SQL as

```
SELECT P1.parent, P1.child
FROM PARENT P1, P2
WHERE P1.child = P2.parent AND P2.child = 'Laure'
```

This shows that logical clauses can easily be transformed into relational algebra formulas or SQL-statements. Discovery systems exploiting this property already exist; see e.g. [7, 8], where a coupling between the ILP-system RDT [6] and the Oracle database system is described. The resulting RDT/DB system makes use of SQL-queries akin to those given further in this paper. Recently, a preliminary version of a coupling between CLAUDIEN and Oracle has also been implemented.

ILP systems, when traversing the search space, check clauses for correctness, and associate heuristic values with them. In the characteristic setting, a clause $B \leftarrow H$ is correct if the query $\leftarrow B \wedge \neg H$ fails. When a clause is incorrect, a heuristic value can be given to it, indicating how close to correctness it is.

The heuristic value of a clause

$$P(\ldots) \leftarrow Q_1(\ldots), \ldots, Q_m(\ldots)$$

is usually computed as a function $f(p, n, c)$ where $p$ is the number of positive examples predicted by the clause to be positive, $n$ is the number of negatives predicted to be positive, and $c$ is the complexity of the clause. It is clear that a clause is closer to correctness when $n$ is smaller; also the usefulness of the clause increases with $p$ (a clause that predicts many positive examples is better than one that predicts few, even if both are correct, i.e. predict no negative examples to be positive).

The computation of $p$ and $n$ is normally done by the ILP system itself. The CLAUDIEN system, for instance, which is implemented in Prolog, will count how many times the body succeeds (by backtracking over the body until all solutions have been found), and how many times the body and head succeed together. If we call these numbers $s_b$ and $s_{bh}$, then this system computes $p$ and $n$ as $\hat{p} = s_{bh}$ and $\hat{n} = s_b - s_{bh}$. In fact, $p = \hat{p}$ and $n = \hat{n}$, only if all the literals in the clause are determinate; otherwise, the number of positive and negative *substitutions* of the clause are counted, and several substitutions can be found for one example.[2] But for the purpose of using them in a heuristic, $\hat{p}$ and $\hat{n}$ work well enough.

Now, if we link the ILP system to a database, all the data are stored in relations, and one relation corresponds to each predicate. The numbers $s_b$ and $s_{bh}$ can then be obtained in SQL using the following queries:

| | |
|---|---|
| $s_b$ | SELECT count(*)<br>FROM Q1, Q2, ..., Qn<br>WHERE *conditions* |
| $s_{bh}$ | SELECT count(*)<br>FROM Q1, Q2, ..., Qn, P<br>WHERE *conditions* |

Although these queries have been written with the CLAUDIEN setting in mind, they can easily be adapted in such a way that they count examples, not substitutions, by changing the queries into:

---

[2] Counting examples is not appropriate in the CLAUDIEN context, where the head of a clause can consist of several literals; the meaning of the term "example" is therefore hard to define here.

| | |
|---|---|
| $s_b$ | SELECT count(distinct *)<br>FROM SELECT A1, ..., Am<br>    FROM Q1, Q2, ..., Qn<br>    WHERE *conditions* |
| $s_{bh}$ | SELECT count(distinct *)<br>FROM SELECT A1, ..., Am<br>    FROM Q1, Q2, ..., Qn, P<br>    WHERE *conditions* |

where the $A_i$ are all the attributes that occur in $P$.

In both cases, the second query will of course be computed using the intermediate relation computed by the first one; the work of joining the $Q_i$ should not be redone. Also note that SQL does not only compute the relations that contain the solutions to the queries $B$ and $B \wedge H$; it immediately counts the tuples in them. This way, the heuristic value of the clause is computed by the database system itself.

If we compare this approach with the previous one (a link to databases on the Prolog level), then there is a considerable efficiency gain:

- Instead of using the database server for each literal in the clause, and backtracking over the clause, which results in a very large number of database accesses, the database is only accessed once for each clause that is to be investigated. This results in much less overhead.
- Database systems have many ways of optimizing queries that generally are not used by Prolog compilers (e.g. performing the most selective queries first, using advanced indexation techniques, ...). This means that the heuristic value can in most cases be computed much more efficiently by the database system than could be done in Prolog.

When compared with the first approach (loading all the data into the Prolog system), there is of course a small disadvantage here, because a database has to be accessed (i.e. data are retrieved from secondary storage instead of main memory), but for large databases, we expect this disadvantage to be outweighed by the efficiency gain obtained by letting an advanced database system compute the heuristic values instead of implementing this in Prolog. We have not yet been able to confirm this experimentally, however.

## 4 Redefining the search space

In the previous sections it was shown that the link between ILP and a relational database can be established on the data level (conversion of data to logical representation), on the Prolog level (database access is completely transparant to the Prolog user), and on the level of the ILP system (transforming whole clauses into SQL queries).

We now go one step further, and in fact hereby leave the area of ILP. What we propose, is that the ILP techniques can be lifted to a search space consisting of database queries, instead of logical clauses. In other words, the discovery system does not use any logical representations anymore, and therefore strictly should not be called an ILP system; but it still uses essentially the same techniques.

In this section, we show how a hypothesis space consisting of relational algebra expressions can be generated and traversed. This section contains mainly ideas for future work; an algorithm is presented, but it has not been implemented yet.

## 4.1 Some results from relational algebra

We first mention some results known from database theory that will be useful later on. These results can be found in most standard works on database theory, e.g. [4].

Several operators are defined in the relational algebra, but it can be proven that they can all be defined using the following five operators (see also [10]):

- the cartesian product of two relations ($R \times S$)
- the union of two relations having the same arity ($R \cup S$)
- the projection of a relation on certain attributes ($\pi_{i_1,\ldots,i_n}(R)$)
- the selection from a relation of those tuples for which the value of two attributes $i_1$ and $i_2$ are the same ($\sigma_{i_1=i_2}(R)$)
- the selection from a relation of those tuples for which the value of two attributes $i_1$ and $i_2$ are different ($\sigma_{i_1 \neq i_2}(R)$)

(We will assume that in a relation, attributes are referred to using the number of the column corresponding to the attribute; e.g. $\sigma_{1=3}$ selects from a relation those tuples which have the same values for the attributes in column 1 and column 3. This way, we can avoid possible problems with renaming of attributes that are irrelevant to our discussion.)

The above implies that there is no loss of generality if we restrict ourselves to expressions that make use of only these operators. It is possible to go even further: every expression using these five operators (and therefore every expression using any relational algebra operator) can be written as a succession of cartesian products, selections, projections and unions, in this specific order. This follows from the following properties:

- if $\pi_A(R \cup S)$ is defined, then $\pi_A(R) \cup \pi_A(S)$ is defined and $\pi_A(R) \cup \pi_A(S) = \pi_A(R \cup S)$
- if $\sigma_C(R \cup S)$ is defined, then $\sigma_C(R) \cup \sigma_C(S)$ is defined and $\sigma_C(R) \cup \sigma_C(S) = \sigma_C(R \cup S)$
- if $(R \cup S) \times T$ is defined, then $(R \times T) \cup (S \times T)$ is defined and $(R \times T) \cup (S \times T) = (R \cup S) \times T$
- if $\sigma_C(\pi_A(R))$ is defined, then $\pi_A(\sigma_C(R))$ is defined, and $\sigma_C(\pi_A(R)) = \pi_A(\sigma_C(R))$
- if $R \times \pi_A(S)$ is defined, then there exists an $A'$ such that $\pi_{A'}(R \times S)$ is defined, and $R \times \pi_A(S) = \pi_{A'}(R \times S)$.
- if $R \times \sigma_C(S)$ is defined, then $\sigma_C(R \times S)$ is defined, and $R \times \sigma_C(S) = \sigma_C(R \times S)$.

The first three properties show that the union operator can always be moved outwards, the following two show that the projection operator can always be moved outwards but not past the union operator, and the last property shows that selection can be moved outwards but not past the projection or union operator. After all the operators have been moved, and considering the fact that consecutive projections can be written as one projection and consecutive selections as one selection, an expression of the form

$$\bigcup_i \pi_{A_i}(\sigma_{C_i}(R_{i,1} \times \cdots \times R_{i,n_i}))$$

emerges.

This property is important because it allows to reduce the size of the search space without giving up completeness. If the search space contains expressions where the operators can occur in any order, then many expressions are investigated that are actually equivalent, but written in a different way. This means that a lot of redundant computations are done. If only expressions of the above form are considered, this redundancy is removed, while the completeness of the search space is preserved.

Note that we write the expressions in this way, only in order to define the search space. When the expression is actually computed for some database instance, the order of the operators will be changed by the database system itself, in such a way that the result can be computed as efficiently as possible. In other words, the database takes care of the efficient computation of one single expression automatically; what we need to worry about, is that no redundant expressions are generated.

## 4.2  An algorithm for finding relationships between relations

ILP systems typically find a set of rules of the form

$$p(X_1, \ldots, X_n) \leftarrow L_1, \ldots, L_n$$

where each rule predicts some facts for $p$, and the set as a whole predicts all the facts of $p$. With this kind of rule corresponds one specific kind of relationship between a relation $R$ (predicate $p$) and a set of relations $R_i$, namely the fact that for some expression $E(R_1, \ldots, R_n)$, it holds that $E(R_1, \ldots, R_n) \subseteq R$. A program consisting of a set of rules $r_i$ is then equivalent to the union of the $E_i$ corresponding to each $r_i$. If the program is complete, then $\bigcup_i E_i(R_{i,1}, \ldots, R_{i,n_i}) = R$.

The algorithm in Figure 1 searches for all the expressions $E_i$ such that

$$E_i(R_1, \ldots, R_n) \subseteq R$$

given as input $R$ and $\mathcal{R} = \{R_1, \ldots, R_n\}$; i.e. it finds a number of (possibly overly specific) descriptions of $R$. These expressions are all of the form $\pi_A(\sigma_C(R_{i,1} \times \cdots \times R_{i,n_i}))$.

The algorithm takes some parameter $N$ as an upper bound on the complexity of the expressions that can be derived. The parameters that define the kind of expressions that can be derived, all together, are called the *language bias* of the algorithm. For this algorithm, $N$ is part of the language bias, as well as the set $\mathcal{R}$.

An exact definition of $R$, if one exists, can be among the $E_i$. If not, $R$ might still be expressible as the union of some or all of the $E_i$. If the union of all the $E_i$ still produces a proper subset of $R$, then $R$ cannot be defined within the language bias used. Since the search space is complete (with respect to given complexity bounds), it follows that if there exists a relationship between $R$ and $\mathcal{R}$ that is expressable in relational algebra, it will be found.

```
find_rules(R, {R₁, ..., Rₙ}, N):
    Sol := ∅
    ∀k = 1, ..., N:
        ∀i₁, ..., iₖ:
            E' := ×ᵏⱼ₌₁Rᵢⱼ
            R' := eval(E')
            P := {πₐ|πₐ(R') ∩ R ≠ ∅ ∧ arity(πₐ(R')) = arity(R)}
            ∀πₐ ∈ P:
                refine(πₐ, E', ∅)

refine(πₐ, E', C):
    if πₐ(σ_C(eval(E'))) ⊄ R then
        ∀i, j where (i = j) ∉ C ∧ (i ≠ j) ∉ C
            refine(πₐ, E', C ∪ {i = j})
            refine(πₐ, E', C ∪ {i ≠ j})
    else
        Sol := Sol ∪ {πₐ(σ_C(E'))}
```

**Fig. 1.** An algorithm for finding relationships between relations

Algorithm 1 works as follows. It considers all subsets of $\mathcal{R}$ of cardinality at most $N$. For each such set, it computes the cartesian product of all the $R_i$ in the subset, and finds all the projections $\pi_A$ onto $r$ attributes (with $r$ the arity of $R$) for which the resulting relation has at least one tuple in common with $R$. (If it has no tuples in common with $R$, then it is not possible to find a subset of this relation that is also a subset of $R$, except the empty relation, which is a trivial case.)

Note that the algorithm will compute *expressions*, not the resulting relations; therefore, when we write $E' := \langle expression \rangle$, this means that the expression itself is stored in $E'$. The evaluation of an expression, when needed, is denoted explicitly using the *eval* function.

For each $R''$ for which $R'' \cap R \neq \emptyset$, it may be possible, using the selection operator $\sigma$, to find a non-empty subset of $R''$ that is also a subset of $R$. However, this selection operator should be applied before the projection operator, not afterwards, in order to preserve the completeness of the search space.

The *refine* procedure in Figure 1 finds every selection $\sigma_C$ for which $\pi_A(\sigma_C(\times_i R_i)) \subseteq R$, and $C$ is a minimal set of conditions (i.e. leaving out one condition from $C$ will not produce a subset of $R$). For each $\sigma_C$ for which this holds, the expression $\pi_A(\sigma_C(\times_i R_i))$ is added to the solution set *Sol*.

This algorithm is written from the point of view of characteristic learning: it returns every expression with which a non-empty subset of $R$ is computed. When the aim is simply to define $R$ in terms of the other relations, using as simple an expression as possible, one can of course first generate all these expressions and then find a minimal subset of them such that the union of the expressions in the subset is complete; but this method, although correct, is quite inefficient. A covering approach, as followed by many ILP algorithms, is often preferable. The algorithm can easily be adapted to this end: using a FOIL-like covering approach, it would select at each time that expression that results in as large a subset of $R$ as possible (not counting the tuples that were already produced by other expressions), and repeatedly traverse the search space in search for such an expression until $R$ has been covered completely. The use of heuristics to guide this search can also easily be incorporated.

## 4.3   Some comments

Although the above algorithm was given for relational algebra, it is obvious that a similar algorithm can be given for SQL statements. An algorithm searching an SQL search space would be of more practical value than one using relational algebra, as most database systems use SQL, not relational algebra. Therefore, an SQL using equivalent of Algorithm 1 seems more worthwhile to be implemented than the algorithm itself. SQL, however, offers many more possibilities than relational algebra, e.g. grouping constructs, counting, ...It seems that a good way to investigate SQL search spaces would be to start from constructs that correspond to those offered by the relational algebra, and then adding more features.

When we take a look at the approach proposed here, some interesting topics are raised:

- The proposed algorithm uses a very simple language bias: there is simply a bound on the complexity, and a specification of the relations that can be used. More elaborate language specifications could be based on those used in ILP systems (e.g. $\mathcal{D}$LAB[3]), but there will probably be enough differences to justify some specific research on, for instance, language specifications for SQL.
- The search space is expected to be organized differently than the clausal logic search spaces. For instance, adding a literal to a clause is considered to be a refinement step in ILP, but in the algorithm we propose, the relations to be used are chosen in advance, and refinement from then on consists of adding selection operators (in logic, this corresponds to unifying variables or adding the condition that they should not be equal). The queries are

equivalent with logical clauses, but ordered differently. This may result in other solutions being found, if only a subset of all the rules is to be returned (as with the covering approach).

- The notion of simplicity of an expression is different in relational algebra than in logic. For instance, when the same variable occurs several times in a logical clause, this is not considered to make the clause more complex (one could even argue that the clause is less complex, as it uses less variables). In relational algebra, on the other hand, unification of variables corresponds to an explicit condition that two values must be equal, and the addition of this condition makes the clause more complex. This is one example of the fact that desirable properties of algebraic expressions may differ from those of logical clauses, and that it is better to work with the expressions themselves instead of with clauses that are equivalent to them.

- Relational algebra is less expressive than first order logic, because there is no equivalent for recursive definitions. We consider this not to be a problem, however, because non-recursive query language such as SQL are used very frequently to query relational databases, and for most databases they have enough expressive power. Moreover, a recursive logical clause cannot be transformed to SQL, so even if a relation could be defined recursively in terms of other relations and itself, there would be no way to write an SQL-view defining this relation.

## 5   Conclusions

Finding an intensional definition for a relation, or investigating which integrity constraints hold in a database, are knowledge discovery tasks that bear a large resemblance to typical ILP classification or discovery tasks. Therefore one expects that ILP-techniques are very suitable for this kind of knowledge discovery.

We have given an overview of several ways in which ILP systems can be linked to relational databases, in order to solve the problems mentioned. These methods range from trivial conversion of relational data to logic, to transferring existing ILP techniques to other domains. We have also discussed some advantages and disadvantages of the different approaches. We are convinced that the more sophisticated approaches will offer several advantages, one of which is efficiency; and this supports our belief that ILP techniques are useful for knowledge discovery in large databases.

Although this paper has only considered some rather specific knowledge discovery tasks, we believe that the advantages discussed here will hold in general, and that efficient methods for general-purpose knowledge discovery in databases can easily be derived from the existing ILP-techniques, without any need for the development of algorithms specifically designed for one task.

# 6 Acknowledgements

Hendrik Blockeel is supported by the Flemish Institute for the Promotion of Scientific and Technological Research in the Industry (IWT). Luc De Raedt is supported by the Belgian National Fund for Scientific Research. This work is also part of the European Community Esprit project no. 20237, Inductive Logic Programming 2.

# References

1. L. De Raedt and L. Dehaspe. Clausal discovery. Forthcoming, 1995.
2. L. De Raedt and W. Van Laer. Inductive constraint logic. In *Proceedings of the 5th Workshop on Algorithmic Learning Theory*, Lecture Notes in Artificial Intelligence. Springer-Verlag, 1995.
3. L. Dehaspe and L. De Raedt. DLAB: a declarative language bias for concept learning and knowledge discovery engines. Technical Report CW-214, Department of Computer Science, Katholieke Universiteit Leuven, October 1995.
4. R. Elmasri and S. B. Navathe. *Fundamentals of Database Systems*. The Benjamin/Cummings Publishing Company, 2nd edition, 1989.
5. U. M. Fayyad and R. Uthurusamy, editors. *Proceedings of the First International Conference on Knowledge Discovery and Data Mining*. AAAI Press, August 1995.
6. J-U. Kietz and S. Wrobel. Controlling the complexity of learning in logic through syntactic and task-oriented models. In S. Muggleton, editor, *Inductive logic programming*, pages 335–359. Academic Press, 1992.
7. G. Lindner. Anwendung des lernverfahrens RDT auf eine relationele datenbank. Master's thesis, Universität Dortmund, August 1994. In German.
8. G. Lindner and K. Morik. Coupling a relational learning algorithm with a database system. In Y. Kodratoff, G. Nakhaeizadeh, and C. Taylor, editors, *Workshop Notes of the MLnet Familiarization Workshop on Statistics, Machine Learning and Knowledge Discovery in Databases*, pages 163–168, 1995.
9. S. Muggleton. Inverse entailment and progol. *New Generation Computing*, 13, 1995.
10. J. Paredaens. On the expressive power of the relational algebra. *Information Processing Letters*, 7(2):107–111, February 1978.
11. J.R. Quinlan. FOIL: A midterm report. In P. Brazdil, editor, *Proceedings of the 6th European Conference on Machine Learning*, Lecture Notes in Artificial Intelligence. Springer-Verlag, 1993.

# Efficient $\theta$-Subsumption Based on Graph Algorithms

Tobias Scheffer, Ralf Herbrich and Fritz Wysotzki

Technische Universität Berlin, Artificial Intelligence Research Group, Sekr. FR 5-8, Franklinstr. 28/29, D-10587 Berlin, email: scheffer@cs.tu-berlin.de

**Abstract.** The $\theta$-subsumption problem is crucial to the efficiency of ILP learning systems. We discuss two $\theta$-subsumption algorithms based on strategies for preselecting suitable matching literals. The class of clauses, for which subsumption becomes polynomial, is a superset of the deterministic clauses. We further map the general problem of $\theta$-subsumption to a certain problem of finding a clique of fixed size in a graph, and in return show that a specialization of the pruning strategy of the Carraghan and Pardalos clique algorithm provides a dramatic reduction of the subsumption search space. We also present empirical results for the mesh design data set.

## 1   Introduction

$\theta$-subsumption [Rob65] is a correct but incomplete, decidable consequence relation, while implication is undecidable in general. A clause $C$ $\theta$-subsumes $D$ ($C \vdash_\theta D$), iff there is a substitution $\theta$, such that $C\theta \subseteq D$.

$\theta$-subsumption is used as a consequence relation in many ILP systems, for the decision if a rule covers an example as well as for the reduction of clauses, e.g. [MF90, vdLNC93, DB93]. Especially the consistency test, i.e. the test if a newly generalized clause covers negative samples, requires a large amount of subsumption tests. Hence, efficient subsumption algorithms that do not come along with restrictions of the hypothesis language, are an important contribution to ILP.

$\theta$-subsumption of two clauses is NP-complete in general [KN86], even if the second clause is fixed [KL94]; the NP-completeness results from the ambiguity of variable identification. As subsumption is performed very often in ILP, the efficiency is crucial to the power of ILP learners; many approaches to speeding up subsumption were studied.

If in a clause a literal can be found, that matches exactly one literal of the other clause, this literal can be matched *deterministically* [DMR92, KL94] and no backtracking needs to be done. Thus, the complexity grows exponentially with the number of remaining, non-deterministic literals. In this paper, we will propose to reduce the number of candidates for each literal using context information, such that for some literals only one candidate remains, and can be matched deterministically.

For the similar problem of graph isomorphism, there are several approaches, [Tin76, Wei76, WSK81, UW81, GW96a, GW96b], to reducing matching candidates using context information. We will adapt a very general approach to the problem of subsumption and show, that characteristic matrices [Soc88] are a special case of this approach. We will present a second approach as well and characterize the set of clauses, that can be subsumed in polynomial time by this algorithm.

Eisinger [Eis81] introduces *S-links* into the framework of the connection graph resolution proof procedure [Kow75, Sic76]. Eisinger further points out that a subsuming substitution exists, if there is a strongly compatible tuple of substitutions in the cartesian product of the literal matches. Kim and Cho [KC92] propose a pruning strategy that reduces the computational effort of finding a compatible substitution. The maximum clique problem is strongly related to the subsumption problem. The clique problem is to find the largest subset of mutually adjacent nodes in a graph. This problem is well known to be NP-complete, e.g. [FGL+91], yet much effort has been spent in the search for algorithms that behave efficient in the average, e.g. [JT96, CP90, GHP96]. We will show, that subsumption can be tested by finding a clique of size $n$, and we will show that a specialization of the Carraghan and Pardalos pruning strategy [CP90] strongly reduces the search space, we will show that this space is smaller than the cartesian product space proposed by Kim and Cho [KC92].

There is a different approach to reducing the complexity of subsumption, that can be combined with all previously mentioned approaches: If a clause contains classes *(locals)* of literals, such that there are no common variables in different classes, then each class can be matched independently and the complexity grows exponentially with the size of the largest local only [GL85, KL94].

In sections 3 and 4, we describe two alternative context based algorithms, while in section 5 we describe our clique based approach. These sections may be read independently.

## 2 The $\theta$-subsumption problem

$\theta$-subsumption [Rob65, Plo70] is an approximation of the logical implication. A clause $C$ $\theta$-subsumes a clause $D$, written $C \vdash_\theta D$, iff there is a substitution $\theta$, such that $C\theta \subseteq D$ and $|C| \leq |D|$. We use the term subsumption instead of $\theta$-subsumption (in contrast to Loveland [Lov78], who defines subsumption as implication).

While implication is undecidable in general for first-order languages, $\theta$-subsumption is decidable but incomplete, i.e. there may exist clauses $C$ and $D$, such that $C \not\vdash_\theta D$ but $C \models D$. This occurs, if $C$ is self-resolving (recursive) or if $D$ is tautological [Got87]. If tautologies and self-resolution are excluded, then $C \vdash_\theta D \Leftrightarrow C \models D$ [Got87, Mug93, KL94].

The $\theta$-subsumption problem is NP-complete in general [KN86]. The worst case time complexity is $O(vars(D)^{vars(C)})$, or $O(|D|^{|C|})$.

**Definition 1.** A substitution is a mapping from variables to terms. We denote substitutions $\theta = \{x_1 \rightarrow t_1, \ldots, x_n \rightarrow t_n\}$.

**Definition 2.** A matching substitution from a literal $l_1$ to a literal $l_2$ is a substitution $\mu$, such that $l_1\mu = l_2$.

**Definition 3.** The matching candidates of a literal $l_C \in C$ is the subset of a clause $D$, such that there is a matching substitution $\mu$ with $l_C\mu = l_D$ and $l_D \in D$.

## 2.1 Deterministic subsumption

One approach to cope with the NP-completeness of $\theta$-subsumption is the deterministic subsumption. A clause is said to be determinate, if for each literal there is exactly one possible match that is consistent with the previously matched literals [MF90] or, more generally, if there is an ordering of literals, such that at each step for each literal there is exactly one match that is consistent with the previously matched literals [KL94].

**Definition 4 deterministic subsumption.** Let $C = c_0 \leftarrow \{c_i\}$ and $D = d_0 \leftarrow d_1, \ldots, d_m$ be Horn clauses. $C$ deterministically $\theta$-subsumes $D$, written $C \vdash_{\theta DET} D$ by $\theta = \theta_0\theta_1 \ldots \theta_n$, iff there exists an ordering $c_1, \ldots, c_n$ of the $c_i$, such that for all $i$, $1 \leq i \leq n$ there exists exactly one $\theta_i$, such that $\{c_1, \ldots c_i\}\theta_0 \ldots \theta_i \subseteq D$.

As Kietz and Lübbe point out [KL94], the definition of determinate subsumption between two clauses is identical to the definition with respect to one clause, a set of background literals and an example [MF90]: if an observation $e$ follows from a clause $C$ and a set of background literals $l_i$, then $C \vdash e \leftarrow \{l_1, \ldots, l_n\}$.

$C \vdash_{\theta DET} D$ can be tested with at most $O(|C|^2 \cdot |D|)$ unification attempts [KL94] by the following algorithm:

1. While there is a literal $l_1 \in C$ that matches exactly one literal $l_2 \in D$ with $l_1\mu = l_2$, substitute $C$ with $\mu$.
2. If there is a literal in $C$ that does not match any literal in $D$, then $C\theta \not\subseteq D$
3. If any literals could not be matched uniquely, start with the clause substituted so far and test for subsumption using a backtracking algorithm.

The main problem of this approach is, that the condition is very strict. In our experiments with the mesh design data set we learned, that almost no literal at all could be matched deterministically, unless the data set was especially prepared (see section 6). Yet, the complexity is reduced dramatically for negative examples ($C \not\vdash_\theta D$). If the number of matching candidates for some literals in $C$ can be reduced, as is done by the following two algorithms, the condition holds more often and the set of clauses, to be subsumed deterministically, grows.

# 3  Reduction of matching candidates using graph context

Wysotzki [WSK81, UW81] proposes an approach to reducing the number of matching candidates for the graph isomorphism problem that is based on results of Weisfeiler [Wei76] and Tinhofer [Tin76]. It was applied to obtaining attribute-value data for machine learning of graph classification rules [GW96a, GW96b]. The approach is based on the idea, that nodes may be matched to those nodes only, that possess the same context, i.e. the same relations up to an arbitrary depth. We will propose an approach to the subsumption problem that reflects this principle. Wysotzki's algorithm is based on the algebraic representation of graphs by adjacency matrices. Each element $A_{ij}$ of an adjacency matrix contains the relation between node $i$ and node $j$. The context of the nodes is computed by multiplying the adjacency matrices.

*Example 1.* Let $G_1$ contain the nodes $x_1$, $x_2$ and $x_3$ labeled with the unary relation $a$ and the relations $r(x_1, x_2)$ and $r(x_2, x_3)$. We can represent $G_1$ by the adjacency matrix

$$A_1 = \begin{pmatrix} a & r & \emptyset \\ \emptyset & a & r \\ \emptyset & \emptyset & a \end{pmatrix}$$

The square of this matrix yields the following:

$$A_1 \cdot A_1 = \begin{pmatrix} aa + r\emptyset + \emptyset\emptyset & ar + ra + \emptyset\emptyset & a\emptyset + rr + \emptyset a \\ \emptyset a + a\emptyset + r\emptyset & \emptyset r + aa + r\emptyset & \emptyset\emptyset + ar + ra \\ \emptyset a + \emptyset\emptyset + a\emptyset & \emptyset r + \emptyset a + a\emptyset & \emptyset\emptyset + \emptyset r + aa \end{pmatrix}$$

It is important to get an understanding of this procedure: While element $A_{ij}$ contains the relation between node $i$ and node $j$, element $A_{ij}^2$ of the multiplied matrix contains a complete enumeration of all paths of length 2 leading from node $i$ to node $j$, each summand representing one path. In general, $A_{ij}^n$ enumerates all paths of length $n$. We shall take a look at element $A_{11}^2$, enumerating paths from node $x_1$ to node $x_1$: the first summand is $aa$, representing a path that consists of two loops through the unary relation $a$. The next summand is $r\emptyset$, representing the relation $r$ leading to node $x_2$ and the empty relation $\emptyset$ back; this might not be considered a path in an intuitive sense because the empty relation was traversed, but it certainly starts from node $x_1$ and leads to node $x_1$. We shall now look at element $A_{12}^2$. Summand $ar$ represents a path that is set up by a loop through the unary $a$ and the binary $r(x_1, x_2)$ relation. Hence the path leads from $x_1$ to $x_2$. The other summands are to be interpreted accordingly

The branching factor for the isomorphism test can be reduced by only matching those nodes, that share the same set of paths of length $k$ for an arbitrary $k$. Note, that the number of paths is $|V|^k$, where $V$ is the set of nodes and $k$ is the context depth, and the comparison of paths is $O(paths^2) = O(|V|^{2k})$. But for not too large a $k$ this is feasible and it showed, that almost any isomorphism test can be performed in polynomial time [Wei76, WSK81, UW81]. It is known, that two nodes cannot match if their context paths do not match, but it is unknown, if a match of the context implies a match of the nodes for any fixed context depth (note that the complexity of the graph isomorphism problem is unknown).

Translating this approach to the problem of $\theta$-subsumption, we have to mind two main differences: The concept of a path does not cover more than binary relations and we do not want to decide the identity of clauses (up to substitution), but the inclusion of clauses (up to substitution) instead. The translation is based on the fact, that for each occurrence of a variable $x_1$ in $C$ there must be a corresponding occurrence of $x_1\theta$ in $D$. We define the occurrence graph to denote the occurrence of identical variables. We firstly focus on datalog clauses, i.e. clauses with terms restricted to variables or constant symbols.

**Definition 5 occurrence graph.** $(C, E_C)$ is the occurrence graph of a datalog clause $C$ with if $(l_i, l_j, \pi_i \leftrightarrow \pi_j) \in E_C$ iff there is a variable $x$ that occurs in literal $l_i$ at argument position $\pi_i$ and in literal $l_j$ at argument position $\pi_j$.

The edges of the occurrence graph are labeled $\pi_i \leftrightarrow \pi_j$, where $\pi_i$ and $\pi_j$ are argument position in which occurrences of the same variable are found.

**Definition 6 graph context.** The graph context of depth $d$ of a literal $l_1$ from a clause $C$, $con_{gra}(l_1, d, C)$, is the set of terms $p_1 \cdot \pi_1 \leftrightarrow \pi_2 \cdot p_2 \cdot \ldots \cdot \pi_{(n-1)} \leftrightarrow \pi_d \cdot p_d$, iff there exists a set $\{(l_1, l_2, \pi_1 \leftrightarrow \pi_2), \ldots, (l_{d-1}, l_d, \pi_{d-1} \leftrightarrow \pi_d)\}$ of edges in the occurrence graph, such that $p_i$ is the predicate symbol of $l_i$ (note that $l_1 = l_d$ is possible, too).

*Example 2.* Let $C = r(x_1, x_2), r(x_2, x_3), q(x_3)$. The occurrence graph contains only two edges: $(r(x_1, x_2), r(x_2, x_3), 2 \leftrightarrow 1)$ and $(r(x_2, x_3), q(x_3), 2 \leftrightarrow 1)$, denoting that there is a variable, that occurs on position 2 of literal $r(x_1, x_2)$ and on position 1 of literal $r(x_2, x_3)$ and a variable on position 2 or $r(x_2, x_3)$ that also occurs on position 1 of $q(x_3)$. The graph context of literal $r(x_1, x_2)$ at depth 1 contains only the term $r \cdot 2 \leftrightarrow 1 \cdot r$. At depth 2 the context contains two paths: $r \cdot 2 \leftrightarrow 1 \cdot r \cdot 2 \leftrightarrow 1 \cdot q$ and $r \cdot 2 \leftrightarrow 1 \cdot r \cdot 1 \leftrightarrow 2 \cdot r$. The first path corresponds to the literal sequence $r(x_1, x_2) - r(x_2, x_3) - q(x_3)$, the second to the sequence $r(x_1, x_2) - r(x_2, x_3) - r(x_1, x_2)$.

**Proposition 7.** *Let $l_1 \in C$, $l_2 \in D$ be literals, let the depth $d$ be any natural number. Let $l_1\mu = l_2$, $\mu$ is a matching substitution. If $con_{gra}(l_1, d, C) \not\subseteq con_{gra}(l_2, d, D)$, then there is no $\theta$, such that $C\mu\theta \subseteq D$.*

That is, a literal must not be matched against another literal, if its context cannot be embedded in the other literal's context.

**Outline of proof 1** *Let $C$ and $D$ be clauses, let $con_{gra}(l_1, d, C)$ and $con_{gra}(l_2, d, D)$ be the context of a literal from $C$ and $D$ respectively, such that $con_{gra}(l_1, d, C) \not\subseteq con_{gra}(l_2, d, D)$. This implies, that there is a sequence of literals of $C$ sharing at least one variable with their neighbors that has no correspondence in $D$. Let $p_a \cdot \pi_a \leftrightarrow \pi_b \cdot p_b$ be the critical part of the path, and $l_a$, $l_b$ the pair of literals, that has no corresponding path in $D$. If there is a $\theta$, such that $C\theta \subseteq D$,* *then $\pi_a(l_a)\theta = \pi_b(l_b)\theta$ where $\pi$ is the argument selector, because the variables at these positions are equal. But $l_a\theta$ and $l_b\theta$ cannot be element of $D$, because they share a common variable and we assumed that there is no corresponding path in $D$.*

The graph context of a literal at depth 1 contains the same amount of information as the characteristic matrix [Soc88] of the literal does. Element $C_{ij}$ of a characteristic matrix of a literal $l$ contains the predicate names of those literals $l_k$, such that there is a variable, that occurs at position $i$ of $l$ and on position $j$ of $l_k$. The graph context in turn contains a path for each literal in which a common variable occurs, consisting of the predicate name and a term $i \leftrightarrow k$, such that the variable occurs at position $i$ and $j$ in either literal. Clearly, this incorporates the same information. The graph context at a larger depth contains more information, namely information about literals that are connected via a chain of common variables. This cannot be represented in the characteristic matrix formalism, because the matrix is indexed with two argument positions, it requires a sequence of pairs of argument positions to represent context information of a higher depth.

The proposed algorithm reduces the number of literals in $D$, a literal in $C$ can be matched with (the matching candidates). There are two interesting cases in which the subsumption can be tested with polynomial effort: If there is a literal $l \in C$ that has no matching candidates left, then $C\theta \not\subseteq D$, and if there is a literal that has exactly one candidate, then we need not perform backtracking for this literal, which is the idea of deterministic subsumption. In these cases, $C \subseteq D$ can be tested in $O(|C|^2 \cdot |D| \cdot 2^{2d})$, because $|C|^2 \cdot |D|$ is the complexity of deterministic subsumption [KL94] and we need to compare $O(2^d)$ paths to test for $con_{gra}(l_i) \subseteq con_{gra}(l_j)$, where $d$ is the fixed depth.

*Example 3.* Let $C = r(x_1, x_2), r(x_2, x_3)$ and $D = r(y_1, y_2), r(y_2, y_3), r(y_1, y_3)$. We want to test if $C\theta \subseteq D$. Note, that the clauses cannot be matched deterministically, nor are there any locals. At depth 1, the context of the first literal $r(x_1, x_2)$ only contains the path $r \cdot 2 \leftrightarrow 1 \cdot r$ ($x_2$ appears at position 2 of $r(x_1, x_2)$ and on position 1 of $r(x_2, x_3)$), the context of $r(x_2, x_3)$ contains $r \cdot 1 \leftrightarrow 2 \cdot r$. The context of $r(y_1, y_2)$ is $\{r \cdot 2 \leftrightarrow 1 \cdot r, r \cdot 1 \leftrightarrow 1 \cdot r\}$, the context of $r(y_2, y_3)$ is $\{r \cdot 1 \leftrightarrow 2 \cdot r, r \cdot 2 \leftrightarrow 2 \cdot r\}$ and of $r(y_1, y_3)$ is $\{r \cdot 1 \leftrightarrow 1 \cdot r, r \cdot 2 \leftrightarrow 2 \cdot r\}$. Now the context of $r(x_1, x_2)$ can only be embedded in the context of $r(y_1, y_2)$, not in any other literal's context; the context of $r(x_2, x_3)$ is only included in the context of $r(y_1, y_2)$. Hence, both literals can be matched deterministically and the substitution was found without backtracking.

If a clause $C$ is not a datalog clause, i.e. the clause contains non-trivial terms, then we compute a datalog clause $C'$ according to [Soc88] and generate the context w.r.t the new datalog clause. For each literal $p(t_1, \ldots, t_n) \in C$, $C'$ contains a literal $p'(x_1, \ldots, x_m)$, such that the $x_i$ are the variables occurring in the $t_i$, in order of their appearance.

# 4 Reduction of matching candidates using the literal context

In this section, we propose another pruning strategy that reduces the number of matching candidates, that is based on the principle, that identical variables in one clause have to be matched on identical variables in the other clause. We define the literal graph in which literals with common variables are adjacent, but in contrast to the occurrence graph we omit the argument positions.

**Definition 8 literal graph.** $(C, E_C)$ is the literal graph of a clause $C$, if and only if $(l_i, l_j) \in E_C$ iff there is a variable $x$ occurring in both, $l_i$ and $l_j$.

The literal context at a depth $d$ of a literal includes all those literals, that can be reached via a path of length $d$.

**Definition 9 literal context.** The context at depth $d$ of a literal $l \in C$ is the clause $con_{lit}(l, C, d)$, that contains exactly those literals, that can be reached via a path of length at most $d$ in the literal graph of $C$.

The size of the context is growing exponentially with the depth but is limited by the size of the clause $C$. We write $con_{lit}(l, C, d, k)$ to limit the size to a fixed $k$, i.e. $con_{lit}(l, C, d, k)$ is a random subset of $con_{lit}(l, C, d)$, of size $k$.

A literal $l_1 \in C$ must not be matched against a literal $l_2 \in D$, if the context of $l_1$ cannot be embedded in the context of $l_2$.

**Proposition 10.** *Let $C$ and $D$ be clauses and $l_1 \in C$ and $l_2 \in D$ be literals, such that $l_1\mu = l_2$. If there is no $\theta$, such that $con_{lit}(l_1, C, d)\mu\theta \subseteq con_{lit}(l_2, D, d)$ then there is no $\theta'$, such that $C\mu\theta' \subseteq D$.*

**Outline of proof 2** *Let $x$ be a variable occurring in more than literal of $C$. These literals only match literals of $D$ containing identical variables $x\theta$ at the corresponding places. This implies that any set of literals of $C$ connected by sequence of pairs of identical variables only matches a set of literals with identical variables in the corresponding pairs of literals. If there is a literal $l_j$ of $C$ in the context of a literal $l_i$ and $l_i$ matches a literal $l'$ of $D$ by a literal match $\mu$, then due to def. 9 it is connected via a chain of variable occurrences and it only matches a literal in the context of $l_i\mu$. If there is no such literal, there can be no global match containing $\mu$.*

We will now focus on the complexity of a match based on the literal context and we will characterize the set of clauses, that can be matched in polynomial time.

Clearly, the size of the context is growing exponentially with the depth, but it is restricted to the size of the clause and furthermore can be restricted to an arbitrary size $k$. Note that, if $C\theta \subseteq D$ is to be tested, the size of the context of the literals of $C$ can be restricted to an arbitrary $k$, while the size of the context of the $D$ literals has to be computed to at least the same depth and cannot be restricted to a random subset of size $k$, because if $A \subset B$, then any subset of $A$ is a subset of $B$ as well, but need not be a subset of a random subset of $B$.

**Definition 11 Generalized determinacy.** Let $C = c_0 \leftarrow \{c_1, \ldots, c_n\}$ and $D = d_0 \leftarrow d_1, \ldots, d_m$ be Horn clauses and let $k$ be the maximum number of literals in any literal's context of an arbitrary lookahead depth $d$. Then $C$ $con(d, k)$-deterministically subsumes $D$ by $\theta = \mu_0 \ldots \mu_n$, written $C \vdash_{\theta dk DET} D$, iff there exists an ordering $l_1, \ldots, l_n$, such that for all $i$, $1 \leq i \leq |C|$, there exists exactly one $\mu$, such that there is a $l' \in D$ and $l_i \mu = l'$ and $con_{lit}(l_i, C, d, k)\mu\theta'_i \subseteq con_{lit}(l', D, d)$.

Clearly, this is a generalization of the determinacy concept, because for the context depth of 0, $con_{lit}(l_i, C, d, k)$ is the empty set and the definition becomes identical to the definition of the deterministic subsumption. For any context depth $d > 0$ and any context size $k > 0$ the context inclusion is an additional condition that reduces the number of candidates, and hence more often there exists exactly one remaining matching candidate.

We know, that the deterministic match can be tested in $O(|C|^2 \cdot |D|)$, we furthermore know, that in general subsumption can be tested in $O(|D|^{|C|})$. Thus, the context inclusion can be tested in $O(|D|^k)$, because the context of the literal from $D$ is restricted by the size of the whole clause, while we can restrict the context of the literal from $C$ to any arbitrary $k$. Since we only have to modify the deterministic matching algorithm in a way that it does not only test the literals for matching substitutions but tests for context inclusion instead, the $con(d, k)$-deterministic match can be tested in $O(|D|^k \cdot |C|^2 \cdot |D|)$.

*Example 4.* Let $C = r(x_1, x_2), r(x_2, x_3)$ and $D = r(y_1, y_2), r(y_2, y_3), r(y_4, y_3)$. We want to test if $C\theta \subseteq D$. Note again, that the clauses cannot be matched deterministically, nor are there any locals. At depth 1, the context of $r(x_1, x_2)$ contains $r(x_2, x_3)$ and vice versa. The context of $r(y_1, y_2)$ contains $r(y_2, y_3)$, the context of $r(y_2, y_3)$ is $\{r(y_1, y_2), r(y_4, y_3)\}$ and the context of $r(y_4, y_3)$ contains $r(y_2, y_3)$. Thus, $r(x_1, x_2)$ matches all literals in $D$ but the context can be embedded in the context of $r(y_1, y_2)$ only; the context of $r(x_2, x_3)$ subsumes the context of $r(y_2, y_3)$. Again we can match the clauses in polynomial time, without any need for backtracking.

# 5  Clique and the general subsumption problem

In this section we show that the subsumption problem can be mapped to the clique problem. We present a specialization of the Carraghan and Pardalos [CP90] pruning strategy.

**Definition 12.** A pair $(V, E)$ of vertices and edges with $E \subseteq V \times V$ we call a graph.

**Definition 13.** A set of nodes $C \subseteq V$ is a *clique* of a graph $(V, E)$, iff $E \supseteq C \times C$, i.e. all nodes are mutually adjacent.

## 5.1 S-link method of subsumption

Eisinger [Eis81] proposes a subsumption test that is based on selecting a compatible tuple of substitutions.

**Definition 14.** Two substitutions $\theta_1$ and $\theta_2$ are called *strongly compatible* iff $\theta_1 \cdot \theta_2 = \theta_2 \cdot \theta_1$, i.e. no variable is assigned different terms in $\theta_1$ and $\theta_2$.

**Definition 15.** $uni(C, l_i, D) = \{\mu | l_i \in C, l_i \mu \in D\}$ is the set of all matching substitutions from a literal $l_i$ in $C$ to to some literal in $D$.

**Proposition 16 Eisinger.** *A clause $C$ subsumes a clause $D$ ($C\theta \subseteq D$), iff there is an n-tuple $(\theta_1, \ldots, \theta_n) \in \times_{i=1}^{n} uni(C, l_i, D)$, where $n = |C|$, such that all $\theta_i$ are pairwise strongly compatible.*

*Example 5.* Let $C = \{P(x, y), P(y, z)\}$ and $D = \{P(a, b), P(b, c), Q(d)\}$. Then $uni(C, P(x, y), D) = \{\{x \to a, y \to b\}, \{x \to b, y \to c\}\}$ and $uni(C, P(y, z), D) = \{\{y \to a, z \to b\}, \{y \to b, z \to c\}\}$. The cartesian product of these sets is $\times_{i=1}^{2} uni(C, l_i, D) = \{\{x \to a, y \to b\} \cdot \{y \to a, z \to b\}, \{x \to a, y \to b\} \cdot \{y \to b, z \to c\}, \{x \to b, y \to c\} \cdot \{y \to a, z \to b\}, \{x \to b, y \to c\} \cdot \{y \to b, z \to c\}\}$, of which only $\{x \to a, y \to b\} \cdot \{y \to b, z \to c\} = \{x \to a, y \to b, z \to c\}$ is a strongly compatible substitution.

To test if there is a compatible substitution, the cartesian product of all matching substitutions has to be enumerated, there are $|D|^{|C|}$ combinations of matching substitutions in the worst case. We now map this problem to the clique problem. We therefore define a graph, the nodes of which are all matching substitutions from any literal of $C$ to some literal in $D$, and the edges of which are given by the compatibility of the substitutions. We augment the substitution with the number of the originating literal in $C$ because we want each clique to contain only one matching substitution for each literal of $C$.

**Definition 17 substitution graph.** Let $C$ and $D$ be clauses and $n = |C|$. Then $(V_{C,D}, E_{C,D})$ is the substitution graph iff $V_{C,D} = \bigcup_{i=1}^{n}(uni(C, l_i, D), i)$ and $((\theta_1, i), (\theta_2, j)) \in E_{C,D}$ iff $\theta_1$ and $\theta_2$ are strongly compatible and $i \neq j$.

**Proposition 18.** *Let $C$ and $D$ be clauses. Then $C\theta \subseteq D$ with $\theta = \theta_1 \cdot \ldots \cdot \theta_n$, iff there is a clique $\{\theta_1, \ldots, \theta_n\}$ of size $|C|$ in the substitution graph of $C$ and $D$.*

**Proof 4** "$\Rightarrow$" *Let $C\theta \subseteq D$. Then each literal $l_i$ of $C$ is embedded in $D$, i.e. we can split $\theta$ into $\theta_1 \cdot \ldots \theta_n$ such that $l_i \in C$, $l_i\theta_i \in D$. The $\theta_i$ are clearly strongly compatible because it $C\theta \subseteq D$, then no variable can be assigned two different terms in $\theta$. Then $(\theta_1, 1), \ldots, (\theta_n, n)$ is a clique in the substitution graph due to def 17. Furthermore, there can exist no clique of size $> n$, because matching substitution for the same literal of $C$ are not adjacent (see def. 17) and there are $n$ literals in $C$ only.*
*"$\Leftarrow$" Let $((\theta_1, 1), \ldots, (\theta_n, n))$ be a clique in the substitution graph. Due to def. 17 the $\theta_i$ are mutually strongly compatible. If $(\theta_i, i)$ and $(\theta_j, j)$ are in the clique, then $i \neq j$, otherwise the nodes had got no edge (see def 17). As there are $n$ matching substitutions for $n$ different literals of $C$ and $n = |C|$, each literal of $C$ is embedded into some literal of $D$, hence for $\theta = \theta_1 \cdot \ldots \cdot \theta_n$ $C\theta \subseteq D$ holds.*

## 5.2 Searching for MAXCLIQUE

Carraghan and Pardalos present the following algorithm to determine the largest clique of a graph [CP90]:

1. Start with initial sets *nodes* containing all nodes, *best-clique*, initially empty, and a recursion *depth*, initially 1.
2. For all nodes $\theta_i$ in *nodes* repeat
   (a) select a new set *nodes'* = *nodes* ∩ *neighbors*($\theta_i$)
   (b) if |*best-clique*| < *depth* + |*nodes'*| (and *nodes'* ≠ ∅), then starting recursively from point (2) with *depth* + 1 and *nodes'*, determine the max clique of *nodes'*.
   (c) If {$\theta_i$}∪ max clique of *nodes'* is larger than the *best-clique*, save the new clique in *best-clique*.
   (d) remove $\theta_i$ *and from nodes* and continue the loop at point 2.
3. return *best-clique*

*Example 6.*

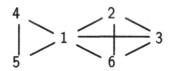

**Fig. 1.** Graph used in example 6

| depth | nodes | $\theta_i$ | nodes' | best-clique | comment |
|---|---|---|---|---|---|
| 1 | 123456 | 1 | 23456 | - | |
| 2 | 23456 | 2 | 36 | - | |
| 3 | 36 | 3 | 6 | - | |
| 4 | 6 | 6 | - | 6 | *nodes'* empty, return |
| 3 | | | | 36 | |
| 2 | | | | 236 | |
| 2 | 3456 | 3 | 6 | 236 | *depth* + *nodes'* = 2 + 1 ≤ 3 → prune |
| 2 | 456 | 4 | 5 | 236 | as above |
| 2 | 56 | 5 | - | 236 | *nodes'* empty, return |
| 1 | | | | 1236 | |
| 1 | 23456 | 2 | 36 | 1236 | *depth* + *nodes'* = 1 + 2 ≤ 4 → prune |
| 1 | 3456 | 3 | 6 | 1236 | *depth* + *nodes'* = 1 + 1 ≤ 4 → prune |
| 1 | 456 | 4 | 5 | 1236 | *depth* + *nodes'* = 1 + 1 ≤ 4 → prune |
| 1 | 56 | 5 | - | 1236 | *nodes'* empty, return 1236. |

The important aspect of this algorithm is point 2b. A current node $\theta_i$ is expanded, only if the number of nodes expanded so far plus the number of nodes not expanded yet, that are neighbors of the current node, exceeds the size of the best clique found so far. Since all nodes in a clique are mutually adjacent, any clique containing node $\theta_i$ cannot include any node that is not a neighbor of $\theta_i$. Obviously, there is no clique containing the current clique and $\theta_i$, that is larger than the current clique plus the neighbors of $\theta_i$ plus 1 (namely $\theta_i$ itself). If the best clique found so far is even larger, we need not further expand $\theta_i$. This pruning strategy provides an optimal reduction, if the best clique known so far is almost as large as the maximum clique in the graph. For the pruning to become mostly efficient, the nodes should be sorted by decreasing output degree, such that large cliques are most likely to be found early. Note that due to point (2a), $nodes \subseteq neighbours(\theta_1) \cap \ldots \cap neighbours(\theta_{n-1})$.

The Carraghan and Pardalos clique algorithm can be used to decide if the substitution graph contains a clique of size $n$. But while this algorithm uses the best clique found so far to decide, if the pruning strategy can be applied, we now know that no clique larger than $|C|$ can exist; thus, we can use the full power of the pruning strategy from the beginning. We can rewrite the pruning strategy in order to find cliques of size $n$:

(2b') if $depth + |nodes'| \geq n$, then starting recursively from point (2) with $depth+1$ and $nodes'$, determine the max clique of $nodes'$.

This rule can still be improved. Remember, that in definition 17 we augmented each substitution with the number of the literal from the left hand side clause. Two nodes of the substitution graph are adjacent, only if their literal numbers are not identical (see def 17 and note, that each literal can be matched to one literal of the right hand side clause only). We can therefore state, that there can be no clique of size $i + j$ which is a superset of a current clique of size $i$, if the set of remaining nodes does not contain at least $j$ different literal numbers.

(2b'') if $depth + |\{i | \exists (\theta_i, i) \in nodes'\}| \geq n$, then starting recursively from point (2) with $depth + 1$ and $nodes'$, determine the max clique of $nodes'$.

We will now compare this algorithm to the algorithm proposed by Kim and Cho [KC92].

1. Generate the set of matching substitutions
2. Delete those substitutions, that are strongly compatible with less than $|C| - 1$ different substitutions
3. enumerate the cartesian product of the remaining substitutions of dimension $n$ and check, if there is a strongly compatible $n$-tuple.

This notation of the algorithm is essentially identical to the algorithm in [KC92], that is expressed in terms of bit vectors. Although this algorithm does not refer to the clique problem, we will explain, that the search space set up by the cartesian product of the remaining matching substitutions is a superset of the search space the clique has to be found in. Since the set of matching substitutions sets up the vertices of the substitution graph and the compatibility relation sets up the edges, any $n$-tuple of pairwise strongly compatible substitutions sets up a clique in the substitution graph. Hence point (3) of the Kim and Cho algorithm performs the search for a clique of size $n$. Point (2) excludes substitutions with less than $|C| - 1$ compatible substitutions, or, in terms of substitution graphs, excludes nodes with an output degree of less than $|C| - 1$. The rewritten rule (2b') in turn does not expand a node $i$, if $depth + |nodes'| < n$, where $nodes' = nodes \cap$ neighbors of $i$. At the top level, where $depth = 1$ and $nodes = V$, both rules are identical. If $depth > 1$ (note that $depth$ is always identical to the number of nodes in the current clique), then obviously $neighbour(\theta_1) \cap \ldots \cap neighbour(\theta_i) \subseteq neighbours(\theta_i)$ (remember, that $nodes' \subseteq neighbour(\theta_1) \cap \ldots \cap neighbour(\theta_i)$). Since $neighbour$ is irreflexive (see def. 17), at least $depth - 1$ nodes (namely $\theta_1, \ldots, \theta_{i-1}$), that are neighbors of $\theta_i$ are missing in $nodes'$, i.e. $depth + |nodes'| \leq depth + |neighbour(\theta_1) \cap \ldots \cap neighbour(\theta_i)| \leq neighbours(\theta_i)$. As $neighbours(\theta_i)$ is the degree of the vertex $\theta_i$ in the substitution graph, the rewritten Carraghan and Pardalos rule is more general than the Kim and Cho rule, i.e. if the Kim and Cho rule fires, this implies that the Carraghan and Pardalos rule fires as well, but not vice versa.

Kim and Cho additionally propose a second pruning strategy: If two incompatible matching substitutions possess an identical set of adjacent nodes, then one of them can be removed. This directly corresponds to a simple symmetry detection in clique search and may increase the performance of the algorithm: if two non-adjacent nodes share the same set of adjacent nodes, then there are at least two cliques of identical size containing exactly one of these nodes, and it is irrelevant, which one of them is chosen.

## 6 Empirical results

Our experiments are based on the well known finite element mesh design data set [BM92]. We used the complete and non-determinate data set, provided by the MLnet server at the GMD. To obtain clauses $C$ of any size, we set up clauses that contained a mesh/2 literal as a head and the set of literals linked to the head via an increasing variable depth as the body. We computed the lgg [Plo70] of two such clauses and drew a random subset of the body literals to more precisely adjust the clause size. The $D$ clauses were generated using a fixed variable depth, they are of approximately the same size (approximately 130 literals). We varied the size of $C$ and tested for $C\theta \subseteq D$. For each curve we used about 5,000 to 10,000 subsumption tests in the positive and up to 25,000 tests in the negative case, taking 140 days of computation time on Sparc20 workstations in total. The matches-deterministic, and the context based algorithms invoke the plain prolog-like matching algorithm after the candidate sets are reduced by the context inclusion criterion. The combination of the graph context and clique algorithm first maximally reduces the set of matching candidates and invokes the clique algorithm to search the remaining substitution space. All algorithms are implemented in "C" and the experiments were performed on sparc stations.

We examined mainly two questions: (1) How does the maximum clique approach compare to a plain subsumption algorithm and (2) How do the context based approaches compare to the deterministic match, especially for negative examples, which are the major problem of the prolog-like algorithms.

The main problem we were facing is the high variance of the measured time. While 95% of the problems can be solved in only a fraction of the average time, very rare cases occur that require several hours up to days to be solved. As we were not able to observe a sufficiently large number of these rare and very expensive cases – which would have required several hundred days – our curves for the positive case are fairly noisy. Yet, we are able to state to state significant results covering 95% of the problems, after we omitted those 5% of cases with the largest deviation from the mean value. Fig. 2 shows the time results in the positive case for 100%, fig. 3 for 95% of the observed problems. The strong similarity between the two diagrams indicates that the exclusion of 5% extrema successfully eliminates the noise but does not influence the obtained results. In contrast to Kietz [KL94] who obtained an improvement of performance using deterministic subsumption (based on an artificial data set), we cannot confirm that deterministic subsumption yields an improvement on the mesh design data set in the positive case. The context based algorithms clearly improve the performance, the curve is shifted by about 10 literals. Although the difference between the algorithms is rather small, the graph context based approach at a depth of 2 yields the best results. While the clique based subsumption shows an impressive behavior, the combination of the graph context and the clique approach produces an even better result. The mean time for 50 literals is only 1 second, while this problem is completely intractable for the plain subsumption algorithm.

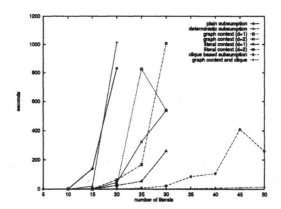

**Fig. 2.** Average time for 100% of the positive samples

Figure 4 shows the results for the negative case ($C\theta \not\sqsubseteq D$). Since the tests are much faster in the negative case, we were able to perform up to 25,000

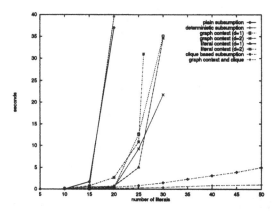

**Fig. 3.** Average time for 95% of the positive samples

tests, hence the curves are less noisy. The deterministic test is significantly faster than the plain subsumption in the negative case, in fact more than 95% of all problems are solved in less than 0.01 second. This occurs, if a literal is found, that does not match any literal of the other clause; otherwise backtracking has to be performed. The most expensive test observed took 34 hours, in contrast the most expensive graph context based test took 4 seconds, the most expensive test done by the combination of the context and clique based algorithm, based on 25,000 observations, took 0.4 seconds.

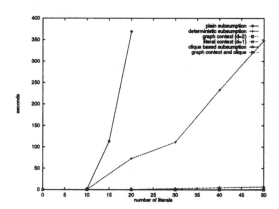

**Fig. 4.** Average time for negative samples

Figure 5 shows the variances $\frac{1}{n}\sum(t_i - \mu_{s_i})^2$, where $t_i$ is the observed time and $\mu_{s_i}$ the mean time for a clause size of $s_i$ literals, for the studied algorithms in the positive and negative case respectively. In the positive case, the variance is very high in general, i.e. most tests require only a fraction of the mean time, the mean value is strongly influenced by a small number of expensive tests. Both, the

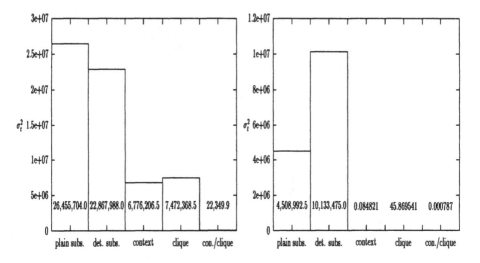

**Fig. 5.** Variance for positive and negative samples

context approach and the pruning strategy of the clique algorithm reduce the number of these expensive tests. The combination of these approaches reduces the variance by a factor of 1000. In the negative case the differences are even larger. The deterministic subsumption shows a very high variance as expected, because more than 95% of all problems are solved instantly. As the candidate elimination procedure leaves only a very small search space (if any), and the pruning strategy works very reliable, the combined algorithm solves all observed problems very fast and shows a very low variance in the time required.

## 7  Conclusion and further research

We proposed two approaches to coping with the complexity of the $\theta$-subsumption problem. One approach is a mapping of the subsumption problem to the problem of the maximum clique and the use of a strongly specialized version of the Carraghan and Pardalos algorithm, that dramatically reduces the search space. We showed that the Kim and Cho algorithm, that enumerates the cartesian product of the matching substitutions operates in a larger search space, due to a much weaker reduction strategy. The other approach is based on a reduction of the matching candidates using context information for each literal. The context is given by occurrences of identical variables or chains of such occurrences. We presented two algorithms, that reflected this idea. We showed that there is a set of clauses, which is a superset of the determinate clauses, that can be tested for subsumption in polynomial time. The approaches are combined to a powerful algorithm: first the candidate sets are reduced using the graph context criterion, the remaining space is searched using the proposed clique algorithm.

Our empirical results, based on the finite element mesh design data set, show that both approaches strongly improve the performance, a combination of both approaches yields the best results, i.e. the least mean time and a small variance.

The determinate subsumption improves the performance in the negative case, although we could not observe an improvement in the positive case. In the negative case, there are very few problems that are extremely expensive.

The proposed combination of the context and the clique based subsumption algorithm can in turn be combined with the $k$-local match [GL85, KL94]. If $C$ contains classes of literals such that there are no common variables in different classes, then each class can be matched independently and the complexity grows exponentially with the size of the largest local only. Each class can be matched using the presented algorithm.

The efficiency of the $\theta$-subsumption test is crucial to the performance of ILP learning algorithms. This is of special importance to generalization based learning algorithms, that usually generate larger clauses and have to test generalized clauses for consistency w.r.t a huge set of samples. Hence, our future work will focus on graph based machine learning algorithms, that make use of the presented efficient matching algorithms. We shortly completed the implementation of a first prototype of our learning system, that requires about 2 minutes to learn a fairly good hypothesis for the mesh design data set.

## ACKNOWLEDGMENT

This work was partially supported by an Ernst-von-Siemens-Fellowship held by Tobias Scheffer. We wish to thank all our colleagues for their patience during the long time we performed our experiments on their workstations.

# References

[BM92]   B. Dolsak and S. Muggleton. The application of inductive logic programming to finite-element mesh design. In *Inductive Logic Programming*, London, 1992. Academic Press.

[CP90]   R. Carraghan and P. Pardalos. An exact algorithm for the maximum clique problem. *Operations Research Letters*, 9:375–382, 1990.

[DB93]   L. DeRaedt and M. Bruynooghe. A theory of clausal discovery. In *Proc. Workshop on ILP*, 1993.

[DMR92]   S. Dzeroski, S. Muggleton, and S. Russel. Pac-learnability of determinate logic programs. In *Proc. 5th ACM Workshop on Computational Learning Theory*, pages 128–135, 1992.

[Eis81]   N. Eisinger. Subsumption and connection graphs. In *Proc. IJCAI*, 1981.

[FGL+91]   U. Feige, S. Goldwasser, L. Lovasz, S. Safra, and M. Szegedy. Approximating the maxclique is almost NP-complete. In *Proc. 32nd IEEE Symp. on Foundations of Comp. Sci.*, 1991.

[GHP96]   L. Gibbons, D. Hearn, and P. Pardalos. A continuous based heuristic for the maximum clique problem. In *Clique, Graph Coloring and Satisfiability: Second DIMACS Implementation Challenge*, 1996.

[GL85]   G. Gottlob and A. Leitsch. On the efficiency of subsumption algorithms. *J. ACM*, 32(2):280–295, 1985.

[Got87]   G. Gottlob. Subsumption and implication. *Information Processing Letters*, 24:109–111, 1987.

[GW96a]   P. Geibel and F. Wysotzki. Learning relational concepts with decision trees. In *Proc. ICML*, 1996.

[GW96b]   P. Geibel and F. Wysotzki. Relational learning with decision trees. In *Proc. ECAI*, 1996.

[JT96]   D. S. Johnson and M. A. Trick, editors. *Clique, Graph Coloring and Satisfiability: Second DIMACS Implementation Challenge*, DIMACS series, 1996.

[KC92]   B. M. Kim and J. W. Cho. A new subsumption method in the connection graph proof procedure. *Theoretical Computer Science*, 103:283–309, 1992.

[KL94]   J.-U. Kietz and M. Lübbe. An efficient subsumption algorithm for inductive logic programming. In *Proc. International Conference on Machine Learning*, 1994.

[KN86]   D. Kapur and P. Narendran. NP-completeness of the set unification and matching problems. In *Proc. 8th International Conference on Automated Deduction*, 1986.

[Kow75]   R. Kowalski. A proof procedure using connection graphs. *J. ACM*, 22(4):572–595, 1975.

[Lov78]   D. W. Loveland. *Automated theorem proving: A logical basis*. Elsevier, North Holland, 1978.

[MF90]   S. Muggleton and C. Feng. Efficient induction of logic programs. In *Proc. 1st Conf. on Algorithmic Learning Theory*, pages 368–381, 1990.

[Mug93]   S. Muggleton. Inverting implication. *Artificial Intelligence Journal*, 1993.

[Plo70]   G. D. Plotkin. A note on inductive generalization. In B. Meltzer and D. Michie, editors, *Machine Intelligence*, volume 5, pages 153–163, 1970.

[Rob65]   J. A. Robinson. A machine-oriented logic based on the resolution principle. *J. ACM*, 12(1):23–41, 1965.

[Sic76]   Sharon Sickel. A search technique for clause interconnectivity graphs. *IEEE Transactions on Computers*, C-25(8):823–835, 1976.

[Soc88]   R. Socher. A subsumption algorithm based on characteristic matrices. In *Proc. 9th Int. Conf. on Automated Deduction*, 1988.

[Tin76]   G. Tinhofer. Zum algorithmischen Nachweis der Isomorphie von endlichen Graphen. In H. Noltemeier, editor, *Graphen, Algorithmen, Datenstrukturen. 2. Fachtagung über Graphentheoretische Konzepte der Informatik*. Carl Hanser Verlag, 1976.

[UW81]   S. Unger and F. Wysotzki. *Lernfähige Klassifizierungssysteme*. Akademie Verlag Berlin, 1981.

[vdLNC93]   P. van der Laag and S. Nienhuys-Cheng. Subsumption and refinement in model inference. In *Machine Learning: ECML*, 1993.

[Wei76]   B. Weisfeiler. *On Construction and Identification of Graphs*. Number 558 in Lecture Notes in Mathematics. Springer Verlag, Berlin, 1976.

[WSK81]   F. Wysotzki, J. Selbig, and W. Kolbe. Concept learning by structured examples – an algebraic approach. In *Proceedings of the 7th International Joint Conference on Artificial Intelligence*, 1981.

# Integrity Constraints in ILP Using a Monte Carlo Approach

Alípio Jorge, Pavel B. Brazdil

LIACC-University of Porto, Rua do Campo Alegre, 823, 4150 PORTO, PORTUGAL.
email: amjorge, pbrazdil@ncc.up.pt http://www.up.pt/liacc/ML

**Abstract.** Many state-of-the-art ILP systems require large numbers of negative examples to avoid overgeneralization. This is a considerable disadvantage for many ILP applications, namely inductive program synthesis where relativelly small and sparse example sets are a more realistic scenario. Integrity constraints are first order clauses that can play the role of negative examples in an inductive process. One integrity constraint can replace a long list of ground negative examples. However, checking the consistency of a program with a set of integrity constraints usually involves heavy theorem-proving. We propose an efficient constraint satisfaction algorithm that applies to a wide variety of useful integrity constraints and uses a Monte Carlo strategy. It looks for inconsistencies by random generation of queries to the program. This method allows the use of integrity constraints instead of (or together with) negative examples. As a consequence programs to induce can be specified more rapidly by the user and the ILP system tends to obtain more accurate definitions. Average running times are not greatly affected by the use of integrity constraints compared to ground negative examples.

## 1 Introduction

An Inductive Logic Programming (ILP) system generates logic programs from incomplete information. This process can either be seen as concept formation from examples [12] or as program synthesis from incomplete specifications [6]. The information given to an ILP system includes positive examples, negative examples, auxiliary logic programs, etc. The output is a logic program that generalizes the positive examples while negative examples are used to reject undesirable solutions, namely overgeneral programs.

Typical ILP systems accept ground negative examples only, and as a result the number of negative examples given to a system tends to be high. To illustrate this problem we give two examples mentioned in the literature: the ILP system FOIL is reported to learn predicate *reverse/2* with 1560 to 92796 negative examples [16]; system CHILLIN [20] is reported to learn the predicate em member/2 with an accuracy of about 50% given more than 80 negative examples. This limits the usability of ILP systems when examples are manually provided by the user, as in the case of program synthesis.

This problem already drew some attention from the ILP community. Some systems like CRUSTACEAN [1] employ a very strong language bias, which restricts the number of necessary negative examples. However, the system seems difficult to extend to handle a wider variety of logic programs. System FOIL [15] allows the use of a closed world assumption (CWA). This technique is not practical in many learning situations since it forces the user to give a complete set of positive examples.

A very promising alternative is the use of integrity constraints. These are first order clauses of the form $a \wedge \ldots \wedge b \rightarrow c \vee \ldots \vee d$ that may also be used as negative information. Such expressive clauses enable the user to provide negative information in a very convenient way. Instead of a long list of negative examples, a few integrity constraints can be given. Luc De Raedt proposed that an ILP system could use integrity constraints by checking that these are satisfied by any generated program [5].

Although integrity constraints are non-Horn clauses, plain SLDNF proof procedure can be applied to check the consistency of a logic program and a constraint by transforming the integrity constraint into a query and posing it to the logic program. This strategy, however, suffers from severe efficiency problems, since finding a violating instance of the constraint may involve trying all its possible instantiations. Other more sophisticated special integrity constraint handlers, like SATCHMO [11], still seem computationally too heavy for pratical use in ILP.

We propose a new method to handle integrity constraints. It enables the use of constraints in ILP systems without high efficiency costs. Experimental results show that we can induce more accurate recursive logic programs quite efficiently this way. In fact, in our experiments, we observed that for the same level of accuracy, our system runs faster with integrity constraints than with negative examples.

Our integrity constraint checker (MONIC) uses a 'Monte Carlo' strategy. To check whether a program $P$ satisfies an integrity constraint $I$, it randomly generates a number of logical consequences of $P$ and tries them against $I$. This is a very efficient way to handle constraints, although incomplete. However, we can control the level of incompleteness by varying the number of logical consequences sampled from $P$.

## 2　Negative Information in ILP

Inductive Logic Programming [12, 10] aims at the synthesis of a logic program P from sparse information. All the positive and negative examples are facts about a predicate $p/k$ ($k$ is the arity of $p$).

---

Given a set of positive examples $E^+$, a set of negative examples $E^-$, a background knowledge program $BK$, and a language $L$ (subset of Horn clause logic), find a program $P \in L$ such that $P \cup BK \models E^+$ and $P \cup BK \cup E^- \not\models \Box$

Fig. 1. The normal ILP setting

Besides the examples and the background knowledge, we also employ type declarations like *type(member(integer, list))* and input/output mode declarations like *mode(member(−, +))* ('+' is input, '−' is output).

## 2.1 Ground Examples

Many ILP systems require an excessive number of positive and negative examples to induce predicate definitions. This a serious problem and a barrier to the usability of ILP systems, especially in a program synthesis context. Regarding positive examples, some systems were proposed recently for the synthesis of logic programs from a small number of positive examples [1, 8]. Our own system SKILit [9] handles the lack of crucial training positive examples (also known as the *sparse* or the *incomplete example set problem*) by generating *properties*. These are clauses that capture regularities within the positive examples, generalize them, and enable the introduction of recursive clauses.

What about negative examples? Giving all the crucial negative examples to an ILP system can also be hard. One ground negative example conveys little information to the system. Besides, the user does not know which negative examples are more appropriate for the synthesis task. Thus he gives the system more negative examples than necessary.

## 2.2 Integrity Constraints

Ground negative examples can be replaced, or complemented, by general clauses that also express negative information. Such clauses can be regarded as negative properties and are called integrity constraints (IC). For example, we can express that no term is a member of the empty list with the integrity constraint *member([ ], X) → false*. The clause *sort(X, Y) → sorted(Y)*, for example, represents an integrity constraint that expresses the condition 'the second argument of the predicate *sort/2* is a sorted list'. Likewise, we can say that list $Y$ is a permutation of $X$ with *sort(X, Y) → permutation(X, Y)*.

Integrity constraints, like negative examples, can be used by an ILP system to detect and reject overgeneral programs. In fact, negative examples can be viewed as a special case of integrity constraints. For instance, *member([ ], 2) → false* represents the negative example *member([ ], 2)*. An integrity constraint stands for a set of negative examples. General constraints represent quite large, possibly infinite sets. Hence, integrity constraints can express the negative information in shorter terms than ground negative examples. We define integrity constraint as follows:

**Definition 1.** An integrity constraint is a first order logic clause of the form $A_1 \vee \ldots \vee A_n \vee \neg B_1 \vee \ldots \vee \neg B_m$. The $A_i$ and the $B_i$ are atoms. The $A_i$ are called positive conditions and the $\neg B_i$ are called negative conditions of the constraint.

Note that $A_1 \vee \ldots \vee A_n \vee \neg B_1 \vee \ldots \vee \neg B_m$ can be written as $B_1 \wedge \ldots \wedge B_m \rightarrow A_1 \vee \ldots \vee A_n$. The integrity constraint $union(A, B, C) \wedge member(X, C) \rightarrow$

*member*$(X, A) \lor$ *member*$(X, B)$ expresses the condition that if $X$ is a member of the third argument of union then it is either a member of the first argument or of the second.

**Constraint Satisfaction** To avoid the induction of an overgeneral program, the typical ILP system periodically checks the candidate programs against the negative information. If a candidate program $P$ satisfies the negative information it passes to the next stage of the inductive process, otherwise $P$ is refined until satisfaction of the negative information is achieved.

When 'negative information' is represented by an integrity constraint $I$, satisfaction means that $P$ is logically consistent with $I$. In the following we define the notions of *satisfaction*, *violation* and *violating instance* [5].

**Definition 2.** Given a constraint $I = B_1 \land \ldots \land B_m \rightarrow A_1 \lor \ldots \lor A_n$ and a program $P$, the constraint is *satisfied* by $P$ if and only if the query $\leftarrow B_1 \land \ldots \land B_m \land \neg A_1 \land \ldots \land \neg A_n$ fails on $P$. If $P$ does not satisfy $I$ we say that $P$ *violates* $I$. If $IT$ is a set of integrity constraints, $P$ satisfies $IT$ if it satisfies every constraint in $IT$.

**Definition 3.** Let $I$ be a constraint $B_1 \land \ldots \land B_m \rightarrow A_1 \lor \ldots \lor A_n$ . $I\theta$ is a *violating instance* of $I$ if and only if $\theta$ is a possible answer substitution for the query $\leftarrow B_1 \land \ldots \land B_m \land \neg A_1 \land \ldots \land \neg A_n$ on $P$.

*Example 1.* Integrity constraint $sort(X, Y) \rightarrow sorted(Y)$ is not satisfied by the program

$\{$ $sort(X, X) \leftarrow list(X)$,
$list([])$,
$list([X|Y]) \leftarrow int(X) \land list(Y)$,
$int(0), \ldots, int(9)$,
$sorted([])$,
$sorted([X])$,
$sorted([X, Y|Z]) \leftarrow X \leq Y \land sorted([Y|Z])\}$

As a violating instance of this integrity constraint we have, e.g.,

$sort([1, 0], [1, 0]) \rightarrow sorted([1, 0])$.

Given Definition 2, we can check whether a program $P$ is satisfied by a constraint (we also say the program and the constraint are consistent) by transforming the constraint into a query and posing that query to $P$, using SLDNF. Although this is a convenient way to check consistency (i.e., to verify that the program satisfies the constraint), it is potentially inefficient. It is convenient because it does not require special theorem provers. Its inefficiency is due to the generate-and-test nature of SLDNF.

*Example 2.* Integrity constraint $sort(X, Y) \rightarrow sorted(Y)$ can be transformed into a query $\leftarrow sort(X, Y) \wedge \neg sorted(Y)$. To check the consistency of the constraint and a program $P$, we pose the query to $P$. SLDNF constructs all possible instantiations of the literal $sort(X, Y)$ and, for each value of $Y$, it tests whether or not it is a sorted list (assuming $X$ and $Y$ range over lists). When an unsorted list is found, we have a violating instance of the constraint. This can be very inefficient. Suppose we are considering that $X$ and $Y$ range over lists of length 0,1,2,3 and 4, with integer elements in $\{0, 1, ..., 9\}$. This represents a universe of more than 10000 lists. To answer such a query, SLDNF may have to try all possible lists. This problem gets exponentially hard as the arity of the predicate in the first literal increases.

Little attention has been given to integrity constraints in machine learning, inductive logic programming included. Luc De Raedt used integrity constraints to enhance system CLINT [5]. The constraint handler used in CLINT employs the strategy defined above. For that reason, the search for a violating instance is inefficient. If a violating instance is found, CLINT tries to determine which predicate definition is wrong with the help of an oracle.

Other constraint handlers exist in the logic programming literature, like SATCHMO [11], and the one by Sadri and Kowalski [18]. The problem with this kind of constraint handlers is their inefficiency.

## 3  MONIC: The Monte Carlo Integrity Checker

In this section we describe MONIC, a Monte Carlo method for handling integrity constraints, which is then used together with our ILP system SKILit. System SKILit [9] induces logic programs from positive examples, negative examples, input/output mode and type declarations, and also from algorithm sketches [3], if available. This system constructs a logic program $P$ by adding one clause $C$ at each cycle to an initial theory $P_0$. At each cycle, program $P$ is also cleaned up for elimination of redundant clauses. The following algorithm is a high level description of SKILit (other systems are covered by this general description).

$P := P_0$
**while** $P$ is not satisfying some stopping criteria
    construct a new clause $C$
    **if** $P \cup \{C\} \cup BK$ is consistent with the negative information
        $P := P \cup C$
    **end if**
**end while**

Algorithm 1: High level description of SKILit.

Within each cycle, after a clause $C$ has been generated, a consistency test is made to the new program $P \cup \{C\}$. This new program is accepted only if it is consistent with the negative information, negative examples included. In fact, in our earlier work, negative information was represented by negative examples only. Now, we extend the meaning of negative information to include integrity constraints as well.

## 3.1 Operational Integrity Constraints

MONIC handles integrity constraints of the form $A_1 \wedge \ldots \wedge A_n \rightarrow B_1 \vee \ldots \vee B_m$ $(n > 0, m \geq 0)$, as defined earlier. On top of that, we make two further restrictions on an integrity constraint $I$ for a program $P$ defining predicate $p/k$.

1. The leftmost literal of the antecedent should be a positive literal of predicate $p/k$.
2. If $I$ is transformed into a query $Q$, and the input arguments of the leftmost literal of $Q$ are bound, then $Q$ should be an acceptable query w.r.t. the input/output modes of the predicates in $Q$ (as noted before every constraint can be turned into a query $\leftarrow A_1 \wedge \ldots \wedge A_n \wedge \neg B_1 \wedge \ldots \wedge \neg B_m$)

A query $\leftarrow p(X_1, \ldots, X_n)$ is acceptable if every input argument $X_i$ is bound. A query $p(X_1, \ldots, X_n) \wedge MoreLiterals$ is acceptable if, after binding all the arguments $X_i$, $\leftarrow MoreLiterals$ is acceptable, where $MoreLiterals$ is a conjunction of literals. Checking the acceptability of a query is straightforward given the input/output mode declarations of the predicates involved in the query.

The first condition guarantees that the integrity constraint restricts predicate $p/k$, since the literal with predicate $p/k$ is in the body of the constraint. The first condition still imposes that the leftmost literal of the antecedent has predicate $p/k$. This guarantees that we can find an instance of the constraint by starting with a logical consequence of program $P$. The integrity constraints we handle are *restrictive* constraints in the sense given in [5]. Such constraints have the literals of the predicate being induced as antecedents. An example of a restrictive constraint for the predicate *union/3* is $union(A, B, C) \wedge member(X, A) \rightarrow member(X, C)$.

The second condition ensures that all goals have ground input arguments before being called (according to the input/output modes declared by the user).

## 3.2 The algorithm for constraint checking

Our consistency checking algorithm (MONIC) takes a program $P$ defining some predicate $p/k$ and a set of integrity constraint $IT$, and gives one of two possible answers. Either $P$ and $IT$ are **inconsistent** (some $I \in IT$ is violated), or $P$ and $IT$ are not found to be inconsistent, and are considered **probably consistent**.

The Monte Carlo method is based on the random generation of facts about the predicate $p/k$ which are logical consequences of the program $P$. Each of these facts is used to search for an instance of some $I \in IT$ which is logically false. If such an instance is found, we can be sure that $P$ and $IT$ are inconsistent. If no fact gives a violating instance of some $I \in IT$, we stop after a limited number of attempts. In that case, $P$ and $IT$ are not found to be inconsistent, but only probably consistent.

The random generation of ground logical consequences of $P$ is central to the algorithm, and deserves some attention. To obtain fact $f$, such that $P \vdash f$, we start with the most general term $p(X_1, \ldots, X_k)$ of $p/k$, $(X_1, \ldots, X_k$ are variables). For ease of presentation we will assume $k = 2$. Let us also suppose $mode(p(+, -))$, and $type(p(type_X, type_Y))$, for a most general term $p(X, Y)$. We now want a query $\leftarrow p(X, Y)$, where $X$ is bound to a term of type $type_X$ (remember that $X$ is an input argument). For that, we assign to $X$ a term $t_{in}$ of type $type_X$. After querying program $P$, variable $Y$ is bound to a term $t_{out}$. Fact $f$ is $p(t_{in}, t_{out})$.

The random nature of $f$ comes from the choice of the input arguments. Each chosen term of a given type is sampled from a population of terms with a fixed distribution.

Given a fact, we unify it with the leftmost literal in the antecedent of each $I \in IT$. The constraint can now be transformed into an acceptable query. The answer obtained by querying $P$ is either 'yes' or 'no'. The positive answer means that a violating instance of $I$ was found, and so $P$ and $I$ are inconsistent. The negative answer means that, although no violating instance was found, $P$ and $I$ can still be inconsistent. However, the more facts fail to violate $I$, the more likely it is that $P$ and $I$ are consistent. Further on, a probabilistic measure of this likeliness is given.

> **input:** program $P$ defining predicate $p/k$ and auxiliary predicates; type and mode declaration of $p/k$ and auxiliary predicates; set of integrity constraints $IT$; integer $n$.
> **output:** one of { inconsistent, probably consistent }

1. generate query $q$
   $p(X, Y)$ is the most general term of $p/k$
   ($X$ represents the input arguments, $Y$ the output ones);
   for each variable $V_i \in X$, randomly instantiate it with $t_i$ of type $type(V_i)$;
   $\quad \theta_{in} = \{V_i/t_i\}$
   $\quad q := \leftarrow P(X, Y)\theta_{in}$
2. pose query $q$ to $P$
   by querying program P with q we get either:
   a) $q$ fails, in this case go back to step 1;
   b) we get an answer substitution $\theta_{out}$
   (if there are alternative answer substitutions,
   we consider each one of them)
3. generate fact $f$
   $f = P(X, Y)\theta_{in}\theta_{out}$
4. query $P$ with each $I \in IT$,
   after unifying the leftmost literal of the antecedent of $I$ with $f$
   if the answer is 'no', go back to step 1
   if the answer is 'yes' then $P$ violates $I$:

store $f$ as negative example;
return 'inconsistent'.
5. After $n$ queries return 'probably consistent'

---

**Algorithm 2**: MONIC: Monte Carlo Integrity Constraint Checker

*Example 3.* Program $P$ below contains an incorrect definition of $rv/2$ which is supposed to reverse the order of the elements of a given list. Type $int$ is the set of integers, and type $list$ is the set of lists of integers (see example 1). Definitions for $append/3$ and $last/2$ are also given as part of the background knowledge. We use Prolog notation for convenience.

$mode(rv(+,-))$.
$type(rv(list,list))$.
$rv([A,B|C],[B,A|C])$.
$rv([A|B],C):-rv(B,D),append(D,[A],C)$.

$mode(append(+,+,-))$.
$type(append(list,list,list))$.
$append([],A,A)$.
$append([A|B],C,[A|D]):-append(B,C,D)$.

$mode(last(+,-))$.
$type(last(list,int))$.
$last([X],X)$.
$last([X|Y],Z):-last(Y,Z)$.

Integrity constraint $I$ imposes that for every fact $rv(X,Y)$, the first element of $X$ is the last element of $Y$.

$rv(X,Y),X=[A|B]\rightarrow last(Y,A)$.

We will follow one iteration of the Constraint Checker (Algorithm 2).

Step 1:  $rv(X,Y)$ is the most general term.
$X$ is the only input argument and has type $list$.
A random choice of a term of type $list$ gives $t=[4,1,5]$.
The query $q$ is $\leftarrow rv([4,1,5],X)$.
Step 2:  Query $q$ succeeds on $P$ and we obtain $\theta_{out}=\{Y/[1,4,5]\}$.
Step 3:  $f$ is rv([4,1,5],[1,4,5]).
Step 4:  $I$ is turned into the query
$\leftarrow rv([4,1,5],[1,4,5]),[4,1,5]=[4|[1,5]],not\ last([4,1,5],4)$.
The answer to such a query is 'yes'. $I$ is violated.
Store $rv([4,1,5],[1,4,5])$ as negative example.
Return 'inconsistent'.

**Types and distributions** Random facts are obtained by randomly generating the input arguments of a query and then querying a program $P$. Each argument is assigned a type. Informally speaking, a type is a set of terms defined by a monadic logic program (all predicates have arity 1).

*Example 4.* The type list (of integers) is defined by the program

$list([])$.
$list([X|Y]) : -int(X), list(Y)$.

In our setting, each set of terms in a type has a pre-defined distribution. This distribution is defined by the ILP system designer or by the user himself. The ideal situation is to free the user from the effort of providing type distributions. For that, the system should have, for each type, an associated predefined distribution.

Currently we define the distribution of a set of terms by specifying the probability of obtaining terms of length 0,1,2, etc. One alternative for the definition of type distributions are stochastic logic programs [13].

*Example 5.* We define a distribution for the set of lists of length 0 to 4, with elements 0 to 9, as follows.

Probability(length of list $L$ is $n$)=0.2 for $n = 0, \ldots, 4$.
Probability(any element of a list $L$ is $d$)=0.1 for $d = 0, \ldots, 9$.

This makes the probability to obtain the empty list equal to 0.2. The probability of obtaining the list [3] is $0.2 \times 0.1 = 0.02$.

## 4 Empirical Evaluation

In [9] we evaluated our system SKILit by synthesizing definitons of predicates like *delete/3*, *append/3*, *rv/2*, *union/3*, among others. The experiments were made by randomly generating training sets, and then testing the produced definitions on randomly generated test sets. The examples in the train sets and the test sets were drawn from the same population with a given distribution. All negative examples were 'near misses' obtained by automatically corrupting random positive examples. Other authors prefer to use totally random negative examples from training and for testing [1, 20]. As an example, the definition of *union/3* synthesized from 5 random positive examples and 25 negative examples (near misses) had an average accuracy rate on a separate test set of more than 80%.

Although this evaluation methodology represents an improvement when compared to earlier work, it has some drawbacks. In the first place, using the same kind of training and testing examples may not give reliable results. Whereas it makes sense to use simple examples for training, the examples in the test set should, in our view, be more demanding, (with longer lists, deeper structures, etc).

In fact, we noticed that theories which had a high accuracy rate on a 'simple' test set were many times obviously wrong. A good test set should rate the theories more or less as a programmer would. We realized that a more complicated test set would serve that purpose. This is why we used such tests also here.

Preliminary experiments using near misses or totally random negative examples showed little differences in SKILit's performance as the number of negative examples increased. In our opinion this fact indicated that these random sets of negative examples lacked crucial negative information. This is why we adopted a different strategy. The results shown in the section are obtained by using negative examples produced by MONIC in previous runs. As we mentioned, the violating facts found by MONIC during learning are kept as negative examples. These examples have a random nature but are also influenced by the way SKILit proceeds in induction.

In our experiments we try to induce logic programs from positive examples and integrity constraints, using the ILP system SKILit extended with MONIC. In these experiments we are interested in measuring the following

a) The effect of the use of integrity constraints on accuracy.
b) The effect of the use of integrity constraints on efficiency.

We chose the tasks of synthezising definitions for the predicates *union/3* and *isort/2*. Predicate *union/3* implements the union of sets, represented as Prolog lists. So, union(A,B,C) means $set(A) \cup set(B) = set(C)$, where $set(X)$ represents the set of elements of list $X$. If each of the lists $A$ and $B$ contains no repetitions, then $C$ should not have repetitions either. We have, for example, $union([2], [3, 2], [3, 2])$ as a positive example, and $union([2], [2], [2, 2])$ as a negative one. The target relation and the integrity constraints used are

**Table 1.** *union/3*: Target relation and integrity constraints.

| target relation |
| --- |
| $type(union(list, list, list))$. |
| $union(A, B, B) : -null(A)$. |
| $union(A, B, C) : -dest(A, D, E), member(D, B), union(E, B, C)$. |
| $union(A, B, C) : -dest(A, D, E), notmember(D, B), union(E, B, F), const(C, A, F)$. |

| height | integrity constraints |
| --- | --- |
| $union(A, B, C) \wedge member(X, A) \rightarrow member(X, C)$. | |
| $union(A, B, C) \wedge member(X, B) \rightarrow member(X, C)$. | |
| $union(A, B, C) \wedge member(X, C) \rightarrow member(X, A) \vee member(X, B)$. | |
| $union(A, B, C) \wedge member(X, A) \wedge member(X, B) \wedge append(A, B, C) \rightarrow false$. | |

where *null/1* is the predicate that succeeds for the empty list, *dest/3* and *const/3* are defined as $dest([A|B], A, B)$ and $const([A|B], A, B)$ respectively, *member*$(X, L)$ succeeds if the element $X$ is in list $L$ and *notmember/2* is the logical negation of *member/2*. The definitions of these predicates are given as background knowledge. Predicate *isort/2* sorts a list. The target relation and constraints are shown below. The predicate *insert/3* inserts an integer into an ordered list maintaining the lists ordered.

**Table 2.** *isort/2*: Target relation and integrity constraints.

| target relation |
| --- |
| *type*(*isort*(*list*, *list*)). |
| *isort*$(A, A) : -null(A)$. |
| *isort*$(A, B) : -dest(A, C, D), isort(D, E), insert(C, E, B)$. |
| integrity constraints |
| *isort*$(X, Y) \rightarrow sorted(Y)$. |
| *isort*$(X, Y) \rightarrow permutation(X, Y)$. |

We generated a pool of positive examples of *union/3* involving input lists of 0,1 and 2 integers ranging from 0 to 9, without repetitions. These examples were generated randomly according to a fixed distribution. Output lists were computed by a definition of the target relation of the predicate being synthesized. Afterwards, we ran SKILit+MONIC (simply referred as SKILit) on 10 different samples of 5,10,15 and 20 positive examples from that pool. As negative information we gave the system the constraints shown above. The first three constraints say that any element of one of the input lists $A$ or $B$ must be an element of the output list $C$, and vice-versa. The fourth constraint says that if $A$ and $B$ have elements in common then the result of *union*$(A, B, C)$ should be different from the list $C$ obtained by simply appending (concatenating) lists $A$ and $B$. The maximum number of random queries generated by MONIC was 100. The input arguments of queries to *union/3* were sampled from a population of lists with equally probable length 0 to 4, and equally probable elements 0 to 9.

The programs synthesised by SKILit were evaluated on a separate test set with 100 randomly drawn positive examples, for reasons that we have explained earlier. The test examples were more complex than the training ones, allowing input lists with up to 10 elements.

Similar experiments were made with 10,20 and 30 negative examples instead of integrity constraints. The pool of negative examples used in training was made of the negative examples stored by SKILit while running with integrity constraints. This means that the pool of negative examples contains all the negative information actually used by SKILit when using integrity constraints. Table 3 shows the overall results obtained by the synthesized programs. Each cell gives an average percentage of covered test examples plus standard deviation.

The results for *isort/2* were obtained in a similar fashion. However, the test set for *isort/2* had 100 positive examples and 100 negative examples which explains the differences in absolute accuracy values between *union/3* and *isort/2*.

Results are shown in Table 3, where '+' and '-exs' are short-type for positive examples and negative examples, respectivelly.

**Table 3.** Experiments with *union/3* and *isort/2*, success rate in percentage. Column headers show the number of positive examples, Row headers show the number of negative examples or indicate the use of integrity constraints (int. const.).

| | union/3 | | | isort/2 | | |
|---|---|---|---|---|---|---|
| | 10+ | 15+ | 20+ | 5+ | 10+ | 15+ |
| 0 -exs | 22.5± 6.1 | 16.1± 7.9 | 17.1± 8.4 | 65.6± 06.8 | 65.2± 06.9 | 64.9± 03.4 |
| 10 -exs | 18.6± 5.3 | 23.0± 12.4 | 31.8± 22.9 | 69.9± 09.5 | 79.3± 12.7 | 82.4± 14.6 |
| 20 -exs | 29.5± 26.3 | 29.0± 8.0 | 41.3± 28.7 | 76.7± 13.1 | 82.6± 14.0 | 84.0± 14.2 |
| 30 -exs | 27.6± 5.8 | 49.2± 33.8 | 50.5± 33.2 | 80.6± 16.2 | 86.9± 15.2 | 86.8± 14.2 |
| int. const. | 27.6± 23.9 | 30.2± 24.2 | 47.6± 35.0 | 74.5± 14.4 | 87.3± 14.6 | 89.2± 13.2 |

The results obtained for *union/3* show that the 4 integrity constraints above replace 20 to 30 informative examples. We believe that a real user would tend to give less informative examples and so more than 30 negative examples, in average, would be necessary to beat the integrity constraints. Experiments with other types of negative examples (totally random, near misses) confirm that many more examples are needed when we give less informative examples. The results with *isort/2* are even better for MONIC. Integrity constraints beat 30 negative examples in two out of three situations.

**Efficiency** In the experiments with *union/3* we measured the average time spent by SKILit in each different learning situation. For a given number of positive examples, in the worst case, SKILit was 3 to 4 times slower with integrity constraints than with 10 negative examples. With 30 negative examples the time spent was about the same as with integrity constraints. With *isort/2*, the average learning time with integrity constraints was less than half the learning time with 30 negative examples.

In another experiment correct definitions of *rv(list, list)* (which reverses lists) and *qsort(list, list)* (which sorts lists) were induced. First the programs were synthesized from manually chosen positive and negative examples. Then they were induced from the same positive examples and integrity constraints. Again we observe that the price we pay for using integrity constraints is negligible or very low. In the case of *rv/2* learning times were practically the same using negative examples or using integrity constraints, and in the case of *qsort/2* using integrity constraints was less than 20% slower than using negative examples. The number of queries generated by MONIC for checking each integrity constraint was 100 (argument *n* in Algorithm 2).

# 5   Related Work

More general procedures for constraint satisfaction exist, like Sadri and Kowalski's [18] and SATCHMO [11]. However, this kind of integrity checkers use a systematic approach to search for inconsistencies. To find a violating instance of an integrity constraint, a large number of different instantiations may have to be tried. The Monte Carlo strategy is non-systematic and drastically reduces the effort in the search for a violating instance of an integrity constraint.

# 6   Discussion

**The number of queries**  Our constraint checking algorithm tries to find one violating instance of an integrity constraint $I$ by generating a limited number of queries. Each query is posed to a program $P$ and facts are obtained. With these facts, we try to find a violating instance of $I$. If a violating instance of the constraint is found, we can be sure that the constraint and the program are inconsistent. Otherwise, we cannot be 100% sure that they are not inconsistent. However, the binomial distribution tells us that the probability, after $n$ queries, of finding no inconsistency is $\alpha = (1 - p)^n$, where $p$ is the probability of any given query posed to $P$ to give a violating instance of $I$. This formula says that the larger the value of $n$, the more likely it is that $P$ and $I$ are consistent in case no inconsistency is found. Likewise for the value of $p$.

Intuitively, the value of $p$ measures the consistency level of the integrity constraint with the program $P$. The true value of $p$ is not known. However, we can choose a lower limit for $p$, meaning that if that if there is an inconsistency then at least $100 \times p\%$ of the queries give a violating instance of $I$. We call this the 'Integrity constraint generality assumption'. After $n$ non-violating queries, and given a value for $p$, we can be $100(1 - \alpha)\%$ sure that $P$ and $I$ are consistent.

Unfortunately, the user cannot tell 'a priori', whether this assumption is going to be violated or not, because that depends on $P$, and $P$ is not known. However, he may have an intuitive notion of how general a given constraint is, and so prefer 'general' constraints, like $sort(X, Y) \rightarrow sorted(Y)$, to more 'particular' ones like $sort([2, 3], [3, 2]) \rightarrow false$.

**Correctness and completeness**  When MONIC finds a violating instance of an integrity constraint that means that the program does not satisfy the constraint. In that sense MONIC is correct or sound. It does not find false inconsistencies. However, we can say that it is only as correct as the proof procedure we are using. To ensure correctness of the proof procedure a safe computation rule must be used [7].

As we saw above MONIC may fail to find a violating instance even if one exists. For that reason it is incomplete. However, when MONIC finds no inconsistency we have an associated level of confidence ($\alpha$). On the other hand, We can control the level of confidence of the answer given by MONIC by choosing the number of sampled queries.

# 7 Limitations and future work

The proposed Monte Carlo Integrity Checker is incomplete. Although incompleteness can be measured and controlled, some integrity constraints are hard to violate with 100 random queries. This is the case of very specific integrity constraints. The more general a constraint is, the easier it is to detect inconsistencies. An example of a specific integrity constraint is a negative example. A random shooting approach to handling negative examples would inefficiently try to guess the negative example. However, it is reasonable to expect that the user provides integrity constraints which cover a large number of negative examples.

Another limitation is the level of abstraction required to write the integrity constraints. We want to produce clauses, but need to provide other clauses instead. This may seem contradictory. However, it makes sense to give the system integrity constraints if they are known. If the user only has negative examples, the system will still be able to run.

On the other hand, integrity constraints can be used to express restrictions which otherwise would have to be built-in into the ILP system as in FFOIL [17]. That is the case when the predicate to synthesize is a function (the output is unique for every different input). For the predicate $sort(+, -)$ this knowledge can be expressed by the integrity constraint $sort(X, Y) \land sort(X, Z) \land \neg Y = Z \rightarrow false$. Our system can handle this constraint following the method described earlier.

MONIC only handles restrictive integrity constraints, since we are interested in the use of integrity constraints as negative information. Extending MONIC to handle any constraint seems quite natural, but it has not been done.

The Monte Carlo strategy for consistency checking solves the problem of efficiently finding an existing violating instance of an integrity constraint, or rapidly come to the conclusion that probably there is no inconsistency. However, this strategy does not seem to help in determining which predicate definition is wrong, when a violating instance is found. This credit assignment problem arises mainly in a multiple predicate learning situation and can be solved with the help of an oracle, as in CLINT or MIS [19]. In single predicate learning situations as the ones considered in this paper only one predicate definition can be wrong.

# 8 Conclusion

Integrity constraints can be efficiently used in ILP using MONIC, the Monte Carlo Integrity Checker we propose. Higher average success rates of synthesized predicates can be obtained with integrity constraints in very resonable time compared to negative examples. In our experiments, runs with integrity constraints were in the worst case four times slower than runs with negative examples.

MONIC is correct (when it finds an inconsistency, there is one), but incomplete (it may fail to find existing inconsistencies. However, its level of incompleteness can be measured and controlled by the user. The algorithm is quite simple to describe and easy to implement.

**Acknowledgments** We would like to thank João Gama and Joaquim Pinto da Costa for many helpful discussions. Part of this work was done under the support of PRAXIS XXI.

# References

1. Aha, D. W., Lapointe, S., Ling, C. X., Matwin S (1994): Inverting Implication with Small Training Sets. Proceedings of the European Conference on Machine Learning, ECML- 94, ed. F. Bergadano and L. De Raedt, Springer Verlag.

2. Bergadano, F., Gunneti, D. and Trinchero, U. (1993): The Difficulties of Learning Logic Programs with Cut. Journal of Artificial Intelligence Research 1, 91-107, AI Access Foundation and Morgan Kaufmann Publishers.

3. Brazdil, P., Jorge, A. (1994): Learning by Refining Algorithm Sketches. Proceedings of ECAI-94, T. Cohn (ed.). Wiley.

4. De Raedt, L., Lavrac, N., Dzeroski, S. (1993): Multiple Predicate Learning. Proceedings of IJCAI-93. Morgan-Kaufmann.

5. De Raedt, L. (1992): Interactive Theory Revision:An Inductive Logic Programming Approach. Academic Press.

6. Deville, Y., Lau, K.,(1994): Logic Program Synthesis. The Journal of Logic Programming, special issue Ten Years of Logic Programming, volumes 19,20, May/July 1994.

7. Hogger, C. J. (1990): Essentials of Logic Programming. Graduate texts in computer science series, Oxford University Press.

8. Idestam-Almquist P (1996) Efficient Induction of Recursive Definitions by Efficient Analysis of Saturations. Advances in Inductive Logic Programming, Ed. by Luc De Raedt, IOS Press/Ohmsha.

9. Jorge, A. and Brazdil, P. (1996): Architecture for Iterative Learning of Recursive Definitions. Advances in Inductive Logic Programming, Ed. by Luc De Raedt, IOS Press/Ohmsha.

10. Lavrac, N. and Dzeroski, S. (1994): Inductive Logic Programming, Techniques and Applications. Ellis Horwood.

11. Manthey, R. and Bry, F. (1988): SATCHMO: a theorem prover implemented in Prolog. Proceedings of CADE 88 (9th Conference on Automated Deduction),Springer-Verlag.

12. Muggleton, S., De Raedt, L., (1994): Inductive Logic Programming. The Journal of Logic Programming. Special issue Ten Years of Logic Programming, volumes 19,20, May/July 1994.

13. Muggleton, S. (1995): Stochastic Logic Programs. Advances in Inductive Logic Programming, Ed. by Luc De Raedt, IOS Press/Ohmsha.

14. Muggleton, S. (1993): Inductive Logic Programming: derivations, successes and shortcomings. Proceedings of ECML- 93, Springer-Verlag.

15. Quinlan, J.R. (1990): Learning logical definitions from relations. Machine Learning 5, 239-266.

16. Quinlan, J.R. (1993): FOIL: A Midterm Report. Proceedings of ECML-93, Springer-Verlag.

17. Quinlan, J.R. (1996): Learning First-Order Definitions of Functions. Journal of Artificial Intelligence Research, to appear.

18. Sadri, F., Kowalski, R. (1988): A Theorem Proving Approach to Database Integrity in Deductive Databases and Logic Programming, ed. by Jack Minker, Morgan Kaufmann Publishers.

19. Shapiro, E. Y., (1982) Algorithmic Program Debugging, MIT Press, Cambridge MA.

20. Zelle J M, Mooney R J, Konvisser J B, (1994): Combining Top-down and Bottom-up Techniques in Inductive Logic Programming. Proceedings of the Eleventh International Conference on Machine Learning ML-94, Morgan-Kaufmann.

# Restructuring Chain Datalog Programs
## (Preliminary Report)

Anke Rieger

FB Informatik LS 8, University of Dortmund
D-44221 Dortmund, Germany
rieger@ls8.informatik.uni-dortmund.de

**Abstract.** The goal of knowledge compilation and program optimization is to transform programs in order to speed up their evaluation. In machine learning, two major approaches to speed-up learning exist: Those which interwine the learning and the optimization process and those which clearly separate them. We follow the latter line of thought and present a new restructuring method for chain Datalog programs which have been learned by ILP algorithms. During the restructuring process, rules for new, intermediate concepts are introduced which are used to modify the original program. We proof that this transformation does not change the coverage of a given set of learned target concepts. We show the details of the implemented algorithm which has been successfully applied to a real-world robot navigation domain. Finally, we show that the restructuring method yields a program which can be evaluated faster than the original one. This speed up is achieved by program decompositions.

## 1  Introduction

In this paper, we work with chain Datalog programs which have been the result of applying inductive logic programs to a robot navigation domain [9]. These rules are to be used by the robot during its performance phase, in order to derive higher level concepts from sensor observations in real time. They contain many redundancies, which are not superfluous in the sense, that they can simply be omitted. Together with ambiguities caused by sensor noise they make the evaluation of the rules via forward inferences slow. Given the real time requirement of the application domain, improvements of both, the program and the inference procedure, are needed. In this paper, we present a method for restructuring chain Datalog programs, such that methods, which are known to speed up their evaluation, can be applied.

The restructuring method transforms the program such that the ambiguities and redundancies are removed. During this process new predicates are invented by combining existing terms into a new combined term. As our main goal for introducing new concepts is to speed up inferences, our approach differs from the demand-driven one proposed by Wrobel [30]. The restructuring method uses inverse resolution (see, e.g., [14], [20], [28]), i.e., it implements the W-operator as inter-construction for chain Datalog rules. Thus, our approach is closely related to the one proposed by Sommer [23], [24]. However, his method **FENDER**, does not yield the result, we are aiming at.

Our restructuring method introduces chain Datalog rules for the newly invented, intermediate concepts. The definitions are used to modify the rules of the original program by folding existing rules with them. Folding is a well-known program transformation operation (see, e.g., [21], [22], [2], [25], [17]). We use this relation to program transformation in order to proof that our method does indeed not change the coverage of a given set of target concepts.

Finally, we show, that the restructuring method yields a program which supports faster evaluations. Dong and Ginsburg introduced in [8] the notion of program decompositions for elementary chain Datalog programs. We give a similar definition for non-elementary chain Datalog programs, and show that our restructuring method is a constructive method which can be used to generate such a decomposition. The purpose of decompositions is to split up the program into components to which the fixpoint operator for calculating the least Herbrand model ([27], [1]) is applied sequentially. This way of proceeding is faster than applying the fixpoint operator to the program as a whole.

## 2 Chain Datalog Programs

In this section, we present the definitions for the syntax and semantics of chain Datalog programs, which have been taken mainly from [26] and [27], [1].

*Syntax* We assume the existence of three pairwise disjoint, finite sets, containing *constant* symbols $(x, y, \ldots)$, *predicate* symbols $(a, b, c, d, p, q)$, and *variables* $(X, Y, \ldots)$. We restrict a *term* to be either a constant or a variable. We consider negation-free Datalog programs, i.e., function-free logic programs with definite clauses $B \leftarrow A_1, \ldots, A_n$, where $B, A_1, \ldots, A_n$ are atoms. Ullman and Gelder (see [26]) distinguish between basic and extended logic programs. A *basic logic program*, $\mathbf{P_I}$, is a finite set of rules containing IDB and EDB predicates. IDB (Intentional Database) predicates appear in rule heads and, possibly, in rule bodies. EDB (Extensional Database) predicates appear in rule bodies only. IDB($\mathbf{P_I}$) and EDB($\mathbf{P_I}$) denote the intensional and extensional database predicates, respectively, of the basic logic program $\mathbf{P_I}$. An *EDB fact* is a ground fact over an EDB predicate. An *EDB instance*, $\mathbf{P_E}$, is a finite set of EDB facts. An *extended logic program*, $\mathbf{P}$, is the union of a basic logic program and an EDB instance, i.e., $\mathbf{P} = \mathbf{P_I} \cup \mathbf{P_E}$.

We consider basic Datalog programs with rules of a special form: An *elementary chain rule* [26] is a rule containing binary predicates of the form $p(X, Y) \leftarrow r_1(X, X_1), r_2(X_1, X_2), \ldots, r_{k+1}(X_k, Y)$, $k > 0$. Let $C$ be a chain rule and $A$ an atom occurring in $C_{body}$, e.g., $r(X, Y)$. Then, we say that $A$ starts at variable $X$ and leads to variable $Y$. Let $from(A)$ denote the function, which maps an arbitrary predicate to its starting variable, and $to(A)$ the function, which maps a predicate to the variable it leads to. Let $X_i, i = 1, \ldots, k$ be the variables occurring in $C_{body}$ and not in $C_{head}$. $X_i$ is called a *chaining variable*, if $C_{body}$ contains two atoms, $A_1$ and $A_2$, such that $to(A_1) = from(A_2)$. Non-elementary chain Datalog rules allow for variables, which are distinct from the chaining variables (see Section 3). In principle, clauses can be considered as sets of literals, whose order of appearance does not matter. In the special case of chain rules, the atoms in the body of the rule can be sorted according to the relation $\ll$, which we define as follows: Let $A_1, A_2$ be two atoms occurring in $C_{body}$. Then, $A_1$ precedes $A_2$, $A_1 \ll A_2$, if $to(A_1) = from(A_2)$. Given the chain rule above, we have $r_1(X, X_1) \ll r_2(X_1, X_2) \ll \ldots \ll r_{k+1}(X_k, Y)$. This relation leads to the definition of a *chain*, which is the ordered sequence of premise atoms of a chain rule, e.g., $r_1(X, X_1), r_2(X_1, X_2), \ldots, r_{k+1}(X_k, Y)$.

*Semantics* The *Herbrand universe* of a Datalog program $\mathbf{P}$, $\mathcal{U}_H(\mathbf{P})$, is the set of all constant symbols appearing in $\mathbf{P}$. The *Herbrand base* of a program $\mathbf{P}$, $\mathcal{B}_H(\mathbf{P})$, is the set of all ground atoms, which can be formed from the predicates in $\mathbf{P}$ and the terms in $\mathcal{U}_H(\mathbf{P})$. A Herbrand *interpretation* $I$ is a subset of $\mathcal{U}_H(\mathbf{P})$. Then, $\mathbf{T_P}$, a mapping from interpretations to interpretations, is defined as

$$\mathbf{T_P}(I) = \{\breve{B} \in \mathcal{B}_H(\mathbf{P}) \mid C\sigma = (\breve{B} \leftarrow \breve{A}_1, \ldots, \breve{A}_m), m \geq 0, \quad \text{is a ground}$$
$$\text{instance of a clause } C \in \mathbf{P} \text{ and } \breve{A}_1, \ldots, \breve{A}_m \in I\}.$$

The least fixpoint of the $\mathbf{T_P}$-mapping, $\mathbf{T_P^\omega}(\emptyset)$, is the least Herbrand model $\mathcal{M}_H(\mathbf{P})$ of $\mathbf{P}$ (see [27], [1]). As we deal with basic logic programs $\mathbf{P_I}$, we use $\mathbf{T_{P_I}^\omega}(\mathbf{P_E})$ to denote the least fixpoint of $\mathbf{T_{P_I}}$ and, thus, the least Herbrand model of the program $\mathbf{P} = \mathbf{P_I} \cup \mathbf{P_E}$. We set $\mathbf{T_{P_I}^0}(\mathbf{P_E}) = \mathbf{P_E}$.

Given an extended logic program $\mathbf{P} = \mathbf{P_I} \cup \mathbf{P_E}$ and a set of target predicates $\mathcal{I} \subseteq \text{IDB}(\mathbf{P_I})$, we define the *coverage* for $\mathcal{I}$ to be the subset of the least Herbrand model, which is restricted to the predicates in $\mathcal{I}$:

$$Cov_\mathbf{P}(\mathcal{I}) = \{p_i(t_1, \ldots, t_s) \mid p_i \in \mathcal{I} \text{ and } p_i(t_1, \ldots, t_s) \in \mathbf{T_{P_I}^\omega}(\mathbf{P_E})\}.$$

Two basic logic programs, $\mathbf{P_I}$ and $\mathbf{P_I'}$, are *equivalent with respect to a set of IDB-predicates* $\mathcal{I}$, if the least Herbrand models of both programs, extended with the same EDB instance, restricted to the predicates in $\mathcal{I}$, are the same ([26]), i.e., $Cov_\mathbf{P}(\mathcal{I}) = Cov_{\mathbf{P'}}(\mathcal{I})$ with $\mathbf{P} = \mathbf{P_I} \cup \mathbf{P_E}$ and $\mathbf{P'} = \mathbf{P_I'} \cup \mathbf{P_E}$.

## 3 The Robotics Domain

Non-elementary chain Datalog rules have been the result of applying inductive logic programming algorithms to a robot navigation domain. We sketch the part of the domain, which is relevant for the methods presented in this paper (for details see [9]). Furthermore, we illustrate the characteristics of the rules, which motivated the development of the restructuring method.

An example of a chain Datalog rule of the domain is

$$\texttt{s\_jump\_parallel}(Tr, S, X, Y) \leftarrow \texttt{stable}(Tr, O, S, X, X_1, G_1),$$
$$\texttt{incr\_peak}(Tr, O, S, X_1, X_2, G_2),$$
$$\texttt{stable}(Tr, O, S, X_2, Y, G_3).$$

It derives so-called sensor features from basic features. Rules of this type are part of an inference hierarchy, that is, the derived sensor features are used in subsequent forward inference steps, in order to derive higher level concepts, which are used for planning. The example rule states: If, during trace $Tr$, sensor $S$ with orientation $O$ perceived **stable** measurements during the interval from time point $X$ to $X_1$, an **incr_peak** during the interval from $X_1$ to $X_2$, and **stable** measurements during the interval from $X_2$ to $Y$, then it has perceived a **jump** during the interval from $X$ to $Y$, while moving **parallelly** along it. The variables $G_i$ denote average gradients of the measurements. Obviously, the $X_i$, which are used to represent the time intervals, are the chaining variables. We define two subsets of the set $PS$ of predicate symbols: Let $PS_{\mathbf{BF}}, PS_{\mathbf{SF}} \subset PS$ with $PS_{\mathbf{BF}} \cap PS_{\mathbf{SF}} = \emptyset$. $PS_{\mathbf{BF}} = \{a, b, c, d, \ldots\}$ and $PS_{\mathbf{SF}} = \{p_1, p_2, p_3, \ldots\}$ represent the predicate symbols, which we use for basic features (EDB predicates) and sensor features (IDB predicates), respectively. In our application domain, only the sensor feature predicates are used in subsequent inference steps of the inference hierarchy. They constitute the set $\mathcal{I}$ of target concepts on which we want to focus, i.e., $\mathcal{I} \subseteq PS_{\mathbf{SF}}$.

The following example program illustrates the features, which motivated the development of the restructuring method. These are the redundancies and ambiguities, which cause the evaluation of the rules to become slow. Consider the basic chain Datalog program $\mathbf{P_I}$

$$p_1(Tr, S, X, Y) \leftarrow a(Tr, O, S, X, X_1, G_1), b(Tr, O, S, X_1, X_2, G_2), \qquad (1)$$
$$c(Tr, O, S, X_2, Y, G_3).$$

$$p_2(Tr, S, X, Y) \leftarrow a(Tr, O, S, X, X_1, G_1), b(Tr, O, S, X_1, X_2, G_2), \qquad (2)$$
$$c(Tr, O, S, X_2, Y, G_3).$$

$$p_3(Tr, S, X, Y) \leftarrow a(Tr, O, S, X, X_1, G_1), b(Tr, O, S, X_1, X_2, G_2), \qquad (3)$$
$$c(Tr, O, S, X_2, X_3, G_3), d(Tr, O, S, X_3, Y, G_4).$$

$$p_4(Tr, S, X, Y) \leftarrow b(Tr, O, S, X, X_1, G_1), c(Tr, O, S, X_1, X_2, G_2), \qquad (4)$$
$$d(Tr, O, S, X_2, Y, G_3).$$

$$p_5(Tr, S, X, Y) \leftarrow b(Tr, O, S, X, X_1, G_1), c(Tr, O, S, X_1, X_2, G_2), \qquad (5)$$
$$d(Tr, O, S, X_2, X_3, G_3), a(Tr, O, S, X_3, X_4, G_4),$$
$$b(Tr, O, S, X_4, Y, G_5).$$

We have EDB($\mathbf{P_I}$)= $\{a, b, c, d\}$ and IDB($\mathbf{P_I}$)= $\{p_1, p_2, p_3, p_4, p_5\}$. We set $\mathcal{I} =$ IDB($\mathbf{P_I}$). All IDB predicates, i.e., the sensor feature predicates, occur only in rule heads. Thus, the program has inference depth one. The program contains rules for several target concepts. In order to illustrate the redundancies, we define a chain $Ch_1$ to be a *prefix (chain)* of a chain $Ch_2$, if there exists a substitution $\sigma$ and a, possibly empty, chain $Ch_3$, such that $Ch_2$ is equal to the concatenation of $Ch_1\sigma$ and $Ch_3$. In our example program $\mathbf{P_I}$, there exist a lot of rules, whose premise chains are prefixes of premise chains of other rules. The chain $a(Tr, O, S, X, X_1, G_1), b(Tr, O, S, X_1, X_2, G_2)$, e.g., is a prefix of Rules (1), (2), and (3). The redundancies and ambiguities (i.e., rules with the same premise chain but different conclusions) cause the effect that during forward inferences, the same input fact may have to be matched redundantly with premise atoms of several rules. Assume a naive forward inference procedure which maps each input or newly derived fact against all premise literals of all rules. Assume, that the robot perceives the sequence of of chronologically ordered basic features, i.e., that the basic logic program $\mathbf{P_I}$ gets as "input" the EDB instance (ground chain) $\mathbf{P_E} = a(t1, 90, s5, 1, 8, 45)$, $b(t1, 90, s5, 8, 10, 26)$, $c(t1, 90, s5, 10, 15, 6)$, $d(t1, 90, s5, 15, 17, -3)$. Then, the first EDB fact, $a(t1, 90, s5, 1, 8, 45)$, matches the first premise atom of Rule (1), (2), and (3). Although it cannot possibly lead to a successful derivation, the fact can, in principle, also be matched to the fourth literal of Rule (5). For the second EDB fact, $b(t1, 90, s5, 8, 10, 26)$, there exists a matching premise atom for every rule of the program $\mathbf{P_I}$. In this case, it also makes no sense to match the fact with the fifth premise literal of Rule (5).

Our goal is, to restructure chain Datalog programs in such a way, that these multiple and superfluous matches are avoided. An important point we want to make is, that here we have the case that the general assumption "The smaller the inference depth, the smaller the answer time.", which motivated EBL ([11], [6]) does not hold. In the next section, we present a restructuring method, which increases the inference depth in order to decrease the answer time.

## 4 Restructuring Chain Datalog Programs

The restructuring method transforms a chain Datalog program into one, which supports fast evaluations via forward inferences. The original program has to satisfy several assumptions: Its IDB predicates have to occur in rule heads only, i.e., its inference depth has to be one. This condition can be easily satisfied by unfolding its rules in all possible ways (see Section 5). Furthermore the premise literals of each rule have to be sorted according to the $\ll$-relation. Before we turn to the restructuring method, we present a method, which sorts automatically the premise literals according to this relation.

### 4.1 Sorting the premise literals of non-elementary chain Datalog rules

Motivated by the application, the goal of sorting is to make the sequence of premise literals reflect the chronological order of the events. The method finds a unique ordering of the premise literals, if the $\ll$-relation is intransitive, irreflexive and asymmetric. Furthermore, no variable may appear in several literals as variable at which they start or to which they leads. The premise $a(X, X_1), b(X_1, X_2)$, $c(X_1, X_3)$, $d(X_3, X_4)$ does not satisfy this requirement. We have $a(X, X_1) \ll b(X_1, X_2)$ and $a(X, X_1) \ll c(X_1, X_3)$. Thus, there is no unique ordering possible. In our application domain, the $\ll$-relation corresponds to the chronological order of the sensor observations. In principle, the above conditions state, that the time intervals of the observations may not overlap.

If we have a rule $C = (C_{head} \leftarrow L_1, \ldots, L_n)$ which satisfies the conditions, then each chaining variable $X_i$ occurs exactly in two predicates, $L_j, L_k \in C_{body}$, such that $from(L_j) = to(L_k) = X_i$. This fact is used to determine possible pairs $(L_i, L_j), i \neq j, i, j \in \{1, \ldots, n\}$, such that $L_i \ll L_j$. These partial chains are then extended to premise chains of length $n$. The details of the algorithm and several examples can be found in [19]. Given a rule $C$, which satisfies the conditions, it returns a rule with sorted premise literals, otherwise it fails.

We developed the sorting method, because we do not get the unique ordering when we try to sort the premise literals according to their depth ([15]) or according to the relation $\leq_P$ between premise literals, which in [12] is defined via the minimum distance of the variables occurring in the literals. This relation was introduced in order to prune the search space during learning. But, given the rule $C_{head} \leftarrow L_1, L_2, L_3$:

$$p_3(Tr, S, X, Y) \leftarrow a(Tr, O, S, X, X_1), b(Tr, O, S, X_1, X_2), c(Tr, O, S, X_2, X_3).$$

the minimum distance of every variable occurring in $L_i, i = 1, 2, 3$ is the same. This is due to the fact, that each literal shares a variable with $C_{head}$. (The same argument applies, if we use the depth). So, for the purpose of hypothesis testing, each permutation of $L_1, L_2, L_3$ would do equally well. Obviously, we do not get deterministically the result, which we need for our purpose.

We could also have used the determinateness ([15]) of the premise literals or mode declarations ([29],[10], [13]). However, in contrast to our method, both would have required the user to specify the mode declarations or to sort the literals according to the determinateness.

## 4.2 The restructuring method

Given a basic chain Datalog program $\mathbf{P_I}$ of inference depth one with rules, whose premise literals are sorted according to the $\ll$-relation, our restructuring method yields a program $\mathbf{P_I'}$, which is equivalent to $\mathbf{P_I}$ with respect to $\mathcal{I} \subseteq \text{IDB}(\mathbf{P_I})$. Remember, that $\mathcal{I}$ is the set of target concepts, which are defined by the rules in $\mathbf{P_I}$.

During the restructuring process, new, intermediate concepts are introduced without changing the coverage of the original target concepts. $\mathbf{P_I'}$ has an inference depth greater than one. Furthermore, $\text{EDB}(\mathbf{P_I}) = \text{EDB}(\mathbf{P_I'})$ and $\text{IDB}(\mathbf{P_I}) \subseteq \text{IDB}(\mathbf{P_I'})$. One of the characteristics of the application domain is, that a lot of premise chains of the rules are prefixes of premise chains of other rules. Given a parameter $m$ and a rule $C = (B \leftarrow A_1, \ldots, A_m, A_{m+1}, \ldots, A_n)$, the basic idea is to take the prefix chain of length $m$, i.e., $A_1, \ldots, A_m$, as a candidate for the definition of a new intermediate concept, e.g., $Q \leftarrow A_1, \ldots, A_m$ with $Q = q(Y_1, \ldots, Y_k)$. The predicate symbol $q$ denotes the new concept, which in our domain is to represent a sequence of observations which occurs frequently in the learned rules. The question is, how to choose the variables

$Y_1, \ldots, Y_k$. One of the goals of defining new concepts is to suppress unnecessary variables, i.e., variables, which occur in $A_1, \ldots, A_m$, but not in $B$ or some $A_i, m < i \leq n$. We denote these *internal variables of* $A_1, \ldots, A_m$ *with respect to* $C$ by $internal\_vars(\{A_1, \ldots, A_m\}|C)$. They are not to appear in the head of the new rule, i.e., we set $\{Y_1, \ldots, Y_k\} = keep\_vars(\{A_1, \ldots, A_m\}|C) = vars(\{A_1, \ldots, A_m\}) - internal\_vars(\{A_1, \ldots, A_m\}|C)$.

---

**restruct**$(m, Rules)$

1. $Done := \emptyset$;
2. $ToDo := Rules$;
3. **while** there exists $C \in ToDo$ with $C = (B \leftarrow A_1, \ldots, A_{m-1}, A_m, \ldots, A_n)$, $n \geq m$, where $A_1, \ldots, A_{m-1}$ are EDB predicates and there exists no $C' \in ToDo$ with a longer premise and the same prefix:
   (a) determine the new head variables:
       **if** $m = 2$ **then** $\{Y_1, \ldots, Y_k\} = vars(\{A_1\})$
           **else** $\{Y_1, \ldots, Y_k\} = vars(\{A_1, \ldots, A_{m-1}\}) - internal\_vars(\{A_1, \ldots, A_{m-1}\}|C)$;
   (b) generate a new predicate symbol $q$
   (c) $Done := Done \cup \{q(Y_1, \ldots, Y_k) \leftarrow A_1, \ldots, A_{m-1}\}$;
   (d) $ToDo := \text{fold}(ToDo, q(Y_1, \ldots, Y_k) \leftarrow A_1, \ldots, A_{m-1})$;
4. **while** there exists $C \in ToDo$ such that either $C = (B \leftarrow A_1, \ldots, A_l)$, $l < m$, or $C = (B \leftarrow A_1, \ldots, A_m, A_{m+1}, \ldots, A_n)$, $n \geq m$ and there exists no $C' \in ToDo$ with a longer premise and the same prefix:
   **if** $C = (B \leftarrow A_1, \ldots, A_l)$
   **then**    (a) $Done := Done \cup \{C\}$;
           (b) $ToDo := ToDo - \{C\}$;
   **else if** there exists no rule $C' \in ToDo$, $C' = (G \leftarrow A'_1, \ldots, A'_m, A'_{m+1}, \ldots, A'_s)$, $s \geq m$, such that $A_1, \ldots, A_m$ and $A'_1, \ldots, A'_m$ are unifiable, but no variants **then**:
       (a) determine the new head variables:
           $\{Y_1, \ldots, Y_k\} = vars(\{A_1, \ldots, A_m\}) - internal\_vars(\{A_1, \ldots, A_m\}|C)$;
       (b) generate a new predicate symbol $q$;
       (c) $Done := Done \cup \{q(Y_1, \ldots, Y_k) \leftarrow A_1, \ldots, A_m\}$;
       (d) $ToDo := \text{fold}(ToDo, q(Y_1, \ldots, Y_k) \leftarrow A_1, \ldots, A_m)$;
       **else return** failure;
5. **return** $Done$;

**Algorithm 1 restruct**

---

Given a basic chain Datalog program $\mathbf{P_I}$ and a value for the parameter $m$, the method **restruct** (see Algorithm 1) puts the rules of the program into a $ToDo$ set. The rules which cannot be transformed any more are put into a set $Done$. The method goes through two main cycles:

In the first initialization cycle, for each prefix chain of length $m - 1$, which consists of EDB predicates only, a new concept is introduced: If $C \in \mathbf{P_I}$, $C =$

$(B \leftarrow A_1, \ldots, A_{m-1}, A_m, \ldots, A_n)$, $n \geq m - 1$, then the rule $Q \leftarrow A_1, \ldots, A_{m-1}$ with $Q = q(Y_1, \ldots, Y_k)$ is introduced, where

$$\{Y_1, \ldots, Y_k\} = \begin{cases} vars(\{A_1\}) & \text{if } m = 2 \\ keep\_vars(\{A_1, \ldots, A_{m-1}\}|C) & \text{if } m > 2. \end{cases}$$

For $m = 2$ and our example program $\mathbf{P}_I^0$ consisting of Rules (1),...,(5), we get

$$q_a(Tr, O, S, X, X_1, G_1) \leftarrow a(Tr, O, S, X, X_1, G_1).$$
$$q_b(Tr, O, S, X, X_2, G_2) \leftarrow b(Tr, O, S, X, X_1, G_2).$$

We replace in $\mathbf{P}_I^0$ each prefix chain of length $m - 1$ by the new concepts and get the folded rules for the intermediate program $\mathbf{P}_I^2$:

$$p_1(Tr, S, X, Y) \leftarrow q_a(Tr, O, S, X, X_1, G_1), b(Tr, O, S, X_1, X_2, G_2), \quad (6)$$
$$c(Tr, O, S, X_2, Y, G_3).$$
$$p_2(Tr, S, X, Y) \leftarrow q_a(Tr, O, S, X, X_1, G_1), b(Tr, O, S, X_1, X_2, G_2),$$
$$c(Tr, O, S, X_2, Y, G_3).$$
$$p_3(Tr, S, X, Y) \leftarrow q_a(Tr, O, S, X, X_1, G_1), b(Tr, O, S, X_1, X_2, G_2),$$
$$c(Tr, O, S, X_2, X_3, G_3), d(Tr, O, S, X_3, Y, G_4).$$
$$p_4(Tr, S, X, Y) \leftarrow q_b(Tr, O, S, X, X_1, G_1), c(Tr, O, S, X_1, X_2, G_2),$$
$$d(Tr, O, S, X_2, Y, G_3).$$
$$p_5(Tr, S, X, Y) \leftarrow q_b(Tr, O, S, X, X_1, G_1), c(Tr, O, S, X_1, X_2, G_2),$$
$$d(Tr, O, S, X_2, X_3, G_3), a(Tr, O, S, X_3, X_4, G_4),$$
$$b(Tr, O, S, X_4, Y, G_5).$$

Using the program transformation terminology, we fold the rules of the program with the new definitions with the restriction that $A_1, \ldots, A_l$ is replaced by $Q$ only where $A_1, \ldots, A_l$ occurs as prefix.

As long as the program contains rules with $m$ or more premise atoms, the second cycle is repeated: We select the rule with the longest premise chain. If there are several rules with the same maximal length, we choose arbitrarily among them. Let the selected rule be $C = (B \leftarrow A_1, \ldots, A_m, A_{m+1}, \ldots, A_n)$. In order to introduce a new concept for $A_1, \ldots, A_m$, the following condition has to be satisfied: For each $C' \in ToDo$, $C' \neq C$, $C' = (G \leftarrow A_1', \ldots, A_m', A_{m+1}', \ldots, A_s')$, $s \geq m$, either $A_1, \ldots, A_m$ and $A_1', \ldots, A_m'$ are variants or they are not unifiable. This condition, together with the principle to consider the rules with the longest premises first, guarantees that the final transformed program $\mathbf{P}_I'$ will be equivalent to $\mathbf{P}_I$ with respect to $\mathcal{I}$. We prove this in Section 5, where we also show the relation of our work to program transformation. If the condition is satisfied, we determine the new head variables $\{Y_1, \ldots, Y_k\} = keep\_vars(\{A_1, \ldots, A_m\}|C) = vars(\{A_1, \ldots, A_m\}) - internal\_vars(\{A_1, \ldots, A_m\}|C)$ and introduce the rule $q(Y_1, \ldots, Y_k) \leftarrow A_1, \ldots, A_m$.

For our example program, we get after the first two iterations of the step 4:

$$q_{ab}(Tr, O, S, X, X_2) \leftarrow q_a(Tr, O, S, X, X_1, G_1), b(Tr, O, S, X_1, X_2, G_2) \quad (7)$$
$$q_{bc}(Tr, O, S, X, X_2) \leftarrow q_b(Tr, O, S, X, X_1, G_1), c(Tr, O, S, X_1, X_2, G_2).$$

We fold each rule of the *ToDo* set, i.e., of $\mathbf{P}_I^2$, if possible with the new rules in the same way as in the initialization step. We get the folded rules of $\mathbf{P}_I^4$:

$$p_1(Tr, S, X, Y) \leftarrow q_{ab}(Tr, O, S, X, X_2), c(Tr, O, S, X_2, Y, G_3). \quad (8)$$
$$p_2(Tr, S, X, Y) \leftarrow q_{ab}(Tr, O, S, X, X_2), c(Tr, O, S, X_2, Y, G_3).$$
$$p_3(Tr, S, X, Y) \leftarrow q_{ab}(Tr, O, S, X, X_2), c(Tr, O, S, X_2, X_3, G_3),$$
$$d(Tr, O, S, X_3, Y, G_4).$$
$$p_4(Tr, S, X, Y) \leftarrow q_{bc}(Tr, O, S, X, X_2), d(Tr, O, S, X_2, Y, G_3).$$
$$p_5(Tr, S, X, Y) \leftarrow q_{bc}(Tr, O, S, X, X_2), d(Tr, O, S, X_2, X_3, G_3),$$
$$a(Tr, O, S, X_3, X_4, G_4), b(Tr, O, S, X_4, Y, G_5).$$

By folding the rules in *ToDo* with the new definitions, their length is reduced more and more. Rules with fewer than $m$ premise atoms are put into the set *Done*. So, if the admissibility condition in step 4 is never violated, the *ToDo* set will finally be empty. In this case the *Done* set contains the transformed program. For our example program, Algorithm 1 yields the program $\mathbf{P}_I'$ consisting of Rules (9), ..., (22):

$$q_a(Tr, O, S, X, Y, G_1) \leftarrow a(Tr, O, S, X, Y, G_1). \quad (9)$$
$$q_b(Tr, O, S, X, Y, G_1) \leftarrow b(Tr, O, S, X, Y, G_1). \quad (10)$$
$$q_{ab}(Tr, O, S, X, Y) \leftarrow q_a(Tr, O, S, X_1, X_2, G_1), b(Tr, O, S, X_2, Y, G_2). \quad (11)$$
$$q_{bc}(Tr, O, S, X, Y) \leftarrow q_b(Tr, O, S, X_1, X_2, G_1), c(Tr, O, S, X_2, Y, G_2). \quad (12)$$
$$q_{abc}(Tr, O, S, X, Y) \leftarrow q_{ab}(Tr, O, S, X_1, X_2), c(Tr, O, S, X_2, Y, G_3). \quad (13)$$
$$q_{bcd}(Tr, O, S, X, Y) \leftarrow q_{bc}(Tr, O, S, X_1, X_2), d(Tr, O, S, X_2, Y, G_3). \quad (14)$$
$$p_1(Tr, S, X, Y) \leftarrow q_{abc}(Tr, O, S, X, Y). \quad (15)$$
$$p_2(Tr, S, X, Y) \leftarrow q_{abc}(Tr, O, S, X, Y). \quad (16)$$
$$p_4(Tr, S, X, Y) \leftarrow q_{bcd}(Tr, O, S, X, Y). \quad (17)$$
$$q_{abcd}(Tr, S, X, Y) \leftarrow q_{abc}(Tr, O, S, X_1, X_2), d(Tr, O, S, X_2, Y, G_4). \quad (18)$$
$$q_{bcda}(Tr, O, S, X, Y) \leftarrow q_{bcd}(Tr, O, S, X_1, X_2), a(Tr, O, S, X_2, Y, G_4). \quad (19)$$
$$p_3(Tr, S, X, Y) \leftarrow q_{abcd}(Tr, S, X, Y). \quad (20)$$
$$q_{bcdab}(Tr, S, X, Y) \leftarrow q_{bcda}(Tr, O, S, X_1, X_2), b(Tr, O, S, X_2, Y, G_5). \quad (21)$$
$$p_5(Tr, S, X, Y) \leftarrow q_{bcdab}(Tr, S, X, Y). \quad (22)$$

$\mathbf{P}_I'$ has an inference depth greater than one. Furthermore, $\mathrm{EDB}(\mathbf{P}_I) = \mathrm{EDB}(\mathbf{P}_I')$ and $\mathrm{IDB}(\mathbf{P}_I) \subseteq \mathrm{IDB}(\mathbf{P}_I')$. Note, that the original program $\mathbf{P}_I$ consisting of Rules (1),...,(5) could be divided into disjunctive sets of rules, such that each set contained the rules for one target concept[1]. Our restructuring method integrates these rules for different concepts by removing the redundancies and decreasing the ambiguities, thus making their evaluation more efficient.

## 5    Program Transformation

The goal of program transformation is to transform a program into one, which can be evaluated more efficiently. In this section, we show the relation of our approach to program transformation, i.e., we show, that our restructuring method implements in a specific way the transformation operations *define* and *fold*, which are known to preserve equivalence under certain conditions. This allows us to prove, that the program $\mathbf{P}'_{\mathrm{I}}$, which results from restructuring $\mathbf{P}_{\mathrm{I}}$, is equivalent to $\mathbf{P}_{\mathrm{I}}$ with respect to a set $\mathcal{I}$ of target concepts.

Unfold/fold transformations have been shown to preserve equivalence with respect to their least Herbrand models [25], the finite failure set by SLD-resolution of a definite program [21], [22], Fitting's semantics [3], and the minimal S-model semantics [2].

In the following, we give a short review of unfold/fold transformations and their properties, in order to formalize our approach in that framework. The unfold and fold operations are defined as follows [21], [22]:

**Definition 1** *(Unfold)*
*Let $\mathbf{P}^i_{\mathrm{I}}$ be a basic program and $C \in \mathbf{P}^i_{\mathrm{I}}$ a clause of the form $B \leftarrow A_1, A_2, \ldots, A_n$. Suppose that $D \in \mathbf{P}_{\mathrm{I}}$ such that $D = (A' \leftarrow R_1, \ldots, R_m)$ and $A'$ is unifiable with $A_1$ with mgu $\theta$. Let $C'$ be the result of applying $\theta$ after replacing $A_1$ in $C$ with the $D_{body}\theta$, i.e., $C' = (B\theta \leftarrow R_1\theta, \ldots, R_m\theta, A_2\theta, \ldots, A_n\theta)$. The unfolding operation, denoted by $\mathrm{unfold}(\mathbf{P}^i_{\mathrm{I}}, C, D)$, has as result the transformed program $\mathbf{P}^{i+1}_{\mathrm{I}} = \mathbf{P}^i_{\mathrm{I}} - \{C\} \cup \{C'\}$.*

The result of, e.g., $unfold(\mathbf{P}'_{\mathrm{I}}, (15), (13))$ is $\mathbf{P}'_{\mathrm{I}} - \{(15)\} \cup \{(8)\}$.

**Definition 2** *(Fold)*
*Let $C, D \in \mathbf{P}^i_{\mathrm{I}}$ be clauses of the form $C = (B \leftarrow A_1, \ldots, A_m, A_{m+1}, \ldots, A_{m+n})$ and $D = (Q \leftarrow A'_1, \ldots, A'_m)$. Furthermore, we require that any terms appearing as internal arguments of $A_1, \ldots, A_m$ be variables. If there exists a substitution $\theta$ satisfying the following applicability conditions*

1. *$A_i = A'_i\theta$ for each $i \in \{1, \ldots, m\}$ ;*
2. *let $X_1, \ldots, X_l$ be the internal variables of $D$, which occur in $D_{body}$, but not in $D_{head}$. Then, each $X_j\theta, 1 \leq j \leq l$ appears neither in $B$ nor in $A_{m+1}, \ldots, A_{m+n}$, and, furthermore, $X_i\theta \neq X_j\theta, i \neq j$ ;*
3. *$D$ is the only clause in $\mathbf{P}_{\mathrm{I}}$, whose head is unifiable with $Q\theta$;*
4. *atom $B$ is one of the target predicates in $\mathcal{I}$.*

---

[1] Rule sets which were actually learned in our domain contain between 50 and 100 rules for 8 target concepts, which means, that there exist on average 5 to 15 rules for one concept.

*Then, let $C' = (B \leftarrow Q\theta, A_{m+1}, \ldots, A_{m+n})$. The* fold *operation, denoted by* fold$(\mathbf{P}_{\mathrm{I}}^i, C, D)$, *has as result the transformed program* $\mathbf{P}_{\mathrm{I}}^{i+1} = \mathbf{P}_{\mathrm{I}}^i - \{C\} \cup \{C', D\}$. *$C$ is called the* folded clause *and $D$ the* folding clause.

The result of, e.g., $fold(\mathbf{P}_{\mathrm{I}}^2, (6), (7))$ is $\mathbf{P}_{\mathrm{I}}^2 - \{(6)\} \cup \{(7), (8)\}$.

**Definition 3** *(Transformation Sequence)*
*Let $\mathbf{P}_{\mathrm{I}}^0$ be an initial basic program and $\mathbf{P}_{\mathrm{I}}^{i+1}, i > 0$ a basic program obtained from $\mathbf{P}_{\mathrm{I}}^i$ by applying either unfolding or folding. Then, the sequence of programs $\mathbf{P}_{\mathrm{I}}^0, \mathbf{P}_{\mathrm{I}}^1, \ldots, \mathbf{P}_{\mathrm{I}}^N$ is called a* transformation sequence *starting from $\mathbf{P}_{\mathrm{I}}^0$.*

Tamaki and Sato have proven the following theorem:

**Theorem 1** *([25]) The least Herbrand model, $\mathcal{M}(\mathbf{P}^i)$, of any program $\mathbf{P}^i = \mathbf{P}_{\mathrm{I}}^i \cup \mathbf{P}_{\mathrm{E}}$, where $\mathbf{P}_{\mathrm{I}}^i$ is a basic program in a transformation sequence starting from the initial program $\mathbf{P}_{\mathrm{I}}^0$, is identical to that of $\mathbf{P}^0 = \mathbf{P}_{\mathrm{I}}^0 \cup \mathbf{P}_{\mathrm{E}}$.*

In our approach, we modify the program by adding rules for newly invented predicates, which are then used as folding clauses. Of course, in that case, the least Herbrand model of the original program $\mathbf{P}^0 = \mathbf{P}_{\mathrm{I}}^0 \cup \mathbf{P}_{\mathrm{E}}$ cannot be identical to the one of $\mathbf{P}^i = \mathbf{P}_{\mathrm{I}}^i \cup \mathbf{P}_{\mathrm{E}}$. But given a set of target concepts $\mathcal{I} \subseteq \mathrm{IDB}(\mathbf{P}_{\mathrm{I}}^0)$, we require the least Herbrand models of $\mathbf{P}^0$ and $\mathbf{P}^i$ restricted to the predicates in $\mathcal{I}$ to be identical, i.e., $Cov_{\mathbf{P}_0}(\mathcal{I}) = Cov_{\mathbf{P}_i}(\mathcal{I})$.

We define our *define*-operation as follows:

**Definition 4** *(Define)*
*Given a parameter $m$ and a rule $C = (B \leftarrow A_1, \ldots, A_m, A_{m+1}, \ldots, A_n), n \geq m$, with ordered premise literals, the result of the* define-operation, *denoted define$(C, m)$, is the rule $D = (Q \leftarrow A_1, \ldots, A_m)$ with $Q = q(Y_1, \ldots, Y_k)$, where $q$ is a new predicate symbol and $\{Y_1, \ldots, Y_k\} = vars(\{A_1, \ldots, A_m\}) - internal\_vars(\{A_1, \ldots, A_m\}|C)$.*

In our method, the new definitions are used as folding clauses. Given a definition $D = (Q \leftarrow A'_1, \ldots, A'_m)$ and a basic program $\mathbf{P}_{\mathrm{I}}$ (i.e., the *ToDo* set in Algorithm 1), we want to replace in every rule $C \in \mathbf{P}_{\mathrm{I}}$ its prefix $A_1, \ldots, A_m$ by $Q\theta$ if $A_1, \ldots, A_m$ and $A'_1, \ldots, A'_m$ are unifiable with mgu $\theta$. We have implemented the $\mathtt{fold}(ToDo, D)$-procedure in Algorithm 1 in this way. But without any further restrictions, some of the applicability conditions for folding (see Definition 2) may not be satisfied, thus, destroying the equivalence of the transformed program. The following examples are to illustrate this point:

**Example 1** $\qquad\qquad \mathbf{P}_{\mathrm{I}}^i = \{C1, C2\}$ with

$C1 : p_2(Tr, S, X, Y) \leftarrow q_{ab}(Tr, \boldsymbol{O}, S, X, X_1), c(Tr, \boldsymbol{O}, S, X_1, Y).$
$C2 : p_3(A, C, D, E) \leftarrow q_{ab}(A, \boldsymbol{B}, C, D, D_1), c(A, \boldsymbol{B}, C, D_1, D_2), d(A, \boldsymbol{B}, C, D_2, E).$

Let $D1$ be the result of $define(C1, 2)$:

$\qquad D1 : q_{abc}(Tr, S, X, Y) \leftarrow q_{ab}(Tr, O, S, X, X_1), c(Tr, O, S, X_1, Y).$

We check the conditions for $fold(\mathbf{P}_{\mathrm{I}}^i, C2, D1)$:
The substitution $\theta = \{Tr/A, O/B, S/C, X/D, X_1/D_1, X_2/E\}$ satisfies applicability condition 1. The internal variables of $D1$ are $O$ and $X_1$. But the substituted variable $B$ occurs in $d(A, B, C, D_2, E)$ of $C2$. Therefore applicability condition 2 is not satisfied. Simple replacement would have yielded

$$C2' : p_3(A, C, D, E) \leftarrow q_{abc}(A, C, D, D_2), d(A, B, C, D_2, E).$$

Unfolding $C2'$ with $D1$ again yields $C2''$, which is more general than the original $C2$:

$$C2'' : p_3(A, C, D, E) \leftarrow q_{ab}(A, O, C, D, D_1), c(A, O, C, D_1, D_2), d(A, B, C, D_2, E).$$

**Example 2**                      $\mathbf{P}_{\mathrm{I}}^i = \{C3, C4\}$ with

$$C3 : p_4(Tr, X, Y) \leftarrow q_a(Tr, O, X, X_1), b(Tr, O, X_1, X_2), c(Tr, O, X_2, Y).$$
$$C4 : p_5(Ar, D, E) \leftarrow q_a(Ar, J, D, D_1), b(Ar, K, D_1, D_2), c(Ar, L, D_2, E).$$

Let $D3$ be the result of $define(C3, 2)$:

$$D3 : q_{ab}(Tr, O, X, X_2) \leftarrow q_a(Tr, O, X, X_1), b(Tr, O, X_1, X_2).$$

We check the conditions for $fold(\mathbf{P}_{\mathrm{I}}^i, C4, D3)$: The chains $q_a(Tr, O, X, X_1)$, $b(Tr, O, X_1, X_2)$ and $q_a(Ar, J, D, D_1)$, $b(Ar, K, D_1, D_2)$ are unifiable with mgu $\sigma = \{Tr/Ar, O/J, X/D, X_1/D_1, X_2/D_2, K/J\}$. But

$$b(Ar, K, D_1, D_2) \neq b(Ar, J, D_1, D_2) = b(Tr, O, X_1, X_2)\sigma.$$

Thus, applicability condition 1 is not satisfied. Simple replacement would have yielded

$$C4' : p_5(Ar, D, E) \leftarrow q_{ab}(Ar, J, D, D_2), c(Ar, L, D_2, E).$$

Unfolding $C4'$ with $D3$ again yields $C4''$, which is more special than the original $C4$:

$$C4'' : p_5(Ar, D, E) \leftarrow q_a(Ar, O, D, D_1), b(Ar, O, D_1, D_2), c(Ar, L, D_2, E).$$

This lets us define admissibility conditions for a definition $D$ in a program $\mathbf{P}_{\mathrm{I}}$:

**Definition 5** *(Admissibility of a definition)*
*Given a basic logic program* $\mathbf{P}_{\mathrm{I}}$ *and a clause* $C \in \mathbf{P}_{\mathrm{I}}$, $C = (B \leftarrow A_1, \ldots, A_m, A_{m+1}, \ldots, A_n)$, *the definition* $D = (Q \leftarrow A_1, \ldots, A_m) = define(C, m)$ *is admissible in* $\mathbf{P}_{\mathrm{I}}$, *if*

1. *there exists no rule* $C' \in \mathbf{P}_{\mathrm{I}}$, $C' = (G \leftarrow R_1, \ldots, R_m, R_{m+1}, \ldots, R_o)$, $o > n$, *such that* $A_1, \ldots, A_m$ *and* $R_1, \ldots, R_m$ *are variants and there exists a substitution* $\theta$, *such that* $R_i = A_i\theta, i = 1, \ldots, m$, *but*

$$internal\_vars(\{A_1\theta, \ldots, A_m\theta\}|C\theta) \supset internal\_vars(\{R_1, \ldots, R_m\}|C');$$

2. *there exists no rule* $C' \in \mathbf{P}_I$, $C' = (G \leftarrow A'_1, \ldots, A'_m, A'_{m+1}, \ldots, A'_s)$, $s \geq m$, *such that* $A_1, \ldots, A_m$ *and* $A'_1, \ldots, A'_m$ *are unifiable, but no variants.*

Applicability condition *1* (*2*) prevents the problem illustrated in Example 1 (2) from occurring. So, admissibility conditions *1* and *2* account for the applicability conditions *1* and *2* for folding. In Algorithm 1, we first consider the rules of maximal length. This guarantees, that admissibility condition *1* is always satisfied. Admissibility condition *2* is checked explicitly. Applicability condition *3* is always satisfied because every folding clause $D$ is a definition which introduces a new predicate symbol. Applicability condition *4* is always satisfied because the *ToDo* set contains only rules for the target predicates in $\mathcal{I}$. So the folding operation implemented in Algorithm 1 is equivalence preserving for the original target concepts.

This leads us to our claim, that our restructuring method generates a transformation sequence whose final element $\mathbf{P}'_I = \mathbf{P}_I^N$ is a program which is equivalent to the original $\mathbf{P}_I = \mathbf{P}_I^0$ with respect to $\mathcal{I}$:

**Theorem 2** *Let* $\mathbf{P}_I$ *be a basic chain Datalog program of inference depth one with rules, whose premise atoms are sorted according to the* $\ll$-*relation. Let* $\mathbf{P}'_I$ *be the program which results from restructuring* $\mathbf{P}_I$. *Then, for a given EDB instance* $\mathbf{P}_E$

$$\{p_i(t_1, \ldots, t_s) \mid p_i \in \mathcal{I} \text{ and } p_i(t_1, \ldots, t_s) \in T^\omega_{\mathbf{P}_I}(\mathbf{P}_E)\}$$

$$=$$

$$\{p_i(t_1, \ldots, t_s) \mid p_i \in \mathcal{I} \text{ and } p_i(t_1, \ldots, t_s) \in T^\omega_{\mathbf{P}'_I}(\mathbf{P}_E)\}$$

*with* $\mathcal{I} \subseteq IDB(\mathbf{P}_I)$, *i.e., the coverage for the target predicates* $p_i \in \mathcal{I}$ *is the same for* $\mathbf{P} = \mathbf{P}_I \cup \mathbf{P}_E$ *and* $\mathbf{P}' = \mathbf{P}'_I \cup \mathbf{P}_E$: $Cov_{\mathbf{P}}(\mathcal{I}) = Cov_{\mathbf{P}'}(\mathcal{I})$.

*Proof* The $\subseteq$-part: The inference depth of $\mathbf{P}_I$ is 1, i.e., $T^\omega_{\mathbf{P}_I}(\mathbf{P}_E) = T^1_{\mathbf{P}_I}(\mathbf{P}_E)$. Let $\breve{B} \in T^1_{\mathbf{P}_I}(\mathbf{P}_E)$. Then, there exists a $C \in \mathbf{P}_I$ such that $C\sigma = (\breve{B} \leftarrow \breve{A}_1, \ldots, \breve{A}_n)$ and $\breve{A}_1, \ldots, \breve{A}_n \in \mathbf{P}_E$. We have to show, that $\breve{B} \in T^\omega_{\mathbf{P}'_I}(\mathbf{P}_E)$. For the rule $C = (B \leftarrow A_1, \ldots, A_n)$, the restructuring method has produced $v + 1$ rules by defining and folding:

$$C_1 = (Q_1 \leftarrow A_1, \ldots, A_{m-1})$$
$$C_2 = (Q_2 \leftarrow Q_1, A_m, \ldots, A_{2(m-1)})$$
$$C_3 = (Q_3 \leftarrow Q_2, A_{2(m-1)+1}, \ldots, A_{3(m-1)})$$
$$\cdots$$
$$C_v = (Q_v \leftarrow Q_{v-1}, A_{(v-1)(m-1)+1}, \ldots, A_n)$$
$$C_{v+1} = (B \leftarrow Q_v),$$

where $v = (n//(m-1)) + \delta(n \bmod (m-1))$. We define $\delta(n \bmod (m-1)) = 0$ if $n \bmod (m-1) = 0$ and 1 otherwise. We use $//$ to denote integer division. As

$\breve{A}_1, \ldots, \breve{A}_{m-1} \in \mathbf{P}_E, \breve{Q}_1 \in T^1_{\mathbf{P}'_I}(\mathbf{P}_E)$, as $\breve{A}_m, \ldots, \breve{A}_{2(m-1)} \in \mathbf{P}_E, \breve{Q}_2 \in T^2_{\mathbf{P}'_I}(\mathbf{P}_E)$, $\ldots$, as $\breve{A}_{(v-1)(m-1)+1}, \ldots, \breve{A}_n \in \mathbf{P}_E, \breve{Q}_v \in T^v_{\mathbf{P}'_I}(\mathbf{P}_E)$, and $\breve{B} \in T^{v+1}_{\mathbf{P}'_I}(\mathbf{P}_E) \subseteq T^\omega_{\mathbf{P}'_I}(\mathbf{P}_E)$.

The $\supseteq$-part: Let $\breve{B} = p_r(t_1, \ldots, t_s) \in \{p_x(t_1, \ldots, t_s) | p_x \in \mathcal{I} \text{ and } p_x(t_1, \ldots, t_s) \in T^{i+1}_{\mathbf{P}'_I}(\mathbf{P}_E)\}$. Then, there is a rule $C \in \mathbf{P}'_I$, such that $C\sigma = (\breve{B} \leftarrow \breve{Q}_l)$ with $\breve{Q}_l \in T^i_{\mathbf{P}'_I}(\mathbf{P}_E)$. We have a sequence of rules

$C_l \in \mathbf{P}'_I$, such that $C_l\sigma_l = (\breve{Q}_l \leftarrow \breve{Q}_{l-1}, \breve{A}_{(l-1)(m-1)+1}, \ldots, \breve{A}_n)$
   with $\breve{A}_{(l-1)(m-1)+1}, \ldots, \breve{A}_n \in \mathbf{P}_E$;

$C_{l-1} \in \mathbf{P}'_I$, such that $C_{l-1}\sigma_{l-1} = (\breve{Q}_{l-1} \leftarrow \breve{Q}_{l-2}, \breve{A}_{(l-2)(m-1)+1} \cdots, \breve{A}_{(l-1)(m-1)})$
   with $\breve{A}_{(l-2)(m-1)+1}, \ldots, \breve{A}_{(l-1)(m-1)} \in \mathbf{P}_E$;

$$\vdots$$

$C_1 \in \mathbf{P}'_I$, such that $C_1\sigma_1 = (\breve{Q}_1 \leftarrow \breve{A}_1, \ldots, \breve{A}_{m-1})$ with $\breve{A}_1, \ldots, \breve{A}_{m-1} \in \mathbf{P}_E$.

Let $C^l$ be the result of unfolding $C$ with $C_l$, $C^{l-1}$ the result of unfolding $C^l$ with $C_{l-1}, \ldots, C^1$ the result of unfolding $C^2$ with $C_1$. $Q_1, \ldots, Q_l$ represent some of the new concepts in $IDB(\mathbf{P}'_I) - \mathcal{I}$. Therefore, there exists only one rule for each of them. So the above unfolding sequence is unique and yields a rule $C^1 = (B \leftarrow A_1, \ldots, A_n)$, which is a member of the original $\mathbf{P}_I$. As $\breve{A}_1, \ldots, \breve{A}_n \in \mathbf{P}_E$, it follows that $\breve{B} \in T^\omega_{\mathbf{P}_I}(\mathbf{P}_E)$. $\square$

# 6   Program Decompositions

The goal of program transformation is to modify a given program, such that it can be evaluated more efficiently. In Section 5, we have proven that our restructuring method preserves equivalence with respect to the target concepts in $\mathcal{I}$. We now show, that the transformed program supports faster evaluations.

Program decompositions of (chain) Datalog programs [7], [8] are known to speed up the process of inferring the least Herbrand model. We introduce a new definition for decompositions of non-elementary chain Datalog programs, which is similar to the one introduced by Dong and Ginsburg [8]:

**Definition 6** *For a given set of IDB predicates* $\mathcal{I} = \{p_1, \ldots, p_v\} \subseteq IDB(\mathbf{P}_I)$ *of a basic logic program* $\mathbf{P}_I$ *a sequence* $\mathbf{P}_{I,1} \ldots \mathbf{P}_{I,n}(n \geq 1)$ *of programs is called a* $\{p_1, \ldots, p_v\}$-*decomposition of* $\mathbf{P}_I$ *if*

$$\{p_i(t_1, \ldots, t_s) \mid p_i \in \mathcal{I} \text{ and } p_i(t_1, \ldots, t_s) \in T^\omega_{\mathbf{P}_{I,n}} \circ \ldots \circ T^\omega_{\mathbf{P}_{I,1}}(I)\}$$
$$=$$
$$\{p_i(t_1, \ldots, t_s) \mid p_i \in \mathcal{I} \text{ and } p_i(t_1, \ldots, t_s) \in T^\omega_{\mathbf{P}_I}(I)\}$$

*for ground terms (constants)* $t_1, \ldots, t_s$ *and interpretations I, which are restricted to be EDB instances of* $\mathbf{P}_I$.

The composition $f \circ g(I)$ is defined as $f(g(I))$. The $\mathbf{P}_{I,i}, i = 1, \ldots, n$ are called *components*. The purpose of decompositions is to divide a program into smaller clusters, in order to speed up its evaluation. Furthermore, they focus on a subset $\mathcal{I}$ of the IDB predicates of the original program $\mathbf{P}_I$.

Given a basic logic program $\mathbf{P}_I$ and two rules $C_1, C_2 \in \mathbf{P}_I$, $C_1$ is said to *depend on* $C_2$ (in $\mathbf{P}_I$), denoted by $C_1 \succ_{\mathbf{P}_I} C_2$, if either the predicate occurring in the head of $C_2$ occurs in the body of $C_1$, or there is a rule $C \in \mathbf{P}_I$, such that $C_1 \succ_{\mathbf{P}_I} C$ and $C \succ_{\mathbf{P}_I} C_2$ [8]. Based on this notion, we can generate components of maximal size by putting into the first component the rules whose bodies contain only EDB predicates. Given a component $\mathbf{P}_{I,i}$, we get $\mathbf{P}_{I,i+1}$ by adding to it all rules which depend directly on a rule in $\mathbf{P}_{I,i}$. We repeat this process until all rules of the original program have been assigned to a component (see Algorithm 2).

---

**max_components($\mathbf{P}_I$)**

1. $\mathbf{P}_{I,1} := \{C | C \in \mathbf{P}_I$ and $C_{body}$ consists of EDB predicates only $\}$;
2. $ToDo := \mathbf{P}_I - \mathbf{P}_{I,1}$;
3. $i := 2$;
4. **while** $ToDo \neq \emptyset$:
   (a) $\mathbf{P}_{I,i} := \{C | C \in ToDo$ and $C \succ_{\mathbf{P}_I} C_j$ directly, with $C_j \in \mathbf{P}_{I,i-1}\}$;
   (b) $ToDo := ToDo - \mathbf{P}_{I,i}$;
   (c) $i := i + 1$;
5. **return** $\mathbf{P}_{I,1} \ldots \mathbf{P}_{I,i-1}$;

**Algorithm 2 max_components**

---

If we apply **max_components** to $\mathbf{P}_I'$, consisting of Rules (9), ..., (22), we get the components $\mathbf{P}_{I,1} = \{(9), (10)\}$, $\mathbf{P}_{I,2} = \{(11), (12)\}$, $\mathbf{P}_{I,3} = \{(13), (14)\}$, $\mathbf{P}_{I,4} = \{(15), (16), (17), (18), (19)\}$, $\mathbf{P}_{I,5} = \{(20), (21)\}$, $\mathbf{P}_{I,6} = \{(22)\}$.

If we calculate $T^{\omega}_{\mathbf{P}_{I,6}} \circ T^{\omega}_{\mathbf{P}_{I,5}} \circ T^{\omega}_{\mathbf{P}_{I,4}} \circ T^{\omega}_{\mathbf{P}_{I,3}} \circ T^{\omega}_{\mathbf{P}_{I,2}} \circ T^{\omega}_{\mathbf{P}_{I,1}}(\mathbf{P}_E)$ according to Definition 6 for $\mathbf{P}_E = a(t1, 90, s5, 1, 8, 45), b(t1, 90, s5, 8, 10, 26), c(t1, 90, s5, 10, 15, 6), d(t1, 90, s5, 15, 17, -3)$, we get

$$I1 = T^{\omega}_{\mathbf{P}_{I,1}}(\mathbf{P}_E) = \mathbf{P}_E \cup \{q_a(t1, 90, s5, 1, 8, 45), q_b(t1, 90, s5, 8, 10, 26)\}$$

$$I2 = T^{\omega}_{\mathbf{P}_{I,2}}(I1) = I1 \cup \{q_{ab}(t1, 90, s5, 1, 10), q_{bc}(t1, 90, s5, 8, 15)\}$$

$$I3 = T^{\omega}_{\mathbf{P}_{I,3}}(I2) = I2 \cup \{q_{abc}(t1, 90, s5, 1, 15), q_{bcd}(t1, 90, s5, 8, 17)\}$$

$$I4 = T^{\omega}_{\mathbf{P}_{I,4}}(I3) = I3 \cup \{p_1(t1, s5, 1, 15), p_2(t1, s5, 1, 15), p_4(t1, s5, 8, 17),$$

$$q_{abcd}(t1, 90, s5, 1, 17)\}$$
$$I5 = T^{\omega}_{\mathbf{P}_{I,5}}(I4) = I4 \cup \{p_3(t1, s5, 1, 17)\}$$
$$I6 = T^{\omega}_{\mathbf{P}_{I,6}}(I5) = I5.$$

So, we have $T^{\omega}_{\mathbf{P}_{I,6}} \circ T^{\omega}_{\mathbf{P}_{I,5}} \circ T^{\omega}_{\mathbf{P}_{I,4}} \circ T^{\omega}_{\mathbf{P}_{I,3}} \circ T^{\omega}_{\mathbf{P}_{I,2}} \circ T^{\omega}_{\mathbf{P}_{I,1}}(\mathbf{P}_E) = I5$. For this example, it is easy to see, that the requirement of Definiton 6 is satisfied, i.e.,

$$\{p_i(t_1, \ldots, t_s) \mid p_i \in \mathcal{I} \text{ and } p_i(t_1, \ldots, t_s) \in T^{\omega}_{\mathbf{P}_{I,6}} \circ T^{\omega}_{\mathbf{P}_{I,5}} \circ \ldots \circ T^{\omega}_{\mathbf{P}_{I,1}}(\mathbf{P}_E)\} =$$
$$\{p_i(t_1, \ldots, t_s) \mid p_i \in \mathcal{I} \text{ and } p_i(t_1, \ldots, t_s) \in T^{\omega}_{\mathbf{P}_I}(\mathbf{P}_E)\} =$$
$$\{p_1(t1, s5, 1, 15), p_2(t1, s5, 1, 15), p_3(t1, s5, 1, 17), p_4(t1, s5, 8, 17)\}.$$

So, $\mathbf{P}_{I,1}\mathbf{P}_{I,2}\mathbf{P}_{I,3}\mathbf{P}_{I,4}\mathbf{P}_{I,5}\mathbf{P}_{I,6}$ is a $\{p_1, p_2, p_3, p_4, p_5\}$-decomposition of $\mathbf{P}_I$. For the general case, we have the following theorem:

**Theorem 3** *Let $\mathbf{P}_I$ be a basic chain Datalog program of inference depth one with rules, whose premise atoms are sorted according to the $\ll$-relation. Let $\mathcal{I} = \{p_1, \ldots, p_v\} \subseteq IDB(\mathbf{P}_I)$. Let $\mathbf{P}'_I$ be the result of applying $\mathtt{restruct}$ to $\mathbf{P}_I$ and $\mathbf{P}_{I,1} \ldots \mathbf{P}_{I,n}$ the sequence of components which is generated by $\mathtt{max\_components}$, i.e., $\mathbf{P}_{I,1} \cup \ldots \cup \mathbf{P}_{I,n} = \mathbf{P}'_I \neq \mathbf{P}_I$. Then, $\mathbf{P}_{I,1} \ldots \mathbf{P}_{I,n}$ is a $\{p_1, \ldots, p_v\}$-decomposition of $\mathbf{P}_I$, i.e.,*

$$\{p_i(t_1, \ldots, t_s) \mid p_i \in \mathcal{I} \text{ and } p_i(t_1, \ldots, t_s) \in T^{\omega}_{\mathbf{P}_I}(\mathbf{P}_E)\}$$
$$=$$
$$\{p_i(t_1, \ldots, t_s) \mid p_i \in \mathcal{I} \text{ and } p_i(t_1, \ldots, t_s) \in T^{\omega}_{\mathbf{P}_{I,n}} \circ \ldots \circ T^{\omega}_{\mathbf{P}_{I,1}}(\mathbf{P}_E)\}.$$

The proof of this theorem is straightforward and can be found in [19]. It is obvious, that calculating the least Herbrand model by applying the fixpoint operator sequentially to the components is more efficient than applying it to the program as a whole. This is due to the fact, that decompositions allow us to consider each rule only after all rules, on which it depends, have been applied. Rule (20), e.g., needs to be considered only after Rule (18) has been applied, which, in turn, is considered after the application of Rule (13). ¿From a parallel processing point of view, the rules of a component, which are independent of each other, can be processed in parallel. Based on these ideas, we have developed an efficient forward inference procedure, which calculates the least Herbrand model of a chain Datalog program (see [18]).

## 7 Related Work

*Program transformation in ILP and deductive databases* Fold and unfold operations have been applied in several EBL approaches, which assume the following scenario: A program $\mathbf{P}$ and a query $G$ are given and usually SLD-resolution is applied in order to find a refutation of $P \cup \neg G$ in a top-down fashion through backward chaining. In this context, the purpose of the transformation is to remove repeated subcomputations [5] or search state redundancies [4] which have the effect that the same consequence which is an instance of $G$ can be derived in more than one way.

In our scenario, we have a program $P$ and we want to derive *all* its consequences in a bottom-up fashion via forward chaining as fast as possible. Redundancies caused by the fact that rule premises share sequences of literals slow down the inference process. So our program transformation method is guided by characteristics of the program in contrast to the EBL approaches which are example-guided.

In the field of deductive databases, a third scenario has been dealt with: A program $P$ and a query $G$ are given and forward chaining methods such as semi-naive evaluation are applied to find a proof for $G$. In this context, the disadvantage of forward chaining methods is that they generate many facts which are irrelevant for the derivation of the query. Magic templates, magic sets, filtering, and counting are some of the methods (for a survey, see [16]) which transform logic programs for a given goal $G$ such that the application of forward inference methods applied to the transformed program do not generate any irrelevant facts. Whereas we share with this scenario the use of forward chaining, our restructuring method is not guided by a query $G$, but by the redundancies.

*Predicate invention by inverse resolution* Inverse resolution has been introduced as a generalization technique for first-order logic theories [14], [28]. Muggleton defined the so-called V- and W-operator (see, e.g., [14]). The latter one can be realized as intra- or inter-construction. Sommer has already shown in [24], that both, intra- and interconstruction, can also be considered as program transformation techniques, which introduce a definition which is then used for folding. Inter-construction is called in [13] an "inductive inference rule"

$$\text{Inter-construction:} \quad \frac{p \leftarrow G, H \qquad q \leftarrow G, K}{p \leftarrow r, H \quad r \leftarrow G \quad q \leftarrow r, K},$$

where $p$ and $q$ represent propositional constants and $G, H$ and $K$ conjunctions of propositional constants. Given the clause above the line, the clauses below the line are generated. Clause $r \leftarrow G$ is the newly introduced definition; $p \leftarrow r, H$ and $q \leftarrow r, K$ result from folding $p \leftarrow G, H$ and $q \leftarrow G, H$ with the definition. In principle, our restructuring method implements the following inter-construction rule for chain Datalog rules

$$\frac{C = (B \leftarrow A_1, \ldots, A_m, A_{m+1}, \ldots, A_n), \quad E \leftarrow A'_1, \ldots, A'_m, D_{m+1}, \ldots, D_r, n \geq r}{B \leftarrow Q, A_{m+1}, \ldots, A_n \quad Q \leftarrow A_1, \ldots, A_m \quad E \leftarrow Q\theta, D_{m+1}, \ldots, D_r},$$

where $Q = q(Y_1, \ldots, Y_k)$ is the newly invented predicate with $\{Y_1, \ldots, Y_k\} = vars(\{A_1, \ldots, A_m\}) - internal\_vars(\{A_1, \ldots, A_m\}|C)$. The substitution $\theta$ is the mgu of $A_1, \ldots, A_m$ and $A'_1, \ldots, A'_m$. We use this specific inter-construction rule not as generalization operator, but as an equivalence preserving program transformation operator.

*Theory restructuring* Sommer was the first one to present in [23],[24] a method for theory restructuring, called **FENDER**, which implements inter-construction as a non example-guided program transformation technique. **FENDER** finds candidates for potential new concept definitions by searching for common partial premises (CPPs), each of which is collected around one variable, which appears only in a rule body. Given a chain Datalog program with rules, such as $p(Tr, S, X, Y) \leftarrow r_1(Tr, O, S, X, X_1), \ldots, r_{k+1}(Tr, O, S, X_k, Y)$, **FENDER** would consider the whole premise chain, collected around the variable $O$, and the set of $k$ overlapping CPPs of the form $r_i(Tr, O, S, X_{i-1}, X_i)$, $r_{i+1}(Tr, O, S, X_i, X_{i+1})$, collected around the chaining variables $X_i, i = 1, \ldots, k$, as candidates for intermediate concepts. Neither of these is what we are aiming at. Furthermore, in contrast to our method, **FENDER** restructures the rules for only one concept, whereas we restructure the rules for several concepts, which share common features. Thus, a side-effect of our method is, that the learned models for several concepts are integrated in such a way, that there dependencies and similarities become more obvious. Thus, the understandability of the learned theory is improved. At the same time, the restructured program supports faster evaluations, thus, improving the performance of inference procedures.

## 8 Conclusion

In this paper, we have been concerned with chain Datalog programs, which have been the result of applying ILP algorithms to a robot navigation domain. Due to the redundancies and ambiguities of the learned rules and due to the requirements of the real-world domain, improvements of both, the programs and their inference procedures were needed.

The contribution of this paper is a new restructuring method, which improves the program in terms of understandability and modularity. The method transforms a given program in such a way, that methods, which are known to speed up inferences, can be applied: It constitutes the main part (besides sorting and determining the maximal components) of a constructive method, which generates a decomposition of non-elementary chain Datalog program, whose components are evaluated sequentially.

The relation of our approach to program transformation helped us to prove, that the restructuring method transforms the program without changing the coverage of a set of target concepts. Thus, the method constitutes a contribution to the field of theory restructuring.

We have pointed out the relation of our approach to inverse resolution, as it implements inter-construction in a specific way. If we generate the rule dependency graph for the transformed program, we get a prefix tree, i.e., each path starting from the root represents a prefix chain occurring in the original rule set. Future work will investigate the use of intra-construction to generate suffix trees, in which each node represents a suffix chain occurring in the original rule set.

The methods for sorting and restructuring depend heavily on the syntactical features of chain Datalog rules. This restricts the applicability of the approach to other domains. But, given the fact, that the $\ll$-relation can be used to reflect the chronological order of events, our method may be applied to any domain involving temporal processes, e.g., language or sequences of images. The application of our methods to domains of this type is a further goal of future work.

*Acknowledgements* The author would like to thank K. Morik for comments on relations to existing ILP approaches.

# References

1. K. R. Apt and M. H. van Emden. Contributions to the theory of logic programming. *Journal of the Association for Computing Machinery*, 29:841–862, 1982.
2. A. Bossi and N. Cocco. Basic transformation operations which preserve computed answer substitutions of logic programs. *Journal of Logic Programming*, 16:47–87, 1993.
3. A. Bossi and S. Etalle. More on unfold/fold transformations of normal programs: Preservation of Fitting's semantics. In L. Fribourg and F. Turini, editors, *Logical Program Synthesis and Transformation - Meta-Programming in Logic*, pages 311–331. Springer-Verlag, 1994.
4. H. Boström. Eliminating redundancy in explanation-based learning. In D. Sleeman and P. Edwards, editors, *Proc. of the Ninth International Workshop on Machine Learning*, pages 37–42, 1992.
5. M. Bruynooghe, L. De Raedt, and D. De Schreye. Explanation-based program transformation. In *Proc. of the Eleventh International Joint Conference on Artificial Intelligence (IJCAI '89)*, pages 407–412. Morgan Kaufmann, 1989.
6. G. DeJong and R. Mooney. Explanation-based learning: An alternative view. *Machine Learning*, 2(1):145–176, 1986.
7. G. Dong and S. Ginsburg. On the decomposition of Datalog program mappings. *Theoretical Computer Science*, 75:143–177, 1990.
8. G. Dong and S. Ginsburg. On decompositions of chain Datalog programs into $p$ (left-)linear 1-rule components. *Journal of Logic Programming*, 23:203–236, 1995.
9. V. Klingspor, K. Morik, and A. Rieger. Learning concepts from sensor data of a mobile robot. *Machine Learning*, 23:305–332, 1996.
10. M. Lübbe. Data-driven learning of syntactical constraints on the hypothesis space for model-based learning. Technical Report 15, University of Dortmund, FB Informatik LS 8, Dortmund, Germany, 1995. in German.
11. T.M. Mitchell, R.M. Keller, and S.T. Kedar-Cabelli. Explanation-based generalization: A unifying view. *Machine Learning*, 1:47–80, 1986.
12. K. Morik, St. Wrobel, J. U. Kietz, and W. Emde. *Knowledge Acquisition and Machine Learning: Theory, Methods, and Applications*. Addison Wesley, 1993.
13. S. Muggleton. Inverse entailment and Progol. *New Generation Computing Journal*, 13:245–286, 1995.
14. S. Muggleton and W. Buntine. Machine invention of first-order predicates by inverting resolution. In S. Muggleton, editor, *Inductive Logic Programming*, pages 261–278. Academic Press, 1992.

15. S. Muggleton and C. Feng. Efficient induction of logic programs. In S. Muggleton, editor, *Inductive Logic Programming*, chapter 13, pages 281–298. Academic Press, 1992.

16. J. F. Naughton and R. Ramakrishnan. Bottom-up evaluation of logic programs. In J. L. Lassez and G. Plotkin, editors, *Computational Logic, Essays in the Honor of Alan Robinson*, pages 640–700. MIT Press, 1991.

17. M. Proietti and A. Pettorossi. Unfolding - definition - folding. In *Proc. of the 3rd International Symp. on Programming Languages Implementation and Logic Programming (PLILP 91)*, number 528 in Lecture Notes in Computer Science, pages 347–358. Spinger Verlag, 1991.

18. A. Rieger. MP: An efficient method for calculating the minimum Herbrand model of chain Datalog programs. In W. Wahlster, editor, *Proc. of the Twelveth European Conference on Artificial Intelligence*, 1996. to appear.

19. A. Rieger. Optimizing chain Datalog programs and their inference procedures. Technical
Report 20, University of Dortmund, FB Informatik LS 8, Dortmund, Germany, 1996. ftp://ftp-ai.informatik.uni-dortmund.de/pub/Reports/report20.ps.Z.

20. C. Rouveirol. Extensions of inversion of resolution applied to theory completion. In *Inductive Logic Programming*, pages 63–92. Academic Press, 1992.

21. H. Seki. Unfold/fold transformation of stratified programs. In *Proc. of the 6th International Conference on Logic Programming*, pages 554–568. MIT Press, 1989.

22. H. Seki. Unfold/fold transformations of stratified programs. *Theoretical Computer Science*, 86:107–139, 1991.

23. E. Sommer. FENDER : An approach to theory restructuring. In N. Lavrač and St. Wrobel, editors, *Proc. of the European Conference on Machine Learning (ECML-95)*, pages 356–359. Springer-Verlag, 1995.

24. E. Sommer. *Theory Restructuring*. PhD thesis, University of Dortmund, 1996.

25. H. Tamaki and T. Sato. Unfold/fold transformation of logic programs. In S. Tarnlund, editor, *Proc. of the Second Internatinal Conference on Logic Programming*, pages 127–138, 1984.

26. J. D. Ullman and A. van Gelder. Parallel complexity of logical query programs. *Algorithmica*, 3:5–42, 1988.

27. M. H. van Emden and R. A. Kowalski. The semantics of predicate logic as programming language. *Journal of the Association for Computing Machinery*, 23:733–742, 1976.

28. R. Wirth. Completing logic programs by inverse resolution. In K. Morik, editor, *Proc. Fourth European Workong Session on Learning (EWSL)*, pages 239–250. Morgan Kaufmann, 1989.

29. R. Wirth. Constraints for predicate invention. In S. Muggleton, editor, *Inductive Logic Programming*, pages 299–317. Academic Press, 1992.

30. S. Wrobel. *Concept Formation and Knowledge Revision*. Kluwer Academic Publishers, 1994.

# Top-down Induction of Logic Programs from Incomplete Samples *

Nobuhiro Inuzuka[1], Masakage Kamo[2], Naohiro Ishii[1],
Hirohisa Seki[1] and Hidenori Itoh[1]

[1] Department of Intelligence and Computer Science, Nagoya Institute of Technology
Gokiso-cho, Showa-ku, Nagoya 466, Japan
E-mail: {inuzuka,ishii,seki,itoh}@ics.nitech.ac.jp
[2] Aishin Seiki Co.,Ltd., Asahi-cho, Kariya-shi, Aichi 448, Japan
E-Mail: mkamo@rd.aisin.co.jp

**Abstract.** We propose an ILP system FOIL-I, which induces logic programs by a top-down method from incomplete samples. An incomplete sample is constituted by some of positive examples and negative examples on a finite domain. FOIL-I has an evaluation function to estimate candidate definitions, the function which is composition of an information-based function and an encoding complexity measure. FOIL-I uses a best-first search using the evaluation function to make use of suspicious but necessary candidates. Other particular points include a treatment for recursive definitions and removal of redundant clauses. Randomly selected incomplete samples are tested with FOIL-I, Quinlan's FOIL and Muggleton's Progol. Compared with others FOIL-I can induce target relations in many cases from small incomplete samples.

## 1 Introduction

Many ILP(Inductive Logic Programming) systems have been proposed recently. They are expected to give a revolutionary function to Software Engineering and Artificial Intelligence. Some researchers aim at practical uses of ILP. Indeed many researches in application areas have been reported[Coh95, DBJ94, DM91, HS92]. To use ILP systems in practical domains development of noise-tolerant ILP systems is one of essential topics. Some researches are worked in this area[DB92, BP91, AP93, Für93, Dže95]. Easiness or tractability of a system is another aspect of practice. The size of a sample of a target logic program requested by a system affects easiness of the system. Reducing the size of samples is one of main topics in ILP as well[MN95, ALLM94a, ALLM94b].

Our system FOIL-I(First Order Inductive Learner from Incomplete samples) basically uses the framework of FOIL[QCJ93, Qui90]. FOIL-I takes an extensional definition of a target relation and background relations described in Horn

---

* This research is partially supported by the Grant-in-Aid for Encouragement of Young Scientists No.08780346 from the Japanese Ministry of Education, Science, Sports and Culture.

clauses. An extensional definition of a target relation consists of examples or tuples that satisfy the target relation and negative examples or tuples that do not satisfy it. The system hopefully outputs an intensional definition of the target relation, that is, a set of Horn clauses that consist of background relations and possibly the target relation recursively. More precisely, we use a restricted version of Prolog language, which is also used in FOIL. The language does not include cuts, fail, disjunctive goals, and functions other than constants, but includes negated literals.

FOIL requires only finite domains. To construct a definition of the membership relation member FOIL maybe needs a domain that consists of three different atoms a, b and c and lists made from the atoms with length 0, 1, 2, or 3. The finite domain makes FOIL need only reasonable numbers of positive and negative examples to induce the target relation. The number is, however, sometimes still large. In this case the number of positive and negative examples are 75 and 85 respectively. In the case of another relation append with the same situation the number of positive and negative examples are 142 and 63,858 respectively. The aim of FOIL-I is to reduce the number of examples required.

We call the set of all positive(negative) examples a *positive(negative) sample*. A sample of target relation is a pair of positive and negative samples, the pair which gives an extensional definition of the target relation. We call a pair of a subset of positive sample and a subset of negative sample an *incomplete sample*. Users can use the system much easier, if an ILP system requires only small incomplete samples, which means incomplete samples consisted of small numbers of positive and negative examples.

## 2 An example of FOIL-I session

Before the details of FOIL-I we show an example of FOIL-I session.

FOIL-I starts with an input of a file which gives information of a finite domain, information of a target relation, positive and negative examples and background relations.

Figure 1 shows an input file. The first three lines give information of a finite domain which consists of atom and list. The following line gives information of a target relation memb or the membership relation(, whose name replaced by memb to avoid conflicting with a Prolog built-in predicate member). The line includes the name, arity, mode, and type. In mode '+'('−') means that the argument at the place should be given with(without, respectively) being bounded. The type specifies possible values of each arguments. The following two lines give an incomplete sample or positive and negative examples. Finally background relations are given with their names, arities, modes, types and their intensional definitions. FOIL-I uses extensional definitions in the system. Intensional definitions are expanded to extensional definitions after FOIL-I reads them. To give intensional definitions is easier than to give lengthy extensional ones.

Figure 2 shows an output from FOIL-I with the file above. The first line is an input by a user that starts the session with a name of the input file. Following to

```
domain(atom,[[],a,b,c]).
domain(list,[[],[a],[b],[c],[a,b],[a,c],[b,a],[b,c],[c,a],[c,b],[a,b,c],
            [a,c,b],[b,a,c],[b,c,a],[c,a,b],[c,b,a]]).

target(memb,2,[+,+],[atom,list]).

positive([[a,[b,a,c]], [b,[c,b,a]], [c,[c,a]], [b,[a,b]],
          [a,[a,c,b]], [b,[b]]]).
negative([[c,[]], [a,[c,b]], [[],[b,c]], [b,[c,a]], [[],[c,a]],
          [c,[b,a]]]).

bg(component,3,[+,-,-],[list,atom,list],[component([A|B],A,B)]).
bg(null,1,[+],[list],[null([])]).
```

**Fig. 1.** An example of input file for FOIL-I.

the title the third line tells the input file. After them lines tell information about evaluation of candidate literals, the information which includes the number of positive and negative examples covered by a literal and its evaluation value. Information for only literals that cover at least one positive example is shown. In this session a literal (d,component,[2,3,4]) is added as a determinate literal, which is described in Sec. 4.2. The lines that start with Candidate(s): show a list of partial clauses saved in the step of induction loop. A literal is shown by a tuple of a sign(p=positive, n=negative and d=determinate), a predicate name and a list of arguments. (p, component, [2,1,3]) denotes a literal 'component($x_2$, $x_1$, $x_3$)', where arguments of head literal are assumed to be a series of variables with subscriptions of consecutive numbers starting from 1, e.g. memb($x_1, x_2$) in this case. If a partial clause covers no negative examples, the clause will be chosen as an induced clause after a redundancy check is done. When every positive example is covered by an induced clause, FOIL-I stops and shows results and some statistics.

# 3 Top-down induction and incomplete samples

FOIL-I uses a top-down induction like Quinlan's FOIL. FOIL tries to constitute clauses which cover some positive examples and no negative examples by generating literals systematically and evaluating their coverage by an information-based function. In this section we show an outline of FOIL and point out problems which we meet when we use an incomplete sample.

## 3.1 FOIL's algorithm

Figure 3 shows an outline of FOIL's algorithm. FOIL starts with a null program(line 1), and repeats a loop in which FOIL searches a clause that covers

```
?-foili('mem.ex').
F O I L - I, v e r. 0.8(July,1996)

Processing a sample file: mem.ex

A determinate literal (d,component,[2,3,4]) is added.
(p,null,[4]) covers 1 pos.and 0 neg.example(s). Evaluation is -3.032
(p,eqatom,[1,3]) covers 3 pos.and 0 neg.example(s). Evaluation is -1.283

Candidate(s):
  Eval.:(Pos.,Neg.) clause
  -1.283:(3,0) [(p,eqatom,[1,3]),(d,component,[2,3,4])]
  -3.032:(1,0) [(p,null,[4]),(d,component,[2,3,4])]

Clause(s):
  memb(X1,X2):-component(X2,X3,X4), eqatom(X1,X3).
is/are induced.

3 positive example(s) remain(s) uncovered

A determinate literal (d,component,[2,3,4]) is added.
(p,memb,[3,2]) covers 3 pos.and 5 neg.example(s). Evaluation is -3.907
(p,memb,[1,4]) covers 3 pos.and 0 neg.example(s). Evaluation is 0.338

Candidate(s):
  Eval.:(Pos.,Neg.) clause
  0.338:(3,0) [(p,memb,[1,4]),(d,component,[2,3,4])]
  -3.907:(3,5) [(p,memb,[3,2]),(d,component,[2,3,4])]

Clause(s):
  memb(X1,X2):-component(X2,X3,X4), memb(X1,X4).
is/are induced.

0 positive example(s) remain(s) uncovered

result((memb(A,B):-component(B,C,_),eqatom(A,C))).
result((memb(A,B):-component(B,_,C),memb(A,C))).

11 literals visited
Runtime: 0.559 sec.
yes
```

**Fig. 2.** An example of output of FOIL-I system

Initialization
1    theory := null program
2    remaining := all tuples belonging to target relation $R$

3 While remaining is not empty
4    clause := "$R(A, B, \cdots) :-$"
5    While clause covers tuples known not to belong to $R$
6        Find appropriate literal(s) $L$
7        add $L$ to body of clause
8    Remove from remaining tuples in $R$ covered by clause
9    Add clause to theory

**Fig. 3.** Outline of FOIL algorithm

only positive examples until every positive example is covered by a set of found clause(lines 3–9). In each iteration of loop FOIL starts to search a clause from the most general clause, a body-less clause(line 4), and makes it specify not to cover any tuples known not to belong to the target relation(lines 5–6). Specification is achieved by adding a literal to the body of the clause(line 6). In the algorithm literals to be added are evaluated from an information-theoretic aspect. A literal is evaluated as a high point if the added literal makes a clause cover a large part of positive tuples than a clause before adding the literal. When a clause covers no negative tuples, the clause is chosen as a part of definition of a target relation(line 9). Positive examples covered by the found clause is removed from sample(line 8), and FOIL returns the loop with the new remaining sample.

## 3.2 'Unknown' examples

FOIL-I system does not assume the Closed World Assumption. A negative sample should be given explicitly. Any examples not given are not known to be positive nor negative. We call examples not given *unknown examples*.

The existence of unknown examples affects the following points.

1. The evaluation function of FOIL should be reconsidered. In FOIL literals are evaluated by an information-based function *Gain*. The function is calculated from the number of positive and negative examples covered by a candidate literals. The function will be reconsidered with the number of unknown examples. Another evaluation measure is also introduced.
2. Some small samples may let a system induce incorrect definitions, because small samples can be covered by unexpected clauses. Plausible literals hence do not always give correct answer. We should reconsider a search strategy.
3. FOIL allows to use a target relation recursively in a clause induced, but treatment of recursive clauses is not sufficient in the case of an incomplete samples. The treatment depends on a given samples, and the size of a sample effects effectiveness of it. We check the treatment of recursive clauses in FOIL and give another procedure.

These points are discussed and we answer them in the following sections.

# 4 Induction from incomplete samples

## 4.1 Evaluation function

The algorithm needs an evaluation function for literals to control the search. As we are going to see it in the following, FOIL uses an evaluation function *Gain* to evaluate literals, while FOIL-I uses an evaluation function to evaluate partial clauses because FOIL-I searches partial clauses instead of literals (see Sec. 4.2).

FOIL-I's evaluation function is composed of two parts. The first one is the function *Gain* of FOIL, which gives information-based estimates of literals. We have to verify effectiveness of this function later. The second part gives an encoding complexity measure.

**Information-based evaluation.** We consider a target relation $R(x_1, \cdots, x_m)$. First a most general clause, i.e., a body-less clause '$R(x_1, \cdots, x_m) :-$' is considered. Let $T$ denote a given sample of $R$ and $T^+$ and $T^-$ denote the numbers of positive and negative examples, respectively. When a literal $L(x_{i_1}, \cdots, x_{i_j})$ is added to the clause, an example $(a_1, \cdots, a_m)$ in the sample $T$ is expanded to examples $(a_1^1, \cdots, a_m^1, a_{m+1}^1, \cdots, a_{m+k}^1), \cdots, (a_1^n, \cdots, a_m^n, a_{m+1}^n, \cdots, a_{m+k}^n)$ if

1. $(a_{i_1}^t, \cdots, a_{i_j}^t)$ is a ground instance of the literal $L(x_{i_1}, \cdots, x_{i_j})$ for $t = 1, \cdots, n$, and
2. $a_1^t = a_1, \cdots, a_m^t = a_m$ for $t = 1, \cdots, m$,

where $\{i_1, \cdots, i_j\} \cup \{1, \cdots, m\} = \{1, \cdots, m+k\}$.

Examples expanded from a positive(negative) sample constitute a new positive(negative) examples, respectively. $T'$ denotes a new sample expanded by the literal, and $T^{++}$ denotes the number of positive examples in $T$ that are expanded to at least one new example in $T'$.

In Quinlan's FOIL the literal $L$ is evaluated by an evaluation function *Gain* that is defined as follows

$$Gain(L) = T^{++} \cdot (I(T) - I(T')), \tag{1}$$

where the function $I(\cdot)$ is defined as follows.

$$I(T) = -\log \frac{T^+}{T^+ + T^-} \tag{2}$$

To apply the function *Gain* for incomplete samples we consider unknown examples. Some of unknown examples are potentially positive. Let $T_I^+ (T_I^-)$ denotes the numbers of all positive(negative) examples including given positive(negative) examples and the potential positive(negative) examples, respectively. $T_I^+$ is estimated as follows.

$$T_I^+ \approx T^+ + W \cdot T^?, \tag{3}$$

where $T^?$ denotes the number of unknown examples, and $W$ is a rate of positive examples in all examples. $W$ is approximated by the following equation.

$$W = \frac{T^+}{T^+ + T^-} \tag{4}$$

Using $T_I^+$ and $T_I^-$, $I(T)$ is estimated as follows.

$$\begin{aligned}
I(T) &= -\log \frac{T_I^+}{T_I^+ + T_I^-} \\
&\approx -\log \frac{T^+ + W \cdot T^?}{T^+ + T^- + T^?} \\
&= -\log \frac{T^+ + (T^+/(T^+ + T^-)) \cdot T^?}{T^+ + T^- + T^?} \\
&= -\log \frac{(T^+T^+ + T^+T^- + T^+T^?)/(T^+ + T^-)}{T^+ + T^- + T^?} \\
&= -\log \frac{T^+}{T^+ + T^-}
\end{aligned}$$

*Gain* for incomplete samples can be approximated by the *Gain* of FOIL. As a side effect we need not to keep unknown examples. This is an advantage in calculation time.

**Encoding complexity-based evaluation.** FOIL uses a kind of encoding length heuristics[Qui90]. It is to deal with noisy domains. In some practical situations it is very difficult to give a precise definition for a given sample. It is the purpose of the heuristics to give a criterion to stop lengthening clauses to fit sample by ignoring small exceptions in noisy domains.

FOIL-I also uses a kind of encoding length heuristics, but there are differences in two points. The first one is its purpose. In FOIL-I the encoding length heuristics does not explicitly intend the treatment of noise. The main purpose is to control search. FOIL-I searches partial clauses instead of literals, and clauses with different lengths are kept in the same list. Short clauses should be visited before lengthy ones.

In second the encoding-length heuristics is implemented as an evaluation function with another heuristics *variable's number heuristics*, that is, the numbers of variables in clauses are measured. An evaluation function for this purpose is defined by the following *Complex* function.

$$Complex(C) = \log\left\{ \binom{\text{the number of}}{\text{body literals in } C} + 1 \right\} + \log\left\{ \binom{\text{the number of}}{\text{variables in } C} + 1 \right\} \tag{5}$$

In FOIL-I, the following function *Eval* that is a composition of *Gain* and *Complex* is used

$$Eval(C) = Gain(L) - Complex(C), \tag{6}$$

where $L$ is a literal in $C$ that is newly chosen.

## 4.2 Search strategy

FOIL's algorithm is basically a greedy method, which means that a literal once chosen by the system is hardly canceled. In the case of incomplete samples, however, it is difficult to give a certain choice. The choice should be postponed. FOIL-I, instead, uses best-first search with restricted expansion of each search step, which is more similar to the search algorithm of Progol[Mug95].

Figure 4 shows the algorithm of FOIL-I. In the same way as FOIL, FOIL-I starts with a null program(line 1) and repeats a loop to find clauses that cover some positive examples but do not cover any negative example(lines 3–12). After some iterations of the loop learning is stopped if every positive example is covered by a found clause(line 3).

In each iteration of the loop, to find clauses the algorithm keeps partial clauses in clauses. At first of steps the most general clause "$R(A, B, \cdots) : -$" is kept in clauses as a partial clause(line 4) and enters a loop to construct clauses(lines 5–10). A partial clause with best evaluation (i.e., the most general clause at the beginning) is picked out from clauses(line 6). FOIL-I generates possible literals to add to the body of the best partial clause(line 7 and 8). The new partial clauses made from the literals generated are evaluated by the evaluation function(line 9). If some clauses of them cover at least one positive example and no negative examples, FOIL-I adds them to theory(line 11), removes positive examples covered by the found clauses from the sample(line 12), and moves to the next iteration of loop(return to line 3). Otherwise FOIL-I sorts the evaluated clauses and the clauses in clauses by their evaluation values and chooses the $m$ new best partial clauses[3] from them(line 10), while FOIL chooses only the best literal. The $m$ clauses do not include any literals that covers no positive examples. The loop is repeated with the best clause from clauses. FOIL-I does not distinguish the new clauses from the others. They and other clauses that have been induced already have the same chance to be chosen.

The major changes in the algorithm of FOIL-I from FOIL include the following points.

1. FOIL-I searches clauses with difference length simultaneously. All partial clauses are kept in clauses without distinguishing their lengths.
2. More than one clauses can be found at the same time.

FOIL prohibits to introduce a zero-gain literal in principle, but some kind of literals are useful even if they are zero-gain. [QCJ93] characterizes such kind of literals by using the idea of determinate literals originally proposed in [MF92]. A determinate literal is a literal that introduces new variables which have exactly one binding for every positive example and for most of negative examples. For example component$(X_2, X_3, X_4)$ gives zero-gain to the following clause, because it only expands $X_2$ to $X_3$ and $X_4$ but $X_3$ and $X_4$ may be useful to construct a definition of the target relation member.

$$\text{member}(X_1, X_2) : -. \tag{7}$$

---

[3] In default the $m$ is ten.

Initialization

1    theory := null program
2    remaining := all tuples belonging to target relation $R$

3  While remaining is not empty
4      clauses := { "$R(A, B, \cdots) :-$" }
5      While there is no clause in clauses that does not cover any tuples
              known not to belong to $R$ (if there exist let them be
              found-clauses)
6          Choose the best clause clause from clauses if clauses is not empty
              and algorithm stops in fail if it is empty
7          Find appropriate literals $\{L_1, \cdots, L_n\}$.
8          Add each literal of $\{L_1, \cdots, L_n\}$ to body of clause to make
              clauses $\{\text{clause}_1, \cdots, \text{clause}_n\}$
9          Evaluate $\{\text{clause}_1, \cdots, \text{clause}_n\}$
10         Choose the best $m$ clauses from $\{\text{clause}_1, \cdots, \text{clause}_n\} \cup$ clauses
              and update clauses to them
11     Add found-clauses to theory
12     Remove from remaining tuples in $R$ covered by found-clauses

**Fig. 4.** Outline of FOIL-I algorithm

A determinate literal sometimes reveals attributes from another one, such as a head and a tail of a given list.

FOIL-I introduces all possible determinate literals before each learning loop, i.e., before Step 7. When a clause is completed a determinate literal that is not referred from others is removed.

### 4.3    Induction of recursive clauses

To use recursive definitions makes ILP systems more powerful. FOIL-I induces recursive definitions by choosing a target predicate in the same manner as other predicates. However, the expansion of examples can not be treated the same as other literals in the case of incomplete samples.

When a target relation is chosen, Quinlan's FOIL expands examples using a given sample itself, because it is an extensional definition of target relation. This expansion is the same as expansion for other relations. For example, let us imagine that FOIL finds a clause:

$$\text{member}(A, B) :-\text{component}(B, C, D), \text{member}(A, D). \tag{8}$$

during learning for a target relation member. Then an example $(b, [a, b, c])$ may be expanded and checked to be covered by this clause using an example $(b, [b, c])$ in a given positive sample.

But it is not effective in the case of incomplete samples, because a given sample is sometimes too small to expand, e.g. the positive example $(b, [b, c])$ may not be included in a given positive sample.

Another method to expand a sample with a recursive clause is to calculate the relation for each example in the sample by using the recursive clause. For example $(b, [a, b, c])$ can be checked by calculation using the clause (8) with the following clause induced before :

$$\mathsf{member}(A, B) : -\mathsf{component}(B, A, C). \tag{9}$$

This method, i.e., calculation using recursive clauses, is effective in small samples, but it is not when a recursive clause is still unfinished. This will happen when a recursive definition is not tail recursive or when more than one recursive clauses are necessary for a definition of a target relation.

FOIL-I takes the following procedure to expand an example by a recursive literal.

1. To check a recursive call FOIL-I checks if a tuple of values bounded by the recursive call is in a given sample.
2. If it fails, FOIL-I processes SLD-resolution using the recursive clause with other clauses induced before.

This method is much effective for small incomplete samples and does not reduce efficiency for complete samples as well.

There are other points on the implementation of processing a recursive definition. They are described in Sec. 5.3.

## 5 Implementation

The current version of FOIL-I is implemented by using SICStus Prolog version 2. Compared with Quinlan's FOIL6, FOIL-I takes time to process induction. One of the reason is that it is implemented on Prolog. The source code will be available on request soon.

In the following sections we discuss implementation issues. The first matter is about redundant clauses. The section gives a method to correctly detect redundant clauses. The second is matters to cut down calculation time. Several topics are discussed. The final section discusses about the treatment of recursive clauses.

### 5.1 Removing redundant clauses

In a theory found by the system, a clause is redundant if every instance of a target relation covered by the clause is covered by other clauses of the theory. In the FOIL-I algorithm there are two cases that redundant clauses can be induced. More than one clauses may be induced in an iteration of learning loop, and some of clauses induced may be redundant. This is the first case. The other case will

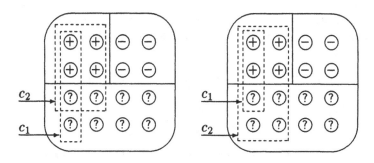

**Fig. 5.** A situation where a clause $c_1$ is mistaken to be redundant against a clause $c_2$(the left) and a situation where $c_1$ is really redundant against $c_2$(the right). $\oplus$, $\ominus$ and $\oslash$ denote a positive example, a negative one and an unknown one, respectively.

happen over iterations of the loop. A clause is induced in an iteration and another one is induced after the iteration. The first clause may not be necessary, that is, every positive example covered by the first clause may be covered by the second one. Note that the second clause is always necessary. Otherwise none of the examples is covered by the second clause, and so the clause must not be induced.

FOIL-I checks redundant clauses and removes them for the first case. To find redundant clauses it is not sufficient to check the subset relation of positive examples covered by clauses, because there are many unknown examples. Figure 5 illustrates that it is not sufficient for detecting redundancy between two clauses to check the subset relation between positive examples covered by the clauses. The left figure of Fig. 5 shows a situation that a clause $c_1$ is mistaken to be redundant against a clause $c_2$. In the right figure, $c_1$ is really redundant against $c_2$.

For each clause induced, FOIL-I calculates a set of all ground instances defined by the clause within a given finite domain. Instead of the subset relation between positive examples covered by clauses, FOIL-I checks the subset relation between the sets of ground instances. In the case of Fig. 5 FOIL-I does not take the $c_1$ as a redundant clause.

Redundant clauses in the second case can be also removed by the same way. This is, however, a time expensive task, because the redundancy check has to be done for all of combinations of clauses. In this version of FOIL-I, redundancy check in the second case is omitted.

## 5.2 Cutting down calculation

**Mode.** FOIL-I uses *mode* to specify each argument to be used as input or output. Mode is specified as a list of '+' or '−' for a target relation and background relations in sample files to be given to the system. '+'('−') specifies that a corresponding argument is an input(output) argument, respectively.

Using mode helps to restrict possible literals to be added to the body of a clause. A literal $(\neg)L(x_{i_1}, \cdots, x_{i_n})$ is a candidate to be added to a partial clause $c$ only if

1. the predicate $L$ has a mode $\mathsf{mode} = (m_1, \cdots, m_n)$, where $m_j = $ '+' or '−' $(j = 1, \cdots, n)$,
2. the partial clause $c$ has variables $\{x_1, \cdots, x_k\}$, and
3. for every variable $x_{i_l}$ in $\{x_{i_1}, \cdots, x_{i_n}\} - \{x_1, \cdots, x_k\}$, $m_l = $ '−'.

Using mode reduces computation time to search for useless literals.

**Type.** To specify a *type* of a predicate is also helpful to reduce computation time and memory. A type is also specified for a target relation and background relations in a sample file as a list of domain names. Each name at a place specifies a domain from which argument at the place can take a value.

A type of a predicate can be extended to a *type of a partial clause* as follows.

1. If a partial clause has no body literal and it has only a target predicate as head literal $P(x_{i_1^1}, \cdots, x_{i_{n_p}^1})$ and the predicate $P$ has type $(d_1^p, \cdots, d_{n_p}^p)$, type $\mathsf{type}_1$ of the partial clause is:

$$\mathsf{type}_1 = (d_{i_1^1}^p, \cdots, d_{i_{n_p}^1}^p) . \tag{10}$$

2. If a partial clause $c$ has variables $x_1, \cdots, x_{m_k}$ and a type $\mathsf{type}_k = (d_1^k, \cdots, d_{n_k}^k)$, a literal $l = (\neg)L(x_{i_1^k}, \cdots, x_{i_{n_k}^k})$ is chosen to be added to $c$, and $L$ has a type $(d_1^L, \cdots, d_{n_L}^L)$, type of a new partial clause made from $c$ by adding $l$ to the body is:

$$\mathsf{type}_{k+1} = (d_1^k, \cdots, d_{n_k}^k, d_{j_1}^L, \cdots, d_{j_{m_k}}^L), \tag{11}$$

where $\{x_{j_1}, \cdots, x_{j_{m_k}}\} = \{x_{i_1^k}, \cdots, x_{i_{n_k}^k}\} - \{x_1, \cdots, x_{n_k}\}$ and $x_{j_1}, \cdots, x_{j_{m_k}}$ occur in $l$ in this order.

The definition above is well-defined only if literals to be added to a clause satisfy the condition of *candidates* which is given in the following.

The specification of types has two effects to reduce computation. The first is to reduce the number of candidates of literals to be added to a partial clauses, which is the same as mode. The second one is to reduce the number of tuples which are generated from positive or negative examples by expansion according to new literals.

The first effect is shown as follows. A literal $(\neg)L(x_{i_1}, \cdots, x_{i_n})$ is a *candidate* to be added to a partial clause $c$ only if

1. the predicate $L$ has a type $\mathsf{type}' = (d_1', \cdots, d_n')$, where $d_j'$ is a domain name $(j = 1, \cdots, n)$,
2. the partial clause $c$ has variables $\{x_1, \cdots, x_k\}$ and a type $\mathsf{type} = (d_1, \cdots, d_k)$, and

3. for every variables $x_{i_l}$ in $\{x_{i_1}, \cdots, x_{i_n}\} \cap \{x_1, \cdots, x_k\}$, $d_{i_l} = d'_l$.

Using type FOIL-I avoids searching for useless literals.

As the second effect, type reduces tuples. A set of possible tuples for a partial clause is a product of domains in the type of the clause.

### 5.3  Induction of recursive clauses

Three points on the implementation of processing recursive definitions are described here. First to induce recursive definition correctly, FOIL-I prohibits to induce a recursive clause before it induces a non-recursive clause. It is because a recursive definition always requires at least one base clause.

Secondly when FOIL-I calculates and finds a tuples to be an instance of a target relation during expansion of an example, the tuple is saved in the system. The saved tuples are used in the same way as given positive examples, which saves processing time in the calculation of recursive clauses.

Finally, we have to pay attention to that a recursive clause may not be completed. Another literal may be necessary to the tail of the clause or even another clause may be required and it and the recursive clause may call each other. In these cases the calculation of the coverage of examples only by a recursive clause is insufficient. After a clause is completed or after another clause is induced, the coverage must be changed. FOIL-I checks the coverage using all of induced clauses again after a clause is completed or after another clause is induced.

## 6  Experimental results

In this section we show experimental results to compare with two ILP systems FOIL and Progol[Mug95]. We used FOIL6.3 written in C language and CProgol Version 4.1 which is also written in C language.

In general FOIL6.3 and CProgol are much faster than our system FOIL-I. We compare their ability to focus on existence of incomplete examples.

Experiments were done for the target relations **member** which checks if an element is a member of a list, **last** which gives the last element of a list. **length** which gives the length of a list, and **nth** which gives the n-th element of a list. Table 1 shows background knowledge used to induce these relations and the numbers of all positive and negative examples of them.

In a 10% samples of **member**, for example, three positive examples and three negative examples are included. Fifty samples of each percentage and of each target relation are generated randomly and automatically, and are given to FOIL-I, FOIL6 and Progol.

Table 2 shows results the of induction of their target relations by the three systems with the incomplete samples. The numbers in the table are the numbers of incomplete samples with which the systems induce correct answers. Some answers include redundant definitions even if they work expectedly. The numbers of samples with which the systems gives exactly correct definitions without redundant clauses are shown as well.

**Table 1.** Target relations and background knowledge tested

| target relation | background knowledge | positive examples | negative examples |
|---|---|---|---|
| member | component($[A|B], A, B$) | 33 | 31 |
| last | component($[A|B], A, B$), null($[]$) | 39 | 121 |
| length | component($[A|B], A, B$), pred($X - 1, X$), zero($0$), null($[]$) | 15 | 45 |
| nth | component($[A|B], A, B$), pred($X - 1, X$), zero($0$) | 33 | 223 |

You can see that FOIL-I is better than FOIL6 and Progol in the point that FOIL-I can induce correct definitions in more cases than others. In particular, FOIL-I is superior to others in lower percentage's samples. Another superiority of FOIL-I is to induce redundant clauses in few cases. Indeed Progol induced very few redundant clauses, but it did not mark high points in lower percentages.

Table 2 shows the average runtime of induction processes as well. FOIL-I is ten times slower than others. A reason of this large runtime is that the system is written in Prolog language. The runtime includes processing time to expand intensional definitions of background relations to extension definitions.

In the experiments, all definitions that can correctly induces all instances of a target relation are classified as correct definitions. FOIL6, however, induces correct but unexpected definitions, for example:

$$\text{memb}(A, B) :- \text{component}(B, A, C).$$
$$\text{memb}(A, B) :- \text{component}(B, C, D), \text{component}(D, A, E). \tag{12}$$
$$\text{memb}(A, B) :- \text{component}(B, C, D), \text{component}(D, E, F), \text{memb}(A, F).,$$

which is not induced by FOIL-I.

As you can see in Table2 the systems fail almost completely in inducing the relation length in lower percentages. Individual outputs from the systems tell that many cases of these failure are caused from the lack of positive examples that suggest the base case of a recursive definition. The relation length has 15 positive examples and 45 negative ones. Only an example ($[], 0$) of all 15 positive examples gives the base clause of length, while in the case of member 15 examples of all 33 give the base clause. Even in the case of last 3 examples of all 39 can give a base definition.

To check the ability of FOIL-I compared with the others more adequately, we made an experiment with samples of length that made from the same samples used before by adding the positive example ($[\ ], 0$). Table 3 shows the results of this experiment. FOIL-I, FOIL6 and Progol gave better results than the samples before adding ($[\ ], 0$). FOIL-I is better than others in this experiment as well, particularly in low percentage's samples.

**Table 2.** Fifty randomly selected (7%) 10%, 20%, 30%, 50%, and 80% incomplete samples are given to FOIL-I, FOIL6, and Progol. The numbers shown are those of samples with which FOIL-I, FOIL6 and Progol induced the correct definitions that may include redundant clauses. The numbers of cases which include no redundancy are shown as well. Runtimes are the average time of induction processes that induced correct definitions.

| samples | FOIL-I correct answer | no redundancy | runtime (msec) | FOIL6 correct answer | no redundancy | runtime (msec) | Progol correct answer | no redundancy | runtime (msec) |
|---|---|---|---|---|---|---|---|---|---|
| **member** | | | | | | | | | |
| 80% | 50 | 50 | 961 | 41 | 6 | 107 | 26 | 26 | 359 |
| 50% | 50 | 50 | 764 | 36 | 5 | 100 | 20 | 20 | 314 |
| 30% | 50 | 50 | 620 | 16 | 1 | 100 | 5 | 5 | 148 |
| 20% | 49 | 49 | 566 | 8 | 5 | 100 | 2 | 2 | 260 |
| 10% | 38 | 38 | 493 | 3 | 3 | 100 | 0 | 0 | - |
| 7% | 22 | 22 | 462 | 0 | 0 | 100 | 0 | 0 | - |
| **last** | | | | | | | | | |
| 80% | 50 | 50 | 4400 | 45 | 2 | 198 | 21 | 17 | 285 |
| 50% | 44 | 44 | 3306 | 24 | 3 | 267 | 6 | 3 | 250 |
| 30% | 33 | 33 | 2580 | 25 | 7 | 232 | 0 | 0 | - |
| 20% | 23 | 23 | 2138 | 13 | 5 | 146 | 0 | 0 | - |
| 10% | 2 | 1 | 2050 | 2 | 2 | 100 | 0 | 0 | - |
| **length** | | | | | | | | | |
| 80% | 38 | 31 | 1810 | 38 | 12 | 113 | 39 | 39 | 87 |
| 50% | 18 | 18 | 1068 | 18 | 11 | 138 | 13 | 13 | 65 |
| 30% | 6 | 6 | 762 | 4 | 4 | 100 | 0 | 0 | - |
| 20% | 4 | 4 | 613 | 2 | 2 | 100 | 0 | 0 | - |
| 10% | 0 | 0 | - | 0 | 0 | - | 0 | 0 | - |
| **nth** | | | | | | | | | |
| 80% | 50 | 50 | 3544 | 0 | 0 | - | 43 | 43 | 1310 |
| 50% | 49 | 49 | 2191 | 6 | 0 | 350 | 43 | 43 | 809 |
| 30% | 46 | 46 | 1559 | 5 | 2 | 160 | 19 | 19 | 510 |
| 20% | 27 | 27 | 1313 | 0 | 0 | - | 0 | 0 | - |
| 10% | 1 | 1 | 1080 | 0 | 0 | - | 0 | 0 | - |

**Table 3.** The results of the target relation length with an example ([ ], 0).

| samples | FOIL-I | | | FOIL6 | | | Progol | | |
|---|---|---|---|---|---|---|---|---|---|
| | correct answer | | | correct answer | | | correct answer | | |
| | | no redundancy | | | no redundancy | | | no redundancy | |
| | | | runtime (msec) | | | runtime (msec) | | | runtime (msec) |
| length | | | | | | | | | |
| 80%+([ ], 0) | 49 | 40 | 1901 | 49 | 19 | 108 | 50 | 50 | 86 |
| 50%+([ ], 0) | 41 | 41 | 1100 | 30 | 21 | 133 | 37 | 37 | 72 |
| 30%+([ ], 0) | 30 | 29 | 769 | 26 | 14 | 108 | 3 | 3 | 50 |
| 20%+([ ], 0) | 18 | 17 | 674 | 9 | 5 | 100 | 2 | 2 | 30 |
| 10%+([ ], 0) | 5 | 5 | 572 | 0 | 0 | - | 0 | 0 | - |

# 7   Conclusions

To reduce the number of examples in samples to be given to an ILP system, we have developed a FOIL-like system FOIL-I. FOIL-I has an ability which deals with large amount of unknown examples. To deal with unknown examples, FOIL-I uses a best-first search with an evaluation function which estimates information-based utilities of literals and encoding complexity. FOIL-I also has an ability to approximately check the redundancy of clauses, which is based on subset relations between sets of tuples covered by the clauses. We implemented this check only partially because it is a time-expensive task. Even with the restricted implementation of the redundancy check, FOIL-I avoids redundant definitions in many cases. Another special point is the careful treatment of recursive clauses in FOIL-I. This is necessary to deal with small incomplete samples.

Experiments show that FOIL-I induces correct definitions of the target relations in more cases of lower percentages than FOIL and Progol. The ability to remove redundant clauses is also shown by the results.

While FOIL's search is basically a greedy method, FOIL-I uses a best-first search, and so it has to keep many nodes, i.e., partial clauses to be visited. This makes memory to be used by the algorithm very large because every node or partial clause is kept with positive examples and negative examples expanded by the partial clauses. Especially the number of negative examples increases rapidly because generally negative examples share much more tuples than positive examples.

The experiment shown in Table 3 tells the importance of examples that give a base definition. FOIL-I can not give correct definitions without such examples as well as FOIL and Progol. It is a future subject to give a correct base clause without such examples.

# References

[ALLM94a] D.W. Aha, S. Lapointe, C.X. Ling, and S. Matwin. Inverting implication with small training sets. In F. Bergadano and L. De Raedt, editors, *Proceedings of the 7th European Conference on Machine Learning*, volume 784 of *Lecture Notes in Artificial Intelligence*, pages 31–48. Springer-Verlag, 1994.

[ALLM94b] D.W. Aha, S. Lapointe, C.X. , and S. Matwin. Learning recursive relations with randomly selected small training sets. In W.W. Cohen and H. Hirsh, editors, *Proceedings of the 11th International Conference on Machine Learning*, pages 12–18. Morgan Kaufmann, 1994.

[AP93]    K.M. Ali and M.J. Pazzani. Hydra: A noise-tolerant relational concept learning algorithm. In R. Bajcsy, editor, *Proceedings of the 13th International Joint Conference on Artificial Intelligence*, pages 1064–1071. Morgan Kaufmann, 1993.

[BP91]    C.A. Brunk and M.J. Pazzani. An investigation of noise-tolerant relational concept learning algorithms. In L. Birnbaum and G. Collins, editors, *Proceedings of the 8th International Workshop on Machine Learning*, pages 389–393. Morgan Kaufmann, 1991.

[Coh95]   W. Cohen. Learning to classify english text with ILP method. In L. De Raedt, editor, *Proceedings of the 5th International Workshop on Inductive Logic Programming*, Scientific report, pages 3–24. Department of Computer Science, Katholieke Universiteit Leuven, 1995.

[DB92]    S. Džeroski and I. Bratko. Handling noise in inductive logic programming. In S. Muggleton, editor, *Proceedings of the 2nd International Workshop on Inductive Logic Programming*, Report ICOT TM-1182, 1992.

[DBJ94]   B. Dolšak, I. Bratko, and A. Jezernik. Finite element mesh design: An engineering domain for ILP application. In S. Wrobel, editor, *Proceedings of the 4th International Workshop on Inductive Logic Programming*, volume 237 of *GMD-Studien*, pages 305–320. Gesellschaft für Mathematik und Datenverarbeitung MBH, 1994.

[DM91]    B. Dolšak and S. Muggleton. The application of ILP to finite element mesh design. In S. Muggleton, editor, *Proceedings of the 1st International Workshop on Inductive Logic Programming*, pages 225–242, 1991.

[Dže95]   S. Džeroski. Learning first-order clausal theories in the presence of noise. In A. Aamodt and J. Komorowski, editors, *Proceedings of the 5th Scandinavian Conference on Artificial Intelligence*, pages 51–60. IOS, Amsterdam, 1995.

[Für93]   J. Fürnkranz. Avoiding noise fitting in a FOIL-like learning algorithm. In F. Bergadano, L. De Raedt, S. Matwin, and S. Muggleton, editors, *Proceedings of the IJCAI-93 Workshop on Inductive Logic Programming*, pages 14–23. Morgan Kaufmann, 1993.

[HS92]    D. Hume and C. Sammut. Applying inductive logic programming in reactive environments. In S. Muggleton, editor, *Inductive Logic Programming*, pages 539–549. Academic Press, 1992.

[MF92]    S. Muggleton and C. Feng. Efficient induction in logic programs. In S. Muggleton, editor, *Inductive Logic Programming*, pages 281–298. Academic Press, 1992.

[MN95]    C. R. Mofizur and M. Numao. Top-down induction of recursive programs from small number of sparse examples. In L. De Raedt, editor, *Proceedings of the 5th International Workshop on Inductive Logic Programming,* Scientific report, pages 161–180. Department of Computer Science, Katholieke Universiteit Leuven, 1995.

[Mug95]   Stephen Muggleton. Inverse entailment and progol. *New Generation Computing,* 3+4:245–286, 1995.

[QCJ93]   J.R. Quinlan and R.M. Cameron-Jones. FOIL: A midterm report. In P. Brazdil, editor, *Proceedings of the 6th European Conference on Machine Learning,* volume 667 of *Lecture Notes in Artificial Intelligence,* pages 3–20. Springer-Verlag, 1993.

[Qui90]   J.R. Quinlan. Learning logical definitions from relations. *Machine Learning,* 5:239–266, 1990.

# Theory

# Least Generalizations under Implication

Shan-Hwei Nienhuys-Cheng and Ronald de Wolf

Erasmus University of Rotterdam, Department of Computer Science, H4-19,
P.O. Box 1738, 3000 DR Rotterdam, the Netherlands,
{cheng,bidewolf}@cs.few.eur.nl

**Abstract.** One of the most prominent approaches in Inductive Logic Programming is the use of *least generalizations* under subsumption of given clauses. However, subsumption is weaker than logical implication, and not very well suited for handling recursive clauses. Therefore an important open question in this area concerns the existence of least generalizations under implication (LGIs). Our main new result in this paper is the existence and computability of such an LGI for any finite set of clauses which contains at least one non-tautologous function-free clause. We can also define implication relative to background knowledge. In this case, least generalizations only exist in a very limited case.

## 1 Introduction

Inductive Logic Programming (ILP) is the intersection of Logic Programming and Machine Learning. It studies methods to induce clausal theories from given sets of positive and negative examples. An inductively inferred theory should imply all of the positive, and none of the negative examples. For instance, suppose we are given $P(0)$, $P(s^2(0))$, $P(s^4(0))$, $P(s^6(0))$ as positive examples, and $P(s(0)), P(s^3(0)), P(s^5(0))$ as negative examples. Then the set $\Sigma = \{P(0), (P(s^2(x)) \leftarrow P(x))\}$ is a solution: it implies all positive, and no negative examples. Note that this set can be seen as a description of the even integers. Thus induction of clausal theories is a form of learning from examples. For a more extensive introduction to ILP, we refer to [6, 10].

One of the most prominent approaches in ILP is the use of least generalizations under subsumption of given clauses, introduced by Plotkin [16, 17]. A clause $C$ is a *least generalization under subsumption* (LGS) of a finite set $S$ of clauses, if $C$ subsumes every clause in $S$, and is subsumed by any other clause which also subsumes every clause in $C$. Plotkin's main result is that any finite set of clauses has an LGS. The construction of such a *least* generalization allows us to generalize the examples cautiously, avoiding over-generalization. Of course, we need not take the LGS of *all* positive examples, which would yield a theory consisting of only one clause. Instead, we might divide the positive examples into subsets, and take a separate LGS of each subset. That way we obtain a theory containing more than one clause.

However, subsumption is not fully satisfactory for such generalizations. For example, if $S$ consists of $D_1 = P(f^2(a)) \leftarrow P(a)$ and $D_2 = P(f(b)) \leftarrow P(b)$, then $P(f(y)) \leftarrow P(x)$ is an LGS of $S$. The clause $P(f(x)) \leftarrow P(x)$, which seems more appropriate as a least generalization of $S$, cannot be found by Plotkin's approach, because it does not subsume $D_1$. As this example also shows, subsumption is particularly unsatisfactory for *recursive* clauses: clauses which can be resolved with themselves.

Because of the weakness of subsumption, it is desirable to consider least generalizations *under implication* (LGIs) instead. Accordingly, we want to find out whether Plotkin's positive result on the existence of LGSs holds for LGIs as well. Most ILP-researchers are inclined to believe that this question has a negative answer, due to the undecidability of logical implication between clauses [8]. If we restrict attention to Horn clauses (clauses with at most one positive literal), the question has indeed been answered negatively: there is no least Horn clause which implies both $P(f^2(x)) \leftarrow P(x)$ and $P(f^3(x)) \leftarrow P(x)$ [10]. However, Muggleton and Page [12] have shown that the *non-Horn* clause $P(f(x)) \vee P(f^2(y)) \leftarrow P(x)$ is an LGI of these two clauses. Therefore we investigate the existence of an LGI in the set of *general* (not necessarily Horn) clauses here.

No definive answer has as yet been given to this more general question, but some work has already been done. For instance, Idestam-Almquist [4] studies least generalizations under *T-implication* as an approximation to LGIs. Muggleton and Page [12] investigate *self-saturated* clauses. A clause is self-saturated if it is subsumed by any clause which implies it. A clause $D$ is a self-saturation of $C$, if $C$ and $D$ are logically equivalent and $D$ is self-saturated. As [12] states, if two clauses $C_1$ and $C_2$ have self-saturations $D_1$ and $D_2$, respectively, then an LGS of $D_1$ and $D_2$ is also an LGI of $C_1$ and $C_2$. This positively answers our question concerning the existence of LGIs for clauses which have a self-saturation. However, Muggleton and Page also show that there exist clauses which have no self-saturation. So the concept of self-saturation cannot solve the general question concerning the existence of LGIs.

In this paper, we prove the new result that if $S$ is a finite set of clauses containing at least one non-tautologous function-free clause (among other clauses which may contain functions), then $S$ has a computable LGI. Our proof is on the one hand based on the Subsumption Theorem for resolution [7, 5, 15], and on the other hand on a modification of some results of Idestam-Almquist [4] concerning T-implication. An immediate corollary of this result is the existence and computability of an LGI of any finite set of function-free clauses. This result does not solve the general question of the existence of LGIs, but it does provide a positive answer for a large class of cases: the presence of one non-tautologous function-free clause in a finite $S$ already guarantees the existence and computability of an LGI of $S$. Because of the prominence of function-free clauses in ILP, this case may be of great practical signifcance.[1] Well-known ILP-systems such as FOIL

---

[1] Note that even for function-free clauses, the subsumption order is still not enough. Consider $D_1 = P(x, y, z) \leftarrow P(y, z, x)$ and $D_2 = P(x, y, z) \leftarrow P(z, x, y)$ (this example is adapted from Idestam-Almquist). $D_1$ is a resolvent of $D_2$ and $D_2$, and $D_2$ is a resolvent of $D_1$ and $D_1$. Hence $D_1$ and $D_2$ are logically equivalent. This means that $D_1$ is an LGI of the set $\{D_1, D_2\}$. However, the LGS of these two clauses is $P(x, y, z) \leftarrow P(u, v, w)$, which is clearly an over-generalization.

[18], LINUS [6], and MOBAL [9], all use only function-free clauses.

Apart from "plain" subsumption, one can also define subsumption relative to background knowledge. The two best-known forms are Plotkin's *relative subsumption* [17], and Buntine's *generalized subsumption* [1]. Similarly, we can generalize implication to *relative* implication, which will be considered in Section 5.

The results of this paper, together with some other results on greatest specializations and the lattice-structure of sets of clauses ordered by subsumption or implication, are described in more detail in our article [14].

## 2 Preliminaries

In this section, we will define the main concepts we need. For the definitions of 'model', 'tautology', 'substitution', etc., we refer to [2]. A *positive literal* is an atom, a *negative literal* is the negation of an atom. A *clause* is a finite set of literals, treated as the universally quantified disjunction of those literals. If $C$ is a clause, then $C^+$ denotes the set of positive literals in $C$, while $C^-$ denotes the set of negative literals.

**Definition 1.** Let $\mathcal{A}$ be an alphabet of the first-order logic. Then the *clausal language* $\mathcal{C}$ *by* $\mathcal{A}$ is the set of all clauses which can be constructed from the symbols in $\mathcal{A}$.

Here we just presuppose some arbitrary alphabet $\mathcal{A}$, and consider the clausal language $\mathcal{C}$ based on this $\mathcal{A}$.

**Definition 2.** Let $\Gamma$ be a set, and $R$ be a binary relation on $\Gamma$.

1. $R$ is *reflexive on* $\Gamma$, if $xRx$ for every $x \in \Gamma$.
2. $R$ is *transitive on* $\Gamma$, if for every $x, y, z \in \Gamma$, $xRy$ and $yRz$ implies $xRz$.
3. $R$ is *symmetric on* $\Gamma$, if for every $x, y \in \Gamma$, $xRy$ implies $yRx$.
4. $R$ is *anti-symmetric on* $\Gamma$, if for every $x, y, z \in \Gamma$, $xRy$ and $yRx$ implies $x = y$.

If $R$ is both reflexive and transitive on $\Gamma$, we say $R$ is a *quasi-order* on $\Gamma$. If $R$ is both reflexive, transitive, and anti-symmetric on $\Gamma$, we say $R$ is a *partial order* on $\Gamma$. If $R$ is reflexive, transitive and symmetric on $\Gamma$, $R$ is an *equivalence relation* on $\Gamma$.

A quasi-order $R$ on $\Gamma$ induces an equivalence-relation $\sim$ on $\Gamma$, as follows: we say $x, y \in \Gamma$ are *equivalent* induced by $R$ (denoted $x \sim y$) if both $xRy$ and $yRx$. Using this equivalence relation, a quasi-order $R$ on $\Gamma$ induces a partial order $R'$ on the set of equivalence classes in $\Gamma$, defined as follows: if $[x]$ denotes the equivalence class of $x$ (i.e., $[x] = \{y \mid x \sim y\}$), then $[x]R'[y]$ iff $xRy$.

We first give a general definition of least generalizations for sets of clauses ordered by some quasi-order.

**Definition 3.** Let $\Gamma$ be a set of clauses, $\geq$ be a quasi-order on $\Gamma$, $S \subseteq \Gamma$ be a finite set of clauses, and $C \in \Gamma$. If $C \geq D$ for every $D \in S$, then we say $C$ is a *generalization* of $S$ under $\geq$. Such a $C$ is called a *least generalization (LG)* of $S$ under $\geq$ in $\Gamma$, if $C' \geq C$ for every generalization $C' \in \Gamma$ of $S$ under $\geq$.

It is easy to see that if some set $S$ has an LG under $\geq$ in $\Gamma$, then this LG will be unique up to the equivalence induced by $\geq$ in $\Gamma$. That is, if $C$ and $D$ are both LGs of some set $S$, then we have $C \sim D$.

We will now define three increasingly strong quasi-orders on clauses: subsumption, implication, and relative implication.

**Definition 4.** Let $C$ and $D$ be clauses, and $\Sigma$ be a set of clauses. $C$ *subsumes* $D$, denoted as $C \succeq D$, if there exists a substitution $\theta$ such that $C\theta \subseteq D$. $C$ and $D$ are *subsume-equivalent* if $C \succeq D$ and $D \succeq C$.

$\Sigma$ *(logically) implies* $C$, denoted as $\Sigma \models C$, if every model of $\Sigma$ is also a model of $C$. $C$ *(logically) implies* $D$, denoted as $C \models D$, if $\{C\} \models D$. $C$ and $D$ are *(logically) equivalent* if $C \models D$ and $D \models C$.

$C$ *implies* $D$ *relative to* $\Sigma$, denoted as $C \models_\Sigma D$, if $\Sigma \cup \{C\} \models D$. $C$ and $D$ are *equivalent relative to* $\Sigma$ if $C \models_\Sigma D$ and $D \models_\Sigma C$.

If $C$ does not subsume $D$, we write $C \not\succeq D$. Similarly we use $C \not\models D$ and $C \not\models_\Sigma D$. 'Least generalization under subsumption' will be abbreviated to LGS. Similarly, LGI is 'least generalization under implication', and LGR is 'least generalization under relative implication'.

If $C \succeq D$, then $C \models D$. The converse does not hold, as the examples in the Introduction showed. Similarly, if $C \models D$, then $C \models_\Sigma D$, and again the converse need not hold. Consider $C = P(a) \vee \neg P(b)$, $D = P(a)$, and $\Sigma = \{P(b)\}$: then $C \models_\Sigma D$, but $C \not\models D$.

We now proceed to define a proof procedure for logical implication between clauses, using resolution and subsumption.

**Definition 5.** Let $C_1$ and $C_2$ be clauses. If $C_1$ and $C_2$ have no variables in common, then they are said to be *standardized apart*.

Given clauses $C_1 = L_1 \vee \ldots \vee L_i \vee \ldots \vee L_m$ and $C_2 = M_1 \vee \ldots \vee M_j \vee \ldots \vee M_n$ which are standardized apart. If the substitution $\theta$ is a most general unifier (mgu) of the set $\{L_i, \neg M_j\}$, then the clause $((C_1 - L_i) \cup (C_2 - M_j))\theta$ is a *binary resolvent* of $C_1$ and $C_2$. $L_i$ and $M_j$ are said to be the literals *resolved upon*.

If $C_1$ and $C_2$ are not standardized apart, we can take a variant $C_2'$ of $C_2$, such that $C_1$ and $C_2'$ are standardized apart. For simplicity, a binary resolvent of $C_1$ and $C_2'$ is also called a binary resolvent of $C_1$ and $C_2$ itself.

**Definition 6.** Let $C$ be a clause, and $\theta$ an mgu of $\{L_1, \ldots, L_n\} \subseteq C$ ($n \geq 1$). Then the clause $C\theta$ is called a *factor* of $C$.

**Definition 7.** A *resolvent* $C$ of clauses $C_1$ and $C_2$ is a binary resolvent of a factor of $C_1$ and a factor of $C_2$, where the literals resolved upon are the literals unified in the respective factors. $C_1$ and $C_2$ are the *parent clauses* of $C$.

**Definition 8.** Let $\Sigma$ be a set of clauses and $C$ a clause. A *derivation* of $C$ from $\Sigma$ is a finite sequence of clauses $R_1, \ldots, R_k = C$, such that each $R_i$ is either in $\Sigma$, or a resolvent of two clauses in $\{R_1, \ldots, R_{i-1}\}$. If such a derivation exists, we write $\Sigma \vdash_r C$.

**Definition 9.** Let $\Sigma$ be a set of clauses and $C$ a clause. We say there exists a *deduction* of $C$ from $\Sigma$, written as $\Sigma \vdash_d C$, if $C$ is a tautology, or if there exists a clause $D$ such that $\Sigma \vdash_r D$ and $D \succeq C$.

The next result, proved in [15], generalizes Herbrand's Theorem:

**Theorem 10.** *Let $\Sigma$ be a set of clauses, and $C$ a ground clause. If $\Sigma \models C$, then there is a finite set $\Sigma_g$ of ground instances of clauses in $\Sigma$, such that $\Sigma_g \models C$.*

The following Subsumption Theorem gives a precise characterization of implication between clauses in terms of resolution and subsumption. It was first proved in [7, 5], and reproved in [15].

**Theorem 11 (Subsumption Theorem).** *Let $\Sigma$ be a set of clauses, and $C$ be a clause. Then $\Sigma \models C$ iff $\Sigma \vdash_d C$.*

The next lemma was first proved by Gottlob [3]. Actually, it is an immediate corollary of the Subsumption Theorem:

**Lemma 12 (Gottlob).** *Let $C$ and $D$ be non-tautologous clauses. If $C \models D$, then $C^+ \succeq D^+$ and $C^- \succeq D^-$.*

*Proof.* Since $C^+ \succeq C$, if $C \models D$, then we have $C^+ \models D$. Since $C^+$ cannot be resolved with itself, it follows from the Subsumption Theorem that $C^+ \succeq D$. But then $C^+$ must subsume the positive literals in $D$, hence $C^+ \succeq D^+$. Similarly $C^- \succeq D^-$. $\qquad\square$

An important consequence of this lemma concerns the *depth* of clauses:

**Definition 13.** Let $t$ be a term. If $t$ is a variable or constant, then the *depth* of $t$ is 1. If $t = f(t_1, \ldots, t_n)$, $n \geq 1$, then the depth of $t$ is 1 plus the depth of the $t_i$ with largest depth. The *depth* of a clause $C$ is the depth of the term with largest depth in $C$.

Suppose $C \models D$, and $D$ is not a tautology. By Gottlob's Lemma, we must have $C^+ \succeq D^+$ and $C^- \succeq D^-$. Since applying a substitution cannot decrease the depth of a clause, it follows that $depth(C) \leq depth(D)$. Hence in case $depth(C) > depth(D)$ and $D$ is not a tautology, we know $C$ cannot imply $D$. For instance, take $D = P(x, f(x, g(y))) \leftarrow P(g(a), b)$, which has depth 3. Then a clause $C$ containing a term $f(x, g^2(y))$ (depth 4) cannot imply $D$.

**Definition 14.** Let $S$ and $S'$ be finite sets of clauses, $x_1, \ldots, x_n$ all distinct variables appearing in $S$, and $a_1, \ldots, a_n$ distinct constants not appearing in $S$ or $S'$. Then $\sigma = \{x_1/a_1, \ldots, x_n/a_n\}$ is called a *Skolem substitution* for $S$ w.r.t. $S'$. If $S'$ is empty, we just say that $\sigma$ is a Skolem substitution for $S$.

**Lemma 15.** *Let $\Sigma$ be a set of clauses, $C$ be a clause, and $\sigma$ be a Skolem substitution for $C$ w.r.t. $\Sigma$. Then $\Sigma \models C$ iff $\Sigma \models C\sigma$.*

*Proof.*

$\Rightarrow$: Obvious.

$\Leftarrow$: Suppose $C$ is not a tautology, and let $\sigma = \{x_1/a_1, \ldots, x_n/a_n\}$. If $\Sigma \models C\sigma$, it follows from the Subsumption Theorem that there is a $D$ such that $\Sigma \vdash_r D$, and $D \succeq C\sigma$. Thus there is a $\theta$, such that $D\theta \subseteq C\sigma$. Note that since $\Sigma \vdash_r D$ and none of the constants $a_1, \ldots, a_n$ appears in $\Sigma$, none of these constants appears in $D$. Now let $\theta'$ be obtained by replacing in $\theta$ all occurrences of $a_i$ by $x_i$, for every $1 \leq i \leq n$. Then $D\theta' \subseteq C$, hence $D \succeq C$. Therefore $\Sigma \vdash_d C$, and hence $\Sigma \models C$. $\square$

## 3 Least Generalizations under Implication

In this section, we show that any finite set of clauses which contains at least one non-tautologous function-free clause, has an LGI in $C$. An immediate corollary is the existence of an LGI of any finite set of function-free clauses. In our usage of the word, a 'function-free' clause may contain constants, even though constants are sometimes seen as functions of arity 0. Note that a clause is function-free iff it has depth 1.

**Definition 16.** A clause is *function-free* if it does not contain function symbols of arity 1 or more.

**Definition 17.** Let $C$ be a clause, $x_1, \ldots, x_n$ all distinct variables in $C$, and $K$ a set of terms. Then the *instance set* of $C$ w.r.t. $K$ is $\mathcal{I}(C, K) = \{C\theta \mid \theta = \{x_1/t_1, \ldots, x_n/t_n\}$, where $t_i \in K$, for every $1 \leq i \leq n\}$. If $\Sigma = \{C_1, \ldots, C_k\}$ is a set of clauses, then the *instance set* of $\Sigma$ w.r.t. $K$ is $\mathcal{I}(\Sigma, K) = \mathcal{I}(C_1, K) \cup \ldots \cup \mathcal{I}(C_k, K)$.

For example, if $C = P(x) \vee Q(y)$ and $T = \{a, f(z)\}$, then $\mathcal{I}(C, T) = \{(P(a) \vee Q(a)), (P(a) \vee Q(f(z))), (P(f(z)) \vee Q(a)), (P(f(z)) \vee Q(f(z)))\}$.

**Definition 18.** Let $S$ be a finite set of clauses, and $\sigma$ a Skolem substitution for $S$. The *term set* of $S$ by $\sigma$ is the set of all terms (including subterms) occurring in $S\sigma$.

A term set of $S$ by some $\sigma$ is a finite set of ground terms. For instance, the term set of $D = P(f^2(x), y, z) \leftarrow P(y, z, f^2(x))$ by $\sigma = \{x/a, y/b, z/c\}$ is $T = \{a, f(a), f^2(a), b, c\}$.

Consider $C = P(x, y, z) \leftarrow P(z, x, y)$, and $D, \sigma$ and $T$ as above. Then $C \models D$, and also $\mathcal{I}(C, T) \models D\sigma$, since $D\sigma$ is a resolvent of $P(f^2(a), b, c) \leftarrow P(c, f^2(a), b)$ and $P(c, f^2(a), b) \leftarrow P(b, c, f^2(a))$, which are in $\mathcal{I}(C, T)$. As we will show in the next lemma, this holds in general: if $C \models D$ and $C$ is function-free, then we can restrict attention to the ground instances of $C$ instantiated to terms in the term set of $D$ by some $\sigma$.

The proof of Lemma 19 uses the following idea. Consider a derivation of a clause $E$ from a set $\Sigma$ of ground clauses. Suppose some of the clauses in $\Sigma$ contain terms not appearing in $E$. Then any literals containing these terms in $\Sigma$ must be resolved away in the derivation. This means that if we replace all the terms in the derivation that are not in $E$, by some other term $t$, then the result will be another derivation of $E$. For example, the left of figure 1 shows a derivation of length 1 of $E$. The term $f^2(b)$ in the parent clauses does not appear in $E$. If we replace this term by the constant $a$, the result is another derivation of $E$ (right of the figure).

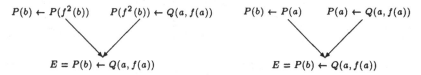

**Fig. 1.** Transforming the left derivation yields the right derivation

**Lemma 19.** *Let $C$ be a function-free clause, $D$ be a clause, $\sigma$ be a Skolem substitution for $D$ w.r.t. $\{C\}$, and $T$ be the term set of $D$ by $\sigma$. Then $C \models D$ iff $\mathcal{I}(C,T) \models D\sigma$.*

*Proof.*
$\Leftarrow$: Since $C \models \mathcal{I}(C,T)$ and $\mathcal{I}(C,T) \models D\sigma$, we have $C \models D\sigma$. Now $C \models D$ by Lemma 15.
$\Rightarrow$: If $D$ is a tautology, then $D\sigma$ is a tautology, so this case is obvious. Suppose $D$ is not a tautology, then $D\sigma$ is not a tautology. Since $C \models D\sigma$, it follows from Theorem 10 that there exists a finite set $\Sigma$ of ground instances of $C$, such that $\Sigma \models D\sigma$. By the Subsumption Theorem, there exists a derivation from $\Sigma$ of a clause $E$, such that $E \succeq D\sigma$. Since $\Sigma$ is ground, $E$ must also be ground, so we have $E \subseteq D\sigma$. This implies that $E$ only contains terms from $T$.

Let $t$ be an arbitrary term in $T$, and let $\Sigma'$ be obtained from $\Sigma$ by replacing every term in clauses in $\Sigma$ which is not in $T$, by $t$. Note that since each clause in $\Sigma$ is a ground instance of the function-free clause $C$, every clause in $\Sigma'$ is also a ground instance of $C$. Now it is easy to see that the same replacement of terms in the derivation of $E$ from $\Sigma$ results in a derivation of $E$ from $\Sigma'$: (1) each resolution step in the derivation from $\Sigma$ can also be carried out in the derivation from $\Sigma'$, since the same terms in $\Sigma$ are replaced by the same terms in $\Sigma'$, and (2) the terms in $\Sigma$ that are not in $T$ (and hence are replaced by $t$), do not appear in the conclusion $E$ of the derivation.

Since there is a derivation of $E$ from $\Sigma$, we have $\Sigma' \models E$, and hence $\Sigma' \models D\sigma$. $\Sigma'$ is a set of ground instances of $C$ and all terms in $\Sigma'$ are terms in $T$, so $\Sigma' \subseteq \mathcal{I}(C,T)$. Hence $\mathcal{I}(C,T) \models D\sigma$. $\qquad\square$

Lemma 19 cannot be generalized to the case where $C$ contains function symbols of arity $\geq 1$, take $C = P(f(x),y) \leftarrow P(z,x)$ and $D = P(f(a),a) \leftarrow P(a,f(a))$.

Then $T = \{a, f(a)\}$ is the term set of $D$, and we have $C \models D$, yet it can be seen that $\mathcal{I}(C, T) \not\models D$. The argument used in the previous lemma does not work here, because different terms in some ground instance need not relate to different variables. For example, in the ground instance $P(f^2(a), a) \leftarrow P(a, f(a))$ of $C$, we cannot just replace $f^2(a)$ by some other term, for then the resulting clause would not be an instance of $C$.

On the other hand, Lemma 19 can be generalized to a *set* of clauses instead of a single clause. If $\Sigma$ is a finite set of function-free clauses, $C$ is an arbitrary clause, and $\sigma$ is a Skolem substitution for $C$ w.r.t. $\Sigma$, then we have that $\Sigma \models C$ iff $\mathcal{I}(\Sigma, T) \models C\sigma$. The proof is almost literally the same as above.

This result implies that $\Sigma \models C$ is reducible to an implication $\mathcal{I}(\Sigma, T) \models C\sigma$ between ground clauses. Since, by the next lemma, implication between ground clauses is decidable, it follows that $\Sigma \models C$ is decidable in case $\Sigma$ is function-free.

**Lemma 20.** *The problem whether $\Sigma \models C$, where $\Sigma$ is a finite set of ground clauses and $C$ is a ground clause, is decidable.*

*Proof.* Let $C = L_1 \lor \ldots \lor L_n$, and $\mathcal{A}$ be the set of all ground atoms occurring in $\Sigma$ and $C$. Now $\Sigma \models C$ iff
$\Sigma \cup \{\neg L_1, \ldots, \neg L_n\}$ is unsatisfiable iff (by Theorem 4.2 of [2])
$\Sigma \cup \{\neg L_1, \ldots, \neg L_n\}$ has no Herbrand model iff
no subset of $\mathcal{A}$ is an Herbrand model of $\Sigma \cup \{\neg L_1, \ldots, \neg L_n\}$.
Since $\mathcal{A}$ is finite, the last statement is decidable. □

**Corollary 21.** *The problem whether $\Sigma \models C$, where $\Sigma$ is a finite set of function-free clauses and $C$ is a clause, is decidable.*

The following sequence of lemmas is adapted, with modifications, from Idestam-Almquist [4], where they are given for T-implication.

**Lemma 22.** *Let $S$ be a finite set of non-tautologous clauses, $V = \{x_1, \ldots, x_m\}$ be a set of variables, and let $G = \{C_1, C_2, \ldots\}$ be a (possibly infinite) set of generalizations of $S$ under implication. Then the set $G' = \mathcal{I}(C_1, V) \cup \mathcal{I}(C_2, V) \cup \ldots$ is a finite set of clauses.*

*Proof.* Let $d$ be the maximal depth of the terms in clauses in $S$. It follows from Lemma 12 that $G$ (and hence also $G'$) cannot contain terms of depth greater than $d$, nor predicates, functions or constants other than those in $S$. The set of literals which can be constructed from predicates in $S$, and from terms of depth at most $d$ consisting of functions and constants in $S$ and variables in $V$, is finite. Hence the set of clauses which can be constructed from those literals is also finite. $G'$ is a subset of this set, so $G'$ is a finite set of clauses. □

**Lemma 23.** *Let $D$ be a clause, $C$ be a function-free clause such that $C \models D$, $T = \{t_1, \ldots, t_n\}$ be the term set of $D$ by $\sigma$, $V = \{x_1, \ldots, x_m\}$ be a set of variables, and $m \geq n$. If $E$ is an LGS of $\mathcal{I}(C, V)$, then $E \models D$.*

*Proof.* Let $\gamma = \{x_1/t_1, \ldots, x_n/t_n, x_{n+1}/t_n, \ldots, x_m/t_n\}$ (it does not matter to which terms the variables $x_{n+1}, \ldots, x_m$ are mapped by $\gamma$, as long as they are mapped to terms in $T$). Suppose $\mathcal{I}(C, V) = \{C\rho_1, \ldots, C\rho_k\}$. Then $\mathcal{I}(C, T) = \{C\rho_1\gamma, \ldots, C\rho_k\gamma\}$. Let $E$ be an LGS of $\mathcal{I}(C, V)$ (note that $E$ must be function-free). Then for every $1 \leq i \leq k$, there are $\theta_i$ such that $E\theta_i \subseteq C\rho_i$. This means that $E\theta_i\gamma \subseteq C\rho_i\gamma$ and hence $E\theta_i\gamma \models C\rho_i\gamma$, for every $1 \leq i \leq k$. Therefore $E \models \mathcal{I}(C, T)$.

Since $C \models D$, we know from Lemma 12 that constants appearing in $C$ must also appear in $D$. This means that $\sigma$ is a Skolem substitution for $D$ w.r.t. $\{C\}$. Then from Lemma 19 we know $\mathcal{I}(C, T) \models D\sigma$, hence $E \models D\sigma$. Furthermore, since $E$ is an LGS of $\mathcal{I}(C, V)$, all constants in $E$ also appear in $C$, hence all constants in $E$ must appear in $D$, so $\sigma$ is a Skolem substitution for $D$ w.r.t. $\{E\}$. Then $E \models D$ by Lemma 15. □

Consider $C = P(x, y, z) \leftarrow P(y, z, x)$ and $D = \leftarrow Q(w)$. Both $C$ and $D$ imply the clause $E = P(x, y, z) \leftarrow P(z, x, y), Q(b)$. Now note that $C \cup D = P(x, y, z) \leftarrow P(y, z, x), Q(w)$ also implies $E$. This holds for clauses in general:

**Lemma 24.** *Let $C$, $D$, and $E$ be clauses such that $C$ and $D$ are standardized apart. If $C \models E$ and $D \models E$, then $C \cup D \models E$.*

*Proof.* Suppose $C \models E$ and $D \models E$, and $M$ be a model of the clause $C \cup D$. Since $C$ and $D$ are standardized apart, the clause $C \cup D$ is equivalent to the formula $\forall(C) \vee \forall(D)$ (where $\forall(C)$ denotes the universally quantified clause $C$). This means that $M$ is a model of $C$ or a model of $D$. Then it follows from $C \models E$ and $D \models E$ that $M$ is a model of $E$. Therefore $C \cup D \models E$. □

Now we can prove the existence of an LGI of any finite set $S$ of clauses which contains at least one non-tautologous and function-free clause. In fact we can prove something stronger, namely that this LGI is a *special* LGI, which is not only implied, but actually *subsumed* by any other generalization of $S$:

**Definition 25.** Let $\mathcal{C}$ be a clausal language, and $S$ be a finite subset of $\mathcal{C}$. An LGI $C$ of $S$ in $\mathcal{C}$ is called a *special* LGI of $S$ in $\mathcal{C}$, if $C' \succeq C$ for every generalization $C' \in \mathcal{C}$ of $S$ under implication.

Note that if $D$ is an LGI of a set containing at least one non-tautologous function-free clause, then by Lemma 12 $D$ is itself function-free, because it should imply the function-free clause(s) in $S$. For instance, $C = P(x, y, z) \leftarrow P(y, z, x), Q(w)$ is an LGI of $D_1 = P(x, y, z) \leftarrow P(y, z, x), Q(f(a))$ and $D_2 = P(x, y, z) \leftarrow P(z, x, y), Q(b)$. Note that this LGI is properly subsumed by the LGS of $\{D_1, D_2\}$, which is $P(x, y, z) \leftarrow P(x', y', z'), Q(w)$. An LGI may sometimes be the empty clause □, for example if $S = \{P(a), Q(a)\}$.

**Theorem 26 (Existence of special LGI in $\mathcal{C}$).** *Let $\mathcal{C}$ be a clausal language. If $S$ is a finite set of clauses from $\mathcal{C}$, and $S$ contains at least one non-tautologous function-free clause, then there exists a special LGI of $S$ in $\mathcal{C}$.*

*Proof.* Let $S = \{D_1, \ldots, D_n\}$ be a finite set of clauses from $\mathcal{C}$, such that $S$ contains at least one non-tautologous function-free clause. We can assume without loss of generality that $S$ contains no tautologies. Let $\sigma$ be a Skolem substitution for $S$, $T = \{t_1, \ldots, t_m\}$ be the term set of $S$ by $\sigma$, $V = \{x_1, \ldots, x_m\}$ be a set of variables, and $G = \{C_1, C_2, \ldots\}$ be the set of all generalizations of $S$ under implication in $\mathcal{C}$. Note that $\square \in G$, so $G$ is not empty. Since each clause in $G$ must imply the function-free clause(s) in $S$, it follows from Lemma 12 that all members of $G$ are function-free. By Lemma 22, the set $G' = \mathcal{I}(C_1, V) \cup \mathcal{I}(C_2, V) \cup \ldots$ is a finite set of clauses. Since $G'$ is finite, the set of $\mathcal{I}(C_i, V)$s is also finite. For simplicity, let $\{\mathcal{I}(C_1, V), \ldots, \mathcal{I}(C_k, V)\}$ be the set of all distinct $\mathcal{I}(C_i, V)$s.

Let $E_i$ be an LGS of $\mathcal{I}(C_i, V)$, for every $1 \leq i \leq k$, such that $E_1, \ldots, E_k$ are standardized apart. For every $1 \leq j \leq n$, the term set of $D_j$ by $\sigma$ is some set $\{t_{j_1}, \ldots, t_{j_s}\} \subseteq T$, such that $m \geq j_s$. ¿From Lemma 23, we have that $E_i \models D_j$, for every $1 \leq i \leq k$ and $1 \leq j \leq n$, hence $E_i \models S$. Now let $F = E_1 \cup \ldots \cup E_k$, then we have $F \models S$ from Lemma 24.

To prove that $F$ is a special LGI of $S$, it remains to show that $C_j \succeq F$, for every $j \geq 1$. For every $j \geq 1$, there is an $i$ ($1 \leq i \leq k$), such that $\mathcal{I}(C_j, V) = \mathcal{I}(C_i, V)$. So for this $i$, $E_i$ is an LGS of $\mathcal{I}(C_j, V)$. $C_j$ is itself also a generalization of $\mathcal{I}(C_j, V)$ under subsumption, hence $C_j \succeq E_i$. Then finally $C_j \succeq F$, since $E_i \subseteq F$. $\square$

**Corollary 27.** *Let $\mathcal{C}$ be a clausal language. Then for every finite set of function-free clauses $S \subseteq \mathcal{C}$, there exists an LGI of $S$ in $\mathcal{C}$.*[2]

*Proof.* Let $S$ be a finite set of function-free clauses in $\mathcal{C}$. If $S$ only contains tautologies, any tautology will be an LGI of $S$. Otherwise, let $S'$ be obtained by deleting all tautologies from $S$. By the previous theorem, there is a special LGI of $S'$. Clearly, this is also a special LGI of $S$ itself in $\mathcal{C}$. $\square$

## 4 The LGI is Computable

In the previous section we proved the *existence* of an LGI in $\mathcal{C}$ of every finite set $S$ of clauses containing at least one non-tautologous function-free clause. In this section, we will establish the *computability* of such an LGI. The next algorithm, extracted from the proof of the previous section, computes this LGI:

**LGI-Algorithm**
**Input:** A finite set $S$ of clauses, at least one of which is non-tautologous and function-free.
**Output:** An LGI of $S$ in $\mathcal{C}$.

---

[2] Niblett [13, p. 135] claims that it is simple to show that LGIs exist in a language with only a finite number of constants and no function symbols. Such a result would imply our corollary. However, Niblett has not provided a proof, and neither has anyone else, as far as we know. We would be rather surprised if a proof exists which is actually much simpler than the proof we have given here.

1. Remove all tautologies from $S$ (a clause is a tautology iff it contains literals $A$ and $\neg A$), call the remaining set $S'$.
2. Let $m$ be the number of distinct terms in $S'$, let $V = \{x_1, \ldots, x_m\}$. (Notice that this $m$ is the same number as the number of terms in the term set $T$ used in the proof of Theorem 26.)
3. Let $G$ be the (finite) set of all clauses which can be constructed from predicates and constants in $S'$ and variables in $V$.
4. Let $\{U_1, \ldots, U_n\}$ be the set of all subsets of $G$.
5. Let $H_i$ be an LGS of $U_i$, for every $1 \leq i \leq n$. These $H_i$ can be computed by Plotkin's algorithm [16].
6. Remove from $\{H_1, \ldots, H_n\}$ all clauses which do not imply $S'$ (since each $H_i$ is function-free, by Corollary 21 this implication is decidable), and standardize the remaining clauses $\{H_1, \ldots, H_q\}$ apart.
7. Return the clause $H = H_1 \cup \ldots \cup H_q$.

The correctness of this algorithm follows from the proof of Theorem 26. First notice that $H \models S$ by Lemma 24. Furthermore, note that all $\mathcal{I}(C_i, V)$s mentioned in the proof of Theorem 26, are elements of the set $\{U_1, \ldots, U_n\}$. This means that for every $E_i$ in the set $\{E_1, \ldots, E_k\}$ mentioned in that proof, there is a clause $H_j$ in $\{H_1, \ldots, H_q\}$ such that $E_i$ and $H_j$ are subsume-equivalent. Then it follows that the LGI $F = E_1 \cup \ldots \cup E_k$ of that proof subsumes the clause $H = H_1 \cup \ldots \cup H_q$ that our algorithm returns. On the other hand, $F$ is a special LGI, so $F$ and $H$ must be subsume-equivalent.

Suppose the number of distinct constants in $S'$ is $c$, and the number of distinct variables in step 2 of the algorithm is $m$. Furthermore, suppose there are $p$ distinct predicate symbols in $S'$, with respective arities $a_1, \ldots, a_p$. Then the number of distinct atoms that can be formed from these constants, variables and predicates, is $l = \sum_{i=1}^{p} (c + m)^{a_i}$, and the number of distinct literals that can be formed, is $2 \cdot l$. The set $G$ of distinct clauses which can be formed from these literals is the power set of this set of literals, so $|G| = 2^{2 \cdot l}$. Then the set $\{U_1, \ldots, U_n\}$ of all subsets of $G$ contains $2^{|G|} = 2^{2^{2 \cdot l}}$ members.

Thus the algorithm outlined above is not very efficient (to say the least). A more efficient algorithm may exist, but since implication is harder than subsumption and the computation of an LGS is already quite expensive, we should not put our hopes too high. Nevertheless, the existence of the LGI-algorithm does establish the theoretical point that the LGI of any finite set of clauses containing at least one non-tautologous function-free clause, is computable.

**Theorem 28 (Computability of LGI).** *Let $\mathcal{C}$ be a clausal language. If $S$ is a finite set of clauses from $\mathcal{C}$, and $S$ contains at least one non-tautologous function-free clause, then the LGI of $S$ in $\mathcal{C}$ is computable.*

## 5  Least Generalizations under Relative Implication

Implication is stronger than subsumption, but implication relative to background knowledge is even more powerful, since background knowledge can be used to model all sorts of useful properties and relations. Here we will discuss least generalizations under implication relative to some given background knowledge $\Sigma$ (LGRs).

We will show that even if $S$ and $\Sigma$ are both finite sets of *function-free* clauses, an LGR of $S$ relative to $\Sigma$ need not exist. Let $D_1 = P(a)$, $D_2 = P(b)$, $S = \{D_1, D_2\}$, and $\Sigma = \{(P(a) \vee \neg Q(x)), (P(b) \vee \neg Q(x))\}$. This $S$ has no LGR relative to $\Sigma$ in $C$.

Suppose $C$ is an LGR of $S$ relative to $\Sigma$. Note that if $C$ contains the literal $P(a)$, then the Herbrand interpretation which makes $P(a)$ true, and which makes all other ground literals false, would be a model of $\Sigma \cup \{C\}$ but not of $D_2$, so then we would have $C \not\models_\Sigma D_2$. Similarly, if $C$ contains $P(b)$ then $C \not\models_\Sigma D_1$. Hence $C$ cannot contain $P(a)$ or $P(b)$ as literals. Now let $d$ be a constant not appearing in $C$. Let $D = P(x) \vee Q(d)$, then $D \models_\Sigma S$. By the definition of an LGR, we should have $D \models_\Sigma C$. Then by the Subsumption Theorem, there must be a derivation from $\Sigma \cup \{D\}$ of a clause $E$, which subsumes $C$. The set of all clauses which can be derived (in 0 or more resolution-steps) from $\Sigma \cup \{D\}$ is $\Sigma \cup \{D\} \cup \{(P(a) \vee P(x)), (P(b) \vee P(x))\}$. But none of these clauses subsumes $C$, because $C$ does not contain the constant $d$, nor the literals $P(a)$ or $P(b)$. Hence $D \not\models_\Sigma C$, contradicting the assumption that $C$ is an LGR of $S$ relative to $\Sigma$ in $C$.

However, we can identify a special case in which the LGR *does* exist. Here $\Sigma = \{L_1, \ldots, L_k\}$ should be a set of function-free ground literals. A notational remark: if $C$ is a clause, we use $C \cup \overline{\Sigma}$ to denote the clause $C \cup \{\neg L_1, \ldots, \neg L_k\}$. Note that $\{C\} \cup \Sigma$ is a *set* of clauses, while $C \cup \overline{\Sigma}$ is a single clause (a set of literals).

**Theorem 29 (Existence of LGR in $C$).** *Let $C$ be a clausal language and $\Sigma \subseteq C$ be a finite set of function-free ground literals. If $S \subseteq C$ is a finite set of clauses, containing at least one $D$ for which $D \cup \overline{\Sigma}$ is non-tautologous and function-free, then $S$ has an LGR in $C$ relative to $\Sigma$.*

*Proof.* Let $S = \{D_1, \ldots, D_n\}$. It can be seen that since $\Sigma$ is a finite set of ground literals, for any clauses $C$ and $D$ we have $C \models_\Sigma D$ (i.e., $\Sigma \cup \{C\} \models D$) iff $C \models (D \cup \overline{\Sigma})$. Hence an LGI in $C$ of $T = \{(D_1 \cup \overline{\Sigma}), \ldots, (D_n \cup \overline{\Sigma})\}$ is also an LGR of $S$ in $C$. The existence of such an LGI of $T$ follows from Theorem 26. $\square$

It is interesting to compare this result with relative *subsumption*. Plotkin [17] proved that any finite set of clauses has a least generalization under relative subsumption, if the background knowledge $\Sigma$ is a set of ground literals. This result forms the basis of GOLEM [11], one of the most prominent ILP systems. Under relative *implication*, the background knowledge should not only be ground, but function-free as well. Moreover, the set $S$ to be generalized should contain at least one $D$ such that $D \cup \overline{\Sigma}$ is non-tautologous and function-free. Thus on the one hand, relative implication is a more powerful order than relative subsumption, but on the other hand, the existence of least generalizations can only be guaranteed in a much more restricted case.

# 6 Conclusion

Implication is more appropriate for least generalizations than subsumption. We have proved here that any finite set of clauses containing at least one non-tautologous function-free clause has a computable LGI. For sets of clauses which all contain functions, the existence of an LGI remains an open question. In case of implication relative to background knowledge, least generalizations need not exist, except for very restricted cases.

## References

1. W. Buntine. Generalized subsumption and its applications to induction and redundancy. *Artificial Intelligence*, 36:149–176, 1988.
2. C.-L. Chang and R. C.-T. Lee. *Symbolic Logic and Mechanical Theorem Proving*. Academic Press, San Diego, 1973.
3. G. Gottlob. Subsumption and implication. *Inf. Process. Lett.*, 24(2):109–111, 1987.
4. P. Idestam-Almquist. Generalization of clauses under implication. *Journal of Artificial Intelligence Research*, 3:467–489, 1995.
5. R. A. Kowalski. The case for using equality axioms in automatic demonstration. In *Proceedings of the Symposium on Automatic Demonstration*, volume 125 of *Lecture Notes in Mathematics*, pages 112–127. Springer-Verlag, 1970.
6. N. Lavrač and S. Džeroski. *Inductive Logic Programming: Techniques and Applications*. Ellis Horwood, 1994.
7. R. C.-T. Lee. *A Completeness Theorem and a Computer Program for Finding Theorems Derivable from Given Axioms*. PhD thesis, University of California, Berkeley, 1967.
8. J. Marcinkowski and L. Pacholski. Undecidability of the horn-clause implication problem. In *Proceedings of the 33rd Annual IEEE Symposium on Foundations of Computer Science*, pages 354–362, Pittsburg, 1992.
9. K. Morik, S. Wrobel, J.-U. Kietz, and W. Emde. *Knowledge Acquisition and Machine Learning: Theory, Methods and Applications*. Academic Press, London, 1993.
10. S. Muggleton and L. De Raedt. Inductive Logic Programming: Theory and methods. *Journal of Logic Programming*, 19–20:629–679, 1994.
11. S. Muggleton and C. Feng. Efficient induction of logic programs. In S. Muggleton, editor, *Inductive Logic Programming*, volume 38 of *APIC Series*, pages 281–298. Academic Press, 1992.
12. S. Muggleton and C. D. Page. Self-saturation of definite clauses. In S. Wrobel, editor, *Proceedings of the 4th International Workshop on Inductive Logic Programming (ILP-94)*, volume 237 of *GMD-Studien*, pages 161–174, Bad Honnef/Bonn, 1994. Gesellschaft für Mathematik und Datenverarbeitung.
13. T. Niblett. A study of generalisation in logic programs. In D. Sleeman, editor, *Proceedings of the 3rd European Working Sessions on Learning (EWSL-88)*, pages 131–138, 1988.
14. S.-H. Nienhuys-Cheng and R. de Wolf. Least generalizations and greatest specializations of sets of clauses. *Journal of Artificial Intelligence Research*, 4:341–363, 1996.

15. S.-H. Nienhuys-Cheng and R. de Wolf. The subsumption theorem in Inductive Logic Programming: Facts and fallacies. In L. De Raedt, editor, *Advances in Inductive Logic Programming*, pages 265–276. IOS Press, Amsterdam, 1996.

16. G. D. Plotkin. A note on inductive generalization. *Machine Intelligence*, 5:153–163, 1970.

17. G. D. Plotkin. A further note on inductive generalization. *Machine Intelligence*, 6:101–124, 1971.

18. J. R. Quinlan and R. M. Cameron-Jones. Foil: A midterm report. In P. B. Brazdil, editor, *Proceedings of the 6th European Conference on Machine Learning (ECML-93)*, volume 667 of *Lecture Notes in Artificial Intelligence*, pages 3–20. Springer-Verlag, 1993.

# Efficient Proof Encoding

Uroš Pompe

University of Ljubljana,
Faculty of Computer and Information Science,
Tržaška 25, SI-1001 Ljubljana, Slovenia
tel: +386-61-1768 386
fax: +386-61-1768 386
e-mail: uros.pompe@fri.uni-lj.si

**Abstract.** This paper proposes a method of storing the proofs of the learning examples in an efficient manner. FOIL-like top down learners usually store the computed answers of a partially induced clause as a set of ground substitutions. The need for the re-computation of the root part of the SLDNF-tree is reduced that way, but the approach is space-inefficient when the literals in the clause are nondeterminate. We introduce a weak syntactic language bias that does not practically restrict the hypothesis space. Further more, we present a proof encoding scheme, using a mesh-like data structure, that exploits the properties of this bias to store the computed answers efficiently. We show that such encoding grows at most linearly with respect to the clause length. The result is not influenced by the presence of nondeterminism in the background knowledge.

## 1 Introduction

Soon after the inception of inductive logic programming (ILP) [10], a subfield of machine learning, it was realized, through the eyes of the theory of learnability [6], that many interesting classes of logic programs are not polynomialy learnable under arbitrary sample distribution. Cohen [1, 2], for instance, showed that most recursive programs are not polynomialy predictable. Kietz [7] proved, that releasing any of the conditions: determinacy of the clause, or the number of literal in its body, leads to an intractability of the learning task. On the positive side, De Raedt and Džeroski [3] showed that range restricted clauses of length at most $k$ and with arity of literals bounded by $j$ are PAC learnable from positive examples only. The proposed learning algorithm has time complexity, which is $n$ to the $n - th$ power in both $j$ and $k$. This limits practical values, especially for $k$, to an unacceptably low values.

The above knowledge led to an increasing interest in heuristically guided learners. FOIL [14], and similar heuristic top-down algorithms, such as mFOIL [5], MILP [8], SFOIL [13]) seem to be a promising step in this direction. They more or less avoid the time trap of exhaustive search but still suffer from the problem of how to efficiently store the partial proof of the training example. It seems at first, that it is not necessary to remember this proof at all, as we can always recompute it from scratch. This can be very expensive time-wise, as we are forced to search the root part of the SLD(NF) tree over and over again. Storing the computed answers of the partial proof, usually as a set of ground tuples, is also impractical in the presence of non-determinate background knowledge. The problem becomes evident when deep lookahead is needed. An introduction of new variables can increase exponentially the number of computed answers. When using ground-tuple based proof encoding scheme this leads to an unmanageable growth of the proof set.

In the following sections, we will show that this problem can be eliminated. We will introduce a weak restriction on the hypothesis language and then exploit the properties of such language bias to store the set of all computed answers in an efficient way, using a mesh like structure instead of usual tuple set. Space-complexity limits of such encoding scheme will be shown. In the conclusions, we will argue that our approach, despite its limitations, is general enough to be of practical importance.

Only sketches of some proofs of the most important assertions are included. More formal discussion can be found in [11].

## 2  Language Bias

For the understanding of the following, text it is assumed that the reader is familiar with the terminology and the basic assertions found in [9]. From now on, when not specified otherwise, our domain of interest are normal programs and normal clauses. We will only consider flat clauses, containing no other terms but variables and constants. Head($C$) denotes an atom occurring in the head of the normal clause $C$. Body($C$) denotes a set of literals from the body of $C$. A set of variables occurring in some literal or set of literals $S$ is denoted by Vars($S$).

The soundness and completeness results for normal programs demand only that the selection rule should be safe. Alternatively, the selection rule could be fixed, left to right for instance as in the standard prolog implementations, while the ordering of literals in the body varies. Again, the soundness and completeness results still hold if the ordering of literals is safe, meaning that no non-ground negative literals should be encountered during the SLDNF resolution. When referring to an **ordered normal clause** in the text below it is assumed that its body is ordered safely, and that the selection rule corresponds to selection of the left most literal in the current goal.

**Definition 1.** A variable $X$ occurring in the ordered normal clause $C = A \leftarrow L_1, \ldots, L_m$ is **linked**, if it is $k$-**linked** for some integer $k$. Variables appearing in the head are 0-linked. Let $L_i \in$ Body($C$) be the first positive literal, starting from the left, such that $Y \in$ Vars($L_i$). The variable $Y$ is $k$-linked if there exists a variable $V \in$ Vars($L_i$) \ $\{Y\} \wedge V \in$ Vars($\{A, L_1, \ldots, L_{i-1}\}$), which is $(k-1)$-linked, and no other variable $Z \in$ Vars($L_i$) \ $\{Y\} \wedge Z \in$ Vars($\{A, L_1, \ldots, L_{i-1}\}$) is more than $(k-1)$-linked.

**Definition 2.** Let $C$ be an ordered normal clause and let $L \in C$ be a literal from either the head or the body of $C$. Literal $L$ is **linked** if there exists a variable $X \in \text{Vars}(L)$, and $X$ is linked. Clause $C$ is **linked** if it contains only linked literals.

*Example 1.* Let us look at the following clauses:

1. $p(X,Y) \leftarrow not(r(Z)), q(Y,Z)$.
2. $p(X,Y) \leftarrow q(Y,Z), not(r(Z)), s(X,V,Z)$.
3. $p(X,Y) \leftarrow q(V,Z), q(Y,Z)$.

Taking into consideration our left-to-right literal selection rule and Definitions 1 and 2, it is easy to see that the first clause is not ordered safely. Variable $V$ in clause 2 is 2-linked, despite the fact that it occurs in the literal together with $X$, which is a 0-linked variable. The third clause is not linked because literal $q(V,Z)$ does not contain any linked variables.

In the remaining text it is assumed that all clauses we are going to consider are linked.

With $\mathcal{D}(X)$ we will denote the **depth** of variable $X$. It represent the length of its linking chain. A literal $L_i$ from the ordered normal clause $C = A \leftarrow L_1, \ldots, L_m$ is called an **open literal** if it introduces new variable(s) in the partial clause $C = A \leftarrow L_1, \ldots, L_{i-1}$. Note that since the ordering is safe, $L_i$ is an atom. The head of the clause is also an open literal. All other literals are **closed**. For example, literal $s(X,V,Z)$ from the second clause of Example 1 is an open literal, while the literal $not(r(Z))$ from the same clause is a closed one.

**Definition 3.** Let $C$ be an ordered normal clause. Variable $X$ **depends** on variable $Y$ if there exists an open literal $L \in C$ such that $X \in \text{Vars}(L)$ and either $Y \in \text{Vars}(L)$ and $\mathcal{D}(X) = \mathcal{D}(Y)$, or there exists a variable $Z \in \text{Vars}(L)$ such that $\mathcal{D}(X) > \mathcal{D}(Z)$ and $Z$ depends on $Y$. Variables $\{X,Y\} \subseteq \text{Vars}(C)$ are **peers** if $X$ depends on $Y$ and $Y$ depends on $X$. This represents an equivalence relation $\mathcal{P}_C \subseteq \text{Vars}(C) \times \text{Vars}(C)$.

It is easy to see that $\mathcal{P}_C$ is indeed an equivalence relation. Since it is induced by the dependency relation, it is reflexive and transitive. The Definition 3 guarantees that it is symmetric. A **factor set** $\text{Vars}_{\mathcal{P}_C}(C) = \text{Vars}(C)/\mathcal{P}_C$ can be obtained from the set of variables in an ordered clause $C$. It represents a set of equivalence classes $\text{Vars}_{\mathcal{P}_C}(C) = \{[X]\}$ where it holds that $Y \in [X]$ iff $X, Y \in \text{Vars}(C)$ and $\langle X, Y \rangle \in \mathcal{P}_C$. Dependency between variables then extends naturally to dependency between the equivalence classes. For all $[X], [Y] \in \text{Vars}_{\mathcal{P}_C}(C)$, $[X]$ depends on $[Y]$ iff $X$ depends on $Y$.

Further definitions and arguments can be expressed easier using another notion, that of variable dependency tree, which represents a skeleton of the variable dependency relation.

**Definition 4.** Let $C$ be an ordered normal clause and $\mathcal{P}_C$ be a peer relation over $\text{Vars}(C)$. Let $G = (V, E)$ be an acyclic directed graph. $V$ is a set of vertices, equivalence classes from $\text{Vars}_{\mathcal{P}_C}(C)$, while $E$ is a set of edges, such that $\langle [Y], [X] \rangle \in$

$E, [X] \neq [Y]$ iff $X$ depends on $Y$ and there exists no $[Z] \in \mathrm{Vars}_{\mathcal{P}_C}(C)$, distinct from both $[X]$ and $[Y]$, such that $[X]$ depends on $[Z]$ and $[Z]$ depends on $[Y]$. The graph $G$ is actually a tree with the the set of head variables at the root. It is called a **variable dependency tree** and denoted by $\mathrm{VDT}(C)$.

*Example 2.* Consider for instance the clause

$$C = p(X, Y) \leftarrow q(Y, Z), r(Z, V, X), q(X, W), p(W, V) \ .$$

Figure 1 shows its variable dependency tree. Every literal from $C$ can be assigned a subtree of $\mathrm{VDT}(C)$, connecting all its variables. The subtree of the literal $p(X, Y)$ in $\mathrm{VDT}(C)$ is emphasized with bold edge, connecting $\{X, Y\}$ and $\{Z\}$. The variable connecting subtree is actually a path in this case but in general, it could be an arbitrary subtree.

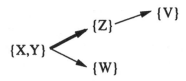

**Fig. 1.** Example of variable dependency tree

Finally, the restriction of the hypothesis language can be given.

**Definition 5.** Let $C$ be an ordered normal clause. A literal $L \in \mathrm{Body}(C)$ is **dependable** iff the set of nodes $\{[X] : X \in \mathrm{Vars}(L)\}$ lies on a path in $\mathrm{VDT}(C)$. $L$ is **$k$-dependable** if it has also the following property:

$$\left( \max_{Y \in \mathrm{Vars}(L)} \mathcal{D}(Y) - \min_{Z \in \mathrm{Vars}(L)} \mathcal{D}(Z) \right) \leq k \ .$$

$C$ is $k$-dependable iff there exists a safe ordering of literals in the body of $C$, such that every literal $L \in C'$, where $C'$ is safely reordered version of $C$, is $k$-dependable. $C'$ is called $k$-**dependable form** of $C$.

As we shall see later, not every clause has a $k$-dependable form. This holds for an arbitrarily large $k$. Let us assume for now that we are dealing with clauses for which such a form exists.

**Definition 6.** A normal program $\mathcal{H}$ is $k$-dependable iff every $C \in \mathcal{H}$ is $k$-dependable. Similarly, $\mathcal{H}'$ is $k$-dependable form of $\mathcal{H}$ iff it is a set of $k$-dependable forms of the clauses from $\mathcal{H}$.

**Definition 7.** Let $B$ be a normal program called **background knowledge** and $p$ be a distinguished predicate from $B$ called **target predicate**. A $k$-**dependable hypothesis language** $\mathcal{L}_k$ is a set of all $k$-dependable hypotheses, built using predicates from $B$, and with predicate $p$ in the head of every clause.

The ordering of literals in the body of the clause obviously does not influence its logical interpretation. From the declarative point of view both, the original normal program $P$ and its $k$-dependable form $P'$ have the same meaning. If $P$ is a normal program and $P'$ is its $k$-dependable form then, a substitution $\theta$ is a correct answer for $comp(P) \cup G$ iff it is a correct answer for $comp(P') \cup G$. By definition of $comp(P)$ [9] it holds that $comp(P) \leftrightarrow comp(P')$. Therefore, $\forall((L_1, \ldots, L_n)\theta)$ is a logical consequence of $comp(P)$ iff $\forall((L_1, \ldots, L_n)\theta)$ is a logical consequence of $comp(P')$.

Reordering of body literals can have quite a dramatic effect on the procedural semantics. Again, it is assumed that the selection rule is the standard left-to-right rule. If the underlying logic programming system is using an unfair search rule then by choosing an unfortunate ordering, incompleteness can be introduced. Fortunately, some properties are still preserved. For instance, if $P$ is a normal program and $P'$ is its $k$-dependable form then $comp(P) \cup G$ is allowed (admissible) iff $comp(P') \cup G$ is allowed (admissible). Similarly, $P'$ is stratified (hierarchical) iff $P$ is stratified (hierarchical). The consequence of these two properties is that the transformation of $P$ to its $k$-dependable form preserves the soundness and completeness of $P$.

The above discussion leads to the conclusion that the declarative and procedural properties are left untouched when $k$-dependable form $P'$ is used instead of the original ordered normal program $P$. It remains to be seen if this form can be always obtained. Unfortunately, it is not hard to prove that for a fixed $k$ the $k$-dependable hypothesis language $\mathcal{L}_k$ is not complete. This is true even if we restrict ourself to a subset of definite hypotheses (programs).

**Proposition 8.** *For some fixed positive integer $k$, let $\mathcal{L}_k$ be a $k$-dependable hypothesis language using predicates from background knowledge $B$. Let $p$ be the target predicate. If $B$ is truly relational (contains also non-target predicates with arity greater than 1 and the target predicate has arity greater than 0) then there exists a normal clause $C_n$ and a definite clause $C_d$, built using predicates from $B$ such that there exist no $k$-dependable forms $C_n'$ and $C_d'$, respectively.*

*Proof.* Let $q$ be a non-target predicate symbol from $B$. Without loss of generality we can assume that $p$ has arity 1, while $q$ has arity 2.

**Normal $C_n$ :** Consider the clause

$$p(X_0) \leftarrow q(X_0, X_1), q(X_0, X_2), \neg q(X_1, X_2) \ .$$

Note that the only other safe ordering of the literals in the body is the clause

$$p(X_0) \leftarrow q(X_0, X_2), q(X_0, X_1), \neg q(X_1, X_2) \ .$$

Variable dependency tree of both the clauses is the same. The last literal
is not $k$-dependable for any $k$, since $X_1$ and $X_2$ are not on the same path
(cross referencing).

**Definite $C_d$ :** Consider the clause

$$p(X_0) \leftarrow q(X_0, X_{1,1}), q(X_{1,1}, X_{1,2}), \ldots, q(X_{1,n-1}, X_{1,n}),$$
$$q(X_0, X_{2,1}), q(X_{2,1}, X_{2,2}), \ldots, q(X_{2,n-1}, X_{2,n}),$$
$$q(X_{1,n}, X_{2,n}) .$$

where $n = \lceil \frac{k}{2} \rceil$. Let $C' = p(X_0) \leftarrow L_1, \ldots, L_{2n+1}$ be its $k$-dependable
form. For $C'$ to be linked, $L_1$ can only be one of the literals $q(X_0, X_{1,1})$,
or $q(X_0, X_{2,1})$. Lets assume for a moment that the former is selected. Since
every variable occurs in exactly two literals of the body, this selection im-
poses a restriction on the ordering of literals $L_{i_1} = q(X_0, X_{1,1}), \ldots, L_{i_n} = q(X_{1,n-1}, X_{1,n})$, such that it must hold $i_1 < i_2 \cdots < i_n$. No ordering of
$C$, that has both $q(X_0, X_{1,1})$ and $q(X_0, X_{2,1})$ as the open literals, can be
$h$-dependable for any $h$. This is true because such clause would have two
leaves in VDT($C'$) but there is always a literal, following both $q(X_0, X_{1,1})$
and $q(X_0, X_{2,1})$, that references variables from both paths from root to those
leaves. This fact imposes additional restrictions on the placement of the rest
of the literals $L_{j_1} = q(X_0, X_{2,1}), \ldots, L_{j_n} = q(X_{2,n-1}, X_{2,n})$. It must hold
that $j_n < \cdots < j_1$. There is actually only one ordering, satisfying both constraints. Let $l$ be the index of literal $q(X_{1,n}, X_{2,n})$ in $C'$. For $C'$ to be linked
it must hold $1 = i_1 < \cdots < i_n < l < j_n < \cdots < j_1 = 2n + 1$.

Similar argument can be made if we pick $q(X_0, X_{2,1})$ as the first literal. The
ordering in this case must be $1 = j_1 < \cdots < j_n < l < i_n < \cdots < i_1 = 2n + 1$.
These two orderings are the only two forms of $C$, such that all variables from
literal $L_i : i \in \{1, \ldots, 2n + 1\}$ lie on the path in VDT($C'$). But, at least one
of the variables $X_{1,1}$ or $X_{2,1}$ has depth equal to $2n + 1 > k$ and it occurs in
the last literal of $C'$ together with $X_0$. This contradicts the assumption that
$C'$ is $k$-dependable. $\qquad\qquad\qquad\qquad\qquad\qquad\qquad\qquad\qquad\qquad\qquad\qquad\qquad\quad$ □

The second part of the proof seems interesting as we were almost able to obtain
a $k$-dependable form of the definite clause $C$. By "almost", we mean that all the
variables occurring in some literal from Body($C'$) were the members of some
nodes on a path in VDT($C'$). Unfortunately, some of them were more than $k$
steps apart, not satisfying by that the second condition of $k$-dependency. It turns
out that, when dealing with definite clauses, we can always obtain such $C'$, which
violates the second condition only. As the following theorem shows, by raising
the integer $k$, we can enlarge the $k$-dependable language to contain an arbitrary
definite program (or its $k$-dependable form).

**Theorem 9.** *Let $C = A \leftarrow B_1, \ldots, B_m$ be a linked finite definite clause. Then,
there exists an integer $k$ and a definite clause $C' \in \mathcal{L}_k$, such that $C'$ is a $k$-
dependable form of $C$.*

*Proof.* The proof is rather long so we are only going to sketch it. The details
can be found in [11]. Note that for any reordering of literals in $C$, maximum

depth of any variable can not exceed $m$. Therefore, we are searching for such an arrangement of literals in the body of $C$ that no literal contains variables, which violate the "lie-on-the-path" constraint of dependable clauses. The proof goes by induction on the length of $C$.

**Base case** $(m = 0)$: Trivial, since a unit clause is a $0$-dependable form of itself.
**Inductive step** $(m - 1 \rightarrow m)$: Assume that for any clause $C$ of length $m - 1$
there exists such $k$ and the $k$-dependable form $C'$. Now let $C$ have length
$m$. Let $B'_m$ be the last literal from Body$(C)$ containing variables from the
deepest leaf of VDT$(C)$. If we remove $B'_m$ from $C$ we obtain a clause with
less than $m$ literals in the body, which by the inductive step assumption has
a $k$-dependable form $C'_{m-1}$. After reinserting $B'_m$ at the end of $C'_{m-1}$, there
are two possibilities. $C'_m$ is $k'$ dependable, or $B'_m$ violates the dependability
constraint. In the latter case, let $N$ denotes the deepest common node on
the paths in the variable connecting subtree of VDT$(C'_m)$ for the variables
in $B'_m$. The body of $C'_m$ can now be split as follows. All the literals in
$C'_m$, following the literal which introduces the variables from $N$, constitute
a set $S_1$ of literals, the rest are kept together in the set $S_2$. Both sets are
non-empty. Both have less then $m$ literals. Clause with head Head$(C)$ and
literals from $S_2$ in the body has a $k$-dependable form, which is a subsequence
of literals in the body of $C'_m$. All the literals in $S_1$ depend on the variables
from $N$, and possibly on those from the path from the root of VDT$(C'_m)$ to
$N$. Since there are less then $m$ literals in $S_1$, we can obtain the $k'$-dependable
ordering of its literals. This sequence can then be appended to $S_2$ to obtain
final $k''$-dependable form of $C$. □

*Example 3.* Let us look at the standard (function free) version of the *quick sort*
relation. Let the background knowledge contains of the following predicates:

$qsort(List, SortedList)$.
$components(List, FirstElement, RestList)$.
$partition(List, Element, SmallerEQ, Greater)$.
$append(PrefixList, List, ConcatenatedList)$.

The variable dependency trees for the three clauses:

(a) $qsort(A, B) \leftarrow components(A, C, D), partition(D, C, E, F), qsort(E, G),$
    $qsort(F, H), components(I, C, H), append(G, I, B)$ .
(b) $qsort(A, B) \leftarrow components(A, C, D), partition(D, C, E, F), qsort(E, G),$
    $append(G, I, B), components(I, C, H), qsort(F, H)$ .
(c) $qsort(A, B) \leftarrow append(G, I, B), components(I, C, H),$
    $components(A, C, D), partition(D, C, E, F), qsort(E, G), qsort(F, H)$ .

are shown in Fig. 2. The first clause is the usual form from the text books.
It is not a dependable clause because of the *append* literal at the end. Forms
(b) and (c) satisfy $k$-dependable criteria. (b) is *4*-dependable while (c) is only
*3*-dependable.

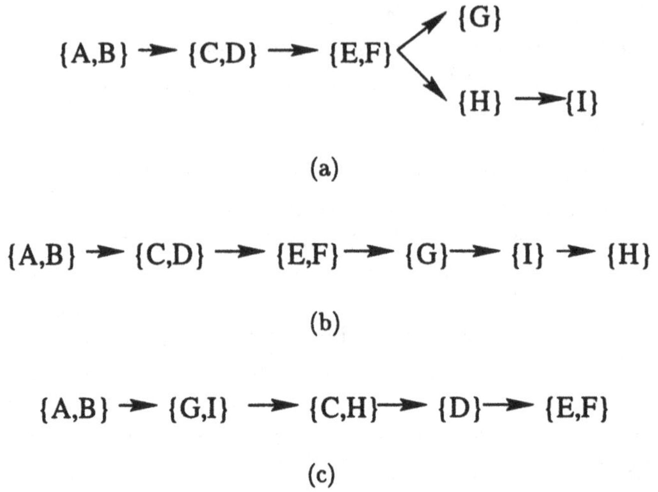

$$\{A,B\} \longrightarrow \{C,D\} \longrightarrow \{E,F\} \diagdown \begin{array}{l} \nearrow \{G\} \\ \searrow \{H\} \longrightarrow \{I\} \end{array}$$

(a)

$$\{A,B\} \longrightarrow \{C,D\} \longrightarrow \{E,F\} \longrightarrow \{G\} \longrightarrow \{I\} \longrightarrow \{H\}$$

(b)

$$\{A,B\} \longrightarrow \{G,I\} \longrightarrow \{C,H\} \longrightarrow \{D\} \longrightarrow \{E,F\}$$

(c)

**Fig. 2.** Variable dependency trees for the various forms of the *qsort* predicate

## 3 PSPACE Limits

Any ILP system that uses $\mathcal{L}_k$, for some fixed positive integer $k$, as its hypothesis language is sometimes not able to learn the correct hypothesis, simply because not every normal (or definite) program has a $k$-dependable form. It is therefore interesting to see what can be gained if $\mathcal{L}_k$ is used. From now on, we are only going to consider the $k$-dependable hypotheses. Let us ignore for a while the incompleteness and show the advantages of our approach. Later, we will argue that the incompleteness does not affect the learners performance from the practical point of view.

Let $B$ be a normal program, background knowledge, and $E$ be a set of ground facts, called the learning examples. Any predicate from $B$, that is allowed to introduce new variables in the clause, must have a finite model and must be able to compute it entirely. For any such $q/r$, the goal $\leftarrow q(X_1, \ldots, X_r)$ must succeed only finitely many times producing only finitely many computed answers $\theta$. Of course, it must be able to compute all the answers in finite time, implying that SLDNF-tree of such goal is finite. Let $q^\theta$ denote the set of all such substitutions. Suppose that $C_i$ is a normal clause $A \leftarrow L_1, \ldots, L_i$ with target predicate in its head. The set of all computed answers, where $A$ matches with one of the examples from $E$, is denoted by $C_i^\theta$. More formally, we can define $C_i^\theta$ recursively as

$$C_0^\theta = \{\theta : A\theta \in E\}$$
$$C_i^\theta = \{\theta\sigma : \theta \in C_{i-1}^\theta \wedge \sigma \text{ is computed answer for } \leftarrow L_i\theta\}, \quad 0 < i \ .$$

Note that for $L_i$ being a closed literal, $\sigma = \epsilon$ when $\leftarrow L_i\theta$ is SLDNF-refutable. By definition of $C_i^\theta$, it is easy to see that for a normal goal $G = \leftarrow L_1, \ldots, L_i$, if $\theta \in C_i^\theta$ then $\theta$ is computed answer for $G$.

Let $L_j \in \text{Body}(C_i)$ be an open literal. Let $\text{Vars}_{\text{new}}(L_j)$ denote the set of variables introduced by $L_j$. These are all the variables that do not occur in any of the literals $L_k \in \text{Body}(C_i) : k < j$, and are also not in the head. Similarly, $\text{Vars}_{\text{old}}(L_j) = \text{Vars}(L_j) \backslash \text{Vars}_{\text{new}}(L_j)$ denotes the set of variables that are already introduced up to the literal $L_j$. Let $S$ be a set of variables and let $\max_{\mathcal{D}}(S)$ and $\min_{\mathcal{D}}(S)$ be defined as

$$\max_{\mathcal{D}}(S) = \left\{ X : X \in S \wedge \mathcal{D}(X) = \max_{Y \in S} \mathcal{D}(Y) \right\}$$

$$\min_{\mathcal{D}}(S) = \left\{ X : X \in S \wedge \mathcal{D}(X) = \min_{Y \in S} \mathcal{D}(Y) \right\}$$

If we look at the variables from $L_j$ and take into account that $L_j$ is a dependable literal it holds that

$$\max_{\mathcal{D}}(\text{Vars}_{\text{new}}(L_j)) \in \text{Vars}_{\mathcal{P}_{C_i}}(C_i)$$

$$\exists [X] \in \text{Vars}_{\mathcal{P}_{C_i}}(C_i) \wedge \max_{\mathcal{D}}(\text{Vars}_{\text{old}}(L_j)) \subseteq [X]$$

For a substitution $\theta$, let $\theta_S$ denote the substitution restricted to the set of variables $S$.

**Definition 10.** Let $C_i = A \leftarrow L_1, \ldots, L_i$ be a normal $k$-dependable clause for some integer $k$. A **variable binding graph** $\text{VBG}_{C_i} = (V_{C_i}, E_{C_i})$ is an acyclic directed graph such that $V_{C_i}$ is a set of vertices defined as

$$V_{C_i} = \left\{ \theta_{[X]} : \theta \in C_i^\theta \wedge [X] \in \text{Vars}_{\mathcal{P}_{C_i}}(C_i) \right\}$$

while $E_{C_i}$ represents the set of edges

$$E_{C_i} = \{ \langle \theta_{[X]}, \theta_{[Y]} \rangle : \theta_{[X]}, \theta_{[Y]} \in V_{C_i} \wedge$$
$$\exists L_j \in \text{Body}(C_i) \wedge X \in \max_{\mathcal{D}}(\text{Vars}_{\text{old}}(L_j)) \wedge Y \in \text{Vars}_{\text{new}}(L_j) \} .$$

Note that $\text{VBG}_{C_i}$ is actually a cascade and each level of nodes corresponds to a level in $\text{VDT}(C_i)$.

*Example 4.* Suppose the background knowledge $B$ contains the definitions of predicates, describing the cube on Fig. 3. The predicates used are those from the well known *finite element mesh design* [4] domain. Let for instance the predicate *neighbour*$(X, Y)$ denotes the neighbouring relation between the edges. Let the atom *equal*$(X, Y)$ denotes that the edge $Y$ is parallel and of similar shape to the edge $X$. Figure 4 shows the description of the cube using the above two predicates. For the convenience, only relevant parts of $B$ are shown. Suppose

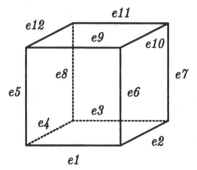

**Fig. 3.** A simple structure for finite element mesh design

```
neighbour(e1,e2). neighbour(e1,e6).
neighbour(e1,e4). neighbour(e1,e5).
neighbour(e2,e1). neighbour(e2,e6).
neighbour(e2,e7). neighbour(e2,e3).
neighbour(e9,e5). neighbour(e1,e12).
neighbour(e1,e6). neighbour(e1,e10).
neighbour(e10,e9). neighbour(e1,e6).
neighbour(e1,e7). neighbour(e1,e11).
    ⋮

equal(e5,e6). equal(e5,e7). equal(e5,e8).
equal(e6,e7). equal(e6,e8). equal(e6,e5).
equal(e7,e8). equal(e7,e5). equal(e7,e6).
equal(e8,e5). equal(e8,e6). equal(e8,e7).
    ⋮
```

**Fig. 4.** Part of the background knowledge describing the cube on Fig. fig:cube

we are given the set of positive learning examples

$$E^+ = \{\, mesh(e1,1), mesh(e2,1), mesh(e3,3), mesh(e4,3),$$
$$mesh(e5,2), mesh(e6,2), mesh(e7,1), mesh(e8,4),$$
$$mesh(e9,1), mesh(e10,1), mesh(e11,3), mesh(e12)\}$$

Negative examples $E^-$ could be obtained using the *closed world assumption*. We should stress that $B$ and $E$ are fictitious and are both adjusted to better support our argument.

For the following partial clause $C_3$:

```
mesh(A,B) :-
        neighbour(A,C),
        equal(C,D),
        neighbour(D,E).
```

a part of the variable binding graph (it is actually a forest) is shown on Fig. 5.

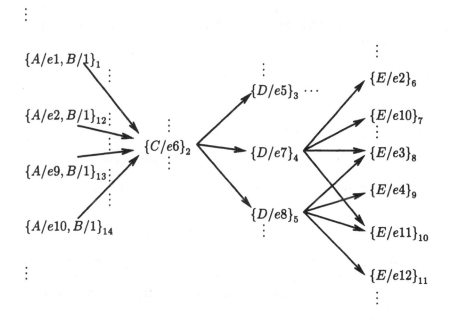

**Fig. 5.** Part of the variable binding graph for the clause in Example 4

$E_{C_i}$ can be viewed as the relation on $V_{C_i} \times V_{C_i}$. Let $E_{C_i}^*$ be its transitive closure. We are particularly interested in nodes of $\mathrm{VBG}_{C_i}$, that can be reached from some $a \in V_{C_i}$. The set of such nodes, denoted by $\mathcal{R}_{C_i}(a)$, is given by

$$\mathcal{R}_{C_i}(a) = \{b : b = a \vee \langle a, b \rangle \in E_{C_i}^*\} \ .$$

In the following definitions we assume that the set of vertices $V_{C_i}$ is enumerated. Each $a \in V_{C_i}$ has a unique index; sometimes we are going to emphasize it by writing it out as an index of $a$. For example, $a_j \in V_{C_i}$ represents a node $a$ with index $j$ according to some fixed enumeration. Let $\mathrm{UT}_{C_i}(a)$ be the set

$$\mathrm{UT}_{C_i}(a) = \{\langle j, l \rangle : \exists b_j, b_l \in V_{C_i} \wedge b_j \in \mathcal{R}_{C_i}(a) \wedge \langle b_j, b_l \rangle \in E_{C_i}\}$$

$\langle j, l \rangle$ is called a **validity tag**. Each tag represents a flag, that indicates if edge $\langle j, i \rangle$ in graph $\mathrm{VBG}_{C_i}$ is valid if we start from node $a$. Let $\mathcal{I}\mathrm{set}(\mathrm{UT}_{C_i}(a), L_j)$

denote a set of all such tags that get invalidated by some literal $L_j \in \text{Body}(C_i)$. This happens if after $L_j$ is included into partial clause, substitutions, that were encoded by a path through $j$ and $i$, are no longer computed. There are two possibilities for $L_j$

$L_j$ **is an open literal:** By definition of $\text{VBG}_{C_i}$ and $\text{UT}_{C_i}(a)$, it is obvious that no binding gets canceled in $\text{UT}_{C_i}(a)$. $\mathcal{I}\text{set}(\text{UT}_{C_i}(a), L_j)$ is therefore an empty set for every $a \in V_{C_i}$.

$L_j$ **is a closed literal:** Let $Y \in \min_{\mathcal{D}}(\text{Vars}(L_j))$ be a variable that all other variables in $\text{Vars}(L_j)$ are reachable from. Such a variable exists because $L_j$ is a dependable literal, so all the variables lie on the path in $\text{VDT}(C_i)$. For any $a \in V_{C_i}, a = \theta_{[X]}$, there are again two possibilities:

$[X] \neq [Y]$

$$\mathcal{I}\text{set}(\text{UT}_{C_i}(a), L_j) = \emptyset$$

$[X] = [Y]$

$$\mathcal{I}\text{set}(\text{UT}_{C_i}(a), L_j) = \{\langle k, l \rangle \; : \; \langle k, l \rangle \in \text{UT}_{C_i}(a) \wedge \theta = path(a, b_l) \wedge$$
$$\wedge \leftarrow L_j\theta \text{ is not refutable}\} \; ,$$

where $path(a, b_l)$ is a substitution obtained recursively by

$$path(a, a) = a$$
$$path(a, b_l) = path(a, b_k) \cdot b_l \; .$$

Note that since no variable is common to any of the substitutions on the path and all the substitutions are ground, the product in the second case does not represent substitution composition, but rather union of the substitutions.

*Example 5.* Suppose the literal $L_4 = not(neighbour(C, E))$ is added to the body of the partial clause $C_3$ from Example 4. By taking into account the indexing scheme from the Fig. 5 and by following the instructions above, it is easy to see that the tags that get invalidated by the literal $L_4$ are for instance $\langle 4, 6 \rangle$ and $\langle 4, 7 \rangle$.

We can now formulate the condition for $\langle b_j, b_k \rangle \in E_{C_i}$ to be valid.

**Definition 11.** For a dependable normal clause $C_i$, let $a$ be a node in $V_{C_i}$. A **binding validity tree** $\text{BVT}_{C_i}(a)$ is a set of the form:

$$\text{BVT}_{C_i}(a) = \text{UT}_{C_i}(a) \setminus [\bigcup_{L_j} \mathcal{I}\text{set}(\text{UT}_{C_i}(a), L_j)]$$

**Definition 12.** Let $a$ be a node in $V_{C_i}$ of the dependable normal clause $C_i$. Then, $\langle b_j, b_k \rangle \in E_{C_i}$ is valid with respect to $a$ in $\text{VBG}_{C_i}$ iff for all $r \in \mathcal{R}_{C_i}(a)$, if $b_j \in \mathcal{R}_{C_i}(r)$ then $\langle j, k \rangle \in \text{BVT}_{C_i}(r)$. $\langle b_j, b_k \rangle \in E_{C_i}$ is valid iff it is valid for any $a \in V_{C_i} \wedge b_j \in \mathcal{R}_{C_i}(a)$.

It is then easy to see:

**Proposition 13.** *Let $C$ be a dependable normal clause. Then, $\theta \in C^\theta$ iff there exists such $U \subseteq V_C$ and $\mathrm{Vars}(C) = \mathrm{Vars}(domain(\theta))$ that it holds $\prod_{u \in U} u = \theta$ and there exists $F \subseteq E_C$, such that graph $(U, F)$ is a valid connected subgraph of the variable binding graph $\mathrm{VBG}_C$.*

*Proof.* If $C$ contains only open literals then the proposition follows immediately from the definition of $\mathrm{VBG}_C$ and the fact that all edges are valid. For any closed literal $L_j$ in $C$, a valid graph $(U, F)$ exists iff $\leftarrow L_j \prod_{u \in U} u$ is refutable. □

**Lemma 14.** *Let $C_i$ be a dependable normal clause. Let $L_{i+1}$ be a literal that is going to be added to the body of $C_i$. Suppose that $L_{i+1}$ is a closed literal. Then it holds*

$$|\mathrm{VBG}_{C_{i+1}}| = |\mathrm{VBG}_{C_i}|$$
$$\forall a |\mathrm{BVT}_{C_{i+1}}(a)| \leq |\mathrm{BVT}_{C_i}(a)|$$

*where $|\mathrm{VBG}_C|$ is the sum of $|V_C|$ and $|E_C|$.*

*Proof.* By definition, $\mathrm{VBG}_C$ is independent of any closed literal $L_j$. Similarly, Definition 11 guarantees that a closed literal $L_j$ can only increase the union of invalidated tags and therefore decrease the size of $\mathrm{BVT}_C(a)$. □

Let the size of any $q^\theta$ be bounded by some constant $M$. This is necessary only for those predicates $q$ from $B$ that we are going to use in open literals.

**Lemma 15.** *Let $C$ be a $k$-dependable normal clause. Let there be some constant $M$, such that for all predicates $q$ from open literals of $C$, it holds $|q^\theta| \leq M$. Then, there exists an encoding $E$ of $a \in V_C$, such that its size satisfies the inequation*

$$|E(\mathrm{BVT}_C(a))| \leq \frac{M^{k+1} - 1}{M - 1} = \mathcal{O}(M^k) \ .$$

*Proof.* Let $E(\mathrm{BVT}_C(a))$ be the set of all validity tags from $\mathrm{BVT}_C(a)$, except those pairs of indices $\langle j, l \rangle$, where the length of the path from $a$ to $b_l$ in $\mathrm{VBG}_C$ exceeds $k$. We adopt the rule that $\langle j, l \rangle \in \mathrm{BVT}_C(a)$ iff there exists a path from $a$ to $b_l$ and the first $k$ are in of this path are in $E(\mathrm{BVT}_C(a))$. Given $\mathrm{VBG}_C$ and $E(\cdot)$, and by taking into account the above rule, we can exactly reproduce $\mathrm{BVT}_C(a)$. Note that this is only possible because $C$ is $k$-dependable. We are in fact exploiting the local influence of literals on the set of computed answers. The literal can only cancel the bindings for those variables that occur as its arguments. All the other bindings are influenced only indirectly, if they can no longer be reached, or are no longer refuted. □

**Lemma 16.** *Let $L_{i+1}$ be an open dependable literal introducing new variables in the dependable clause $C_i$. Let $q$ be the predicate in $L_{i+1}$ from background knowledge $B$, such that $|q^\theta| \leq M$ for some constant $M$. Then it holds*

$$|V_{C_{i+1}} \setminus V_{C_i}| \leq q^\theta \leq M$$
$$|E_{C_{i+1}} \setminus E_{C_i}| \leq |\{\theta_{[X]} : \theta_{[X]} \in V_{C_i} \wedge \mathrm{Vars}_{old}(L_{i+1}) \subset [X]\}| \leq M \ .$$

*Proof.* The first inequation is obvious. The projection of any set of correct substitutions on the variables $\mathrm{Vars}_{\mathrm{new}}(L_{i+1})$ can never exceed $q^\theta$. The second inequality is not as transparent, but again we can take into account the local influence of $L_{i+1}$. Values of $\theta_{[X]}$ from the previous cascade actually partition the values of new bindings into equivalence classes. Smart encoding of $E_{C_{i+1}}$ would take this property into account and therefore store only one edge per equivalence class. The number of such edges is obviously bounded by the number of nodes in the previous cascade, which is in turn bounded by $M$. □

And finally, we can state the following result.

**Theorem 17.** *Let $B$ be a normal program, a background knowledge with a property that every predicate $q$ from $B$ which is considered to be used in open literals of $k$-dependable language $\mathcal{L}_k$, has a finite set $q^\theta$. Then there exists a constant $N$, such that for every $k$-dependable normal clause $C$, it holds*

$$|\mathrm{VBG}_C| + \sum_{a \in V_C} |\mathrm{BVT}_C(a)| \leq N \cdot i .$$

*Proof.* Follows directly from Lemmas 16 and 15. □

## 4 Conclusions

The imminent complexity of learning within the first order logic forces us to use various heuristic techniques to alleviate the problem. This paper is concerned primarily with the encoding of proofs that are needed, when evaluating some partially induced theory. First, an interesting declarative bias (syntactic) on the hypothesis language is introduced. Despite its incompleteness for the normal program setting, it is still able to express, to our knowledge, all the hypotheses in the standard ILP domains. Even more, most of the hypotheses, known to be correct, are $k$-dependable for relatively small value of $k$ ($k \leq 3$). In the case when definite hypotheses are our concern, any program can be expressed if $k$ is raised appropriately.

The paper also shows how this bias is used to encode the computed answers of some clause $C$ in such a way, that the stored proof grows linearly with respect to the clause length. That way, the problem of deep search, many literals introducing new variables, becomes tractable. The space problem of proof encoding is nonexistent if we compute a proof of the learning examples each time from scratch. We argue that this might be too expensive when the computation of the proof is a costly operation. Our approach demands that the proof is computed only once.

We implemented this proof encoding scheme in our ILP system ILP-R [12] (limited to 2-dependable language). Empirically, it proved to be efficient for many artificial and real world domains by both, being able to express the target hypothesis, and to compute the proofs efficiently (time-wise).

Finally, this new approach to the proof encoding could lead to a substantially improved learning algorithms. The introduction of new variables and their bindings comes at no additional cost. This can encourage much more thorough search through structures found in the engineering and chemical domains, for example. These domains have usually finite, but quite often highly non-determinate background knowledge. The deep search through such a space still presents an unmanageable obstacle for the current learners using traditional proof handling.

## Acknowledgments

Most of all, I would like to thank my mentor Igor Kononenko for the encouragement he gave me, that made this work possible. He and my colleague Marko Robnik-Šikonja contributed many valuable suggestions that helped me improve this paper. I am also grateful to the Slovenian Ministry of Science and Technology for financially supporting my studies.

## References

1. W. W. Cohen. Learnability of restricted logic programs. In S. Muggleton, editor, *Proceedings of The Third International Workshop on Inductive Logic Programming ILP'93*, pages 41–71, Bled, Slovenia, Apr. 1993.
2. W. W. Cohen. Pac-learning a restricted class of recursive logic programs. In S. Muggleton, editor, *Proceedings of The Third International Workshop on Inductive Logic Programming ILP'93*, pages 73–86, Bled, Slovenia, Apr. 1993.
3. L. De Raedt and S. Džeroski. First order jk-clausal theories are pac-learnable. In S. Wrobel, editor, *Proceedings of the Fourth International Workshop on Inductive Logic Programming*, Bad Honnef/Bonn, Germany, Sept. 1994.
4. B. Dolšak and S. Muggleton. The application of inductive logic programming to finite elements mesh design. In S. Muggleton, editor, *Inductive Logic Programming*. Academic Press, 1992.
5. S. Džeroski. Handling noise in inductive logic programming. Master's thesis, University of Ljubljana, Faculty of electrical engineering and computer science, Ljubljana, Slovenia, 1991.
6. M. J. Kearns and U. V. Vazirani. *An Introduction to Computational Learning Theory*. MIT Press, Cambridge, Massachusetts, 1994.
7. J.-U. Kietz. Some lower bounds for the computational complexity of inductive logic programming. In *Proceedings of Sixth European Conference on Machine Learning*, pages 115–123, Berlin, Germany, 1993. Springer Verlag.
8. M. Kovačič. *Stochastic inductive logic programming*. PhD thesis, University of Ljubljana, Faculty of electrical engineering and computer science, Ljubljana, Slovenia, 1995.
9. J. W. Lloyd. *Foundations of Logic Programming*. Springer Verlag, Berlin, Germany, second edition, 1987.
10. S. Muggleton. *Inductive Logic Programming*. Academic Press, London, England, 1992.
11. U. Pompe. Restricting the hypothesis space, guiding the search, and handling of redundant information in inductive logic programming. Master's thesis, University of Ljubljana, Faculty of Computer and Information Science, Ljubljana, Slovenia, May 1996.

12. U. Pompe and I. Kononenko. Linear space induction in first order logic with relief. In R. Kruse, R. Viertl, and G. Della Riccia, editors, *CISM Lecture notes, (to appear)*. Springer Verlag, Udine, Italy, Sept. 1994. Presented at: International School for the Synthesis of Expert Knowledge.

13. U. Pompe, M. Kovačič, and I. Kononenko. Sfoil: Stochastic approach to inductive logic programming. In *Proceedings of the Second Electrotechnical and Computer Science Conference ERK'93*, pages 189–192, Portorož, Slovenia, Sept. 1993.

14. J. R. Quinlan. Learning logical definitions from relations. *Machine Learning*, 5:239–266, 1990.

# Learning Logic Programs with Random Classification Noise

Tamás Horváth[1]*, Robert H. Sloan[2]**, and György Turán[3]***

[1] Dept. of Applied Informatics, József A. University, Szeged 6720, Hungary
[2] Dept. of EE & Computer Science, University of Illinois at Chicago
851 S. Morgan St. Rm 1120, Chicago, IL 60607-7053, USA
[3] Dept. of Mathematics, Stat., & Computer Science, University of Illinois at Chicago,
Research Group on Artificial Intelligence, Hungarian Academy of Sciences

**Abstract.** We consider the learnability of classes of logic programs in the presence of noise, assuming that the label of each example is reversed with a fixed probability. We review the polynomial *PAC* learnability of nonrecursive, determinate, constant-depth Horn clauses in the presence of such noise. This result is extended to an analogous class of recursive logic programs that consist of a recursive clause, a base case clause, and ground background knowledge. Also, we show that arbitrary nonrecursive Horn clauses with forest background knowledge remain polynomially *PAC* learnable in the presence of noise. We point out that the sample size can be decreased by using dependencies among the literals.

## 1 Introduction

Learnability in the presence of noise is a major issue in machine learning. Its importance in inductive logic programming (ILP) is illustrated by the great emphasis given to noise handling mechanisms in Lavrač and Džeroski's book [16], and by numerous papers (e.g., [15, 17, 22]). Noise-tolerant heuristics often depend on probabilities estimated from the training set. Such heuristics usually work because a moderate amount of noise typically alters these estimates only slightly.

Computational learning theory has also long recognized that noise is of central importance for learnability. Several formal models have been developed based on different assumptions about the noise occurring in the data. In this paper, we consider the *random classification* noise model [1]: each labeled example has its label reversed with the same fixed probability. Kearns's *statistical query* method [12, 14] gives a general approach for the construction of *provably*

---

\* Partially supported by OTKA grant T-14228 and Phare TDQM grant 9305-02/1022 (ILP2/HUN). Email: `thorvath@sol.cc.u-szeged.hu`.
\*\* Partially supported by NSF grant CCR-9314258. Email: `sloan@eecs.uic.edu`.
\*\*\* Partially supported by NSF grant CCR-9208170, OTKA grant T-14228 and Phare TDQM grant 9305-02/1022 (ILP2/HUN). Email: `U11557@uicvm.uic.edu`.

noise-tolerant learning algorithms in the random classification model. The statistical query method is based on estimating probabilities and thus it may be viewed as a formalization of the heuristics referred to above.

Most Boolean concept classes that are known to be *PAC*-learnable can be shown to be *PAC*-learnable with random classification noise using the statistical query method. Also, several predicate-logic learning problems have been shown to be *PAC*-learnable in the noise-free model by using a reduction to a learning problem in propositional logic. Results of these two types can be combined to prove the *PAC*-learnability of predicate-logic learning problems in the presence of random classification noise. (Most positive results about the learnability of logic programs apply to nonrecursive Horn clauses with ground background knowledge. The usual approaches to these problems, such as least general generalizations, assume that the data are noiseless and thus cannot be used in the present context.)

Gennaro [8] obtained the first theoretical results on learnability in predicate logic in the presence of noise, using the basic argument outlined above. His results apply to nonrecursive Horn clauses of constant locality. Džeroski [6], besides proving related results, gave positive results in the framework of *nonmonotonic ILP*. Both discussed the learnability of restricted *multiple clause* nonrecursive logic programs with noise [6, 8], although mostly not in the *PAC* setting studied in this paper, where we assume that the hypothesis class and the concept class are the same, and permit arbitrary probability distributions on the examples.

In this paper we provide further positive results about the learnability of restricted classes of logic programs in the random classification noise model. We consider single *unrestricted* nonrecursive clauses with restricted background knowledge, and restricted recursive clauses.

In Sects. 3 and 4 we present the statistical query model and the standard algorithm for learning Boolean conjunctions with statistical queries. Section 5 discusses nonrecursive determinate constant-depth Horn clauses (defined by Muggleton and Feng [19]). This class was shown to be *PAC*-learnable by Džeroski, Muggleton, and Russell [7]. We review the algorithm to learn this class with random classification noise [6, 8], using the framework and the description of the noise-free learning algorithm given by Cohen [3]. The noisy learning algorithm proceeds by building a large set of literals that contains all possible literals that might occur in the body of the target clause, and then applying the noisy conjunction learning algorithm to find the body of the hypothesis clause.

In Sect. 6 we consider *nonrecursive Horn clauses with forest background knowledge*. This is a class of unrestricted clauses with a single binary background predicate that was proven to be *PAC*-learnable by Horváth and Turán [11]. Although these clauses are not necessarily determinate, one can still view the body of such a clause as a conjunction of literals (corresponding to *new* predicates) depending only on the variables occurring in the head. An example of such a predicate is "the height of element $x$ in the tree is at least 3". When this predicate is translated back to the original background predicate, new *nondeterminate* literals will occur that cannot be evaluated directly for a given example.

Thus the probability estimates in the learning algorithm will refer to the new predicates.

In several logic learning problems, the number of literals is quite large in terms of the learning parameters. Thus, for the sake of efficiency, it is desirable to find learning algorithms that use a smaller sample size than the one obtained by a direct reduction to learning Boolean conjunctions. The case of forest background knowledge shows that in some cases this is indeed possible. We make use of the fact that there are *dependencies* between the different literals. For example, "$x$ has height at least 3" implies "$x$ has height at least 2", and "$x$ and $y$ have distance 2" excludes "$x$ and $y$ have distance 3". These dependencies can be used to show that the probabilities needed may be estimated with a *larger tolerance* than in the general case. As the sample size depends *quadratically* on the inverse of the smallest tolerance, this results in a significant decrease in the sample size.

In Sect. 7 we consider the learnability of *recursive* logic programs in the presence of random classification noise. Cohen's results [3, 4] establish a sharp boundary for those classes of recursive logic programs that are *PAC*-learnable. In particular, he shows that a restricted class of logic programs consisting of a determinate recursive clause, a nonrecursive clause, and ground background knowledge is *PAC*-learnable. The details of these restrictions are given in Sects. 2.2 and 7.

We show that this class also remains *PAC*-learnable with random classification noise. We note that although the learnability of recursive logic programs in the presence of noise is a topic of interest in itself, from the practical point of view the nonrecursive case appears to be more important. The reason for this is that target concepts for application domains with noisy data appear to be nonrecursive (see e.g., Cohen [3]). The learning algorithm presented in Sect. 7 selects the literals to be included in the body of the recursive target clause using statistical queries, similarly to the nonrecursive case. In this case, however, the queries become considerably more complicated as they have to take into account the behavior of the literal on the recursive calls, similarly to Cohen's original algorithm.

Section 8 contains a review of additional noise models from computational learning theory, and some possible directions for further research. In Appendix A, we give some mathematical details for the statistical query method.

## 2 Preliminaries

Let $P$ be the *target* predicate of arity $m$, and $R_1, \ldots, R_r$ be the *background* predicates of arities $m_1, \ldots, m_r$. The *constants* are denoted by $a_1, \ldots, a_n$.

An *atomic formula* or *atom* is of the form $P(t_1, \ldots, t_m)$ or $R_i(t_1, \ldots, t_{m_i})$, where the $t$'s are *terms* (i.e., variables or constants). An atom is called a *P-atom* (or an *$R_i$-atom*) if its predicate symbol is $P$ (resp. $R_i$). An atom is *ground* if it contains no variables. Ground atoms are also referred to as *facts*.

The *background knowledge* $B$ used in the learning process is assumed to consist of ground atoms of the background predicates.

In this setting, a *concept* will be a set of ground atoms of the target predicate. A *concept class* is a set of concepts. *Positive* and *negative examples* are ground atoms of the target predicate $P$, labeled according to their classification by a $+$ or $-$.

## 2.1 Nonrecursive Logic Programs and Determinateness

A *definite, nonrecursive Horn clause* is of the form

$$A \longleftarrow B_1, \ldots, B_l ,$$

where $A$ is a $P$-atom and each $B_i$ is a background predicate atom.

Given a background knowledge $\mathcal{B}$, a definite, nonrecursive Horn clause $C$ represents the concept $C_\mathcal{B}$ consisting of all the ground atoms of the target predicate that are implied by the logic program $(C, \mathcal{B})$.

Now we turn to determinate clauses. In this case the atoms in the body are assumed to be *ordered*. Consider a clause $A \longleftarrow B_1, \ldots, B_l$. The *input variables* of an atom $B_i$ are those variables which occur in at least one of the atoms preceding $B_i$. Its other variables are called *output variables*.

An atom $B_i$ in the body is *determinate* if the following holds. Let $\sigma$ be a substitution that maps $A$ to some $P$-fact and maps the atoms $B_1, \ldots, B_{i-1}$ to facts in $\mathcal{B}$. Then there is *at most one* binding of the output variables in $B_i$ that maps $B_i$ to some fact in $\mathcal{B}$. A clause is determinate (with respect to the background knowledge $\mathcal{B}$) if all atoms in its body are determinate.

Determinate clauses are often assumed to have constant depth. The *depth* of a variable is defined as follows. Variables in the head have depth 0. Assume that we determined the depth of all variables in $B_1, \ldots, B_{i-1}$, and let $x$ be an output variable of $B_i$. Thus, $B_i$ is the first atom where $x$ occurs. Let $d$ be the maximum depth of the input variables of $B_i$. Then the depth of $x$ is $d + 1$.

It is a hard problem to decide if a clause is determinate with respect to a background knowledge. The problem in general can be shown to be co-NP-complete. Cohen introduced natural additional conditions that lead to a nice syntactic class of determinate clauses [3].

The *mode* of an atom is a partition of its variables into *input* and *output* variables. For example, if Father$(x, y)$ is a binary predicate corresponding to "the father of $x$ is $y$", then [Father, $+, -$] is a mode. A *mode constraint* $M$ is a set of modes. Each predicate must have a unique mode. A clause *satisfies* a mode constraint, if for each of its atoms, the division of its variables into input and output variables is consistent with a mode in the mode constraint. We assume that the predicate Equal with mode [Equal, $+, +$] is part of $\mathcal{B}$ and $M$. Our results remain valid *without* the assumptions about the unique mode and the Equal predicate [3].

Now, a mode for a given predicate $R$ is *determinate with respect to a background knowledge* $\mathcal{B}$ if the $R$-facts in $\mathcal{B}$ form a (partial) function mapping the input variables to the output variables. For example, the mode [Father, $+, -$] is determinate with respect to databases representing family relationships. A mode constraint is determinate with respect to $\mathcal{B}$ if all its modes are determinate with respect to $\mathcal{B}$. We note that for every fixed set of background predicates it can be checked efficiently whether a given mode constraint is determinate with respect to a given background knowledge.

Then, it is clear from the definitions that any clause satisfying a determinate mode constraint with respect to $\mathcal{B}$ is determinate with respect to $\mathcal{B}$.

Let $M$ be a determinate mode constraint with respect to the background knowledge $\mathcal{B}$. We denote by $\mathcal{C}_{\mathcal{B},d,M}$ the class of concepts with background knowledge $\mathcal{B}$ that are represented by Horn clauses of depth at most $d$ satisfying $M$.

The parameters measuring the size of a learning problem are $m$, the *arity of the target predicate*, and $n$, the *number of constants* in $\mathcal{B}$. We assume throughout that the arity of every background predicate is bounded by a constant.

## 2.2 Recursive Logic Programs

Now we describe a modification of the framework above that is suitable for determinate *recursive* clauses, due to Cohen [3].

The basic objects are assumed to come from an infinite set, such as $\{0,1\}^*$ or $\mathbb{N}^*$, replacing the constants $a_1, \ldots, a_n$. The *size* of a string or a sequence is its length and the size of a ground atom is the sum of the sizes of its arguments.

A *recursive* clause differs from a nonrecursive clause in that its body may contain $P$-atoms. These are called the *recursive literals* of the body. We will restrict ourselves to closed linear recursive clauses. A recursive clause is *linear* if its body contains exactly one recursive literal, and it is *closed* if its recursive literals have no output variables.

Examples are now labeled *extended instances* consisting of a labeled ground $P$-atom and a set of ground atoms of the background predicates, forming a *description* of the ground $P$-atom. For instance, a positive example of the target concept *append* is

**Labeled fact**: (append($l12, l3, l123$), +)
**Description**: {components($l12, 1, l2$), components($l2, 2, $nil),
components($l123, 1, l23$), components($l23, 2, l3$), components($l3, 3, $nil)}

The size of an extended instance is the sum of the sizes of its ground atoms.

One reason for this formalism is to allow us to discuss recursive structures, such as lists, without using function symbols. Also, this modification provides a framework for learning predicates of *constant arity* from an *exponential-size concept class* over an exponential-size or infinite domain. The arity of the target predicate and the arities of the background predicates are assumed to be fixed. (We know how to *PAC* learn recursive clauses only when the arity of the target predicate is constant.) The relevant parameters for the learning problem are the *bound on the size of the examples* and the *sizes of the background knowledge* and the *mode declaration*. Note that only part of the background knowledge is given explicitly in $\mathcal{B}$. Further facts from the background knowledge are given in the descriptions of the extended examples. Determinateness is required for each example with respect to $\mathcal{B}$ and its description.

## 2.3  *PAC* Learning and Random Classification Noise

Now we give a brief definition of *PAC*-learnability. Our description is informal; more details are given, for example, in Kearns and Vazirani [14].

It is assumed that there is a probability distribution on the set of all ground *P*-atoms. A learning algorithm first draws a sequence of random examples and then it outputs a *hypothesis* from the target class. The *error* of a hypothesis is the probability of the set of misclassified instances.

A family of learning problems is *polynomially PAC-learnable* if there is a learning algorithm with inputs $\epsilon$, $\delta$, and the background knowledge, and access to examples, such that the following hold. First, there is a polynomial in $1/\epsilon$, $1/\delta$, and the other relevant learning parameters that bounds the time of the learning algorithm. Second, for every learning problem that belongs to the family, for every $\epsilon, \delta > 0$, for every target concept and for every probability distribution on the domain, Pr(error of the hypothesis output by the algorithm $> \epsilon) \leq \delta$. (In the introduction, the term "polynomially," which refers to the running time, was omitted for simplicity.)

Formally, one speaks of the training data coming from an oracle EXAMPLES, which draws ground *P*-atoms from a fixed but unknown probability distribution, and returns the atoms together with the proper label. To study *random classification noise with rate* $\eta < 1/2$, we define a noisy oracle, EXAMPLES$^\eta$, which gets labeled examples from EXAMPLES, and for each example reverses the label independently with probability $\eta$. We say that a family of learning problems is *polynomially PAC-learnable with random classification noise* if the definition of polynomial *PAC*-learnability is met with the EXAMPLES oracle replaced by the noisy oracle EXAMPLES$^\eta$. Notice that formally the performance of the learning algorithm is measured against the correct labels; the noise occurs only in the training set. In fact, a hypothesis that more closely matches the true labels will also more closely match the labels given by the noisy oracle.

# 3  *PAC* Learning with Statistical Queries

In this section, we present a method for *PAC* learning a concept class from data with random classification noise. Kearns's *statistical query method* [12, 14] allows one to learn most, although not all, *PAC*-learnable concept classes with noisy data of this type.

Here we will present an overview of the method. In Appendix A we will prove some of the specific bounds on sample size. Our presentation generally follows Kearns and Vazirani's textbook [14], although we provide explicit, and slightly different, bounds on sample size instead of big-O bounds. Another proof of Theorem 1, below, is given by Aslam and Decatur [2].

Let us assume that we are trying to learn target concept $C$ on instance space $X$, with distribution $D$. A *statistical query learning algorithm* has access to the STAT oracle instead of the usual EXAMPLES oracle. The STAT oracle will tell us statistical properties of labeled examples, instead of giving us a sample of labeled examples.

More precisely, a query $(\chi, \tau)$ to the STAT oracle asks for an approximation to $\Pr_D(\chi(x, C(x)) = 1)$ with additive *tolerance* $\tau$. Here $\chi : X \times \{0, 1\} \to \{0, 1\}$ is a $\{0, 1\}$-function of labeled examples that can be computed in polynomial time. Thus, if $X = \{0, 1\}^n$ we can ask the oracle questions such as, "What fraction of examples have the second bit off and a label $+$?" We get back an answer that is guaranteed to be accurate to within $\tau$.

A family of learning problems is *polynomially learnable from statistical queries* if there is a learning algorithm $L$ running in time polynomial in $1/\epsilon$ and the learning parameters, such that all of $L$'s queries have tolerance bounded by the inverse of a polynomial of $1/\epsilon$ and the learning parameters, and $L$ outputs a hypothesis with error at most $\epsilon$. The main result is the following.

**Theorem 1 (Kearns).** *Any concept class that is polynomially learnable from statistical queries can be polynomially PAC learned with random classification noise.*

We give an outline of the proof. We show how to simulate the answer to a statistical query $(\chi, \tau)$ with noisy examples. The key idea is to partition the instance space $X$ into $X_1$ and $X_2$, where $X_1$ is the subset of $X$ for which $\chi(x, 0) \neq \chi(x, 1)$. That is, $X_1$ is the part of $X$ where the answers to query $\chi$ depend on the label of the example, and $X_2$ is the part where the answers do not depend on the label. Notice that for any example we can determine whether it is in $X_1$ or $X_2$, because we can evaluate $\chi$.

Let $p_1$ and $p_2$ be the total probability weight that $D$ assigns to $X_1$ and $X_2$, respectively, and let $D_1$ and $D_2$ be the probability measures induced on $X_1$ and $X_2$, respectively, by $D$. (Thus $D_1 = D/p_1$ and $D_2 = D/p_2$. We will see in (1) and (2) that we never use $D_2$ directly, and we do not use $D_1$ when $p_1$ is 0.)

We wish to estimate $\Pr_D(\chi(x, C(x)) = 1)$; we will abbreviate this quantity by $\Pr_D(\chi = 1)$. Now

$$\Pr_D(\chi = 1) = p_1 \Pr_{D_1}(\chi = 1) + \Pr_D(\chi = 1 \wedge x \in X_2) . \tag{1}$$

One can estimate $p_1$ directly from the noisy oracle. The same holds for $\Pr_D(\chi = 1 \wedge x \in X_2)$, since we can determine whether an instance is in $X_2$, and if it is, then the label of the example is irrelevant for computing $\chi$.

We also need to show how to estimate $\Pr_{D_1}(\chi = 1)$. Let us use $\Pr_{D,\eta}(E)$ to denote the probability of event $E$ with respect to examples drawn from the random classification noise oracle with noise rate $\eta$ and distribution $D$ on the instances. We show how to calculate $\Pr_{D_1}(\chi = 1)$ given $\eta$ and $\Pr_{D_1,\eta}(\chi = 1)$.

Now $\Pr_{D_1,\eta}(\chi = 1) = \eta + (1 - 2\eta) \Pr_{D_1}(\chi = 1)$. Thus we can rewrite (1) as

$$\Pr_D(\chi = 1) = p_1 \frac{\Pr_{D_1,\eta}(\chi = 1) - \eta}{1 - 2\eta} + \Pr_{D,\eta}(\chi = 1 \wedge x \in X_2) . \tag{2}$$

Notice that all the quantities except $\eta$ on the right-hand side of (2) can be estimated directly from the noisy oracle.

Consider a fixed algorithm SQA that learns from statistical queries. Given the noise rate $\eta$, we could simulate Algorithm SQA, by drawing a sufficiently large sample of say, $m_1$ examples, and for each query asked by Algorithm SQA, using that sample to estimate the quantities on the right-hand side of Equation 2. This algorithm, which we will call Algorithm GENERATEHYPOTHESIS($\eta$), would give the correct answer with high probability. There is some chance for error because it might be that one of the quantities that we estimated empirically was badly estimated. We note that this is the point where the confidence parameter $\delta$ enters the estimates, as $\delta$ is not a parameter of a statistical query algorithm.

Now, given an upper bound $\eta_b$ on the noise rate $\eta$, we could simply run Algorithm GENERATEHYPOTHESIS on inputs $0, \Delta, 2\Delta, 3\Delta, \ldots (\eta_b/\Delta)\Delta$, for some appropriate small value of $\Delta$. Each run would generate a hypothesis. We then draw another sample of $m_2$ examples, and measure the empirical error rate of each hypothesis on this sample. One can show that even with examples from the noisy oracle, the lower the actual error rate of a hypothesis, the lower the expected observed error rate. (Of course, with examples from the noisy oracle, the minimum error rate will be $\eta$, not 0.) Thus, we can use the hypothesis with the lowest error rate as our final output.

To make our algorithm complete, we need to specify the values of $m_1$, $m_2$, and $\Delta$. We assume that we have a statistical query algorithm that draws all its queries from a finite set $\mathcal{Q}$, and that the smallest tolerance that it ever uses in any query is $\alpha$. We also assume we are given an upper bound $\eta_b$ on the actual noise rate. (Kearns [12] shows how to remove this assumption.) Moreover, our final goal is to *PAC* learn with the usual parameters $\epsilon$ and $\delta$.

We use $\Delta \leq \alpha(1 - 2\eta_b)^2/16$ [14].[4] The other two values are

$$m_1 = \frac{32}{\alpha^2(1 - 2\eta_b)^2} \ln\left(\frac{12|\mathcal{Q}|}{\delta}\right) \tag{3}$$

$$m_2 = \frac{2}{\epsilon^2(1 - 2\eta_b)^2} \ln\left(\frac{16}{(1 - 2\eta_b)^2\alpha\delta}\right) . \tag{4}$$

The total number of samples required is $m_1 + m_2$. Justification for these values is given in Appendix A.

*Note:* The value $\alpha$ should be a lower bound for the smallest tolerance used by a statistical query algorithm that learns with an accuracy of $\epsilon/2$ (not $\epsilon$), for reasons we sketch in Appendix A.

## 4 Learning Conjunctions from Noisy Data

Angluin and Laird [1] gave the first algorithm for *PAC* learning conjunctions from data with random classification noise. Their algorithm can be modified using the statistical query method to get an improved bound on the sample size.

Let us assume that our target concept $C$ is a conjunction of some subset of a set of $n$ given variables. (That is, negation is not allowed. It is easy to generalize

---

[4] Kearns and Vazirani [14] show that $\Delta = c_0\alpha'(1 - 2\eta)^2/2$, where $\alpha'$ is a parameter smaller than $\alpha$ which we show in Appendix A can be safely set to $\alpha/8$. It is easy to fill in the missing details and see that setting the leading constant $c_0 = 1/2$ works.

to allow negation.) For a fixed target concept, a distribution $D$ on the instances, and a variable $v$, let us define $p_{01}(v)$ to be $\text{Pr}_D(\text{positive instances with } v \text{ false})$. We call variable $v$ *harmful* if $p_{01}(v) > K$, where for now we set $K = \epsilon/n$.

Notice that if $v$ is actually in the target concept, then $p_{01}(v) = 0$. Any conjunction that includes all variables with $p_{01} = 0$ and no harmful variables will differ from the target conjunction by at most $\epsilon$ [1]. Thus a statistical query learning algorithm for conjunctions is to ask for $p_{01}(v)$ for every variable $v$ with tolerance $K/2$, and include all those variables where the query is answered with a value of $K/2$ or less.

This gives a sample complexity of

$$\frac{1}{\epsilon^2(1 - 2\eta_b)^2} \left( 128n^2 \ln\left(\frac{12n}{\delta}\right) + \ln\left(\frac{2n}{(1 - 2\eta_b)^2 \epsilon \delta}\right) \right) \ .$$

Typically, when the conjunctions we are learning are the bodies of Horn clauses, we would prefer a smaller conjunction to a larger conjunction as the output of the learning algorithm. We can sometimes get such a reduction in the size of the learned conjunction by omitting those variables that are almost always 1.

Let us call a variable *insignificant* (or *irrelevant* in the terminology of Lavrač and Džeroski [16]) if the probability that it is false in any example is less than $\epsilon/2n$. If our learning algorithm omits all insignificant variables from its output, it increases its error rate by at most $\epsilon/2$. We can discard some insignificant variables by asking for the probability that each variable is off with tolerance $\epsilon/4n$, and discarding those where the answer is at most $\epsilon/4n$. We also need to adjust the value of $K$ to $\epsilon/2n$, so the error in our learner's hypothesis from including (nonharmful) variables not in the target concept is at most $\epsilon/2$.

This modification does not change the asymptotic sample complexity of the algorithm, but the constants do increase so the sample complexity becomes

$$\frac{1}{\epsilon^2(1 - 2\eta_b)^2} \left( 2048n^2 \ln\left(\frac{24n}{\delta}\right) + \ln\left(\frac{8n}{(1 - 2\eta_b)^2 \epsilon \delta}\right) \right) \ .$$

## 5 Nonrecursive Determinate Constant-Depth Clauses

We present a version of the algorithm to learn nonrecursive, determinate constant-depth Horn clauses with random classification noise [6, 8]. We use Cohen's approach [3] to the noise-free case as a starting point.

We assume that we are given a background knowledge $\mathcal{B}$, a depth bound $d$, and a mode constraint $M$ that is determinate with respect to $\mathcal{B}$. We are trying to learn a target concept from $\mathcal{C}_{\mathcal{B},d,M}$.

One can construct a clause $\text{BOTTOM}_d^*(P, m, M)$ in polynomial time such that the target clause must be semantically equivalent to one of its subclauses [3].

We could almost view the body of this clause as a large conjunction, and apply the algorithm of Sect. 4, with the atoms in the clause's body playing the role of the variables. The reason we write "almost" is because any given atom in the body might be true, false, or undefined for a particular binding of the variables in the head. Thus the notions of *harmful* and *insignificant* of Sect. 4 must be modified by replacing "false" by "false or undefined".

For an ordered clause $A \longleftarrow B_1, \ldots, B_l$, we say an atom $B_i$ (or $A$) *directly supports* atom $B_j$, if some output variable of $B_i$ is an input variable of $B_j$. Atom $B_i$ *supports* atom $B_j$ if there is a (possibly empty) sequence of atoms $C_1, \ldots, C_s$ such that $B_i$ directly supports $C_1$, each $C_k$ directly supports $C_{k+1}$, for $1 \leq k \leq s-1$, and $C_s$ directly supports $B_j$.

Now we could modify our statistical query conjunction learning algorithm from Sect. 4 to inquire about the atoms in order. Whenever an atom is to be deleted, also delete all atoms it supports. This will in fact work for the first algorithm we gave (the one that considers only harmfulness and not significance). We get an algorithm that *PAC* learns nonrecursive determinate constant-depth Horn clauses, with the drawback that it will always learn as large a body as possible.

However, we cannot simply apply the significance modification of the conjunction algorithm, and discard all insignificant atoms and all atoms supported by them. The difficulty is that an insignificant atom might support a significant atom.

Thus we are led to the following statistical query algorithm. Let $\text{BOTTOM}_d^*(P, m, M)$ be $P(\mathbf{x}) \leftarrow L_1, \ldots, L_k$. Define the probabilities

$p_i = \Pr(P(\mathbf{x})$ is positive and $L_i$ is false or undefined with binding
   induced by $\mathbf{x})$

$q_i = \Pr(L_i$ is false or undefined) .

**Algorithm DET.**

1. Compute $S := \text{BOTTOM}_d^*(P, m, M)$. Put $T = \epsilon/4k$.
2. For each literal $L_i$ in order, obtain an estimate $\hat{p}_i$ of $p_i$ with tolerance $T$.
   If $\hat{p}_i \leq T$ then retain $L_i$ in $S$. Otherwise, delete $L_i$ and all atoms supported by $L_i$ from $S$.[5]
3. For each remaining literal $L_j$ in $S$, obtain an estimate $\hat{q}_j$ of $q_j$ with tolerance $T$.
   If $q_j \leq T$, then label $L_j$ insignificant.
4. Delete from $S$ all insignificant literals that do not support any significant literals.

**Theorem 2.** *Algorithm DET is a polynomial statistical query algorithm for the concept class $\mathcal{C}_{\mathcal{B},d,M}$. Thus, the concept class $\mathcal{C}_{\mathcal{B},d,M}$ is polynomially PAC learnable with random classification noise with sample size*

$$O\left(\frac{1}{\epsilon^2(1 - 2\eta_b)^2}\left((2m|M|)^{2a^{d+1}} \ln\left(\frac{(2m|M|)^{a^{d+1}}}{\delta}\right) + \ln\left(\frac{(2m|M|)^{a^{d+1}}}{(1 - 2\eta_b)^2 \epsilon \delta}\right)\right)\right),$$

---

[5] Notice that some literals may be deleted before we can calculate $\hat{p}_i$ for them.

*where $|M|$ is the number of modes in $M$, and constant $a$ is the maximum arity of any predicate in $\mathcal{B}$.*

*Proof.* The theorem follows from the previous discussion and the following lemma. Let the target concept be $C$ and let $H$ be the concept represented by the output of Algorithm DET.

**Lemma 3.** $\Pr(C \triangle H) \leq \epsilon$.

*Proof of lemma.* Suppose $C(\mathbf{a})$ is 0 but $H(\mathbf{a})$ is 1. Then there is a literal $L_j$ in the body of the target clause that does not belong to the body of the hypothesis clause. It must be that $p_j = 0$, so $\hat{p}_j \leq T$. Similarly, $\hat{p}_\ell \leq T$ for all literals $L_\ell$ supporting $L_j$. Thus we could not have removed $L_j$ in Step 2. We must have removed $L_j$ because it was an insignificant literal that supports only insignificant literals. Thus $\hat{q}_j \leq \epsilon/4k$, and $q_j \leq \epsilon/2k$, so the error contributed by $L_j$ is at most $\epsilon/2k$. Hence the total error in $H$ from all such missing literals is at most $\epsilon/2$.

Now assume that $C(\mathbf{a})$ is 1 but $H(\mathbf{a})$ is 0. Clearly in this case there is a literal $L_h$ in $H$ that does not occur in $C$. We know that $\hat{p}_h \leq T$ and therefore $p_h \leq 2T = \epsilon/2k$. The total error contributed by $L_h$ is at most $\epsilon/2k$, and the total error contributed by all such literals is at most $\epsilon/2$.

Thus the total error of $H$ is at most $\epsilon$, as desired. $\qquad\square$

We can calculate that $\text{BOTTOM}_d^*(P, m, M)$ has at most $(2m|M|)^{a^{d+1}}$ literals in its body, and this gives us the sample complexity. $\qquad\square$

## 6    Forest Background Knowledge

In this section we assume that there is a single binary background predicate $R$. The facts $R(a_i, a_j)$ belonging to the background knowledge $\mathcal{B}$ may be viewed as a directed graph with edges $(a_i, a_j)$. Horváth and Turán [11] showed that if this graph is a forest with edges directed towards the roots, then a single non-recursive Horn clause is polynomially $PAC$-learnable. Their algorithm is based on computing least general generalizations, and thus it is not noise tolerant. In this section, we give a noise-tolerant learning algorithm for this problem.

First let us introduce some notations. If $a$ is a node then $f(a)$ denotes its parent and $f^{(i)}(a) = f(f^{(i-1)}(a))$ denotes its $i$th parent ($f^{(i)}(a)$ may be undefined). The *height* of $a$, denoted by $h(a)$, is the number of edges on the longest directed path ending at $a$. If $f^{(i)}(a)$ is undefined then we define $h(f^{(i)}(a))$ to be 0. A path is a $(d_1, d_2)$-*path* if it consists of $d_1$ forward edges followed by $d_2$ backward edges.

Let $\mathbf{x} = (x_1, \ldots, x_m)$ be an $m$-tuple of variables. We define the following predicates:

$$E_{u,v,d_1,d_2}(\mathbf{x}) \Leftrightarrow \text{ there is a } (d_1, d_2)\text{-path from } x_u \text{ to } x_v$$

for $1 \leq u < v \leq m$ and $0 \leq d_1, d_2 \leq n$,

$$F_{u,l,k}(\mathbf{x}) \Leftrightarrow h(f^{(l)}(x_u)) \geq k$$

for $1 \leq u \leq m$, $0 \leq l < n$, and $1 \leq k < n$, and

$$I_{u,j}(\mathbf{x}) \Leftrightarrow x_u = a_j$$

for $1 \leq u \leq m$ and $1 \leq j \leq n$.

We note that the predicates $E_{u,v,d_1,d_2}(\mathbf{x})$ and $F_{u,l,k}(\mathbf{x})$ introduce new, usually nondeterminate, variables when written out in terms of the background predicate.

Every concept defined by a nonrecursive Horn clause has a definition of the form $P(\mathbf{x}) \longleftarrow L_1(\mathbf{x}), \ldots, L_s(\mathbf{x})$, where each literal in the body is of the form $E_{u,v,d_1,d_2}(\mathbf{x})$, $F_{u,l,k}(\mathbf{x})$, or $I_{u,j}(\mathbf{x})$ [11]. Furthermore, for every $u$ and $v$ there is at most one literal of the form $E_{u,v,d_1,d_2}(\mathbf{x})$, for every $u$ and $l$ there is at most one literal of the form $F_{u,l,k}(\mathbf{x})$, and for every $u$ there is at most one literal of the form $I_{u,j}(\mathbf{x})$ in the body.

Thus learning a nonrecursive Horn clause can be viewed as learning a conjunction of the literals $E_{u,v,d_1,d_2}(\mathbf{x})$, $F_{u,l,k}(\mathbf{x})$ and $I_{u,j}(\mathbf{x})$. The number of all these literals together is of the order $m^2 n^2$. The statistical query learning algorithm described in Sect. 4 for learning a conjunction can be adapted to this case as well, similarly to the case of determinate clauses discussed in the previous section. The dependence of the sample size of this algorithm on $m$ and $n$ is of the form $m^4 n^4$. (In this paragraph, we ignore log factors.) In order to improve this rather large sample size, one may observe that the target conjunction contains at most $m^2 + mn$ of the $m^2 n^2$ literals. Kearns [12] showed that the sample size can be improved if the conjunctions are known to contain few literals. The bound of [12] applied to our case is of the order $(m^2 + mn)^3$. We now give another statistical query learning algorithm for this particular case. The sample size provided by this algorithm is of the order $m^4 n^2$. This is never worse than the bound for Kearns's algorithm referred to above and it is better, for example, when $n$ (the number of constants in the database) is much larger than $m$ (the arity of the target predicate), which is usually expected to be the case.

**Theorem 4.** *Assume that there is a single binary background predicate and the ground atoms in the background knowledge form a forest. Then a nonrecursive Horn clause is polynomially PAC learnable with random classification noise with sample size*

$$O\left( \frac{m^4 n^2}{\epsilon^2 (1 - 2\eta_b)^2} \ln\left( \frac{m^2 n^2}{\delta} \right) + \frac{1}{\epsilon^2 (1 - 2\eta_b)^2} \ln\left( \frac{m^2 n}{\delta \epsilon (1 - 2\eta_b)^2} \right) \right) .$$

*Proof.* Let us define the following probabilities:

$$p = \Pr(\mathbf{x} \text{ is a positive example}) ,$$

$$p_{u,v,d_1,d_2} = \Pr(\mathbf{x} \text{ is a positive example and } E_{u,v,d_1,d_2}(\mathbf{x})) ,$$

$$p_{u,l,k} = \Pr(\mathbf{x} \text{ is a positive example and } \overline{F_{u,l,k}(\mathbf{x})}) , \text{ and}$$

$$p_{u,j} = \Pr(\mathbf{x} \text{ is a positive example and } I_{u,j}(\mathbf{x})) .$$

In each case the probability is with respect to $\mathbf{x}$. The ranges for the subscripts are the same as those for the corresponding predicates. Let $M = \binom{m}{2}n$ if $m > 1$ and $M = 1$ if $m = 1$. Then the algorithm works as follows.

**Algorithm** FOREST.

1. Obtain an estimate $\hat{p}$ of $p$ with tolerance $\epsilon/12M$. If $\hat{p} \leq \frac{5}{6}\frac{\epsilon}{M}$, stop and output the hypothesis that $P$ is always false.
   Otherwise, initialize the hypothesis clause $S := P(\mathbf{x}) \leftarrow$.
2. For $1 \leq u \leq m$, $0 \leq l < n$ and $1 \leq k < n$, obtain an estimate $\hat{p}_{u,l,k}$ of $p_{u,l,k}$ with tolerance $\epsilon/6mn$.
   Include $F_{u,l,k}(\mathbf{x})$ in the body of $S$ for the largest $k$ (if any) such that $\hat{p}_{u,l,k} \leq \epsilon/6mn$.
3. If $m > 1$, for $1 \leq u < v \leq m$, $0 \leq d_1, d_2 < n$ obtain an estimate $\hat{p}_{u,v,d_1,d_2}$ of $p_{u,v,d_1,d_2}$ with tolerance $\epsilon/12M$.
   Include in the body of $S$ all $E_{u,v,d_1,d_2}(\mathbf{x})$ such that $|\hat{p}_{u,v,d_1,d_2} - \hat{p}| \leq \epsilon/6M$ (if any).
4. For $1 \leq u \leq m$, $1 \leq j \leq n$, obtain an estimate $\hat{p}_{u,j}$ of $p_{u,j}$ with tolerance $\epsilon/12M$.
   If there is a $j$ such that $|\hat{p}_{u,j} - \hat{p}| \leq \epsilon/6M$, then include in the body of $S$ the $I_{u,j}(\mathbf{x})$ such that $|\hat{p}_{u,j} - \hat{p}|$ is as small as possible.

We note that the literals included in $S$ have to be expanded into literals of the background predicate in order to get a clause of the required form. For example, $F_{u,1,2}(\mathbf{x})$ is transformed into $R(x_u, y_1), R(y_2, y_1), R(y_3, y_2)$, corresponding to $h(f^{(1)}(x_u)) \geq 2$. Similarly, $E_{u,v,2,1}(\mathbf{x})$ is transformed into $R(x_u, z_1), R(z_1, z_2), R(x_v, z_2)$, describing a $(2,1)$-path form $x_u$ to $x_v$. All the new variables introduced should be different.

Let $C$ be the target concept, and let $H$ be the concept represented by the output of Algorithm FOREST. The correctness of the algorithm follows from the following lemma.

**Lemma 5.** $H \subseteq C$ and $\Pr(C \setminus H) \leq \epsilon$.

*Proof of lemma.* First, if $\hat{p} \leq \frac{5}{6}\frac{\epsilon}{M}$ in Step 1 of the algorithm, then $p \leq \left(\frac{5}{6} + \frac{1}{12}\right)\frac{\epsilon}{M} \leq \epsilon$. Thus the statement of the lemma holds in this case. In the remainder of the argument, we assume $\hat{p} > \frac{5}{6}\frac{\epsilon}{M}$.

Now we show that $\Pr(C \setminus H) \leq \epsilon$.

If a literal of the form $F_{u,l,k}(\mathbf{x})$ is included in $S$, then the conditions of Step 2 imply that the probability weight of positive examples not satisfying $F_{u,l,k}(\mathbf{x})$ is $p_{u,l,k} \leq \hat{p}_{u,l,k} + \frac{\epsilon}{6mn} \leq \frac{\epsilon}{3mn}$. Summing up for all possible values of $u$ and $l$, it follows that the probability weight of the positive examples lost by the inclusion of these literals is at most $\epsilon/3$.

Now let us assume that a literal of the for $E_{u,v,d_1,d_2}(\mathbf{x})$ is included in $S$. Then by definition, $|\hat{p}_{u,v,d_1,d_2} - \hat{p}| \leq \epsilon/6M$. As the tolerance is $\epsilon/12M$, this implies that $|p_{u,v,d_1,d_2} - p| \leq \epsilon/3M$. As we assume that $\hat{p} \geq \frac{5}{6}\frac{\epsilon}{M}$, it follows that $p \geq \frac{3}{4}\frac{\epsilon}{M}$, and so $\epsilon/3M < p/2$. Thus it holds that $p_{u,v,d_1,d_2} > p/2$. We now argue that we cannot include both $E_{u,v,d_1,d_2}(\mathbf{x})$ and $E_{u,v,d_3,d_4}(\mathbf{x})$ for $d_3 - d_4 \neq d_1 - d_2$. If both those literals were included, then $p_{u,v,d_1,d_2} > 1/2$ and $p_{u,v,d_3,d_4} > 1/2$. This would imply that there is a positive example $\mathbf{x}$ with both $E_{u,v,d_1,d_2}(\mathbf{x})$ and $E_{u,v,d_3,d_4}(\mathbf{x})$ true, but from the properties of trees, that is impossible.

Thus only literals $E_{u,v,d_5,d_6}(\mathbf{x})$ with $d_5 - d_6 = d_1 - d_2$ can be included in the hypothesis. There are at most $n$ such literals. For these literals it holds that $|\hat{p}_{u,v,d_5,d_6} - \hat{p}| \leq \epsilon/6M$, and so $|p_{u,v,d_5,d_6} - p| \leq \epsilon/3M$. Hence, summing over all possible values of $u$ and $v$, we get that the probability weight of positive examples lost by the inclusion of literals of the form $E_{u,v,d_1,d_2}(\mathbf{x})$ is at most $\epsilon/3$.

Similarly to the first case, if a literal of the form $I_{u,j}(\mathbf{x})$ is included in $S$, then $|\hat{p}_{u,j} - \hat{p}| \leq \epsilon/6M$, and so $|p_{u,j} - p| \leq \epsilon/3M$. Thus again, the probability weight of positive examples lost by the inclusion of literals of the form $I_{u,j}(\mathbf{x})$ is at most $\epsilon/3$. Considering the three cases together, it follows that $\Pr(C \setminus H) \leq \epsilon$.

It remains to be shown that $H \subseteq C$.

If there is a literal of the form $F_{u,l,k'}(\mathbf{x})$ in the body of the target clause, then $p_{u,l,k'} = 0$. Hence $\hat{p}_{u,l,k'} \leq \epsilon/6mn$. Therefore $k'$ was a candidate in Step 2 and so there must be a literal $F_{u,l,k}(\mathbf{x})$ in $S$ such that $k' \leq k$. But $F_{u,l,k}(\mathbf{x})$ implies $F_{u,l,k'}(\mathbf{x})$, so no new positive examples are included in $H$ by replacing $F_{u,l,k'}(\mathbf{x})$ by $F_{u,l,k}(\mathbf{x})$.

In the other two cases, every literal that occurs in the body of the target clause will also occur in $S$. If a literal of the form $E_{u,v,d_1,d_2}(\mathbf{x})$ is contained in the body of the target clause, then $p_{u,v,d_1,d_2} = p$ and so $|\hat{p}_{u,v,d_1,d_2} - \hat{p}| \leq \epsilon/6M$. Thus $E_{u,v,d_1,d_2}(\mathbf{x})$ is included in $S$.

If a literal of the form $I_{u,j}(\mathbf{x})$ is contained in the body of the target clause, then $p_{u,j} = p$, and so $|\hat{p}_{u,j} - \hat{p}| \leq \epsilon/6M$. On the other hand, $p_{u,k} = 0$ for all $k \neq j$, and $\hat{p}_{u,k} \leq \epsilon/12M$. With $\hat{p} \geq \frac{5}{6}\frac{\epsilon}{M}$, this implies $|\hat{p}_{u,k} - \hat{p}| \geq \frac{2}{3}\frac{\epsilon}{M}$. Thus indeed $I_{u,j}(\mathbf{x})$ is included in $S$. $\qquad\square$

The bound for the sample complexity follows by noting that the algorithm asks $O(m^2 n^2)$ queries and the finest tolerance is $\Omega(\epsilon/m^2 n)$. $\qquad\square$

As noted above, Algorithm FOREST is more efficient in terms of sample size than a direct reduction to learning Boolean conjunctions because we were able to use larger tolerances. When looking at statistical query algorithms, one may also try to increase their efficiency by *decreasing the number of statistical queries asked*.

In our case it appears to be possible to decrease the number of queries by performing binary searches on the probabilities in order to determine which one should be included in the hypothesis conjunction. Indeed, one can give an algorithm that uses $O((mn + m^2)\log n)$ statistical queries with tolerances of the same order of magnitude as Algorithm FOREST.

However, it is an interesting feature of statistical query learning algorithms that this improvement in query complexity does *not* lead to an improvement in sample size for the following reason (also observed by Aslam and Decatur [2]).

The queries of Algorithm FOREST are *non-adaptive* in the sense that they can all be asked at the same time, without depending on the results of the other queries. Thus in this case one can use Hoeffding's Inequality (described in Appendix A) to *evaluate each query simultaneously* from a *single* sample that has size depending only *logarithmically* on the number of queries. On the other hand, the queries of the binary search algorithm are *adaptive*—that is, the outcome of a query will determine which query is asked next. So the queries are *dependent* and we need a different sample for the evaluation of each query. Thus in this case the sample size will depend *linearly* on the number of queries asked by the algorithm.

## 7 The Recursive Case

In this section, we show how to learn a linear closed recursive Horn clause that is determinate and constant depth together with a simple base case and ground background knowledge. Our concepts will be of the form

$$P(\mathbf{x}) \leftarrow B_1, \ldots, B_\ell, P(\mathbf{y})$$
$$P(\mathbf{x}) \leftarrow D_1, \ldots, D_s \ , \tag{5}$$

where $s$ is constant and the $D_i$ are atoms of the background predicates (which, recall, include Equal) instantiated with variables from the head and/or constants from a specified polynomial-size set of constants. (For learning problems involving $\mathbb{N}$, that set of constants might be $\{0, 1\}$; for learning problems involving lists that set might contain only the empty list.) For example, the base case for append would be $\text{append}(x, y, z) \leftarrow \text{Equal}(y, \text{nil}), \text{Equal}(x, z)$.

We call base cases meeting these assumptions *simple base cases*. Simple base cases are actually a special case of Cohen's "base case oracle" [3] that we believe can handle many practical logic programs. (Our assumptions can be slightly weakened; for instance, we could allow a constant number of such clauses.)

In this section, for $\text{BOTTOM}_d^*(P, m, M)$ we will just write BOTTOM, and we denote the literals of BOTTOM by $L_1, \ldots, L_k$. (Notice that $k$ is polynomial in all the relevant parameters.) We will write BOTTOM($\mathbf{z}$) for the BOTTOM clause built starting with the variables $\mathbf{z}$ as the arguments to the target predicate. We write $\mathbf{z}'$ for the full set of variables in BOTTOM($\mathbf{z}$), and with some abuse of notation we can write $\mathbf{z} \subset \mathbf{z}'$. Notice that by determinateness the values of $\mathbf{z}$ determine the values of $\mathbf{z}'$. (Of course, some of the values of $\mathbf{z}'$ may be undefined.)

In the concept definition (5), each $B_i = L_{j_i}$, for some $1 \leq j_i \leq k$. We use $\mathcal{L}$ to denote the conjunction of all the nonrecursive literals in the recursive clause, and BASE to denote the body of the nonrecursive clause. Finally, we use $\mathbf{x}^*$ to denote the arguments to the first recursive call of $P$ starting from $P(\mathbf{x})$, for some $\mathbf{x}^* \subset \mathbf{x}'$. Thus we can rewrite (5) as a logic program of the form

$$P(\mathbf{x}) \leftarrow \mathcal{L}(\mathbf{x}'), P(\mathbf{x}^*)$$
$$P(\mathbf{x}) \leftarrow \text{BASE}(\mathbf{x}) \ . \tag{6}$$

We define $\mathbf{x}^{(0)} = \mathbf{x}$ and $\mathbf{x}^{(i)} = (\mathbf{x}^{(i-1)})^*$.

Now we are ready to discuss learning recursive programs in the presence of noise. Let the target logic program, of the form of (6), be $\Pi$.

Observe that if $P(\mathbf{a})$ and $\overline{\text{BASE}(\mathbf{a})}$ hold, then $\mathcal{L}(\mathbf{a}')$ must be true. More generally, $P(\mathbf{a}), \overline{\text{BASE}(\mathbf{a}^{(0)})}, \ldots, \overline{\text{BASE}(\mathbf{a}^{(i)})}$ together imply $\mathcal{L}((\mathbf{a}^{(0)})'), \ldots, \mathcal{L}((\mathbf{a}^{(i)})')$. Since $P(\mathbf{a})$ is a positive example, $\Pi$ must derive $P(\mathbf{a})$. Now $\overline{\text{BASE}(\mathbf{a}^{(0)})}, \ldots,$

$\overline{\text{BASE}(\mathbf{a}^{(i)})}$ implies that $\Pi$ cannot derive $P(\mathbf{a})$ with $i$ or fewer recursive calls. Hence the recursive clause of $\Pi$ must succeed on the first $i$ calls, and so $\mathcal{L}((\mathbf{a}^{(0)})')$, ..., $\mathcal{L}((\mathbf{a}^{(i)})')$ must succeed.

Let us use $\mathbf{z}'(j)$ to denote the subset of the variables $\mathbf{z}'$ that are arguments to literal $L_j$ of the recursive clause of $\Pi$. Now if $P(\mathbf{a})$ is positive and $L_j$ occurs in $\Pi$'s body, then for all $i$, the argument above shows that

$$\left(\overline{\text{BASE}(\mathbf{a}^{(0)})} \wedge \cdots \wedge \overline{\text{BASE}(\mathbf{a}^{(i)})}\right) \Rightarrow \left(L_j((\mathbf{a}^{(0)})'(j)) \wedge \cdots \wedge L_j((\mathbf{a}^{(i)})'(j))\right) .$$
$$(7)$$

An equivalent formulation of (7) would keep only the last $L_j$. Switching to probability notation this gives

$$\Pr\left(P(\mathbf{x}) \wedge \bigvee_{i=0}^{\infty} \left(\bigwedge_{\ell=0}^{i} \overline{\text{BASE}(\mathbf{x}^{(\ell)})} \wedge \overline{L_j((\mathbf{x}^{(i)})'(j))}\right)\right) = 0 .$$

Here, as in Sect. 5, falseness is taken to mean false or undefined.

Now for any literal $L_j \in \text{BOTTOM}$, put

$$p_j = \Pr\left(P(\mathbf{x}) \wedge \bigvee_{i=0}^{\infty} \left(\bigwedge_{\ell=0}^{i} \overline{\text{BASE}(\mathbf{x}^{(\ell)})} \wedge \overline{L_j((\mathbf{x}^{(i)})'(j))}\right)\right) .$$
$$(8)$$

We say that literal $L_j$ is *harmful* if $p_j > \epsilon/2k$.

**Lemma 6.** *Let $C$ be a concept represented by a closed linear recursive logic program $\Pi$ of the form given by (6) that is determinate and constant depth. Let the hypothesis $H$ have a logic program $\Pi'$ of the form*

$$P(\mathbf{x}) \leftarrow \mathcal{A}(\mathbf{x}), P(\mathbf{x}^*)$$
$$P(\mathbf{x}) \leftarrow \text{BASE}(\mathbf{x}) ,$$

*where $P(\mathbf{x}^*)$ and $\text{BASE}(\mathbf{x})$ are correct, and $\mathcal{A}$ contains all the literals in $\mathcal{L}$ and no harmful literals. Then $\Pr(C \triangle H) \leq \epsilon/2$.*

*Proof.* Since $\mathcal{A}$ contains all the literals in $\mathcal{L}$, $H \subseteq C$. So we need to show only that $\Pr(C \setminus H) \leq \epsilon/2$. Without loss of generality, say that the literals in $\mathcal{A}$ but not in $\mathcal{L}$ are $L_1, \ldots, L_r$.

$$\Pr(\mathbf{x} \in C \setminus H) = \Pr\left(\bigvee_{i=0}^{\infty} (\Pi \text{ derives } \mathbf{x} \text{ in } i \text{ steps but } \Pi' \text{ doesn't derive } \mathbf{x})\right) .$$
$$(9)$$

Notice that $\Pi$ and $\Pi'$ make the same recursive calls, so BASE holds for both programs at exactly the same time. Thus the only way $\mathbf{x}$ can be in $C \setminus H$ is for $\Pi'$ to have an extra literal that disqualifies $\mathbf{x}$ at some level of the recursion before $\Pi$ accepts $\mathbf{x}$. The quantity in (9) is equal to

$$\Pr\left(\mathbf{x} \in C \wedge \bigvee_{i=0}^{\infty} \left(\bigwedge_{\ell=0}^{i} \overline{\text{BASE}(\mathbf{x}^{(\ell)})} \wedge \overline{L_j((\mathbf{x}^{(i)})'(j))}\right) \text{ for some } j \leq r\right) .$$
$$(10)$$

Now the quantity in (10) is at most $(\epsilon/2k)r \leq \epsilon/2$, completing the proof. $\square$

Lemma 6 proves the correctness of the heart of the following algorithm, which we only sketch. The formal details are broadly similar to the nonrecursive case. Recall that BOTTOM is $P(\mathbf{x}) \leftarrow L_1, \ldots L_k$. Besides the usual inputs, the following algorithm must also be given a set of constants to use in constructing possible base cases.

**Algorithm REC.**

1. Compute $S := \text{BOTTOM}$. Put $T = \epsilon/4k$.
2. Compute the sets $U_B$ of all possible base cases and $U_r$ of all possible instantiations of the recursive literal with variables from BOTTOM.
3. Using one sample of examples, run the following algorithm on that sample for all possible choices of a base case from $U_B$ and a recursive literal from $U_r$. (Each run will output its own hypothesis.)
   - For each nonrecursive literal $L_j$ of the recursive clause, determine an estimate $\hat{p}_j$ of $p_j$ as in (8), with accuracy $T$ .
     If $\hat{p}_j > T$, delete it and all literals that it supports. (This is very similar to the algorithm of the nonrecursive case in Sect. 5.)
4. Draw a new sample of examples. Test each hypothesis from the previous stage on this sample. Output the hypothesis with the lowest error rate.

**Theorem 7.** *Algorithm REC is a polynomial statistical query algorithm for the class of of determinate, constant-depth closed linear recursive logic programs with simple base cases and ground background knowledge. Hence those logic programs are polynomially PAC learnable with random classification noise.*

*Remark.* Recall that for recursive logic programs, the definition of *polynomial PAC* learnability, given in Sect. 2.2, is different from the one used elsewhere in this paper.

*Proof idea.* To apply Lemma 6, we must show that for the right choice of the recursive literal and the base case, our algorithm included all literals in the body of $\Pi$'s recursive clause, and no harmful literals. This is true because if $L_j$ occurs in the body of $\Pi$'s recursive clause, then $p_j = 0$, and our estimate $\hat{p}_j$ must be less than or equal to $\epsilon/4k$. The same applies to literals that support $L_j$. Conversely, for any harmful literal $L_h$, we know $p_h > \epsilon/2k$, and therefore $\hat{p}_h > \epsilon/4k$.

We also must show that the statistical query can be evaluated in polynomial time. A simple counting argument shows that there is a polynomial bound on the depth of recursion of $\Pi$ such that if $\Pi$ goes beyond this bound, then it will never succeed [3]. Thus the limit $\infty$ in (8) can be replaced by a polynomial bound.

In Step 4, we will need the correct Step 3 hypothesis to have error $\epsilon/2$. The reason for this is explained in Appendix A.2.

Beyond the use of Lemma 6, the key points are that the sets $U_B$ and $U_r$ are of polynomial size. Recall that BOTTOM has only polynomially many literals.

The number of choices for the recursive literal ($|U_r|$) is the number of ways of choosing $m$ variables from all the variables mentioned in BOTTOM. The arity of the background predicates is a constant, so the total number of variables in BOTTOM, which is at worst the number of literals times the number of variable per literal, is polynomial. We have assumed that $m$ is constant.

The base case contains only up to some constant $s$ literals, and every literal is chosen from the background knowledge and instantiated with either some of the $m$ variables in the head and/or constants from a polynomial-size set. Thus $U_B$ is clearly polynomial in size. □

# 8 Remarks

## 8.1 Learning Theory Results on Noise

As noted in the introduction, we have studied random classification noise in some detail because for that noise model, there is a nontrivial procedure for coping with the noise.

We now present a brief overview of other models of noise in the learning theory literature. Some models that make the most sense from the point of view of ILP include *malicious* noise [23], *malicious classification* noise [21], and *random attribute* noise [20, 21].

With malicious noise, an omnipotent, omniscient adversary (i.e., the adversary has unlimited computing time, and knowledge of the learner's algorithm) gets to alter a small fraction of the training examples in any way he chooses. Kearns and Li [13] show that the fraction of the examples the adversary alters (i.e., the noise rate) must be less than $\epsilon/(1 + \epsilon)$ (where $\epsilon$ as usual is the desired accuracy) for *PAC* learning to be possible. They also provide a meta-algorithm that converts any ordinary *PAC* learning algorithm into one that tolerates a small amount of malicious noise. For conjunctions, that meta-algorithm can tolerate a noise rate up to $O(\epsilon/n)$, where $n$ is the number of variables. For recent work on the $\Theta(1/n)$ gap between that rate and the lower bound, see [5, 18]. Džeroski discusses the application of the model to ILP [6].

In the case of malicious classification noise, the omnipotent, omniscient adversary can alter the label of some fraction of the training data, but not the instances. The difference between this model and random classification noise is that the adversary may choose not to alter the labels of some examples. For example, malicious classification noise can model the case where "boundary" instances are frequently misclassified but "core" instances are never misclassified. The statistical query method relies heavily on the independence of instances and label noise, and, as far as we know, does not work at all for random misclassification noise. (If computational efficiency is not an issue, then it suffices to choose the hypothesis that has minimal disagreement with the training data [21], but this is almost always NP-hard.)

With random attribute noise, the label is always accurate, but the value of each Boolean variable in each training instance is flipped with some probability. If this noise is *uniform*, then each variable is altered with the same probability; with *product* random attribute noise, there is a distinct probability $p_i$ of each variable $i$ being flipped. For some simple classes including conjunctions, large amounts of uniform random attribute noise can be tolerated [9, 20]. For the more realistic case of product random attribute noise, the noise rate (i.e., maximum probability that any bit is flipped) must be less than $\epsilon$ for $PAC$ learning to be possible [9]. Thus, somewhat surprisingly, the $PAC$ algorithms situation for product random attribute noise is essentially the same as for malicious noise.

## 8.2 Further Research

The bounds of Sect. 6 can perhaps be improved by considering Step 3 of Algorithm FOREST more carefully. One could also consider the query complexity of the algorithm mentioned at the end of Sect. 6 in more detail.

It is an open problem whether a monotone Boolean conjunction of $n$ variables is polynomially $PAC$-learnable with random classification noise using sample size *less than quadratic* in $n$. If computation time is not taken into account, then it is sufficient to take a sample of size linear in $n$ and output a hypothesis that makes the least number of errors in the training set [1].

Another topic for further work is noise models between the random and the malicious classification models. For example, Kearns [14] considers the case where the noise rate may be different for each round of drawing a random example, but it is still assumed that in each round the error probability is the same for each instance. He showed that statistical query algorithms generalize to this model. It would be interesting to study models where the error probabilities of different instances may differ, as appears to be the case in practice.

Another issue is to study types of noise that are specific to learning in predicate logic, such as noise in the background knowledge. Gennaro [8] presents an initial proposal in this direction.

# Acknowledgments

We thank an anonymous referee for calling our attention to references [6] and [8]. We thank Jorge Lobo for useful discussions.

# References

1. D. Angluin and P. Laird. Learning from noisy examples. *Machine Learning*, 2(4):343–370, 1988.
2. J. A. Aslam and S. E. Decatur. Improved noise-tolerant learning and generalized statistical queries. Technical Report TR-17-94, Center for Research in Computing Technology, Division of Applied Sciences, Harvard University, 1994.
3. W. W. Cohen. Pac-learning recursive logic programs: efficient algorithms. *J. AI Research*, 2:501–539, 1995.
4. W. W. Cohen. Pac-learning recursive logic programs: negative results. *J. AI Research*, 2:541–573, 1995.

5. S. E. Decatur. Statistical queries and faulty PAC oracles. In *Proc. 6th Annu. Workshop on Comput. Learning Theory*, pages 262–268. ACM Press, New York, NY, 1993.

6. S. Džeroski. Learning first-order clausal theories in the presence of noise. In *Proc. 5th Scandinavian Conf. on Artificial Intelligence*, Amsterdam, 1995. IOS Press.

7. S. Džeroski, S. Muggleton, and S. Russell. PAC-learnability of determinate logic programs. In *Proc. 5th Annu. Workshop on Comput. Learning Theory*, pages 128–135. ACM Press, New York, NY, 1992.

8. R. Gennaro. PAC-learning PROLOG clauses with or without errors. Tech. Memo 500, MIT Laboratory for Computer Science, 1994.

9. S. A. Goldman and R. H. Sloan. Can PAC learning algorithms tolerate random attribute noise? *Algorithmica*, 14:70–84, 1995.

10. W. Hoeffding. Probability inequalities for sums of bounded random variables. *Journal of the American Statistical Association*, 58(301):13–30, Mar. 1963.

11. T. Horváth and G. Turán. Learning logic programs with structured background knowledge. In L. De Raedt, editor, *5th Int. Workshop on Inductive Logic Programming*, pages 53–76, 1995. Also in *Advances in Inductive Logic Programming* (ed. L. De Raedt). IOS Press, 1996, pages 172–191. (IOS Frontiers in AI and Appl.).

12. M. Kearns. Efficient noise-tolerant learning from statistical queries. In *Proc. 25th Annu. ACM Sympos. Theory Comput.*, pages 392–401. ACM Press, New York, NY, 1993.

13. M. Kearns and M. Li. Learning in the presence of malicious errors. *SIAM J. Comput.*, 22:807–837, 1993.

14. M. J. Kearns and U. V. Vazirani. *An Introduction to Computational Learning Theory*. The MIT Press, Cambridge, Massachusetts, 1994.

15. N. Lavrač and S. Džeroski. Inductive learning of relations from noisy examples. In S. H. Muggleton, editor, *Inductive Logic Programming*, pages 495–514, London, 1992. Academic Press.

16. N. Lavrač and S. Džeroski. *Inductive Logic Programming: Techniques and Applications*. Ellis Horwood, New York, 1994.

17. N. Lavrač, S. Džeroski, and I. Bratko. Handling imperfect data in inductive logic programming. In L. De Raedt, editor, *Advances in Inductive Logic Programming*, pages 48–64. IOS Press, 1996.

18. Y. Mansour and M. Parnas. On learning conjunctions with malicious noise. In *Israel System and Theory Computer Symposium (ISTCS 96)*, 1996. (To appear).

19. S. Muggleton and C. Feng. Efficient induction of logic programs. In S. Muggleton, editor, *Inductive Logic Programming*, pages 281–298. Academic Press, 1992.

20. G. Shackelford and D. Volper. Learning k-DNF with noise in the attributes. In *Proc. 1st Annu. Workshop on Comput. Learning Theory*, pages 97–103, San Mateo, CA, 1988. Morgan Kaufmann.

21. R. H. Sloan. Four types of noise in data for PAC learning. *Inf. Process. Lett.*, 54:157–162, 1995.

22. A. Srinivasan, S. H. Muggleton, and M. Bain. Distinguishing exceptions from noise in non-monotonic learning. In *Proc. Second International Workshop on Inductive Logic Programming*, Tokyo, Japan, 1992. ICOT TM-1182.

23. L. G. Valiant. Learning disjunctions of conjunctions. In *Proceedings of the 9th International Joint Conference on Artificial Intelligence, vol. 1*, pages 560–566, Los Angeles, California, 1985. International Joint Committee for Artificial Intelligence.

# A   Sample complexity of statistical query simulation

We now derive the sample complexity values specified in (3) and (4).

## A.1   Bound on $m_1$

We need to do a sensitivity analysis of (2), which we can rewrite as

$$\Pr_D(\chi = 1) = p_1 \Pr_{D_1,\eta}(\chi = 1)\left(\tfrac{1}{1-2\eta}\right) - p_1\eta\left(\tfrac{1}{1-2\eta}\right) + \Pr_{D,\eta}(\chi = 1 \wedge x \in X_2) \ .$$
(11)

We need to figure out how much error we can allow in each of the three terms of the sum so that the total error in the value of $\Pr_D(\chi = 1)$ is at most $\alpha$. In fact, we want to know how much additive error in the basic quantities $p_1$, $\Pr_{D_1,\eta}(\chi = 1)$, $\Pr_{D,\eta}(\chi = 1 \wedge x \in X_2)$, and $\eta$ we can allow. Notice that all those quantities have values strictly between 0 and 1, although $1/(1 - 2\eta)$ does not.

Kearns [12, 14] suggests how to find an estimate $\widehat{\tfrac{1}{1-2\eta}}$ of $1/(1 - 2\eta)$ that has additive error at most $\tau$. Now consider two quantities $0 < A, B < 1$, and two estimates of them, $\hat{A}$ and $\hat{B}$, such that $A - \tau(1 - 2\eta_b) \leq \hat{A} \leq A + \tau(1 - 2\eta_b)$, and similarly for $\hat{B}$.

What is the maximum additive error in the estimate $\hat{A}\hat{B}\widehat{\tfrac{1}{1-2\eta}}$ of $AB/(1-2\eta)$? We have

$$\hat{A}\hat{B}\frac{\hat{1}}{1 - 2\eta} \leq (A + \tau(1 - 2\eta_b))(B + \tau(1 - 2\eta_b))\left(\frac{1}{1 - 2\eta} + \tau\right)$$

$$\leq AB/(1 - 2\eta) + 3\tau + 4\tau^2 \ .$$

We get something smaller for the lower bound, so the additive error in this estimate is at most $3\tau + 4\tau^2$.

Now taking $A = p_1$ and $B = \Pr_{D_1,\eta}(\chi = 1)$, we see that if we estimate $A$, $B$, and $1/(1 - 2\eta)$ to the stated accuracies, then the total additive error in the first term of the sum in (11) would be at most $3\tau + 4\tau^2$. The same error bound holds for the second term. The third term of (11) obviously has additive error at most $\tau$. Thus the total additive error in (11) is at most $7\tau + 8\tau^2$.

Now, if we estimate each of $p_1$, $\Pr_{D_1,\eta}(\chi = 1)$, $\eta$, and $\Pr_{D,\eta}(\chi = 1 \wedge x \in X_2)$ to within additive error $\alpha(1 - 2\eta_b)/8$, and $1/(1 - 2\eta)$ to within additive error $\alpha/8$, then the the additive error of our estimate of $\Pr_D(\chi = 1)$ is at most $\alpha$.

The value of $\Delta$ was chosen to give the desired accuracy on $\eta$ and $1/(1 - 2\eta)$ [14]; we will make our sample size $m_1$ big enough to guarantee the other accuracies with high probability.

We are going to estimate all three quantities $p_1$, $\Pr_{D_1,\eta}(\chi = 1)$, and $\Pr_{D,\eta}(\chi = 1 \wedge x \in X_2)$ for all queries $\chi$ from the same large sample of $m_1$ examples. Thus, the total number of quantities to estimate is at most three times the maximum number of queries; that is, $3|\mathcal{Q}|$. We want the probability that all of those estimates are within $\alpha(1 - 2\eta_b)/8$ of the true value to be at least $1 - \delta/2$. We will achieve this if the probability that any one estimate is more than $\alpha(1 - 2\eta_b)/8$ away from its true value is at most $\delta/6|\mathcal{Q}|$.

To ensure this, we will need Hoeffding's Inequality [10], which is as follows.

Let $X_1, X_2, \cdots, X_m$ be independent 0-1 random variables each with probability $p$ of being 1. Let $S = \sum_1^m X_i$. Then for any positive $t$, $\Pr(|S - pm| \geq tm) \leq 2e^{-2mt^2}$.

Thus we need $2e^{-2m_1(\alpha(1-2\eta_b)/8)^2} \leq \delta/(6|\mathcal{Q}|)$, which we can solve for $m_1$ getting

$$m_1 \geq \frac{32}{\alpha^2(1-2\eta_b)^2} \ln\left(\frac{12|\mathcal{Q}|}{\delta}\right) .$$

As we are about to explain, $\alpha$ should be chosen so that the statistical query algorithm achieves an error rate of at most $\epsilon/2$.

## A.2  Bound on $m_2$

We test all our hypotheses on one sample of $m_2$ examples from the noisy oracle. For every hypothesis $H_i$ we get an empirical estimate $\hat{\gamma}_i$ of $\gamma_i$, which we define to be the probability that $H_i$ disagrees with the label of an example from the random classification noise oracle. We pick a large enough sample so that $|\hat{\gamma}_i - \gamma_i| \leq (1 - 2\eta_b)\epsilon/4$ with probability at least $1 - \delta/2$.

If a hypothesis has error rate $r$ on noise-free examples, then its error rate on examples with random classification noise will be $\eta + (1 - 2\eta)r$ [12].

We know that there is a "good" hypothesis $H_g$ with error at most $\epsilon/2$. For this hypothesis, (with high probability)

$$\gamma_g \leq \eta + (1 - 2\eta)\epsilon/2 + (1 - 2\eta_b)\epsilon/4 \leq \eta + \frac{3\epsilon(1-2\eta_b)}{4}$$

For any "bad" hypothesis $H_b$ with error greater than $\epsilon$, (with high probability)

$$\gamma_b > \eta + (1 - 2\eta)\epsilon - (1 - 2\eta_b)\epsilon/4 \geq \eta + \frac{3\epsilon(1-2\eta_b)}{4}$$

Thus, if our estimates $\hat{\gamma}_i$ all meet our desired accuracy with high probability, and we choose as our final output the hypothesis with the smallest $\hat{\gamma}_i$, then with high probability we will have chosen a hypothesis with error less than $\epsilon$.

We have $\eta_b/\Delta$ possible hypotheses, and $\eta_b < 1/2$, so we have at most $1/2\Delta = 8/\alpha(1 - 2\eta_b)^2$ hypotheses and estimates. It is sufficient if the probability that any one estimate is too far off is at most $\delta\alpha(1 - 2\eta_b)^2/8$.

By Hoeffding's Inequality, we need $2e^{-2m_2(\epsilon(1-2\eta_b)/2)^2} \leq \delta\alpha(1 - 2\eta_b)^2/8$. Solving for $m_2$ gives

$$m_2 \geq \frac{2}{\epsilon^2(1-2\eta_b)^2} \ln\left(\frac{16}{\delta\alpha(1-2\eta_b)^2}\right) .$$

# Handling Quantifiers in ILP

M.-Elisabeth GONCALVES

Université de Paris Sud,
Laboratoire de Recherche en Informatique,
Bâtiment 490,
91405 Orsay Cedex, France
email: goncalve@lri.fr

**Abstract.** An important research area in the field of Inductive Logic Programming (ILP) is concerned with predicate learning. Recently, many predicate learners have been developed whose task consists in learning a definition of a concept from positive and negative examples. In most of them, the definition of the concept is represented by a set of definite (or normal) clauses. The variables that appear in the head of a clause (the head-variables) are universally quantified, and the variables that appear only in the body of the clause (the body-variables) are existentially quantified. Some predicate learners described in the ILP literature are able to deal with such existential (body-)variables, using some language bias like ij-determinacy (see [11]). However, as far as the authors know, no ILP system is able to deal with clauses in whose body both existential and universal body-variables appear. Moreover, there exists no generalisation and no specialisation operator that handle such body-variables.

In this paper, we first present a set of generalisation/specialisation rules devoted to deal with existential and universal variables that appear only in the body of the clauses. We then highlight some properties of these rules, essentially correctness and completeness theorems. We do not explicit any type of control that could permit to exploit practically these rules in an ILP system, however we give some ideas of how to integrate them in different sorts of systems with minor modifications and without increasing the search space too greatly.

Following the motivation of ILP systems with respect to more classical machine learning ones, an important motivation of these rules is to extend the expressiveness of the ILP representation formalism (clauses without any Skolem functions, i.e. with only existential body-variables). Moreover, a significant interest of the q-operators presented in this paper is that several existing ILP systems can be adapted (with some modifications) to process quantifiers in the body of clauses and thus increase their expressiveness.

## 1 Introduction

A predicate learner is an ILP system intended to learn a definition of a concept from positive and negative evidence, see among others [11],[9],[17]. For most of the existing systems, the representation formalism of such a definition is a set of definite (or normal —see [2],[17],[19]—) clauses. Each clause is interpreted as follows: the predicate of the head of the clause represents the concept to be learned and the conjunction of the literals of its body represents the sequence of necessary conditions[1] to be respected to belong to this concept. In this formalism, the classical ILP systems, as far as the authors know, do not take into account Skolem terms and therefore the quantification of every variable is universal. Note that we consider here the prenex form of the formulae. Recent learners allow for the occurrence, in the body of a clause, of variables which do not appear in the head of the clause. The accepted way of designating such variables is as *existential variables*. Note that these variables correspond to universal variables in the prenex form of the formulae. Therefore, the classical ILP representation formalism cannot simulate the occurrence of existential variables and all the less so a sequence of both existential and universal quantifiers. We aim at extending the expressivity of the classical ILP representation formalism, by allowing for the occurrence of any sequence of quantifiers in the body of the clauses. In order to illustrate the growth of expressivity, let us consider the following two formulae which define the concept *bound*.

$$\forall X \ (bound(X) \leftarrow \forall Y \ less(X, Y))$$
$$\forall X \ (bound(X) \leftarrow \forall Y \ less(Y, X))$$

X is a bound if X is an upperbound —every Y is less than X—, or if X is a lowerbound —X is less than every Y. Such a definition cannot be represented in classical ILP formalisms using only the predicate *less*.

Let us consider a more elaborate example. The aim is to define the concept —that we name *cross*—, of a picture crossed by a horizontal and a vertical line. The picture is represented by the coordinates of its pixels and the status (*on* or *off*) of each pixel. The picture represented in Fig. 1 is an example of the concept *cross*.

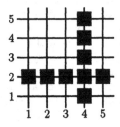

**Fig. 1.** Example of the concept *cross*.

In the following formula, defining the concept *cross*, $on(X, Y, P)$ is true if, in the picture P, the pixel, whose coordinates are (X,Y), is on.

$$\forall P \ (cross(P) \leftarrow \exists X_1 \forall Y_1 \ on(X_1, Y_1, P) \wedge \exists X_2 \forall Y_2 \ on(X_2, Y_2, P))$$

---

[1] these conditions are logically sufficient but are turned into necessary ones by some completion procedure

The reader will note that all the previous formulae may be implemented by Horn clauses via skolemisation. The difference between the resulting formulae and classical ILP clauses, is that the former clauses contain Skolem terms whereas the latter ones do not.

To handle such clauses with Skolem terms, it is necessary for predicate learners to have at their disposal generalisation or specialisation operators specifically devoted to deal with these terms. We name such operators *q-operators* —for quantification-operators— and in the same vein, we will use the term *q-rules*. To be operational in an ILP system, these operators have to satisfy some interesting properties shared by the majority of ILP operators, like correctness and completeness.

In this paper, we first present a set of seven generalisation/specialisation q-rules, which satisfies some desirable properties. The generality relation we consider is the logical implication. We then propose three generalisation q-operators based on these q-rules. Two of these operators are globally complete with regard to the chosen generality relation. The third operator is locally complete.

We also propose the dual operators: three specialisation q-operators.

This paper is structured as follows. In Section 2, we define the general form of a q-rule. Section 3 presents then the seven generalisation/specialisation q-rules, whose properties are described in Section 4. Section 5 proposes three generalisation q-operators based on these q-rules and analyses their properties. In a similar way, Section 6 presents and analyses three specialisation q-operators. In Section 7, we investigate, in an intuitive manner, possible ways to integrate these operators in existing ILP systems. Finally, Section 8 concludes with a brief discussion of the advantages of the presented operators, as well as some remarks and open problems concerning these operators.

For the proofs of the theorems defined in Sections 4, 5 and 6, the reader will refer to [6].

## 2 What the Q-Rules Are

After stating the notations used throughout this paper in Table 1, we will describe the general form of the q-rules and we will try to enlighten the reader on their purpose before accurately presenting each of them in the next section.

Our aim is to extend the classical representation formalism in the following way. A definition of a concept is represented by a set of formulae of the form: $\overrightarrow{\forall V_h} \left( C \left( \overrightarrow{V_h} \right) \leftarrow \overrightarrow{Q V_b} \, F \left( \overrightarrow{V_b}, \overrightarrow{V_h^b} \right) \right)$. Recall that such a formula may be easily translated into a Horn clause by skolemisation.

To handle these formulae, we define seven q-rules. There exists much more such q-rules, but we are interested only in (and we present only) the minimal ones[2].

---

[2] The property of minimality is defined in Section 4.

**Table 1.** Notations Used

**For a particular clause:** $C\left(\overrightarrow{V_h}\right) \leftarrow F\left(\overrightarrow{V_h^b}, \overrightarrow{V_b}\right)$

| | |
|---|---|
| F: | the conjunction of literals of its body. $head \leftarrow \bigwedge_{i=1}^n l_i\left(\overrightarrow{t_i}\right)$ becomes $head \leftarrow F\left(\overrightarrow{t_1}, \ldots, \overrightarrow{t_n}\right)$, where, for each $i \in [1 \ldots n]$, $\overrightarrow{t_i}$ is the vector of terms of the litteral $l_i$. |
| $\overrightarrow{V_h}$ : | the vector of the variables of its head. |
| $\overrightarrow{V_h^b}$ : | the vector of the variables that appear both in its head and in its body. |
| $\overrightarrow{V_b}$ : | a vector of domain constants and variables that appear only in its body. |
| C: | the predicate denoting the concept to be learned. |

**More generally:**

| | |
|---|---|
| $\overrightarrow{QV}$: | the sequence of quantifiers that quantify the variables of the vector $\overrightarrow{V}$. If $\overrightarrow{V} = V_1, \ldots, V_n$ then $\overrightarrow{QV} = q_1 V_1 \ldots q_n V_n$, where for each i, $q_i \in \{\forall, \exists\}$. |
| $\overrightarrow{\forall V}$ (resp. $\overrightarrow{\exists V}$) | : a sequence of universal (resp. existential) quantifiers that quantify the variables of the vector $\overrightarrow{V}$. If $\overrightarrow{V} = V_1 \ldots V_n$ then $\overrightarrow{\forall V} = \forall V_1 \ldots \forall V_n$ (resp. $\overrightarrow{\exists V} = \exists V_1 \ldots \exists V_n$) |
| d: | a particular constant of the domain. |
| $\overrightarrow{d}$ : | a vector whose all the components are equal to the same domain constant $d$, $\overrightarrow{d} = (d, \ldots, d)$. |
| $V, X, Y, Z$: | variables. |

A q-rule transforms a formula of the form: $\overrightarrow{\forall V_h}\left(C\left(\overrightarrow{V_h}\right) \leftarrow \overrightarrow{QV_b} F\left(\overrightarrow{V_b}, \overrightarrow{V_h^b}\right)\right)$ into a formula of the form: $\overrightarrow{\forall V_h}\left(C\left(\overrightarrow{V_h}\right) \leftarrow \overrightarrow{Q'V_b'} F\left(\overrightarrow{V_b'}, \overrightarrow{V_h^b}\right)\right)$, where the prime denotes a modification. From a formula to its transformation by a q-rule, the modification concerns only the domain constants of the body of the formula, its variables and their quantification. The generality relation we consider is the logical implication.

As we will see in Section 4.4, the q-rules that we present are such that the set of formulae of the form $\overrightarrow{\forall V_h}\left(C\left(\overrightarrow{V_h}\right) \leftarrow \overrightarrow{QV_b}\, F\left(\overrightarrow{V_b}, \overrightarrow{V_h^b}\right)\right)$ (up to variable

renaming) where $C$, $F$, $\overrightarrow{V_h}$ and $\overrightarrow{V_h^b}$ are fixed, forms a lattice. To help the reader to understand the next section, we present from now on in Fig. 2 a simplified form of this lattice for formulae of the form $\overrightarrow{\forall V_h}\left(C\left(\overrightarrow{V_h}\right) \leftarrow \overrightarrow{QX}\, F\left(X_1, X_2, \overrightarrow{V_h^b}\right)\right)$.

For the sake of simplicity and readability of the figure, we do not consider the formulae whose two first arguments of $F$ are domain constants. To permit this simplification we denote $\Re_3^\forall$ the composition of the two q-rules $\Re_D^\forall$ and $\Re_D^\exists$, and, in order to bring out the modifications of the formulae induced by the application of the rules, we replace in Fig. 2 each formula by the sequence of quantifiers of its body. Two nodes of the figure are connected by a rule $\Re_i^j$ if the generalisation (resp. specialisation) q-rule $\Re_i^j$ transforms minimally the formula represented in the higher (resp. lower) node into the formula represented in the lower (resp. higher) node.

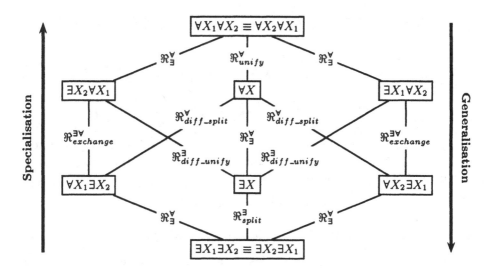

**Fig. 2.** Simplified Lattice

## 3 The Generalisation/Specialisation Q-rules

In this section, we first give a formal description of each q-rule and then illustrate it by an example. The only purpose of the example is to persuade the reader that a generalisation/specialisation step is realised by applying a q-rule. The applicability of the q-rules is conditioned by the form of the formula to be generalised/specialised, up to a logical equivalence. A q-rule is presented in terms of its precondition of application and its postcondition. The precondition describes the form of the formula to be generalised/specialised and the postcondition corresponds to the transformed formula (i.e. the generalised/specialised formula). For the sake of readability, we present each rule in a quantified form. The reader can find the skolemised form in [6].

Without loss of generality, we choose an arbitrary fixed order for the arguments of the formulae.

Given the reversibility of the generalisation and specialisation rules, we arbitrarily choose to describe only the generalisation ones.

## 3.1 The Q-rule $\Re_D^\forall$

**Definition.** The q-rule $\Re_D^\forall$ is applicable only when the first element of the sequence of quantifiers in the body of the formula is universal. $\Re_D^\forall$ consists in removing this universal quantifier and replacing all the occurrences of the variable it quantifies by a constant of the domain. The chosen constant may already appear in the initial formula.

**Formally:**

$$precondition : \overrightarrow{\forall V_h} \left( C\left(\overrightarrow{V_h}\right) \leftarrow \forall X \overrightarrow{QV_b} F\left(X, \overrightarrow{V_b}, \overrightarrow{V_h^b}\right)\right)$$

$$\downarrow \Re_D^\forall$$

$$postcondition : \overrightarrow{\forall V_h} \left( C\left(\overrightarrow{V_h}\right) \leftarrow \overrightarrow{QV_b} F\left(d, \overrightarrow{V_b}, \overrightarrow{V_h^b}\right)\right)$$

**Illustration.** In the following example, the domain is constituted by the positive integers. The semantics of the predicate *less_or_equal* is: *less_or_equal* $(X, Y)$ is true if $X$ is less than or equal to $Y$.

$$\forall V \left( C\left(V\right) \leftarrow \forall X less\_or\_equal\left(V, X\right)\right)$$
$$\downarrow \Re_D^\forall$$
$$\forall V \left( C\left(V\right) \leftarrow less\_or\_equal\left(V, 7\right)\right)$$

The only integer covered by the first formula is the least element 0, whereas the second formula covers all the integers belonging to the interval $[0, 7]$. In this example, the second formula clearly generalises the first one with regard to the logical implication, since the latter covers a bounded interval and the former covers a point.

## 3.2 The Q-rule $\Re_D^\exists$

**Definition.** The q-rule $\Re_D^\exists$ is the dual q-rule of $\Re_D^\forall$. $\Re_D^\exists$ is applicable only if a constant of the domain occurs in the body of the formula. $\Re_D^\exists$ consists in transforming one or more occurrences of a domain constant in an existential variable, the existential quantifier beginning the sequence of body-quantifiers. This rule is often used in classical ascendant learners during the generation of the starting clause. Indeed, the first step of the learning task is usually the variabilisation of the positive example.

**Formally:**

$$precondition: \quad \overrightarrow{\forall V_h}\left(C\left(\overrightarrow{V_h}\right) \leftarrow \overrightarrow{QV_b}\, F\left(\overrightarrow{d}, \overrightarrow{V_b}, \overrightarrow{V_h^b}\right)\right)$$

$$\downarrow \Re_D^{\exists}$$

$$postcondition: \overrightarrow{\forall V_h}\left(C\left(\overrightarrow{V_h}\right) \leftarrow \exists X \overrightarrow{QV_b}\, F\left(X, \overrightarrow{V_b}, \overrightarrow{V_h^b}\right)\right)$$

**Illustration.** In the following example, the domain is the same as previously and the predicate *less_or_equal* has the same semantics.

$$\forall V\,(C\,(V) \leftarrow less\_or\_equal\,(V, 7))$$

$$\downarrow \Re_D^{\exists}$$

$$\forall V\,(C\,(V) \leftarrow \exists X less\_or\_equal\,(V, X))$$

$\Re_D^{\exists}$ clearly generalises the first formula into the second one since the first one covers only the integers belonging to the bounded interval $[0, 7]$, whereas the second one covers all the integers belonging to the infinite interval $[0, +\infty[$.

## 3.3 The Q-rule $\Re_{unify}^{\forall}$

**Definition.** The q-rule $\Re_{unify}^{\forall}$ consists in simply unifying two distinct successive universal variables that appear in a same literal. The new universal quantifier replaces the two initial ones at the same position in the sequence of body-quantifiers.

**Formally:**

$$precondition: \quad \overrightarrow{\forall V_h}\left(C\left(\overrightarrow{V_h}\right) \leftarrow \overrightarrow{QV_b^1}\forall X_1 \forall X_2 \overrightarrow{QV_b^2}\, F\left(X_1, X_2, \overrightarrow{V_b^1}, \overrightarrow{V_b^2}, \overrightarrow{V_h^b}\right)\right)$$

$$\downarrow \Re_{unify}^{\forall}$$

$$postcondition: \quad \overrightarrow{\forall V_h}\left(C\left(\overrightarrow{V_h}\right) \leftarrow \overrightarrow{QV_b^1}\forall X \overrightarrow{QV_b^2}\, F\left(X, X, \overrightarrow{V_b^1}, \overrightarrow{V_b^2}, \overrightarrow{V_h^b}\right)\right)$$

where $X_1$ and $X_2$ appear in a same literal.

Notice that if $X_1$ and $X_2$ do not appear in a same literal then the formulae are logically equivalent.

**Illustration.** In the following example, the domain is constituted by a plane. The semantics of the predicate *straight_line* is: *straight_line* $(X_1, X_2, Y_1, Y_2, Z_1, Z_2)$ is true if there exists a straight line that contains the three points of respective coordinates $(X_1, X_2), (Y_1, Y_2)$ and $(Z_1, Z_2)$.

$$\forall V_1 \forall V_2 \left( C\left(V_1, V_2\right) \leftarrow \forall X_1 \forall X_2 \, straight\_line\left(V_1, V_2, X_1, X_2, 0, 0\right)\right)$$
$$\downarrow \Re^{\forall}_{unify}$$
$$\forall V_1 \forall V_2 \left( C\left(V_1, V_2\right) \leftarrow \forall X \, straight\_line\left(V_1, V_2, X, X, 0, 0\right)\right)$$

The only point of the plane, that can be an example of the concept C defined by the first formula, is the origin point —since it has to belong to every straight line which contains the origin point.

Moreover, every point of the diagonal of the plane is covered by the second formula —since such a point is always contained by any straight line which goes through the origin point and any point of the diagonal.

Hence, applying $\Re^{\forall}_{unify}$ to the initial formula clearly entails a generalisation step.

## 3.4 The Q-rule $\Re^{\exists}_{split}$

**Definition.** The q-rule $\Re^{\exists}_{split}$ is the dual q-rule of $\Re^{\forall}_{unify}$. It consists in splitting two occurrences of an existential variable. The new existential quantifiers replace the initial one at the same position in the sequence of body-quantifiers.

Since $\Re^{\exists}_{split}$ concerns only existential body-variables, it is not surprising that this rule is sometimes used in existing predicate learners, see [8].

**Formally:**

$$precondition: \quad \overrightarrow{\forall V_h}\left(C\left(\overrightarrow{V_h}\right) \leftarrow \overrightarrow{QV_b^1}\exists X \overrightarrow{QV_b^2} F\left(X, X, \overrightarrow{V_b^1}, \overrightarrow{V_b^2}, \overrightarrow{V_h^b}\right)\right)$$
$$\downarrow \Re^{\exists}_{split}$$
$$postcondition: \overrightarrow{\forall V_h}\left(C\left(\overrightarrow{V_h}\right) \leftarrow \overrightarrow{QV_b^1}\exists X_1 \exists X_2 \overrightarrow{QV_b^2} F\left(X_1, X_2, \overrightarrow{V_b^1}, \overrightarrow{V_b^2}, \overrightarrow{V_h^b}\right)\right)$$

**Illustration.** In the following example, the domain is constituted by a plane. The semantics of the predicate $top\_left$ is: $top\_left\left(X_1, X_2, Y_1, Y_2\right)$ is true if the point of coordinates $(X_1, X_2)$ is situated on the top left-hand side of the point of coordinates $(Y_1, Y_2)$. That is, $X_1$ is less than or equal to $Y_1$ and $X_2$ is greater than or equal to $Y_2$.

$$\forall V_1 \forall V_2 \left( C\left(V_1, V_2\right) \leftarrow \exists X \, top\_left\left(V_1, V_2, X, X\right)\right)$$
$$\downarrow \Re^{\exists}_{split}$$
$$\forall V_1 \forall V_2 \left( C\left(V_1, V_2\right) \leftarrow \exists X_1 \exists X_2 \, top\_left\left(V_1, V_2, X_1, X_2\right)\right)$$

The first formula covers every point of the half plane that is above the diagonal, since a covered point has to be situated on the top left-hand side of some point of the diagonal (i.e. $V_2 \geq V_1$).

The second formula covers every point of the plane, since a covered point has to be situated on the top left-hand side of some point of the plane.

Due to these remarks, it is clear that the second formula generalises the first one with regard to the logical implication.

## 3.5 The Q-rule $\mathfrak{R}^{\forall}_{diff\_split}$

**Definition.** The q-rule $\mathfrak{R}^{\forall}_{diff\_split}$ amounts to splitting two occurrences of a universal variable into two variables distinguished by their quantifiers, the first quantifier being universal and the second one existential. The introduced quantifiers replace the initial universal quantifier at the same position in the sequence of body-quantifiers. $\mathfrak{R}^{\forall}_{diff\_split}$ is applied only if the transformed universal quantifier cannot be preceded by a universal one in the sequence of body-quantifiers[3].

**Formally:**

$$precondition: \quad \overrightarrow{\forall V_h}\left(C\left(\overrightarrow{V_h}\right) \leftarrow \overrightarrow{QV_b^1}\exists Y \forall X \overrightarrow{QV_b^2} F\left(X, X, Y, \overrightarrow{V_b^1}, \overrightarrow{V_b^2}, \overrightarrow{V_h^b}\right)\right)$$

$$\downarrow \mathfrak{R}^{\forall}_{diff\_split}$$

$$postcondition: \overrightarrow{\forall V_h}\left(C\left(\overrightarrow{V_h}\right) \leftarrow \overrightarrow{QV_b^1}\exists Y \forall X_1 \exists X_2 \overrightarrow{QV_b^2} F\left(X_1, X_2, Y, \overrightarrow{V_b^1}, \overrightarrow{V_b^2}, \overrightarrow{V_h^b}\right)\right)$$

where $\exists Y$ is optional when the vector $\overrightarrow{QV_b^1}$ is empty.

**Illustration.** In the following example, the domain is constituted by the top right quarter of a plane, i.e. the portion of the plane defined by the inequalities: $X \geq 0$ and $Y \geq 0$.

The semantics of the predicate *bottom_left* is: *bottom_left* $(X_1, X_2, Y_1, Y_2)$ is true if the point of coordinates $(X_1, X_2)$ is situated on the bottom left-hand side of the point of coordinates $(Y_1, Y_2)$. That is, $X_1$ is less than or equal to $Y_1$ and $X_2$ is less than or equal to $Y_2$.

$$\forall V_1 \forall V_2 \left(C\left(V_1, V_2\right) \leftarrow \forall X \, bottom\_left\left(V_1, V_2, X, X\right)\right)$$
$$\downarrow \mathfrak{R}^{\forall}_{diff\_split}$$
$$\forall V_1 \forall V_2 \left(C\left(V_1, V_2\right) \leftarrow \forall X_1 \exists X_2 \, bottom\_left\left(V_1, V_2, X_1, X_2\right)\right)$$

The first formula covers only the origin point, since a covered point has to be situated on the bottom left-hand side of every point of the diagonal.

The second formula covers every point of the ordinate axis, since a covered point has to be situated on the bottom left-hand side of a point of each straight line parallel with the ordinate axis.

As the first set of examples is included in the second one, a generalisation step has been realised.

## 3.6 The Q-rule $\mathfrak{R}^{\exists}_{diff\_unify}$

**Definition.** The q-rule $\mathfrak{R}^{\exists}_{diff\_unify}$ is the dual q-rule of $\mathfrak{R}^{\forall}_{diff\_split}$. $\mathfrak{R}^{\exists}_{diff\_unify}$ unifies two differently quantified variables, such that both quantifiers are successive in the sequence of body-quantifiers, the first one being existential and

---

[3] This constraint ensures the minimality of the rule, see Section 4.

the second one universal. The quantifier resulting from the unification is existential and replaces the initial quantifiers at the same position in the sequence of body-quantifiers. $\Re^{\exists}_{diff\_unify}$ is applied only if the preceding quantifier of the two modified ones is not existential[4].

**Formally:**

$$precondition: \overrightarrow{\forall V_h}\left(C\left(\overrightarrow{V_h}\right) \leftarrow \overrightarrow{QV_b^1}\forall Y \exists X_1 \forall X_2 \overrightarrow{QV_b^2} \, F\left(X_1, X_2, Y, \overrightarrow{V_b^1}, \overrightarrow{V_b^2}, \overrightarrow{V_h^b}\right)\right)$$

$$\downarrow \Re^{\exists}_{diff\_unify}$$

$$postcondition: \quad \overrightarrow{\forall V_h}\left(C\left(\overrightarrow{V_h}\right) \leftarrow \overrightarrow{QV_b^1}\forall Y \exists X \overrightarrow{QV_b^2} \, F\left(X, X, Y, \overrightarrow{V_b^1}, \overrightarrow{V_b^2}, \overrightarrow{V_h^b}\right)\right)$$

where $\forall Y$ is optional when the vector $\overrightarrow{QV_b^1}$ is empty.

**Illustration.** In the following example, the domain is the same as above and the predicate $bottom\_left$ has the same semantics.

$$\forall V_1 \forall V_2 \left(C\left(V_1, V_2\right) \leftarrow \exists X_1 \forall X_2 bottom\_left\left(V_1, V_2, X_1, X_2\right)\right)$$
$$\downarrow \Re^{\exists}_{diff\_unify}$$
$$\forall V_1 \forall V_2 \left(C\left(V_1, V_2\right) \leftarrow \exists X bottom\_left\left(V_1, V_2, X, X\right)\right)$$

The first formula covers the points of the abscissa axis $(X_1 \geq 0)$, since there must exist a straight line parallel with the ordinate axis whose each point is situated on the top right-hand side of a covered point.

The second formula covers every point of the domain (a quarter of plane), since a covered point has to be situated on the bottom left-hand side of some point of the diagonal.

So, $\Re^{\exists}_{diff\_unify}$ generalises the first formula into the second one.

## 3.7   The Q-rule $\Re^{\exists\forall}_{exchange}$

**Definition.** The q-rule $\Re^{\exists\forall}_{exchange}$ exchanges an existential and a universal quantifiers. A condition of application of this rule is that in the initial formula, the existential quantifier immediately precedes the universal quantifier.

**Formally:**

$$precondition: \overrightarrow{\forall V_h}\left(C\left(\overrightarrow{V_h}\right) \leftarrow \overrightarrow{QV_b^1}\exists X_1 \forall X_2 \overrightarrow{QV_b^2} \, F\left(X_1, X_2, \overrightarrow{V_b^1}, \overrightarrow{V_b^2}, \overrightarrow{V_h^b}\right)\right)$$

$$\downarrow \Re^{\exists\forall}_{exchange}$$

$$postcondition: \overrightarrow{\forall V_h}\left(C\left(\overrightarrow{V_h}\right) \leftarrow \overrightarrow{QV_b^1}\forall X_2 \exists X_1 \overrightarrow{QV_b^2} \, F\left(X_1, X_2, \overrightarrow{V_b^1}, \overrightarrow{V_b^2}, \overrightarrow{V_h^b}\right)\right)$$

---

[4] See Footnote 3.

**Illustration.** In the following example, the domain is constituted by all the real numbers. The semantics of the predicate *product_equal* is: *product_equal* $(X, Y, Z)$ is true if and only if $Z$ is the result of the product of $X$ and $Y$.

$$\forall V \left( C\left( V \right) \leftarrow \exists X_1 \forall X_2 product\_equal\left( V, X_1, X_2 \right) \right)$$
$$\downarrow \Re_{exchange}^{\exists \forall}$$
$$\forall V \left( C\left( V \right) \leftarrow \forall X_2 \exists X_1 product\_equal\left( V, X_1, X_2 \right) \right)$$

No real number is covered by the first formula. Indeed, if there exists a number $v$ covered by the first formula, then there exists a number $n$ such that the product of $v$ by $n$ is equal to every real number, and this is impossible. In the second formula, the existential variable $X_1$ depends on the universal variable $X_2$. So, one can always choose $X_1$ such that $X_1$ is the result of the division of $X_2$ by $V$. Hence, all the real numbers except $0.0$ are examples of the concept $C$ defined by the second formula, and therefore $\Re_{exchange}^{\exists \forall}$ clearly generalises the initial formula.

### 3.8   The Specialisation Q-rules

The specialisation q-rules are the reverse ones of the generalisation q-rules. They are obtained by exchanging the pre- and the postconditions of the previous rules. To differentiate the generalisation and the specialisation rules, we will add to their names a superscript letter: $G$ for generalisation and $S$ for specialisation.

## 4   Properties of the Presented Q-rules

### 4.1   Correctness

Every presented generalisation and specialisation q-rule is correct with regard to the logical implication.

**Theorem : correctness of the generalisation q-rules.** *Let $Fs$ and $Fg$ be two formulae of the form:* $\overrightarrow{\forall V_h}\left( C\left( \overrightarrow{V_h} \right) \leftarrow \overrightarrow{QV_b} F\left( \overrightarrow{V_b}, \overrightarrow{V_h^b} \right) \right).$
*For every generalisation q-rule $^G\Re$ introduced above, if $^G\Re$ transforms the formula $Fs$ into the formula $Fg$, then $Fg$ logically and strictly entails $Fs$.*

$$\left\{ ^G\Re\left( Fs \right) = Fg \right\} \Longrightarrow \left\{ \begin{array}{l} Fg \vdash Fs \\ Fs \nvdash Fg \end{array} \right\}$$

The dual theorem exists for the specialisation q-rules.

**Theorem : correctness of the specialisation q-rules.** *Let $Fs$ and $Fg$ be two formulae of the form:* $\overrightarrow{\forall V_h}\left( C\left( \overrightarrow{V_h} \right) \leftarrow \overrightarrow{QV_b} F\left( \overrightarrow{V_b}, \overrightarrow{V_h^b} \right) \right).$
*For every specialisation q-rule $^S\Re$ introduced above, if $^S\Re$ transforms the formula $Fg$ into the formula $Fs$, then $Fg$ logically and strictly entails $Fs$.*

$$\left\{ ^S\Re\left( Fg \right) = Fs \right\} \Longrightarrow \left\{ \begin{array}{l} Fg \vdash Fs \\ Fs \nvdash Fg \end{array} \right\}$$

## 4.2 Minimality

Every generalisation and specialisation q-rule is also minimal for the logical implication.

**Theorem : minimality of the generalisation q-rules.** *Let* $Fs$ *and* $Fg$ *be two formulae of the form:* $\overrightarrow{\forall V_h}\left(C\left(\overrightarrow{V_h}\right) \leftarrow \overrightarrow{QV_b}\, F\left(\overrightarrow{V_b}, \overrightarrow{V_h^b}\right)\right).$

*For every generalisation q-rule* $^G\mathfrak{R}$ *introduced above, if* $^G\mathfrak{R}$ *transforms the formula* $Fs$ *into the formula* $Fg$, *then* $Fg$ *minimally entails* $Fs$.

   *Let* $F$ *be any formula.*

   *If* $F$ *is entailed by* $Fg$ *and entails* $Fs$, *then* $F$ *entails* $Fg$ *or* $F$ *is entailed by* $Fs$.

$$\{^G\mathfrak{R}(Fs) = Fg\} \Longrightarrow \left\{\left(\begin{array}{c} Fg \vdash F \\ \wedge \\ F \vdash Fs \end{array}\right) \Longrightarrow \left(\begin{array}{c} F \vdash Fg \\ \vee \\ Fs \vdash F \end{array}\right)\right\}$$

The dual minimality theorem exists for the specialisation q-rules.

**Theorem : minimality of the specialisation q-rules.** *Let* $Fs$ *and* $Fg$ *be two formulae of the form:* $\overrightarrow{\forall V_h}\left(C\left(\overrightarrow{V_h}\right) \leftarrow \overrightarrow{QV_b}\, F\left(\overrightarrow{V_b}, \overrightarrow{V_h^b}\right)\right).$

*For every specialisation q-rule* $^S\mathfrak{R}$ *introduced above, if* $^S\mathfrak{R}$ *transforms the formula* $Fg$ *into the formula* $Fs$, *then* $Fg$ *minimally entails* $Fs$.

   *Let* $F$ *be any formula.*

$$\{^S\mathfrak{R}(Fg) = Fs\} \Longrightarrow \left\{\left(\begin{array}{c} Fg \vdash F \\ \wedge \\ F \vdash Fs \end{array}\right) \Longrightarrow \left(\begin{array}{c} F \vdash Fg \\ \vee \\ Fs \vdash F \end{array}\right)\right\}$$

The property of minimality is at the origin of the constraints concerning the applicability of the q-rules. For example, we have seen in Section 3.6 that the generalisation q-rules $^G\mathfrak{R}^\exists_{diff\_unify}$ is applied only if the preceding quantifier of the two modified ones in the sequence of body- quantifier is not existential. Indeed, the following diagram illustrates the non-minimality of $^G\mathfrak{R}^\exists_{diff\_unify}$ when the modified quantifiers are preceded by an existential one.

$$\boxed{\begin{array}{c} \overrightarrow{\forall V_h}\left(C\left(\overrightarrow{V_h}\right) \leftarrow \exists Y \exists X_1 \forall X_2\, F\left(X_1, X_2, Y, \overrightarrow{V_h^b}\right)\right) \\ \downarrow^{G}\mathfrak{R}^{\exists\forall}_{exchange} \\ \overrightarrow{\forall V_h}\left(C\left(\overrightarrow{V_h}\right) \leftarrow \exists X_1 \forall X_2 \exists Y\, F\left(X_1, X_2, Y, \overrightarrow{V_h^b}\right)\right) \\ \downarrow^{G}\mathfrak{R}^{\exists}_{diff\_unify} \\ \overrightarrow{\forall V_h}\left(C\left(\overrightarrow{V_h}\right) \leftarrow \exists Y \exists X\, F\left(X, X, Y, \overrightarrow{V_h^b}\right)\right) \end{array}}$$

   The first formula of the diagram would be transformed in the last one by $^G\mathfrak{R}^\exists_{diff\_unify}$ if its constraint of applicability did not exist, but we can see in this figure that an intermediate formula exists. So ${}^{G}\mathfrak{R}^{\exists}_{diff\_unify}$ would be non-minimal without its constraint of applicability. The reader will note in this figure that the q-rules are applicable up to a logical equivalence.

## 4.3 Unicity

Every other generalisation and specialisation q-rule, that one could propose, is not minimal.

**Theorem : unicity of the minimal presented generalisation q-rules.** *Let* $\mathfrak{R}_{Gener}$ *be any correct generalisation q-rule. There exists an equivalent composition of presented specialisation q-rules.*

$$\mathfrak{R}_{Gener} = {}^{G}\mathfrak{R}_1 \circ \cdots \circ {}^{G}\mathfrak{R}_n$$

*where:* $\forall i \in [1 \ldots n]$,

$${}^{G}\mathfrak{R}_i \in \{ {}^{G}\mathfrak{R}^{\forall}_D, {}^{G}\mathfrak{R}^{\exists}_D, {}^{G}\mathfrak{R}^{\forall}_{unify}, {}^{G}\mathfrak{R}^{\exists}_{split}, {}^{G}\mathfrak{R}^{\forall}_{diff\_split}, {}^{G}\mathfrak{R}^{\exists}_{diff\_unify}, {}^{G}\mathfrak{R}^{\exists\forall}_{exchange} \}$$

**Theorem : unicity of the minimal presented specialisation q-rules.** *Let* $\mathfrak{R}_{Spec}$ *be any correct specialisation q-rule. There exists an equivalent composition of presented specialisation q-rules.*

$$\mathfrak{R}_{Spec} = {}^{S}\mathfrak{R}_1 \circ \cdots \circ {}^{S}\mathfrak{R}_n$$

*where:* $\forall i \in [1 \ldots n]$,

$${}^{S}\mathfrak{R}_i \in \{ {}^{S}\mathfrak{R}^{\forall}_D, {}^{S}\mathfrak{R}^{\exists}_D, {}^{S}\mathfrak{R}^{\forall}_{unify}, {}^{S}\mathfrak{R}^{\exists}_{split}, {}^{S}\mathfrak{R}^{\forall}_{diff\_split}, {}^{S}\mathfrak{R}^{\exists}_{diff\_unify}, {}^{S}\mathfrak{R}^{\exists\forall}_{exchange} \}$$

## 4.4 Lattice

As a consequence of these theorems, the set of formulae of the form $\overrightarrow{\forall V_h} \left( C \left( \overrightarrow{V_h} \right) \leftarrow \overrightarrow{QV_b} F \left( \overrightarrow{V_b}, \overrightarrow{V_h^b} \right) \right)$ (up to variable renaming) where $C$, $F$, $\overrightarrow{V_h}$

and $\overrightarrow{V_h^b}$ are fixed, forms a lattice. Any two formulae have a unique least general q-generalisation, and any two formulae have a unique least special q-specialisation.

We present in Fig. 3 the form of this lattice for formulae of the form $\overrightarrow{\forall V_h} \left( C \left( \overrightarrow{V_h} \right) \leftarrow \overrightarrow{QX} F \left( X_1, X_2, \overrightarrow{V_h^b} \right) \right)$ , where $\overrightarrow{QX}$ denotes the sequence of

quantifiers quantifying the first and the second argument of $F$ (i.e. $X_1$ and $X_2$). The only purpose of this figure is to give to the reader an intuitive idea of the form of the lattice.

For the sake of simplicity and readability of the figure, we do not consider the formulae whose two first arguments of $F$ are domain constants. The reader interested in the representation of the complete lattice will refer to [6].

In Fig. 3, $\mathfrak{R}^{\forall}_{\exists}$ denotes the composition of the two q-rules $\mathfrak{R}^{\forall}_D$ and $\mathfrak{R}^{\exists}_D$.

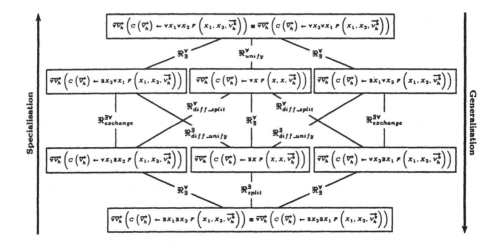

**Fig. 3.** Lattice

# 5 Generalisation Q-operators

In this section, we present three generalisation q-operators which satisfy the completeness property. These operators are based on the presented generalisation q-rules, and more precisely they are made up of a disjunction of generalisation q-rules.

Therefore, they inherit the properties of correctness and minimality of the q-rules.

## 5.1 The Generalisation Q-operators GCGO1 and GCGO2[5]

The first generalisation q-operator we consider is made up of by the disjunction of the q-rules $\Re_D^\forall$, $\Re_D^\exists$, $\Re_{unify}^\forall$ and $\Re_{exchange}^{\exists\forall}$. We denote it by GCGO1.

$$GCO1 = {}^G\Re_D^\forall \vee {}^G\Re_D^\exists \vee {}^G\Re_{unify}^\forall \vee {}^G\Re_{exchange}^{\exists\forall}$$

Applying the q-operator GCGO1 to a formula consists in applying to the formula the q-rule $\Re_D^\forall$ or the q-rule $\Re_D^\exists$ or the q-rule $\Re_{unify}^\forall$ or the q-rule $\Re_{exchange}^{\exists\forall}$.

---

[5] for Globally Complete Generalisation Operator 1 and 2.

The second generalisation q-operator we consider is formed by the disjunction of the q-rules ${}^{G}\mathfrak{R}_{D}^{\forall}$, ${}^{G}\mathfrak{R}_{D}^{\exists}$, ${}^{G}\mathfrak{R}_{unify}^{\forall}$ and ${}^{G}\mathfrak{R}_{diff\_split}^{\forall}$. We denote it by GCGO2.

$$GCO2 = {}^{G}\mathfrak{R}_{D}^{\forall} \vee {}^{G}\mathfrak{R}_{D}^{\exists} \vee {}^{G}\mathfrak{R}_{unify}^{\forall} \vee {}^{G}\mathfrak{R}_{diff\_split}^{\forall}$$

**Notation.** Let $\mathcal{L}_{\forall\exists}$ be the infinite set of languages $L_{\forall\exists}^{i}$, such that for each i $L_{\forall\exists}^{i}$ is a language composed by formulae of the form $\overrightarrow{\forall V_{h}}\left(C\left(\overrightarrow{V_{h}}\right) \leftarrow \overrightarrow{QV_{b}}\, F\left(\overrightarrow{V_{b}}, \overrightarrow{V_{h}^{b}}\right)\right)$ where $C$, $F$, $\overrightarrow{V_{h}}$ and $\overrightarrow{V_{h}^{b}}$ are fixed.

The generalisation q-operators GCGO1 and GCGO2 are both globally complete (see [12]) for any language $L_{\forall\exists}$ of $\mathcal{L}_{\forall\exists}$. That is, one can obtain, from the most specific formula, any formula of the language $L_{\forall\exists}$ (and no other one) by recursively applying GCGO1 or by recursively applying GCGO2.

**Theorem : global completeness of GCGO1 and GCGO2.** *Let $L_{\forall\exists}$ be a particular language of the set of languages $\mathcal{L}_{\forall\exists}$. Let $MSF$ be the most specific formula of the language $L_{\forall\exists}$.*

$$MSF = \overrightarrow{\forall V_{h}}\left(C\left(\overrightarrow{V_{h}}\right) \leftarrow \overrightarrow{\forall V_{b}}\, F\left(\overrightarrow{V_{b}}, \overrightarrow{V_{h}^{b}}\right)\right)$$

*Let GCGO1\* be the reflexive and transitive closure of GCGO1 and GCGO2\* be the reflexive and transitive closure of GCGO2.*

$$GCGO1*(MSF) = L_{\forall\exists} \quad and \quad GCGO2*(MSF) = L_{\forall\exists}.$$

## 5.2 The Generalisation Q-operator LCGO[6]

The third operator we consider is formed by the disjunction of all the generalisation q-rule introduced above. We denote it by LCGO.

$$LCGO = {}^{G}\mathfrak{R}_{D}^{\forall} \vee {}^{G}\mathfrak{R}_{D}^{\exists} \vee {}^{G}\mathfrak{R}_{unify}^{\forall} \vee {}^{G}\mathfrak{R}_{split}^{\exists} \vee {}^{G}\mathfrak{R}_{diff\_split}^{\forall} \vee {}^{G}\mathfrak{R}_{diff\_unify}^{\exists} \vee {}^{G}\mathfrak{R}_{exchange}^{\exists\forall}$$

The generalisation q-operator LCGO is locally complete (see [12]) for any language $L_{\forall\exists}$ of $\mathcal{L}_{\forall\exists}$. That is, by applying LGCO to a given formula of the language, one obtains every formula of the language (up to a logical equivalence) which is a minimal generalisation of the given formula.

**Theorem : local completeness of the generalisation q-operator LCGO.**
*Let $L_{\forall\exists}$ be a particular language of the set of languages $\mathcal{L}_{\forall\exists}$.*
*Let $F$ be any formula of the language $L_{\forall\exists}$.*

$$LCGO(F) = \{F' \in L_{\forall\exists} \mid F' \text{ is a minimal generalisation of } F\}$$

---

[6] for Locally Complete Generalisation Operator.

# 6 Specialisation Q-operators

In this section, we present three specialisation q-operators, the dual ones of the generalisation q-operators of the previous section. As the previous ones, these specialisation operators are made up of a disjunction of specialisation q-rules.

Therefore, they also inherit the properties of correctness and minimality of the q-rules.

## 6.1 The Specialisation Q-operators GCSO1 and GCSO2[7]

The first specialisation q-operator we consider is formed by the disjunction of the q-rules $^S\Re_D^\forall, ^S\Re_D^\exists, ^S\Re_{split}^\exists$ and $^S\Re_{exchange}^{\exists\forall}$. We denote it by GCSO1.

$$GCSO1 = ^S\Re_D^\forall \vee ^S\Re_D^\exists \vee ^S\Re_{split}^\exists \vee ^S\Re_{exchange}^{\exists\forall}$$

The second specialisation q-operator we consider is formed by the disjunction of the q-rules $^S\Re_D^\forall, ^S\Re_D^\exists, ^S\Re_{split}^\exists$ and $^S\Re_{diff\_unify}^\exists$. We denote it by GCSO2.

$$GCSO2 = ^S\Re_D^\forall \vee ^S\Re_D^\exists \vee ^S\Re_{split}^\exists \vee ^S\Re_{diff\_unify}^\exists$$

The specialisation q-operators GCSO1 and GCSO2 are both globally complete for any language $L_{\forall\exists}$ of the set of languages $\mathcal{L}_{\forall\exists}$ defined in Section 5.1. That is, from the most general formula, one can obtain any formula of the language (and no other one) by recursively applying GCSO1 or by recursively applying GCSO2.

**Theorem : global completeness of GCSO1 and GCSO2.** *Let $L_{\forall\exists}$ be a particular language of the set of languages $\mathcal{L}_{\forall\exists}$.*
*Let $MGF$ be the most general formula of the language $L_{\forall\exists}$.*

$$MGF = \overrightarrow{\forall V_h} \left( C\left(\overrightarrow{V_h}\right) \leftarrow \overrightarrow{\exists V_b} F\left(\overrightarrow{V_b}, \overrightarrow{V_h^b}\right)\right)$$

*Let $GCSO1^*$ be the reflexive and transitive closure of GCSO1 and $GCSO2^*$ be the reflexive and transitive closure of GCSO2.*

$$GCSO1 * (MGF) = L_{\forall\exists} \, and \, GCSO2 * (MGF) = L_{\forall\exists}$$

## 6.2 The Specialisation Q-operator LCSO[8]

The third specialisation q-operator we consider is formed by the disjunction of every presented specialisation q-rule. We denote it by LCSO.

$$LCSO = ^S\Re_D^\forall \vee ^S\Re_D^\exists \vee ^S\Re_{unify}^\forall \vee ^S\Re_{split}^\exists \vee ^S\Re_{diff\_split}^\forall \vee ^S\Re_{diff\_unify}^\exists \vee ^S\Re_{exchange}^{\exists\forall}$$

The specialisation q-operator LCSO is locally complete for any language $L_{\forall\exists}$ of the set of languages $\mathcal{L}_{\forall\exists}$. That is, by applying LGSO to a given formula of the language, one obtains every formula of the language (up to a logical equivalence) which is a maximal specialisation of the given formula.

---

[7] for Globally Complete Specialisation Operator 1 (and 2).
[8] for Locally Complete Specialisation Operator.

**Theorem : local completeness of the specialisation q-operator LCSO.**
*Let $L_{\forall\exists}$ be a particular language of the set of languages $\mathcal{L}_{\forall\exists}$.*
*Let $F$ be any formula of the language $L_{\forall\exists}$.*

$$LCSO\,(F) = \{F' \in L \mid F' \text{ is a maximal specialisation of } F\}$$

# 7 Integration of the Q-operators in Existing ILP Systems

In this section, we describe three different ways to integrate our q-operators in existing predicate learners, and thus to allow such systems to handle Skolem terms modelling a sequence of body-quantifiers. We discuss then in a fourth subsection the difficulties induced for the task of theorem proving.

In our representation formalism (definite or normal clauses with Skolem terms), the most specific clause among the formulae of the form $\overrightarrow{\forall V_h}\left(C\left(\overrightarrow{V_h}\right) \leftarrow \overrightarrow{QV_b}\, F\left(\overrightarrow{V_b}, \overrightarrow{V_h^b}\right)\right)$ where $C$, $F$, $\overrightarrow{V_h}$ and $\overrightarrow{V_h^b}$ are fixed, is the formula $\overrightarrow{\forall V_h}\left(C\left(\overrightarrow{V_h}\right) \leftarrow \overrightarrow{\forall V_b}\, F\left(\overrightarrow{V_b}, \overrightarrow{V_h^b}\right)\right)$. The most general formula is $\overrightarrow{\forall V_h}\left(C\left(\overrightarrow{V_h}\right) \leftarrow \overrightarrow{\exists V_b}\, F\left(\overrightarrow{V_b}, \overrightarrow{V_h^b}\right)\right)$. Thus the formulae classically used in ILP are the most general ones with regard to our formalism, and so the purpose of our q-operators, with regard to the clauses without Skolem terms, is only to specialise them.

On the basis of this remark, we propose two first ways to handle quantifiers in existing ILP systems. Both these ways allow us to minimally modify the systems and to minimally increase their search space. But, they are only applicable to particular systems: the only operators of these systems have to be the deletion/addition of a literal from/in the body of a clause and the addition/deletion of a clause.

The third way we propose is more complete but more complicated, and its elaboration is in perspective. Due to the increase of the search space, the complexity is also highly increased. Therefore, the definition of methods of control is necessary, but this is outside of the scope of this paper.

## 7.1 First Way of Integration

The systems we consider here are the ascendant systems whose generalisation operator is the deletion of a literal from the body of a clause or the addition of a clause to the theory (see among others [18],[20]). In such systems, a completion phase (cf. [1],[14],[15]) often occurs after the calculus of the starting clause. This phase produces a clause more general than or simply equivalent to the starting clause. Unfortunately, this completed clause can already be too general for the concept to be learned. For example, the task of learning the concept of upperbound from an example by using the predicate *greater_than*[9], is impossible

---

[9] With the same semantics as defined in Section 3.

without predicate invention, since any usual starting clause is already too general. As a solution, one can use the generalisation q-operators presented above, during the completion phase. By this way, one obtains a clause more specific than the starting clause and not too general for the concept to be learned. Beginning the learning task from a clause containing Skolem terms, it is then possible to use both the chosen generalisation q-operator and the deletion of a literal from the body of the clause.

## 7.2 Second Way of Integration

The systems we consider here are the descendant systems whose specialisation operator is the addition of a literal to the body of a clause or the deletion of a clause from the theory. Since the formulae used in classical ILP systems are more general than every similar clause containing Skolem terms, one can integrate the specialisation q-operators during the refinement phase (see [23], [3], [16], [5], [22], [13]). This phase occurs when a negative example is covered by the current clause defining the concept to be learned and when the specialisation operators employed are unable to discriminate the positive from the negative examples. In such a case, it can be useful to test a specialisation q-operator.

## 7.3 Third Way of Integration

This way allows for the integration of our q-operators into systems whose operators are not particular, for example into systems described in [10],[21] (the operator is the inversion of resolution), in [11] (rlgg), or in [7] (inversion of implication).

If we allow the theory and the positive and negative evidences to be constituted by definite or normal clauses with Skolem terms, then we can couple our q-operators with existing correct and complete operators (for example, deletion of a literal or inversion of the resolution). Indeed, the set of definite or normal reduced clauses with Skolem terms forms a lattice, and a q-operator coupled with a correct and complete operator for clauses without Skolem terms forms a correct and complete operator, for the considered language. The lattice formed in this way includes the lattice of reduced clauses without Skolem terms of classical ILP. With this way of integration, the search space is highly increased.

## 7.4 Theorem Proving

The representation formalism we adopt in this paper (clauses with mixed quantifiers) can be easily translated into classical definite (or normal) clauses containing Skolem terms. Owing to this translation, resolution processes can be used for theorem proving tasks. However, in this case, the closed world assumption can not be made, and a litteral with universally quantified variables can be proved only if it effectively appears in the background theory.

One could then propose, to permit a closed world assumption, to use a "negation as failure"-like approach. That is : $\forall X \overrightarrow{Q\overrightarrow{V}} F\left(X, \overrightarrow{V}\right)$ is provable if, for each possible instanciation $t_i$ of $X$, $\overrightarrow{Q\overrightarrow{V}} F\left(t_i, \overrightarrow{V}\right)$ is provable and $\exists X \overrightarrow{Q\overrightarrow{V}} F\left(X, \overrightarrow{V}\right)$ is provable if there exists an instanciation $t_i$ of $X$ such that $\overrightarrow{Q\overrightarrow{V}} F\left(t_i, \overrightarrow{V}\right)$ is provable. But this method induces a prohibitive increase of the complexity.

So, an important perspective of our work is to propose a modified efficient resolution algorithm able to deal with Skolem terms (or mixed quantifiers) with some closed world assumption.

# 8 Conclusion

In this paper, we have extended the representation formalism used in classical ILP systems, by allowing for a sequence of quantifiers quantifying the variables that appear only in the body of clauses. For this, we have presented a set of q-rules specifically devoted to deal with Skolem terms (these terms modelling the sequence of quantifiers). The chosen generality relation is the logical implication. We have then described the properties of correctness and minimality of the presented q-rules. On the basis of these q-rules, we have proposed two generalisation q-operators and two specialisation q-operators, which are globally complete for any language constituted by clauses of the form $\overrightarrow{\forall V_h}\left(C\left(\overrightarrow{V_h}\right) \leftarrow \overrightarrow{QV_b} F\left(\overrightarrow{V_b}, \overrightarrow{V_h^b}\right)\right)$

where $C$, $F$, $\overrightarrow{V_h}$ and $\overrightarrow{V_h^b}$ are fixed. We have also proposed one more generalisation q-operator and one more specialisation q-operator which are locally complete for the considered language. We have finally made a brief study of possible ways to integrate our formalism and our q-operators into existing ILP systems. A resulting remark of this study is that it is possible to integrate them without a prohibitive increase of the search space if the system does not use inversion of resolution and if the clauses of the theory do not contain Skolem terms. In the more general case where every clause of the system adopts our representation formalism and where any operator is allowed, the complexity increase may become prohibitive, so a necessary control is induced, which is out of the scope of this paper. We have finally pointed out the problem of the cover testing tasks. If no closed world assumption is made, classical resolution algorithms can be used, since the presented clauses with mixed quantifiers can be easily translated into classical clauses with Skolem terms. Then, after the learning process, to present the resulting definition of the target concept in a quantified form instead of in the less readable skolemised form, we can use the algorithm of Cox and Pietrzykowski intended to reverse Skolemisation (see [4]).

As far as the authors know, no system of the ILP literature handles mixed body-quantifiers. Nevertheless, for a very particular form of the list of body-quantifiers, the formalism described here is related with negation as failure (see for examples of systems using the negation as failure process, the systems $FOIL$ [17] and $TRACY^{not}$ [2]). Indeed, if the list of body-quantifiers is reduced to a unique universal quantifier and if the closed world assumption is made, then the universal quantifier can be treated as the negation of an existantial quantifier. For example, $\forall X (bound(X) \leftarrow \forall Y\ less(X, Y))$ can be equivalently expressed by $bound(X) \leftarrow not\ greater\_or\_equal(X, Y)$.

The perspectives of this work are various. They firstly include defining an efficient method of resolution that takes into account the Skolem terms and some closed world assumption. A second perspective is to precisely study the complexity induced by our q-operators and, finally, to effectively integrate our formalism into an existing ILP learner and to provide real-world tests.

## Acknowledgements

Special thanks go to Christine Froidevaux who supervised this work and more particularly provided us with insightful comments on this paper.

Thanks are due to Céline Rouveirol and Claire Nedellec for helpful discussions on the work presented in this paper and particularly on its integration in existing ILP systems.

The authors would like to thank their anonymous referees for their useful comments.

Thanks finally to Lidia Fraczak, Marie-Rose Gonçalves and Françoise Tort for commenting an earlier version of this paper.

## References

1. Ade, H., De Raedt, L., and Bruynooghe, M., 1995: Declarative Bias for Specific-to-General ILP Systems. Machine Learning, Volume 20, pp. 119–154.
2. Bergadano, F., Gunetti, D., Nicosia, M. and Ruffo, G., 1995: Learning Logic Programs with Negation as Failure. In De Raedt, L., editor, Proceedings of the 5th International Workshop on Inductive Logic Programming, pp. 33–51. Leuven, Belgium.
3. Cain, T., 1991: The DUCTOR: A Theory Revision System for Propositional Domains. In Proceedings of the 5th. International Machine Learning Workshop, Evanston.
4. Cox, P. T., and Pietrzykowski, T., 1984: A Complete, Nonredundant Algorithm for Reversed Skolemisation. In Theoretical Computer Science, volume 28, pp. 239–261.
5. Ginsberg, A., 1989: Theory Revision via Prior Operationalisation. In Proceedings of the National Conference on Artificial Intelligence, pp. 590–595.
6. Goncalves, E., 1996: Traitement des Quantificateurs en ILP. In Technical Report, LRI-Orsay, to appear.
7. Lapointe, S., and Matwin, S., 1992: Sub-Unification: A Tool for Efficient Induction of Recursive Programs. In Proceedings of the 9th International Machine Learning Conference, Morgan-Kaufmann, Los Altos, CA.
8. Michalski, R.S., 1983: Learning from Observation: Conceptual Clustering. In Michalski, R.S., Carbonell, G., and Mitchell, T.M., editors, Machine Learning: An Artificial Intelligence Approach, pp. 361–363.

9. Muggleton, S., 1995: Inverse Entailment and Progol. In New Generation Computing, Volume 13, pp. 245–286.

10. Muggleton, S., and Buntine, W., 1988: Machine Invention of First-Order Predicates by Inverting Resolution. In Morgan Kaufmann, editor, Proceedings of the 5th International Conference on Machine Learning, pp. 339–352.

11. Muggleton, S., and Feng, C., 1990: Efficient Induction of Logic Programs. In Proceedings of the Workshop on Algorithmic Learning Theory. Ohmsha publishers, Tokyo.

12. Muggleton, S., and De Raedt, L., 1994: Inductive Logic Programming: Theory and Methods. In Journal of Logic Programming, Volume 19,20, pp 626–679.

13. Nedellec, C., 1992: How to Specialise by Theory Refinement. In B. Neumann, editor, Proceedings of ECAI, pp. 474–478. Wiley.

14. Nedellec, C., and Rouveirol, C., 1993: Biases for Incremental Hypothesis-Driven Systems. In the AAAI Spring Symposium on Training Issues in Incremental Learning, Standford University.

15. Nedellec, C., and Rouveirol, C., 1994: Specifications of the HAIKU System. In technical report, LRI, Number 928.

16. Ourston, D., and Mooney, R.J., 1990: Changing the Rules: A Comprehensive Approach to Theory Refinement. In Proceedings of National Conference on Artificial Intelligence, pp. 815–820.

17. Quinlan, J. R., and Cameron-Jones, R. M., 1993: FOIL: a Midterm Report. In Pavel B. Brazdil, editor, Machine Learning: ECML-93. Vienna, Austria. Springer Verlag.

18. De Raedt, L., 1992: Interactive Theory Revision, an Inductive Logic Programming Approach. In Academic Press Limited.

19. De Raedt, L., and Bruynooghe, M., 1993: A Theory of Clausal Discovery. In Proceedings of the 13th. IJCAI, Morgan Kaufmann.

20. Rouveirol, C., 1992: Extensions of Inversion of Resolution Applied and Theory Completion. In Muggleton, S., editor, Inductive Logic Programming, pp. 64–92, Academic Press.

21. Sammut, C., and Banerji, R.B., 1986: Learning Concepts by Asking Questions. In Michalski, R., Carbonnel, J., and Mitchell, T., editors, Machine Learning: An Artificial Intelligence Approach, Volume 2, Kaufmann, Los Altos, CA, pp. 167–192.

22. Shapiro, E.Y., 1983: Algorithmic Program Debugging. MIT Press.

23. Wrobel, S., 1993: On the Proper Definition of Minimality in Specialisation and Theory Revision. In Pavel B. Brazdil editor, Proceedings of the European Conference on Machine Learning, pp. 65–82, Springer-Verlag, Vienna.

# Learning from Positive Data

Stephen Muggleton

Oxford University Computing Laboratory,
Parks Road,
Oxford, OX1 3QD,
United Kingdom.

**Abstract.** Gold showed in 1967 that not even regular grammars can be exactly identified from positive examples alone. Since it is known that children learn natural grammars almost exclusively from positives examples, Gold's result has been used as a theoretical support for Chomsky's theory of innate human linguistic abilities. In this paper new results are presented which show that within a Bayesian framework not only grammars, but also logic programs are learnable with arbitrarily low expected error from positive examples only. In addition, we show that the upper bound for expected error of a learner which maximises the Bayes' posterior probability when learning from positive examples is within a small additive term of one which does the same from a mixture of positive and negative examples. An Inductive Logic Programming implementation is described which avoids the pitfalls of greedy search by global optimisation of this function during the local construction of individual clauses of the hypothesis. Results of testing this implementation on artificially-generated data-sets are reported. These results are in agreement with the theoretical predictions.

## 1 Introduction

Gold's [5] seminal paper not only formed the foundations of learnability theory but also provided an important negative result for the learnability of grammars. It was shown that not even the class of all regular languages could be *identified in the limit* from an arbitrary finite sequence of positive examples of the target language. In the same paper Gold pointed out the implications for theories of language acquisition in children. He notes that psycholinguistic studies by McNeill and others had shown that

> ... children are rarely informed when they make grammatical errors and those that are informed take little heed.

Gold's negative results have been taken by [14] as theoretical support for Chomsky's theory [4] of innate human linguistic abilities.

In this paper Gold's requirements for exact identification of a language are replaced by a need to converge with arbitrarily low error. In a previous paper [10] the author derived a function for learning logic programs from positive examples only. In the present paper the Bayes' function for maximising posterior probability is derived. The solution is representation independent, and therefore equally applicable to grammar learning, scientific theory formation or even automatic programming. The expected error of an algorithm which maximises this function over a high prior probability segment of the hypothesis space is analysed and shown to be within a small additive term of that obtained from a mixture of positive and negative examples.

An implementation of this approach within the Inductive Logic Programming (ILP) system Progol4.2 is described. A novel aspect of this implementation is the use of global optimisation during local construction of individual clauses of the hypothesis. The technique avoids the local optimisation pitfalls of cover-set algorithms. Experiments on three separate domains (animal taxonomy, KRK-illegal and grammar learning) are shown to be in accordance with the theoretical predictions.

This paper is organised as follows. In Section 2 a Bayes' framework is described which is compatible with the U-learnability framework [9, 13]. The Bayes' function for the posterior probability of hypotheses given positive examples only is derived in Section 3. The expected error of an algorithm which maximises the Bayes' function over a high prior probability segment of the hypothesis space is given in Section 4. In Section 5 the ILP system Progol4.2, which implements this function is described. An experiment is presented in Section 6, in which Progol4.2 is tested on varying amounts of randomly generated data for three target concepts. The results of these experiments are discussed in Section 7. The paper is concluded in Section 8 by a comparison to related work and a discussion of directions for future research.

## 2 Bayes' positive example framework

The following is a simplified version of the U-learnability framework presented in [9, 13]. $X$ is taken to be a countable class of instances and $\mathcal{H} \subseteq 2^X$ to be a countable class of concepts. $D_X$ and $D_H$ are probability distributions over $X$ and $\mathcal{H}$ respectively. For $H \in \mathcal{H}$, $D_X(H) = \sum_{x \in H} D_X(x)$ and the conditional distribution of $D_X$ associated with $H$ is as follows.

$$D_{X|H}(x) = D_X(x|H) = \frac{D_X(x \cap H)}{D_X(H)} = \begin{cases} 0 & \text{if } x \notin H \\ \frac{D_X(x)}{D_X(H)} & \text{otherwise} \end{cases}$$

The teacher randomly chooses a target theory $T$ from $D_H$ and randomly and independently chooses a series of examples $E = \langle x_1, .., x_m \rangle$ from $T$ according to $D_{X|T}$. Given $E$, $D_H$ and $D_X$ a learner $L$ chooses an hypothesis $H \in \mathcal{H}$ for which all elements of $E$ are in $H$. The teacher then assesses Error($H$) as $D_X(H \setminus T) + D_X(T \setminus H)$.

Unlike the setting in U-learnability it is assumed in the present paper that $L$ is given $D_H$ and $D_X$.

## 3  Bayes' posterior estimation

Gold's negative result for identification of the regular languages over the symbol set $\Sigma$ is based on the fact that for any sequence of positive examples $E$ there will always be at least two possible candidate hypotheses, 1) $\Sigma^*$, the language containing all possible sentences and 2) the language corresponding to elements of $E$ alone. It is clear that 1) is the most general hypothesis, and has a compact finite automaton description, while 2) is the least general hypothesis and has a complex finite state automaton description. Since neither of these two extremes seems attractive it would seem desirable to find a compromise between the size of the hypothesis description and the generality of the hypothesis. Size and generality of an hypothesis can be defined within the Bayes' framework of the previous section as follows.

$$sz(H) = -\ln D_H(H)$$
$$g(H) = D_X(H)$$

Bayes' theorem allows us to derive a tradeoff between $sz(H)$ and $g(H)$. In its familiar form, Bayes' theorem is as follows.

$$p(H|E) = \frac{p(H)p(E|H)}{p(E)}$$

With respect to the Bayes' framework of the previous section $p(H|E)$ is interpreted from the learner's perspective as the probability that $H = T$ given the example sequence is $E$. Similarly, $p(H)$ is defined as the probability that $H = T$, which is

$$p(H) = D_H(H).$$

Meanwhile $p(E|H)$ is the probability that the example sequence is $E$ given that $H = T$. Since examples are chosen randomly and independently from $D_{X|H}$ then for any consistent hypothesis this is as follows.

$$p(E|H) = \prod_{i=1}^{m} D_{X|H}(x_i)$$
$$= \prod_{i=1}^{m} \frac{D_X(x_i)}{D_X(H)}$$

The prior $p(E)$ is the probability that the example sequence is $E$ irrespective of $T$. This is as follows.

$$p(E) = \sum_{T \in \mathcal{H}} D_H(T) \prod_{j=1}^{m} D_{X|T}(x_j)$$

The Bayes' equation can now be rewritten as follows.

$$p(H|E) = \frac{D_H(H) \prod_{i=1}^{m} \frac{D_X(x_i)}{D_X(H)}}{p(E)}$$

Since $\frac{\prod_{i=1}^{m} D_X(x_i)}{p(E)}$ is common to all consistent hypotheses, it will be treated as a normalising constant $c_m$ in the following.

$$p(H|E) = D_H(H) \left(\frac{1}{D_X(H)}\right)^m c_m$$

$$\ln p(H|E) = m \ln \left(\frac{1}{g(H)}\right) - sz(H) + d_m$$

In the above $d_m = \ln c_m$. The tradeoff between size and generality of an hypothesis can be seen in the final equation above. The function $\ln p(H|E)$ decreases with increases in $sz(H)$ and $g(H)$. Additionally, as $m$ grows, the requirements on generality of an hypothesis become stricter. A function with similar properties was defined in [10] and it was shown there that for every hypothesis $H$ except $T$ there is a value of $m$ such that for all $m' > m$ it is the case that $f_{m'}(H) < f_m(T)$. This result indicates a form of convergence, somewhat different from Gold's identification in the limit.

## 4 Analysis of expected error

In [7] Haussler et al. argue the advantages of analysing expected error over VC dimension analysis. Analysis of expected error is the approach taken below.

It is assumed that class membership of instances is decidable for all hypotheses. Also the hypotheses in $\mathcal{H}$ are assumed to be ordered according to decreasing prior probability as $H_1, H_2, \ldots$. For the purposes of analysis the distribution $D_H(H_i) = \frac{a}{i^2}$ is assumed, where $a$ is a normalising constant. This is similar to the prior distribution assumptions used in Progol4.1 [10] and is a smoothed version of a distribution which assigns equal probability to the $2^b$ hypotheses describable in $b$ bits, where the sum of the probabilities of such hypotheses is $2^{-b}$. Within this distribution $i$ has infinite mean and variance. It is also assumed that the hypothesis space contains only targets $T$ for which $D_X(T) \leq \frac{1}{2}$. This assumption, which holds for most target concepts used in Inductive Logic Programming, is not a particularly strong restriction on the hypothesis space since if $\overline{T}$ is the complement of $T$ and $D_X(T) > \frac{1}{2}$ then clearly $D_X(\overline{T}) \leq \frac{1}{2}$.

The following theorem gives an upper bound on the expected error of an algorithm which learns from positive examples only by maximising the Bayes' posterior probability function over the initial $am$ hypotheses within the space.

**Theorem 1. Expected error for positive examples only.** *Let $X$ be a countable instance space and $D_X$ be a probability distribution over $X$. Let $\mathcal{H} \subseteq 2^X$ be a countable hypothesis space containing at least all finite subsets of $X$, and for which all $H \in \mathcal{H}$ have $D_X(H) \leq \frac{1}{2}$. Let $D_H$ be a probability distribution over $\mathcal{H}$. Assume that $\mathcal{H}$ has an ordering $H_1, H_2, \ldots$ such that $D_H(H_i) \geq D_H(H_j)$ for all $j > i$. Let $D_H(H_i) = \frac{a}{i^2}$ where $\frac{1}{a} = \sum_{i=1}^{\infty} \frac{1}{i^2} \approx \frac{1}{0.608}$. Let $\mathcal{H}_n = \{H_i : H_i \in \mathcal{H} \text{ and } i \leq n\}$. Let $f(H) = D_H(H)(\frac{1}{D_X(H)})^m$. $T$ is chosen randomly*

*from $D_H$ and the $x_i$ in $E = \langle x_1, .., x_m \rangle$ are chosen randomly and independently from $D_{X|T}$. $L$ is the following learning algorithm. If there are no hypotheses $H \in \mathcal{H}_n$ such that $H \supseteq H_E = \{x_1, .., x_m\}$ then $L(E) = H_E$. Otherwise $L(E) = H_n(E) = H$ only if $H \in \mathcal{H}_n$, $H \supseteq H_E$ and for all $H' \in \mathcal{H}_n$ for which $H' \supseteq H_E$ it is the case that $f(H) \geq f(H')$. The error of an hypothesis $H$ is defined as $Error(H, T) = D_X(T \setminus H) + D_X(H \setminus T)$. For $n = am$ the expected error of $L$ after $m$ examples, $EE(m)$, is at most $\frac{2.33 + 2\ln m}{m}$.*
**Proof.** *Given in Appendix A.* □

Note that this result is independent of the choice of $D_X$ and that $L$ considers only $O(m)$ hypotheses to achieve an expected error of $O(\frac{\ln m}{m})$. For comparison a similar algorithm which learns from a mixture of positive and negative examples is analysed for the same choice of $D_H$.

**Theorem 2. Expected error for positive and negative examples.** *Let $X$ be a countable instance space and $\mathcal{H} \subseteq 2^X$ be a countable hypothesis space containing at least all finite subsets of $X$. Let $D_H$, $D_X$ be probability distributions over $\mathcal{H}$ and $X$. Assume that $\mathcal{H}$ has an ordering $H_1, H_2, \ldots$ such that $D_H(H_i) \geq D_H(H_j)$ for all $j > i$. Let $D_H(H_i) = \frac{a}{i^2}$ where $\frac{1}{a} = \sum_{i=1}^{\infty} \frac{1}{i^2}$. Let $\mathcal{H}_n = \{H_i : H_i \in \mathcal{H}$ and $i \leq n\}$. Let $f(H) = D_H(H)$. $T$ is chosen randomly from $D_H$. Let $ex(x, H) = \langle x, v \rangle$ where $v = True$ if $x \in H$ and $v = False$ otherwise. Let $E = \langle ex(x_1, T), .., ex(x_m, T) \rangle$ where each $x_i$ is chosen randomly and independently from $D_X$. $H_E = \{x : \langle x, True \rangle$ in $E\}$. Hypothesis $H$ is said to be consistent with $E$ if and only if $x_i \in H$ for each $\langle x_i, True \rangle$ in $E$ and $x_j \notin H$ for each $\langle x_j, False \rangle$ in $E$. $L$ is the following learning algorithm. If there are no hypotheses $H \in \mathcal{H}_n$ consistent with $E$ then $L(E) = H_E$. Otherwise $L(E) = H_n(E) = H$ only if $H \in \mathcal{H}_n$, $H$ consistent with $E$ and for all $H' \in \mathcal{H}_n$ consistent with $E$ it is the case that $f(H) \geq f(H')$. The error of an hypothesis $H$ is defined as $Error(H, T) = D_X(T \setminus H) + D_X(H \setminus T)$. For $n = am$ the expected error of $L$ after $m$ examples, $EE(m)$, is at most $\frac{1.51 + 2\ln m}{m}$.*
**Proof.** *Given in Appendix A.* □

Note that this is within a small additive term of the bound for learning from positive examples only. Again the result is independent of the choice of $D_X$ and again $L$ considers only $O(m)$ hypotheses to achieve an expected error of $O(\frac{\ln m}{m})$.

## 5 Implementation

The Bayes' function $f_m$ has been implemented to guide the search of the ILP system Progol [10] when learning from positive examples only. The new version, Progol4.2, is available by anonymous ftp from ftp.comlab.ox.ac.uk in directory pub/Packages/ILP/progol4.2. The earlier version, Progol4.1, uses a cover-set algorithm to construct the set of clauses, but for each clause does a pruned admissible search to maximise compression. Progol4.2 has a similar overall search algorithm, but when constructing each clause carries out an admissible search which optimises a global estimate of $f_m$ for the complete theory containing the clause under construction. The basis for this global estimate is as follows. Suppose a clause $C_i$ has been constructed as the $i$th clause of an overall theory (set of clauses) $H_n = \{C_1, .., C_n\}$. It is found that $H_i = C_1, .., C_i$ implies $p$ more of the $m$ positive examples than $H_{i-1}$. Figure 1 shows this situation with respect

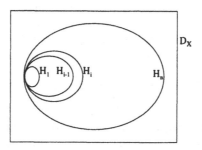

**Fig. 1.** Generality of partial theories

to the sample distribution $D_X$. According to the Law of Large Numbers when $m$ is large

$$\frac{g(H_i) - g(H_{i-1})}{g(H_n)} \approx \frac{p}{m}$$

and therefore

$$g(H_n) \approx \frac{m}{p}(g(H_i) - g(H_{i-1})).$$

The surprising conclusion is that for large $m$ it is possible to estimate the generality of $H_n$ from $p$, $m$, $g(H_i)$ and $g(H_{i-1})$.

By assuming that the size of an hypothesis can be measured in bits for any hypothesis and that the number of examples covered per bit of an hypothesis is approximately uniform the following should also hold.

$$sz(H_n) \approx \frac{m}{p} \; sz(C_i)$$

In Progol4.2 the value of $sz(C_i)$ is measured crudely as the number of atoms in the clause.

Since it is possible to estimate both $sz(H_n)$ and $g(H_n)$ during the local construction of each individual clause, it is possible to maximise an estimate of $f_m(H_n)$ during the construction of each of the clauses. The polynomial time-complexity bounds on the search carried out by Progol4.1 [10] are unaltered for Progol4.2.

## 5.1 Estimation of $g(H_i)$

The function $g(H_i)$ in the above is estimated in Progol4.2 using Stochastic Logic Programs (SLPs) [11]. An SLP is a range-restricted logic program $P$ with numeric labels associated with each of the clauses. An SLP can be used to randomly derive elements of the Herbrand Base of $P$ using SLD derivation with a stochastic selection rule. In order to estimate $g(H_i)$ an SLP, representing $D_X$, is used to randomly generate a sample of size $s$ from the domain of the predicate $p/n$ being learned. If $s'$ of these instances are entailed by $p/n$ then the Laplace corrected estimate of $g(H_i)$ is $\frac{s'+1}{s+2}$.

In order to construct the SLP for the domain of $p/n$, Progol4.2 uses the *modeh* declaration of $p/n$ (see [10]). For instance, suppose in a chess domain the mode declaration is modeh(1,move(+piece,pos(+file,+rank),pos(+file,+rank))). Then Progol4.2 will construct the following generating clause for the domain.

'*move'(A,pos(B,C),pos(D,E)) :- piece(A), file(B), rank(C),
file(D), rank(E).

The clauses of the SLP consist of the above clause and the definitions of *piece/1*, *file/1* and *rank/1*. The labels for the SLP are built up by recording the total number of times each clause is visited in the derivations of the positive examples of *move/3*. In this way it is possible to estimate the distribution $D_X$ from the examples themselves. For instance, in the example set we might find that half the examples involve the queen, a quarter involve rooks and the other quarter involve bishops. When randomly generating examples from the conditioned SLP these proportions are maintained.

## 6 Experiment

### 6.1 Experimental hypotheses

The experiments described in this section will test the following two hypotheses.

1. **Upper bound.** In every domain $EE(m) \leq \frac{2.33+2\ln m}{m}$.
2. **Positive versus positive and negative data.** In every domain error is of a similar order when learning from positives examples only compared to learning from a mixture of positive and negative examples.

### 6.2 Materials

The experimental hypotheses will be tested using Progol4.2 on the following target theories.

**Animal taxonomy.** Figure 2 shows the target and form of examples for the animal taxonomy domain.

**KRK illegality.** Figure 3 shows the target and form of examples for the KRK illegality domain (originally described in [12]).

**Natural language grammar.** Figure 4 shows the target and form of examples for the natural language grammar domain.

Examples sets and background knowledge for the domains above are available from the ftp site described in Section 5.

**Examples.**

class(dog,mammal). class(dolphin,mammal).
class(trout,fish).    class(eel,fish).
class(lizard,reptile). class(snake,reptile).
class(eagle,bird).    class(penguin,bird).

**Target.**

class(A,mammal) :- has_milk(A).
class(A,fish) :- has_gills(A).
class(A,bird) :- has_covering(A,feathers).
class(A,reptile) :- has_covering(A,scales),
                    not has_gills(A).

**Fig. 2.** Animal taxonomy

**Examples.**

illegal(3,5,6,7,6,2). illegal(3,6,7,6,7,4).
illegal(5,1,2,1,2,1). illegal(4,3,1,1,4,2).

**Target.**

illegal(A,B,A,B,_,_).
illegal(_,_,A,B,A,B).
illegal(A,B,_,_,C,D) :- adj(A,C), adj(B,D).
illegal(A,_,B,_,B,_) :- not A=B.
illegal(_,A,_,B,_,B) :- not A=B.
illegal(_,A,B,C,B,D) :- A<C, A<D.
illegal(_,A,B,C,B,D) :- A>C, A>D.
illegal(A,_,B,C,D,C) :- A<B, A<D.
illegal(A,_,B,C,D,C) :- A>B, A>D.

**Fig. 3.** KRK illegality

**Examples.**

s([every, nice, dog, barks], []).
s([the,man,hits,the,ball,at,the,house],[]).
s([the,dog,walks,to,the,man],[]).

**Target.**

s(A,B) :- np(A,C), iverb(C,B).
s(A,B) :- np(A,C), vp(C,D), np(D,B).
s(A,B) :- np(A,C), tverb(C,D), np(D,E),
        prep(E,F), np(F,B).

**Fig. 4.** Natural language grammar

## 6.3 Method

For the first two domains instances were generated randomly using the appropriate SLP (see Section 5.1) with uniform values of labels on all clauses. In the grammar domain it was found that only around 4 in 10,000 randomly generated sentences were positive examples of the target grammar $T$. Thus the distribution $D_X$ was skewed so that $D_X(T) = D_X(\overline{T}) = 0.5$. In all domains instances were classified according to the target theory in order to construct training and test sets. In the case of learning from positive examples only, training sets had all negative examples removed.

For each domain Progol4.2 was tested on 1) learning from positive examples only and 2) learning from a mixture of positive and negative examples. In both cases $m$ was varied according to the series $m = 5, 10, 20, 40, 80, 160, 320, 640, 1280$. For each size of sample the predictive accuracy of the hypothesis returned by Progol4.2 was estimated on a test set of size 10,000. For each $m$ the estimate of predictive accuracy was averaged over 10 repeat resamplings of the same sized training set. The series was discontinued for a particular domain if the estimate error was 0 for several successive values of $m$.

## 7 Results

### 7.1 Predictive accuracy versus bound

The results of testing the first experimental hypothesis (expected error upper bound) are graphed in Figures 5, 6 and 7. Labels on these graphs have the following meanings.

**P.** The predictive accuracy of learning from positive examples only is shown as the mean and standard deviation (error bars) of the 10 retrials for each value of $m$.

**L(P).** The theoretical lower bound on positive examples only accuracy from Theorem 1 (Accuracy= $100(1 - EE(m))$).

**M.** Majority class for domain $(100D_X(T))$.

Since each data point in each of the three domains lies above the bound, the first experimental hypothesis of Section 6 is confirmed [1].

### 7.2 Positive versus positive and negative

The results of testing the second experimental hypothesis (similar expected error for positive versus positive and negative) are graphed in Figures 8, 9 and 10. Labels on these graphs have the following meanings.

---

[1] The non-monotonic behaviour of **P** in Figure 5 was found to be caused by large fluctuations in errors of commission. This is due to the gradual allowance of larger theories by the Bayes' function as $m$ grows, together with the fact that generality does not vary monotonically with increasing size of a clausal theory.

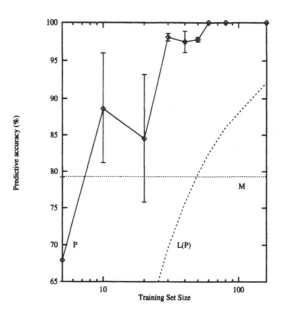

**Fig. 5.** Predictive accuracy versus bound for animal taxonomy

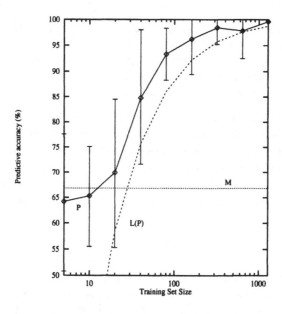

**Fig. 6.** Predictive accuracy versus bound for KRK illegal

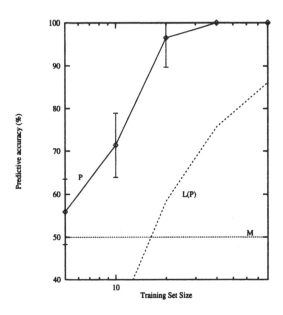

**Fig. 7.** Predictive accuracy versus bound for natural language grammar

**P.** The predictive accuracy of learning from positive examples only, shown as the mean of the 10 retrials for each value of $m$.

**P+N.** The predictive accuracy of learning from a mixture of positive and negative examples, shown as the mean of the 10 retrials for each value of $m$.

**L(P+N).** The theoretical lower bound on positive examples only accuracy from Theorem 2 (Accuracy= $100(1 - EE(m))$).

**M.** Majority class for domain $(100D_X(T))$.

In the taxonomy and grammar domains (Figures 8 and 10) learning from positive examples only requires consistently fewer examples for any given $\epsilon$ than learning from a mixture of positive and negative examples. In the KRK-illegality domain the converse is true. In every domain accuracy for all values of $m$ is comparable when learning from positive examples compared to learning from a mixture of positive and negative examples. This confirms the experimental hypothesis.

## 8  Conclusion

In 1967 Gold demonstrated negative results for learnability in the limit of various classes of formal languages. This has provided a strong impetus for the investigation of constrained hypothesis languages, within which learning from positive examples is possible. For instance, Plotkin [15] demonstrated the existence of unique least general generalisations of positive examples represented as first-order clauses. Biermann and Feldman [2] and later Angluin [1] demonstrated

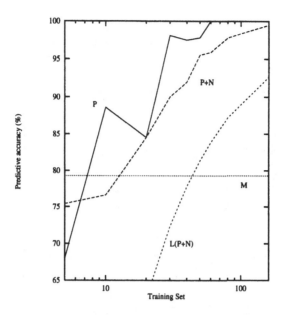

**Fig. 8.** Positives versus positives and negatives for animal taxonomy

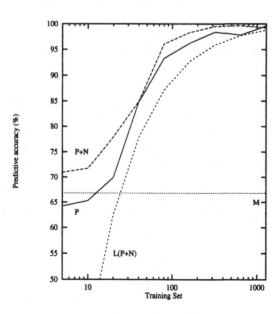

**Fig. 9.** Positives versus positives and negatives for KRK illegal

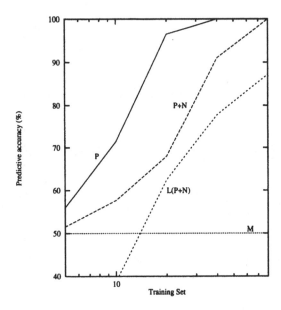

**Fig. 10.** Positives versus positives and negatives for natural language grammar

that certain parameterised subsets of the regular languages could be identified in the limit from positive examples only. Within the framework of PAC-learning Valiant demonstrated [19] that k-CNF propositional logic formulae are learnable from positive examples. More recently Shinohara [18] demonstrated that certain size-bounded classes of elementary formal systems are identifiable in the limit from positive examples.

Unlike the approaches above, the techniques used in this paper for learning from positive examples are representation independent. That is to say, the representation of hypotheses does not play a part either in the development of the Bayes' function (Section 3) or the analysis of expected error (Section 4). It might legitimately be claimed that two strong assumptions are made in Section 2: 1) that the learner knows $D_H$ and 2) that the learner can estimate $D_X$ by conditioning a Stochastic Logic Program. The second assumption seems less pernicious since it only requires a logic program which defines the Herbrand base. The first assumption is more worrying. Further research is required to analyse the effect of discrepancy between the learner's prior $p(H)$ and the teacher's distribution $D_H$.

Various researchers including [3, 6] have advocated and demonstrated the use of Bayesian analysis in machine learning. The success of the Bayesian solution to learning from positive examples reinforces this trend.

Several techniques [16, 17, 8] for learning from positive examples only have been investigated within Inductive Logic Programming. However, all these approaches differ from this paper in assuming some form of completeness within the example set.

In the light of the results in this paper it would seem worth reconsidering the degree of support that Gold's learnability results provide for Chomskian linguistics. Clearly, Chomsky's theory of innate linguistic ability is consistent with the results in this paper. However, the results in this paper show that weaker assumptions concerning the innate properties of natural language can be made than those suggested by Gold's results.

## Acknowledgements

The author would like to thank David Haussler for influential discussions on the topic of learning from positive examples. The author's investigations with David Haussler of PAC upper-bound results for learning from positive examples will be reported elsewhere. Many thanks are due to my wife, Thirza Castello-Cortes, who has shown me great support during the writing of this paper. The author is grateful to Nick Chater of the Experimental Psychology Department in Oxford for pointing out the relevant literature on language learning in children. Thanks also for useful discussions on the topics in this paper with Donald Michie, John McCarthy, Tony Hoare, David Page, Ashwin Srinivasan and James Cussens. This work was supported partly by the Esprit Long Term Research Action ILP II (project 20237), EPSRC grant GR/J46623 on Experimental Application and Development of ILP, EPSRC grant GR/K57985 on Experiments with Distribution-based Machine Learning and an EPSRC Advanced Research Fellowship held by the author. The author is also a Research Fellow at Wolfson College Oxford.

## References

1. D. Angluin. Inference of reversible languages. *Journal of the ACM*, 29:741–765, 1982.
2. A.W. Biermann and J.A. Feldman. On the synthesis of finite-state machines from samples of their behaviour. *IEEE Transactions on Computers*, C(21):592–597, 1972.
3. W. Buntine. *A Theory of Learning Classification Rules*. PhD thesis, School of Computing Science, University of Technology, Sydney, 1990.
4. N. Chomsky. *Knowledge of language: its nature, origin and use*. Praeger, New York, 1986. First published 1965.
5. E.M. Gold. Language identification in the limit. *Information and Control*, 10:447–474, 1967.
6. D. Haussler, M Kearns, and R. Shapire. Bounds on the sample complexity of Bayesian learning using information theory and the VC dimension. In *COLT-91: Proceedings of the 4th Annual Workshop on Computational Learning Theory*, pages 61–74, San Mateo, CA, 1991. Morgan Kauffmann.
7. D. Haussler, M Kearns, and R. Shapire. Bounds on the sample complexity of Bayesian learning using information theory and the VC dimension. *Machine Learning Journal*, 14(1):83–113, 1994.

8. R.J. Mooney and M.E. Califf. Induction of first-order decision lists: Results on learning the past tense of english verbs. *Journal of Artificial Intelligence Research*, 3:1–24, 1995.

9. S. Muggleton. Bayesian inductive logic programming. In M. Warmuth, editor, *Proceedings of the Seventh Annual ACM Conference on Computational Learning Theory*, pages 3–11, New York, 1994. ACM Press.

10. S. Muggleton. Inverse entailment and Progol. *New Generation Computing*, 13:245–286, 1995.

11. S. Muggleton. Stochastic logic programs. In L. De Raedt, editor, *Advances in Inductive Logic Programming*. IOS Press/Ohmsha, 1996.

12. S. Muggleton, M.E. Bain, J. Hayes-Michie, and D. Michie. An experimental comparison of human and machine learning formalisms. In *Proceedings of the Sixth International Workshop on Machine Learning*, Los Altos, CA, 1989. Kaufmann.

13. S. Muggleton and C.D. Page. A learnability model for universal representations. Technical Report PRG-TR-3-94, Oxford University Computing Laboratory, Oxford, 1994.

14. S. Pinker. *Language learnability and language development*. Harvard University Press, Cambridge, Mass., 1984.

15. G.D. Plotkin. A note on inductive generalisation. In B. Meltzer and D. Michie, editors, *Machine Intelligence 5*, pages 153–163. Edinburgh University Press, Edinburgh, 1969.

16. J.R. Quinlan and R.M. Cameron. Induction of logic programs: FOIL and related systems. *New Generation Computing*, 13:287–312, 1995.

17. L. De Raedt and M. Bruynooghe. A theory of clausal discovery. In *Proceedings of the 13th International Joint Conference on Artificial Intelligence*. Morgan Kaufmann, 1993.

18. T. Shinohara. Inductive inference of monotonic formal systems from positive data. In *Proceedings of the first international workshop on algorithmic learning theory*, Tokyo, 1990. Ohmsha.

19. L.G. Valiant. A theory of the learnable. *Communications of the ACM*, 27:1134–1142, 1984.

# A   Proof of Theorems 1 and 2

**Theorem 1. Expected error for positive examples only.** *Let $X$ be a countable instance space and $D_X$ be a probability distribution over $X$. Let $\mathcal{H} \subseteq 2^X$ be a countable hypothesis space containing at least all finite subsets of $X$, and for which all $H \in \mathcal{H}$ have $D_X(H) \leq \frac{1}{2}$. Let $D_H$ be a probability distribution over $\mathcal{H}$. Assume that $\mathcal{H}$ has an ordering $H_1, H_2, \ldots$ such that $D_H(H_i) \geq D_H(H_j)$ for all $j > i$. Let $D_H(H_i) = \frac{a}{i^2}$ where $\frac{1}{a} = \sum_{i=1}^{\infty} \frac{1}{i^2} \approx \frac{1}{0.608}$. Let $\mathcal{H}_n = \{H_i : H_i \in \mathcal{H} \text{ and } i \leq n\}$. Let $f(H) = D_H(H)(\frac{1}{D_X(H)})^m$. $T$ is chosen randomly from $D_H$ and the $x_i$ in $E = \langle x_1, \ldots, x_m \rangle$ are chosen randomly and independently from $D_{X|T}$. $L$ is the following learning algorithm. If there are no hypotheses $H \in \mathcal{H}_n$ such that $H \supseteq H_E = \{x_1, \ldots, x_m\}$ then $L(E) = H_E$. Otherwise $L(E) = H_n(E) = H$ only if $H \in \mathcal{H}_n$, $H \supseteq H_E$ and for all $H' \in \mathcal{H}_n$ for which $H' \supseteq H_E$ it is the case that $f(H) \geq f(H')$. The error of an hypothesis $H$ is defined as $Error(H, T) = D_X(T \setminus H) + D_X(H \setminus T)$. For $n = am$ the expected* *error of L after m examples, EE(m), is at most* $\frac{2.33 + 2\ln m}{m}$.

**Proof.** *Consider the case in which* $T \in \mathcal{H}_n$ *(case 1). Then by definition* $L(E) = H_n(E) = H$. *Since* $H = H_n(E)$ *has the maximum value of* $f$ *in* $\mathcal{H}_n$ *it follows that*

$$D_H(H) \left( \frac{1}{D_X(H)} \right)^m \geq D_H(T) \left( \frac{1}{D_X(T)} \right)^m. \tag{1}$$

*Also* $D_X(T \cap H) = D_X(T) - D_X(T \setminus H) = D_X(H) - D_X(H \setminus T)$ *and therefore*

$$D_X(H) - D_X(T) = D_X(H \setminus T) - D_X(T \setminus H). \tag{2}$$

*Furthermore consider the case in which* $D_X(H) > D_X(T)$ *(case 1a). Rearranging (1) and taking logs we get*

$$m(\ln D_X(H) - \ln D_X(T)) \leq \ln D_H(H) - \ln D_H(T). \tag{3}$$

*Since* $D_X(H) > D_X(T)$ *let* $D_X(H) = D_X(T) + \Delta$ *where* $0 < \Delta \leq 1$. *Also let* $r(D_X(T), \Delta) = \frac{\ln (D_X(T) + \Delta) - \ln D_X(T)}{\Delta} = \frac{\ln D_X(H) - \ln D_X(T)}{D_X(H) - D_X(T)}$. *We now show that for* $0 \leq D_X(T) < D_X(H) \leq \frac{1}{2}$ *it is the case that* $r(D_X(T), \Delta) \geq 2$. *First note that* $r(D_X(T), \Delta)$ *decreases monotonically in* $D_X(T)$ *since* $\frac{\partial}{\partial D_X(T)} r(D_X(T), \Delta) = \frac{1}{\Delta^2}(\ln \frac{D_X(H)}{D_X(T)} - \frac{D_X(H)}{D_X(T)} + 1) < 0$ *for* $\Delta > 0$. *But within the given ranges* $\Delta$ *approaches 0 as* $D_X(T)$ *approaches* $\frac{1}{2}$ *and therefore* $\lim_{D_X(T) \to \frac{1}{2}} r(D_X(T), \Delta) = \frac{\partial}{\partial D_X(T)} \ln D_X(T) = \frac{1}{D_X(T)} = 2$. *Thus* $r(D_X(T), \Delta) > 2$ *for* $0 \leq D_X(T) < D_X(H) \leq \frac{1}{2}$ *from which it follows that* $\ln D_X(H) - \ln D_X(T) > 2(D_X(H) - D_X(T))$. *Combining this with (2) and (3) gives*

$$2m(D_X(H \setminus T) - D_X(T \setminus H)) \leq \ln D_H(H) - \ln D_H(T)$$

*and therefore*

$$D_X(H \setminus T) \leq \frac{-\ln D_H(T)}{2m} + D_X(T \setminus H). \tag{4}$$

*Now consider the case in which* $D_X(H) \leq D_X(T)$ *(case 1b). From (2) it follows that* $D_X(H \setminus T) \leq D_X(T \setminus H)$. *Thus (4) holds in both case 1a and case 1b, and therefore from the definition of Error in the theorem for all of case 1 we get*

$$Error(H(E), T) \leq \frac{-\ln D_H(T)}{2m} + 2D_X(T \setminus H). \tag{5}$$

*Lastly consider the case in which* $T \notin \mathcal{H}_n$ *(case 2). In this case we have the trivial bound*

$$Error(H, T) \leq 1. \tag{6}$$

*We are now in a position to bound* $EE(m)$. *First we define* $T^1 = T$ *and* $T^m = T \times T^{m-1}$. *Now*

$$EE(m) = \sum_{T \in \mathcal{H}} D_H(T) \sum_{E \in T^m} D_X(E|T) Error(L(E), T).$$

*Splitting the sum into case 1 and case 2 and making use of (6) gives the following.*

$$EE(m) \leq \sum_{T \in \mathcal{H}_n} D_H(T) \sum_{E \in T^m} D_X(E|T) Error(H_n(E), T) + \sum_{T \in \mathcal{H} \setminus \mathcal{H}_n} D_H(T).1$$

*But since* $D_H(H_i) = \frac{a}{i^2}$,

$$\sum_{T \in \mathcal{H} \setminus \mathcal{H}_n} D_H(T) = \sum_{i=n+1}^{\infty} \frac{a}{i^2} \leq \int_{i=n}^{\infty} \frac{a}{i^2} = \frac{a}{n}.$$

*This together with (5) gives*

$$EE(m) \leq \frac{a}{n} + \sum_{T \in \mathcal{H}_n} D_H(T) \sum_{E \in T^m} D_X(E|T) \left( \frac{-\ln D_H(T)}{2m} + 2D_X(T \setminus H) \right)$$

$$= \frac{a}{n} - \frac{1}{2m} \sum_{T \in \mathcal{H}_n} D_H(T) \ln D_H(T)$$

$$+ 2 \sum_{T \in \mathcal{H}_n} D_H(T) \sum_{E \in T^m} D_X(E|T) D_X(T \setminus H)$$

*But*

$$-\frac{1}{2} \sum_{T \in \mathcal{H}_n} D_H(T) \ln D_H(T) \leq -\frac{1}{2} \sum_{i=1}^{\infty} \frac{a}{i^2} \ln \left( \frac{a}{i^2} \right) < 0.82.$$

*Letting* $\tau_{mn}(\epsilon) = \{E : E \in T^m \text{ and } D_X(T \setminus H_n(E)) \leq \epsilon D_X(T)\}$ *and remembering that* $D_X(T \setminus H) \leq D_X(T) \leq \frac{1}{2}$ *gives*

$$\sum_{T \in H_n} D_H(T) \sum_{E \in T^m} D_X(E|T) D_X(T \setminus H)$$

$$= \sum_{T \in H_n} D_H(T) \sum_{E \in \tau_{mn}(\epsilon)} D_X(E|T) D_X(T \setminus H)$$

$$+ \sum_{T \in H_n} D_H(T) \sum_{E \in T^m \setminus \tau_{mn}(\epsilon)} D_X(E|T) D_X(T \setminus H)$$

$$\leq \frac{\epsilon}{2} + \sum_{T \in H_n} D_H(T) \sum_{E \in T^m \setminus \tau_{mn}(\epsilon)} D_X(E|T) \frac{1}{2}$$

$$= \frac{\epsilon}{2} + \frac{1}{2} \sum_{T \in H_n} D_H(T) Pr(\text{for random } E, D_X(T \setminus H_n(E)) > \epsilon D_X(T))$$

$$\leq \frac{\epsilon}{2} + \frac{Pr(\exists H \in \mathcal{H}_n . D_X(T \setminus H) > \epsilon D_X(T) \text{ and } x_1, .., x_m \in (T \cap H))}{2}$$

$$\leq \frac{\epsilon + n(1 - \epsilon)^m}{2}$$

$$\leq \frac{\epsilon + ne^{-\epsilon m}}{2}$$

*Thus*

$$EE(m) \leq \frac{a}{n} + \frac{0.82}{m} + \epsilon + ne^{-\epsilon m}$$

*Optimal values of n and ε are found by successively setting to zero the partial derivatives of $n, \epsilon$ and solving. This gives $\epsilon = \frac{\ln nm}{m}$ and $n = am$. Substituting gives*

$$EE(m) \leq \frac{1 + 0.82 + 2\ln m + \ln a + 1}{m}$$
$$< \frac{2.33 + 2\ln m}{m}.$$

□

**Theorem 2. Expected error for positive and negative examples.** *Let X be a countable instance space and $\mathcal{H} \subseteq 2^X$ be a countable hypothesis space containing at least all finite subsets of X. Let $D_H$, $D_X$ be probability distributions over $\mathcal{H}$ and X. Assume that $\mathcal{H}$ has an ordering $H_1, H_2, \ldots$ such that $D_H(H_i) \geq D_H(H_j)$ for all $j > i$. Let $D_H(H_i) = \frac{a}{i^2}$ where $\frac{1}{a} = \sum_{i=1}^{\infty} \frac{1}{i^2}$. Let $\mathcal{H}_n = \{H_i : H_i \in \mathcal{H}$ and $i \leq n\}$. Let $f(H) = D_H(H)$. T is chosen randomly from $D_H$. Let $ex(x, H) = \langle x, v \rangle$ where $v = True$ if $x \in H$ and $v = False$ otherwise. Let $E = \langle ex(x_1, T), .., ex(x_m, T) \rangle$ where each $x_i$ is chosen randomly and independently from $D_X$. $H_E = \{x : \langle x, True \rangle$ in $E\}$. Hypothesis H is said to be consistent with E if and only if $x_i \in H$ for each $\langle x_i, True \rangle$ in E and $x_j \notin H$ for each $\langle x_j, False \rangle$ in E. L is the following learning algorithm. If there are no hypotheses $H \in \mathcal{H}_n$ consistent with E then $L(E) = H_E$. Otherwise $L(E) = H_n(E) = H$ only if $H \in \mathcal{H}_n$, H consistent with E and for all $H' \in \mathcal{H}_n$ consistent with E it is the case that $f(H) \geq f(H')$. The error of an hypothesis H is defined as $Error(H, T) = D_X(T \setminus H) + D_X(H \setminus T)$. For $n = am$ the expected error of L after m examples, EE(m), is at most $\frac{1.51 + 2\ln m}{m}$.*
**Proof.** *Let $T^m = \{\langle ex(x_1, T), .., ex(x_m, T) \rangle : x_i \in T\}$. The expected error can be bounded in a similar way to that used in the proof of Theorem 1.*

$$EE(m) = \sum_{T \in \mathcal{H}} D_H(T) \sum_{E \in T^m} D_X(E|T) Error(L(E), T)$$

$$\leq \sum_{T \in \mathcal{H}_n} D_H(T) \sum_{E \in T^m} D_X(E|T) Error(H_n(E), T) + \sum_{T \in \mathcal{H} \setminus \mathcal{H}_n} D_H(T).1$$

$$\leq \frac{a}{n} + \sum_{T \in \mathcal{H}_n} D_H(T) \sum_{E \in T^m} D_X(E|T) Error(L(E), T)$$

*Letting $\tau_{mn}(\epsilon) = \{E' : E' \in T^m$ and $Error(H_n(E'), T) \leq \epsilon\}$ gives*

$$\sum_{T \in H_n} D_H(T) \sum_{E \in T^m} D_X(E|T) Error(L(E), T)$$

$$= \sum_{T \in H_n} D_H(T) \sum_{E \in \tau_{mn}(\epsilon)} D_X(E|T) Error(L(E), T)$$

$$+ \sum_{T \in H_n} D_H(T) \sum_{E \in T^m \setminus \tau_{mn}(\epsilon)} D_X(E|T) Error(L(E), T)$$

$$\leq \epsilon + Pr(\exists H \in \mathcal{H}_n . Error(H, T) > \epsilon \text{ and } x_1, .., x_m \in (T \cap H))$$

$$\leq \epsilon + n(1 - \epsilon)^m$$

$$\leq \epsilon + n e^{-\epsilon m}$$

*Thus*

$$EE(m) \leq \frac{a}{n} + \epsilon + n e^{-\epsilon m}$$

*Again optimal values of $n$ and $\epsilon$ are found by successively setting to zero the partial derivatives of $n, \epsilon$ and solving. This gives $\epsilon = \frac{\ln nm}{m}$ and $n = am$. Substituting gives*

$$EE(m) \leq \frac{1 + 2 \ln m + \ln a + 1}{m}$$

$$< \frac{1.51 + 2 \ln m}{m}.$$

$\square$

# λ-Subsumption and Its Application to Learning from Positive-only Examples*

Zdravko Markov

Institute for Information Technologies – Bulgarian Academy of Sciences
Acad.G.Bonchev St. Block 29A, 1113 Sofia, Bulgaria
Email: markov@iinf.bg

**Abstract.** The general aim of the present paper is to show the advantages of the model-theoretic approach to Inductive Logic Programming. The paper introduces a new generality ordering between Horn clauses, called λ-subsumption. It is stronger than θ-subsumption and weaker than generalized subsumption. Most importantly λ-subsumption allows to compare clauses in a *local* sense, i.e. with respect to a partial interpretation. This allows to define a non-trivial upper bound in the λ-subsumption lattice without the use of negative examples. An algorithm for concept learning from positive-only examples, based on these ideas, is described and its performance is empirically evaluated in the paper.

## 1 Introduction

Most of the techniques in Inductive Logic Programming (ILP) are based on search in the space of clauses. To make the search process tractable the search space is often structured as a subsumption lattice by some generality ordering. Two types of orderings are mostly used – θ-subsumption and subsumption under implication. The former is preferable, since there exist simple algorithms for computing least general generalizations (lgg) of clauses. However θ-subsumption is weaker than implication and thus it restricts too much the search space. Furthermore, as logical implication is the base of deduction, the use of full scale induction requires the counterpart of logical implication – inverted implication. There are many approaches in this direction, including inverse resolution ([9]), inverse clausal implication ([12]), inverse entailment ([13]). Many of these approaches basically are trying to invert the resolution procedure, as the latter is seen as an efficient technique for deductive inference.

However, as noted in [13], approaching the problems from the direction of model theory rather than resolution proof-theory can clarify and simplify matters. The basic reason for this is that the concept learning problem which is addressed in ILP is inherently connected with ground data (examples) and their interpretation with respect to the background knowledge.

The aim of the present paper is to show that using the model-theoretic approach gives another important advantage. It allows to investigate generality

---

* This work was partially supported by contract I-523/95 with Bulgarian Science Fund.

orderings between clauses in a *local* sense, i.e. with respect to a partial interpretation of the background knowledge.

A new local generality ordering, called $\lambda$-subsumption, is proposed in the paper. It falls between $\theta$-subsumption and generalized subsumption and most importantly it allows the comparison of clauses in a local sense. Consequently, the locality of $\lambda$-subsumption allows to search for clauses, which are correct with respect to a small subset of the set of atoms they generally cover. This allows the building of predicate definitions using positive-only examples.

The paper is organized as follows. The next section introduces the basic notions of $\lambda$-subsumption and its connections with $\theta$-subsumption and logical implication. An approach to learning from positive-only examples based on $\lambda$-subsumption is discussed in Section 3. Sections 4 gives a performance evaluation of the approach using a number of well-known data sets. Sections 5 discusses related work and Section 6 contains concluding remarks.

## 2 $\lambda$-Subsumption

Though some terms from *lambda calculus* are used in this section, the mathematical background is purely first order logic. The ideas and notions discussed in the section are not based on deep results from lambda calculus. Rather, the $\lambda$-terminology is a way to make things clearer and to simplify the notation.

The need of $\lambda$-notation arises when describing the model of a first order expression with respect to a single variable occurring within it. For this purpose we adopt the approach taken in [15].

### 2.1 Basic definitions

**Definition 1 ($\lambda$-model of an expression).** Let $E$ be a closed first order expression and $\lambda$ – a substitution. Denote by $\lambda_x$ the substitution $\lambda$, where the binding $x/t$ is removed, i.e. $\lambda_x = \lambda \backslash \{x/t\}$. Now considering the expression $E\lambda_x$ as a function of $x$ we can use the $\lambda$-notation to represent its semantics. That is, we have the function $f(x) = \lambda x E\lambda_x$, which maps constants (bindings of $x$) onto truth values $\{T, F\}$ w.r.t. some Herbrand interpretation $I$. The set of all constants which map onto $T$ w.r.t. $I$ form the $\lambda$-*calculus model* of $\lambda x E\lambda_x$:

$$\|\lambda x E\lambda_x\| = \{t | \exists \sigma, \lambda x E\lambda_x \sigma(t) = T \ in \ I\}, \tag{1}$$

where $\sigma$ is a substitution grounding $E\lambda$. Actually the expression $\lambda x E\lambda_x \sigma$ is a one-argument predicate. Thus $\|\lambda x E\lambda_x\|$ is a *model* of this predicate in the normal first order sense.

The $\lambda$-calculus model of an expression can be found by using *implicit* or *explicit* interpretations $I$. The implicit interpretation is given by the intended semantics of the predicates in the expression. For example, knowing the meaning of the *member* predicate we can find that:

$$\|\lambda x \ member(x, [a, b, c])\| = \{t | \lambda x \ member(x, [a, b, c])(t) = T\} = \{a, b, c\}$$

The explicit interpretation is given by the extensional definition of the predicates in the $\lambda$-expression. For example, given that $p(a,b), p(b,a), p(c,d), p(d,e)$ are true, we can conclude that:

$$\|\lambda y\ (p(x,y), p(y,x))\| = \{b, a\}$$

There are two special cases of definition 1. The first one is when no grounding substitution $\sigma$, making $E\lambda\sigma$ true in $I$, can be found. Then all $\lambda$-models of $E\lambda$ are empty, i.e. $\|\lambda x E\lambda_x\| = \oslash, \forall x \in E$. The second special case is when there exists a grounding substitution $\sigma$ making $E\lambda\sigma$ true in $I$ (the first special case does not apply) however the $\lambda$-variable does not occur in the expression, i.e. $x \notin E$. Then clearly $\|\lambda x E\lambda_x\| = U_E$, where $U_E$ is the Herbrand universe for the language of $E$.

The intuition behind the notion of $\lambda$-model is to express explicitly the allowable bindings of a variable in an expression with respect to some *partial interpretation* (determined by the substitution $\lambda$). The expression, where the variable occurs, defines the constraints on its bindings. Thus we can compare expressions (and hence clauses) by generality knowing only partially their models. The latter is very important for the open world systems typically used in ML.

**Definition 2 ($\lambda$-subsumption of clauses).** Let $C$ and $D$ be clauses with identical heads ($C_{head} = D_{head}$) and $\lambda$ – a grounding substitution for $C_{head}$ and $D_{head}$. Clause $C$ $\lambda$-subsumes clause $D$, denoted $C \geq_\lambda D$, if for any Herbrand interpretation $I$ such that $C_{head}\lambda$ and $D_{head}\lambda$ are true in $I$:

$$\|\lambda x\ C_{body}\lambda_x\| \supseteq \|\lambda x\ D_{body}\lambda_x\|, \forall x \in C_{head} \tag{2}$$

The substitution $\lambda$ plays an important role in the definition. Clearly the substitution $\sigma$, giving the truth value of the $\lambda$-expression w.r.t. $I$, depends greatly on the choice of $\lambda$. Thus $\lambda$ determines the part of $I$ actually used for comparing $C$ and $D$. This allows to make this comparison without knowing the complete interpretation $I$.

Let us discuss examples of $\lambda$-subsumption of clauses.

*Example 1.* Consider the following two clauses:

$C = \text{member(X,[Y|T])} \ \text{:- member(X,T)}$
$D = \text{member(X,[Y|T])} \ \text{:- T=[Z|V],member(X,V)}$

Let $I$ be the intended interpretation of the **member** predicate (list membership) including also the interpretation of a standard equality theory (needed to define the semantics of the equality atom T=[Z|V]).

Since both clauses are true in $I$, to determine the substitution $\lambda$ we can use an instance of the **member** predicate, for example **member(c,[a,b,c])**. Then $\lambda = \{X/c, Y/a, T/[b,c]\}$. Now we have

$\|\lambda X\ C_{body}\lambda_X\| = \{b, c\}$
$\|\lambda Y\ C_{body}\lambda_Y\| = U_{member}$
$\|\lambda T\ C_{body}\lambda_T\| = \{L|c \in L\}$

$$\|\lambda X\ D_{body}\lambda_X\| = \{c\}$$
$$\|\lambda Y\ D_{body}\lambda_Y\| = U_{member}$$
$$\|\lambda T\ D_{body}\lambda_T\| = \{L|L = [\_|L_1], c \in L_1\},$$

where $U_{member}$ is the Herbrand universe for the language of **member**. Now, comparing the sets of allowable bindings of each of the head variables we see that each of the $\lambda$-models of $D_{body}$ is a subset of the corresponding $\lambda$-model of $C_{body}$. Thus according to condition (2) $C \geq_\lambda D$.

Note that $C$ implies $D$ (easily shown by self-resolution of $C$), but $C$ does not $\theta$-subsume $D$.

*Example 2.* Consider now two clauses with different heads:

$C = $ member(X,[Y|T]) :- member(X,T)
$D = $ member(X,[Y,Z|V]) :- member(X,V)

Since $C_{head} \neq D_{head}$ definition 2 does not apply. In that case we can used a technique which is a special case of flattening ([16]) to transform clause $D$ in a clause $D'$ such that $D'_{head} = C_{head}$. The basic idea of this transformation is to apply flattening, but only to the sub-terms which make $D_{head}$ different from $C_{head}$. That is, we have to flatten only the term [Z|V] by introducing a new variable $T$ and the corresponding flattening predicate $f_p(Z, V, T) :- T = [Z|V]$. Thus we obtain the clause

$D' = $ member(X,[Y|T]) :- member(X,V), f_p(Z,V,T).

This clause along with the definition of the flattening predicate $f_p$ determines the same $\lambda$-models as those of clause $D$ in the previous example. Thus $C \geq_\lambda D'$. Furthermore it is known that flattening does not change the semantics of the clauses. In our case this means that for any atom $A$

$$D \vdash A \text{ iff } D' \wedge (f_p(Z, V, T) :- T = [Z|V]) \wedge ET \vdash flat(A),$$

where $ET$ is a standard equality theory and $flat(A)$ is a partial flattening of $A$ according to the above described idea.

Generally it might be necessary to flatten both clauses $C$ and $D$ to make their heads identical. In the worst case their heads have to be completely flattened to achieve function-free form. A natural way to minimize the flattening steps is to use the $lgg_\theta$ of the clause heads as a pattern for flattening of each of the clauses.

Formally we can define a procedure called $flat(C, D)$ which returns the flattened clause $C$ such that $flat(C, D)_{head} = lgg_\theta(C_{head}, D_{head})$. (Clearly the functor and arity of $C_{head}$ and $D_{head}$ must be the same.) This procedure is a slightly modified version of the standard flattening algorithm defined in [16]. The difference is that the standard algorithm is performed for clause $C$ and *only* for those functions which occur in $C_{head}$ and do not occur in $lgg_\theta(C_{head}, D_{head})$ (to ensure that $flat(C, D)_{head} = lgg_\theta(C_{head}, D_{head})$ proper renaming of the variables might be also necessary). The following properties of $flat(C, D)$ are obvious:

1. $flat(C, D)_{head} = flat(D, C)_{head}$

2. if $C_{head} = D_{head}$ then $flat(C, D) = C$ and $flat(D, C) = D$
3. Let $C \geq_\theta D$, i.e. $\exists \theta$ such that $C\theta \subseteq D$, where $\theta_{head} \subseteq \theta$, $C_{head}\theta_{head} = D_{head}$ and $\theta_{head} = \{v_1/f_1(t_1), ..., v_n/f_n(t_n)\}$. Then $flat(D, C) = C_{head} :- D_{body} \cup \{p_{f_1}(t_1, v_1), ..., p_{f_n}(t_n, v_n)\}$, where $p_{f_i}(t_i, v_i) :- v_i = f_i(t_i)$ for $i = 1, ..., n$ are the definitions of the flattening predicates (generally $t_i$ may be a tuple of terms and $f_i$ may be a constant as well).

The use of above defined flattening technique suggests to extend the scope of $\lambda$-subsumption to clauses with different heads too.

**Definition 3 (generalised $\lambda$-subsumption).** Let $C$ and $D$ be clauses with same predicates at the head (same head functor and arity). $C$ $\lambda$-subsumes $D$ iff $flat(C, D) \geq_\lambda flat(D, C)$ by definition 2.

## 2.2 Relation to other generality orderings

The examples discussed in the previous section suggest that $\lambda$-subsumption is a stronger generality ordering than $\theta$-subsumption and weaker than the subsumption under implication. The following theorems formally show the connection between $\lambda$-subsumption and $\theta$-*subsumption* and between $\lambda$-subsumption and a weaker version of logical implication – *generalized subsumption* ([2]).

**Theorem 4.** *Let $C$ and $D$ be clauses and let $C$ $\theta$-subsume $D$. Then $C \geq_\lambda D$.*

*Proof.* (1) $C_{head} = D_{head}$. In this case $C \geq_\theta D$ means that there exists a substitution $\theta$ such that $D_{body} = (C_{body} \cup D_1)\theta$, where $D_1\theta$ is a part of $D_{body}$. Applying substitutions to an expression or adding conjuncts to it reduces the number of interpretations in which it is true. Thus the model of such an expression is getting smaller. Formally this means that $\|\lambda x C_{body}\lambda_x\| \supseteq \|\lambda x C_{body}\theta\lambda_x\| \supseteq \|\lambda x (C_{body} \cup D_1)\theta\lambda_x\| = \|\lambda x D_{body}\lambda_x\|$ for $\forall x \in C_{head}$ (note that $x$ does not occur in the domain of $\theta$ since $C_{head} = D_{head}$ by the current assumption and $C_{head}\theta = D_{head}$ by the assumption of the theorem), i.e. $C \geq_\lambda D$ by definition 2.

(2) $C_{head} \neq D_{head}$. Let $D' = flat(D, C)$ and $(C \cup D_1)\theta = D$, where $D_1\theta$ is a part of $D_{body}$ and $\theta_{head} \subseteq \theta$, $C_{head}\theta_{head} = D_{head}$, $\theta_{head} = \{v_1/f_1(t_1), ..., v_n/f_n(t_n)\}$. Then, according to property 3 of the $flat(D, C)$ procedure, we obtain $D' = C_{head} :- D_{body} \cup \{p_{f_1}(t_1, v_1), ..., p_{f_n}(t_n, v_n)\}$. Then $D'_{body} = (C_{body} \cup D_1)\theta \cup \{p_{f_1}(t_1, v_1), ..., p_{f_n}(t_n, v_n)\}$. Ignoring the details we have that $D'_{body}$ is obtained from $C_{body}$ by adding conjuncts and applying substitutions. Thus similarly to (1) we can conclude that $C \geq_\lambda D'$ and according to definition 3 $C \geq_\lambda D$. $\square$

Example 1 shows that the converse of Theorem 4 does not hold. Thus we have shown that $\lambda$-subsumption is a *strictly* stronger generality ordering than $\theta$-subsumption.

**Theorem 5.** *Let $C$ and $D$ be clauses. If $C$ $\lambda$-subsumes $D$ for any $\lambda$ then $C \geq_P D$, where "$\geq_P$" means generalised subsumption.*

*Proof.* (1) $C_{head} = D_{head}$. Let $P$ be a program which is true in $I$ and let $A$ be an atom from the Herbrand base of $P$, $C$ and $D$, which is covered by clause $D$. This means that there exists a substitution $\lambda$, such that $D_{head}\lambda = A$ and $\exists \gamma$, $D_{body}\lambda\gamma$ is true in $I$. Let $t \in \|\lambda x \ D_{body}\lambda_x\|$ for some $x \in C_{head}$. Then according to condition (2) of definition 2, $t \in \|\lambda x \ C_{body}\lambda_x\|$. By definition 1 the latter means that $\exists \sigma$ such that $\lambda x \ C_{body}\lambda_x\sigma(t)$ is true in $I$, i.e. $C_{body}\lambda\sigma$ is true in $I$. Thus $C$ covers $A$ and by the definition of generalized subsumption, $C \geq_P D$.

(2) $C_{head} \neq D_{head}$. Let $C' = flat(C, D)$, $D' = flat(D, C)$, $A$ is covered by $D$ and $B = flat(C, D)_{head}$. Using the "if" and the "only-if" parts of Rouveirol's Theorem 4 ([16]) and (1) of the present theorem we have: $flat(D, C)$ covers $flat(A, B)$, $flat(C, D)$ covers $flat(A, B)$ and $C$ covers $A$. That is, $C \geq_P D$. □

Theorem 5 shows that $\lambda$-subsumption is a weaker generality relation than the generalized subsumption. As noted in [2], $C \geq_P D$ means informally that the body of $D$ implies the body of $C$ in the context of $P$. In this terms $\lambda$-subsumption reads "the body of $D$ implies the body of $C$ in the context of $P$ for some partial interpretation, given by the substitution $\lambda$". Thus $\lambda$-subsumption can be viewed as a local instance of generalized subsumption.

## 2.3 $\lambda$-Subsumption test

Though $\lambda$-subsumption is weaker that generalized subsumption and logical implication the $\lambda$-subsumption test is still semi-decidable. As for generalized subsumption this test is decidable if the program contain no recursion or the language is restricted to contain no functions (DATALOG). Practically the condition $C \geq_\lambda D$ can be checked in two ways:

- *Model-based.* This is the case when the interpretation $I$ is known (fully of partially). Then the corresponding $\lambda$-models (sets of bindings) can be explicitly computed and compared for set inclusion (as shown in Example 1). Thus the $\lambda$-subsumption test is straightforward in case of *ground* background knowledge.
- *Resolution proof-based.* If instead of $I$ we are given a logic program $P$ and a deductive system (e.g. Prolog) then the test comes to showing the resolution proof equivalent of condition (2) of definition 2. That is, in the context of $P$ for $\forall x \in C_{head}$ we must have:

$$D_{body}\lambda_x \vdash C_{body}\lambda_x \tag{3}$$

Note that this condition is easier to show than $D_{body} \vdash C_{body}$ (required by generalized subsumption) or $C \vdash D$ (subsumption by implication).

Practically to check the condition $C \geq_\lambda D$ we have to evaluate the goals $C_{body}\lambda_x$ and $D_{body}\lambda_x$ in the presence of program $P$ (asserted in the database) finding all answer substitutions for the variables $x \in C_{head}$. For example the answer "yes" of the following Prolog query indicates that $C \geq_\lambda D$ (care should taken to handle the two special cases of definition 1):

$$? - C_{head} = ..[\_|L],$$
$$not((member(X, L),$$
$$not((setof(X, call(C_{body}\lambda_x), M_C),$$
$$setof(X, call(D_{body}\lambda_x), M_D),$$
$$subset(M_D, M_C))))).$$

Furthermore we can extend the $\lambda$-subsumption test to recursive clauses (as defined in [2] the generalized subsumption does not apply to recursive clauses). For this purpose the model of the head atom $C_{head}$ must be added as a set of ground facts to the program $P$. This will avoid the need to resolve the clause head while evaluating the clause body.

Despite its undecidability in general, the $\lambda$-subsumption test can be very useful for practical ML algorithms basically due to the substitution $\lambda$, which "focuses" the test on some partial (known) interpretations or on easier to prove goals. This aspect of $\lambda$-subsumption is further explored in the paper.

### 2.4 $\lambda$-Subsumption Hierarchy

The $\lambda$-subsumption ordering determines a lattice. For any two clauses $C_1$ and $C_2$ their least upper bound $lub(\{C_1, C_2\})$ is a clause $C$ such that $\|\lambda C_{body}\lambda_x\| = \|\lambda(C_1)_{body}\lambda_x\| \cup \|\lambda(C_2)_{body}\lambda_x\|$ for $\forall x \in (C_1)_{head}$. Obviously $lub(\{C_1, C_2\})$ exists because such a clause is $(C_1)_{head} : - C_{body}$, where $C_{body}$ is defined as follows: $C_{body} : - (C_1)_{body} \vee (C_2)_{body}$. (In case of $(C_1)_{head} \neq (C_2)_{head}$ the *flat* procedure described in 2.2 can be used.) Similarly the greatest lower bound $glb(\{C_1, C_2\})$ is a clause $C$ such that $\|\lambda C_{body}\lambda_x\| = \|\lambda(C_1)_{body}\lambda_x\| \cap \|\lambda(C_2)_{body}\lambda_x\|$ for $\forall x \in (C_1)_{head}$ (e.g. $C = (C_1)_{head} : - (C_1)_{body} \wedge (C_2)_{body}$).

The top element of the $\lambda$-subsumption lattice is the clause with distinct head variables and no body literals. If the functor of the clause head is $p$ with arity $n$ then this clause is $p(x_1, x_2, ..., x_n)$, where $x_i \neq x_j$, for $i \neq j$. Clearly the $\lambda$-model of this clause for any of the variables $x_i$ is the Herbrand universe for the language used. By adding body literals we can constrain the possible bindings of the head variables, thus obtaining $\lambda$-specializations of the clauses in the lattice. Thus for a particular $\lambda = \{x_1/t_1, x_2/t_2, ..., x_n/t_n\}$ the bottom element of this lattice is the clause $p(x_1, x_2, ..., x_n) : - x_1 = t_1, x_2 = t_2, ..., x_n = t_n$.

Let us discuss an example of ordered by $\lambda$-subsumption clauses.

*Example 3.* Let $I$ be the set of all correct instances of the member(X,Y) predicate in the domain of up to two element lists built out of the constants $a$ and $b$. Let us also choose the instance member(b,[a,b]) to determine the substitution $\lambda = \{X/b, Y/[a, b]\}$. A chain of $\lambda$-subsumed clauses for the member predicate is shown in Table 1.

Each of the upper clauses $\lambda$-subsumes the lower ones in the table. Note however that none of these clauses $\theta$-subsumes others, except for clause $\top$, which $\theta$-subsumes all the rest.

The test of two clauses for $\theta$-subsumption or for generalized subsumption generally requires a number of operations, applied repeatedly to the more general

**Table 1.** Clauses ordered by $\lambda$-subsumption

| | C | $\|\lambda X\ C_{body}\lambda_X\|$ | $\|\lambda Y\ C_{body}\lambda_Y\|$ |
|---|---|---|---|
| ⊤ | member(X,Y) | {a,b} | {[],[a],[b],[a,a],[a,b],[b,a],[b,b]} |
| 1 | member(X,Y):-Y=[A\|B],member(A,Y) | {a,b} | {[a],[b],[a,a],[a,b],[b,a],[b,b]} |
| 2 | member(X,Y):-Y=[A\|B],member(X,B) | {a,b} | {[a,b],[b,b]} |
| 3 | member(X,Y):-Y=[a,b],member(X,Y) | {a,b} | {[a,b]} |
| ⊥ | member(X,Y):-X=b,Y=[a,b] | {b} | {[a,b]} |

clause until it is converted into the more specific one. These operations are as follows (the corresponding generality ordering is shown in brackets):

1. Applying substitutions to the whole clause ($\theta$-subsumption).
2. Substituting individual variables (generalized subsumption).
3. Adding body literals ($\theta$-subsumption and generalized subsumption).
4. Resolving body atoms with clauses of the background knowledge (generalized subsumption)

In contrast the test for $\lambda$-subsumption is straightforward. As shown in section 2.3, it can be performed by a logic programming system and extended to recursive clauses as well (as in the example above).

The operations 1-4 can be used to generate clauses $\lambda$-subsumed by a given clause, i.e. these are specialisation operators for moving downward along the lattice structure induced by $\lambda$-subsumption. For example, the clauses in Table 1 are produced from ⊤ by applying operations 3, 2, 2 and 4, resulting in clauses 1, 2, 3 and ⊥ correspondingly.

## 3 Learning from Positive-only Examples

### 3.1 Locally consistent clauses

The model-theoretic view on a Horn clause as implication means that any model of the clause body should be also a model of the clause head. In terms of $\lambda$-models this is expressed in the following way: for clause $C$, substitution $\lambda$ and interpretation $I$, such that $C_{head}\lambda$ is true in $I$, we must have:

$$\|\lambda x\ C_{body}\lambda_x\| \subseteq \|\lambda x\ C_{head}\lambda_x\|, \forall x \in C_{head} \qquad (4)$$

(In [8] this is called $\lambda$-model of a clause.) The substitution $\lambda$ can be determined by an instance $E_i \in I$ of the clause head $C_{head}$, i.e. $E_i = C_{head}\lambda$. Thus $E_i$ also determines the $\lambda$-models $\|\lambda x\ C_{head}\lambda_x\|$ for $\forall x \in C_{head}$. We call the later $\lambda$-extension of $E_i$ and $E_i$ itself – seed example.

Let us consider Table 1 again. The $\lambda$-extension of $E_i = $ member(b,[a,b]) actually defines the head model of the clauses in the table w.r.t. $I$ (the intended interpretation of the member predicate). These models are:

$$\|\lambda X \ C_{head}\lambda_X\| = \{a, b\}$$
$$\|\lambda Y \ C_{head}\lambda_Y\| = \{[a, b], [b, a], [b, b], [b]\}$$

Now using condition (4) we can check the clauses for correctness (i.e. for being true in $I$). Thus clauses $\top$ and 1 are incorrect, and clauses 2,3 and $\bot$ are correct. Furthermore as the clauses are ordered by $\lambda$-subsumption we can select clause 2 as the *most general* correct one. That is, the $\lambda$-extension of $E_i$ determines an *upper bound* for the correct clauses in the $\lambda$-subsumption lattice.

Though induced *locally* (using a partial interpretation) clause 2 is *globally* valid (this is the recursive clause of the standard definition of member). The set of examples used for building the corresponding $\lambda$-models is {member(a, [a, b]), member(b, [b, a]), member(b, [a, b]), member(b, [b, b]), member(b, [b])}. Note that this set is not the coverage of clause 2. Furthermore we do not need negative examples to check the clauses for correctness. In other words the $\lambda$-approach to correctness is different from the traditional ones based on completeness (covering positive examples) and consistency (not covering negative examples). This is the basic motivation to introduce the notion of *locally consistent*[2] clause and to use this notion as a replacement of the *strong consistency* requirement (based on the use of negative examples) in the definition of the learning task.

**Definition 6 (locally consistent clause).** Let $E$ be a set of examples and $BK$ – background knowledge. $C$ is locally consistent with $E$ and $BK$ iff there exists an example $E_i \in E$ such that $C$ is correct in terms of condition (4), where $I$ is such that $BK$ and $E$ are true in $I$ and $\lambda$ is determined by $C_{head}\lambda = E_i$.

### 3.2 Setting for $\lambda$-ILP

The problem we address is defined as follows. Let $BK$ (Background Knowledge) and $H$ (Hypothesis) be logic programs, and $E$ (Examples) – a set of ground facts. The conditions for construction of $H$ are:

1. *Necessity:* $BK \nvdash E$
2. *Weak consistency:* $BK \cup E \cup H \nvdash \Box$
3. *Sufficiency:* $BK \cup H \vdash E$
4. *Local consistency:* $\forall C \in H$, $C$ is locally consistent (definition 4)

The standard ILP task includes conditions 1-3 and usually instead of (4) we have $BK \cup H \nvdash E^-$ (strong consistency). The conditions 1-3 alone are not sufficient because in that case the task is highly underconstrained and hence generally there are an infinite number of hypotheses that meet these conditions. The problem is how to reject the useless hypotheses laying between $\top$ and $\bot$ within the lattice structure induced by the generality relation over the hypotheses. The over-specific hypotheses can be rejected on the basis of their coverage,

---

[2] The same term is introduced in [4] to denote the locality of the examples for one predicate w.r.t. the whole set of examples in the multiple predicate learning task. We use this term here because it reflects a similar notion of local consistency – the consistency w.r.t. a subset of the whole set of examples.

i.e. by preferring those of them covering more examples. To reject over-general hypotheses however one needs negative examples (e.g. the strong consistency requirement). Many approaches (e.g. FOIL) use combined evaluation functions (e.g. information gain) which account both for excluding the negative coverage and for maximizing the positive coverage.

For the approaches based on positive coverage the use of negative examples is essential. Consequently these approaches are very sensitive to the particular choice of negative examples. This is because in many cases the negative examples not only reject the inconsistent hypothesis, but also guide the search in the hypothesis space, i.e. they play the role of an inductive bias. Recently most of the approaches try to avoid this by using other preference criteria for the hypotheses. One often used criterion is the Occam's principle which gives preference to the simpler hypotheses. The diversity of Occam based approaches comes from the various interpretations of the notion of simplicity.

In contrast, the local consistency approach is also based on coverage, however at a local level. The locality is expressed by the $\lambda$-extensions of the examples which in fact model the input/output behavior of the target predicate, considered as fixed number one-argument functions (as many as the arity of the predicate).

## 3.3   Basic $\lambda$-ILP algorithm

At the outermost level the algorithm $\lambda$-ILP consists of the following basic steps:

1. Choose a seed example $E_i \in E$.
2. Find a clause $C_i = P : -Q_1, ..., Q_m$, $m > 0$, which is correct in terms of condition (4) w.r.t. the $\lambda$-extension of $E_i$ and satisfies the proof complexity preference criterion (described in section 3.4).
3. Remove from $E$ the instances covered by $C_i$.
4. If $E \neq \oslash$ then go to 1.
5. Remove the clauses $\lambda$-subsumed by other clauses (to determine the substitution $\lambda$ required for the $\lambda$-subsumption test an example covered by both tested clauses is used). The remaining clauses form the hypothesis $H$ conforming to the requirements of the $\lambda$-ILP problem (section 3.2).

In step 1 the seed example is chosen without any preference, in the order they are supplied.

The candidate clauses in step 2 are generated by using a *top-down* search strategy. The basic argument for this choice is the special case of learning functional relations [16]. The head $\lambda$-model of a clause defining a functional relation consists of only one element for every head variable. The problem is that this is also the $\lambda$-model of the most specific clause $\bot$. Thus the search space in the bottom-up approach is reduced to all clauses equivalent to $\bot$ under $\lambda$-subsumption. To choose a clause in this space we need a preference criterion, based on some other (not $\lambda$-subsumption) ordering. Therefore we have adopted a top-down approach, which uses $\lambda$-subsumption essentially in the search process. The approach can be briefly described as follows: First, build the $\lambda$-extension of $E_i$, i.e. the sets $\|\lambda x_1 C_{head} \lambda_{x_1}\|, ..., \|\lambda x_n C_{head} \lambda_{x_n}\|$, where $C_{head}\lambda = E_i$ and $x_j \in C_{head}$ for $j = 1, ..., n$. Then for each $x_j$ find an atom $L_j$ (with functor and arity from $BK$, $x_j = x_k$ or $x_j = constant$) containing at least one occurrence of $x_j$ and satisfying the condition:

$$\|\lambda x_j C_{head} \lambda_{x_j}\| \supseteq \|\lambda x_j L \sigma_{x_j}\| \tag{5}$$

The substitution $\sigma$ is such that $L_j\sigma$ is true w.r.t. $BK$ and $E$, i.e. $BK \cup E \vdash L\sigma$. If for some $x_j$ a single atom $L_j$ satisfying condition (5) cannot be found, conjunctions of such atoms are searched. Clearly, the $\lambda$-models of these conjunctions will be smaller than those of the individual atoms and thus finally they will satisfy (5).

A special case in step 2 of the algorithm is when no one of the generated clauses is correct in terms of condition (4) w.r.t. the $\lambda$-extension of $E_i$. Such a situation may happen because of the restricted number (by the arity of the clause head) of body literals. In this case the clause body is first built by one or more *determinate literals* and then the above algorithm is applied to complete the clause body. However in addition to the original head variables $x_1, ..., x_n$, the variables of the determinate literals are also considered in the search for body literals. This actually extends the number of arguments of the clause head, allowing in such a way more choice for the body literals. This technique is applied to the one-argument predicates too.

Further we collect all clauses produced in the above-described way and employ a preference criterion to choose one.

## 3.4 Preference criteria

Most of the systems that learn from positive-only examples employ preference criteria based on *complexity measures*. The use of complexity measures is motivated by the Occam's principle stating that "entities should not be multiplied beyond necessity". That is, simpler hypotheses are to be preferred. In the ILP framework generally three types of complexity measures are considered ([11, 3]): *proof complexity, model complexity* and *syntactic (coding) complexity*. The proof complexity estimates the computational complexity of inferring the examples by a given theory. It is defined as the sum of the logarithm of the choice-points involved in the SLD-derivation of the examples covered by the theory. The model complexity ([3]) estimates the *empirical content* of a theory, i.e. the intersection of the model of the theory (logical consequences of the theory) and the given set of examples (observable consequences of the theory). Finally, the coding complexity is defined as the length of the message (in bits) necessary to transmit the theory itself across a noiseless channel.

The coding complexity is used basically when estimating the *data compression*. The data compression accounts for the code length of the coverage of the hypothesis compared to the code length of the hypothesis itself. Since however the emphasis of our approach is not on the positive coverage this kind of complexity is not considered.

The model complexity is calculated as the logarithm of the ratio between the total number of examples and those of them covered by the theory. However no information is available for the examples covered by a particular clause of the theory (moreover the theory itself is unknown). Therefore, as we are evaluating not a theory but a single clause, the model complexity measure in inapplicable.

Following the above mentioned reasons we have chosen the proof complexity ($PC$) measure in our approach. For each clause induced for a given seed example $E_i$, we consider the *proof complexity* (PC) to derive $E_i$. Let $C = P : -L_1, ..., L_n$, then:

$$PC(E_i, C) = \sum_{j=1}^{n} log_2(k_j + 1),$$

where $k_j$ is the number of choice-points in the SLD-derivation of the goal $L_j\lambda$ ($\lambda$ is obtained by unification of $C_{head}$ and $E_i$, i.e. $C_{head}\lambda = E_i$). In case of background knowledge represented as ground facts, $k_j$ is equal to the number of background facts that unify with $L_j\lambda$. Note that a one is added to the number of choice-points. This is done to ensure preference of the shortest clause when comparing clauses with no choice for proving their body literals.


## 4  Empirical evaluation

### 4.1  Experiments

The $\lambda$-ILP algorithm[3] is implemented in Prolog and runs on Poplog-Prolog for SPARC station 10. The algorithm is empirically evaluated on several test data sets shown in Table 2. Some characteristics of these data sets and the runtimes of the algorithm are given in Table 3. Generally three types of domains are considered:

- Recursive domains. These are mainly list processing predicates in Prolog as list membership, appending lists etc. The popular "can_reach" predicate (path finding in a directional graph) and adding integer numbers (the predicate "plus") are also tested. In all tests the standard definitions are found.
- Non-recursive relational domains. These are the well-known data sets: family relationships, legal chess moves and illegal chess endgame positions ("krki" domain). The family data are the same used by Quinlan to test FOIL ([14]). The "krki" domain is usually tested by random samples since it contains $8^6$ examples. $\lambda$-ILP approach allows small number of examples, however they should meet some requirements (discussed in the next section). Therefore we have chosen two samples ("krki1" and "krki2") with different number of positive examples (18 and 355), where the second data are generated by the first one by adding random data. The idea is to compare the run times on the two data sets and the performance of the algorithm with redundant

---

[3] The source text of the Prolog implementation of $\lambda$-ILP along with the test data sets are available by anonymous ftp from ftp.gmd.de, directory /MachineLearning/ILP/public/software/lilp.

information. The result shows that the two data sets produce the same target concept (the one produced by FOIL) for comparable runtimes.

- Propositional data sets. These are problems often used to evaluate propositional learners – the task of classifying various animals, and the Michalski's MONK's and train problems. All these problems have been tested with the same training sets as used to test other learning systems (the "train" and "animals" data are taken from the Progol [13] package, and "monk1" is the original MONK's training set), but without the negative examples. In all cases the λ-ILP system produced correct target concepts.

## 4.2 Discussion

The experiments show that in *any* domain correct definitions can be achieved with varying number of positive-only examples, ranging from only one example (**insert**) to complete sets of examples (**member2** and **conc2**). Tests with non-ground background knowledge have been also performed (**member3** and **conc3**). As the algorithm does not distinguish ground from non-ground $BK$ special care should be taken when defining non-ground $BK$ predicates. They must work properly when called with only one non-ground argument (this restriction comes from the way of searching literals and calculating λ-models). The general use of non-ground $BK$ will require user-specified *mode declarations* and *argument types*. These features can be easily introduced in the λ-ILP algorithm by extending its technique for searching literals. Moreover this will increase the efficiency of the algorithm because the search space of literals will be reduced.

An important feature of the λ-ILP algorithm is that it normally induces the *most general* locally correct hypothesis. This is illustrated by the experiments with the **min** predicate. The problem arises when with the supplied positive-only examples the algorithm induces the definition of **member**. Actually this is correct because the examples for **min** if considered without the background knowledge for comparing numbers, in fact define the **member** relation. The algorithm induces the more general definition (the minimal element of a list is a member of this list, i.e. **member(X,Y)** subsumes **min(Y,X)**). There are cases, however (as with **min**) when the more specific definition is preferred. That is the place to use *negative examples*. As shown in Table 3, two negative examples are sufficient to reject the definition of **member** and thus to build the more specific definition of **min**. The negatives supplied are **min([3,2,1],3)** and **min([1,2],2)**, the first one rejecting the base case and the second one – the recursive clause of **member**. The basic λ-ILP algorithm is extended to use negative examples by modifying step 2 where the candidate clauses covering negative examples are rejected.

It is important to note that this use of negative examples is different from the way they are used in the traditional ILP systems. Here the negatives do not reject an incorrect hypothesis, rather they reflect the user preference to one of several competing correct explanations of the supplied positive examples. Of course, choosing such kind of negative examples is a difficult task in the general case, when no information about the intended predicate is available.

**Table 2.** Test domains for λ-ILP

| Data set | Description |
|----------|-------------|
| member1 | list membership with 3 examples |
| member2 | list membership with complete set of examples |
| member3 | list membership using non-ground BK |
| member4 | list membership using conc/3 |
| member5 | list membership using del/3 |
| conc1 | appending lists with 4 examples |
| conc2 | appending lists with complete set of examples |
| conc3 | appending lists using non-ground BK |
| qsort | sorting lists with quick sort algorithm |
| min | finding the minimal element of a list |
| reverse | reversing lists |
| del | deleting one element from a list |
| insert | inserting an element into a list |
| sublist | sublist relation |
| subset | subset relation on ordered lists |
| permutation | permutations of a list |
| palindrome | a list is a palindrome (using reverse/2) |
| palindrome1 | a list is a palindrome (using conc/3) |
| evenlength | a list has even number of elements |
| last1 | finding the last element of a list (using conc/3) |
| last2 | finding the last element of a list |
| can_reach | check for a path in a graph |
| plus | adding integer numbers |
| family | family relationships |
| chess | legal chess moves |
| krki1 | illegal chess endgame positions with 18 positives |
| krki2 | illegal chess endgame positions with 355 positives |
| animals | descriptions of various animals |
| monks1 | Michalski's MONK's problem #1 |
| train1 | Michalski's train problem with 10 BK predicates |
| train2 | Michalski's train problem with 6 BK predicates |

Another use of negative examples can be found in the task for inducing the definition of the predicate **move**. The point here is that as described the λ-ILP algorithm searches for body literals corresponding to *every one* of the head arguments $x_1, ..., x_n$. If however the actual predicate definition requires singleton head variables (i.e. don't care variables) the algorithm may fail to find a relevant literal for such a variable. The automatic detection of such a variable is a difficult task because it must be shown that the predicate is true for *any* binding of this variable, i.e. the corresponding λ-model must include the whole Herbrand universe of the language. Clearly this will require a large number of examples.

**Table 3.** Results of running λ-ILP. The run times are given in seconds for a Poplog-Prolog implementation running on SPARC station 10

| Data set | Predicate | $|E|$ | $|E^-|$ | $|BK|$ | $|H|$ | Time |
|----------|-----------|-------|---------|--------|-------|------|
| member1 | member/2 | 3 | - | 10 | 2 | 0.18 |
| member2 | member/2 | 12 | - | 19 | 2 | 0.15 |
| member3 | member/2 | 11 | - | 15 | 2 | 0.13 |
| member4 | member/2 | 7 | - | 34 | 1 | 0.23 |
| member5 | member/2 | 6 | - | 25 | 1 | 0.12 |
| conc1 | conc/3 | 4 | - | 11 | 2 | 0.08 |
| conc2 | conc/3 | 20 | - | 27 | 2 | 0.54 |
| conc3 | conc/3 | 4 | - | 8 | 2 | 0.09 |
| qsort | qsort/3 | 6 | - | 29 | 2 | 2.01 |
| min | min/2 | 13 | 2 | 31 | 3 | 0.48 |
| reverse | reverse/2 | 11 | - | 216 | 2 | 1.59 |
| del | del/3 | 4 | - | 11 | 2 | 0.30 |
| insert | insert/3 | 1 | - | 20 | 1 | 0.12 |
| sublist | sublist/2 | 11 | - | 37 | 2 | 0.44 |
| subset | sub/2 | 10 | - | 17 | 3 | 0.31 |
| permutation | permutation/2 | 7 | - | 55 | 2 | 0.44 |
| palindrome | palindrome/1 | 5 | - | 19 | 1 | 0.04 |
| palindrome1 | palindrome/1 | 6 | - | 43 | 3 | 0.34 |
| evenlength | evenlength/1 | 5 | - | 15 | 2 | 0.16 |
| last1 | last/2 | 6 | - | 33 | 1 | 0.30 |
| last2 | last/2 | 6 | - | 13 | 2 | 0.15 |
| can_reach | can_reach/2 | 4 | - | 14 | 2 | 0.13 |
| plus | plus/3 | 7 | - | 14 | 2 | 0.68 |
| family | husband/2 | 5 | - | 56 | 1 | 0.06 |
|  | father/2 | 6 | - | 56 | 1 | 0.18 |
|  | son/2 | 6 | - | 56 | 2 | 0.86 |
|  | brother/2 | 3 | - | 56 | 1 | 0.17 |
|  | uncle/2 | 4 | - | 56 | 2 | 0.85 |
| chess | move/5 | 26 | 3 | 26 | 11 | 9.49 |
| krki1 | illegal/6 | 18 | 6 | 22 | 4 | 0.76 |
| krki2 | illegal/6 | 355 | 6 | 22 | 4 | 2.37 |
| animals | class/2 | 16 | - | 78 | 5 | 0.24 |
| monks1 | monks1/1 | 61 | - | 744 | 2 | 0.27 |
| train1 | eastbound/1 | 5 | - | 211 | 1 | 1.25 |
| train2 | eastbound/1 | 5 | - | 91 | 1 | 0.19 |

A way to solve this problem is to use negative examples to indicate which head arguments are important (not don't care type) for a particular seed example. For example if we define a move of the queen by move(queen,b,2,e,2), the negative example "move(queen,b,2,e,3)" will show that in this case the last argument is important and the system will try to find a literal for it. Thus the clause move(queen,_,A,_,B):-A=B will be induced. This kind of negative examples are necessary for the data sets **chess** and **krki**. As shown in Table 3 a very restricted number on negatives is sufficient in these cases.

In most of the experiments a relatively small number of positive examples are chosen. A reasonable question at this point is how have these examples been chosen? In many inductive learning systems the examples are chosen randomly. This is the case in most of the empirical ILP systems (such as FOIL for example), where either completeness of the positive examples or large number of negative examples is required. Other ILP systems (mostly those based on inverse resolution and *lgg*) need special care to prepare the set of examples. In most cases (especially in the recursive domains) the examples should be chosen from a single resolution chain, should belong to the *basic representative set* ([6]) or form an *h-easy* ground model ([10]). All these approaches to find "good" examples however require some prior knowledge about the target theory. In contrast the $\lambda$-ILP approach introduces some requirements to the data, which can be ensured without intensional knowledge about the target theory. Furthermore these requirements have clear semantics in most domains and can be expressed in extensional terms (by the examples themselves). The basic idea is that the data supplied to the $\lambda$-ILP system should contain *locally complete* descriptions of domain cases corresponding to individual clauses in the theory. A locally complete description must contain one seed and its *complete $\lambda$-extension* w.r.t. the background knowledge.

For example, in the case of learning correct knight moves, described in terms of rank and file differences (the background knowledge) we have two typical cases: moving two positions along the rank and then one along the file, and moving two positions along the file and then one along the rank. These two types of moves can be shown be two examples correspondingly: move(knight,b,1,a,3) and move(knight,f,1,h,2). The complete $\lambda$-extension of move(knight,b,1,a,3) is then the set {move(knight,b,1,c,3),move(knight,b,5,a,3)}, i.e. *all* moves from position b1 and *all* moves to position a3. Similarly the complete $\lambda$ extension of move(knight,f,1,h,2) is {move(knight,f,1,d,2),move(knight,f,3,h,2)}. (Note that we have chosen the periphery of the chess board and thus the corresponding $\lambda$-models are smaller.)

This shows that the preparation of the examples does not require any knowledge about the rules of chess playing in the form of clauses. Supplied only with the above six examples – the two seeds and their extensions (the complete set of examples for the knight moves consists of 336 examples) *without any negative examples* the $\lambda$-ILP algorithm will produce the two clauses for the correct knight moves:

```
move(knight,A,B,C,D) :- diff(A,C,2),diff(B,D,1)
move(knight,A,B,C,D) :- diff(A,C,1),diff(B,D,2)
```

The local completeness requirement is necessary only in case of complete background knowledge. If the background knowledge in not complete, then the seed extensions can contain smaller number of examples. The selection of these examples however would be more difficult. Actually this is the case of recursive predicates, where the examples of the target predicate are also a part of the background knowledge. In this case the examples of the target predicate should contain the *basic representative set* of the theory and the complete λ-extensions of the instances on the clause heads.

## 4.3 Limitations of the algorithm and possible improvements

The current version of the λ-ILP algorithm may fail to induce clauses for some predicates. This may happen when the learned predicate require clauses with many body literals (e.g. more that the arity of their head). In that case the algorithm uses determinate literals. However such literals may not exist for the current background knowledge. In other cases the use of determinate literals may lead to a large number of new variables and consequently to a large number of candidate clauses to be evaluated for λ-correctness and proof complexity.

Here is an example of a predicate not learnable with λ-ILP. The target clause is p(A,D):-q(A,B),r(B,C),s(C,D), $E = \{p(a,d)\}$ and $BK = \{q(a,b),q(a,c),$ r(b,c),s(c,d),s(e,d)\}. Note that the problem here is not in the λ-correctness of the clause (it satisfies condition (4)), but rather in the restriction of determinate literals (the special case in step 2 in the algorithm) – the literals q(A,B) and s(C,D) are not determinate (before adding r(B,C)).

Two possible solutions of the problem are being currently studied:
- Abandoning the restriction of determinate literals.
- Using a FOIL-like search strategy.

The first option is actually an exhaustive search with a restriction on the candidate literals only (the condition (5)). The provisional experiments showed however that this approach is computationally too expensive. The second option which is now under development seems more promising. The basic idea here is to use a greedy search strategy with a kind of information gain heuristics for the choice of candidate literals. The information gain is defined similarly as in FOIL, where the key notion is the information provided by signaling that a binding of the λ-variable makes the clause $C$ correct in terms of condition (4). That is:

$$I = - \sum_{x \in C_{head}} log_2(\frac{p_x}{n_x}),$$

where $p_x$ is the number of elements in $\|\lambda x \ (C_{head} \wedge C_{boby})\lambda_x\|$ and $n_x$ – the number of elements in $\|\lambda x \ C_{body}\lambda_x\|$.

Another advantage of using the information gain or other similar heuristics for evaluating candidate clauses (e.g. accuracy) is that the necessity for negative examples in some special cases (discussed in the previous section) could be avoided. The λ-ILP algorithm as described in section 3.3 searches for the shortest (and thus for the most general) clauses conforming to the local consistency condition. By using the above heuristics the search for clauses can be directed alternatively towards maximizing the information (or accuracy) gain. In this way any target predicate can be learned with a proper choice of positive only examples. Furthermore this will allow weakening of the stopping condition for the search for literals (the local consistency condition employed in step 2 of the algorithm) by choosing not only the strictly consistent clauses but rather those with high information (accuracy) gain. Thus the scope of application of the $\lambda$-ILP approach could be extended to noisy domains.

# 5 Related Work

The approach presented in the paper can be traced back to [7], where the so called determinate ground clauses were introduced. These are ground clauses which preserve the types of their head arguments when variabilised. This notion is now extended and theoretically justified. Furthermore the proof complexity measure used in the present approach seems to be better than the clustering measure employed in [7]. The lambda model of clauses, which is the basis of the $\lambda$-ILP approach is introduced in [8].

The system FILP ([1]) can learn functional relations from positive-only examples. Additionally it uses mode declarations and existential queries to the user about missing examples. The system INDICO ([17]) also can learn from positive examples by determining the types of the target predicate arguments. Both systems use a similar idea of determining the allowable output bindings of the target predicate given fixed inputs and use this to search for appropriate body literals. The outputs can be found by asking the user or applying ILP techniques to induce its type.

A more general approach also based on the above idea is proposed in [18]. It is not restricted to functional relations and provides a way of quantifying the negative coverage without explicit negative examples. This is achieved by the assumption of *output completeness*, which the supplied positive examples should meet. The set of examples is said to be output complete, if for any set of inputs present in an example all correct outputs are also present in the training set. All other outputs generated for an input are assumed as negative examples.

The idea of output completeness is close to the notion of the complete $\lambda$-extension introduced in the present paper. The latter however is *more general*, because it does not assume mode declarations. Furthermore as the complete $\lambda$-extension is required for at least one example for a given case, it is a *weaker* constraint on the training data. In the $\lambda$-ILP approach the notion of negative coverage is avoided and instead a complexity measure for the candidate clauses is employed. This is a way to introduce some kind of a priori (data-independant) knowledge about the inductive hypotheses. Another advantage of the $\lambda$-ILP approach is that the $\lambda$-extension is used directly in the search for body literals, which makes this search more efficient, while the implicit negative examples are used just to evaluate the inductive hypothesis, already generated by another method.

Another line of research in learning from positive-only data is based on the Occam's principle, formally expressed by MDL and various complexity or data compression measures. In most of the ILP approaches this principle just complements the underlying inductive mechanism by introducing some preference on the induced hypotheses. In Progol ([13]), for example the clause with maximal compression is searched in the subsumption lattice for each example. There are also direct approaches based only on complexity measures. The one described in [3] uses a model complexity measure to evaluate theories (sets of clauses) and to choose the best one. This approach though allowing to choose the best hypothesis using positive-only data, does not propose a particular algorithm to generate theories (moreover such an algorithm would be computationally hard, since the search space of theories is much larger than the search space of clauses).

# 6 Conclusion and future work

The proposed $\lambda$-ILP approach actually extends the functional approaches based on output completeness and combines them with the Occam based approaches. The performance evaluation shows that the $\lambda$-ILP algorithm can be applied successfully to recursive, relational and propositional domains. Some of the test problems solved are the same as used by other ILP systems, however with the set of negative examples skipped. This shows that in many cases negative examples are redundant. i.e. they are required by the learning system to work properly but are not inherent for the problem domain.

The $\lambda$-ILP task as defined in the paper and the results of the $\lambda$-ILP algorithm may seem contradicting some fundamental learnability results. According to Gold [5] many concept classes are not identifiable in the limit from positive-only examples. Identification in the limit is a strong property of the learning algorithms which ensures the convergence to the intended theory given an infinite supply of positive examples. The latter however is not the case we are investigating. Rather we are interested in inducing predicate definitions from small sets of examples conforming to the requirement of local completeness (section 4.2). Nevertheless the fact that in most cases the locally consistent clauses appear to be globally consistent too is interesting and needs further justification. This is one of the direction for future work.

Another direction for further work is the extension of the $\lambda$-ILP algorithm suggested in section 4.3. Along this line of research the well-known heuristics for noise handling in empirical ILP (e.g. the information gain and the various probability estimates) can be adapted for the purposes of *local evaluation* (w.r.t. the seed extension) of the quality of the candidate clauses, i.e. they can provide a quantitative measure of the local consistency of the clauses. These measures could be useful not only for the improvement of the $\lambda$-ILP algorithm discussed in the paper. In our opinion they have also a potential in the area of *knowledge discovery in databases (KDD)* as estimations of the "interestingness" or utility of the discovered clauses.

### Acknowledgements

I am grateful to my colleague Christo Dichev for the interesting and very helpful discussions on the lambda models. I owe also many tanks to the anonymous referees for the valuable comments and suggestions for improvement on the paper.

# References

1. Bergadano, F., Gunetti, D.: Functional Inductive Logic Programming with Queries to the User. In *Proceedings of ECML-93*, LNAI, Vol.667, Springer-Verlag, 1993, 323-328.
2. Buntine, W.: Generalized Subsumption and Its Application to Induction and Redundancy, *Artificial Intelligence*, Vol. 36 (1988), 149-176.
3. Conklin, D., Witten, I.: Complexity-Based Induction, *Machine Learning*, Vol. 16 (3), 1994, 203-225.
4. De Raedt, L., Lavrac, N., Dzeroski, S.: Multiple Predicate Learning. In: *Proceedings of IJCAI-93*, Chambery, France, August 28 – September 3, 1993, 1037-1042.
5. Gold, E.M.: Language Identification in the Limit. *Information and Control*, Vol.10, 1967, 447-474.
6. Ling, C.X.: Logic Program Synthesis from Good Examples. In S. Muggleton (ed.), Inductive Logic Programming, Academic Press, 1992, 113-129.
7. Markov, Z.: Relational Learning by Heuristic Evaluation of Ground Data. In S. Wrobel (Ed.), *Proceedings of Fourth Int. Workshop on ILP (ILP-94)*, September 12-14, 1994, Bad Honnef/Bon, Germany, GMD-Studien Nr.237, 337-349.
8. Markov, Z.: A Functional Approach to ILP. In Luc De Raedt (Ed.), *Proceedings of the Fifth Int. Workshop on ILP (ILP-95)*, 4-6 Sept. 1995, Leuven, Scientific report, Department of Computer Science, K.U. Leuven, September, 1995, 267-280.
9. Muggleton, S., Buntine, W.: Machine invention of first-order predicates by inverting resolution. In *Proceedings of the Fifth Int. Conference on Machine Learning*, Morgan Kaufmann, 1988, 339-352.
10. Muggleton, S., Feng, C.: Efficient induction of logic programs. In S. Muggleton (ed.), Inductive Logic Programming, Academic Press, 1992, 281-298.
11. Muggleton, S., Srinivasan, A., Bain, M.: Compression, significance and accuracy. In D. Sleeman, P. Edwards (eds.), *Proceedings of the Ninth Int. Conference of Machine Learning (ML92)*, Morgan Kaufmann, 1992, 338-347.
12. Muggleton, S., Page, C.D.: Self-saturation of definite clauses. In S. Wrobel (Ed.), *Proceedings of Fourth Int. Workshop on ILP (ILP'94)*, September 12-14, 1994, Bad Honnef/Bon, Germany, GMD-Studien Nr.237, 161-174.
13. Muggleton, S.: Inverse Entailment and Progol, *New Generation Computing*, 13 (1995), 245-286.
14. Quinlan, J.R.: Learning logical definitions from relations. *Machine Learning*, 5 (1990), 239-266.
15. Ramsay, A.: Formal Methods in Artificial Intelligence, Cambridge University Press, 1991.
16. Rouveirol, S.: Extensions of Inversion of Resolution Applied to Theory Completion. In S. Muggleton (ed.), Inductive Logic Programming, Academic Press, 1992, 63-92.
17. Stahl, I., Tausend, B., Wirth, R.: Two Methods for Improving Inductive Logic Programming Systems. In *Proceedings of ECML-93*, LNAI, Vol.667, Springer-Verlag, 1993, 41-55.
18. Zelle, J., Thompson, C., Califf, M., Mooney, R.: Inducing Logic Programs without Explicit Negative Examples. In Luc De Raedt (Ed.), *Proceedings of the Fifth Int. Workshop on ILP (ILP-95)*, 4-6 Sept. 1995, Leuven, Scientific report, Department of Computer Science, K.U. Leuven, September, 1995, 403-416.

# Author Index

# Lecture Notes in Artificial Intelligence (LNAI)

# Lecture Notes in Computer Science